STRONGER VICTIMS' RIGHTS IN EU LAW?

This collection looks at the protection of victims' rights in EU law.

Taking a four-part approach, it firstly focuses on the Victims' Right Directive and the proposal for a Directive on combating violence against women. It then explores victims' rights in the national laws of the Member States, including France, Germany, Hungary, the Netherlands, Romania, Lithuania and Ireland. Finally it analyses the main challenges in the field and the need for coherence between the different competing interests.

Volume 22 in the series Hart Studies in European Criminal Law

Hart Studies in European Criminal Law

Series Editors: Professor Valsamis Mitsilegas, Queen Mary University of London; Professor Katalin Ligeti, University of Luxembourg; Professor Anne Weyembergh, Brussels Free University

Since the Lisbon Treaty, European criminal law has become an increasingly important field of research and debate. Working with the European Criminal Law Academic Network (ECLAN), the series will publish works of the highest intellectual rigour and cutting edge scholarship which will be required reading for all European criminal lawyers.

The series is happy to consider both edited and single authored titles. The series defines 'European' and 'criminal law' in the broadest sense so books on the European criminal law, justice and policy will be considered. The series also welcomes books which offer different methodological approaches.

Volume 1: *EU Criminal Law after Lisbon: Rights, Trust and the Transformation of Justice in Europe*
Valsamis Mitsilegas

Volume 2: *Challenges in the Field of Economic and Financial Crime in Europe and the US*
Edited by Vanessa Franssen and Katalin Ligeti

Volume 3: *Chasing Criminal Money: Challenges and Perspectives On Asset Recovery in the EU*
Edited by Katalin Ligeti and Michele Simonato

Volume 4: *Limits to EU Powers: A Case Study of EU Regulatory Criminal Law*
Jacob Öberg

Volume 5: *The Needed Balances in EU Criminal Law: Past, Present and Future*
Edited by Chloé Brière and Anne Weyembergh

Volume 6: *Redefining Organised Crime: A Challenge for the European Union?*
Edited by Stefania Carnevale, Serena Forlati and Orsetta Giolo

Volume 7: *White Collar Crime: A Comparative Perspective*
Edited by Katalin Ligeti and Stanislaw Tosza

Volume 8: *Criminal Liability of Managers in Europe: Punishing Excessive Risk*
Stanisław Tosza

Volume 9: *The European Union and Deprivation of Liberty: A Legislative and Judicial Analysis from the Perspective of the Individual*
Leandro Mancano

Volume 10: *The Legitimacy of EU Criminal Law*
Irene Wieczorek

Volume 11: *The Fight Against Impunity in EU Law*
Edited by Luisa Marin and Stefano Montaldo

Volume 12: *Controlling Immigration Through Criminal Law: European and Comparative Perspectives on 'Crimmigration'*
Edited by Gian Luigi Gatta, Valsamis Mitsilegas, and Stefano Zirulia

Volume 13: *The Principle of Mutual Trust in EU Criminal Law*
Auke Willems

Volume 14: *Surveillance and Privacy in the Digital Age: European, Transatlantic and Global Perspectives*
Edited by Valsamis Mitsilegas and Niovi Vavoula

Volume 15: *The External Dimension of the EU's Policy against Trafficking in Human Beings*
Chloé Brière

Volume 16: *Criminal and Quasi-criminal Enforcement Mechanisms in Europe: Origins, Concepts, Future*
Edited by Vanessa Franssen and Christopher Harding

Volume 17: *Data protection, Migration and Border Control: The GDPR, the Law Enforcement Directive and Beyond*
Teresa Quintel

Volume 18: *Corporations and the Privilege against Self-Incrimination*
Stijn Lamberigts

Volume 19: *EU Enforcement Authorities: Punitive Law Enforcement in a Composite Legal Order*
Edited by Michiel Luchtman, Katalin Ligeti and John Vervaele

Volume 20: *Admissibility of Evidence in EU Cross-Border Criminal Proceedings: Electronic Evidence, Efficiency and Fair Trial Rights*
Edited by Lorena Bachmaier Winter and Farsam Salimi

Volume 21: *Proportionality of Criminal Penalties in EU Law*
Edited by Stefano Montaldo, Valsamis Mitsilegas and Lorenzo Grossio

Volume 22: *Stronger Victims' Rights in EU Law? Assessment and Prospects*
Edited by Julia Burchett and Anne Weyembergh

Stronger Victims' Rights in EU Law?

Assessment and Prospects

Edited by
Julia Burchett
and
Anne Weyembergh

•HART•
OXFORD • LONDON • NEW YORK • NEW DELHI • SYDNEY

HART PUBLISHING

Bloomsbury Publishing Plc

Kemp House, Chawley Park, Cumnor Hill, Oxford, OX2 9PH, UK

1385 Broadway, New York, NY 10018, USA

Bloomsbury Publishing Ireland Limited, 29 Earlsfort Terrace, Dublin 2, D02 AY28, Ireland

HART PUBLISHING, the Hart/Stag logo, BLOOMSBURY and the Diana logo are trademarks of Bloomsbury Publishing Plc

First published in Great Britain 2025

A catalogue record for this book is available from the British Library.

A catalogue record for this book is available from the Library of Congress.

Library of Congress Control Number: 2025930494

ISBN: HB: 978-1-50997-535-8
ePDF: 978-1-50997-537-2
ePub: 978-1-50997-536-5

Typeset by Compuscript Ltd, Shannon

For product safety related questions contact productsafety@bloomsbury.com

To find out more about our authors and books visit www.hartpublishing.co.uk. Here you will find extracts, author information, details of forthcoming events and the option to sign up for our newsletters.

FOREWORD

The work of legal academics is key for a well-functioning EU justice system. When it comes to evaluating the need for stronger regulations, legal academics play an important role in assessing needs and benefits. During the legislative process, they make an essential contribution to the development of the law. In the field of EU criminal law in particular, the work and expertise of legal academics is indispensable. They provide for dedicated research and a critical evaluation of the law. Legal academics have not only accompanied the evolution of EU criminal law, they have shaped it.

When it comes to cross-cutting areas like victims' rights, it is essential to take into account different points of view and to include different areas of expertise. Hence, legal academics, practitioners and civil society play a complementary role. This is why a network like the European Criminal Law Academic Network (ECLAN) plays such a vital role in the assessment of victim' rights in EU law. It brings together expertise from researchers, academia, practitioners, and civil society from across the whole EU which is instrumental in facilitating the exchange of ideas and thoughts. Likewise, this publication consolidates a broad range of expertise. It allows a wider audience to benefit from the valuable discourse and conclusions of the ECLAN Conference – I highly welcome it.

Stronger Victims' Rights in EU Law? – This publication deals with a very important question which is worth further analysing. It can be understood as posing the question whether victims' rights are stronger in EU law, or whether they should rather be left to national law?

Crime knows no borders. This is not only true for perpetrators, but it is equally valid for victims. It is particularly important in the European Area of Freedom, Security and Justice, which is characterised by the absence of any internal borders. That is why – since the Lisbon Treaty – victims' rights have a clear legal basis in the Union law.

EU rules on victims' rights are an essential part of the Union criminal law. Together with the EU rules on procedural rights of suspects and accused, victims' rights are indispensable to establish the mutual trust in other Member States' judicial schemes and thus to facilitate judicial cooperation in criminal matters. For that, trust in equal access to victims' rights independently of where in the EU the crime happened is essential.

As a consequence, the EU level indeed is the right place to establish minimum standards on victims' rights. This does not mean however, that Member States on their own, should stop developing their rules and practices on victims' rights. On the contrary: EU Member States are always encouraged to go beyond the EU minimum standards.

Stronger Victims' Rights in EU Law? – This title can also be understood as posing a different or an additional question: Do we need any stronger rules on victims' rights in the EU? We already have a strong set of rules on victims' rights in the EU. They are composed notably of the 2012 Victims' Rights Directive – the main horizontal instrument on victims' rights. It lays down rights for all victims of all crimes, including the right to information, the right to support and protection in accordance with victims' individual needs, procedural rights and the right to receive a decision on compensation from the offender at the end of criminal proceedings.

In addition, the EU set of rules on victims' rights comprises the 2004 Compensation Directive and the EU rules on protection orders. These instruments are also of a horizontal nature and are applicable to all victims of crime.

The EU *acquis* on victims' rights also includes sectorial legislation composed of several instruments addressing the specific needs of victims of certain categories of crimes, such as the 2011 Directive on Preventing and Combating Trafficking in Human Beings and Protecting its Victims and the 2017 Directive on Combating Terrorism.

Furthermore, the Commission continues to improve the existing rules on victims' rights. In 2022, the Commission adopted two proposals in the field of sectorial legislation: a proposal for a Directive on combating violence against women and domestic violence as well as a proposal to revise the Directive on Preventing and Combating Trafficking in Human Beings and Protecting its Victims.

On 12 July 2023, the Commission adopted the proposal for a Directive amending the 2012 Victims' Rights Directive. The proposal for the revision is based on the evaluation of the Directive which shows that overall, the instrument has been successful and has considerably improved the situation of victims in the EU. Nonetheless it has also found that punctual amendments are necessary to ensure its optimal effectiveness. The issues relate to the five main victims' rights: access to information, improved support and protection, improved participation in criminal proceedings and facilitated access to compensation. Hence, there is some need for stronger rules on victims' rights in the EU. The revision of the Victims' Rights Directive further strengthens the rights of victims of crime in the EU by providing for such punctual targeted amendments.

With the revision of the Directive, the Commission proposes to ensure that:

1) victims have the information they need to be able to exercise their rights – thanks to the provision of victims' helplines,
2) victims' needs for protection are met accordingly – via strengthened individual assessment,
3) victims are better supported – via enhanced support for the most vulnerable victims, notably child victims,
4) victims can more effectively participate in a criminal proceeding – with the right to challenge the decision that concern victims directly and the right to legal remedies,
5) victims have more adequate access to compensation from the offender – thanks to improved state support in executing compensation from the offender.

With the proposed revision, the Commission aims to ensure that there are stronger rules to further improve the rights of victims of crime in the EU.

Stronger Victims' Rights in EU Law? – To deal with this question in depth it is imperative to take into account all relevant points of view. Who could be better equipped to conduct such an assessment than a network like ECLAN? This publication brings together various highly regarded experts to look at the state of play of victims' rights at EU and national levels, at main challenges as well as prospects. Its valuable assessment plays a vital role in continuing the discourse on victims' rights in EU law and bringing the discussion to the next level.

Didier Reynders
Former EU Commissioner for Justice, European Commission

Electronically signed on 22/12/2023 14:39 (UTC+01) in accordance with Article 11 of Commission Decision (EU) 2021/2121.

ACKNOWLEDGEMENTS

This collective book stems from the 2023 European Criminal Law Academic Network (ECLAN) Annual Conference entitled 'Stronger Victims' Rights in EU Law? Assessment and Prospects', held at the European Commission on 18 April 2023. It serves as the cornerstone of a four-year research project (2020–2024) funded by the Belgian Fund for Scientific Research (*Fonds National pour la Recherche Scientifique* – FNRS), aimed at conducting a comprehensive analysis of the current state of victims' rights protection in the EU, identifying gaps and challenges in the implementation of EU instruments.

The editors would like to extend their gratitude to all those who supported the organisation of the Conference, notably the *Fonds National pour la Recherche Scientifique* (FNRS) and the European Commission. Their appreciation also goes out to those behind the scenes who contributed to making this event a success, particularly the services of the Directorate General for Justice and the Directorate General for interpretation (SCIC) of the European Commission, along with the dedicated members of the ECLAN Brussels team. Their heartfelt thanks also go to Marta Ramat, a former ECLAN intern, for her significant contribution to the organisation of the Conference. The editors would like to thank all Conference participants and the authors of this collective work. Special thanks are also owed to Julian Hale and Iris Tolgonay for their invaluable assistance in finalising the manuscript.

The editors wish to highlight that the manuscript was completed in August 2024, and therefore the discussions in this volume do not reflect developments that occurred afterwards.

CONTENTS

Foreword ... *vii*
Acknowledgements ... *xi*
List of Contributors ... *xvii*
List of Abbreviations ... *xix*

PART I
INTRODUCTION

1. *Victims' Rights in EU Law – Coming of Age?* ... *3*
Julia Burchett

PART II
THE PROTECTION OF VICTIMS' RIGHTS IN EU LAW AND INSIGHTS FROM REGIONAL AND INTERNATIONAL INSTRUMENTS

2. *Victims' Rights in the EU: Boosting the Recognition and Participation of Victims in Criminal Proceedings* ... *19*
Chara Chioni-Chotouman

3. *Protecting Vulnerable Victims: An Analysis of the EU Legal Framework for Victims of Gender-Based Violence* ... *35*
Cristina Sáenz Pérez

4. *The Flood that Never Came: Case Law of the Court of Justice on the Victims' Rights* Acquis ... *55*
Adam Łazowski

5. *Being 'Fair and Appropriate' to Victims of Violent Crime: Evaluating the Provision of State Compensation in the European Union* ... *75*
Liam O'Driscoll

6. *Eurojust's Role in Enhancing Victims' Rights in Cross-Border Criminal Cases* ... *95*
Julieta Carmona Bermejo and Eric Fréjabue

7. *Council of Europe Instruments and the Case Law of the ECtHR on Victims' Rights: What Influence on EU Law?* ... *121*
Lorena Bachmaier Winter

8. *Victim Participation in International Criminal Trials: A Way Forward?* ... *139*
Vaios Koutroulis and Marie-Laurence Hébert-Dolbec

PART III
SELECTED NATIONAL PERSPECTIVES ON VICTIMS' RIGHTS ACROSS THE EU: MAJOR TRENDS AND EU LAW IMPACT

9. *Victims' Rights in Belgian Law: Significant Progress Due to the Influence of EU Law but Still Gaps to be Filled* 173
Maryse Alié and Clémentine Samri

10. *Victim Rights in the Netherlands: Unconditional Compliance or Pursuing the National Agenda?* 193
Suzan van der Aa

11. *Victims' Rights in Romania: The Gap between the Adoption of Legal Texts and their Effective Implementation* 209
Diana Ionescu

12. *The Status of the Victim in Latvian Criminal Procedure Law – When the Most Urgent Thing is to Strengthen Active Participation with Effective Protection* 233
Kristīne Strada-Rozenberga and Ārija Meikališa

13. *Impact of EU Law Instruments Regarding Victims' Rights on Lithuania's Criminal Procedure* 249
Gintaras Švedas

14. *The Protection of Victims of Crime in the Italian Criminal Justice System* 267
Valeria Scalia

15. *An Evaluation of the Impact of the EU Victims' Rights Directive on the Scope of Victims' Rights in Ireland* 289
Gerard Conway

PART IV
KEY CHALLENGES: ENSURING COHERENCE, CRISIS RESPONSES AND BALANCING COMPETING INTERESTS

16. *(Human Trafficking) Victims on the Margins of Protection: The (In)coherence of Sectoral Instruments?* 317
Amy Weatherburn

17. *Do Victims' Rights and Defendants' Rights Really have to be Equal?* 335
Kristīne Strada-Rozenberga

18. *Prospects of Increasing Victims' Rights in Criminal Proceedings: The Fault Lines in the EU Procedural Fairness Mode* 351
Laure Baudrihaye-Gérard

19. *The Protection of Victims at EU Level: The Need for Cross-Border Cooperation and Coordination* 371
Aniella Ferenczi

PART V
CONCLUSION AND REFLECTIONS

20. *Transforming EU Victims' Laws into Reality for Victims: Developing a Strategic Framework for the Implementation of Victims' Rights* *381*
Levent Altan

21. *Exploring the Emergence of an EU Model for Victims' Rights: Progress and Challenges* *401*
Chloé Brière

Index *419*

LIST OF CONTRIBUTORS

EDITORS

Julia BURCHETT – PhD in Law, Université Libre de Bruxelles and Université Grenoble-Alpes. Postdoctoral Researcher, Centre for European Law, Université Libre de Bruxelles.

Anne WEYEMBERGH – Prof Dr Law, Professor, Université Libre de Bruxelles. Vice-Rector for External Relations and Development Cooperation, Université Libre de Bruxelles.

CONTRIBUTORS

Maryse ALIÉ – Lawyer at the Brussels Bar. Guest Expert at the Université Libre de Bruxelles Assistant Lecturer at UCLouvain-Saint-Louis.

Levent ALTAN – Executive Director, Victim Support Europe.

Lorena BACHMAIER WINTER – Prof Dr Law, Professor of Justice Systems and Procedural Law, Complutense University of Madrid. International legal expert for the Council of Europe and other international organisations. Member of the European Commission's Expert Group on European Criminal Law Policy.

Laure BAUDRIHAYE-GÉRARD – Researcher, Faculty of Law and Criminology, Université Libre de Bruxelles. Former Legal Director, Fair Trials Europe (2018–2023).

Chloé BRIÈRE – Prof Dr Law, Professor of EU Law, Université Libre de Bruxelles. Director of the Institute for European Studies, Université Libre de Bruxelles.

Julia BURCHETT – PhD in Law, Université Libre de Bruxelles and Université Grenoble-Alpes. Postdoctoral Researcher, Centre for European Law, Université Libre de Bruxelles.

Julieta CARMONA BERMEJO – Senior Officer, Head of the Legal Affairs Unit, a.i., Eurojust. Former Associate Trial Lawyer, Office of the Prosecutor, International Criminal Court.

Chara CHIONI-CHOTOUMAN – PhD in Law, National Kapodistrian University of Athens. Postdoctoral Researcher, Aristotle University of Thessaloniki.

Gerard CONWAY – PhD in Law, Brunel University London. Senior Lecturer in Law, Brunel University London.

Aniella FERENCZI – Lawyer, Executive Manager, Association of the European Network on Victims' Rights.

Eric FRÉJABUE – Judicial Cooperation Officer, Eurojust.

Marie-Laurence HÉBERT-DOLBEC – PhD in Law, Université Libre de Bruxelles. Lecturer in International Law, Université Libre de Bruxelles and Université Catholique de Lille.

Diana IONESCU – PhD in Law, Babeş-Bolyai University. Lecturer in Law, Faculty of Law, Babeş-Bolyai University in Cluj-Napoca.

Vaios KOUTROULIS – Prof Dr Law, Professor of Public International Law, International Law Centre, Faculty of Law, Université Libre de Bruxelles.

Adam LAZOWSKI – Prof Dr Law, Professor of EU Law, Westminster Law School, University of Westminster, London. Visiting Professor at the College of Europe (Natolin) and at Ivan Franko University of Lviv (Ukraine).

Ārija MEIKALIŠA – Prof Dr Law, Head of Department of Criminal Law at the Faculty of Law, University of Latvia.

Liam O'DRISCOLL – PhD Researcher, Dublin City University.

Didier REYNDERS – Former EU Commissioner for Justice, European Commission.

Cristina SÁENZ PÉREZ – PhD in Law, University of Leicester. Lecturer in Law, University of Leeds.

Clémentine SAMRI – Lawyer at the Brussels Bar.

Valeria SCALIA – Prof Dr Law, Professor of Criminal Law, Department of Law of the University of Catania.

Kristine STRADA-ROZENBERGA – Prof Dr Law, Professor of Law, Department of Criminal Law, University of Latvia. Vice Rector for Studies, University of Latvia.

Gintaras ŠVEDAS – Prof Dr Law, Professor of Law, Faculty of Law, Vilnius University.

Suzan VAN DER AA – Prof Dr Law, Professor of Criminal Law and Criminal Procedure, Department of Criminal Law and Criminology, Maastricht University.

Amy WEATHERBURN – PhD in Law, Vrije Universiteit Brussel and Tilburg University. Postdoctoral Fellow Fonds de la Recherche Scientifique (F.R.S-F.N.R.S).

LIST OF ABBREVIATIONS

AFSJ	Area of Freedom, Security and Justice
APS	Advanced Payment Scheme
CC	Criminal Code
CCP	Code of Criminal Procedure
CEDAW	Convention on the Elimination of All Forms of Discrimination against Women
CICS	Criminal Injuries Compensation Scheme
CICr	Code d'instruction criminelle
CICT	Criminal Injuries Compensation Tribunal
CISA	Convention Implementing the Schengen Agreement
CJEU	Court of Justice of the European Union
CJIB	Centraal Justitieel Incassobureau (Central Judicial Collection Agency of the Netherlands)
CJ(VC)A	Criminal Justice (Victims of Crime) Act of Ireland
CoE	Council of Europe
CP	Code pénal
CPE	Code of Punishment Execution (G.Svedas)
DIAV	Inter-Ministerial Delegate for Victim Support
DPP	Office of the Director of Public Prosecutions
EAW	European Arrest Warrant
EC	European Commission
ECHR	European Convention on Human Rights
ECtHR	European Court of Human Rights
ECLAN	European Criminal Law Academic Network
EIGE	European Institute for Gender Equality
EIO	European Investigation Order

EJR	Eurojust Regulation
ENVR	European Network on Victims' Rights
EP	European Parliament
EPM	Protection measures for victims taken in civil matters
EPRS	European Parliamentary Research Service
EPO	European Protection Order
EU	European Union
FRA	European Union Agency for Fundamental Rights
FWD	Framework Decision
GDSACP	General Directorates for Social Assistance and Child Protection
JHA	Justice and Home Affairs
JIT	Joint Investigation Teams
LIBE	Civil Liberties, Justice and Home Affairs Committee
MS	Member States
NGO	Non-governmental organisation
OCG	Organised criminal group
OECD	Organisation for Economic Cooperation and Development
OLAF	The European Anti-Fraud Office
POHCCJ	Prosecutors' Office attached to The High Court of Cassation and Justice of Romania
ROJ	Romanian Official Journal
SCPVOT	European Union Network of Single Contact Points for Victims of Terrorism
TEU	Treaty on the European Union
TFEU	Treaty on the Functioning of the European Union
TPCPP	Titre préliminaire du Code de procedure pénale
UK	United Kingdom
UN	United Nations
VRD	Victims' Rights Directive
VSE	Victim Support Europe
WHO	World Health Organisation

PART I

Introduction

1

Victims' Rights in EU Law – Coming of Age?

JULIA BURCHETT

Initially overlooked but later emerging as a pivotal focus in the EU's area of criminal justice in the early 2000s, the situation of crime victims has steadily gained prominence in the EU's agenda over the past 20 years. Between 2001 and 2013, several major legislative initiatives were introduced, underscoring the EU's commitment to addressing the rights and needs of crime victims through a comprehensive approach developed primarily within the Area of Freedom, Security and Justice (AFSJ). While the EU's efforts to strengthen the role of victims in criminal justice systems have been unwavering, progress has not followed a straightforward path. As with many initiatives in the criminal justice domain, the EU's approach continues to be heavily shaped by the diverse national perspectives that collide on these sensitive issues. To lay the groundwork for the discussion in this collective book, it is essential to provide a brief chronological account of the key milestones that have shaped the EU's legal framework for the protection of victims' rights (section I). Rather than examining these milestones in exhaustive detail – already the subject of significant scholarly work – this overview aims to present a comprehensive picture that highlights the main achievements, challenges and current trends in the field. It will be shown that, while the Lisbon Treaty certainly reinvigorated the EU's efforts in this area, the framework for victims' rights is now entering a new phase, meriting renewed scholarly attention (section II).

I. The Evolving Landscape of Victims' Rights in EU Law

A. A Longstanding Commitment to Advance Victims' Rights and Interests

It is hard to overemphasise just how topical the subject matter addressed in this collective book is. Long considered the 'forgotten party' in criminal proceedings, the resurgence of the subject of victims' rights in the criminal justice arena, which was already observed in the 1970–80s,[1] appears to be gaining renewed momentum. The EU, which is central to this work, may not have been the first actor to have addressed the subject of victims' rights,[2] yet it has undeniably played a significant role in this regard. At a time when the European Community had no competence over criminal matters, the European Parliament[3] and the Court of Justice of the European Union (CJEU)[4] made the issue of compensation for victims of cross-border crime a central concern, closely tied to the principles of free movement and non-discrimination. While the plight of victims in criminal proceedings did not receive ample attention in the early stages of the EU's work on criminal matters, the focus on it has increased since the early 2000s and it now very much has its place on the EU agenda. Several factors have contributed to this shift. The establishment of the AFSJ, as envisioned by the Treaty of Amsterdam, paved the way for a diversification of concerns in the criminal justice sector, characterised notably by greater focus on the protection of individuals, particularly suspects and victims. A political consensus on setting minimum standards for the protection of victims of crime can be traced back in the conclusions of the European Council of Tampere,[5] with the former third pillar serving as the foundation for significant initiatives in this regard. One of the most noteworthy is Council Framework Decision 2001/220/JHA of 15 March 2001 on the standing of victims in criminal proceedings, which represented the first hard law instrument dedicated to safeguarding the rights of victims of crime, and one of the few at that time dedicated to harmonising procedural rights in criminal matters.[6] It is also worth noting some legislation that has considered the specific needs of vulnerable victim categories as part of the EU's efforts to harmonise substantive criminal law in specific crime sectors.[7] Notwithstanding the importance of the measures adopted under the third pillar, European Community law, in particular the principle of free movement as interpreted by the CJEU, has played a crucial role in advancing victims' rights and interests. To ensure that victims of cross-border crime can receive fair and appropriate compensation regardless of where they move in the EU, the EU legislator adopted

[1] See J Doak, *Victims' Rights, Human Rights and Criminal Justice. Reconceiving the Role of Third Parties* (Hart Publishing, 2008) 7 ff.

[2] From the 1980s onwards, significant instruments were adopted at international and European level with the aim of improving the position of victims in the criminal justice system. For an account of the Council of Europe instruments on victims' rights and the case law of the European Court of Human Rights (ECtHR), see in this volume the contribution by L Bachmaier, 'Council of Europe Instruments and the Case Law of the ECtHR: What Influence on EU Law?' in chapter 7. For an overview of pioneering international instruments recognising victims' rights in criminal proceedings, see in this volume the contribution by V Koutroulis and M-L Hébert-Dolbec, 'The Participation of Victims in International Criminal Trials: A Way Forward?' in chapter 8.

[3] Resolution of the European Parliament on compensation for victims of acts of violence, 13 March 1981; Resolution of the European Parliament on compensation for victims of violent crimes, 12 September 1989.

[4] Case 186/87 *Cowan* EU:C:1989:47.

[5] Presidency Conclusions, Tampere European Council, 15 and 16 October 1999, para 32.

[6] Council Framework Decision 2001/220/JHA of 15 March 2001 on the standing of victims in criminal proceedings [2001] OJ L82/1.

[7] See former Council Framework Decision of 18 July 2002 on combating trafficking in human beings [2002] OJ L203/1; former Council Framework Decision 2004/68/JHA of 22 December 2003 on combating the sexual exploitation of children and child pornography [2004] OJ L13/44; Council Framework Decision of 13 June 2002 on combating terrorism [2002] OJ L164/3.

Directive 2004/80/EC relating to compensation for victims of crime,[8] thereby codifying the CJEU's decision in the *Cowan* case.[9]

The abolition of the pillar structure by the Treaty of Lisbon along with the introduction of a new legal basis in Article 82(2)(c) of the Treaty on the Functioning of the European Union (TFEU), explicitly granting the EU competence to establish minimum rules regarding the rights of victims of crime, has certainly provided fresh impetus to the EU's engagement in this sector. Since then, the situation of victims of crime has gradually become a political priority for the EU, with the EU calling for better consideration of their rights within national criminal justice systems while ensuring that their needs for protection, support and access to justice are met.[10] A significant milestone in this direction was reached in 2012 with the adoption of the landmark Directive 2012/29/EU establishing minimum standards on the rights, support and protection of victims of crime, and replacing the Framework Decision of 2001.[11] Alongside this major development, the goal of ensuring that victims of crime can move safely and enjoy effective protection within a common area of justice has led to the adoption of two key instruments based on the principle of mutual recognition. These include Directive 2011/99/EU of 13 December 2011 on the European protection order,[12] which was adopted on the legal basis of Article 82(1)(a) and (d) TFEU and applies to protection measures adopted in criminal matters. The disparities in the nature of protection measures across national legislations necessitated the adoption of a second complementary instrument, Regulation (EU) 606/2013 of June 2013 on the mutual recognition of protection measures in civil matters[13] based on Article 81(2)(a)(e) and (f) TFEU.

Recent decades have therefore seen significant initiatives demonstrating the EU's commitment to ensuring that the needs and interests of victims of crime are duly considered within the development of the AFSJ. The EU's efforts extend beyond merely addressing the plight of victims of crime in cross-border situations. Indeed, the broader ambition to contribute to the enhancement of the position of victims in criminal proceedings is particularly notable and has remained a constant focus of the EU's work. A holistic approach is furthermore traceable in the means mobilised by the EU to support victims' rights, encompassing not only legislative instruments but also funding opportunities and awareness raising activities. Despite the EU's consistent efforts to enhance the position of victims within national criminal justice systems, with tangible progress achieved, assessments reveal persistent gaps preventing crime victims from fully exercising their rights.

[8] Council Directive 2004/80/EC of 29 April 2004 relating to compensation to crime victims (Compensation Directive) [2004] OJ L261/15.

[9] *Cowan* (n 4).

[10] European Council, 'The Stockholm Programme – An Open and Secure Europe Serving and Protecting Citizens' [2010] OJ C115/1.

[11] Directive 2012/29/EU of the European Parliament and of the Council of 25 October 2012 establishing minimum standards on the rights, support and protection of victims of crime, and replacing Council Framework Decision 2001/220/JHA (2012) OJ L315/57 (Victims' Rights Directive).

[12] Directive 2011/99/EU of the European Parliament and of the Council on the European protection order [2011] OJ L338/2.

[13] Regulation (EU) 606/2013 of June 2013 on mutual recognition of protection measures in civil matters [2013] OJ L181/4.

B. Entering a New and More Mature Phase?

i. *A Renewed Push for Action Driven by the Need to Address Persistent Gaps*

Significant shortcomings have been identified concerning the Victims' Rights Directive, which has been the focus of numerous evaluation reports produced by EU institutions and bodies between 2017 and 2022.[14] If incomplete and/or incorrect transposition were identified as an important part of the problem, gaps were also attributed to practical difficulties encountered by Member States in implementing certain rights outlined in the Directive, as well as deficiencies stemming from the lack of clarity in some of its provisions, to name but a few.[15] Overall, it is widely acknowledged that, while the Victims' Rights Directive has expanded and strengthened minimum standards in relation to victims' rights compared to the largely ineffective 2001 Framework Decision, the results are still not fully satisfactory, and there is still room for improvements in many respects.[16] Several experts have also made key contributions on these issues, identifying weaknesses in relation to other instruments that are part of the EU's *acquis* on victims' rights. In spite of that all Member States now have a State compensation scheme in place, the implementation of Directive 2004/80/EC remains somewhat inadequate, and compensation of victims in cross-border situations continues to face numerous obstacles, as highlighted by the former Special Adviser to the President of the Commission[17] and several scholars.[18] One recurring criticism lies in the leeway left to Member States in interpreting certain key terms in the Directive in a narrow way, resulting in some crime victims being excluded from the benefits of State compensation provisions under EU law.[19] While the CJEU cannot fill in all the gaps left by the EU legislator, it has gradually played a crucial role in curtailing Member States' discretion, thereby preventing interpretations that would render the cooperation mechanism established under Directive 2004/80/EC ineffective.[20] This has required the Court to navigate ambiguous

[14] See, ie, A Scherrer and I Kristo, 'The Victims' Rights Directive 2012/29/EU. European Implementation Assessment' (2017) European Parliamentary Research Service, PE 611.022; European Parliament Resolution of 30 May 2018 on the implementation of Directive 2012/29/EU establishing minimum standards on the rights, support and protection of victims of crime, P8_TA (2018)0229; European Union Agency for Fundamental Rights (FRA), 'Victims' Rights as Standards of Criminal Justice. Justice for Victims of Violent Crime Part I' (2019); Commission, 'Report from the Commission to the European Parliament and the Council on the implementation of Directive 2012/29/EU' COM(2020) 188 final; Commission Staff Working Document, 'Evaluation of Directive 2012/29/EU of the European Parliament and of the Council of 25 October 2012 establishing minimum standards on the rights, support and protection of victims of crime, and replacing Council Framework Decision 2001/220/JHA' SWD (2022) 179 final.

[15] See, notably, in this volume, the contribution by L Altan, 'Transforming EU Victims' Laws into Reality for Victims: Developing a Strategic Framework fro the Implementation of Victims' Rights' in chapter 20.

[16] For a discussion on gaps in the harmonisation of crime victims' rights see A Lazowski, '"Tra il dire e il fare c'è di mezzo il mare": Harmonisation of Victims' Rights in EU Criminal Law' in K Lenaerts and et al. (eds), *Shaping a Genuine Area of Freedom, Security and Justice. Perspective on AFSJ Developments as a Driving Force of EU Law. Essays in Honour of Lars Bay Larsen* (Hart Publishing, 2024) 219–229.

[17] J Milquet, 'Strengthening Victims' Rights: from Compensation to Reparation' (Report European Commission, 2019); Also see Council of the European Union, 'Draft Council Conclusions on Victims' Rights' [2019] 14056/19.

[18] See E Sellier and A Weyembergh (eds), *Criminal Procedures and Cross-Border Cooperation in the EU Area of Criminal Justice. Together but Apart?* (l'Université Libre de Bruxelles, 2020) 397–400.

[19] Case 122/13 *Paola C v Presidenza del Consiglio dei Ministri* ECLI: EU:C:2014:59.

[20] Case 601/14 *European Commission v Italian Republic* ECLI: EU:C:2016:759; Case 129/19 *Prezidenza del Consiglio dei Ministri* ECLI: EU:C:2020:566; Case 126/23 *Burdene* ECLI:EU:C:2024:937.

concepts and vague provisions – often the result of delicate political compromises.[21] Despite the Court's case law in this area remaining relatively limited, its potential to positively influence national compensation systems should not be underestimated, as demonstrated by some contributions in this book.[22]

Similarly, several empirical studies have highlighted the ineffectiveness of mutual recognition instruments applicable to victim protection in cross-border cases, largely due to a lack of awareness among victims and practitioners coupled with practical difficulties in their use.[23] Evaluating the overall coherence of the measures adopted by the EU, some comparative studies have also revealed a problematic disconnect among various instruments within the EU's 'toolbox' for victims' rights.[24] Efforts to address these deficiencies and make the implementation of EU minimum rules on victims' rights more effective have been a central priority for the European Commission since 2020. This commitment has prompted an initial series of measures, mobilising a range of tools at its disposal, from infringement proceedings, to softer measures such as financial support, while also considering the possibility of legislative action. Additionally, steps have been taken to enhance coordination among stakeholders involved in this sector and to engage in a collective reflection on potential long-term improvements. These efforts culminated in the adoption of the first EU Strategy on victims' rights for 2020–2025[25] along with the creation of the position of the Commission Coordinator for victims' rights in 2020. From this non-exhaustive overview, it becomes evident that fresh impetus is being injected into the victims' rights sector at the EU level. Recent crises and societal changes detrimental to victims' rights appear to have further underscored the necessity to modernise the EU's legal framework on victims' rights.

ii. Societal Challenges as Catalysts for Developing a Modern and Resilient EU Framework for Victims' Rights

According to the European Commission, around 75 million people in the EU are victims of crime every year.[26] One of the most recent surveys by the EU's Agency for Fundamental Rights (FRA) states that more than 22 million people experienced physical violence in one year in the EU.[27] Moreover, due to increasing intra-EU mobility, many of such cases present a cross-border element, posing additional challenges to

[21] See in this volume the contribution by A Łazowski, 'The Flood that Never Came: Case Law of the Court of Justice on the Victims' Rights Acquis' in chapter 4.

[22] See in this volume the contribution by L O' Driscoll, 'Being "Fair and Appropriate" to Victims of Violent Crime: Evaluating the Provision of State Compensation in the European Union' in chapter 5.

[23] Sellier and Weyembergh (n 17) 406 ff; Research report ARTEMIS, 'Promoting the Right of Women through the Application of the EC Directive 2011/99/EU and the European Protection Order' (2020). See also in this volume the contribution by J Carmona Bermejo and E Fréjabue, 'Eurojust's Role in Enhancing Victims' Rights in Cross-Border Criminal Cases' in chapter 6.

[24] Sellier and Weyembergh (n 17) 399, 412–15, 429–30.

[25] Communication from the Commission to the European Parliament, the Council, the European Economic and Social Committee and the Committee of the Regions, 'EU Strategy on Victims' Rights (2020-2025)' COM(2020) 258 final.

[26] See the dedicated page on the European Commission's website to victims' rights in the EU, availableathttps://commission.europa.eu/strategy-and-policy/policies/justice-and-fundamental-rights/criminal-justice/protecting-victims-rights/victims-rights-eu_en.

[27] FRA, 'Crime, Safety and Victims' Rights' (Fundamental Rights Survey, 2021) 18.

victims and judicial authorities.[28] Victims may, for instance, experience further difficulties when seeking to assert their rights in another State than their country of residence due to language barriers and/or lack of understanding of the foreign judicial system.[29] In complex cross-border cases involving a large number of victims, obstacles may arise in terms of identifying them and organising their participation in different trials without running the risk of secondary victimisation.[30] The issues faced by crime victims have gained increasing visibility in recent years due to several factors that have tested their protection. In this regard, Europol reports that the Covid-19 pandemic lockdowns saw a significant surge in domestic violence, child sexual abuse and cybercrime.[31] The evolution of criminal activities, particularly the increase in crimes facilitated by new technologies, also presents new challenges for effectively protecting victims.[32] Additionally, the resurgence of conflicts affecting a large number of civilians in several regions in and near Europe contributes to increasing attention on victims' needs. Although external to the EU, conflict situations typically involve a significant number of vulnerable migrants seeking protection within the EU, necessitating greater coordination among EU Member States.[33] These factual elements highlight the timeliness of issues concerning the protection of victims' rights and the evolving nature of the challenges associated with it.

While the EU has long demonstrated a commitment to ensuring that the interests of victims are duly considered in criminal justice systems, this commitment has only strengthened in recent years. European institutions have made the protection of victims' rights one of the top priorities on the EU's agenda, as evidenced by ongoing legislative initiatives aimed at enhancing the EU legal framework for the protection of victims' rights, coupled with major awareness-raising campaigns.[34] Notable among these initiatives is the adoption of a proposal for a Directive specifically dedicated to combating violence against women and domestic violence by the Commission on 8 March 2022.[35] This was recently adopted on 14 May 2024,[36] representing the first-ever binding EU legal instrument to combat violence against women and domestic violence. Additionally,

[28] As stated by Eurojust's factsheet on 'Eurojust's Role in Safeguarding Victims' Rights in Cross-Border Crime' (2022), the complexity of cross-border cases makes it especially difficult for judicial authorities to protect victims' rights; also see 'Report on Eurojust's Casework on Victims' Rights. A Contribution to the European Commission Coordinator for Victims' Rights Mapping Exercise'(2022).

[29] See in this volume the contribution by A Ferenczi, 'The Protection of Victims at EU Level: The Need for Cross-Border Cooperation and Coordination' in chapter 19.

[30] See the dedicated page on Eurojust, available at www.eurojust.europa.eu/annual-report-2021/safeguarding-victims-rights.

[31] Europol, 'Exploiting Isolation: Offenders and Victims of Online Child Sexual Abuse' (2020); Europol, 'Catching the Virus. Cybercrime, Disinformation and the Covid-19 Pandemic' (2020); Europol 'How COVID-19-related Crime Infected Europe during 2020' (2020).

[32] Eurojust, Overview Report, 'Challenges and Best Practices from Eurojust's Casework in the Area of Cybercrime' (2020). Also see Council of the European Union, 'Draft Council Conclusions on Victims' Rights' (n 16); N Lomba, C Navarra and M Fernandes, 'Combating Gender-Based Violence: Cyberviolence. European Added Value Assessment' (European Parliamentary Research Service, 2021).

[33] See FRA, 'Fundamental Rights Implications for the EU of the War in Ukraine' (2023).

[34] See European Commission's campaign website 'Keep Your Eyes Open', available at https://victims-rights.campaign.europa.eu/en/about.

[35] European Commission, 'Proposal for a Directive of the European Parliament and of the Council on combating violence against women and domestic violence' COM(2022) 105 final.

[36] Directive (EU) 2024/1385 of the European Parliament and of the Council of 14 May 2024 on combating violence against women and domestic violence [2024] OJ L2024/1385.

the European Commission's ambition to revise the Victims' Rights Directive, which currently stands as the flagship instrument for victim protection within the EU, materialised through a concrete initiative on 12 July 2023.[37] Negotiations regarding this latest initiative are still ongoing, with the adoption of the Council's General Approach[38] paving the way for the opening of trilogues.

II. A Changing Landscape Calling for Renewed Reflection

In light of these new dynamics, this collective reflection seeks to provide some answers to the questions that prompted this research project. Foremost among these is whether the EU's approach to victims' rights is coherently aligned with its established objectives and develops in accordance with the framework set by the treaties and the fundamental principles of EU criminal law. This inquiry has highlighted the necessity to explore several research avenues, including whether the coexistence of a variety of EU instruments, spanning different generations, with both horizontal and sectoral scope – sometimes mobilising legal bases outside the realm of EU criminal law – constitutes an adequate and coherent framework for the protection of victims' rights. This scattered landscape inevitably called for a comprehensive evaluation, considering both approximation efforts and the mutual recognition and cooperation instruments specifically focused on victims' rights, as well as related instruments adopted within the wider AFSJ. To recreate a unified and integrated vision that enhances understanding of the EU framework for the protection of victims' rights – its strengths and remaining loopholes – the perspective of national law also proved to be an essential component of this analysis. This led to the critical question of what lessons can be drawn about the integration of European texts into national legal systems? The insights gained from this research aim to foster broader discussions on the possible emergence of a European model in the field of victims' rights, one capable of ensuring adequate protection for all crime victims while respecting the key principles and balances underlying the EU's area of criminal justice.

While these initial questions have greatly shaped the lines of reflections proposed in this collective work, both the acceleration of EU legislative initiatives in this field, along with the discussions held during the European Criminal Law Academic Network (ECLAN) 2023 Annual Conference, have further influenced the direction of this collective book. Indeed, despite over 20 years of efforts to make victims' rights a core dimension of the AFSJ, the new surge of mobilisation to address persistent gaps raises the question as to whether the EU's actions in this field are reaching a new and more mature phase. In this respect, it is worth considering whether the current EU reforms are sufficiently ambitious and what their implications might be: are we witnessing a

[37] European Commission, Proposal for a Directive of the European Parliament and of the Council amending Directive 2012/29/EU establishing minimum standards on the rights, support and protection of victims of crime, and replacing Council Framework Decision 2001/220/JHA, COM(2023) 424 final.

[38] Council of the European Union, Proposal for a Directive of the European Parliament and of the Council amending Directive 2012/29/EU establishing minimum standards on the rights, support and protection of victims of crime, and replacing Council Framework Decision 2001/220/JHA – General approach, 11260/24 (2024).

mere strengthening of the EU minimum standards on victims' rights, or are we entering a new phase characterised by greater prominence of victims within criminal justice systems across Europe? To what extent do the proposed legislative changes risk affecting the balancing of interests in criminal proceedings, and what impact might they have on the overall coherence of European criminal law? These are just a few of the key questions that this book explores.

The need for renewed reflection on these questions is further underscored by the limited scholarly attention devoted to this fast evolving area of EU law.

A. An Opportunity to Fill Scholarly Gaps

Despite advancements in victims' position across various criminal justice systems and strong EU support for this trend, it is notable that the topic has not consistently received attention in European criminal law literature. Beyond a few seminal works tracing the progressive development of victims' rights in EU law,[39] along with some collective reflections exploring the implications of the rise of the victim in the criminal scene in Europe,[40] research in this area remains uneven and does not reflect the most recent developments. Given that the issue of victims' rights touches on sensitive matters and may challenge the traditional understanding of modern criminal justice, in which a criminal trial is mainly perceived as a de-privatised conflict between the State and the accused,[41] it does not enjoy unanimous support within legal scholarship and legal practitioners. Indeed, while some academics advocate for strengthening victims' rights, others see it as a potential threat to the fairness of the criminal proceedings.[42]

Regardless of the diverging doctrinal perspectives on these issues, it is interesting to see that a number of observations made several years ago still resonate today. The first pertains to the acknowledgment of a complex and fragmented landscape. While this piecemeal approach arises mainly from the evolving EU institutional framework, in addition to the overlapping of horizontal and sectoral instruments applicable to victims, and the need to account for the diversity of national legal systems, it is not without challenges. The identification of a disconnect between harmonisation instruments and texts related to cooperation and mutual recognition has prompted some

[39] S De Biolley and A Weyembergh, 'L'espace pénal européen et les droits des victimes' (2005) 31 *Revue de la Faculté de droit de l'ULB* 93–122; L Lupària and J Della Torre, 'Victims of Crime in the Area of Freedom, Security and Justice' in I Sànchez and M-G Pascual (eds), *Fundamental Rights in the EU Area of Freedom Security and Justice* (Cambridge University Press, 2021) 312–29; C Saas, 'La progression d'un statut des victimes en droit de l'Union européenne' (2016) 38 *Les cahiers de la sécurité et de la justice* 88–96.

[40] G Giudicelli-Delage and C Lazerges, *La victime sur la scène pénale en Europe* (Presses Universitaires de France, 2008); L Lupária, *Victims and Criminal Justice. European Standards and National Good Practices* (Wolters Kluwer, 2015).

[41] See K Braun, *Victims' Participation Rights. Variation Across Criminal Justice Systems* (Palgrave Studies in Victims and Victimology, Palgrave Macmillan, 2019) 20.

[42] A Klip, 'On Victim's Rights and Its Impact on the Rights of the Accused' (2015) 23 *European Journal of Crime, Criminal Law and Criminal Justice* 177–90; FRA, 'Justice for Victims of Violent Crimes, Part I' (2019) 9. For another skeptical perspective, see P Caeiro, 'Introduction (or: every criminal procedure starts with a bill of rights)' in P Caiero et al (eds), *The European Union Agenda on Procedural Safeguards for Suspects or Accused Persons: The "Second Wave" and its Predictable Impact on Portuguese Law* (Law Institute University of Coimbra, 2015) 14.

researchers to call for a more inclusive and integrated approach.[43] Greater alignment in this regard is even more desirable given that Article 82(2) TFEU establishes a functional link between these two mechanisms, conditioning the use of harmonisation as a means to facilitate mutual recognition. Ensuring complementarity within the EU toolbox for victims' rights becomes especially acute in the current legislative context, marked by the proliferation of sectoral instruments coupled with the ambition to elevate the minimum standards derived from horizontal instruments. Feeding into prior reflections, various themes discussed in this volume will aim to explore the potential for these legislative developments to result or not in a more comprehensive and integrated framework. Marking a step in this direction, some of the proposed amendments to the Victim's Rights Directive appear to establish new links with the Compensation Directive, which is to be welcomed. However, is this truly sufficient to overcome the difficulties faced by victims in obtaining compensation for the harm that they have suffered? This might trigger further scrutiny of the decision to revise the horizontal instrument represented by the Victims' Rights Directive while leaving the Compensation Directive untouched.[44] Recent legislative developments aimed at preventing and combating domestic and gender-based violence, due to their connections with other existing instruments applicable to this particularly vulnerable category of victims, also warrant special attention. As shown by some contributions in this volume, despite major advances, the persistent lack of common minimum standards regulating cross-border protection measures seems to be the missing piece of a comprehensive EU framework for the protection of victims of gender-based violence.[45]

The Victims' Rights Directive has been widely described as the most comprehensive and advanced EU instrument in the field,[46] justifying the central attention it receives in this book.[47] It undoubtedly serves as the cornerstone of the EU's framework for protecting victims' rights, reflecting the EU's commitment to addressing victims' issues through a holistic approach. This is particularly evident in the scope of this instrument, both in terms of the rights recognised and the victims covered. The Directive establishes a series of rights applicable to all victims of crime, excluding legal persons or the State,[48] within and at the periphery of criminal proceedings. Thus, the minimum standards set by this instrument do not only aim at enhancing the victim's position within the criminal proceedings, but also, more broadly, at facilitating their access to justice by obligating Member States to provide them with appropriate information and support measures (also known as 'service rights' or 'peripherical rights'). In this respect, it is noteworthy that while the EU and the Council of Europe (CoE) appear to be moving in a similar

[43] See Sellier and Weyembergh (n 17) 399, 412–15, 429–30.

[44] See O' Driscoll (n 21).

[45] See in this volume the contribution by C Sáenz Pérez, 'Protecting Vulnerable Victims: An Analysis of the EU Legal Framework for Victims of Gender-Based Violence' in chapter 3.

[46] See Lupária (n 39) 323.

[47] See notably the contribution in this volume by C Chioni-Chotouman, 'Victims' Rights in the EU: Boosting the Recognition and Participation of Victims in Criminal Proceedings' in chapter 2.

[48] This exclusion, which can be inferred from Art 2(1) of the Victims' Rights Directive (n 11), was confirmed by the CJEU in case 603/19, *TG and UF*, ECLI: EU:C:2020:774. As clarified by the Court, Art 2(1) of the Victims' Rights Directive, ibid, must be interpreted as meaning that that Directive does not apply to legal persons or to the State, even if national law confers on them the status of injured party in criminal proceedings.

direction, the holistic approach promoted by the latter seems to go even further by seeking to develop and expand victims' rights and services not only within the context of criminal proceedings, but also before, after, or irrespective of such proceedings.[49] Another key feature highlighting the wide scope of the Victims' Rights Directive can be found within the definition of victims. In this regard, the approach taken by the EU legislator is clearly more inclusive than that of the previous 2001 Framework Decision, though it appears somewhat more restrictive in certain aspects compared to international law definitions.[50] Particularly notable of this inclusive approach is the fact that the Victims' Rights Directive applies not only to EU citizens. As stated in Recital 10, 'Member States must ensure that the rights conferred by the directive are not dependent on the victim's residence status on their territory or on the victim's citizenship or nationality'. Furthermore, Recital 13 specifies that the said Directive confers rights on victims of extra-territorial offences provided that these are in relation to criminal proceedings taking place in the Union. This clarification is of particular significance in a context where international conflicts create numerous victims seeking refuge within the EU, placing them in a vulnerable situation to enforce and protect their rights. Increased recognition of the vulnerable situation of non-EU resident victims appears to be reflected in the proposed revision of the Victims' Rights Directive, suggesting potential new synergies between EU law and international law.[51] However, as highlighted in some contributions in this volume, victims of war crimes and warfare may encounter significant barriers in asserting their status as direct victims under the Victims' Rights Directive, raising questions about the extent of protection offered to them under EU law.[52] Although this transversal instrument, along with sectoral instruments for specific vulnerable groups, represent substantial progress towards a comprehensive framework for protecting all crime victims regardless of where the crime took place, there remains room to question whether certain aspects of victims' rights are still neglected, leaving loopholes in the EU's approach.[53]

The second observation lies in the relatively modest level of ambition in the European texts adopted in this sector, leaving significant leeway for Member States in transposing certain key provisions – a critique often recurring in the scholarly debate.[54] The aspiration for unity while accomodating diversity is a familiar tension in the EU's area of criminal justice,[55] and it is especially pronounced when it comes to victims' rights. Differences between Member States' legal regimes are particularly strong here and must

[49] See the contribution in this volume by Bachmaier (n 2).

[50] See the contribution in this volume by V Koutroulis and M-L Hébert-Dolbec, 'The Participation of Victims in International Criminal Trials: A Way Forward?' in chapter 8.

[51] ibid.

[52] See Bachmaier (n 2).

[53] See in this regard S van der Aa, 'Post-Trial Victims' Rights in the EU: Do Law Enforcement Motives Still Reign Supreme' (2015) 21 *European Law Journal* 239–56; See also the contribution in this volume by A Weatherburn, '(Human Trafficking) Victims on the Margins of Protection: The (In)coherence of Sectoral Instruments?' in chapter 16.

[54] See F Catteau, 'Les droits procéduraux des personnes poursuivies et des victimes de criminalité devant la Cour de justice de l'Union européenne. Vers un droit européen de la procédure pénale?' (2020) *Cahiers de droit européen* 485–547.

[55] See A Weyembergh, *L'harmonisation des législations : condition de l'espace pénal européen et révélateur de ses tensions* (l'Université de Bruxelles, 2004) 38–39.

be taken into account by the EU legislator, inevitably impacting the content and scope of the final EU acts adopted. This has resulted in significant flexibility in EU cross-border cooperation instruments to reconcile these national differences. Similarly, the challenges involved in harmonising widely varying legal systems have compelled the EU legislator to find a conciliatory approach, largely reflected in the wording of some provisions and the decision not to alter the role of the victim as defined by national law. Hence, despite the fact that the Victims' Rights Directive is a second generation instrument making a significant step forward, it has been widely criticised for allowing too much leeway to the Member States and for being overly willing to compromise,[56] which rather suggests an approximation 'en trompe l'oeil'.[57] This collective reflection is intended to further enhance the understanding of the challenges surrounding the integration of EU texts into national legal systems through the lens of national law perspectives.[58] By offering a representative overview of the various national models currently in place, this book highlights how the prevailing diversity adds an additional layer of fragmentation to the European landscape of victims' rights. This is notably evident when considering the definition of a 'victim', which is crucial for determining who can qualify as such and claim the rights associated with such a status. The Court of Justice has recently elevated this notion to the status of an 'autonomous concept' of EU law, ensuring that it is interpreted consistently across EU instruments in accordance with the definition set out in Article 2 of the Victims' Rights Directive.[59] Despite the progressive construction of a victim status in European law, the victim emerges as a multifaceted figure without a clearly defined overall image. Even in Member States where the term 'victim' has a legal basis, it is enshrined in a variety of sources and lacks a unified definition.[60] Besides, the blurred distinctions with related concepts such as 'injured person' or 'aggrieved party' – each granting variable prerogatives – further complicate the emergence of a clear victim figure. This situation has not only been identified as creating legal uncertainty to the detriment of the protection of victims,[61] but also raises the fundamental question: who is considered a victim in EU criminal law?

This overview of national approaches will prompt consideration of the varying influence of EU law on national legal systems, highlighting the low level of harmonisation achieved and the gaps that sometimes exist between formal compliance with EU texts and their practical implementation. While recent legislative initiatives seem to open up new avenues towards clearer and higher standards of protection, the need to accommodate the vast diversity of national legal systems continues to influence their negotiations

[56] FRA (n 41).

[57] See D Flore, 'Droit pénal et Union européenne' in G de Kerchove et A Weyembergh (eds), *Quelles réformes pour l'espace pénal européen?* (l'Université de Bruxelles, 2003) 73.

[58] See 'Part III: Selected National Perspectives on Victims' Rights Across the EU: Major Trends and EU Law Impact' in this volume.

[59] Case 126/23 *Burdene* ECLI: EU:C:2024:937.

[60] See in particular the contribution in this volume by M Alié and C Samri, 'Victims' Rights in Belgian Law: Significant Progress due to the Influence of EU law but Still Gaps to be Filled' in chapter 9. Also see the contribution by S van der Aa on Dutch law, 'Victim Rights in the Netherlands: Unconditional Compliance or Pursuing the National Agenda?' in chapter 10.

[61] See Alié and Samri, ibid.

markedly.[62] This is likely due to the fact that some proposed innovations seem to imply a significant shift for certain national legal systems, and the financial costs involved in these reforms remain a major concern for Member States.[63] Hence, recent developments aimed at enhancing the EU legal framework for the protection of victims' rights require a careful analysis to better assess the extent and implications of these changes.

A third area of reflection, which continues to generate significant debate, concerns the balance between victims' rights and the rights of suspects and defendants in criminal proceedings. Indeed, the rising prominence of the victim inevitably raises questions about its impact on the interests and equilibrium at play in criminal trials. Beyond the doctrinal perspectives that clash over these issues – some advocating for strengthening the victim's position, while others view it as a threat to the fairness of criminal proceedings – there is a need to consider this issue in light of the coherent development of the EU area of criminal justice. In this regard, several commentators regret that these two dimensions of harmonisation of procedural rights, concerning victims' rights and suspects' rights respectively, have developed largely independently of one another despite being intertwined[64] – a situation that persists today.[65] The connections between victims' rights and suspects' rights are not entirely absent from EU instruments – and despite its limited contribution, the CJEU has had an opportunity to balance the interests of victims and suspects in interpreting the Victims' Rights Directive[66] – but they remain relatively tenuous. The Victims' Rights Directive conditions certain rights recognised for victims on the requirement that they do not prejudice the fairness of the proceedings and the rights of the defence,[67] leaving some ambiguity as to which rights prevail in case of conflict. Conversely, references to victims are largely absent from the directives on the rights of suspects and the accused.[68] By way of comparison, while the EU addressed victim's rights well before it tackled the rights of suspects, the former were enshrined in much vaguer terms, allowing greater latitude for Member States.

[62] See Altan (n 15). Also see Council of the European Union, Proposal for a Directive of the European Parliament and of the Council amending Directive 2012/29/EU establishing minimum standards on the rights, support and protection of victims of crime, and replacing Council Framework Decision 2001.220/JHA – General approach (n 37).

[63] See van der Aa (n 59).

[64] Klip (n 41) 177–89; Also see Catteau (n 53) 526–43.

[65] See in this volume the contribution by L Baudrihaye-Gérard, 'Towards More Rights for Victims to Participate in Criminal Proceedings? Reflections from the Implementation Experience of EU Defence Rights' in chapter 18.

[66] Case 38/18 *Gambino and Hyka* ECLI:EU:C:2019:628.

[67] See notably Victims' Rights Directive, Arts 7(6), 18, 20 and 23.

[68] Directive 2010/64/EU of the European Parliament and of the Council of 20 October 2010 on the right to interpretation and translation in criminal proceedings [2010] OJ L280; Directive 2012/13/EU of the European Parliament and of the Council of 22 May 2012 on the right to information in criminal proceedings [2012] OJ L142; Directive 2013/48/EU of the European Parliament and of the Council of 22 October 2013 on the right of access to a lawyer in criminal proceedings and in European arrest warrant proceedings, and on the right to have a third party informed upon deprivation of liberty and to communicate with third persons and with consular authorities while deprived of liberty [2013] OJ L294; Directive 2016/343 of the European Parliament and of the Council of 9 March 2016 on the strengthening of certain aspects of the presumption of innocence and of the right to be present at the trial in criminal proceedings [2016] OJ L65; Directive 2016/800 of the European Parliament and of the Council of 11 May 2016 on procedural safeguards for children who are suspects or accused persons in criminal proceedings [2016] OJ L132; Directive 2016/1919 of the European Parliament and of the Council of 26 October 2016 on the legal aid for suspects and accused persons in criminal proceedings and for requested persons in European arrest warrant proceedings [2016] OJ L297.

Similarly, with the exception of certain areas such as the exchange of evidence, the alignment between harmonisation and mutual recognition is much more pronounced with regard to suspects' rights. While it is not a matter of placing victims' rights and defence rights on an equal footing in criminal proceedings,[69] it is nevertheless crucial to ensure that European criminal procedural law develops in a coherent direction, paying equal attention to the fair and adequate protection of all parties involved. This latter concern warrants even more attention as a third-generation instrument for the protection of victims' rights is about to be adopted – while procedural safeguards for suspects and accused persons remained governed by first-generation EU instruments. A more in-depth examination of the adequacy of procedural safeguards for suspects and victims is equally important in light of the current transformations in criminal procedure and trials.[70]

B. Bridging Divides: Building a Cohesive Understanding Shifting from a 'Siloed' Approach

As the title suggests, this book primarily adopts an EU perspective, focusing first and foremost on the EU legal framework applicable to victims' rights, while not limited solely to it. To provide complementary insights, it takes into account other national and supranational legal systems that have worked towards the victim being granted a greater role in criminal proceedings. In order to overcome the fragmentation of the existing EU framework, this collective book will move away from an instrument-by-instrument approach to adopting a comprehensive perspective. Special attention will be paid to the need to ensure complementarity among the various instruments in the EU 'toolbox' while also maintaining coherence with other policies beyond the AFSJ. The book does not claim to cover all sectoral directives containing provisions applicable to victims, nor does it seek to exhaustively address the myriad issues associated with the rights of victims of transnational crimes. Instead, it rather aims to provide a global understanding of the EU framework for the protection of victims' rights, its achievements and challenges, examined in light of the most recent developments.

This book is structured into four main parts, each contributing to its central theme: the evolution of the EU framework for the protection of victims' rights, its implications for developing a coherent model of victim protection within the EU, and its impact on the overall coherence of EU criminal law.

To start with, Part I will underscore the significance of the issue addressed in this book: the evolution towards stronger victims' rights in EU law. The question at hand prompts not only an initial consideration of whether the EU is best positioned to address these issues but also whether stronger EU rules are needed in this field. To set the stage of the ensuing discussion, this introductory part will trace back some major

[69] For an in-depth reflection on these issues see in this volume the contribution by K Strada Rozenberga, 'Do Victims' Rights and Defence Rights Really have to be Equal?' in chapter 17.

[70] Baudrihaye-Gérard (n 64).

developments in the area, emphasising the necessity of initiating a fresh discussion on these issues, integrating various complementary perspectives.

Part II will examine several key EU horizontal and sectoral instruments for the protection of victims' rights, highlighting both the advancements and the limitations of the EU's *acquis* in this field. This will include exploring the opportunities created by recent legislative initiatives adopted by the EU, their ability to redress certain gaps and their contribution to establishing a more coherent and integrated framework. As a complementary perspective, this part will emphasise the significant contribution of instruments adopted within other regional and international legal frameworks, while also identifying mutual interactions with instruments adopted at the EU level.

Following this, Part III will provide an overview of the variety of national legal systems coexisting within the EU regarding the rights of victims. Based on a selection of national cases, this part will seek to gauge the extent to which the role attributed to the victim may vary according to the legal traditions of the Member States, resulting in considerable diversity. In addition to the specificities that may be observed from one national model to another, the aim will be to examine the diverging impact of EU law across national legal systems.

Part IV will shift the attention onto several challenges in the field, emphasising the need for coherence in the interplay of relevant EU instruments and policies, as well as the importance of striking an appropriate balance between victims' rights and other crucial interests. This part will provide an opportunity to highlight potential problematic disconnects among the instruments comprising the EU toolbox and to identify certain gaps that reveal 'forgotten victims' who remain on the margins of the protection provided by European standards. Incorporating a practical perspective, it will also offer an overview of the mechanisms established to facilitate EU-wide cooperation and coordination, including in the context of crisis situations.

Finally, Part V will present a forward-looking perspective on the EU framework for the protection of victims' rights. Building on the gaps identified in both the law and in practice, the aim will be to explore avenues for future improvements. This concluding part will also initiate a deeper reflection, examining whether the EU has succeeded in elaborating a comprehensive model for victims' rights providing all victims with the assistance they need.

PART II

The Protection of Victims' Rights in EU Law and Insights from Regional and International Instruments

2

Victims' Rights in the EU: Boosting the Recognition and Participation of Victims in Criminal Proceedings

CHARA CHIONI-CHOTOUMAN

I. Introduction

The content of the EU directives in the field of criminal law adopted following the entry into force of the Lisbon Treaty reflects a general shift in the European Union's (EU) policy towards the individual. As indicated in the Stockholm Programme, the interests and needs of citizens constitute a priority for the European Council.[1] The first post-Lisbon EU directives aimed to ensure respect for fundamental freedoms while guaranteeing security. In this context, it is evident that safeguarding the rights of citizens who fall victim to crime could not be absent from the legislative agenda, as also emphasised in the Budapest Roadmap on strengthening the rights, support and protection of victims.[2]

With the Lisbon Treaty the word 'victim' was included for the first time in primary law.[3] Article 82(2)(c) of the Treaty on the Functioning of the EU (TFEU) established an explicit legal basis for adopting minimum rules regarding the rights of victims of crime, although limited by the need to consider the differences between the legal systems and traditions of EU Member States.[4] While the rules adopted pertain, as expressly provided in Article 82, to cases of a cross-border nature aiming at facilitating mutual recognition, they entail an obligation to reform the national legal system, thereby also affecting cases that are purely domestic in nature.[5] Restricting their application to cross-border cases

[1] European Council, 'The Stockholm Programme – An Open and Secure Europe Serving and Protecting Citizens' (2010/C 115/01) 1.1.

[2] Resolution of the Council of 10 June 2011 on a Roadmap for strengthening the rights and protection of victims, in particular in criminal proceedings (2011/C 187/01).

[3] See also KM Helmken, *Das Opfer im Strafverfahrensrecht* (Peter Lang, 2019) 55.

[4] See, for those differences, M Daury-Fauveau, 'Le statut de la victime en quête de cohérence' in S Corioland, E Letouzey (eds), *La transposition des directives en droit pénal interne: l'intégration d'un corps étranger* (CEPRISCA-Lextenso, 2017) 158.

[5] See Judgment of the Court of 13 June 2019, Case 646/17 *Moro* ECLI:EU:C:2019:489, paras 30–37, A Wanitschek, *Die Grundrechtecharta der Europäischen Union im Strafverfahren* (Springer, 2018) 205; V Mitsilegas, *EU Criminal Law*, 2nd edn (Hart Publishing, 2022) 258.

would indeed have resulted in the operation of two parallel procedural systems within the same State, with the parties involved in purely national cases finding themselves at a disadvantage.[6] Furthermore, it is difficult to determine from the outset whether a case has a cross-border dimension. Competent authorities shall be able to treat the decisions of judicial authorities in other Member States as equivalent to their own if a cross-border dimension arises, which is facilitated by applying the EU directives' provisions to all cases.[7]

Directive 2012/29,[8] establishing minimum standards on the rights, support and protection of victims of crime (hereinafter 'Directive 2012/29') is therefore affecting national criminal proceedings aiming towards establishing, if not a victim-centered, at least a victim-inclusive justice, in the framework of which victims are not only protected but also informed and heard.

In this chapter, this aspect of Directive 2012/29 aiming at victims' participation in the proceedings will be explored, taking into account the Proposal for a Directive amending Directive 2012/29/EU.[9] Directive 2012/29 includes rights aimed at ensuring that victims are informed, supported, protected and have access to compensation from the offender. It does not treat victims' rights merely as a means to facilitate criminal repression but includes detailed provisions on providing assistance and protection. The following analysis will focus on those rights that have a direct impact on national criminal proceedings, which will be examined alongside the choices included in the Proposal to amend Directive 2012/29, in order to reflect the options at the EU level providing victims with rights that enhance their position and participation in national proceedings. In this framework, two main areas of rights are identified, those related to and facilitating the access to information and those directly ensuring the participation of victims in criminal proceedings. In particular, after a brief description of the legislative evolution leading up to Directive 2012/29, the rights related to providing victims with information, thereby enabling them to actively participate in the proceedings, will be analysed. Subsequently, the rights aiming at ensuring the participation of victims will be examined.

II. Tracing the Path to Directive 2012/29: A Brief Overview

The characteristics of the legal instrument available under the old pillar system, namely the framework decisions, resulted in reduced enforcement of the relevant measures and, ultimately, less protection for victims.[10] After the entry into force of the Lisbon

[6] S van der Aa, 'Post-Trial Victims' Rights in the EU: Do Law Enforcement Motives Still Reign Supreme?' (2015) 21(2) *European Law Journal* 239, 253.

[7] See also *Moro* (n 5) para 35.

[8] Directive 2012/29/EU of the European Parliament and of the Council of 25 October 2012 establishing minimum standards on the rights, support and protection of victims of crime, and replacing Council Framework Decision 2001/220/JHA (2012) OJ L315/57.

[9] Proposal for a Directive of the European Parliament and of the Council amending Directive 2012/29/EU establishing minimum standards on the rights, support and protection of victims of crime, and replacing Council Framework Decision 2001/220/JHA, Brussels, 12.7.2023, COM (2023) 424 final.

[10] EU Citizenship Report 2010, 27.10.2010, COM(2010) 603, 6–7.

Treaty, a legislative initiative to enhance the position of victims within national criminal justice systems through a Directive was announced in the Commission's 2011 Work Programme.[11] The need to analyse and mitigate the differences between EU Member States regarding the protection of victims had already been expressed in 2010.[12] The Commission subsequently presented, in the second quarter of 2011, a proposal for a Directive on the rights, support and protection of victims of crime.[13] It was accompanied by a proposal for a Regulation on mutual recognition of protection measures in civil matters, reflecting a shift toward a more holistic approach to protection.[14] The proposal for a Directive was rather restrained, based on rights already provided in several systems, despite the fact that EU Member States have responded positively and recognised the need to protect victims.[15] Nevertheless, the difference in addressing victims' needs between the former Framework Decision 2001/220 on the standing of victims in criminal proceedings (hereinafter 'the Framework Decision') and the Proposal for a Directive is already evident from the latter's title. Instead of regulations on 'the status of victims in criminal proceedings', the proposal opts for a holistic approach. In particular, an attempt was made to incorporate the five categories of victims' needs, consisting of the need for recognition and appropriate treatment, protection, support, access to justice, as well as compensation and reparation. It is a stance followed in all subsequent actions regarding legislation on crime victims.[16] This approach, which is largely based on the one outlined in CoE Recommendation Rec(2006)8 on assistance to crime victims, served as the basis for Directive 2012/29.

The purpose of Directive 2012/29, as outlined in its first Article, is to ensure that victims are properly informed, supported, protected and able to participate in the criminal proceedings concerning them. It extends beyond an instrumental approach, guaranteeing more than just rights directed to promote criminal repression, by including specific provisions for granting support from specialised services and securing protection during criminal proceedings.[17] This analysis will focus on the provisions that are relevant and have a direct impact on criminal proceedings. Therefore, based on the preceding categorisation, particular emphasis will be placed on the need for recognition and appropriate treatment, as well as access to justice. Reference will also be made to the Proposal for amending Directive 2012/29, which is indicative of the willingness to establish clearer and higher standards for victims' rights at EU level.

[11] Communication from the Commission to the European Parliament, the Council, the European Economic and Social Committee, and the Committee of the Regions, COM (2010) 623 final Vol I, section 3.

[12] Communication from the Commission to the European Parliament, the Council, the European Economic and Social Committee, and the Committee of the Regions, 20.04.2010, COM (2010) 171.

[13] Proposal for a Directive of the European Parliament and of the Council establishing minimum standards on the rights, support and protection of victims of crime, 18.5.2011, COM (2011) 275 final.

[14] Proposal for a Regulation of the European Parliament and of the Council on mutual recognition of protection measures in civil matters, 18.5.2011, COM (2011) 276 final.

[15] B Schünemann, 'Die Vorschläge der Europäischen Kommission für eine Opferschutzrichtlinie' (2011) 12 (3) ERA Forum 445, 458; S Buczma, 'An Overview of the Law Concerning Protection of Victims of Crime in View of the Adoption of the Directive 2012/29/EU Establishing Minimum Standards on the Rights, Support and Protection of Victims of Crime in the European Union' (2013) 14 (2) ERA Forum 235, 242.

[16] Communication from the Commission to the European Parliament, the Council, the Economic and Social Committee, and the Committee of the Regions, 18.5.2011, COM (2011) 274 final.

[17] See also van der Aa (n 6) 240.

III. Access to Information

The first set of rights relates to providing victims with information thereby enabling them to assert their rights and actively participate in the proceedings. Access to information is a key right, as indicated by the fact that this wording is also found in subsequent directives.[18] It was also provided for by the former Framework Decision yet not adequately implemented by EU Member States.[19] Its importance is also highlighted in the Commission's Proposal to amend Directive 2012/29, where Article 3a includes a duty to establish a helpline for victims, ensuring that information can be easily accessed. Directive 2012/29 establishes a duty of substantial disclosure of information that extends throughout the criminal proceedings. To this end, rights related to the facilitation of effective communication between competent authorities and victims, such as the right to interpretation and translation are also provided.[20]

A. The Right to Understand and be Understood

Article 3 establishes the right to effective communication from the victim's first contact with competent authorities. While Directive 2012/29 does not define the term 'competent authority', it can be interpreted as including police, port, and judicial authorities. Entities like hospitals, which may be the first place a victim resorts to, cannot be included, as they have no jurisdiction or formal role in the context of criminal proceedings.[21] Article 3 can be linked to Article 7 on the right to interpretation and translation. The latter requires active participation by competent authorities in ensuring that the victim understands what is being said and can be understood. In this context, the language used should be as simple as possible, taking into account any special circumstances (gender, age, maturity, psychological condition) of the victim.

The victim is also permitted to be accompanied by a person of their choice, yet only during the first interaction with the competent authority. This right pertains to the aftermath of a recent crime which often prevents victims from expressing themselves freely without the presence of a relative, a friend or a competent social worker due to fear and anxiety. It also covers cases where the victim is accompanied by a stranger who assisted them in addressing the authorities and remains there due to the emotional stress.[22] This provision also allows victims to be accompanied by their own interpreters, a common

[18] See Directive (EU) 2019/713 of the European Parliament and of the Council of 17 April 2019 on combating fraud and counterfeiting of non-cash means of payment and replacing Council Framework Decision 2001/413/JHA [2019] OJ L 123/18 and, in particular, Art 16, which includes the provisions of Art 4 of Directive 2012/29 (n 8). See also JM Göhler, *Strafprozessuale Rechte des Verletzten in der Europäischen Union* (Duncker & Humblot, 2019) 130.

[19] R Letschert and M Groenhuijsen, 'Global Governance and Global Crime – Do Victims Fall in Between?' in R Letschert, J van Dijk (eds), *The New Faces of Victimhood: Globalization, Transnational Crimes and Victim Rights* (Springer, 2011) 24.

[20] C Chioni-Chotouman, *Victim's Rights in Criminal Procedure* (in Greek, Nomiki Bibliothiki, 2021) 70.

[21] DG JUSTICE, Guidance Document related to the transposition and implementation of Directive 2012/29/EU, December 2013, 13. See, for the importance of this document in interpreting the Directive's provisions: R Müller-Piepenkötter, 'Die EU-Opferschutz-Richtlinie 2012/29/EU: Handlungsbedarf bei Unterstützungsdiensten in Deutschland' (2016) 28 *Neue Kriminalpolitik* 9, 13.

[22] DG JUSTICE Guidance Document, ibid 12. See also Helmken (n 3) 75.

practice prompted by the economic implications for the Member States in offering interpretation at police stations, particularly for less widely spoken languages. Providing the right for the victim to be accompanied by a person of their choice cannot be denied unless it contradicts the victim's interests or impedes the progress of the proceedings, such as in cases involving a conflict of interests (eg a victim of domestic violence appearing with an intimate partner), which will be determined by the competent authority.[23]

The aim is to guarantee that victims can obtain the necessary information to exercise their rights in criminal proceedings. Although it covers the victim's first contact with the competent authorities, it should be combined with Article 20(c), which allows victims to be accompanied by their legal representative and a person of their choice during criminal investigations.

B. The Right to Receive Information

The right to receive information can be found in different provisions. It is a right where the need to reconcile the diverse national legal systems results in Member States being granted a wide margin of discretion in providing information after the initiation of criminal proceedings.

Article 4 outlines the victims' right to receive information without undue delay when they have a first contact with competent authorities. The relevant information that must be provided to victims is specified in Directive 2012/29, thereby enhancing the applicability of the right. Such applicability is also facilitated by the fact that providing the information is not contingent upon a request from the victim.[24]

The information that should be available to the victims can be put into two main categories: those concerning victim protection and support and those relating to criminal proceedings. Firstly, victims should be informed about the possibility of receiving support, in accordance with the requirement of Article 8(2) of the said Directive for referral to relevant bodies. Additionally, they need to be informed about the procedure for reporting a criminal offence and the role that they can acquire under the national criminal justice system. The competent authorities must also provide information on available protection measures, the conditions for obtaining legal assistance or other types of advice, and how to obtain compensation and reimbursement of any costs. Paragraph 23 of the Preamble emphasises the importance of providing information about the possibility of reimbursement, such as through a leaflet. Although generally the Directives' preambles are not legally binding, this choice reflects a desire to ensure that victims are not deterred from reporting criminal offences due to financial consequences.[25] Victims should also be informed about their right to interpretation and

[23] See DG JUSTICE Guidance Document, ibid 13.

[24] See S Bock, 'Das europäische Opferrechtspaket: zwischen substantiellem Fortschritt und blindem Aktionismus' (2013) 4 *ZIS* 201, 205, who stresses that it is not sufficient for information to be available, for example, on the Internet. See also C Rasquete, A Ferreira and F Moyano Marques, 'Why Do We Need Concrete Measures for Victims at EU Level? A View from the Coalface' (2014) 15(1) *ERA Forum* 119, 124.

[25] On the non-binding character of preambles see Case C-136/04 *Deutsches Milch-Kontor GmbH* ECLI:EU:C:2005:716, [2005] ECR I-10095, para 32, Case C-287/17 *Česká pojišťovna a.s. v WCZ spol. s r.o.* ECLI:EU:C:2018:707, para 33.

translation, as well as more specific information on the applicable protection procedures if they reside in another Member State and are not familiar with the legal system of the State where the offence was committed. Information on complaint procedures in the event of a violation of their rights should also be available, along with communication channels through which victims can receive updates about their case. Finally, information should be provided about the restorative justice services that are available.

This information should also be accessible by telephone if that is how the first contact takes place and they are not contingent upon filing a formal complaint.[26] The level of detail is determined by factors such as the type of crime and the specific characteristics of the victim, with the possibility of providing additional details at a later stage.[27] Competent authorities are thus expected to adopt an individualised approach and to ensure that the victim understands the information. The introduction of an obligation to document the fact that information was provided could also enhance the practical enforcement of this right, as recommended by the Commission.[28]

Article 6 further elaborates on the right to receive information, specifying the information that the victim is entitled to once criminal proceedings are initiated following a complaint. Information should be provided regarding any decision not to proceed with the investigation or prosecution. According to paragraph 3, such a decision must be reasoned and communicated to the victim. Access to the reasoning of such decisions is essential both procedurally, allowing victims to challenge them, and in terms of the need for respect and recognition.[29] Member States are also invited to provide victims with information on the final decision and the status of the criminal proceedings, insofar as this does not hinder the course of the proceedings. However, such information is not provided *ex officio*. Victims have to actively seek it, and each Member State has the flexibility to adapt these obligations to its criminal justice system. This margin of appreciation is of particular importance for criminal justice systems, which provide for a formal procedural status, such as being a civil party. In jurisdictions outlining a distinct formal role for victims opting for it, the legislator may limit the provision of the above information solely to victims who have taken on that role. For instance, a civil party may be notified of the final decision or informed about the status of proceedings, without this being required when the victim chooses not to acquire this procedural status.

By way of innovation, the Proposal for amending Directive 2012/29 aims, through Article 10a, at providing, in addition to emotional support, information at the court premises. It is a provision that aims to address the needs of victims who come to the court premises to testify or attend the proceedings. It increases the openness of a process that can be confusing or intimidating to victims and enhances their active participation.

Finally, as provided under Article 6(5) of Directive 2012/29, victims should be allowed to obtain information regarding the release or escape of the offender, along

[26] DG JUSTICE Guidance Document (n 21) 14. See, however, about enforcement issues, Evaluation of Directive 2012/29/EU of the European Parliament and of the Council of 25 October 2012 establishing minimum standards on the rights, support and protection of victims of crime, and replacing Council Framework Decision 2001/220/JHA, Brussels, 28.6.2022, SWD(2022) 179 final.

[27] Directive 2012/29 (n 8) Art 4, para 2.

[28] See DG JUSTICE Guidance Document (n 21) 15.

[29] ibid 19.

with any protective measures implemented by the competent authorities. This information should be provided upon request, at least in cases where there is a risk to their safety. When assessing the risk, factors such as the nature of the offence and any risk of retaliation should be taken into consideration. Paragraph 33 of the Preamble encourages Member States to ensure that the victim is aware of any right under national law to lodge an appeal against the release decision. It was a topic that sparked heated debates prior to the adoption of the Directive. Consequently, it was decided not to include it in the text as a binding provision and therefore no such right is conferred upon victims.[30]

C. Rights Relating to Filing a Complaint

One of the most important steps in the initiation of criminal proceedings is the lodging of a complaint. Authorities rely heavily on victims' complaints to address the crime. At the same time it constitutes, for victims, an appeal to the State for assistance.

According to Article 5, the victim has the right to obtain a copy of the complaint filed. This right applies whether the victim has contacted the authorities in person or by any other means of communication but, only if the complaint is formal. The necessary elements of this document are specified in the Preamble and include the type, location and time of the offence as well as the file number and the time and place of the complaint.[31] The document should also include any physical or mental-emotional harm, as well as any financial losses. This documentary evidence constitutes a minimum requirement under Directive 2012/29 ensuring transparency and facilitating the pursuit of civil claims.[32]

Regarding the filing of a complaint, the Directive aims to make it easier for victims who don't speak or understand the language of the proceedings. Special measures should also be in place for victims residing in another Member State.[33] Given the importance of establishing adequate reporting mechanisms that ensure a prompt criminal response and improve victim satisfaction with the system, enhancing reporting mechanisms is at the heart of new initiatives. The Proposal for a Directive on combating violence against women and domestic violence gives further concrete form to Member States' obligations by providing, in Article 16, that reporting offences covered therein should be facilitated also by the use of information and communication technologies. Article 17 also implies an obligation for the competent authorities to secure the filing of an official complaint following a report. Aligning with this modern framework, the proposed amendments to Directive 2012/29 include the establishment of communication channels facilitating contact between victims and competent authorities through, *inter alia*, communication technologies.[34]

[30] For discussions within some Member States, see ibid.
[31] Directive 2012/29 (n 8) Preamble, para 24.
[32] See also Helmken (n 3) 80.
[33] Directive 2012/29 (n 8) Art 17.
[34] Proposal for a Directive amending Directive 2012/29/EU (n 9) Art 5a. See also Art 26b.

D. The Right to Translation and Interpretation

The right to interpretation and translation is outlined in Article 7 of Directive 2012/29 for victims who do not speak or understand the language of the proceedings. Victims are entitled to interpretation, which should be provided free of charge at least during their examination in criminal proceedings. This includes questioning by police officers and members of the judiciary as well as testimony during the main hearing. The right is provided to victims 'in accordance with their role in the relevant criminal justice system'. This phrase is not particularly problematic in systems where victims cannot acquire the role of a party in the proceedings, as interpretation will be provided during their examination as witnesses. However, in procedural systems where a distinct formal role is provided for the victim, the question arises as to whether they are entitled to an interpreter when choosing not to acquire this role. The answer should not be negative, as the enjoyment of translation and interpretation is simply linked to the formal role that the victim is entitled to acquire under national law.[35] The status of the witness also constitutes a formal role. As discussed regarding the right to receive information, a victim choosing not to participate as a party in the proceedings still retains the right to interpretation and translation, although to a lesser extent. For instance, a victim appearing as a witness is not entitled to receive a translated document only provided to the civil party. The same rationale should be applied during the main hearing. For a victim participating solely as a witness, access to an interpreter should be provided only during their testimony. Although this approach may affect the victim's right to recognition and respect, as they wouldn't be able to follow the proceedings without the interpreter, it represents a balanced choice, since assuming the formal role remains an option. Moreover, according to the proposed amendments, victims should be able to challenge decisions on interpretation during court hearings.[36] The right to review such decisions is granted in accordance with their procedural status. However, it should not be completely excluded in case victims do not participate as a party.

A limitation based on the victim's role is logically absent at the stage of filing a complaint. According to Article 5(2), victims are entitled to linguistic assistance, for example, from a person accompanying them or a police officer capable of understanding and aiding the victim in expressing themselves. Operational reasons, driven by the imperative to promptly understand the victim and respond to the incident in a timely fashion, allow the involvement of non-professional interpreters.[37] While the presence of a qualified interpreter is not obligatory at this stage, Member States can opt to offer this possibility. However, due to the associated costs, it is common for victims to be accompanied to the police station by a relative or acquaintance who can interpret. Yet, if this option is not available, police stations should act as referral bodies according to Article 8(2), and refer the victim to protection organisations capable of providing an interpreter. Alternatively, victims should have the option to file the complaint in

[35] DG JUSTICE Guidance Document (n 21) 21 where it is stated that the right is only granted to victims who have a formal role in the proceedings.
[36] Proposal for a Directive amending Directive 2012/29/EU (n 9) Art 10b.
[37] See DG JUSTICE Guidance Document (n 21) 21.

a language that they understand, with the complaint subsequently translated into the language of the Member State.

Interpretation may also be provided through electronic means as long as it does not prejudice the rights of the accused or impede communication with the victims, as determined by the competent authority. While this possibility was also provided for in the former Framework Decision, Directive 2012/29 explicitly emphasises the need to consider the rights of the defence. This evolution highlights that Directive 2012/29 is now integrated into a broader framework of European procedural law, where conflicting interests are carefully weighed up to balance the system and to ensure procedural fairness for all parties.

The language in which interpretation is provided does not necessarily have to be the victim's mother tongue. The purpose of the right is to ensure effective communication between the victim and the competent authorities. It is a procedural and not a linguistic right.[38] Therefore, if the victim understands the language of the procedure to a sufficient degree, it may be that an interpreter is not provided. Moreover, if the victim's mother tongue is not widely spoken and providing interpretation in that language would cause significant delay and cost, interpretation may be provided in another widely spoken language that the victim understands.

In addition to providing free interpretation to victims under the conditions outlined above, written translation of information essential for the exercise of their other rights should be provided upon request. The Directive clarifies the vague phrase 'essential information' by specifying its minimum content. The latter is directly linked to Article 6, which, as explained, guarantees the victim's right to receive information about the case concerning them and it includes at least any decision terminating the criminal proceedings. Upon further request, the reasons, or at least a brief summary of the reasons for that decision, shall also be provided, unless such reasons are not provided under national law. If requested, a written translation about the time and place of the main proceedings must be provided. The same applies to proceedings at the second instance.[39] If the victim considers it necessary to have another document translated, they may request, with a reasoned application, the characterisation of a document as essential, following the procedure outlined in national law. However, even if the request is granted, there is no obligation to translate passages deemed non-essential. It is up to the competent authority to decide, illustrating the wide margin of appreciation provided by Directive 2012/29.

The right to translation for victims is further constrained by paragraph 6, allowing for the replacement of written with oral translation. It is even possible to have an oral summary of the documents, provided that in both cases the fairness of the proceedings is not affected. The question that arises is whether the fairness of the proceedings should be considered from the perspective of the victim or the accused.[40] Opting for an oral translation aims at conserving both financial resources and time. Thus, one objective

[38] See also C Chioni-Chotouman, 'The Right to Translation and Interpretation in Criminal Proceedings: Providing a Common Code Between the Defendant and the Court' (2018) 1 *Cambridge Law Review* 66, 68.

[39] Directive 2012/29 (n 8) Preamble, para 31.

[40] A Klip, 'On Victim's Rights and its Impact on the Rights of the Accused' (2015) 23 *European Journal of Crime Criminal Law & Criminal Justice* 177, 186.

of this regulation is already to ensure an aspect of fairness that concerns the defendant, namely that the case is heard within a reasonable period of time.[41] It is thus reasonable to consider fairness from the victim's perspective, who is directly affected.

The right is left to the will and initiative of the victim. However, whenever the victim expresses such a need, it would be good practice to record this to ensure transparency.[42] According to paragraph 7, competent authorities are responsible for evaluating such requests and determining the necessity of providing interpretation during the examination of victims by police or judicial authorities, as well as translation of essential documents. Victims have the right to challenge this decision in accordance with national law. The Proposal for amending Directive 2012/29 aims to further enhance this aspect, promoting control over the decision not to grant interpretation. According to Article 10b of the said Proposal, the victim should not only be informed about such a decision but should have the right to request its review, yet only during court proceedings.

However, no specific guidelines are provided for the competent authority to determine when the assistance of an interpreter is necessary. The issue is easily resolved when the victim is entirely unfamiliar with the language spoken in the Member State. In such instances, competent authorities should arrange for an interpreter *ex officio* to facilitate communication, as contact would otherwise be impossible. No further action should be required from the victim, as their presence alone means seeking assistance from the State, including the removal of language barriers. Any other interpretation would violate the victim's right to be respected, the foreign-language-speaking victim being already at a serious disadvantage. Difficulties arise in cases where the victim speaks or partially understands the language of the proceedings but still requests the appointment of an interpreter. In such instances, competent authorities must assess whether the victim's linguistic competence enables them to adequately express themselves and understand the proceedings, particularly if their role in the proceedings is extensive. The language of criminal procedure, according to sociolinguistics, constitutes a distinct sublanguage markedly different from everyday speech. It features specialised phraseology and linguistic structures that may be unfamiliar even to native speakers.[43] Therefore, if a victim requests interpretation, supported by objective evidence such as not many years of residence in the country, difficulty in finding appropriate vocabulary or frequent requests for clarification, it should be provided, unless it entails significant delays or costs. In case of doubt about the victim's linguistic competence, an interpreter should be appointed, with a parallel effort either to use electronic means or opt for interpretation in a widely spoken language to reduce costs.

The preceding analysis indicates that Member States have significant discretion, which may lead to restrictions in national law to reduce expenses. It is also evident that victims have a much more limited right to translation and interpretation in comparison with the accused, who, according to Article 2 of Directive 2010/64 on the right to interpretation and translation in criminal proceedings, enjoys the right to free interpretation

[41] While the victim also has a general interest in the timely conclusion of the proceedings, any delay in this context serves primarily their benefit.

[42] See DG JUSTICE Guidance Document (n 21) 21.

[43] Chioni-Chotouman (n 38) 76.

during all interactions with authorities, as well as when communicating with their lawyer in preparation for procedural actions.[44]

IV. Rights Ensuring the Participation of Victims in Criminal Proceedings

The Directive's third chapter includes rights that promote victim participation in criminal proceedings without fundamentally altering their role under national law. While resulting in a somewhat fragmented structure of rights, this choice reflects the need to ensure conformity with the heterogeneous national procedural systems.

A. The Right to be Heard

The right to be heard is closely linked to the recognition of the victim.[45] To accommodate differences in national procedural systems, the right is drafted in Article 10 in a way that does not alter the role reserved for victims under national law. Accordingly, the scope of the right and the rules on evidence are regulated by national law. However, Directive 2012/29 requires that victims must have at least the right to address the court and provide evidence.[46] More generally, the construction of the right encompasses the victim's right to provide information, express thoughts and opinions, and provide evidence,[47] without however focusing on providing them orally.[48]

It is not specified at which procedural stage the victim should be heard, ie whether the exercise of the right can be limited to the sentencing stage. Furthermore, there is also no mention of whether this right should also be granted at the second instance. Regarding the first issue, it should be noted that the purpose of the Directive was not to alter the practice of victim impact statements at the sentencing stage, particularly in Anglo-Saxon law, while maintaining the cooperation of the prosecution and the victim at the evidence-gathering stage. Moreover, it should be considered that if under national law the victim has a broad role at the stage determining the defendant's guilt, the right to be heard should be retained to the same extent at the second instance hearing, provided a substantive review of the case occurs.

B. Right to Request a Review of the Decision not to Prosecute

In some Member States, prosecution is governed by the principle of legality, whereas in others it is governed by the principle of opportunity, conferring discretionary power on

[44] Directive 2010/64/EU of the European Parliament and of the Council of 20 October 2010 on the right to interpretation and translation in criminal proceedings [2010] OJ L280/1.

[45] See, for this aspect, also Göhler (n 18) 143.

[46] See, in this respect, also Case C-404/07 *György Katz v István Roland Sós* ECLI:EU:C:2008:553, [2008] ECR I-7607, para 47; G Ahlfeld, *Die Nebenklage im Lichte spätmoderner Herausforderungen* (Duncker & Humblot, 2024) 185.

[47] See Directive 2012/29 (n 8) Preamble, para 41.

[48] Göhler (n 18) 146.

the competent body. The involvement of victims in the prosecution has been debated, with some arguing that enabling victims' interests and emotions to affect the initiation of proceedings undermines the objectivity and impartiality of the procedure.[49] Directive 2012/29 does not establish a right of consultation between victims and prosecuting authorities. Instead, the EU legislature provides victims with the opportunity to request a review of decisions not to prosecute. Concerns about allowing victims to influence or request the review of decisions at this stage originate from the recognised public interest in punishing crimes and ensuring fair and consistent treatment of alleged perpetrators. Notably, this right was absent from the former Framework Decision despite the contrasting trend in CoE Recommendation Rec (2000)19. However, the interests of a party that contributes substantially to the prosecution of crimes by providing evidence cannot be excluded.[50] The European legislator has therefore, for the first time, granted a right to review the actions of prosecuting authorities through the possibility of requesting a review of the decision not to prosecute.

This right reflects the right to be heard in the field of prosecution of crimes and complements Article 6 establishing a right to information on any decision not to prosecute. However, because of the aforementioned reservations and the significant disparity between the practices followed in the Member States, where, in some cases, even private prosecution is provided for, the right is granted in line with the victim's role in the national criminal justice system and the procedural rules for review are also determined by national law.

To mitigate the general wording of the provision, which is more akin to an exhortation, efforts were made to reduce the margin of discretion of Member States, as reflected in Article 11(2), by providing that the right should be granted to victims of serious crimes. However, the concept of 'serious crime' mentioned in this Article is rather vague, with its content not specified in Directive 2012/29. In the absence of an explicit reference to Member States' national regulations, the question arises regarding the definition of 'serious crimes' for which Member States should provide the right to review, even if national law does not give a formal role to the victim at the pre-prosecution stage. It can be argued either that there is a margin of discretion left to Member States to define what these serious crimes are under their national law or that it constitutes an autonomous concept.[51]

[49] L Campbell, A Ashworth, and M Redmayne, *The Criminal Process*, 5th edn (Oxford University Press, 2019) 51.

[50] See also, for other relevant non-binding international legal acts, D Marko, 'Reasons for a Decision not to Institute or to Discontinue an Inquiry – Remarks on the Effectiveness of the Right of the Victim of Crime to a Review of a Decision not to Prosecute in the Light of Polish Implementation of the Article 11 of the Directive 2012/29/EU' (2020) 2 *European Criminal Law Review* 218, 220.

[51] It is an autonomous concept according to Klip (n 40) 182; Göhler (n 18) 150. For autonomous concepts, see Mitsilegas (n 5) 292 et seq; V Mitsilegas, 'Autonomous Concepts, Diversity Management and Mutual Trust in Europe's Area of Criminal Justice' (2020) 57 (1) *Common Market Law Review* 45, 70; E Rubi Cavagna, 'La transposition des directives de l'Union européenne en droit pénal français' (2019) 41 *Archives de politique criminelle* 147, 164–65. A Novokmet, 'The Right of a Victim to a Review of a Decision not to Prosecute as Set out in Article 11 of Directive 2012/29/EU and an Assessment of its Transposition in Germany, Italy, France and Croatia' (2016) 12(1) *Utrecht Law Review* 86, 91 argues that it should be interpreted by Member States. According to the DG JUSTICE Guidance Document (n 21), 30 existing European criminal law and international standards could be taken into account when interpreting the concept at national level.

Moreover, Article 11(3) includes an obligation to provide information within a reasonable period before the expiration of the time limit under national law for submitting a request for review. It is a right contingent upon the victim's request. Furthermore, upon request, the victim should be provided with sufficient information to decide whether to request a review. This provision should be combined with Article 6(3) regarding the right to receive the reasoning of the decision concerned, a key element in deciding whether to request a review. A right to access the case file, a possibility that is generally absent from Directive 2012/29, is difficult to infer from this though. Nevertheless, such a practice should be promoted at the national level as it ensures that victims make informed decisions and enhances efficiency by allowing them to carefully consider their options.[52] The right to request a review does not pertain to court decisions and is not available in case the decision of the prosecuting authority leads to an out-of-court settlement if a warning or an obligation is imposed on the offender.[53]

To ensure impartiality, the decision should be reviewed by a different individual or authority from the one that issued the original decision. However, if it was made by a higher prosecuting authority whose decision is not subject to review under national law, the same authority may conduct the review. In the latter case, to safeguard the Directive's objectives, precautions should be taken to ensure that the review does not involve the same individuals.[54] Directive 2012/29 does not require the review to be conducted by a court, which typically meets the requirements of independence and impartiality.[55] Hence, the review may be conducted, for example, by another prosecutor of the same rank or by a senior prosecutor.[56]

A final question that arises is whether the victim is also granted this right if the competent authority decides, after the prosecution has been brought, to refrain from continuing the prosecution. This was the interpretation given in the UK in *R v Killick*, where the relevant provision of the proposal of Directive 2012/29 was interpreted. In the literature, it is also assumed that the right extends to decisions that end an ongoing prosecution.[57]

C. Right to Legal Aid

The right to legal aid in the case of the accused constitutes a prerequisite for the effective exercise of other rights and aims to address the inequality between them and the

[52] See also M Endler, *Die Doppelstellung des Opferzeugen* (Nomos, 2019) 128.

[53] Directive 2012/29 (n 8) Preamble, paras 43, 45. See also Helmken (n 3) 104 who argues against the application in the case of involvement of a judge.

[54] Novokmet (n 51) 92.

[55] Bock (n 24) 206.

[56] Novokmet (n 51) 91, Helmken (n 3) 106.

[57] S Allegrezza, 'Victim's Statute within Directive 2012/29/EU' in L Lupária (ed), *Victims and Criminal Justice. European Standards and National Good Practices* (Wolters Kluwer, 2015) 14, 91; I Wieczorek, 'A Needed Balance between Security, Liberty and Justice. Positive Signals Arrive From the Field of Victims' Rights' (2012) 2 (2) *European Criminal Law Review* 141, 153. See also DG JUSTICE Guidance Document (n 21) 30.

State and to ensure the fairness of the proceedings. Victims, however, are not only not confronted with the State, but their interests often align with those of the prosecution. In the case of victims, the right to legal aid is intended to increase their participation in the proceedings, ensuring that their interests are considered and that they can avail themselves of the opportunities and rights provided.[58]

Access to legal aid is only mandatory when the victim has assumed the status of a party according to national law. The chosen wording may prevent victims from accessing free legal advice in situations where they can acquire the formal role at a later stage. It would therefore be more appropriate, in the light of the justificatory basis of the right, to provide access to free legal assistance at least when the victim can, under national law, assume the role of the party in criminal proceedings. In that way, they would not be deprived of the legal information necessary to make an informed decision about assuming such a role. Thus, it would be more appropriate to grant access to free legal aid, at a minimum, when victims can potentially take on, under national law, the role of the party in criminal proceedings.[59]

D. Proposing a Right to Receive a Decision on Compensation in Criminal Proceedings

Receiving compensation is usually a strong motive for victims to engage in criminal proceedings. The right to receive a decision on compensation from the offender is recognised in Directive 2012/29. However, due to the heterogeneity of national procedural systems, Article 16 exceptionally allows for compensation to be provided in other legal proceedings rather than in criminal proceedings. It is a choice that, although minimises the impact on national criminal proceedings, can result in the victim engaging in lengthy parallel proceedings. To secure better access to compensation, the Proposal for amending Directive 2012/29 opts for securing the right to receive a decision on compensation from the offender only in the course of criminal proceedings. It is a choice that even though does not directly alter the status of victim's participation, may result in enhancing the institution of the civil party in Member States that are familiar with it. More generally, the introduction of the right to compensation exclusively within the context of criminal proceedings will enhance the interest and, ultimately, the active participation of the victim in them. To this end works also the proposed amendment according to which compensation will be paid to the victim immediately after the judgment by the State, which will subsequently seek reimbursement from the offender. The proposed version of Article 16, paragraph 2 constitutes a paradigm shift, as, although it implies the allocation of recourses to this end, it makes the State the guarantor of providing compensation and thus enhances victims' confidence that they will be compensated through criminal proceedings.

[58] See also I Edwards, 'An Ambiguous Participant' (2004) 44(6) *The British Journal of Criminology* 967, 972.

[59] Chioni-Chotouman (n 20) 91. Contra B Schünemann, 'Protection of Children and Other Vulnerable Victims Against Secondary Victimisation: Making It Easier to Testify in Court' (2009) *ERA Forum* 387, 389.

V. Conclusions

Directive 2012/29 laid the framework for recognising basic rights aiming at enhancing engagement and participation in criminal proceedings, subject though to the need to respect the differences between national legal systems. A lot of choices regarding rights that directly enhance victim participation were influenced by the limited possibility of compromising it with the adversarial structure of criminal proceedings.[60] Even after Brexit, discrepancies regarding the victim's status in criminal proceedings persist among Member States. Yet the decline in the use of the common law element may potentially enhance the participation of victims.

Regarding the proposed amendments to Directive 2012/29, it can be said that they indicate an effort to secure enforcement of basic information and participatory rights by, *inter alia*, turning to electronic means of communication that do not entail delays and high costs.[61] Furthermore, efforts are being made to address the lack of sanctions and mechanisms for appeal and redress in cases of rights infringement.[62] Overall, Directive 2012/29 and the proposed amendments reveal a cautious attempt to balance the heterogeneity of national legal systems alongside the absence of a concrete theoretical framework for the necessity and nature of victims' rights and victim participation in the context of a complex system, where the much more entrenched rights of the accused prevail.

[60] See Göhler (n 18) 89.
[61] Proposal for a Directive amending Directive 2012/29/EU (n 9) Art 26b.
[62] ibid.

3

Protecting Vulnerable Victims: An Analysis of the EU Legal Framework for Victims of Gender-Based Violence

CRISTINA SÁENZ PÉREZ

I. Introduction

Since the 1970s, EU Member States have increasingly recognised the role of victims within the criminal justice system.[1] In this context, most EU Member States have either constitutionally protected or considered victims' rights as fundamental rights within the domestic legal framework.[2] Although the specific rights recognised across the EU and their status in criminal proceedings varies, these have become essential in understanding the functioning of the criminal justice system across the Member States. The EU, in turn, is a latecomer to the recognition of these rights and setting of minimum standards in this area. This can be partially attributed to the late development of competences within the Area of Freedom, Security and Justice (AFSJ), which were only fully 'communitarised' with the Treaty of Lisbon.

Within the AFSJ, Directive 2012/29/EU establishing minimum standards on the rights, support and protection of victims of crime[3] (hereinafter 'the Victims' Rights Directive') constitutes the first truly comprehensive instrument adopted by the Union setting minimum standards within the field of victims' rights. This came to replace the Framework Decision on the standing of victims in criminal proceedings[4] which, despite

[1] On the evolution of victims' rights in Europe: M Engelhart, 'Victims and the European Convention on Human Rights' in G Forti (ed), *Victims and Corporations. Legal Challenges and Empirical Findings* (Wolters Kluwer Italia, 2018); S Walklate et al, 'Victim Stories and Victim Policy: Is there a Case for a Narrative Victimology?' (2019) 15(2) *Crime, Media, Culture* 199.

[2] E Sellier and A Weyembergh, *Criminal Procedural Law across the European Union: A Comparative Analysis of Selected Main Differences and the Impact they Have Over the Development of EU Legislation* (LIBE Committee, 2018) 144.

[3] Directive 2012/29/EU of the European Parliament and of the Council of 25 October 2012 establishing minimum standards on the rights, support and protection of victims of crime, and replacing Council Framework Decision 2001/220/JHA (Victims' Rights Directive) [2012] OJ L315/57.

[4] Council Framework Decision 2001/220/JHA of 15 March 2001 on the standing of victims in criminal proceedings [2001] OJ L82/1.

introducing for the first time 'hard-law' to set minimum victim rights' standards, faced significant implementation challenges that questioned its adequacy and challenged its effectiveness.[5] Regardless of the progress represented by the Victims' Rights Directive, the evidence available shows that the rights recognised by this instrument are not fully available to all victims of crime, with cross-border victims holding the weakest position in this area.[6] In this context, the European Commission adopted, on 24 June 2020, its first EU strategy on victims' rights that will cover the period 2020–2025.[7] In it, the Commission stated that particular attention would be paid to the protection of the rights of victims of gender-based violence.[8] Since then, the EU adopted a Directive on combatting violence against women and domestic violence (hereinafter 'Directive on Domestic Violence'),[9] proposed a revision of the Victims' Rights Directive[10] and included fighting domestic and gender-based violence as a priority within its Equality Strategy 2020–2025,[11] whilst the Council has ratified the Istanbul Convention.

Efforts to improve the rights of victims and, more particularly, victims of gender-based violence have centred on developing a comprehensive framework of rights that encompasses protection measures, access to support, and access to justice. This chapter will critically analyse the initiatives adopted within this area and will evaluate whether the harmonisation of minimum standards under the Victims' Rights Directive (and its proposed revision) and the proposed Directive on Domestic Violence may improve access of victims of gender-based violence to protection, support measures, and justice. This analysis seeks to critically examine the effectiveness of the EU's approach to harmonising victims' rights under Article 82(2)c Treaty on the Functioning of the European Union (TFEU), which links harmonisation efforts in the field of criminal law to 'facilitating mutual recognition of judgments and judicial decisions and police and judicial cooperation in criminal matters having a cross-border dimension'. This chapter will consider how this instrumental understanding of victims' rights limits the EU's harmonisation efforts to the adoption of (sometimes) vague standards that facilitate the persistence of disparities across the domestic criminal justice systems.

This analysis will proceed as follows. Section II will examine one of the EU's first attempts to legislate within the field of domestic violence, namely Article 13 of the Citizenship Directive,[12] and will expose the limited scope of this initiative that was

[5] See A Pemberton and C Rasquete, 'Victims in Europe – Assessment of the Implementation of the Framework Decision on the Standing of Victims in Criminal Proceedings: Preliminary Results' in J Hartmann (ed), *Perspektiven professioneller Opferhilfe: Theorie und Praxis eines interdisziplinären Handlungsfelds* (Springer, 2010); Victim Support and APAV, *Victims in Europe: Implementation of the EU Framework Decision on the standing of victims in the criminal proceedings in the Member States of the European Union* (2009) 123–33.

[6] European Commission, 'EU Strategy on Victims' Rights (2020-2025)' COM(2020) 258 final.

[7] ibid.

[8] ibid 1.

[9] Directive (EU) 2024/1385 of the European Parliament and of the Council of 14 May 2024 on combating violence against women and domestic violence (Directive on Domestic Violence) [2024] OJ L/1385.

[10] Proposal for a Directive of the European Parliament and of the Council amending Directive 2012/29/EU establishing minimum standards on the rights, support and protection of victims of crime, and replacing Council Framework Decision 2001/220/JHA, COM/2023/424 final (Proposal amending the Victims' Rights Directive).

[11] European Commission, 'A Union of Equality: Gender Equality Strategy 2020-2025' COM/2020/152.

[12] Directive 2004/38/EC of the European Parliament and of the Council of 29 April 2004 on the right of citizens of the Union and their family members to move and reside freely within the territory of the Member

linked to the fulfilment of economic aims. Then, section III will focus on EU horizontal instruments for the protection of victims' rights and will critically examine how these have improved (and failed) the protection of the rights of victims, with sections III.A and III.B examining the Victims' Rights Directive and the Directive on the European Protection Order, whilst section III.C will evaluate the limitations of this framework and the need for reform to guarantee the rights of victims across the EU. Finally, section IV will focus on measures that increase the protection of victims of gender-based violence, namely the Council's decision to ratify the Istanbul Convention (section IV.A) and the Commission's proposals for new instruments within the field of victims' rights, particularly the Directive on Domestic Violence (section IV.B). These sections will evaluate the changes introduced/proposed by these instruments, whilst section IV.C will consider the need to expand the list of Euro crimes to incorporate an offence of gender violence and will evaluate whether such an approach could contribute to fulfilling the goals set by the Commission in its Strategy on Victims' Rights 2020–2025.

II. Article 13 of the Citizenship Directive: An Analysis of the Early Initiatives to Fight against Domestic Violence

The Declaration accompanying Article 8 TFEU included the elimination of gender inequalities and combatting domestic violence as EU-wide objectives within the Treaty of Lisbon.[13] Since then, the European Commission has adopted a number of strategies that have sought to implement this goal. The latest one is the Gender Equality Strategy 2020–2025, which incorporates the compromise to present a new Victims' Rights Strategy addressing the specific needs of victims of gender-based violence.[14]

But even before the adoption of the TFEU, the EU legal framework contained measures aimed at providing a certain level of protection to victims of domestic violence. For instance, Article 13 of the Citizenship Directive includes a rule that permits third country national victims of domestic violence to retain residency rights after marriage has ended. However, this right is very limited and merely establishes an exception that is far from being part of a comprehensive strategy for vulnerable victims, namely migrant women victims of domestic violence. Instead, this Directive seeks to guarantee the effective exercise of the free movement rights of EU citizens, which might be impeded if these cannot move together with their third country family members. In the context of this provision, Article 13(2)c introduces a limit to this teleological approach by which the rights of third country nationals are linked to their EU spouses, when the third country national is a victim of domestic violence. Despite this limitation, and even within the context of the new Directive on Domestic Violence, victims of domestic abuse continue

States amending Regulation (EEC) No 1612/68 and repealing Directives 64/221/EEC, 68/360/EEC, 72/194/EEC, 73/148/EEC, 75/34/EEC, 75/35/EEC, 90/364/EEC, 90/365/EEC and 93/96/EEC (Citizenship Directive) [2004] OJ L158/77.

[13] Consolidated Version of the Treaty on the Functioning of the European Union [2012] OJ C326/47, Declaration on Article 8.

[14] Gender Equality Strategy 2020–2025 (n 11) 3–4.

to be in the most vulnerable position, with limited measures introduced to protect their status as victims and residency rights.[15]

Article 13(2)c can be seen as introducing some (albeit limited) 'social sensibility'[16] into legislation designed to prioritise economic goals, ie the exercise of free movement rights within the internal market. These additional residency rights are only granted to third country nationals who are victims of domestic violence and linked to mobile EU citizens, whilst third country nationals in similar situations but in purely domestic scenarios would fall under the competence of Member States. Limited additional measures have been introduced by the Directive on Domestic Violence despite the obligations acquired under the Istanbul Convention.[17]

An added problem of this provision is that its application is not open to all victims of gender-based violence. Instead, it is limited to victims of domestic violence only who must fulfil an additional economic requirement to retain residency rights: they must qualify as workers or self-employed individuals or have sufficient resources to support themselves as well as comprehensive sickness insurance.[18] These requirements disregard the situation of victims of domestic violence who may have been victims of different types of abuse, including financial, physical, and psychological abuse and degrees of controlling and abusive behaviour that prevent them from actively participating in the labour market and having access to financial resources.[19] Third country nationals who would have, in many cases, arrived in the EU through an abusive relationship might lack the necessary skills (whether linguistic, economic or employability) to actively participate in the labour market. In order to do so, they would require extensive support to heal and be able to integrate fully in the Member State of residency. Conversely, the provision of specialised services for victims to recover from violence (irrespective of their nationality) is part of the compromises acquired by the signatories of the Istanbul Convention[20] and is part of the rights granted to all victims under the Victims' Rights Directive.[21] At the same time, the limited scope of protection offered to third country national victims of domestic violence under the Citizenship Directive is at odds with the Gender Equality Strategy 2020–2025, which acknowledges the intersectional nature of

[15] Amnesty International, Recommendations on the proposal for a directive of the European Parliament and of the Council on combating violence against women and domestic violence (2023) 6, available at www.amnesty.eu/wp-content/uploads/2023/06/TIGO_IOR_10_2023_4160_AI-Position-Paper-VAW-Directive.pdf.

[16] A Weiss, 'Transnational Families in Crisis: An Analysis of the Domestic Violence Rule in E.U. Free Movement Law' (2009) 30 *Michigan Journal of International Law* 841, 871.

[17] Council of Europe Convention on preventing and combating violence against women and domestic violence, Istanbul, 11 May 2011, Art 4 (Istanbul Convention).

[18] Case C-930/19 *X v the Belgian State* ECLI:EU:C:2021:657; Case C-115/15 *Secretary of State for the Home Department v N.A.* ECLI:EU:C:2016:487; Case C-218/14 *Kuldip Singh and others v Minister for Justice and Equality* ECLI:EU:C:2015:476.

[19] On the impact of domestic violence on the economic stability and self-sufficiency of victims, see: AE Adams, 'Measuring the Effects of Domestic Violence on Women's Financial WellBeing' (2011) *CFS Research Brief* 2011-5.6; M Ford-Gilboe, J Wuest et al, 'Modelling the Effects of Intimate Partner Violence and Access to Resources on Women's Health in the Early Years after Leaving an Abusive Partner' (2009) 68 *Social Science & Medicine* 1021.

[20] Istanbul Convention (n 17) Arts 4, 20 and 22.

[21] Victims' Rights Directive (n 3) Art 9.

gender inequality and violence against women and establishes that this intersectionality shall be incorporated into all EU policies and Commission initiatives.[22]

III. An Overview of the Legal Safeguards for Victims of Gender-Based Violence

A. The Victims' Rights Directive as a Framework

The emergence of groups that support or represent victims of crime has grown in importance across European states,[23] particularly in Nordic states that have been at the forefront of the development of victim policy-making in Europe.[24] Nevertheless, the harmonisation of the rights of victims within criminal proceedings at EU level took a back seat due to the relatively late development of Justice and Home Affairs as a field of EU competence and the security-driven conception of this area that devoted limited efforts to the harmonisation of rights until the Treaty of Lisbon.

Early attempts to recognise victims' rights within criminal proceedings precede the Lisbon Treaty and can be found in the Framework Decision on Victim Participation from 2001 (hereinafter 'the Framework Decision').[25] The Framework Decision was the first legal instrument at EU level that partially recognised victims' rights already contained in other international instruments, including Council of Europe recommendations.[26] Despite the ambitious rights included within it, the deficient implementation of this instrument and the different standards that persisted at Member State level meant that victims were not sufficiently protected or supported, lacked access to justice, and had insufficient access to compensation or restorative justice initiatives.[27] These limitations can be partially explained by the lack of explicit competences present in the treaties to legislate within the field of victims' rights. Within this legal framework, victims' rights were conceived in a very limited manner as linked to the rights of cross-border victims

[22] Gender Equality Strategy 2020–2025 (n 11) 2, 15–16.

[23] S Walklate, JM Maher et al, 'Victim Stories and Victim Policy: Is there a Case for a Narrative Victimology?' (2019) 15 *Crime, Media, Culture* 199, 200; V Barker, 'The Politics of Pain: A Political Institutionalist Analysis of Crime Victims' Moral Protests' (2007) 41 *Law & Society Review* 619.

[24] M Helminen, 'We Need to Make Sure that We are Always Something Else': Victim Support Organisations and the Increasing Responsibility of the State in Supporting Crime Victims in Finland and Norway' (2019) 25 *International Review of Victimology* 157; F Holm, 'Successful Human Rights Implementation? Victims of Crime and the Swedish Example' (2022) 40 *Nordic Journal of Human Rights* 529; H Tham, A Rönneling, and LL Rytterbro, 'The Emergence of the Crime Victim: Sweden in a Scandinavian Context' (2011) 40 *Crime and Justice* 555.

[25] Council Framework Decision 2001/220/JHA on the standing of victims in criminal proceeding [2001] OJ L82/1.

[26] For an in-depth analysis of the EU Framework Decision on Victims of Crime, see MS Groenhuijsen and A Pemberton, 'The EU Framework Decision for Victims of Crime: Does Hard Law Make a Difference? (2009) 17 *European Journal of Crime, Criminal Law and Criminal Justice* 43; A Pemberton and C Rasquete, 'Victims in Europe – Assessment of the Implementation of the Framework Decision on the Standing of Victims in Criminal Proceedings: Preliminary Results' in J Hartmann (eds), *Perspektiven professioneller Opferhilfe. VS Verlag für Sozialwissenschaften* (Springer, 2019).

[27] M Insight and A Elffers Felix, 'A Study for an Impact Assessment on Ways of Improving the Support, Protection and Rights of Victims across Europe' (European Commission, 2010).

who were negatively affected by the absence of a harmonised framework in this area when exercising their free movement rights.[28]

The Treaty of Lisbon changed this, elevating the construction of the AFSJ to an objective with the same standing as the completion of the internal market, and conferring the EU the competence to harmonise minimum standards in the field of victims' rights.[29] The setting of these minimum standards, nonetheless, remains instrumental to the attainment of security goals: victims' rights shall be harmonised only 'to the extent necessary to facilitate mutual recognition of judgments and judicial decisions and police and judicial cooperation in criminal matters'.[30] In other words, the harmonisation of victims' rights post-Lisbon is primarily linked to the attainment of security aims, such as the strengthening of judicial and police cooperation in criminal matters. In this context, Article 82(2)c TFEU ties the harmonisation of minimum standards in the field of victims' rights to the need to guarantee the smooth functioning of mutual recognition instruments that advance these security goals.

Despite the requirements imposed by Article 82(2) TFEU, the entry into force of the Treaty of Lisbon facilitated the adoption of the first comprehensive strategy approved by the Commission for the protection of victims' rights.[31] This Strategy recognises the need to adopt minimum standards in the field of victims' rights as an essential step to enhance the trust of EU citizens in the notion of justice.[32] Furthermore, it explicitly refers to the victims of domestic abuse and domestic violence, with the Commission acknowledging that 'there is a gender dimension to victims' rights' that needs to be addressed.[33] This gender perspective is present in the two main action points that the Commission adopted in this Strategy: a Directive establishing minimum standards on the rights, support and protection of victims of crime[34] and a Regulation on mutual recognition of protection measures in civil matters.[35] Both of these instruments aim at guaranteeing rights that are essential to all victims but, particularly, to vulnerable victims, such as victims of gender-based violence.

The Victims' Rights Directive is the most relevant horizontal instrument adopted in this area and recognises a number of rights for victims that can be broadly classified as right to information and support, right to participate in criminal proceedings, and right to protection. Nevertheless, its most relevant feature is its capacity to produce direct effect, which overcomes some of the limitations that characterised the deficient implementation of the former 2001 Framework Decision. The use of framework decisions within the field of Justice and Home Affairs before Lisbon, together with the European Commission's inability to initiate infringement proceedings for this lack of

[28] MJ Lehmkuhl, 'The Value of Legal Provisions for an Adequate Treatment of Victims of Crime: Does the Victims' Rights Directive of the European Union Set a New Benchmark?' in J Joseph and S Jergenson, *An International Perspective on Contemporary Developments in Victimology* (Springer, 2020) 185.

[29] TFEU Art 82(2)c.

[30] ibid Art 82(2).

[31] European Commission, 'Strengthening Victims' Rights in the EU' COM(2011) 274 final.

[32] ibid 2–3.

[33] ibid 1.

[34] Victims' Rights Directive (n 3).

[35] Regulation (EU) No 606/2013 of the European Parliament and of the Council on mutual recognition of protection measures in civil matters [2013] OJ L181/4.

domestic implementation, resulted in a deficient implementation of this instrument.[36] The Lisbonisation of the AFSJ, together with the capacity of this Directive to produce direct effect, set the potential for a more robust legal framework in the field of victims' rights.

Although the Directive does not contain specific measures for victims of gender-based violence, the harmonisation of minimum standards to safeguard the right to protection and access to support services also benefit this category of victim. The protection of particularly vulnerable victims, such as victims of gender-based violence, had already been incorporated into the Stockholm Programme,[37] which recognised the needs of these victims to access support and legal protection within all Member States.[38] Although protection rights recognised under the Directive grant a lot of leeway to Member States, the need to carry out an individual assessment to identify specific protection and support needs of victims meets a traditional demand of victims of gender-based violence across the EU.[39] However, the analysis becomes more complex when considering the implementation of this right to access support services or victims' access to justice at Member State level. In these areas, the Directive provides extensive flexibility to the Member States, and the minimum standards that they have to implement are quite vague. This can be explained by a variety of factors that range from the financial costs required to modify these aspects within the domestic justice systems,[40] particularly when analysing support services, to the different characteristics of national criminal justice systems and the status of victims within these procedures.[41]

Overall, the Victims' Rights Directive incorporated a wide range of rights for all victims of crime, considering their individual needs and including measures to prevent their re-victimisation and secondary victimisation (a priority for victims of gender-based violence). Nevertheless, the reports commissioned by the European Commission and European Parliament have shown that 'the full potential of the Directive has not been reached yet' due to the incomplete and/or incorrect transposition of this instrument at Member State level.[42] These limitations have been found to affect, particularly, provisions concerning access to information, the quality of support services, and the availability of protection measures necessary to satisfy victims' individual needs.[43] These issues, in turn, are likely to affect vulnerable victims, such as victims of gender-based violence, more severely, as these are likely to require more extensive support and protection. At the same time, this Directive provides significant leeway to the Member States when regulating victim participation rights due to the persistent differences in national

[36] M McDonald, *Guide for Lawyers to the Victims Directive and the Criminal Justice Act 2017* (Irish Council for Liberties, 2018) 4.

[37] European Council, The Stockholm Programme – An open and secure Europe serving and protecting citizens [2010] OJ C115/1 (Stockholm Programme).

[38] ibid para 2.3.4.

[39] Victims' Rights Directive (n 3) Art 22.

[40] ibid.

[41] Report from the Commission to the European Parliament and the Council on the implementation of Directive 2012/29/EU of the European Parliament and of the Council of 25 October 2012 establishing minimum standards on the rights, support and protection of victims of crime, and replacing Council Framework Decision 2001/220/JHA, COM(2020) 188 final, 10.

[42] ibid 9.

[43] ibid 10.

legal systems and the financial costs that any reforms in this area may involve.[44] This challenges the effective realisation of justice rights and shows that despite the innovative nature of the Victims' Rights Directive, further harmonisation is required to guarantee that all victims can effectively access and exercise their rights.

B. Mutual Recognition as a Tool to Expand Rights: The Case of the European Protection Order

One of the key action points in the EU's strategy on victims' rights was the adoption of a Regulation on mutual recognition of protection measures for victims taken in civil matters (hereinafter 'the EPM Regulation'), which was later included in the Council's Roadmap on victims' rights.[45] However, the EPM Regulation was not approved until 2013,[46] two years after the Union approved the Directive on the European Protection Order (hereinafter 'the EPO Directive'),[47] which regulates the mutual recognition of these protection measures adopted in the context of criminal proceedings. This instrument became the first one within the package on victims' rights that, despite applying to all types of victims of violent crime, had victims of domestic and gender-based violence as their primary focus.[48] But, overall, the EPM Regulation and the EPO Directive addressed a category of victim whose rights to protection have been identified as particularly difficult to guarantee, namely cross-border victims.[49] Cross-border victims who may have a protection order in a Member State but move to another one (either temporarily or permanently) usually struggle to see these protection orders recognised in their new state of residence.

The EPO Directive was the first initiative in this area, launched under the Spanish Presidency of the Council in 2010 to ensure that protection measures issued in a Member State (in the context of criminal proceedings) would be applied across the EU irrespective of the Member State in which the victim may be resident. This instrument did not set minimum standards for these protection measures nor did it seek to harmonise the type of instruments used in this field. Indeed, the EPO Directive states that '[it] does not create obligations to modify national systems for adopting protection measures nor does it create obligations to introduce or amend a criminal law system for executing a European protection order'.[50] Instead, it focuses on mitigating the impact that intra-EU mobility may have on victims of crime, by facilitating the mutual recognition of these measures in other Member States. Consequently, the EPO Directive focuses on

[44] Lehmkuhl (n 28) 196.

[45] Resolution of the Council on a Roadmap for strengthening the rights and protection of victims, in particular in criminal proceedings [2011] OJ C187/1 (Roadmap on Victims' Rights).

[46] Regulation No 606/2013 (n 35).

[47] Directive 2011/99/EU of the European Parliament and of the Council on the European protection order (EPO Directive) [2011] OJ L338/2.

[48] ibid Rec 9.

[49] Report from the Commission to the European Parliament and the Council on the implementation of Directive 2011/99/EU of the European Parliament and of the Council of 13 December 2011 on the European protection order, COM(2020) 187 final, 2–3.

[50] ibid Rec 8.

cross-border victims who have moved from a Member State and seek the recognition of the protection in their new Member State of residency. The EPM Regulation pursues similar aims and utilises mutual recognition to recognise protection orders across the EU, but it refers to civil protection measures rather than those approved in the course of criminal proceedings.

Although the existence of two instruments (ie the EPM Regulation and the EPO Directive) tries to cover the different national regimes at Member State level, with some Member States using civil law and others criminal justice proceedings to impose protection measures, this has created significant confusion in their application.[51] The main problem here arises when the executing Member State requires a proceeding that is completely different in nature to the one foreseen by the issuing Member State. For instance, Spain would not be able to execute the EPM requests for protection measures and would only accept EPO certificates, as protection measures are criminal in nature and require the guarantees of a criminal procedure in the issuing Member State to be recognised.[52] This is not exceptional, and the persistence of a dual regime, together with the lack of standardisation of protection measures in the EU, raises important questions about the operability of the system, with some scholars going as far as to call it 'a waste of time'.[53]

An additional question that arises when examining these instruments concerns the adequacy of mutual recognition as a governance principle used to expand the use of protection measures across borders. Mutual recognition has been relatively successful in advancing security goals in areas such as criminal law, with the European Arrest Warrant as the paradigmatic example of this process. Nevertheless, mutual recognition in criminal matters has not operated in a vacuum, being highly 'managed' through extensive harmonisation of standards in a number of areas,[54] such as defence rights or the regulation of *in absentia* proceedings. Despite the lessons learnt in this area, which highlight that a minimum level ground is necessary for mutual recognition to operate, the EU's strategy in the field of victims' rights has prioritised the preservation of legal diversity[55] at the expense of sacrificing the effective enforcement of protection orders across the EU.

These limitations have resulted in significant delays to transpose and implement both the EPO Directive and EPM Regulation, with the last Member State (Belgium)

[51] D Porcheron, 'Le principe de reconnaissance mutuelle au service des victimes de violences. Règlement (UE) n° 606/2013 du Parlement et européen et du Conseil du 12 juin 2013 relatif à la reconnaissance mutuelle des mesures de protection en matière civile' (2016) 2 *Revue critique de droit international privé* 267, 270; Sellier and Weyembergh (n 2) 164.

[52] Sellier and Weyembergh (n 2) 165; R Borges Blazquez, 'La orden de protección europea y su aplicación en España' (2020) 41 *Revista jurídica de la Universidad Autónoma de Madrid* 93.

[53] S van der Aa and J Ouwerkerk, 'The European Protection Order: No Time to Waste or a Waste of Time?' (2011) 19 *European Journal of Crime Criminal Law & Criminal Justice* 267, 287.

[54] On the notion of 'managed' mutual recognition and the need of ex-ante harmonisation of minimum standards, see: C Janssens, *The Principle of Mutual Recognition in EU Law* (Oxford University Press, 2013) Ch 4; M Möstl, 'Preconditions and Limits of Mutual Recognition' (2010) 47 *Common Market Law Review* 405; S Schmidt, 'Mutual Recognition as a New Mode of Governance' (2014) 14 *Journal of European Public Policy* 667, 673.

[55] EPO Directive (n 47) Rec 8.

transposing the EPO Directive in May 2017, two years after the deadline.[56] Although there is limited data available regarding the protection measures issued and executed under both instruments,[57] it seems clear that their use is very limited, showing that these have not addressed the problems that victims face when moving across borders. Based on the data provided by Member States, only 37 EPOs had been issued in the period 2015–2018 and only 15 of these had been executed.[58] Furthermore, there were 10 Member States during this period that did not issue, execute or recognise any EPOs.[59] This is particularly striking if compared with the data of a single Member State, Spain, which, in 2022, had 71,357 protection measures registered as 'active' in its Central Register for the Protection of Victims of Domestic Violence (*Registro Central para la Protección de las Víctimas de Violencia Doméstica y de Género*).[60]

This analysis demonstrates that cross-border cooperation in criminal matters based on mutual recognition without the approximation of minimum standards tends to be ineffective and does not help cross-border victims. The persistence of different legal regimes at Member State level make protection measures issued in a Member State nearly impossible to execute in another state. Faced with this situation, reports have concluded that it is easier for cross-border victims to apply for national protection measures when they move to a different Member State despite the cost, time, and difficulties that they may experience in this process.[61] Based on this analysis, it seems clear that it is necessary to reform the protection system of cross-border victims (a system that is essential to victims who have a close relationship with the abuser, such as victims of gender-based violence) to ensure that these can exercise their free movement rights without jeopardising their security. If mutual recognition is favoured in these reforms, the Commission should consider the need to approximate protection measures at Member State level to facilitate the unimpeded operation of this governance principle and the free movement of protection orders across borders.

C. Revisiting the Current Framework for Victims' Rights: An Analysis from the Perspective of Victims of Gender-Based Violence

The strengthening of victims' rights has been a priority for the EU since the Stockholm Programme.[62] This priority is in line with other international obligations adopted by the Member States, including the UN's Sustainable Development Goals which include

[56] Sellier and Weyembergh (n 2) 166.
[57] ibid; Artemis Network, 'Promoting the Right of Protection of Women through the Application of the EC Directive 2011/99/EU and the European Protection Order' (2020); E Cerrato, T Freixes et al, 'European Protection Order Directive 2011/99/EU: European Implementation Assessment' (European Parliamentary Research Service, 2017) 17–18.
[58] Artemis Network, ibid 7.
[59] ibid.
[60] Instituto Nacional de Estadística de España, Estadística de Violencia Doméstica y Violencia de Género (EVDVG) de 2022 (31 May 2023), available at www.ine.es/prensa/evdvg_2022.pdf.
[61] Weyembergh and Seller (n 51) 99.
[62] Stockholm Programme (n 37).

a duty to promote appropriate legislation, policies and actions on victims' rights[63] and the Istanbul Convention, which includes the obligation of parties to incorporate 'measures to protect the rights of victims'[64] (in this case, victims of gender-based violence). As explained in previous sections, these obligations crystallised in the Victims' Rights Directive, as the main instrument setting the minimum standards for victims' rights across the EU. Additionally, the EU has developed other instruments, such as the EPO Directive and EPM Regulation to strengthen the right to protection of cross-border victims.

Nevertheless, most evaluation projects have shown that neither the Directive nor the EPO Directive or EPM Regulation have been effective in guaranteeing victims' rights to protection, with standards in this area varying from country to country.[65] The latest report conducted by the Commission on the Victims' Rights Directive refers specifically to the lack of measures available in many Member States to prevent contact between the victim and offender.[66] This affects, particularly, victims of domestic violence who due to the close relationship with the offender and, in many cases, the maintenance of long-term ties due to children visitation rights require specific measures to protect their safety and prevent their re-victimisation. Equally, it has been concluded that the lack of adequate standards for support services across Member States means that these services vary greatly across the EU and, in many cases, cannot guarantee the right to access support services contained in the Directive.[67] This affects, particularly, vulnerable victims, such as victims of gender-based violence who require extensive physical, psychological and sometimes financial support to recover from the consequences of the violence experienced.

The lack of harmonisation initiatives in these areas and the limited financial support available to develop support services have resulted in the Victims' Directive not developing its full potential.[68] At the same time, the reliance on domestic protection mechanisms and mutual recognition instruments to guarantee the protection of cross-border victims has been incapable of guaranteeing that they can effectively exercise their rights. As a result, in its analysis of the protection of victims' rights in Europe, VOCIARE found that 'protection measures (in the EU) only rarely function for victims who need them'.[69] The Commission acknowledged some of these failings and proposed a Directive (now adopted) on combatting violence against women and domestic violence and a Directive revising the Victims Rights' Directive, which reinforce the right to access protection across the EU. The following sections will assess these proposals, considering their

[63] UN Sustainable Development Goals, Goal 16, target 16.3.

[64] Istanbul Convention (n 17) Art 4.

[65] Commission Staff Working Document: Evaluation of Directive 2012/29/EU of the European Parliament and of the Council of 25 October 2012 establishing minimum standards on the rights, support and protection of victims of crime, and replacing Council Framework Decision 2001/220/JHA [2022] SWD(2022) 179 final, 20.

[66] ibid.

[67] ICF, 'Study to Support the Evaluation of Directive 2012/29/EU Establishing Minimum Standards on the Rights, Support and Protection of Victims of Crime' (2021) final report, 44.

[68] Victim Support Europe, Victims of Crime Implementation Analysis of Rights in Europe (VOCIARE), October 2019, 59; Commission Staff Working Document (n 65) 12.

[69] VOCIARE, ibid, 136.

capacity to deliver on the compromises adopted by the EU and the Member States under the Istanbul Convention.

IV. Towards a Legal Framework for Victims of Gender-Based Violence

A. The Istanbul Convention as a Milestone

The Istanbul Convention (hereinafter 'the Convention') is considered a milestone for the elimination of violence against women and girls in Europe.[70] It entered into force on 1 August 2014, with the main objective of preventing all forms of gender-based violence, including domestic violence, which affects women disproportionately.[71] The Convention builds on the case law of the European Court of Human Rights[72] and develops the standards elaborated under the Convention on the Elimination of All Forms of Discrimination against Women (CEDAW) to prevent and tackle gender-based violence.[73]

Although all EU Member States and the EU itself have signed it, its ratification has not been equally completed across the EU. Bulgaria, for instance, decided not to ratify the Convention, as the Constitutional Court of this country considered the term 'gender' in this instrument incompatible with the constitutional understanding of 'sex'.[74] Additionally, this Member State stated that the Convention threatens traditional values and leads to the legalisation of same-sex marriage and the recognition of transgender rights.[75] On the other hand, Poland and Hungary have also indicated their intention to withdraw from the Convention due to their disagreements over the origins of violence against women and girls.[76] Hungary has gone a step further and criticised the Convention for being rooted on 'destructive gender ideologies'.[77] Other Member States, such as Slovakia, refused to ratify it due to its alleged incompatibility with the constitutional definition of marriage as a union between a man and a woman.[78] In response

[70] Council Decision on the conclusion, on behalf of the European Union, of the Council of Europe Convention on preventing and combating violence against women and domestic violence with regard to institutions and public administration of the Union (2023) Doc 5514/23, para 1.

[71] Istanbul Convention (n 7) Art 2.

[72] ibid Preamble.

[73] UN Convention on the Elimination of all Forms of Discrimination against Women, Resolution 34/180 of 18 December 1979 (CEDAW).

[74] On the position of Bulgaria regarding the Istanbul Convention, see: M Ilcheva, 'Bulgaria and the Istanbul Convention – Law, Politics and Propaganda vs. the Rights of Victims of Gender-Based Violence' (2020) 3 *Open Journal of Legal Studies* 49; R Vassileva, 'Bulgaria's Constitutional Troubles with the Istanbul Convention' (*Verfassungsblog*, 20 Aug 2018), available at https://verfassungsblog.de/bulgarias-constitutional-troubles-with-the-istanbul-convention/.

[75] Ilcheva, ibid.

[76] W Grzebalska and A Pető, 'The Gendered Modus Operandi of the Illiberal Transformation in Hungary and Poland' (2018) 68 *Women's Studies International Forum* 164, 166–67.

[77] Hungarian Parliament, 'Political Declaration on the Protection of Women and Children' (5 May 2020).

[78] P Guasti, 'Same Same, but Different: Domestic Conditions of Illiberal Backlash Against Universal Rights in the Czech Republic and Slovakia' in A Lorenz and LH Anders, *Illiberal Trends and Anti-EU Politics in East Central Europe* (Palgrave MacMillan, 2021) 180–81.

to these allegations, the Council of Europe issued a legal opinion[79] clarifying that 'the Istanbul Convention does not imply the obligation to legally recognise a third sex or to provide legal recognition of same-sex marriages'.[80] Despite these clarifications, some Member States are still withholding ratification, which has made EU accession to this instrument all the more relevant to achieve the goals of the Convention.

The EU signed the Convention on 13 June 2017 and, despite the disagreements that some Member States have introduced in the debate, the Council requested the consent of the European Parliament to adopt a decision on the conclusion of the Convention in February 2023. On 1 June 2023, the European Council issued a decision on the accession to the Istanbul Convention and, on 28 June 2023, the instrument of accession was deposited with the Secretary General of the Council of Europe. This decision followed the Court of Justice of the European Union's (CJEU) reasoning in Opinion 1/19,[81] in which the Court clarified that following the requirements laid down in Articles 218(2), (6), and (8) of the TFEU, the Council could not add a further step in the conclusion process based on reaching a common agreement between the Member States.[82] However, nothing prevented it from waiting before adopting the decision of accession to achieve unanimity within the Council.[83] In other words, the Council could wait until Member States reached a unanimous agreement to accede to the Istanbul Convention, but it could not add an additional requirement of unanimity to the Council decision. Following the CJEU's Opinion, the Council's decision to move ahead with ratification without this unanimous agreement was a positive development in the advancement of EU goals in the field of gender.[84] In parallel, the Commission has already adopted a series of measures, such as the proposal of a Directive on Domestic Violence (now adopted), to achieve the goals of the Convention at EU and Member State level.

Nevertheless, the EU's decision to ratify the Convention has a disadvantage: this remains a mixed agreement, where some Member States have still not ratified the Convention and have not agreed on the Council's decision to ratify it. This permits that Member States that have not ratified the Convention are bound by it only when EU competences are exercised.[85] Despite this limitation, the Istanbul Convention is likely to become a key standard for the interpretation of EU law, including the protection of EU fundamental rights and equality laws.[86] This includes the protection of the rights of victims of gender-based violence. As seen earlier, the EU already has competences and has developed legislation in this area, for which the Convention has now become a key interpretative tool.

[79] Council of Europe, 'Convention on Preventing and Combating Violence against Women and Domestic Violence (CETS No 210) – Scope of Obligations' (11 January 2018).

[80] ibid para 18.

[81] Opinion 1/19 of the Court (Grand Chamber) of 6 October 2021, ECLI:EU:C:2021:198.

[82] ibid para 254–58.

[83] ibid para 253.

[84] Gender Equality Strategy 2020-2025 (n 11) 4.

[85] On the difficulties of mixed agreements, see: P Koutrakos, 'Confronting the Complexities of Mixed Agreements-*Opinion 1/19* on the Istanbul Convention' (2022) 47 *European Law Review* 247; F Castillo de la Torre, 'El *Dictamen 1/19* del TJUE sobre el Convenio de Estambul sobre la Prevención y Lucha contra la Violencia contra la Mujer y la Violencia Doméstica: entre el rigor y el pragmatismo' (2023) 84 *Revista Española De Derecho Europeo* 93.

[86] K Nousiainen and C Chinkin, Legal Implications of EU Accession to the Istanbul Convention (European Commission, December 2015) 84.

Overall, the Istanbul Convention advances the EU's strategy in the field of victims' rights, particularly in the field of protection. The Convention develops a comprehensive framework of protection and support to victims of gender-based violence; mandates the criminalisation of various forms of gender-based violence; emphasises the principles of non-discrimination and gender equality as fundamental to addressing violence against women, and promotes preventative initiatives to change cultural and societal norms that perpetuate this violence. The Directive on Domestic Violence builds on these goals closely, albeit in a more limited manner, and becomes an essential instrument to operationalise these obligations at Member State level.

B. The Commission's Proposals on Victims' Rights: An Analysis of their Impact on Victims of Gender-Based Violence

The Directive on Domestic Violence is an essential instrument to fulfil the Commission's Presidency guidelines, which included ending violence against women, widening protection for victims of these offences, and punishing offenders as priorities for the period 2020–2025.[87] The adoption of this Directive relies on criminal justice competences under Articles 83(1) and 82(2) TFEU, which is consistent with the main goals of the proposal that combines the criminalisation of certain offences that target women disproportionately and the strengthening of the rights of such victims.[88] This initiative was followed, in July 2023, by the presentation of a legislative initiative to amend the Victims' Rights Directive.[89] This proposal incorporates reforms in areas that are essential for victims of domestic violence and gender-based violence, such as improvements in crime reporting; access to specialist support for vulnerable victims; increased participation of victims in criminal proceedings; access to compensation for victims, and the development of victims' protection measures based on an assessment of victims' needs. This section will consider how these two initiatives seek to address some of the gaps identified in the exercise of the rights to protection and access to justice by victims of domestic and gender-based violence.

Overall, the Directive on Domestic Violence is a step in the right direction to achieve the objectives of the Istanbul Convention, particularly in harmonising the definition of certain offences (eg female genital mutilation or forced marriage). However, the final version of this Directive has also removed essential parts of the harmonisation of offences. For instance, the version of the proposal for a Directive on Domestic Violence presented by the Commission in March 2022 harmonised the definition of rape, by making the lack of consent the essential element of this offence and eliminating the

[87] President U Von der Leyen, 'A Union that Strives for More: My Agenda for Europe' (Political Guidelines for the next European Commission 2019–2024) 11.

[88] Proposal for a Directive of the European Parliament and of the Council amending Directive 2012/29/EU establishing minimum standards on the rights, support and protection of victims of crime, and replacing Council Framework Decision 2001/220/JHA, COM/2023/424 final, Explanatory Memorandum para 1.

[89] Proposal amending the Victims' Rights Directive (n 10). For an analysis of this proposal, see T Wahl, 'Commission Proposes Reform of Victims' Rights Directive' (EUCrim, 22 September 2023), available at https://eucrim.eu/news/commission-proposes-reform-of-victims-rights-directive/.

requirement of violence or intimidation that some Member States still maintain within their domestic legislations.[90] This definition is in line with Article 36(1)a of the Istanbul Convention, which considers the lack of consent essential to the fulfilment of the *actus reus* of all sexual offences. This provision, nonetheless, did not consider other types of non-consensual acts of a sexual nature that are also criminalised under Article 36(1).[91] In other words, the Commission's proposal left out instances of sexual abuse and sexual assault without penetration, implementing a very restrictive reading of the Convention and the centrality of consent and women's autonomy that it imposes. This list has been further restricted in the adopted Directive, which focusses on the harmonisation of cyber offences, forced marriage, and female genital mutilation.

On the other hand, when discussing victims' rights, it is noteworthy that the Directive on Domestic Violence does not regulate the right of victims of gender-based violence to participate in criminal proceedings. Chapter 3 of the Directive includes 'access to justice' within its title, but references to victims' standing and access to justice in criminal proceedings are very limited. As explained in section III.A, victims' access to justice and their standing in criminal trials is recognised as a right of victims under the Victims' Rights Directive.[92] Nevertheless, differences concerning the legal status of victims across Member States and their capacity to participate in proceedings and access remedies persist. For instance, in some Member States, victims have full status as a third party during criminal proceedings whilst, in others, they are only considered witnesses during trial.[93] These differences, together with the limited harmonisation impact under the Victims' Rights Directive, means that significant differences persist across the EU in the guarantee of this right.[94]

The revision of the Victims' Rights Directive seeks to fix some of these issues by expanding on the right to access information and support in court[95] and reinforcing the right of victims to challenge decisions that affect their rights, independently of their formal status under national law in the criminal proceedings.[96] This reform, if adopted, would expand on the right of victims to have access to effective remedies at Member State level when judicial decisions affect their rights, provided that strict requirements are met. However, little is proposed in terms of facilitating their full participation in criminal proceedings, a significant gap identified in this area and explained above. Articles 10a and b explicitly acknowledge the differences that persist in terms of victims' formal status at Member State level and does not seek to address these divergencies.

In turn, Chapter 3 of the Directive on Domestic Violence focuses on the regulation of protection measures and the individual needs' assessment as an essential instrument in assessing these. The inclusion of an obligation upon Member States to provide protection

[90] Proposal for a Directive on combating violence against women and domestic violence, COM/2022/105 final.

[91] Amnesty International Recommendations (n 15) 6–7.

[92] Victims' Rights Directive (n 3) Chapter 3.

[93] Lehmkuhl (n 28) 196.

[94] Women Against Violence Europe (WAVE), 'Public Statement on the Proposal for a Directive on Combating Violence Against Women and Domestic Violence' (November 2022) 2, available at https://wave-network.org/wp-content/uploads/151122_WAVE_RedLinesNovember_F.pdf.

[95] Proposal amending the Victims' Rights Directive (n 10) Art 10a.

[96] Directive on Domestic Violence (n 9) Art 25.

measures for victims of gender-based violence[97] and the regulation of the individualised assessment as a tool to identify these needs is a welcome development that mirrors the obligations adopted under the Convention.[98] On the other hand, the proposal to reform the Victims' Rights Directive reinforces the importance of the individual needs' assessment and its role in determining physicial protection needs from the first contact with the authorities.[99] This reform supports the steps taken by the Directive on Domestic Violence in terms of guaranteeing the safety of victims of domestic violence, but does not address the problems faced by cross-border victims due to the persistence of different regulations and protection measures across the EU. These disparities are particularly problematic when seeking the cross-border enforcement of protection orders, as examined in the context of the EPO Directive and the EPM Regulation in section III.B.[100] Cross-border victims, in turn, are particularly vulnerable to secondary victimisation and re-victimisation, and access to protection is more difficult for them to obtain, but none of these proposals address this particular problem. These proposals do not incorporate harmonisation of minimum standards for protection measures, which means disparities across the EU are likely to remain, perpetuating the difficulties encountered for the cross-border enforcement of protection measures.[101]

Additionally, some organisations have criticised the lack of appropriate protection measures that take into account the specific needs faced by victims of domestic violence in the Directive on Domestic Violence, particularly when offender and victim have children in common.[102] The Istanbul Convention, in its Article 31, requires that judicial authorities consider violent criminal offences, including instances of gender-based violence within the scope of the Convention, before granting visitation rights to the abuser. The Commission's proposal to reform the Victims' Rights Directive, on the other hand, does not include any reference to this situation and only incorporates references to children as victims, in terms of reporting crime (Article 5a) and their access to adequate support (Article 9a). To guarantee the physical protection of victims and wellbeing of children it would be important that the Commission include a provision linking the protection of the victim of gender-based violence, the existence of that violence, and the visitation rights of the accused in the Directive on Domestic Violence. These are all issues that the judicial authority should consider to ensure that the protection of both the child and the victim are guaranteed in accordance with their individual needs. In this context, some authors (and some Member States) have gone further to suggest that a provision should be added 'obliging Member States to ensure that violence by an intimate partner is a decisive factor when determining custody and visitation rights'.[103]

Overall, the Directive on Domestic Violence and the proposal for a reform of the Victims' Rights Directive have clarified the scope of application of some of the rights that are essential to victims of gender-based and domestic violence and strengthened

[97] ibid Art 15.
[98] ibid Art 17.
[99] Proposal amending the Victims' Rights Directive (n 10) Art 10b(10).
[100] See section III.B.
[101] ibid.
[102] WAVE (n 94) 5–6.
[103] ibid 6.

the binding nature of such rights, particularly the rights to access support services or protection. Nevertheless, very little has been done to address some of the issues surrounding their implementation and harmonisation at Member State level, particularly when discussing the rights of cross-border victims. The proposal to reform the Victims' Rights Directive has gone a step further in this area by clarifying the obligation of States to provide physical protection measures from the first contact and by incorporating the duty of States to establish and revise such measures according to the assessment of individual needs. However, the absence of minimum standards regulating protections measures facilitates that very different standards persist across the EU, restricting the effectiveness of protection orders.

C. Gender-Based Violence as a Euro Crime

The Directive on Domestic Violence focuses on the criminalisation of a number of criminal offences, including the practice of female genital mutilation, and certain forms of cyber violence, such as cyber stalking, cyber harassment, cyber incitement to violence or hatred against women, and the non-consensual sharing of intimate or manipulated material. These conducts are amongst those included in the Istanbul Convention, but this Directive has left out other forms of gender-based violence especially recognised by this instrument, such as the denial of sexual and reproductive rights (Article 38 of the Istanbul Convention). This limitation could have been overcome by either broadening the offences incorporated in the proposed Directive on Domestic Violence or by criminalising all conducts constitutive of gender-based violence under Article 83(1) TFEU. The latter is a possibility supported by non-governmental organisations that have examined this proposal and favoured an approach that would permit an easier adaptation of this legislation to changing times.[104]

Article 83(1) TFEU would facilitate this flexibility by including gender-based violence within the list of the so-called 'Euro crimes', namely particularly serious offences that have a cross-border dimension and pose a significant threat to the interests of the EU as a whole. If the requirements of gravity (serious offence) and cross-border nature are met, Article 83(1) permits the establishment of minimum standards for the definition of such offences and their sanctions. Some examples of gender-based violence are already criminalised as Euro crimes under Article 83(1) TFEU, such as the sexual exploitation and trafficking of women and children.[105] Nevertheless, extending this list to encompass all instances of gender-based violence would require widening the exhaustive list of criminal offences for which the European Parliament and the Council may establish minimum rules.[106] The European Parliament has shown support for this possibility.

[104] Amnesty International Recommendations (n 15) 8–9.

[105] TFEU Art 83(1); Directive 2011/36/EU of the European Parliament and of the Council of 5 April 2011 on preventing and combating trafficking in human beings and protecting its victims, and replacing Council Framework Decision 2002/629/JHA [2011] OJ L101/1.

[106] According to TFEU, Art 83(1), this list includes: terrorism, trafficking in human beings and sexual exploitation of women and children, illicit drug trafficking, illicit arms trafficking, money laundering, corruption, counterfeiting of means of payment, computer crime and organised crime.

On 16 September 2021, it supported the possibility of extending such a list and adopted a legislative proposal by 427 votes in favour, 119 against, and 140 abstentions to list gender-based violence as a new Euro crime under Article 83(1) TFEU.[107]

However, Article 83(1) TFEU requires that the Council adopts a decision identifying areas of particularly serious crime with a cross-border dimension due to their nature or impact or from the need to combat such offences. And this might be a particularly high standard to incorporate gender-based violence within the list of Article 83(1) TFEU. As seen in section IV.A, some Member States are reluctant to recognise the structural and widespread nature of gender-based violence as defined by the Istanbul Convention. This might restrict the possibilities of obtaining unanimity in the Council to broaden the list of Euro crimes and explain the preference of the Commission for the selective approach explained above. This, however, does not explain why it excluded two key offences under the Istanbul Convention: forced marriage and the denial of sexual and reproductive rights.

In the long-term, Article 83(1) TFEU continues to provide an alternative to harmonise all types of gender-based violence in line with the main objectives of the Istanbul Convention. On the one hand, these offences meet the threshold of 'particularly serious offence'. Gender-based violence covers a broad range of conducts that range from the most serious of offences, namely femicide, which affects an average of two women daily across the EU,[108] to other types of sexual, physical, financial, or psychological violence, which affects one in two women across the EU.[109] The statistics show the structural nature of these fundamental rights violations that represent one of the most prevalent examples of gender inequality across EU Member States.[110] From the consequences that this type of violence can have, which range from chronic mental and physical health problems to labour market exclusion, poverty, and even the loss of life, it is clear that these types of conduct meet the threshold of 'particularly serious offences'. On the other hand, the statistics analysed above demonstrate the 'cross-border element' of gender-based violence. Gender-based violence is prevalent across all Member States examined, and it is estimated that it has a cost of over €366 billion for the European Union (approx €175 billion correspond to domestic or intimate partner violence).[111] At the same time, this violence has an impact on women's exercise of fundamental rights and fundamental freedoms, including their right to move freely across the EU and their capacity to exercise their citizenship rights.

[107] European Parliament, 'Make Gender-Based Violence a Crime under EU Law, MEPs Say' (Press Release, 19 September 2021), available at www.europarl.europa.eu/news/en/press-room/20210910IPR11927/make-gender-based-violence-a-crime-under-eu-law-meps-say.

[108] European Institute for Gender Equality, 'Gender Equality Index Report 2023: Towards a Green Transition in Transport and Energy' (Publications Office of the European Union, 2023).

[109] EU Agency for Fundamental Rights, 'Crime, Safety and Victims' Rights: Fundamental Rights Survey' (2021) 18–19.

[110] On the prevalence and characteristics of gender-based violence in Europe, see: C Bradbury-Jones, JV Appleton et al., 'A Profile of Gender-Based Violence Research in Europe: Findings From a Focused Mapping Review and Synthesis' (2019) 20 *Trauma, Violence and Abuse* 470; G Malgesini, L Cesarini Sforza and M Babović, *Gender-based Violence and Poverty in Europe* (European Anti Poverty Network, 2019).

[111] European Institute for Gender Equality, 'The Costs of Gender-Based Violence in the European Union' (Publications Office of the European Union, 2021) 21.

Ultimately, the criminalisation of gender-based violence, although not providing a definite solution to all of these issues (the Istanbul Convention and the Directive on Domestic Violence recognise the necessity to tackle the root causes of inequality as the only long-term solution to this violence), would provide a powerful tool to combat gender-based violence across the EU. At the same time, this would meet the EU's obligations under Chapter V of the Istanbul Convention, which should set a benchmark in the fight against gender-based violence.

V. Conclusions

Traditionally, victims have had a secondary role in criminal proceedings limited to them acting as witnesses from which facts could be extracted to obtain the conviction of the accused. In other words, victims lacked specific rights and did not play any relevant role in criminal proceedings.[112] This traditional vision of the criminal justice system started changing in the EU in the early 2000s with the adoption of the Framework Decision on the standing of victims in criminal proceedings. Since then, the EU has adopted, amongst other instruments, the EPO Directive, the EPM Regulation and the Victims' Rights Directive aiming at standardising the rights of victims in criminal proceedings and guaranteeing their access to support, protection, justice, and compensation across the EU. Nevertheless, the success of these efforts has been limited, particularly when considering the position of vulnerable victims such as victims of gender-based violence.

The EU lacked a specific approach towards the rights of victims of gender-based violence until the Commission adopted the Gender Equality Strategy 2020–2025 and the EU Strategy on Victims' Rights 2020–2025. These strategies have permitted the drafting of a Directive on Domestic Violence, which develops a series of rights that are essential for all victims but, particularly, for victims of gender-based violence. This proposal, together with the Commission's proposal to reform the Victims' Rights Directive, has reinforced the binding nature of, *inter alia*, the right of access to protection measures, access to justice, or access to support services. Despite these advances, this chapter has shown the difficulties that these victims still face when trying to exercise them. These difficulties continue to exist due to the differences across Member States, the financial difficulties in implementing some of the measures introduced by the Victims' Rights Directive, the differences across Member State criminal justice systems, and the limited harmonisation impact in this area. These difficulties continue to affect, particularly, cross-border victims, who are more likely to be re-victimised and whose rights to free movement are likely to be affected by the lack of effective cross-border protection measures.

The Council's accession to the Istanbul Convention and the Directive on Domestic Violence have been seen as a turning point that may provide a comprehensive framework to end gender-based violence and overcome these difficulties. Nevertheless, this chapter has shown that, whilst these instruments are essential to promote an EU-wide approach

[112] VE Gaviria Londoño, 'Estado actual de los derechos de las víctimas en el proceso penal: evolución (¿involución?) dogmática, jurisprudencial y legislativa' (2009) 30 *Derecho Penal y Criminología* 37, 39.

to this type of violence, the Directive on Domestic Violence falls short of the commitments adopted by the EU and most Member States under the Istanbul Convention. For instance, it fails to criminalise all instances of gender-based violence incorporated in this instrument and does not address the protection needs of these victims. Despite the difficulties examined in section IV.C, the criminalisation of this offence as a Euro crime could help address some of these limitations, help the Commission fulfil some of its commitments in the field of combatting gender-based violence and contribute to the development of a truly comprehensive framework to combat these offences.[113]

[113] Amnesty International Recommendations (n 15) 3.

4

The Flood that Never Came: Case Law of the Court of Justice on the Victims' Rights *Acquis*

ADAM ŁAZOWSKI

I. Introduction

It was 11 June 1982, a late summer night in otherwise peaceful Paris. Ian William Cowan, a British citizen, had exited the *Métro* and – much to his surprise – faced a rather adversary environment. While a traditional *bonsoir* would have been more agreeable, sadly, he was assaulted and robbed. Alas, the perpetrators fled the crime scene, leaving him seriously injured and short of 150 French Francs.

This is not a brief description of a new instalment of a TV crime series, but, in a nutshell, the summary of a criminal offence committed over 40 years ago in one of the *arrondissements* of Paris. At first sight, it may look like nothing out of the ordinary. As deploring as the reality may be, such crimes are committed daily in every corner of the planet. For the purposes of this chapter it is interesting to note that the victim's next actions laid the foundations for a piece of contemporary EU *acquis* on the rights of victims. To begin with, Mr Cowan filed his request for compensation with the French *Commission d'indemnisation des victimes d'infraction*, which – in turn – proceeded with a reference for preliminary ruling to the Court of Justice. The Court ruled that the general prohibition of discrimination on grounds of nationality, which – at the time – was regulated in Article 7 EEC (now Article 18 Treaty on the Functioning of the European Union (TFEU)), precluded the French legislation that limited the right to receive compensation for harm caused by a crime to the French citizens or third country nationals who possessed residence permits, or their countries of nationality had reciprocal agreements with France.[1] Both Advocate General (AG) Lenz[2] and the Court of Justice sang from the same hymn sheet.[3]

[1] Case 186/87 *Ian William Cowan v Trésor public* ECLI:EU:C:1989:47.

[2] Case 186/87 *Ian William Cowan v Trésor public* ECLI:EU:C:1988:526, Opinion of AG Lenz.

[3] See further, *inter alia*, S Weatherill, 'Case 186/87, Cowan v. Le Tresor Public. Preliminary reference under Art. 177 EEC by the Commission d'indemnisation des vicfimes des infraction du Tribunal de Grande Instance

Since then a lot of water has passed under the bridges on the river Seine. The judgment in *Cowan* became one of the inspirations for the adoption of Directive 2004/80 on compensation to crime victims.[4] Irrespective of Mr Cowan and his unpleasant adventures, a series of EU criminal law instruments were also approved with the aim of either holistically dealing with the victims' rights,[5] or regulating them as part and parcel of legislation providing frameworks, for instance, for combatting of trafficking in human beings or violence against women.[6] Against this backdrop it is intriguing to explore to what extent the transposition of these legal acts and their application in national courts have triggered jurisprudence of the Court of Justice. The existing evidence as to the delayed or – at best – partial transposition could, perhaps, make one expect the Court's docket to be filled with infringement cases brought by the European Commission or references for preliminary ruling submitted by national courts.[7] In fact, such a flood of cases has never materialised. In other words, the case law of the Court of Justice on victims' rights is sparce. The reasons are manifold and attributable to a variety of factors of a legal and non-legal nature.

To start with, at the time when Framework Decision 2001/220 and Directive 2004/80on the standing of victims in criminal proceedings were approved, the European Union was taking baby steps in regulating victims' rights. In more general terms, those were also the very early days of EU criminal law and thus, it only remained on the radars of true *afficionados*. Consequently, for many lawyers, in particular those on the Bench

de Paris, on the interpretation of Art. 7 EEC. Decision of the European Court of Justice of 2 February 1989' (1989) 26 *CML Rev* 563; J Mertens de Wilmars, 'L'arret Cowan' (1990) 26 *Cahiers de droit européen* 393.

[4] Council Directive 2004/80/EC of 29 April 2004 relating to compensation to crime victims [2004] OJ L261/15. See Recital 2 of the Preamble. As noted in the academic literature, one of the reasons why victims' rights appeared on the EU agenda, and why this area received such priority treatment, was the status of 'cross-border victims'. See MS Groenhuijsen and A Pemberton, 'The EU Framework Decision for Victims of Crime: Does Hard Law Make a Difference?' (2009) 17 *European Journal of Crime, Criminal Law and Criminal Justice* 43, 44.

[5] Council Framework Decision 2001/220/JHA of 15 March 2001 on the standing of victims in criminal proceedings [2001] OJ L82/1; Directive 2012/29/EU of the European Parliament and of the Council of 25 October 2012 establishing minimum standards on the rights, support and protection of victims of crime, and replacing Council Framework Decision 2001/220/JHA [2012] OJ L315/57.

[6] Directive 2011/99/EU of the European Parliament and of the Council of 13 December 2011 on the European protection order [2011] OJ L338/2; Regulation (EU) No 606/2013 of the European Parliament and of the Council of 12 June 2013 on mutual recognition of protection measures in civil matters [2013] OJ L 181/4; Directive 2011/36/EU of the European Parliament and of the Council of 5 April 2011 on preventing and combating trafficking in human beings and protecting its victims, and replacing Council Framework Decision 2002/629/JHA [2011] OJ L 101/1; Directive 2011/93/EU of the European Parliament and of the Council of 13 December 2011 on combating the sexual abuse and sexual exploitation of children and child pornography, and replacing Council Framework Decision 2004/68/JHA [2011] OJ L335/1; Directive (EU) 2017/541 of the European Parliament and of the Council of 15 March 2017 on combating terrorism and replacing Council Framework Decision 2002/475/JHA and amending Council Decision 2005/671/JHA [2017] OJ L88/6; Directive (EU) 2019/713 of the European Parliament and of the Council of 17 April 2019 on combating fraud and counterfeiting of non-cash means of payment and replacing Council Framework Decision 2001/413/JHA [2019] OJ L123/18; Directive (EU) 2024/1385 of the European Parliament and of the Council of 14 May 2024 on combating violence against women and domestic violence [2024] OJ L2024/1385.

[7] For an analysis see, *inter alia*, A Łazowski, 'Tra il dire e il fare c'è di mezzo il mare. Harmonisation of Victims' Rights in EU Criminal Law' in K Lenaerts, E Regan, U Neergaard and K Engsig Sørensen (eds), *Shaping a Genuine Area of Freedom, Security and Justice. Perspectives on AFSJ Developments as a Driving Force of EU Law* (Hart Publishing, 2024).

and at the Bar, this was a *terra incognita*.[8] Another reason, which is discussed later in this chapter, is the fact that initially the jurisdiction of the Court of Justice in the then Third Pillar was limited. Then there is the non-legal side of the story. Unlike the rights of defendants, which are likely to be relied on by those subject to prosecution, the rights of victims apply to those who, by definition, are in a vulnerable position. Of course, some will be more vulnerable than others and many crimes will remain unreported. When push comes to shove and a case ends up in the national court, victims are likely to testify as witnesses and express a desire to keep the ordeal as brief as possible. Under such circumstances, a prospect of putting on hold the domestic proceedings to clarify a nuance of EU law with the Court of Justice would not be, by any stretch of the imagination, a tempting proposition.[9] Those are, of course, just examples of reasons why the number of cases that have so far reached the Court of Justice is not spectacular. And yet, one should not be misled by statistical data itself and jump to conclusions without looking at the substance of the cases which have landed in the Courts' docket. In other words, one needs to remember about the limited power of bare numbers. As noted by M Bobek and J Adams-Prassl, 'numbers in and of themselves do not tell much of a story, of course, especially in the law'.[10] The reality is that some of the cases which reached the Luxembourg courtrooms have laid a firm mark either on the application of EU criminal law at large, or on the interpretation of the legal acts on rights of victims. With this in mind, the aim of this chapter is to shed light on these fairly rare occasions when the advocates general and judges of the Court of Justice were called upon to take a closer look at victims' rights.

The analysis starts with the evolution of jurisdiction of the Court of Justice in criminal matters (section II). In section III the jurisprudence on Framework Decision 2001/220 and Directive 2012/29, the two flagship EU instruments on victims' rights, is put under the microscope. In turn, section IV is dedicated to case law based on Directive 2004/80.[11] Conclusions are offered in section V.

II. Evolving Jurisdiction of the Court of Justice to Adjudicate on Victims' Rights

Since 1989 when the *Cowan* judgment was handed down by the Court of Justice, its jurisdiction to deal with victims' rights has considerably evolved. For the sake of clarity,

[8] A bit of anecdotal evidence may be fitting at this juncture. The author of the present chapter was involved as a country correspondent in several studies prepared for the European Commission by the European Criminal Law Academic Network (ECLAN). For that purpose, a plethora of interviews was conducted with various stakeholders. Frequently, conversations would start with a blunt opening line explaining that it was the first time the interlocutors were hearing about such EU legal acts ('Framework what?'/ 'Would you, as a starting point, kindly tell me something about the EU legal act this conversation is supposed to be about?').

[9] I am grateful to participants of the ECLAN Annual Conference ('Stronger Victims' Rights in EU Law? Assessment and Prospects') held in Brussels on 18 April 2023 for drawing my attention to this very valid point.

[10] M Bober and J Adams-Prassl, 'Conclusions' in M Bobek, J Adams-Prassl (eds), *The EU Charter of Fundamental Rights in the Member States* (Hart Publishing, 2020) 559, 560.

[11] It is not accidental that the present analysis is limited to Framework Decision 2001/220, Directive 2012/29, and Directive 2004/80. As things stood when the present chapter was last updated (27 November 2024),

it should be emphasised that the changes which have been made in the intervening time were not tailored specifically to the area of our interest but rather they have been a consequence of the general evolution of the Court's jurisdiction in the Area of Freedom, Security and Justice (AFSJ). In graphic terms, this can be compared to two separate motorways originating in two geographical locations, which – however – are separated by a considerable distance. One has its starting point in a remote corner of the country, the other one commences somewhere much closer to the junction where they merge into a single motorway taking travellers to a common destination.

Cowan as well as Directive 2004/80 have travelled on the first of those two motorways. Article 7 EEC (now Article 18 TFEU), which served as the anchor in *Cowan*, as well as the Directive in question, that was based on Article 308 EC (now Article 352 TFEU), have always fallen under the general rules on the jurisdiction of the Court. Thus both the infringement procedures, as well as the preliminary ruling procedure have applied fully and from the day these legal acts entered into force. Consequently, the European Commission and national courts have had the full jurisdiction to trigger the respective types of Court procedures, just as they have had in all other areas falling under the former first pillar of the European Union. In particularly pressing cases, the expedited procedure could have been put into action, albeit subject to a positive decision of the Court.[12]

Things were completely different with the Framework Decision 2001/220, which – just like other EU criminal law instruments adopted in the pre-Lisbon Treaty era – suffered from very limited jurisdiction of the Court.[13] This second motorway on which it travelled was full of diversions and potholes, precluding a smooth ride. To begin with, the main tools for public enforcement of EU law, that is the infringement procedures, did not apply in relation to such legal acts until 1 December 2014.[14] A direct consequence of that enforcement deficiency was that the late or partial transposition of framework decisions went unpunished for years. Without the sword of Damocles over their heads, the Member States proceeded at their leisure, making deficiencies in transposition a general rule, not an exception. The reports of the European Commission on transposition of Framework Decision 2001/220 have shown the scale of the problem.[15] Private enforcement in national courts had its limits, too. Firstly, since the entry into force of the Treaty of Amsterdam, the jurisdiction to send references for preliminary

cases on the victims' rights regulated in other EU legal acts had yet to reach the Court of Justice, or – in one instance – were declared to be manifestly inadmissible (see case C-241/24 *Tsenochev* ECLI:EU:C:2024:931).

[12] See Arts 105–106 of the Rules of Procedure of the Court of Justice [2012] OJ L265/1.

[13] See, *inter alia*, A Hinarejos, *Judicial Control in the European Union. Reforming Jurisdiction in the Intergovernmental Pillars* (Oxford University Press, 2009) 14–121. See also A Łazowski, 'Stepping into Uncharted Waters No More: The Court of Justice and EU Criminal Law' in C Brière and A Weyembergh (eds), *The Needed Balances in EU Criminal Law. Past, Present and Future* (Hart Publishing, 2018).

[14] The end of the transition period laid down in Article 10 of Protocol no 36 introduced by the Treaty of Lisbon.

[15] Report from the European Commission on the basis of Article 18 of the Council Framework Decision of 15 March 2001 on the standing of victims in criminal proceedings COM (2004) 54 final; Report from the Commission pursuant to Article 18 of the Council Framework Decision of 15 March 2001 on the standing of victims in criminal proceedings (2001/220/JHA) COM (2009) 166 final.

ruling under the then Article 35 Treaty on European Union (TEU) was limited only to the extent that it was recognised by the Member States.[16] With only some Member States allowing their courts to proceed with references, many national judges were left to their own devices. It is notable, though, that a dedicated fast lane was provided. As of 2008, a new tailor-made fast track procedure for the handling of references on the AFSJ (Urgent Preliminary Ruling Procedure, PPU for short) was added to the Court's procedural toolkit.[17] Secondly, a fundamental tenet of EC law: the doctrine of direct effect did not (and still does not) apply to framework decisions and decisions adopted under the Third Pillar legal bases.[18] As will be shown in section III of this chapter, against these limitations, the Court of Justice came to the rescue in *Pupino* by extending the doctrine of indirect effect to framework decisions (a judgment, which dealt with the interpretation of Framework Decision 2001/220).[19] All of the above, combined with the simple fact that EU criminal law was in its early formative years, and the knowledge about it was anything but widespread, translated into a restricted involvement of the Court of Justice.[20]

An important qualitative change came with the entry into force of the Treaty of Lisbon and expiry of the transition period laid down therein. As of 1 December 2014, the special regimes regulating the Courts' jurisdiction in the AFSJ are no more. In other words, both the standard infringement procedures and the general regime for preliminary ruling apply to legal acts forming EU criminal law. Since then, the motorways have been, therefore, merged.

III. *Pupino* and All the Rest: Case Law on Framework Decision 2001/220 and Directive 2012/29

A. Introduction

Framework Decision 2001/220 was the first EU legal instrument to regulate the rights of victims.[21] It was a novelty in the EU law book in more than one way, however. After framework decisions were added to the suite of secondary legislation by the Treaty of

[16] See Information concerning the declarations by the Republic of Hungary, the Republic of Latvia, the Republic of Lithuania and the Republic of Slovenia on their acceptance of the jurisdiction of the Court of Justice to give preliminary rulings on the acts referred to in Article 35 of the Treaty on European Union [2008] OJ C69/1.

[17] See, *inter alia*, S Iglesias Sánchez, 'The Urgent Preliminary Ruling Procedure and the European Arrest Warrant' in A Łazowski and V Mitsilegas (eds), *Coming of Age? The European Arrest Warrant at Twenty* (Hart Publishing, forthcoming in 2025).

[18] Case C-573/17 *Criminal Proceedings against Daniel Adam Popławski* ECLI:EU:C:2019:530. For an academic appraisal of this judgment, see D Miąsik and M Szwarc, 'Primacy and Direct Effect – Still Together: Popławski II, Case C-573/17, Criminal Proceedings against Daniel Adam Popławski' (2021) 58 *CML Rev* 571.

[19] Case C-105/03 *Criminal proceedings against Maria Pupino* ECLI:EU:C:2005:386.

[20] The Court of Justice itself was navigating unchartered waters as criminal law was a relative novelty. See further, *inter alia*, Łazowski (n 13).

[21] See further, *inter alia*, Groenhuijsen and Pemberton (n 4).

Amsterdam, this was the first EU legal act of that type to ever be adopted.[22] One can debate if it has generated the voltage necessary to turn the rights of victims regulated therein into a reality. Many of its provisions have been vaguely formulated, raising a legitimate question of its added value.[23] Furthermore, as already alluded to, it suffered from patchy and delayed transposition into national laws of the Member States. And yet, despite all, it has served as a foundation for several judgments of the Court of Justice. Its successor, Directive 2012/29, has fared better, even though the Member States have been rather economical with transposition to domestic law.[24] This legal act, too, has paid several visits to the courtrooms at Kirchberg, though not as many as one could, perhaps, expect.

However, in the great scheme of things, one judgment based on Framework Decision 2001/220 has outgrown all other case law developments: *Pupino*. This decision as well as its broader impact are analysed in turn (section III.B). In section III.C a series of judgments based on Framework Decision 2001/220 is looked at. Section III.D puts under the microscope Court of Justice of the European Union (CJEU) jurisprudence on Directive 2012/29.

B. Judgment in *Pupino* and its Impact on Enforcement of EU Criminal Law

Pupino was a milestone, the *Van Gend en Loos* moment of EU criminal law. It was one of those serendipitous judicial developments, which had the effects going well beyond the actual case and paved the way for a breakthrough in enforcement of post-Amsterdam Third Pillar legislation. *Pupino* has been addressed extensively in the academic literature, thus there is little point in going over all its details.[25] It suffices to remind readers that the crux of the issue was whether the provisions of the Italian Criminal Procedure Code governing testimony, should have been interpreted in the light of Framework Decision 2001/220 to allow for special treatment of vulnerable victims of crime. *In casu*, the victims were a group of small children who had been exposed to rather brutal and unorthodox teaching methods employed by their former kindergarten teacher. The matter raised in the reference for preliminary ruling, apart from the

[22] See further on framework decisions, *inter alia*, A Łazowski and B Kurcz, 'Two Sides of the Same Coin? Framework Decisions and Directives Compared' (2006) 25 *Yearbook of European Law* 177; MJ Borgers, 'Implementing Framework Decisions' (2007) 44 *CML Rev* 1361.

[23] For examples, see Łazowski (n 7).

[24] That is so even despite the guidelines on transposition provided by the European Commission. See European Commission, 'Report from the Commission to the European Parliament and the Council on the implementation of Directive 2012/29/EU of the European Parliament and of the Council of 25 October 2012 establishing minimum standards on the rights, support and protection of victims of crime, and replacing Council Framework Decision 2001/220/JHA' COM (2020) 188 final; European Commission, 'DG Justice Guidance Document related to the transposition and implementation of Directive 2012/29/EU of the European Parliament and of the Council of 25 October 2012 establishing minimum standards on the rights, support and protection of victims of crime, and replacing Council Framework Decision 2001/220/JHA' available at https://commission.europa.eu/system/files/2019-02/13_12_19_3763804_guidance_victims_rights_directive_eu_en.pdf.

[25] See, *inter alia*, M Fletcher, 'Extending "Indirect Effect" to the Third Pillar: The Significance of Pupino?' (2005) 30 *EL Rev* 862; E Spaventa, 'Opening Pandora's Box: Some Reflections on the Constitutional Effects

obvious issue of criminal law, was a fundamental question about constitutional principles applicable in the Third Pillar. On the one hand, it was clear from the then Article 34 TEU, and definition of framework decisions provided therein, that they could not produce direct effect. Yet did this also extend to other tenets governing enforcement of EU law, for example the doctrine of indirect effect? In its answer to questions submitted by the judge in charge of preliminary enquiries at the *Tribunale di Firenze*, the Court of Justice, sitting in the Grand Chamber composition, famously ruled that indirect effect applied to the area in question. Unlike AG Kokott, who provided a robust opinion in the case, the Court of Justice was – sadly though not surprisingly – quite economical in its reasoning.[26] The reaction of the Member States and the academic commentariat was mixed. Yet, looking at the entire story with the benefit of hindsight, one has to agree with Eleanor Sharpston who, in her Sir Thomas More Lecture 2008, aptly noted that '[s]omething that seems to cause surprise (if not downright consternation) is how often the ECJ merely applies established principles of construction known from EC law to AFSJ questions […]'.[27] And indeed, since Article 34 TEU precluded only direct effect, it did mean something that the Member States added neither the doctrine of indirect effect, nor the state liability to the mix. This was a garden gate left ajar, which the Court of Justice, not surprisingly for those who are familiar with the way it operates, decided to open.

The extension of indirect effect to Third Pillar instruments gave a very much needed thrust to their enforcement but, at the same time, it came with all limits that the doctrine in question inherently carries. The obligation to interpret national law in the light of EU law is required only as far as it is possible and, among others, it may not lead to interpretation *contra legem*.[28] This was set in stone in relation to directives, and so it has become also as far as indirect effect of framework decisions was concerned. In subsequent jurisprudence, the Court of Justice made clear in *Popławski II* that application of the doctrine of indirect effect to framework decisions does not trigger the *Simmenthal* mandate requiring the domestic judges to set aside conflicting national laws.[29] This can only be applicable in case of direct effect, which – all those years later – remains precluded in relation to framework decisions which are still in force. While many of them have indeed been replaced by directives (Framework Decision 2001/220 being a good example), some pre-Lisbon framework decisions remain in force. This includes Framework Decision 2002/584 on the European Arrest Warrant which, for over two

of the Decision in Pupino' (2007) 3 *European Constititional Law Review* 5; M Fletcher, 'Impact of the Pupino Decision on EU Law' in V Mitsilegas, A di Martino and L Mancano (eds), *The Court of Justice and European Criminal Law. Leading Cases in a Contextual Analysis* (Hart Publishing, 2019).

[26] Case C-105/03 *Criminal proceedings against Maria Pupino* ECLI:EU:C:2004:712, Opinion of AG Kokott.

[27] E Sharpston, 'The Area of Freedom, Security and Justice (AFSJ) in the EU. The Story So far and (Some of) the Challenges Ahead' in E Ligere (ed), *Lincoln's Inn Lectures on European Law and Human Rights* (Wildy, Simmonds & Hill Publishing, 2010) 103, 119.

[28] See, *inter alia*, Case 80/86 *Criminal proceedings against Kolpinghuis Nijmegen BV* ECLI:EU:C:1987:431, [1987] ECR 3969. See further L Martin, 'The General Principles of European (Criminal) Law as Limitation to the Enforcement of EU Law: The Kolpinghuis Nijmegen Rule' in Mitsilegas, di Martino, Mancano (n 25); S Prechal, *Directives in EC Law*, 2nd edn (Oxford University Press, 2005) 193–210.

[29] Case 106/77 *Amministrazione delle Finanze dello Stato v Simmenthal SpA* ECLI:EU:C:1978:49, [1978] ECR 629. See further, *inter alia*, K Lenaerts and Piet Van Nuffel, *EU Constitutional Law* (Oxford University Press, 2021) 635–39.

decades now, has remained the flagship of mutual recognition in criminal matters.[30] If one wished to assess the impact of *Pupino*, that would be a place to go.

C. *Beyond Pupino*: Jurisprudence on Framework Decision 2001/220 on the Standing of Victims in Criminal Procedure

Pupino, as already alluded to, was not the only judgment of the Court of Justice focusing on Framework Decision 2001/220. It was followed by several references for preliminary ruling aiming at clarification of the scope of application of the legal act in question and its relationship with national law. From the procedural point of view, these references had several things in common. Firstly, all of them were allocated by the Court to the five judges chambers. In other words, none of the cases – according to the Court – merited to be handled by the Grand Chamber. Secondly, in all cases it was decided at the *Réunion Générale* that an opinion of an Advocate General would be required. Thirdly, none of the cases were given a fast lane treatment (expedited procedure or, when it became available, the PPU).[31] The standard procedure applied. Fourthly, for reasons unknown to outsiders, many of the discussed references originated in Italian courts.

The starting point was case *Giovanni Dell'Orto*, which was submitted by the *Tribunale di Milano* against a particularly convoluted factual and legal background.[32] For the purposes of the present chapter, it suffices to say that the heart of the matter was repayment of considerable amounts of money which *Mr Dell'Orto* embezzled from an undertaking called *Saipem*. The question was whether *Saipem*, as a legal person, could rely on the right laid down in Article 9(3) of Framework Decision 2001/220, which provided that 'recoverable property belonging to victims which is seized in the course of criminal proceedings shall be returned to them without delay'. Both AG Kokott and the Court of Justice concluded that the legal act in question applied only to victims who were natural persons, therefore – as far as EU law was concerned – it did not apply to legal persons like *Saipem*.[33] That interpretation was confirmed a little over three years later, albeit in the context of Article 10(1) of Framework Decision 2001/220 (creating an obligation on the Member States to promote mediation), in *Emil Eredics*.[34] Here too, the Court of Justice and AG Kokott were on the same page, confirming that legal persons were not considered as victims that could benefit from Framework Decision 2001/220.[35]

[30] Council Framework Decision 2002/584/JHA of 13 June 2002 on the European arrest warrant and the surrender procedures between Member States [2002] OJ L190/1. See further, *inter alia*, Łazowski and Mitsilegas (n 17).

[31] Interestingly, several of these cases had judge Cunha Rodrigues on duty as *juge rapporteur* and Juliane Kokott as the Advocate General.

[32] See Case C-467/05 *Criminal proceedings against Giovanni Dell'Orto* ECLI:EU:C:2007:395. For the factual background see paras 16–30.

[33] AG Kokott in her opinion provided an extensive analysis of how Framework Decision 2001/220 should be interpreted in case, by the power of national law, the rights laid down therein were to be applied to legal persons. This issue, however, was not picked by the Court of Justice in its judgment. See *Dell'Orto* (n 32) Opinion of AG Kokott paras 73–96.

[34] Case C-205/09 *Criminal proceedings against Emil Eredics and Mária Vassné Sápi* ECLI:EU:C:2010:623.

[35] Case C-205/09 *Criminal proceedings against Emil Eredics and Mária Vassné Sápi* ECLI:EU:C:2010:396, Opinion of AG Kokott.

Another interesting issue as to the scope of application of Framework Decision 2001/220 was raised in *Katz*.[36] This time a reference was submitted by *Fővárosi Bíróság*, the Budapest Metropolitan Court in case of substitute private prosecution brought by Mr Katz against Mr Sós, who was accused of financial fraud. In the course of these proceedings, the applicant requested to be heard as a victim with the view of providing testimony. This request, however, was not entertained by the Hungarian court which drew a parallel to public prosecution where a prosecutor may not be heard as a witness in the same case. This paved the way to the reference and the question whether the Hungarian law was compatible with the Framework Decision 2001/220. Both AG Kokott and the judges concluded that due to its vagueness, the Framework Decision 2001/220 itself did not require granting in such circumstances the status of a victim. However, should that not be possible under the national law, it should allow for the possibility to provide testimony which – in turn – would have the status of evidence. This was an important clarification, which has boosted the rights of victims.[37]

A peculiar scenario of victims pleading for a more lenient penalty for the perpetrators was dealt with in *Gueye* and *Sánchez*.[38] Both references were submitted by the Spanish *Audiencia Provincial de Tarragona* in the course of criminal proceedings against two men who were being charged with breach of an ancillary penalty which had been imposed on them for domestic abuse. Both convicts were ordered not to contact the victims and or be in their vicinity. What happened in turn has, however, put them in an even greater deal of trouble. It is unclear from the facts whether their partners' blind love prevailed, or they opted to take the high road and forgive. Yet, each couple moved in together and cohabited, apparently peacefully, until one fine day when the two men in question were apprehended by law enforcement authorities for breach of that ancillary penalty. At the national court, both women – who were the men's partners and victims of domestic abuse – testified that the arrangements were voluntary and decisions in this regard were taken consciously. This chain of events triggered a number of important questions which were raised by the national court dealing with an appeal from the decision of the lower instance court finding *Magatte Gueye* and *Valentín Salmerón Sánchez* guilty as charged. As some of them dealt with interpretation of Framework Decision 2001/220, the *Audiencia Provincial de Tarragona* proceeded with references for preliminary ruling. Due to the similarity of cases, the Court opted to take an efficiency measure and deal with them together. The first legal issue was whether the Spanish law which – under the circumstances of the case – made such an ancillary penalty compulsory was, in fact, in compliance with Framework Decision 2001/220. The point of departure for the Court of Justice were two constatations: the legal act in question did not deal with penalties imposed by the Member States and it merely provided for minimum standards of victims' protection.[39] Articles 2, 3, and 8 of Framework Decision 2001/220 envisaged the right to be heard and express an opinion, which did not amount to the right

[36] Case C-404/07 *György Katz v István Roland Sós* ECLI:EU:C:2008:553.
[37] ibid paras 47–50.
[38] Joined Cases C-483/09 and C-1/10 *Criminal proceedings against Magatte Gueye (C-483/09) and Valentín Salmerón Sánchez (C-1/10)* ECLI:EU:C:2011:583.
[39] ibid paras 51–52.

to choose a penalty for the offender.[40] The choice of the most suitable protection for the victim, as per Article 8, was not restricting the discretion given to the Member States.[41] Last but not least, the fact that the Spanish law precluded use of mediation in cases of domestic violence, was not in breach of Article 10 of Framework Decision 2001/220 which provided a twofold obligation for the Member States in this respect (to promote mediation and to ensure that agreements reached during mediation can be taken into account in criminal proceedings). It is notable that the Court of Justice has been, again, on the same page as AG Kokott.[42] The judgment in question, unlike the decisions discussed earlier in the present section, has led to academic commentary.[43] This is hardly surprising bearing in mind the underlying legal and social issues of combating violence against women.[44] At the same time, it raised a fundamental issue of division of powers between the European Union and its Member States. *In casu*, the Court drew a demarcation line between Framework Decision 2001/220 and policy choices available to the Member States. Looking at this judgment with the benefit of hindsight makes one appreciate how far the European Union has travelled since. Seen from that perspective, the recent adoption of Directive (EU) 2024/1385 on combating violence against women and domestic violence, despite some imperfections, is a big turning point.[45]

Discretion of the Member States left by the EU legislator was again tested in *Criminal Proceedings against X*.[46] This time a reference was submitted by *Tribunale di Firenze* (the same referring court as in *Pupino*) and the legal issue at stake was whether Italian rules governing a special procedure for taking early evidence (the *incidente probatario*) was compatible with the rights enshrined in Framework Decision 2001/220. The matter in question was raised in the course of a court battle between a minor victim of sexual crime and the prosecutor who wished to close the case against the victims' father, the alleged perpetrator. The crux of the issue was whether the flexibility given to the prosecutor to seek the *incidente probatario* and, in case of the negative decision, the lack of the right to appeal available to the victim, were permissible under Articles 2, 3, and 8 of Framework Decision 2001/220. AG Cruz Villalón and the Court of Justice concluded that such arrangements as made in the Italian law were compatible with Framework Decision 2001/220 and fell within discretion granted to the Member States.[47]

Tribunale di Firenze requested assistance of the Court of Justice in one more case dealing with the Framework Decision 2001/220. *Giovanardi* dealt with the rights of

[40] ibid paras 59–60.

[41] ibid paras 66–68.

[42] See Joined Cases C-483/09 and C-1/10 *Criminal proceedings against Magatte Gueye (C-483/09) and Valentín Salmerón Sánchez (C-1/10)* ECLI:EU:C:2011:297, Opinion of AG Kokott.

[43] See R Lamont, 'Joined Cases C-483/09 and C-1/10, Gueye and Salmerón Sánchez, Judgment of the Court of Justice (Fourth Chamber) of 15 September 2011' (2012) 49 *CML Rev* 1443; RJA McQuigg, 'Domestic Violence and the ECJ: Joined Cases C-483/09 and C-1/10 Magatte Gueye and Valentin Salmeron Sanchez' 2012 (18) *European Public Law* 645.

[44] See the contribution in this volume by C Sáenz Pérez, 'Protecting Vulnerable Victims: An Analysis of the EU Legal Framework for Victims of Gender-Based Violence' in chapter 3.

[45] Directive 2024/1385 on combating violence against women and domestic violence (n 6). For criticism see, *inter alia*, M Dell'Aquila, 'Omitting Rape from the EU's Directive on Combating Violence against Women is a Huge Mistake' (*CEPS*, 28 March 2024), available at www.ceps.eu/omitting-rape-from-the-eus-directive-on-combating-violence-against-women-is-a-huge-mistake/?mc_cid=fca4336bd5&mc_eid=435e3b9424.

[46] *Criminal proceedings against X* ECLI:EU:C:2011:873.

[47] *Criminal proceedings against X* ECLI:EU:C:2011:682, Opinion of AG Cruz Villalón.

victims of accidents in the workplace resulting from negligence of employees of an Italian railway company (*Rete Ferroviaria Italiana SpA*).[48] Under Italian law applicable at the time, the criminal liability of the employees was unquestionable and so was the right to seek compensation from them. At the same time, the legal persons which were employers would only be subjected to administrative liability. Therefore, according to the referring court, the question arose if compensation could be also sought under criminal law from the employer. The Court of Justice ruled that since the actions of the legal persons in the case at hand were classified by the Italian law as administrative offences, the victims could not benefit from Article 9 of Framework Decision 2001/220 which applied only to criminal proceedings. In this instance, the reasoning of the Court of Justice was rather shallow, especially when contrasted with the rich and multifaced opinion of AG Sharpston.[49]

D. The Flood that is Yet to Come? Case Law on Directive 2012/29 on Victims' Rights

The adoption of Directive 2012/29 on victims' rights was an important milestone in the development of EU criminal law.[50] However, as already alluded to, the replacement of a general and basic Framework Decision 2001/220 with a comprehensive directive has not been unproblematic. Many delays and cases of partial transposition have been on the European Commission's radar for several years, yet none of the many infringement procedures opened against the Member States led to submission of cases to the Court of Justice.[51] In other words, the infraction procedures were closed at the administrative stages showing that dialogue and the persuasive power of the European Commission may in some cases suffice to achieve satisfactory levels of compliance.[52] The Court also clarified that Directive 2012/29 does not apply to its own proceedings.[53] As far as the preliminary ruling procedure is concerned, one would – perhaps – assume that the

[48] Case C-79/11 *Maurizio Giovanardi and Others* ECLI:EU:C:2012:448.

[49] Case C-79/11 *Maurizio Giovanardi and Others* ECLI:EU:C:2012:297, Opinion of AG Sharpston.

[50] See the introductory remarks in this volume by J Burchett, 'Victims' Rights in EU Law – Coming of Age?, in chapter 1 and by C Chioni-Chotouman, 'Victims' Rights in the EU: Boosting the Recognition and Participation of Victims in Criminal Proceedings' in chapter 2.

[51] European Commission, 'Report from the Commission to the European Parliament and the Council on the implementation of Directive 2012/29/EU of the European Parliament and of the Council of 25 October 2012 establishing minimum standards on the rights, support and protection of victims of crime, and replacing Council Framework Decision 2001/220/JHA' COM (2020) 188 final; European Commission, 'Commission Staff Working Document. Evaluation of Directive 2012/29/EU of the European Parliament and of the Council of 25 October 2012 establishing minimum standards on the rights, support and protection of victims of crime, and replacing Council Framework Decision 2001/220/JHA' SWD (2022) 179 final.

[52] This was not to the liking of everyone. A German citizen, Anthony Andrew King, filed a complaint to the European Commission requesting triggering the infraction procedure against Luxembourg. Unsatisfied with the outcome, he submitted an action for failure to act (Article 265 TFEU) against the Commission. Both, the General Court and the Court of Justice in the appeal dismissed his actions as, respectively, manifestly inadmissible and unfounded. See Case T-810/17 *Anthony Andrew King v European Commission* ECLI:EU:T:2018:191; Case C-412/18 P *Anthony Andrew King v European Commission* ECLI:EU:C:2018:947.

[53] See Case C-702/19 P *Silver Plastics GmbH & Co. KG and Johannes Reifenhäuser Holding GmbH & Co. KG v European Commission* ECLI:EU:C:2020:857.

compulsory jurisdiction of the Court of Justice, combined with the application of all fundamental tenets to Directive 2012/29, including the doctrine of direct effect, would generate queries from national courts. Alas, so far it has been exactly the opposite.

The first reference on the interpretation of Directive 2012/29 to arrive in Luxembourg was submitted by *Guidice di pace di Taranto* (Justice of the Peace of Taranto) in *Semeraro*.[54] Sadly, it has joined the pantheon of references that should never have landed in the CJEU's docket in the first place. The criminal proceedings in the national court dealt with a person who got involved in a physical and verbal ding-dong during a football match. For reasons which are rather unclear, the Italian judge found it fitting to ask the Court of Justice whether the re-classification of an insult from a criminal offence to a civil offence was compatible with Directive 2012/29. Not surprisingly, the Court of Justice proceeded with a reasoned order concluding that the questions asked lacked a link with EU law and, therefore, the reference was inadmissible.

The next case to reach the Court at Kirchberg plateau fared better, at least in terms of its admissibility. In *TG*,[55] the Slovakian *Špecializovaný trestný súd* (the Special Criminal Court) submitted a reference touching upon interpretation of several EU legal acts, including Directive 2012/29. Two defendants in the case at hand were accused of financial fraud against EU financial interests. While it would go beyond the scope of the present chapter to analyse this decision in greater detail, it suffices to highlight that whether the notion of 'victim' within the meaning of the Directive in question extended also to legal persons if, under national law, they benefited from the status of 'injured person'. One should not be blamed for having a slight *déjà vu* at this juncture, as several references on interpretation of Framework Decision 2001/220 were along the same lines. While the statutory definition of the term in question has evolved and became more precise in Directive 2012/29, one thing, however, has remained unchanged. The notion of 'victims' is limited to natural persons, and the Court has ruled accordingly.

The third and, so far, the latest reference on the interpretation of Directive 2012/29 has arrived from *Tribunale di Bari* (District Court in Bari) in *Massimo Gambino and Shpetim Hyka*.[56] The request was made in the course of criminal proceedings relating to fraud and money laundering. Two victims on this case gave evidence during a hearing in front of the referring court, sitting on that occasion in a chamber of three judges. However, at a later stage one of the judges was replaced by another member of the Bench. When the composition of a chamber changes, in accordance with Italian law and its interpretation by the *Corte suprema di cassazione* (Court of Cassation), a party to proceedings may file a request for the oral proceedings to be repeated to allow the new member of the Bench to hear the testimony. Such a request was, in the case at hand, submitted by one of the defendants. The question raised by the referring court was whether the discussed procedural arrangement was compatible with the rights of victims laid down in Articles 16, 18, and 20(b) of Directive 2012/29. The centre of gravity in the analysis conducted by AG Bot and the Court of Justice were the first two of the listed provisions, with Article 20(b) dealing with the rights during the investigation

[54] Case C-484/16 *Criminal Proceedings against Antonio Semeraro* ECLI:EU:C:2016:952.
[55] Case C-603/19 *TG and UF* ECLI:EU:C:2020:774.
[56] Case C-38/18 *Criminal procedure against Massimo Gambino and Shpetim Hyka* ECLI:EU:C:2019:628.

stage not being terribly relevant for the case at hand.[57] The underlying legal issue was the human rights principle of fair trial and its requirement that 'the interests of the defence are balanced against those of witnesses or victims called upon to testify'.[58] The balancing act done by the Court of Justice involved taking a closer look not only at EU law itself but also the jurisprudence of the European Court of Human Rights.[59] The conclusion reached by AG Bot and the Court was that neither Article 16 nor Article 18 of Directive 2012/29 precluded the Italian law at stake. However, should the national court decide that a victim has to testify again, an examination of the needs of the victims is a *conditio sine qua non* and, when required, protection measures envisaged by Articles 23–24 of Directive 2012/29 should be made available.

IV. Directive 2004/80 on Trial: Filling the Gaps and Ambiguities Left by the European Union Legislator

A. Introduction

As *cliché* as it may be, it is important to start the analysis of case law based on Directive 2004/80 with a reminder that badly drafted laws frequently end up in courts which have the enviable task of deciphering the results of political compromises.[60] Alas, the European Union is no different in this respect to its Member States or, for that matter, countries at large. There is an abundance of examples in the European Union legal order that could be employed to prove this point. Directive 2004/80 qualifies as a good example due to lack of clarity as to its scope of application, lack of statutory definitions as well as vaguely defined parameters of what compensation should entail. All these issues have been addressed by the Court of Justice and will be presented in turn (sections IV.B and C). For the sake of completeness, section IV.D looks into two judgments of the Court of Justice rendered in infringement proceedings against Greece.[61]

B. Scope of Application: Purely or Not So Purely Internal Situations?

Determination of the scope of application of any piece of legislation, be it EU or domestic, is of fundamental importance for those to whom it applies, and to those who are in charge of its enforcement. This is where the desideratum propagated by Seneca – *legem enim brevem esse oportet*[62] is at times not the most fortunate guiding

[57] ibid, paras 30–35.
[58] ibid, para 41.
[59] ibid, paras 38–59.
[60] Directive 2004/80 on compensation to crime victims (n 4).
[61] Case C-26/07 *Commission of the European Communities v Hellenic Republic* ECLI:EU:C:2007:461; Case C-407/09 *Commission of the European Communities v Hellenic Republic* ECLI:EU:C:2011:196.
[62] 'The law should be brief'.

principle for the lawmakers. Directive 2004/80 is, without a doubt, an example of what such brevity may lead to. This is particularly the case when one makes an effort to compare a more elaborate draft proposed by the European Commission[63] with the final text adopted (unanimously) by the Council of the European Union. The crux of the issue is as follows. Does Directive 2004/80 apply only to situations comparable to *Cowan*, that is to nationals of EU Member States who become victims of crime in a country that is neither a Member State of their nationality nor of their residence? Or, in the alternative, does it, in particular Article 12 thereof, apply also to purely internal situations? In other words, can this provision of Directive 2004/80 be relied on by a victim in his/her own Member State. Before the present analysis is taken further it is worth reproducing Articles 1 and 12 of Directive 2004/80 which are at the heart of the problem. The former provides:

> Member States shall ensure that where a violent intentional crime has been committed in a Member State other than the Member State where the applicant for compensation is habitually resident, the applicant shall have the right to submit the application to an authority or any other body in the latter Member State.

It should be added that the provision in question found its home in Chapter I of the Directive which is titled 'Access to compensation in cross-border situations'. This, put together with several other provisions grouped in Chapter I, as well as numerous recitals of the Preamble, would suggest that indeed the scope of Directive 2004/80 does not encompass purely domestic cases. However, the situation becomes rather confusing when Article 12 is added to the equation. It is a sole provision in Chapter II of the Directive, aptly titled 'National schemes on compensation'. It reads:

> 1. The rules on access to compensation in cross-border situations drawn up by this Directive shall operate on the basis of Member States' schemes on compensation to victims of violent intentional crime committed in their respective territories.
> 2. All Member States shall ensure that their national rules provide for the existence of a scheme on compensation to victims of violent intentional crimes committed in their respective territories, which guarantees fair and appropriate compensation to victims.

This provision, *prima facie*, contradicts what has been said above. Alas, it is just the tip of the iceberg. The picture is equally *Monetesque* even if one ploughs through all preparatory acts, including the explanatory note annexed to the original proposal of the European Commission. It is impressionistically blurred, with only general contours visible. In the words of AG Bobek, 'it is rarely the case that after having explored the text, context, purpose, legislative history, as well as arguments relating to the legal basis of an EU law instrument, one finds oneself pretty much where one started: lost'.[64] Thus, it is hardly surprising that the determination of the scope of Directive 2004/80 had to, eventually, reach the Kirchberg courtrooms. Sadly, the approach of the Court of Justice has not been consistent throughout.

[63] European Commission, 'Proposal for a Council Directive on compensation to crime victims' COM (2002) 562 final.

[64] Case C-129/19 *Presidenza del Consiglio dei Ministri v BV* ECLI:EU:C:2020:375, Opinion of AG Bobek, para 100.

The starting point were cases *Dell'Orto* and *Giovanardi*.[65] While, as already discussed, they dealt extensively with interpretation of the Framework Decision 2001/220, the Court – somewhat *en passant* – concluded that the scope of Directive 2004/80 was limited to victims of cross-border crimes only.[66] This was followed by a reference for preliminary ruling in case *Paola C v Presidenza del Consiglio dei Ministri*.[67] It was submitted in the course of proceedings pending at the *Tribunale ordinario di Firenze* in which the applicant, who was a victim of sexual assault, claimed damages for breach of EU law, in particular the failure to transpose Directive 2004/80 to Italian law.[68] The Court of Justice ruled that due to the purely internal character of the dispute, it had no jurisdiction to deal with the case and, therefore, the reference in question was not admissible. It is worth noting that the Court proceeded not with a judgment but with a reasoned order (which is traditionally, though not exclusively, reserved for such occasions). The decision was taken by a small chamber of three judges without a hearing or opinion of an Advocate General. While details of *délibéré* remain secret, the way cases internally travel at the Court of Justice may give ground for a few assumptions. To begin with, after the initial allocation of the case to the Sixth Chamber and to AG Bot, both must have produced *rapport préalable*, which then must have been presented at the weekly *Réunion Générale* of the entire Court. Key procedural decisions must have been taken at this stage, leaving the chamber of three the liberty to finish the text of the reasoned order. It is essential to mention that as this case was pending at the Court of Justice, the European Commission proceeded with the infringement procedure against Italy for failure to comply with Article 12(2) of Directive 2004/80.[69] This led to the judgment of the Court in case C-601/14 *Commission v Italy*,[70] a decision which started to turn tables when it comes to the scope of application of Directive 2004/80. Due to its fundamental importance, it deserves a closer look.

In its application to the Court, the European Commission argued that Italy was in breach of Directive 2004/80 resulting from its incomplete transposition to domestic law.[71] The crux of the problem was the way in which the Italian authorities dealt with the above cited Article 12(2) of the Directive. The wording of the provision in question is

[65] *Dell'Orto* (n 32) and *Giovanardi* (n 48).

[66] *Dell'Orto* (n 32) para 59 and *Giovanardi* (n 48) para 37. See also *Dell'Orto* (n 32) Opinion of AG Kokott, paras 61–72.

[67] Case C-122/13 *Paola C v Presidenza del Consiglio dei Ministri* ECLI:EU:C:2014:59.

[68] For an account of the factual background, see ibid paras 6–9.

[69] It is notable that during the administrative phase of the infringement procedure, the Italian Government has tried to put the proceedings on hold until the Court of Justice ruled in *Paola C v Presidenza del Consiglio dei Ministri* (n 67). This request was not entertained by the European Commission, which – however – with submission of the infringement case to the Court until the judges declared the reference inadmissible (for a detailed account see Case C-601/14 *European Commission v Italian Republic* ECLI:EU:C:2016:249, Opinion of AG Bot, paras 14–21). Furthermore, the European Commission submitted written observations in the case referred by *Tribunale ordinario di Firenze*. Without access to the file, it is impossible to find out what exactly it argued for as the Court did not find it fitting to summarise written observations submitted by the European Commission (to which the judges vaguely referred to in para 17 of the Order) and by the Italian, Spanish, and Dutch Governments.

[70] Case C-601/14 *European Commission v Italian Republic* ECLI:EU:C:2016:759.

[71] It is notable that already in 2007, the Court of Justice ruled that Italy, in general terms, failed to transpose Directive 2004/80 into national law. See Case C-112/07 *European Commission v Italian Republic* ECLI:EU:C:2007:742.

not terribly helpful to begin with. It requires the Member States to set up compensation schemes for victims of 'violent intentional crimes'. This is a rather abstract notion, which in the eyes of EU legislators, did not deserve a statutory definition, therefore leaving to the Member States, perhaps, more discretion that one would consider as agreeable. In its implementing rules, the Italian authorities opted for a narrow interpretation including *Cosa Nostra* related crimes, but excluding, among others, sexual offences. According to the applicant, this was not a correct way to transpose Article 12(2) to national law. Both AG Bot and the Grand Chamber of the Court of Justice agreed with the European Commission and ruled accordingly. Unfortunately, in doing so, they added to the list of ambiguities that this Directive has created. Having attentively read the judgment, readers will be none the wiser whether the previous jurisprudence of the Court was still considered to be a good law or not. An attempt at explanation provided in the judgment is a textbook case of a constructive ambiguity. The relevant passage reads:

> [...] the Court merely stated that the system of cooperation established by Directive 2004/80 solely concerns access to compensation in cross-border situations, without however excluding that Article 12(2) of that directive requires each Member State, for the purposes of securing the objective pursued by it in such situations, to adopt a national scheme guaranteeing compensation for victims of any violent intentional crime on its territory.[72]

The truth is that Article 12(2) was mentioned neither in the judgment in *Dell'Orto*, nor in *Giovanardi*. In *Paola C* the purely domestic character of the case was the *raison d'être* behind the decision to declare the reference for preliminary ruling as inadmissible with, again, Article 12(2) not being explored properly. While here the Court has thrown a ball in the air, it has still failed to rule what exactly the scope of application of the Directive was. As noted by AG Bobek, in this being an infringement case, the judges were simply bound by the scope of application submitted by the European Commission.[73] This may explain why in the operative part, the Court ruled that the failure amounted to incomplete cover of violent intentional crimes in cross-border situations. It is understandable but confusing, nevertheless. It is also puzzling that the Court of Justice ruled on the breach of Article 12(2) by Italy to the limitation of the scope of domestic compensation scheme only to some violent intentional crimes. Yet, the judges ruled so without any reflection in the judgment as to the scope of that critical notion, leaving the catalogue of such crimes open ended. On the one hand, it is true that the Court should avoid making the mistakes like in the case of *Sturgeon*, where – against the advice of AG Sharpston – it stepped on a territory reserved for the legislature.[74] In other words, it is not the task of the Court to rewrite EU legislation even if it results from an episode of constructive ambiguity in the name of reaching an agreement by the EU legislator. On the other hand, the principle of legal certainty dictates that more clarity would be desired. With

[72] ibid para 49.

[73] *Presidenza del Consiglio dei Ministri v BV* (n 64) para 99 of the Opinion of AG Bobek.

[74] Joined cases C-402/07 and C-432/07 *Christopher Sturgeon, Gabriel Sturgeon and Alana Sturgeon v Condor Flugdienst GmbH (C-402/07) and Stefan Böck and Cornelia Lepuschitz v Air France SA (C-432/07)* ECLI:EU:C:2009:716; Joined cases C-402/07 and C-432/07 *Christopher Sturgeon, Gabriel Sturgeon and Alana Sturgeon v Condor Flugdienst GmbH (C-402/07) and Stefan Böck and Cornelia Lepuschitz v Air France SA (C-432/07)* ECLI:EU:C:2009:416, Opinion of AG Sharpston.

the above in mind, it is no surprise that a reference from one of the national courts requesting further clarification followed.

In case *BV* a reference for preliminary ruling was submitted by the *Corte suprema di cassazione* (the Supreme Court of Cassation) from Italy.[75] Even a cursory look at the questions sent to the Court of Justice, and reasoning provided in the reference itself demonstrates, not surprisingly, a fair deal of confusion caused by the EU legislator and, sadly, also with the help of the Court of Justice. The arising issues were very extensively discussed in the already mentioned Opinion of AG Bobek.[76] The Grand Chamber of the Court of Justice followed the AG and ruled that the compensation schemes required by Directive 2004/80 should cover 'all victims of violent intentional crime committed on their territory and not only those victims that are in a cross-border situation'.[77] This has come as a long-awaited clarification as to the scope of application of Directive 2004/80. Furthermore, the Court of Justice also confirmed that non-compliance of national law with Article 12(2) of Directive 2004/80 may be the ground for submission of state liability claims to national courts.[78] This has opened the door, albeit subject to application by domestic judges of a triparty test established by the Court in *Brasserie du Pecheur*, to compensation for those victims of crime who have been deprived of it before the ruling of the Court of Justice in *BV*.[79] It is notable though, that the Court did not specify whether failure to comply with Article 12(2) constituted a sufficiently serious breach of EU law, which is the second limb of the state liability test.[80] Furthermore, the Court was neither asked, nor opted *ex officio*, to limit the temporal scope of the judgment, therefore such claims may go back to 1 January 2006 (the deadline for transposition of Directive 2004/80).[81] It may, potentially, lead to an increase of litigation in national courts and, by ricochet, also references for preliminary ruling. Time will tell whether this supposition has merits or not.

C. What is Meant by 'Fair and Appropriate Compensation'?

Apart from the notorious question of the scope of application of Directive 2004/80, two other matters have been, thus far, referred to the CJEU. To begin with, in compliance with the principle of procedural autonomy of the Member States, the decision as to the available remedies has been left to the domestic legislator. In case of Directive 2004/80, the Member States were given ample flexibility to determine the main parameters of

[75] Summary of the request for a preliminary ruling pursuant to Art 98(1) of the Rules of Procedure of the Court of Justice, available at https://curia.europa.eu/juris/showPdf.jsf?text=&docid=219900&pageIndex=0&doclang=en&mode=lst&dir=&occ=first&part=1&cid=3462156.

[76] *Presidenza del Consiglio dei Ministri v BV* (n 64) Opinion of AG Bobek.

[77] ibid para 52.

[78] ibid para 56.

[79] Joined Cases C-46/93 and C-48/93 *Brasserie du Pêcheur SA v Bundesrepublik Deutschland and The Queen v Secretary of State for Transport, ex parte: Factortame Ltd and others* ECLI:EU:C:1996:79.

[80] See, in particular, Joined cases C-178/94, C-179/94, C-188/94, C-189/94 and C-190/94 *Erich Dillenkofer, Christian Erdmann, Hans-Jürgen Schulte, Anke Heuer, Werner, Ursula and Trosten Knor v Bundesrepublik Deutschland* ECLI:EU:C:1996:375.

[81] In case of Bulgaria, Romania, and Croatia the deadlines were dates of accession to the European Union (respectively, 1 January 2007 and 1 July 2013).

compensation schemes, including the calculation methods as well as potential caps. Article 12(2) of Directive 2004/80 provides only for a vague, and prone to various interpretations, benchmark of required 'fair and appropriate compensation'. Not surprisingly, questions have been asked whether domestic law of the Member States meets this generically defined standard.[82] In *BV* the Court had, for the first time, an opportunity to deal with the matter in question. It concluded that the fixed rate of compensation available to victims of sexual offences in Italy was not meeting the benchmark as it was:

> [...] fixed without taking into account the seriousness of the consequences, for the victims, of the crime committed and does not therefore represent an appropriate contribution to the reparation of the material and non-material harm suffered.[83]

While this shed light on how the discretion given to the Member States should be exercised, it raised further doubts, for instance, as to what may fall under the 'non-material' damage. It has already returned the Court in two cases, one of which was still pending at the time of writing of the present chapter. To begin with, yet another reference was submitted by an Italian court (on this occasion, *Tribunale Ordinario di Venezia*) in *Burdene*.[84] It raises two important points of law. Firstly, the Court of Justice has been asked a fundamental question as to the interpretation of the term 'victim' employed in Directive 2004/80 and the extent it applies to different types of family members of a victim of murder. In particular, the question raised by the referring Court was whether the Italian law was compliant with Directive 2004/80. It limited the right to compensation of victims' parents and siblings to the following situations. Parents could only be entitled to compensation if the victim had no spouse or children, while siblings' entitlement was restricted merely to the absence of both, family of victim and their parents. As it was already noted, Directive 2004/80 fails to provide any statutory definitions, therefore it leaves the meaning of the most crucial term laid down therein unclear. Furthermore, it fails to cross refer either to other EU secondary legislation where such a definition is provided or, for that matter, to national law. According to AG de la Tour, all of this means that the term 'victim' is an autonomous term of EU law which should be interpreted consistently with other EU legal instruments governing the rights of victims.[85] Inevitably, it leads to Directive 2012/29 which, as already discussed in the previous section of the chapter, has the status of a legal act of horizontal application. With that in mind, as argued by AG de la Tour in his Opinion, Directive 2004/80 should be interpreted in the light of Directive 2012/29. This led to the conclusion that Italian law was not compatible with Directive 2004/80 by restricting the right to compensation in a manner summarised above. In its judgment of 7 November 2024, the Court followed AG de la Tour and ruled accordingly.[86] Both AG de la Tour and the Court of Justice also concluded that a request for further clarification of the notion of 'fair and

[82] See further the contribution in this volume by L O'Driscoll, 'Being "Fair and Appropriate" to Victims of Violent Crime: Evaluating the Provision of State Compensation in the European Union' in chapter 5.

[83] *Presidenza del Consiglio dei Ministri v BV* (n 64) para 69.

[84] See Summary of reference for a preliminary ruling pursuant to Article 98(1) of the Rules of Procedure of the Court of Justice (n 75).

[85] Case C-126/23 *Burdene* ECLI:EU:C:2024:396, Opinion of AG de la Tour, para 37.

[86] ibid 937. See further J Burchett, 'Compensation for Victims of Violent Intentional Crime. Narrowing the Member States's Discretion under Directive 2004/80/EC' (*Verfassungsblog*, forthcoming in 2024).

appropriate compensation' (the second question) was not admissible, as the referring court has failed to explain its relevance to the case. This, however, is at the heart of the second case which was in the Courts' docket when the present chapter was completed. In *LD*, the High Court of Ireland has asked for clarification of the *BV* judgment, in particular the conclusion reached by the Court of Justice that the compensation should extend to 'material and non-material harm'.[87] The Opinion of the Advocate General (if, at the *Réunion Générale* the Court decided to ask for one) and the judgment of the Court are currently in the making.

D. Keeping the Pressure On: Infringement Cases

Thus far the European Commission has brought a total of four infringement cases in relation to Directive 2004/80 to the Court of Justice. Two judgments finding Italy to be in breach of EU law have been already discussed (section IV.B above). This leaves us with two remaining judgments, both against Greece. Both were relatively pedestrian and therefore do not merit much attention. It suffices to point out that in the first case the Court of Justice found Greece to have failed to transpose Directive 2004/80 on time.[88] Further delays in transposition led to the submission of the second request as per Article 260 TFEU, this time requesting the Court to impose financial penalties: a periodical payment of €72 532.80 for each day of delay, supplemented by a lump sum of €10 512 per day counted from the day of the first judgment of the Court, to the day of the second judgment. Since Greece has transposed the Directive in question as the case was sitting in the Court's docket, the first of those requests was dropped by the applicant. However, the European Commission opted not to withdraw the action entirely and maintained that the Court should impose a lump sum as a penalty for delay in implementation of the first judgment. This request was entertained by the Court which, having heard AG Mazák,[89] imposed a lump sum penalty of €3 000 000.[90]

V. Conclusions

Tour d'horizon offered in this chapter leads to several conclusions. To begin with, while the number of cases on EU victims' *acquis* which have reached the Court of Justice thus far may be lower than in case of some other EU criminal law instruments, most of the decisions have been anything but pedestrian. Good evidence to prove it is that, except for very rare occasions, all these cases have received a Roll's Royce treatment with opinions of Advocates General. This means that they raised new points of law which required extra attention of the Court at Kirchberg plateau. Many cases that have reached the Court of Justice, in particular in relation to Directive 2004/80 and Framework Decision

[87] See Case C-284/24 Request for a preliminary ruling, available at https://curia.europa.eu/juris/showPdf.jsf?text=&docid=287127&pageIndex=0&doclang=en&mode=lst&dir=&occ=first&part=1&cid=7446584.

[88] *Commission of the European Communities v Hellenic Republic* (n 61).

[89] *Commission of the European Communities v Hellenic Republic* (n 61) Opinion of AG Mazák.

[90] ibid.

2001/220, were inevitable consequences of very poor drafting of the legal acts in question. It is little wonder that national judges were in a pickle, trying to figure out what the constructive ambiguity resulting from political compromises could mean. As for the Court of Justice, despite the jurisdictional limits, the judges at Kirchberg plateau have put a firm mark not only on interpretation of EU victims' *acquis* and its relationship with national law, but also on the application of pre-Lisbon Third Pillar instruments at national level. In this respect, both, the opinion of AG Kokott and the judgment of the Court (despite poor reasoning) in *Pupino* stand out. Having said that, not everything has been as one would wish. Alas, the Court of Justice itself contributed to the one fine mess created by Directive 2004/80 and lack of clarity as to the scope of its application. While this has been eventually sorted, it took a number of Court judgments for that to happen. Last but not least, this story is not over, and more episodes are likely to be produced. Yet, the story thus far already shows how far the European Union, its legislation, and jurisprudence of its Court, have travelled from that fateful night of 11 June 1982 when Mr Cowan had his unfortunate adventures in Paris.

5

Being 'Fair and Appropriate' to Victims of Violent Crime: Evaluating the Provision of State Compensation in the European Union

LIAM O'DRISCOLL*

I. Introduction

This chapter considers the rights and entitlements of victims of violent crime in the European Union (EU) to State compensation. Specifically, the chapter evaluates the judgment of the Court of Justice of the European Union (CJEU) in *Presidenza del Consiglio dei Ministri v BV*,[1] and the manner in which this judgment has impacted the provision of State compensation in one EU Member State, Ireland. The *BV* proceedings at the CJEU concerned the correct interpretation of Article 12(2) of Directive 2004/80/EC (the 'Compensation Directive'), which obligates Member States to put in place a State compensation scheme 'which guarantees fair and appropriate compensation to victims'.[2] In *BV*, the CJEU held that the right to compensation under Article 12(2) applies to all victims of violent crime in the EU and not just those exercising their freedom of movement rights, as previously indicated by the CJEU.[3] Additionally, it was held that compensation must not be 'purely symbolic or manifestly insufficient having regard to the gravity of the consequences' on the victim, and must 'compensate to an appropriate extent the suffering to which [victims] have been exposed'.[4] At the core of the Advocate General's Opinion in *BV* was the application of the EU Charter of Fundamental Rights (the 'EU Charter') to the interpretation of the Compensation Directive, particularly Article 1 in respect of the right to human dignity.[5] *BV* has been

* Dublin City University, Ireland.

[1] C-129/19 *Presidenza del Consiglio dei Ministri v BV* ECLI:EU:C 220:566.

[2] Directive 2004/80/EC of 29 April 2004 Relating to Compensation to Crime Victims [2004] OJ L261/15, Art 12(2).

[3] *BV* (n 1) para 55.

[4] ibid para 63.

[5] Opinion of the Advocate General in C-129/19 *BV* ECLI:EU:C:2020:375 paras 107–109.

heralded as a seminal decision which establishes a right to State compensation for all victims of violent intentional crime in the EU.[6] Whilst State compensation schemes for victims have been in existence across most EU Member States even prior to the adoption of the Compensation Directive in 2004, there still exists significant disparities across the Member States.[7] Furthermore, national schemes have been criticised for excluding victims unfairly, primarily due to the limited scope of available compensation and the strict application of the various criteria to individual victims.[8] The *BV* judgment, therefore, presents an opportunity to improve national schemes for all victims in a fair and just manner.

This chapter seeks to examine the developments arising from the *BV* judgment and discusses future legislative and policy priorities concerning victims of crime and their right to State compensation at the EU and Member State level. It is imperative to comprehensively understand these developments in light of the European Commission's (Commission) 2023 Proposal to amend Directive 2012/29/EU (the 'Victims' Rights Directive').[9] Instead of recommending reform of the Compensation Directive through the putting in place of minimum standards at the EU level, the Commission's 2023 Proposal seeks to amend the Victims' Rights Directive to obligate Member States to pay any compensation awarded in the criminal trial (from the offender) directly to the victim, and then recoup the amount from the offender after the conclusion of the criminal process. Importantly, the Proposal, if adopted, will not impact the operation of the Compensation Directive and national compensation schemes. The impact, if any, of the Proposal on the rights of both victims and offenders requires clarification.[10] An example of a mechanism such as this, where the State pays compensation directly to the victim and recoups the amount from the offender, is the Advanced Payment Scheme (APS) in the Netherlands.[11] This chapter commences by discussing the background and provisions of the Compensation Directive itself, which the CJEU in *BV* were called upon to interpret. I then outline the relevant case law of the CJEU concerning the Compensation Directive. The impact of these decisions in the Member States is then examined, with a particular focus on Ireland. Finally, future reform of compensation provision for victims in the EU is considered. Overall, I conclude that the *BV* judgment has the potential to positively impact the provision of State compensation in the Member States. Despite

[6] Irish Law Reform Commission, *Consultation Paper: Compensating Victims of Crime* (LRC CP 67 – 2022) para 3.6.

[7] These disparities are well documented and will not be discussed in detail here. For more information, see J Milquet, *Strengthening Victims' Rights: from Compensation to Reparation* (European Commission, 2019) 23–24; N Elbers et al, *Fair and Appropriate? Compensation of Victims of Sexual Violence in EU Member States: Greece, Italy, Latvia, the Netherlands and Spain: Part II: State and Offender Compensation: Survey, Good Practices and Recommendations* (European Commission, 2020).

[8] Milquet, ibid.

[9] Directive 2012/29/EU of the European Parliament and of the Council of 25 October 2012 Establishing Minimum Standards on the Rights, Support and Protection of Victims of Crime, and Replacing Council Framework Decision 2001/220/JHA [2012] OJ L315/57.

[10] European Commission, Proposal for a Directive of the European Parliament and of the Council Amending Directive 2012/29/EU Establishing Minimum Standards on the Rights, Support and Protection of Victims of Crime, and Replacing Council Framework Decision 2001/220/JHA COM(2023) 424 final 29, 17–18 ('Commission's 2023 Proposal').

[11] JP Kuipers, *Evaluation of the Advanced Payment Scheme for Sex Crimes and Violent Crimes and the Collection of Damage Compensation* (Cebeon, 2018).

this, I also conclude that it is disappointing that the Commission has not proposed any reform of the Compensation Directive.

II. The Background and Provisions of the Compensation Directive

The Compensation Directive contains three Chapters. Chapter I relates to the obligations on Member States to put in place cooperation mechanisms to facilitate access to national compensation schemes for victims of crime in a cross-border situation such as tourists or business travellers who are subject to a violent crime in a Member State different to the one they normally reside in (cooperation mechanisms). Chapter II sets out obligations in relation to the operation of national schemes on compensation and Chapter III provides for implementing measures in respect of Chapter I and Chapter II. Whilst the Chapter I obligations in relation to the cooperation mechanisms for cross-border victims are important, this contribution focuses on the provision of Chapter II as it is this provision which the *BV* judgment addressed. Specifically, *BV* concerned the interpretation of Article 12(2), which provides that '[a]ll Member States shall ensure that their national rules provide for the existence of a scheme on compensation to victims of violent intentional crimes committed in their respective territories, which guarantees fair and appropriate compensation to victims'. Additionally, whilst Chapter I contains rules regulating access to compensation in cross-border situations, the importance of comprehensively understanding Article 12(2) cannot be overstated. This is because the 'fair and appropriate compensation' requirement is, in fact, the only minimum standard contained in the Compensation Directive which Member States must ensure is reflected in their national compensation schemes.

Despite this, the Compensation Directive, as originally proposed by the Commission, contained comprehensive minimum standards. These standards included rules in relation to the type and amount of compensation available and the permissible procedural and eligibility criteria which Member States could impose, for example in relation to time limits to submit applications and police reporting requirements.[12] If adopted, these comprehensive minimum standards would have contributed to the harmonisation of the various rules and procedures concerning national compensation schemes throughout the EU. Unfortunately, however, due to the budgetary concerns of Member States, these comprehensive minimum standards were dropped from the Compensation Directive prior to its adoption.[13] As well as budgetary concerns, there were also concerns in respect of the chosen legal basis for the legislation, which was ex-Article 308 of the Treaty on European Union (TEU), now Article 352 of the Treaty on the Functioning of the European Union (TFEU). Some Member States expressed concerns that this

[12] European Commission, Proposal for a Council Directive on Compensation to Crime Victims COM(2002) 562 ('Commission's 2002 Proposal').

[13] Council of the European Union, Note from the Presidency of the Council to the Council on the Proposal for a Council Directive on Compensation to Crime Victims dated 26 March 2004 7752/04 JUSTCIV 49 para 4.

provision of the EU Treaties, known as the flexibility clause, did not permit the EU to put in place minumum standards in respect of national compensation schemes.[14] As the flexibility clause requires unanimity at the Council of the EU, the comprehensive minimum standards had to be removed.[15] In their place, the 'fair and appropriate compensation' requirement was added to ensure that at least some level of harmonisation in respect of national compensation schemes was provided for in the legislation.[16] The precise meaning of this minimum standard will now be examined.

III. Defining 'Fair and Appropriate Compensation' at the CJEU

As stated above, the *BV* judgment has been described as a seminal CJEU decision in that the 'fair and appropriate compensation' requirement under Article 12(2) of the Compensation Directive now applies to all victims of violent intentional crime in the EU, regardless of whether there exists a cross-border element.[17] Additionally, the CJEU in *BV* set down guidelines for Member States as to the minimum amount of compensation that should be available to victims of violent crime and the manner in which this compensation should be calculated.[18] Prior to *BV*, the requirement that national compensation schemes provide 'fair and appropriate compensation' was understood only to apply to cross-border victims. This understanding was in keeping with the fact that the other provisions of the Compensation Directive, the provisions governing access to compensation in Chapter I, clearly applied only to victims in a cross-border situation. Indeed, the CJEU made a number of statements confirming this position. First, the CJEU judgment in *Dell'Orto* arose as a result of a preliminary reference issued from the Italian courts, the facts of which involved criminal proceedings concerning embezzlement and the unlawful financing of political parties. The question referred concerned the correct interpretation of the term 'victim' under Article 1 of the 2001 Council Framework Decision on the Standing of Victims in Criminal Proceedings (the '2001 Framework Decision').[19] The judgment, therefore, primarily did not involve the correct interpretation of Article 12(2) of the Compensation Directive. Despite this, the Advocate General, without referring specifically to Article 12(2), commented that '[t]he Directive governs compensation where the crime has been committed in another Member State'.[20] In line with the Opinion of the Advocate General, the CJEU, again not referring specifically to Article 12(2), held that the Compensation Directive 'provides for compensation only where a violent intentional crime has been committed in a Member State other than that in which the victim is habitually resident'.[21] The CJEU largely

[14] ibid paras 11–12.
[15] ibid paras 15–16.
[16] Opinion of Advocate General in *BV* (n 5) para 83.
[17] *BV* (n 1) para 55.
[18] ibid para 63.
[19] Council Framework Decision of 15 March 2001 On the Standing of Victims in Criminal Proceedings 2001/220/JHA [2001] OJ L82/1.
[20] Opinion of the Advocate General in C-467/05 *Dell'Orto* ECLI:EU:C:2007:395 para 61.
[21] C-467/05 *Dell'Orto* ECLI:EU:C:2007:395 para 59.

repeated itself in *Giovanardi and Others*, another Italian reference concerning the interpretation of the 2001 Framework Decision. Here, the Advocate General stated that the application of the Compensation Directive was limited to cross-border situations.[22] The CJEU relied on Article 1 of the Compensation Directive, which states that victims have a right to apply for compensation in their Member State of residence in situations where they are victimised in another Member State, to find that the Compensation Directive itself applies merely to cross-border scenarios.[23]

The same approach was taken by the CJEU in the *Paola C* proceedings, which arose as a result of a reference from the Italian courts in the context of a sexual assault inflicted on the victim in Italy.[24] Here, the applicability of the Compensation Directive was a crucial issue as the victim was in a purely internal situation. In other words, she was victimised in her Member State of residence and was not exercising her freedom of movement rights in a Member State different to her Member State of residence. For this reason, the CJEU held that it did not have jurisdiction to answer the question posed, as to whether Member States can limit the eligibility for national compensation schemes to certain categories of offences, as purely internal situations do not fall within the scope of the Compensation Directive.[25] Whilst in *Paola C*, the CJEU stated that it did not have jurisdiction to answer the question posed, the CJEU in *Commission v Italy* attempted to clarify the situation.[26] This ruling arises from infringement proceedings initiated by the Commission against Italy due to its failure to transpose the Compensation Directive. Specifically, the proceedings related to the fact that Italian law to date had only provided for State compensation for victims of terrorism and organised crime, to the exclusion of other victims of violent crimes, including victims of sexual violence.[27] In ruling that Italy was in breach of its obligations under the Compensation Directive,[28] the CJEU held that Member States cannot limit the scope of Article 12(2) to victims of certain violent intentional crimes.[29] Additionally, the CJEU clarified its prior jurisprudence in relation to the distinction between cross-border victims and victims in purely internal situations and stated that its prior judgments merely held that the cooperation mechanisms obligated under the Compensation Directive apply only to cross-border victims. The CJEU further held that its prior rulings which refer to the Compensation Directive do not permit Member States to adopt national compensation schemes which exclude victims of certain violent intentional crime.[30] In this regard, the CJEU's decision is consistent with the Advocate General's Opinion, where it is stated that '[t]he EU legislature … considered that it was necessary for all the Member States to have such a compensation scheme in order to facilitate access to such schemes in cross-border situations'.[31]

[22] Opinion of the Advocate General in C-79/11 *Giovanardi & Others* ECLI:EU:C:2012:448 para 31.
[23] C-79/11 *Giovanardi & Others* ECLI:EU:C:2012:448 para 37.
[24] C-122/13 *Paola C v Presidenza del Consiglio dei Ministri* ECLI:EU:C:2014:59 para 7.
[25] ibid paras 13 14.
[26] C-601/14 *Commission v Italy* ECLI:EU:C:2016:759.
[27] ibid para 20.
[28] ibid para 54.
[29] ibid para 46.
[30] ibid para 49.
[31] Opinion of the Advocate General in C-601/14 *Commission v Italy* ECLI:EU:C:2016:759 para 77.

It is interesting to note that the Advocate General in *BV* stated that the CJEU in *Commission v Italy* in fact had left the question open as to whether Article 12(2) applies to internal situations.[32] In this regard, the Advocate General stated that *Commission v Italy* provided no clarification as to whether Article 12(2) requires Member States to introduce a national compensation scheme that covers all victims of violent intentional crimes committed in their respective territories, including victims in a purely domestic situation. Whilst it is correct to state that the nature of the infringement proceedings in *Commission v Italy* did not require clarification of this point, and indeed that the point was not posed in the proceedings themselves,[33] I disagree with the Advocate General in *BV* that the decision in *Commission v Italy* was 'ambiguous' on the point.[34] I maintain that the CJEU was clear, albeit not as part of the core reasoning of the decision, that Article 12(2) does not apply to purely internal situations. How, then, did the CJEU shift its position in *BV*? In this regard, the crucial factor is discussed in the Advocate General's Opinion were it is stated that Article 1, in relation to the right to human dignity and Article 6, in relation to the right to liberty and security, of the EU Charter can be used as 'an interpretative tiebreaker' in relation to two equally plausible interpretations of Article 12(2).[35] According to the Advocate General, one interpretation, based on the text itself and select recitals of the Compensation Directive, suggests that Article 12(2) does apply to purely internal situations.[36] A second interpretation, based on the legislative history of the Compensation Directive and other recitals,[37] suggests that purely internal situations are not covered by the provision.[38] Using the EU Charter as a 'tiebreaker' and holding that favouring an interpretation to the 'detriment of the individuals concerned' would be 'problematic',[39] the Advocate General stated that Article 12(2) must apply to purely internal situations.[40]

Overall, the CJEU agreed with the Opinion of the Advocate General and held that Article 12(2) does apply to such situations. In effect, the CJEU held that Article 12(2) grants all victims of violent crime in the EU a right to 'fair and appropriate' State compensation.[41] Whilst this is a welcome result for victims and the Advocate General's use of the right to human dignity in the EU Charter is of note, it is concerning that the CJEU did not itself engage with EU Charter based arguments in respect of Article 12(2). Of further concern is that, in relying on the EU Charter in this manner, the Advocate General stated that he did 'not think that it is even necessary to discuss in any great depth the individual Charter rights that would militate against opting for the narrowest scope of Article 12(2) possible'.[42] In other words, even the Advocate General did not engage in much detail on the correct scope of the EU Charter. Whilst it is standard practice for the CJEU not to mirror the level of analysis contained in the opinions of

[32] Opinion of the Advocate General in *BV* (n 5) para 98.
[33] Opinion of the Advocate General in *Commission v Italy* (n 31) para 99.
[34] Opinion of the Advocate General in *BV* (n 5) para 98.
[35] ibid paras 105–107.
[36] ibid para 101.
[37] See L O'Driscoll, 'Towards a Rights-based Approach: Victims of Violent Crime, State-funded Compensation and the European Union' (2023) 14(3) *New Journal of European Criminal Law* 303–26.
[38] Opinion of the Advocate General in *BV* (n 5) para 101.
[39] ibid para 123.
[40] ibid para 124.
[41] *BV* (n 1) para 55.
[42] Opinion of the Advocate General in *BV* (n 5) para 107.

Advocates General,[43] at the very least the Advocate General should be conducting such a detailed analysis.[44] Despite this, the CJEU went on to make a number of findings in relation to the scope of the 'fair and appropriate compensation' requirement. It was held that fixed rates of compensation are allowed but must account for the seriousness of the consequences for the victim of the particular injuries sustained.[45] In this regard, the CJEU stated that Member States must 'compensate to an appropriate extent the suffering to which [victims] have been exposed'.[46] On the specific facts of the case at hand, it held that '[a] fixed rate of €4,800 for the compensation of a victim of sexual violence does not appear, at first sight, to correspond to "fair and appropriate compensation"'.[47] Importantly, also, the CJEU held that State compensation does not have to equal full compensation available from offenders in civil or criminal proceedings.[48]

The precise meaning of these statements from the CJEU remain somewhat unclear and are giving rise to new requests for preliminary rulings, particularly in relation to the extent to which Member States must grant non-material damages to victims.[49] On the CJEU's use of the EU Charter as an interpretative tool, the key question is whether the use of the EU Charter, particularly the right to human dignity, 'was a necessary premise or a cosmetic addition' to the proceedings?[50] In evaluating the CJEU's use of the right to human dignity generally, Petrić maintains that whilst there are 'hardly any situations in which [the right to human dignity] appear[s] to have a vital importance for the outcome of individual cases',[51] it is often an 'indispensable building block' for the CJEU in these types of proceedings.[52] In the context of *BV*, I argue that the EU Charter, and the right to human dignity especially, was of vital importance. Further detail from the CJEU on its use of the EU Charter would, therefore, have been welcome. Regardless, it is clear that as a result of its use of the EU Charter in *BV*, the right to human dignity particularly is a 'powerful extension of the CJEU's institutional authority and judicial powers'.[53] In the context of *BV* and the development of the right to fair and appropriate compensation for all victims of violent crime, the influence and impact of the CJEU's authority and power is clear. In this regard, the next section will analyse this impact in the context of the national courts in Ireland.

IV. The Impact of the CJEU Jurisprudence in the Member States: Ireland as a Case Study

Ireland was one of the first EU Member States to establish a State compensation fund for victims of violent crime. The Criminal Injuries Compensation Scheme (CICS),

[43] D Petrić, 'Different Faces of Dignity': A Functionalist Account of the Institutional Use of Concept of Dignity in the European Union' (2019) 26(6) *Maastricht Journal of European and Comparative Law* 792, 797.
[44] ibid 799.
[45] *BV* (n 1) para 63.
[46] ibid para 64.
[47] ibid para 68.
[48] ibid para 60.
[49] *Blanco v Criminal Injuries Compensation Tribunal* High Court Record No 2019 6174P.
[50] Petrić (n 43) 808.
[51] ibid 800.
[52] ibid 808.
[53] ibid 801.

administered by the Criminal Injuries Compensation Tribunal (CICT), was established in 1974 and operates on an administrative basis within the Department of Justice. Despite there being no primary or secondary legislation underpinning the CICS, it is the mechanism by which Ireland has transposed its obligations under the Compensation Directive. Additionally, despite the adoption of the Compensation Directive in 2004, the CICS has only ever been amended twice since its establishment. First, in 1986, where the payment of compensation for non-material losses was removed due to budgetary constraints.[54] Second, in 2021, where operational amendments were introduced to improve decision-making efficiency, the bar on domestic violence victims applying to the CICS was removed,[55] along with other amendments.[56] There have been several legal challenges in the Irish courts against the manner in which the CICT operates. These legal challenges primarily focus on the procedural rules at the CICT and the process by which the CICT makes decisions in individual applications. Whilst there were several occasions where the Irish courts found in favour of applicants in these legal challenges,[57] rarely did substantive change result in the procedure and practice of the CICT. Additionally, the Irish courts were clear that such procedure and practice was a policy matter, entirely within the remit of the Irish Government.[58] With the CJEU judgment in *BV* and its interpretation of Article 12(2) of the Compensation Directive as applying to all victims of violent crime in the EU, I argue that the position taken by the Irish courts has shifted and indeed will continue to evolve. Up until *BV*, legal challenges against the CICT focused on domestic law arguments. However, with *BV*, EU law could now be invoked against the CICT by victims of crime in a purely internal situation. Indeed, this has successfully occurred on two occasions so far, with further litigation pending in the Irish courts. Both of these occasions will now be examined in turn.

V. The Need for Transparent Decision-Making: *Doyle and Kelly v CICT*

The first, at least partly, successful challenge occurred as a result of the judgment of the Court of Appeal in *Doyle and Kelly v Criminal Injuries Compensation Tribunal and Others*.[59] These judicial review proceedings arose following separate applications submitted by the applicants to the CICT for compensation in respect of injuries sustained

[54] Memorandum for the Government dated 12 July 1985, 8/399/31, National Archives of Ireland, 2015.88.612.

[55] L O'Driscoll, 'The Criminal Injuries Compensation Tribunal and the "Same Roof" Rule in Ireland: Exclusion, Inclusion and Reform' (2022) 6(2) *Irish Judicial Studies Journal* 60.

[56] Department of Justice, 'Minister McEntee Announces Reforms to the Criminal Injuries Compensation Scheme' (Press Release, 20 April 2021).

[57] *State (Creedon) v Criminal Injuries Compensation Tribunal* [1989] ILRM 104; *Hill v Criminal Injuries Compensation Tribunal* [1990] ILRM 36; *Gavin v The Criminal Injuries Compensation Tribunal* [1997] 1 IR 132; *Tomlinson v Criminal Injuries Compensation Tribunal* [2006] 4 IR 321; *Byrne v Criminal Injuries Compensation Tribunal* [2017] IEHC 28; *Vonkova v Criminal Injuries Compensation Tribunal* [2019] IEHC 13.

[58] *AD v Ireland* [1994] IR 369.

[59] *Doyle v Criminal Injuries Tribunal, The Minister for Justice and Equality, Ireland and The Attorney General & Kelly v Criminal Injuries Tribunal, The Minister for Justice and Equality, Ireland and The Attorney General* [2020] IECA 342.

in the course of two separate and unrelated violent criminal assaults in Ireland.[60] At the time the judicial review proceedings were taken, the CICT had not made decisions in relation to the applications,[61] however, there were a number of grounds of complaint raised by the applicants concerning the manner in which the CICT was processing their applications. First, it was argued that the CICS was in breach of Ireland's obligations under EU law to put in place 'fair and appropriate compensation' under the Compensation Directive, by not providing for compensation in respect of non-material losses. Second, it was argued that the Court should declare that the CICT should assume responsibility for the legal costs of the applicants' claims for compensation under the CICS in accordance with the access to justice provisions of the EU Charter. Third, it was argued that the provision of the CICS which allows the CICT to deny or reduce an award of compensation based on the conduct, character and way of life of victims is contrary to the 'fair and appropriate compensation' requirement under the Compensation Directive. Finally, it was submitted that the CICT should be compelled to make available to the applicants prior CICT decisions in relation to the application of the conduct, character and way of life provision and that there should be a preliminary mechanism in place at the CICT to determine such issues in advance of the applications proceeding to a full determination.[62]

In the High Court determination of the action, Murphy J dismissed the proceedings and found against the applicants on the basis that there was no right to State compensation under both Irish constitutional law and EU law, specifically under the Compensation Directive.[63] It should be said that between the High Court determination of the action and the matter concluding before the Court of Appeal, the CJEU judgment in *BV* was handed down. As a result of the *BV* judgment, the Court of Appeal in *Doyle and Kelly* held that '[t]here is no longer any doubt that the Directive does indeed confer an EU law right to compensation from the State upon the victim of a violent intentional crime in a wholly domestic situation'.[64] The use of *BV* in *Doyle and Kelly* is significant in terms of the particular rulings made by the Court of Appeal. In this regard, Ní Raifeartaigh J held that the CICS 'must now be seen as the means by which the State gives effect to its obligations under the Directive both as regards cross-border and purely domestic scenarios'.[65] In relation to the applicants' arguments that their legal costs should be paid by the CICT, or provided to them under the provisions of the legal aid scheme, the Court of Appeal relied on various CJEU judgments and judgments of the European Court of Human Rights (ECtHR), to dismiss this particular pleading.[66]

A similar conclusion was reached by the Court of Appeal in respect of the applicants' arguments concerning the exclusion of compensation for non-material losses. In this regard, the Court of Appeal stated that this question might well require a reference to the CJEU in order to be definitively determined.[67] However, the Court of Appeal refused to do so in this instance as the CICT had yet to make a decision in relation to

[60] ibid paras 5–19.
[61] ibid para 27.
[62] ibid para 15 and 25.
[63] ibid para 33. *Doyle & Kelly v CICT* [2019] IEHC 265.
[64] *Doyle & Kelly* (n 59) para 69.
[65] ibid para 81.
[66] ibid paras 94–115.
[67] ibid para 129.

the applicants' applications for compensation.[68] In addition to this holding, the Court of Appeal refused to make any declaration in relation to the conduct, character and way of life provisions of the CICS, again as no actual CICT decision was in issue. In relation to victims' right of access to prior decisions of the CICT, the Court of Appeal held that:

> The complete absence of any information which might assist both decision-maker and claimant in ensuring that the claimant gets the benefit of a consistent approach, and has notice as to what that approach is, seems to me to be fundamentally unfair. I consider it to be both a breach of constitutional fair procedures and a failure to protect, effectively, the exercise of an EU right.[69]

In coming to this conclusion, and ordering the CICT to publish a select number of decisions in relation to the conduct, character and way of life provision,[70] the Court of Appeal held that the CICT 'should strive for a measure of consistency in the application of [the conduct, character and way of life provision of the CICS], even if it currently does not', as decisions of the type made by the CICT should be 'fair rather than arbitrary' to applicants.[71] As a result of this ruling, the Court of Appeal ordered a select number of CICT decisions to be published.[72] In addition to complying with this order, the CICT has now published a wider range of decisions on different aspects of the CICS.

With the High Court initially dismissing the proceedings, there can be doubt as to the influential role played by the *BV* judgment in the proceedings. Whilst the applicants did not succeed on most points raised, perhaps most significantly in relation to the non-payment of non-material losses, the influential role of EU law is clear from the Court of Appeal judgment. In this regard, Murphy states that, whilst the absence of non-material losses in the CICS received a 'temporary stay of execution' in *Doyle and Kelly*, future litigation, relying on *BV*, will hopefully lead to the introduction of both compensation for non-material losses and the placing of the CICS on a statutory footing,[73] which would be a significant development from its current administrative and non-statutory basis.

VI. The Need for a Reasonable Time Limit: *Bowes and Brophy v CICT*

The influence of *BV* is further demonstrated when the judgment of the High Court in *Bowes and Brophy v Criminal Injuries Compensation Tribunal and Others* is considered.[74] These proceedings arose as a result of two separate incidents in Ireland whereby

[68] ibid para 131.

[69] ibid para 162.

[70] *Doyle v Criminal Injuries Tribunal, The Minister for Justice and Equality, Ireland and The Attorney General & Kelly v Criminal Injuries Tribunal, The Minister for Justice and Equality, Ireland and The Attorney General* [2021] IECA 131.

[71] *Doyle & Kelly* (n 59) para 158.

[72] *Doyle & Kelly* (n 70) para 20.

[73] MW Murphy, 'The Right under EU Law to Compensation for Injuries Criminally Inflicted: The Implications of BV for Irish Law' (2021) 23(1) *Irish Journal of European Law* 219, 238–48.

[74] *Bowes & Brophy v Criminal Injuries Compensation Tribunal* [2022] IEHC 703. See also L O'Driscoll, 'Victims of Crime and the Right to State Compensation under EU Law in Light of the High Court Judgment in Bowes & Brophy v Criminal Injuries Compensation Tribunal' (2023) 25(1) *Irish Journal of European Law* 63.

Mr Bowes and Mr Brophy were assaulted and seriously injured by persons unknown to them. Both men submitted applications to the CICT and were rejected by virtue of the claims being submitted outside the applicable time limit under the CICS.[75]

The time limit is set out in paragraph 20 of the CICS and provides that applications must be submitted within three months of the incident. From the establishment of the CICS in 1974, the CICT had discretion to extend this three-month time limit if circumstances existed which justified exceptional treatment of a particular application. There was no upper limit on this discretion, meaning applications could be submitted and accepted, if exceptional treatment was justified, many years after the original incident. This was particularly beneficial for victims of non-recent or historical crimes of violence. Despite this, in April 2021, the Irish Government amended this section of the CICS and placed a two-year upper limit on the CICT's discretion to extend the time limit. As a result, applications relating to crimes of violence which occurred more than two years prior to the date of application could not now be admitted by the CICT. Victims, therefore, had their entitlements restricted under the amended CICS.[76] With the assaults inflicted on Mr Bowes and Mr Brophy occurring more than two years prior to April 2021, December 2018 and April 2019 respectively, they were essentially cut off from accessing the CICS, hence why their applications were rejected by the CICT.[77] As a result, Mr Bowes and Mr Brophy, along with other victims impacted by the 2021 amendment, issued judicial review proceedings in the High Court challenging the operation of the two-year element of the time limit. A number of grounds were argued before Holland J, based both on Irish administrative law principles and EU law. The principle domestic legal argument maintained that the 2021 amendment breached the common law presumption against the retrospective application of law.[78] The EU law arguments maintained that the 2021 amendment breached the EU law principles of effectiveness and equivalence, with reference to Mr Bowes' and Mr Brophy's right to compensation under Article 12(2) of the Compensation Directive, as interpreted by the CJEU in *BV*. On the EU principle of effectiveness, Mr Bowes and Mr Brophy submitted that the 2021 amendment did not afford them an opportunity to comply with the new legal framework through transitional measures, thereby depriving them of the effective enjoyment of their EU law right to compensation.[79] Additionally, it was argued that the two-year element of the time limit itself breached the equivalence principle as it is a significantly lower time limit than that provided for in relation to equivalent domestic legal proceedings, in this instance assault and battery actions through the civil process, where the time limit to bring a claim is six years.[80]

For the purposes of this chapter, the interesting point is that the victims in these proceedings, Mr Bowes and Mr Brophy, failed in their domestic law arguments, but succeeded in relation to the arguments on the effectiveness principle under EU law. In relation to their arguments that the 2021 amendment breached the common law presumption against the retrospective application of law, Holland J held that existing

[75] *Bowes & Brophy*, ibid para 6.
[76] Department of Justice Press Release (n 56).
[77] *Bowes & Brophy* (n 74) para 99.
[78] ibid para 80.
[79] ibid para 131.
[80] ibid.

rights and obligations were impaired by the 2021 amendment, in that Mr Bowes and Mr Brophy lost their right to apply to the CICS.[81] However, he further held that a literal interpretation of the relevant provision in the CICS suggests that such an impairment was deliberate on the part of the Irish Government so that such applications would be excluded.[82] Therefore, the presumption in relation to retrospectivity was displaced and the domestic law argument failed. On equivalence, Holland J ruled that assault and battery actions are not an appropriate comparator for the purposes of the equivalence principle as, whilst State and civil compensation are similar in some respects, there are also notable differences, as recognised by the CJEU in *BV*,[83] which result in the equivalence principle not applying.[84] However, on effectiveness, Holland J held that there was a breach of the effectiveness principle as the 2021 amendment did not afford Mr Bowes and Mr Brophy a genuine opportunity, via transitional arrangements, to adapt to the new legal circumstances brought about as a result of the new two-year time limit.[85]

As a result of this High Court ruling, the Irish Government has amended the CICS to take account of the effectiveness principle.[86] These proceedings, along with *Doyle and Kelly*, demonstrate that the development of an EU right to compensation, as provided for by the CJEU in its interpretation of Article 12(2), has the potential to significantly improve access to State compensation for victims of violent crime. In *Doyle and Kelly*, the Court of Appeal used the Article 12(2) right to compensation, in conjunction with the effectiveness principle, to hold that applicants to the CICT have a right to access the CICT's prior decisions in the context of the conduct, character and way of life provisions of the CICS. Since the judgment, the CICT has now published a wide range of decisions on various aspects of the CICS which contributes to a more effective understanding of decision-making at the CICT, which allows applicants to better put forward their claims.[87] In *Bowes and Brophy*, the High Court judgment resulted in the CICT's strict time limit being set aside on the basis of EU law. As mentioned previously, the Irish courts were generally deferential to the Irish Government in relation to the CICT's procedures. As a result of both *Doyle and Kelly* and *Bowes and Brophy*, this has now changed and applicants to the CICT now have a substantive legal basis on which to challenge CICT decisions. This is as a direct result of an EU minimum standard, as interpreted by the CJEU. With the Commission opting not to expand these minimum standards in its proposed revision of the EU Victims' Rights Directive, the development of the *BV* jurisprudence at the CJEU and national court level is more important than

[81] ibid para 100.
[82] ibid paras 128–29.
[83] *BV* (n 1) para 60.
[84] *Bowes & Brophy* (n 74) para 216.
[85] ibid paras 163–66. In this regard, J Holland relied on the CJEU judgments in C-62/00 *Marks & Spencer PLC v Customs and Excise Commissioners* EU:C:2002:435, on transitional arrangements, and C 429/15 *Danqua v Minister for Justice and Equality* EU:C:2016:789, in relation to providing a genuine opportunity.
[86] 'Criminal Injuries Compensation Scheme to Temporarily Allow Very Late Applications' *Irish Legal News* (1 February 2024).
[87] See *Earls v Criminal Injuries Compensation Tribunal* [2022] IEHC 679 paras 78–81 where the High Court incorrectly, in my view, held that the publication of prior decisions made no difference to the applicant's ability to put forward her claim. For more information, see L O'Driscoll, 'Just Another Victim' *Law Society Gazette* (6 April 2023).

ever.[88] Its importance, and indeed the need for increased minimum standards at the EU level, is further highlighted when the shortcomings in the Commission's 2023 Proposal are highlighted. The next section will examine this issue.

VII. Reforming Compensation Provision for Victims of Crime in the EU

A. Commission's 2023 Proposal

With the adoption of the Lisbon Treaty in 2009,[89] legislative protection in respect of victims' rights in the EU was strengthened. In this regard, the 2001 Framework Decision was replaced with the Victims' Rights Directive in 2012 which provides victims with a comprehensive set of rights and support throughout the criminal process. The right of victims to State compensation and the development of comprehensive minimum standards for national schemes was thought not to be necessary in the immediate post-Lisbon context.[90] Reform of the Compensation Directive and doubt as to the available legal bases for doing so continues to be an issue as evidenced in the Commission's 2023 Proposal. Here, the Commission again rejects reform of the Compensation Directive and the imposition of comprehensive minimum standards, as such action cannot be achieved under the EU Treaty provisions in respect of judicial cooperation in civil and criminal matters and would again require the exercise of the flexibility clause, now Article 352 TFEU.[91] As minimum standards in respect of State compensation cannot be achieved using the ordinary legislative procedure provided for by the Lisbon Treaty under Article 82(2) TFEU in respect of judicial cooperation in criminal matters, and unanimity would have to achieved under Article 352 TFEU,[92] the Commission concluded that the imposition of minimum standards through amendments to the Compensation Directive would not be worthwhile.[93] The Commission stated that the EU 'currently lacks a clear legal basis to revise the Compensation Directive' and the necessary amendments needed to put in place comprehensive minimum standards would be 'particularly costly' for Member States.[94] Instead, the Commission opted for amendments to the Victims' Rights Directive obligating Member States to pay directly

[88] It is clear from the Law Reform Commission process that the development of an EU right to compensation is having a broader impact in the context of legal and policy reforms. For more information, see Law Reform Commission (n 6).

[89] Lisbon Treaty [2007[OJ C306/1.

[90] European Commission, Commission Staff Working Paper: Impact Assessment Accompanying the Document Proposal for a Directive of the European Parliament and of the Council Establishing Minimum Standards on the Rights, Support and Protection of Victims of Crime SEC(2011) 580, 6–7.

[91] European Commission, Commission Staff Working Document: Impact Assessment Report Accompanying the Document Proposal for a Directive of the European Parliament and of the Council Amending Directive 2012/29/EU Establishing Minimum Standards on the Rights, Support and Protection of Victims of Crime, and Replacing Council Framework Decision 2001/220/JHA SWD(2023) 246 final 48–49.

[92] ibid 49.

[93] ibid 50.

[94] ibid.

to the victim any compensation awarded in the criminal trial from the offender and then recoup the amount from the offender after the conclusion of the criminal process.[95]

In this regard, I argue that it is not that Article 352 TFEU does not provide a clear legal basis, rather the problem lies in the unanimity requirement. As the legal basis for the Commission's 2023 Proposal falls under the ordinary legislative procedure under Article 82(2) TFEU, due to it being dependent on an award of compensation being made in the context of criminal proceedings, the absence of a unanimity requirement perhaps explains the Commission's reasoning here as to its preferred proposal. Whilst the Commission's reasoning is understandable from a political viewpoint, I am not convinced that the provisions in relation to judicial cooperation in civil and criminal matters exclude completely legislative action in relation to minimum standards for national compensation schemes. In relation to civil matters under Article 81 TFEU, why this provision is limited 'to rights or obligations between individuals',[96] as argued by the Commission Proposal for a Council Directive on Compensation to Crime Victims, is not clear. On criminal matters under Article 82 TFEU, whilst national compensation schemes differ from offender compensation in the context of criminal proceedings, these two issues are not completely unrelated and overlap quite significantly in many respects. This is particularly the case should the Commission's 2023 Proposal be adopted in that compensation awarded in criminal proceedings will become payable to victims by Member States, albeit with the condition that Member States can recoup such amounts from the offender. If the EU can obligate Member States to 'do' State compensation by grounding such an obligation in the criminal trial, why can't the EU obligate Member States to provide improved State compensation, through comprehensive minimum standards, via a mechanism which already exists in the Member States, ie national compensation funds? The Commission's exclusion of Articles 81 and 82 TFEU as legal bases is, therefore, not completely convincing. Ultimately, this question warrants further consideration for future research.

In justifying its proposal in relation to the role of Member States paying and recouping compensation, the Commission stated that the measure, if implemented, would reduce the uncertainty, costs and time associated with victims themselves executing compensation judgments against offenders, thereby reducing secondary victimisation.[97] Additionally, the Commission maintains that the measure is consistent both with other amendments proposed in the 2023 Proposal and also with the Proposal for a Directive on Violence Against Women. In relation to the other amendments, the Commission's 2023 Proposal also imposes obligations on Member States to ensure that victims of crime have a right to receive compensation from the offender in the course of criminal proceedings, thereby removing the exception contained in the Victims' Rights Directive which allowed Member States not to do so if compensation could be obtained in other proceedings.[98] Furthermore, in relation to the proposed Violence Against Women Directive, Article 26 proposes to obligate Member States to do likewise in relation to this category of victim, along with putting in place specific minimum standards in

[95] Commission's 2023 Proposal (n 10).
[96] Commission's 2002 Proposal (n 12) para 5.1.
[97] Impact Assessment Report (n 91) 47.
[98] ibid 49.

relation to such proceedings.[99] Finally, in its 2023 Proposal, the Commission maintains that obligating Member States to pay offender compensation upfront will improve trust in the justice system.[100] On the financial costs to Member States of the measure,[101] the Commission argue that as compensation can be recouped from the offender, which typically does not occur in relation to national compensation schemes, significant costs will not be incurred.[102] The Commission point to the Netherlands as a jurisdiction where such a measure, the APS, operates. In this regard, the Commission highlight that of the 3,531 payments made to victims by the Dutch Government since 2017 under the APS in respect of violent and sexual offences, 2,888 (82 per cent) payments were collected in full (2,795) or in part (93) from offenders.[103] Whilst this demonstrates success in many respects, it is important to clarify that the remaining 18 per cent of non-recouped payments amounts to a not insignificant financial burden on the Dutch State. For example, approximately €7.5 million was advanced to victims of violent and sexual offences in 2017 with approximately only €3 million collected from offenders.[104] Despite this, it is important to acknowledge that recouped amounts will increase year-on-year as offenders continue to pay off their debts, thereby reducing the financial burden on the Dutch State. In this regard, the next subsection will examine the APS in more detail.

B. The APS in the Netherlands

Under the relevant Dutch legal framework, victims can receive compensation from the offender through the criminal courts by way of a compensation order. Victims can also receive compensation from the offender through civil proceedings. In relation to the compensation order, whilst compensation is awarded as part of the criminal proceedings, whereby the victim is joined to the proceedings as a party for the purposes of the compensation claim, the criminal court utilises the relevant rules used in the context of civil proceedings to determine whether to award compensation and the amount of compensation if awarded.[105] Importantly, if the criminal court determines that the compensation claim is too complicated to be assessed as part of the criminal proceedings, then it will be deemed inadmissible and the victim must then file civil proceedings in order to pursue their compensation claim.[106] If compensation is awarded by the

[99] ibid. European Commission, 'Proposal for a Directive of the European Parliament and of the Council on Combating Violence Against Women and Domestic Violence' COM(2022) 105 final.

[100] Impact Assessment Report (n 91) 50.

[101] In this regard, the Irish Government's concerns are of note, see D Kent, 'Government Raises Concerns with EU over "Problematic" Crime Directive' *Irish Examiner* (16 August 2023). See also Opinion of Regulatory Scrutiny Board, 'Proposal for a Directive of the European Parliament and of the Council Amending Directive 2012/29/EU Establishing Minimum Standards on the Rights, Support and Protection of Victims of Crime, and Replacing Council Framework Decision 2001/220/JHA' SEC(2023) 270 final 2.

[102] Impact Assessment Report (n 91) 47.

[103] ibid.

[104] M Hebly et al, *Compensatie en Verhaal van Schade door Strafbare Feiten Verkenning van Bronnen, Volumes en Publieke Kosten: Summary* (Erasmus Law School, 2020) 4.

[105] I Giesen et al, 'The Dutch Crush on Compensating Crime Victims' in M Dyson, *Comparing Tort and Crime* (Cambridge University Press, 2015) 346.

[106] ibid 341.

criminal court and the amount is not paid to the victim by the offender within an eight-month period, then the APS steps in and pays the relevant compensation.[107] The APS was established in 2011 and at first it applied only to violent and sexual offences. From 2016, the APS applied to all victims of crime but with a cap of €5,000 for non-violent and non-sexual offences.[108] Once the APS has paid out the relevant compensation, the Central Justitieel Incassobureau or the Central Judicial Collection Agency (CJIB) of the Dutch Government seeks repayment of the amount from the offender.[109] The CJIB has operated in the Netherlands prior to the introduction of the APS and collects a wide range of court and administrative fines on behalf of the Dutch Government, including traffic fines. The CJIB can take several measures to enforce payment including agreeing with the offender to repay the amount in instalments. In the case of non-cooperation from the offender, the offender can have his assets seized by the CJIB. Furthermore, proceedings can be commenced to imprison the offender as a measure of last resort if he refuses to pay the awarded compensation.[110] Importantly, the APS and the CJIB framework is not available in the context of compensation awarded during the civil process.[111]

Whilst the Dutch Government is generally successful at recouping compensation from the offender, there has been controversy in recent years as to whether the APS is an appropriate use of public funds. As a result, the Dutch Government committed itself to reviewing the operation of the APS. This review process, named the Donner Committee, reported in 2021 and recommended that the APS should be reformed. Specifically, it was recommended that victims of violent and sexual offences should be treated in the same manner as all other victims of crime in that amounts of compensation for all offences should be limited to what the CJIB expects to collect from the offender. The uncapped amount for violent and sexual offences would, therefore, be replaced with a capped amount calculated by the CJIB.[112] The maximum amount proposed for all offences would be approximately €15,000.[113] In addition to this proposal, the review also recommended that the eight-month time limit should be abolished, and the advance payment be paid straight away after the judgment.[114] Whilst these recommendations were broadly welcomed by the Dutch Government, the Ministry of Justice and Security decided to reject the proposals in relation to capped amounts as this would result in a significant reduction in the amount of compensation available to victims of violent and sexual offences. According to the Ministry of Justice and Security, retaining uncapped amounts for these victims is consistent with Government policy in respect of safeguarding these victims and recognising the unique harm caused to victims' integrity as a result of violent and sexual crimes. Despite rejecting this proposal, the Ministry

[107] Donner Committee to Investigate the System for Compensating Victims of Criminal Offences, *Coming to Terms: Towards a Balanced, Consistent and Affordable System for the Compensation of Victims of Criminal Offences in the Netherlands* (2021) para 5.6.3.

[108] ibid.

[109] ibid.

[110] ibid para 2.3.3.5.

[111] ibid para 5.6.2.

[112] ibid para 6.4.3.3.

[113] Ministry of Justice and Security, *Letter to the Speaker of the House of Representatives of the States General in Response to Report of Committee to Investigate the System for Compensating Victims of Criminal Offences* (2023).

[114] Donner Committee (n 107) para 3.3.5.3.

committed to expanding the APS to violent offences which were previously excluded, including arson resulting in serious bodily injury or death.[115]

C. The Need for Minimum Standards

Despite the relative success of the APS in the Netherlands and the Commission's preference for Member States to adopt a similar framework in their respective jurisdictions, I maintain that there is still a need for comprehensive minimum standards at the EU level in respect of State compensation schemes.[116] Such minimum standards might detail the type of victims who qualify for State compensation, the applicable violent offences included, along with the appropriate minimum time limit which victims must abide by when applying. Furthermore, these standards might include details on the minimum amount of compensation available, the types of losses covered and various other eligibility rules including police reporting requirements and the manner in which compensation can be denied or reduced should the victim be responsible in some way for the offence. As mentioned earlier, issues such as these were addressed in the 2002 Commission Proposal.[117] Despite problems in relation to the legal bases for such minimum standards, I argue for such standards due to the inherent limitations of advance payment frameworks operating in the context of criminal trials, including the APS. One such limitation includes that the criminal court will often dismiss the compensation claim if such a determination is too complicated for the criminal court to assess. Victims are then left to issue civil proceedings where they must prosecute the case, secure evidence and enforce any judgments made themselves, without the possibility of an advanced payment.[118] In the Netherlands, according to the Ministry of Justice and Security, two-thirds of compensation claims made by natural persons in the criminal courts are deemed inadmissible. This amounts to 20,000 claims per year, 8,000 of which are claims involving violent and sexual offences.[119] A further limitation relates to the fact that there is no guarantee that a criminal trial will take place, for example, if the offender cannot be identified or if the prosecution decides not to proceed with charging an individual for the offence due to an absence of evidence. If such a trial does take place, there is no guarantee that there will be a conviction. Victims might not ever be granted a compensation order and no advanced payment can, therefore, be made. As in criminal cases where the matter is dismissed, victims are forced to issue civil proceedings. With the civil process posing significant challenges for victims, as referred to above, the national compensation scheme is often the only realistic option for victims who do not wish to pursue a civil claim against the offender.[120]

[115] Letter from Ministry of Justice and Security (n 113).
[116] As argued in a recent study completed for the European Parliament; see E Sellier and A Weyembergh, *Criminal Procedural Laws across the European Union – A Comparative Analysis of Selected Main Differences and the Impact they have over the Development of EU Legislation* (European Parliament, 2018) 156.
[117] Commission's 2002 Proposal (n 12) para 5.1.
[118] Donner Committee (n 107) para 3.3.2.
[119] Letter from Ministry of Justice and Security (n 113).
[120] Donner Committee (n 107) para 2.4.5.

For this reason, the Commission's 2023 Proposal in relation to the advanced payment framework has limitations. Whilst the Commission stated that this Proposal will bring 'considerable improvement to victims' standards on compensation from the offender',[121] and acknowledged that some Member States will need to considerably adapt their justice systems to effectively operate such a framework,[122] the Commission did not consider in detail the various difficulties raised above. In fact, the Commission based the Proposal on an assumption that 'if the prosecution wins the criminal case … then the victim will be entitled to compensation'.[123] As demonstrated with the APS in the Netherlands, this is not necessarily the case. In fact, compensation claims are often dismissed due to their complexity, even where offenders have been convicted.[124] Furthermore, the fact that a criminal trial or conviction might often not occur in Member States was not considered by the Commission. In fact, the Commission's 2023 Proposal seeks to force Member States to provide a compensation procedure in the criminal courts only, removing the current exception in the Victims' Rights Directive which allows Member States not to do so if another procedure exists elsewhere, such as civil proceedings. In putting forward this proposal, it is not clear whether the Commission considered the fact that no criminal procedure or conviction occurs in many instances. Finally, there is then the issue of the impact of enforcing compensation orders on the rights of offenders. The enforcement of such orders, especially where an advance payment has been made to the victim and the Member State in question is taking measures to recoup the amount from the offender, could potentially be understood as a further punishment on offenders which might impact their rehabilitation. This issue is amplified by the fact that such measures might be imposed on offenders many years after the final judgment of the criminal court.[125] Ultimately, the impact, if any, of such an approach warrants further study in advance of becoming a core part of the EU victims' rights landscape. Considering the limitations with advanced payment frameworks in the criminal trial and with minimum standards in respect of national compensation schemes being rejected by the Commission, despite the significant disparities present across the national schemes of Member States, the meaning of 'fair and appropriate compensation' under the Compensation Directive is, therefore, more important than ever.

VIII. Conclusion

This chapter has examined the current legal framework for State compensation at the EU and Member State levels, focusing in particular on the Irish and Dutch compensation regimes. Overall, whilst the Commission's Proposal in relation to compensation is to be welcomed, I argue that there is still a necessity for reform of the Compensation Directive and the development of more comprehensive minimum standards in respect

[121] Impact Assessment Report (n 91) 50.
[122] ibid 47.
[123] ibid 107.
[124] Giesen (n 105) 343.
[125] Donner Committee (n 107) para 3.3.4.4.

of national compensation funds. I submit that these minimum standards are needed, despite concerns as to the applicable legal bases, as it is clear that significant disparities exist across the national compensation funds of Member States. Additionally, I argue that there is still a need for the development of more comprehensive minimum rules as the Proposal from the Commission is limited and will not reach every violent crime victim, especially as the criminal trial is often not the appropriate place for compensation claims to be determined and a criminal trial or conviction often does not take place. I also submit that it is imperative that the Commission reconsider its proposals in light of concerns as to the impact on the rights of offenders. Overall, with the minimum standard of 'fair and appropriate compensation' having a positive impact on compensation provision for victims in Ireland, I argue that minimum standards, expressed through appropriate EU legal instruments, is the optimum method to improve victims' access to compensation.

6

Eurojust's Role in Enhancing Victims' Rights in Cross-Border Criminal Cases

JULIETA CARMONA BERMEJO AND ERIC FRÉJABUE*

I. Introduction

The last decades of the twentieth century marked a paradigm shift in the position of the victim in criminal proceedings. As many authors point out,[1] traditionally, criminal proceedings were seen exclusively as a dispute between the State and the defendant. The role of the victim was limited to that of witness or informant with no further function.[2] However, the 1960s and 1970s marked a turning point in the role of victims in criminal proceedings.[3] A number of authors have noted this paradigm shift,[4] which was also taken up by the European Court of Human Rights (ECtHR)[5] and eventually the

* The opinions expressed in this publication are those of the authors. They do not purport to reflect the opinions or views of Eurojust. We would like to express our sincere gratitude to Ms Hilde Vandevoorde, Mr Vincent Jamin, Ms Federica Curtol and Mr Thomas Labrosse for their kind support in the elaboration of this contribution.

[1] See, for all, F Vacas Fernández, *El estatuto jurídico internacional de las víctimas en crímenes internacionales*, (*The International Legal Status of Victims in International Crimes*) (Tirant lo Blanch, 2023) 23 *passim*, and the authors cited in it, particularly J Doak, *Victim's Rights, Human Rights and Criminal Justice. Reconceiving the Role of Third Parties* (Hart Publishing, 2008).

[2] To cite Doak (n 1) 7, quoted by Vacas (n 1) 32: 'There has been a clear historical pattern whereby the victim has been gradually excluded from both the investigation and trial stages of the criminal process. Centuries of centralization led to the emergence of a public criminal law administered by the State, and later by lawyers. As a result, the contemporary criminal justice is normatively and structurally built around a contest between the State and the accused, which inherently excludes the rights and interest of the victim.'

[3] P Rock, 'On Becoming a Victim' in C Hoyle and R Young (eds), *New Visions of Crime Victims* (Bloomsbury Publishing, 2002) 1 *passim*.

[4] Quoting Vacas (n 1) among these authors MCH Bassiuoni, 'International Recognition of Victims' Rights' (2006) 6 *Human Rights Law Review* 2, 210–11; N Roth-Arriaza,'Combating Impunity: Some Thoughts on the Way Forward' (1996) 59 *Law and Contemporary Problems* 93-012, 93; A Karmen, 'Who is Against Victims' Rights?' (1992) 157 8 *St. John's Journal of Legal Commentary* 159; F Klug, 'Human Rights and Victims' in E Cape (ed), '*Reconcilable Rights? Analysing the Tension between Victims and Defendants* (Legal Action Group, 2004); or G Konrád, 'The Viewpoint of the Victim' (1990) 2 *Cardozo Studies in Law and Literature* 9.

[5] See, eg, *Doorson v The Netherlands* App no 20524/92 (ECtHR, 26 March 1996), para 70: 'It is true that Article 6 [of the European Convention on Human Rights] does not explicitly require the interest (…) of victims (…) to be taken into consideration. However, their life, security, or person may be at stake, as may interests coming generally within the ambit of Article 8 of the Convention. Such interests of witnesses and

European Union (EU) with the adoption of the Council Framework Decision 2001/220/JHA of 15 March 2001, on the statute of victims in criminal proceedings.[6] The poor results of the implementation of this Framework Decision[7] led to the adoption of the current Directive 2012/29/EU establishing minimum standards and protection of victims of crime[8] (hereafter the VRD).

The VRD establishes minimum standards on the rights, support and protection of victims of crime and ensures that persons who have fallen victim to crime are recognised and treated with respect. Today, thanks to this legislative development, victims of crime in the EU are entitled to a range of rights, regardless of their nationality, place of residence, the type of crime or the place where the crime was committed. These rights are enshrined in a number of EU directives and international conventions and include, for example, the right to be heard, the right to information, the right to protection and the right to compensation.

The complexity of cross-border crimes exacerbates the difficulties in protecting the victims in cases involving different jurisdictions. The procedural rights of victims cannot always be fully guaranteed. Difficulties range from the identification of all victims to the complexity of organising their participation in trials in different countries without running the risk of secondary victimisation, for example. In addition, the right to restitution and compensation cannot always be adequately implemented due to the large number of victims, for example, or the lack of full harmonisation and implementation of the legislative framework.

Experience shows that prosecutors and investigative judges are often at the forefront of identifying and solving problems related to the exercise of victims' rights in a cross-border context.

Eurojust (henceforth referred to as 'the Agency') mitigates these difficulties by ensuring timely and efficient coordination between the various countries and actors involved. It does this by ensuring that the dimension of victims' rights is considered on

victims are in principle protected by other, substantive provisions of the Convention, which imply that contracting States should organise their criminal proceedings in such a way that those interest are not unjustifiably imperilled. Against this background, principles of fair trial also require that in appropriate cases the interest of the defence are balanced against those of witnesses or victims called upon to testify'.

[6] Council Framework Decision (FWD) of 15 March 2001 on the standing of victims in criminal proceedings (2001/220/JHA) [2001] OJ L82/1. The adoption of this FWD can be seen in the context of the previous steps taken after the Treaty of Amsterdam, namely the Action Plan of the Council and the Commission on how best to implement the provision of the Treaty of Amsterdam on an area of freedom, security and justice (text adopted by the Justice and Home Affairs Council of 3 December 1998 (1999/C 19/01) [1999] OJ C19/1, see in particular paras 19 and 51). Acting in conformity with this Action Plan, on 14.7.99 the EC published a communication on crime victims in the European Union (COM (1999) 349 final, Communication from the Commission to the Council, the European Parliament and the Economic and Social Committee: 'Crime Victims in the European Union. Reflexions on Standards and Actions' (CELEX Number 51999DC0349). See also the conclusions of the European Council held in Tampere on 15–16 October 1999 (para 32).

[7] According to JL Gómez Colomer, *Estatuto Jurídico de las Víctimas del Delito ('Legal Status of Crime Victims')* (Thomson Reuters, 2015), 173, the improvement of this FWD was a failure, as none of the Member States transposed it properly, leading the EU to consider it as merely a recommendation following Recommendation (85) 11 of 28 June 1985 on victims' standing in criminal proceedings and Recommendation (87) of 17 September 1987 on assistance to victims and prevention of victimisation.

[8] Directive 2012/29/EU of the European Parliament and of the Council of 25 October 2012 establishing minimum standards on the rights, support, and protection of victims of crime, and replacing Council Framework Decision 2001/220/JHA (hereafter the 'VRD') [2012] OJ L315/57.

its own merits, according to the specificities of the given case that the Agency is providing support for.

By bringing together the prosecutors and judges in charge of cross-border cases involving victims, Eurojust can contribute to greater convergence and coherence of national efforts in this field.

This chapter presents Eurojust's mandate in the fight against the most serious forms of cross-border crime and how the Agency interacts with the EU's legal and institutional architecture governing victims' rights (section II) when assisting national judicial authorities in the implementation of judicial cooperation (section III) and the challenges faced by practitioners and the perspectives arising from the revision of key pieces of EU legislation (section IV).

II. Eurojust and its Role in the Implementation of the EU Strategy on Victims' Rights

A. Eurojust's Contribution to Safeguarding Victims' Rights in Cross-Border Cases: Multifaceted Support

Eurojust is the European Union Agency for Criminal Justice Cooperation, which coordinates investigations into serious cross-border crime in Europe and beyond. Eurojust provides hands-on support to national authorities by promoting the exchange of information, developing prosecutorial strategies, facilitating the use of judicial cooperation tools and implementing joint actions.

Eurojust assists national judges and prosecutors to take due account of the needs and legitimate interests of the victims beyond their national jurisdiction when deciding on a common prosecutorial strategy in cross-border cases. At the request of its national members or acting as a College, Eurojust issues recommendations, joint recommendations or requests[9] on which jurisdiction should prosecute in a given case, whether the proceedings should be transferred to another country or what to do when confronted with competing requests for surrender and extradition.

Eurojust has designed a series of practical judicial tools and instruments aimed at facilitating the work of national practitioners in the context of cross-border crime cases involving victims.

[9] Under the Eurojust Decision (Council Decision 2002/187/JHA of 28 February 2022, setting up Eurojust with a view to reinforcing the fight against serious crime [2002] OJ L63/1), Eurojust recommendations were issued either by its national members (Art 6(a)) or by the College of Eurojust (Art 7(a)). The 2009 amendments to the Eurojust Decision did not modify this provision (Council Decision 2009/426/JHA of 16 December 2008 on the strengthening of Eurojust and amending Decision 2002/187/JHA setting up Eurojust with a view to reinforcing the fight against serious crime [2009] OJ L138/14). Since 12 December 2019, the Eurojust Regulation (Regulation (EU) 2018/1727 of the European Parliament and of the Council of 14 November 2018 on the European Agency for Criminal Justice Cooperation (Eurojust), and replacing and repealing Council Decision 2002/187/JHA (hereafter 'EJR') [2018] OJ L295/138), enables Eurojust to issue recommendations in Art 4(2)(b).

One pivotal element in relation to judicial cooperation is the timely and effective exchange of information. Coordination meetings are designed to bring together the judicial and law enforcement authorities of the countries involved to reach agreement on their cooperation and/or the coordination of investigations and prosecutions at national level. If appropriate, participants may exchange information on the identity and status of the victims, the nature and extent of their damage, and possible remedial actions such as protection or compensation.

In addition, Eurojust also provides financial support to Joint Investigation Teams (JITs). A JIT is a legal agreement between competent authorities of two or more States for the purpose of carrying out criminal investigations. Once a JIT has been set up, the partners can exchange information and evidence directly, cooperate in real time and carry out joint operations. JITs could be used to discuss the interests of the victims, their identification and how their statements will be taken to ensure that they are admissible in the jurisdictions concerned, thus avoiding the need for them to be interviewed again. JITs can also facilitate discussions on the legal requirements to ensure that victims can be compensated, possibly making it one of the objectives of the JIT.

Finally, coordination centres are another judicial tool created by Eurojust to support action days where arrests, searches, interviews of suspects and witnesses, seizure of evidence and freezing of assets are carried out in several countries simultaneously. Before, during and after the organisation of a coordination centre, practitioners are invited to consider the means to support and protect victims. This is crucial, for instance, when action days are organised to take down organised crime groups involved in human trafficking. In such cases, the timely provision of a safe shelter, protection measures and support services are key.

B. The EU Architecture for Protecting Victims' Rights and the Role of Eurojust

Supporting and protecting all victims of crime is currently enshrined as a priority policy within the EU. Nevertheless, as acknowledged by the European Commission,[10] the practical implementation of the VRD by the Member States (MS) presents a number of shortcomings and inadequacies.[11] In this context, the European Commission

[10] Communication from the Commission to the European Parliament, the Council, the Economic and Social Committee, and the Committee of the Regions, adopted on 24 June 2020, Doc COM (2020) 258 final. After this Communication, a deeper implementation appraisal was produced by the European Parliamentary Research Service (EPRS) on the implementation of existing EU legislation in practice (see EPRS, 'Victims' Rights in the EU Revision of Directive 2012/29/EU' (July 2023), available at www.europarl.europa.eu/RegData/etudes/BRIE/2023/747432/EPRS_BRI(2023)747432_EN.pdf. Another extremely interesting survey on the extent of violence in Europe was produced by the European Union Agency for Fundamental Rights (FRA) in 2021 under the title 'Crime, Safety and Victims' Rights' (2021), available at https://fra.europa.eu/sites/default/files/fra_uploads/fra-2021-crime-safety-victims-rights_en.pdf. This later survey was preceded by a string of reports in the 'Justice for Victims of Violent Crimes' series, all of them available on the FRA website.

[11] As a matter of fact, the EU opened infringement proceedings, on several occasions between 2016 and 2021 against MS that had not communicated their transposition measures or had not fully transposed the VRD.

elaborated its first EU Strategy on victims' rights for the period 2020–2025[12] (hereafter 'the Strategy') to ensure that victims of all crime, no matter where in the EU or under what circumstances the crime took place, can fully rely on the protection of their rights. To this end, the Strategy outlines actions to be taken by the European Commission, MS and civil society. The Strategy has become one of the EU's top policy priorities and is based on a two-pronged approach: empowering victims of crime and working together to promote victims' rights.

Guaranteeing victims' effective access to justice to ensure that they are aware of their rights, understand them and are able to participate in proceedings is crucial. However, the cross-border nature of all cases supported by Eurojust presents specific challenges in terms of protecting these victims' rights. The right to information is one of them. For example, in a case supported by Eurojust, the victims of different nationalities other than the one where a terrorist attack was commited, were informed of their procedural rights shortly after the attack and in a language they could understand. Another topical example relates to cases of cyber fraud, involving large numbers of victims located in various jurisdictions. Their identification can be facilitated by Eurojust, as a list of victims can be drawn from the information of the countries involved in the case. The mere identification of as many victims as possible is a prerequisite to inform them on their rights.

In response, policymakers have sought to ensure that victims' rights are consistently protected, regardless of their location, nationality or where the crime took place. The EU uses various means to protect the procedural rights of victims of cross-border crimes. This includes general (the VRD) and specific Directives (victims of terrorism, of trafficking in human beings) and policy documents such as the Strategy. As a result, an extensive legal and institutional framework has been developed over the past 20 years. Eurojust plays a critical role in this architecture.

Article 17 of the VRD is a key provision from a judicial cooperation perspective as it governs the rights of victims when they reside in another MS. This Article provides guidance to MSs to ensure that victims can be heard. This entails for example the possibility to take a statement from the victim immediately after the victim has made a complaint in the country where the offence was committed. Also, there have been cases at Eurojust concerning a complaint made by a victim in the MS of the victim's residence. The latter however had not yet exercised jurisdiction over crimes committed abroad to the MS where the criminal offence occurred in accordance with Article 17, paragraph 3. This provision gives the obligation to transmit the complaint of the victim to the authorities where the crime was committed.

The VRD is complemented by sectoral legislative instruments. These latter instruments aim to respond to the needs of victims of specific crimes.

Firstly, it is worth mentioning the Anti-Trafficking Directive.[13] On 19 December 2022, the European Commission proposed a Revision to this Directive to strengthen the

[12] Communication from the Commission to the European Parliament, the Council, the European Economic and Social Committee, and the Committee of the Regions, of 24.6.2020 'EU Strategy on Victims' Rights (2020–2025)' COM (2020) 258 final.

[13] Directive 2011/36/EU of the European Parliament and of the Council of 5 April 2011 on preventing and combating trafficking in human beings and protecting its victims, and replacing Council Framework Decision 2002/629/JHA [2011] OJ L101/1.

EU rules to prevent and combat trafficking in human beings and protecting its victims.[14] The revised Directive was adopted on 27 May 2024.

Eurojust practice offers numerous examples in which the provisions of this Directive are used to protect victims' rights. This is notably the case of the provisions aimed at limiting the unnecessary repetition of interviews during investigation, prosecution and trial (Art 12 (4)(a) or the provision of support to child victims (Art 14). The Eurojust Report on Trafficking in Human Beings[15] identified a series of best practices stemming from the obligations set in the Directive. For example, Eurojust encourages the use of video conferencing and the seconding of specialised officers to interview potential victims and take into consideration the particularities of child victims of human trafficking. Eurojust disseminates these recommendations to practitioners during dedicated meetings and when supporting cases.

A second important instrument for protection of the rights of specific vulnerable victims is the Directive on combating the sexual abuse and sexual exploitation of children and child pornography.[16] Emblematic of the prime interest of the victims is the reference that the child's best interests must be a primary consideration when carrying out any measures to combat the offences sanctioned in the Directive. In addition, a series of procedural guarantees are provided in Article 20 of the Directive. It should be noted that on 11 May 2022, the Commission proposed new rules to prevent and combat child sexual abuse.

The best practices identified in Eurojust's Report on Trafficking in Human Beings are applicable, in particular when it comes to minimising the risk of secondary victimisation and providing adequate support.

Third, the EU Directive on combating terrorism[17] provides inter alia that MSs should ensure that all victims of terrorism have access to information about victims' rights, available support services and compensation schemes in the MS where the terrorist offence was committed. Eurojust is actively involved in identifying, promoting and implementing best practices in relation to victims of terrorism. For example, after the 2017 terrorist attacks in Barcelona and Cambrils, in Spain, which affected victims of 34 nationalities, Eurojust assisted the Spanish authorities in preparing and transmitting a specially designed template informing victims of their rights.

A fourth EU sectoral instrument designed to meet the specific needs of certain categories of victims is the Directive on combating fraud and counterfeiting of non-cash means of payment.[18] The Directive provides that when such fraud involves, for example,

[14] Proposal for a Directive of the European Parliament and of the Council amending Directive 2011/36/EU on preventing and combating trafficking in human beings and protecting its victims COM/2022/732 final.

[15] 'Eurojust Report on Trafficking in Human Beings Best Practice and Issues in Judicial Cooperation' (February 2021).

[16] Directive 2011/93/EU of the European Parliament and of the Council of 13 December 2011 on combating the sexual abuse and sexual exploitation of children and child pornography, and replacing Council Framework Decision 2004/68/JHA [2011] OJ L335/1.

[17] Directive 2017/541/EU of the European Parliament and of the Council of 15 March 2017 on combating terrorism and replacing Council Framework Decision 2002/475/JHA and amending Council Decision 2005/671/JHA [2017] OJ L88/6.

[18] Directive 2019/713/EU of the European Parliament and of the Council of 17 April 2019 on combating fraud and counterfeiting of non-cash means of payment and replacing Council Framework Decision 2001/413/JHA [2019] OJ L123/18.

identity theft, its consequences are often aggravated by reputational and professional damage, damage to an individual's credit rating and serious emotional harm. The Directive therefore provides that MSs should adopt assistance, support and protection measures aimed at mitigating these consequences.

Finally, the Council Directive relating to compensation to crime victims[19] applies more generally to all victims of a violent intentional crime committed in a MS other than the MS where the applicant for compensation is habitually resident. The Directive provides that the applicant shall have the right to submit the application to an authority or any other body in the latter MS. The rules on access to compensation are governed by the MSs' national schemes on compensation to such victims. Compensation will be examined below.

In addition to the legislative framework, several policy documents and institutional structures were established to enhance the protection of victims, including those identified in cross-border cases.

This is the case in the above-mentioned first EU Strategy on Victims' Rights,[20] for example. One of the Strategy's objectives is to strengthen cooperation and coordination between relevant actors and strengthen the international dimension of victims' rights. In this context, Eurojust's role is mentioned in relation to its cooperation with the European Union Agency for Fundamental Rights, the European Institute for Gender Equality and the European Network on Victims' Rights.[21] However, the cross-border dimension of judicial cooperation remains marginal in the Strategy. The Strategy concludes that 'the EU must do more to protect victims of crime'.

Eurojust cooperates with the European Commission Coordinator for Victims' Rights. The Coordinator synchronises the activities of other actors at EU level in the field of victims' rights, in particular where relevant for the application of the VRD. Eurojust maintains regular contact with the Coordinator and her staff regarding cross-border issues arising from Eurojust projects and operational activities.

Eurojust participates in the Victims' Rights Platform, which was established in September 2020. It brings together all relevant actors at EU level in the field of victims' rights. The Commission regularly organises *ad hoc* meetings of the Victims' Rights Platform on specific topics in the framework of the Strategy.

In this context, Eurojust set up the Victims' Rights Working Group to bring together the Agency's expertise in this field. The Group consists of representatives from all Eurojust crime-based Working Groups and is responsible for compiling, monitoring and analysing victim-related issues reported by practitioners working on Eurojust-referred cases. Through its targeted approach for practitioners, Eurojust advises on the most effective ways to protect victims' rights. The Agency offers an overview of best practices to overcome victim-related challenges in various EU priority crime areas.

The expertise developed by Eurojust is used when implementing judicial cooperation instruments, as shown in section III, and is informed by the issues encountered

[19] Council Directive 2004/80/EC of 29 April 2004 relating to compensation to crime victims [2004] OJ L261/15.

[20] EU Strategy on Victims' Rights (2020–2025) (n 12).

[21] See ibid 20.

while supporting MSs, as indicated in section IV.A, for example. This expertise is directed primarily at judges and prosecutors and also to policymakers, thus feeding the policy and legislative work on this topic, while supporting practitioners by providing best practices and disseminating information.

III. Implementation of Judicial Cooperation Instruments from a Victims' Rights Perspective

Experience shows that prosecutors and investigative judges are at the forefront of identifying and solving issues related to the exercise of victims' rights in a cross-border context. However, the complexity of cross-border cases can make it particularly difficult for judicial authorities to protect victims' rights in isolation.

Drawing on its extensive operational expertise, Eurojust's casework[22] demonstrates the value of incorporating a victims' rights perspective when designing investigation and prosecution strategies to tackle cross-border crime. To this end, Eurojust is developing guidelines for judicial practitioners.

This section analyses the main judicial cooperation instruments and how Eurojust contributes to their implementation to preserve victims' rights in cross-border cases.

A. Preventing Conflicts of Jurisdiction

Stemming from Article 85(1)(c) TFEU,[23] Eurojust's role in the resolution of conflicts of jurisdiction was provided for by Article 6(1)(a)(ii) and Article 7(1)(a)(ii) of the Eurojust Decision[24] and is kept in Article 4(2)(b) of the Eurojust Regulation (hereafter 'EJR').[25] Under Article 21(6)(a) EJR, there is an obligation to inform Eurojust, through its national members, of cases where a conflict of jurisdiction has arisen or is likely to arise.

The fact that Eurojust is well placed to provide assistance in resolving conflicts of jurisdiction[26] led to the publication, as early as 2003,[27] of Guidelines for deciding 'Which Jurisdiction Should Prosecute?' (hereafter, 'the Guidelines' in this section). The Guidelines, which set out a number of criteria to assist the competent national authorities in reaching a consensus on a conflict of jurisdiction, led to the adoption of Council Framework Decision 2009/948/JHA of 30 November 2009 on prevention and settlement of conflicts of exercise of jurisdiction in criminal proceedings[28] (hereafter 'FWD').

[22] For an overview of Eurojust's casework, please refer to www.eurojust.europa.eu/crime-types-and-cases/casework.

[23] Consolidated version of the Treaty on European Union and the Treaty of the Functioning of the European Union [2012] OJ C326/47.

[24] ibid note 9.

[25] EJR (n 9).

[26] See Recital 14 to the Council Framework Decision 2009/948/JHA of 30 November 2009 on the prevention and settlement of conflicts of exercise of jurisdiction in criminal proceedings [2009] OJ L328/42.

[27] The Guidelines were published in the Eurojust Annual Report 2003, 60–66, available at www.eurojust.europa.eu/publication/eurojust-annual-report-2003.

[28] Council Framework Decision 2009/948/JHA (n 26) 42–47. See in particular Recital 14 and Art 12.

This was the first instrument in EU law on the prevention and resolution of conflicts of jurisdiction.

The role of Eurojust as a facilitator in resolving conflicts of jurisdiction, whether positive or negative, in its area of competence, is recognised in Article 12 of the FWD, which is 'complementary and without prejudice to the Eurojust Decision'.[29] This Framework Decision provides for direct consultations between the judicial authorities of the Member States concerned with a view to reaching consensus as soon as one of these competent authorities has reasonable grounds to believe that parallel proceedings are being conducted in another MS.[30] When this consensus cannot be reached, the matter shall, where appropriate, be referred to Eurojust by any of the competent authorities of the MS concerned, if Eurojust is competent to act under Article 3(1) EJR.[31] In the eyes of the EU legislator, 'the referral of a case to Eurojust should be a usual step'.[32]

Under Article 4(2)(b) of the EJR, Eurojust may, giving its reasons, ask the competent authorities of the MS concerned to accept that one of them is better placed to investigate or prosecute certain acts. Eurojust shall assist the competent national authorities in preventing and resolving conflicts of jurisdiction.[33]

Among the criteria provided by the Guidelines to help national authorities resolve cross-border conflicts of jurisdiction, 'the interests of victims' should be taken into account to avoid adverse consequences, either from parallel proceedings in two or more countries or from no proceedings at all. In this respect, the said Guidelines call for due consideration to be given to 'the possibility of victims claiming compensation'. The Framework Decision on conflicts of jurisdiction[34] echoes this (non-binding) requirement, explicitly referring to 'the significant interests of victims and witnesses' as a relevant criterion to be taken into consideration when seeking consensus to solve conflicts of jurisdiction as provided for in its Recital 9.

The Guidelines were revised in 2016,[35] aligning this criterion with the provisions of the VRD[36] by introducing the element of protection. Chapter 4 of the VRD acknowledges that 'Member States shall ensure that measures are available to protect victims',[37] and advocates for the protection of crime victims 'from secondary and repeat victimisation, from intimidation and from retaliation'.[38] The updated Eurojust Guidelines extend

[29] ibid Art 12.

[30] See ibid Art 10. This FWD obliges the judicial authorities to establish direct contact and exchange information with a view to reaching a consensus. The FWD explicitly aimed to avoid the risk of *ne bis in idem*, without including any criteria about which jurisdictions could be considered best placed to investigate or prosecute.

[31] Eurojust Decision (n 9) former Art 4(1). See Council Framework Decision 2009/948/JHA (n 26) Art 12.

[32] Council Framework Decision 2009/948/JHA (n 26) Recital 14.

[33] In accordance with EJR (n 9) Art 21(6)(a), '[t]he competent national authorities shall inform their national members of cases in which conflicts of jurisdiction have arisen or are likely to arise'. See also Framework Decision 2002/584/JHA on the European Arrest Warrant [2002] OJ L190 (Art 16), Framework Decision 2008/841/JHA on the fight against organised crime [2008] OJ L300 (Art 7) and Directive 2017/541 on combating terrorism (n 17) (Art 19(3)), which include relevant provisions that might lead to Eurojust's involvement in the area of conflicts of jurisdiction for the facilitation of cooperation between judicial authorities and the coordination of their actions. See 'Report on Eurojust's Casework in the Field of Prevention and Resolution on Conflicts of Jurisdictions' (updated February 2018.)

[34] Council Framework Decision 2009/948/JHA (n 26).

[35] 'Guidelines for Deciding "Which Jurisdiction Should Prosecute?"' (2016) *ISBN*: 978-92-9490-139-2.

[36] VRD (n 8).

[37] ibid Arts 18–24.

[38] ibid Recital 9.

this criterion of victim's protection beyond the strict procedural rights of the victim to include their protection.[39] In cases of human trafficking, the victims' interests and protection are particularly important.[40]

It is worth noting that the Guidelines 'do not constitute binding rules and are without prejudice to applicable national, EU and international law'.[41] Moreover, the national laws transposing the FWD on conflicts of jurisdiction or regulating the prevention and resolution of conflicts of jurisdiction do not provide any hierarchical criteria. Hence, the factors therein should be considered on a case-by-case basis according to the specific merits of each case and in the best interest of justice.[42]

Eurojust's written requests (or recommendations) are issued by its national members to assist national authorities when jurisdictional issues arise between two or more MSs. The requests usually take the form of joint requests, issued jointly by two or more national members involved in a case. Occasionally, if the case involves a third country that has signed a cooperation agreement with Eurojust, the liaison prosecutors of that third country will join the request. With a joint request, the national members ask their respective competent authorities to accept that one of them is responsible for investigating or prosecuting certain acts.

The conclusion included in the joint request is based on a thorough assessment of the legal and factual circumstances of the case and is developed in accordance with the Eurojust Guidelines on Jurisdiction.

National authorities can therefore rely on a non-binding opinion of Eurojust, supported by a reasoned legal assessment. Authorities may only refuse to comply with such requests if doing so would harm essential national security interests, jeopardise the success of an ongoing investigation or jeopardise the safety of an individual.[43]

For example, victims' rights were a key factor in identifying the best jurisdiction to prosecute in the 'Prestige' (oil spill) case[44] (2006). The Prestige, a 26-year-old oil tanker owned by a Greek firm and registered in the Bahamas, broke up off the coast of Galicia in 2002, spilling 77,000 tonnes of heavy fuel, the worst ever oil spill in European waters. The oil spill fueled thousands of kilometres of mostly Spanish coastline and forced the closure of Spanish and French fishing grounds.

Following a recommendation from Eurojust, it was apparent that only one legal proceeding should take place and, given the large number of victims involved, since the widest and most severe ecological damage had been done in Spanish sea and shores, Spain was in the best position to conduct the investigations and hold the trial while giving the appropriate guarantees to the French victims.

This case is emblematic of the way in which a conflict of jurisdiction has been resolved, with the best interest of the victims in obtaining adequate compensation being

[39] 'Guidelines for Deciding "Which Jurisdiction Should Prosecute?"' (n 35) 3.

[40] Art 22(3) of the VRD also provides for due consideration to be given to 'victims of terrorism, organised crime, human trafficking, gender-based violence, violence in close relationships, sexual violence, exploitation or hate crimes, and victims with disabilities'.

[41] 'Guidelines for Deciding "Which Jurisdiction Should Prosecute?"' (n 35) 1.

[42] ibid 2.

[43] As interpreted from EJR (n 9) Art 8(5).

[44] College Recommendation of 24 February 2006. Ref: Eurojust Annual Report 2021, available at www.eurojust.europa.eu/annual-report-2021/eurojust-twenty-years-timeline.

the determining factor.[45] The Prestige case also illustrates how the protection of victims has been at the core of Eurojust's activities from the outset.

As mentioned above, the FWD on conflicts of jurisdiction was explicitly aimed at preventing an infringement of the principle of *ne bis in idem*. This instrument encourages MSs to take into consideration the interests of the victim when solving conflicts of jurisdiction. In a recent preliminary ruling by the Court of Justice of the European Union (hereafter 'CJEU' or 'Court'),[46] the Court gave an unprecedented judgment on the qualification of the condition of *idem* in the application of the principle *ne bis in idem*, provided for in Article 55(1)(b) of the Convention Implementing the Schengen Agreement (CISA),[47] in cross-border crimes committed by organised crime groups intending to undermine the security or other equally essential interests of a MS. The case triggering this preliminary ruling concerned a massive online investment fraud allegedly perpetrated by a criminal organisation and affecting investors in various European countries, including Germany and Austria. The German judge asked the CJEU to what extent the judgment already rendered by Austria for fraud committed against victims residing in Austria could be considered to cover the same acts as those for which the same person was being prosecuted in Germany, where the proceedings concerned fraud committed against victims residing in Germany.[48]

The Court held that

> it cannot be concluded that the earlier definitive Austrian decision concerning the applicant in the main proceedings related to the same acts as those covered by the prosecution brought against him in Germany. At most, that earlier decision might be considered to have related to *similar acts*, which, however, is *not sufficient for the 'idem' condition to be regarded as being satisfied* (emphasis added).[49]

With this preliminary ruling, the CJEU provides victims of cross-border crime, involved in sophisticated *modus operandi*, with the possibility that justice will be done and that their financial losses will be compensated, as provided for in Article 16 of the VRD.

B. Transfer of Proceedings

Transfer of proceedings is often the natural way forward when direct contacts between the national authorities concerned have led to a successful agreement or consensus on

[45] See 'Report on Eurojust's Casework on Victims' Rights. A Contribution to the European Commission Coordinator for Victims' Rights Mapping Exercise (February 2022) 14.

[46] Case C-365/21 *Generalstaatsanwaltschaft Bamberg* ECLI:EU:C:2023:236.

[47] Convention Implementing the Schengen Agreement of 14 June 1985 between the Governments of the States of the Benelux Economic Union, the Federal Republic of Germany and the French Republic on the gradual abolition of checks at their common borders [2000] OJ L239, 19.

[48] *Generalstaatsanwaltschaft Bamberg* (n 46) paras 16 and 29. Acknowledging that the principle of *ne bis in idem* is a fundamental right of EU law, enshrined in Art 50 of the Charter of Fundamental Rights of the European Union (hereafter 'the Charter'), that it derives from the constitutional traditions common to the MS, and based on settled case law where the relevant criterion is identity of the facts, the CJEU recalled that 'the "idem" condition requires that the material facts be identical'. 'Yet, as the Court has made clear, identity of the material facts is understood to mean a set of concrete circumstances stemming from events which are, in essence, the same, in that they involve the same perpetrator and are inextricably linked together in time and space' (para 38, with further references).

[49] ibid para 43.

the chosen forum, as one of the conflicting jurisdictions accepts to relinquish its jurisdiction and to transfer to the other MS the results and documents gathered so far in the investigation or prosecution of its own opened case.

The transfer of proceedings to another MS has far-reaching consequences on the position of suspects and victims, both in terms of the procedural rights that they may be entitled to during the criminal proceedings and the substantive criminal law applicable to the offence.

While the future EU legislation governing transfer of proceedings between EU MSs is well advanced, at the time of writing, there is, however, currently no EU legal instrument governing transfer of proceedings between EU MSs. In 2019, the Romanian Presidency of the Council evaluated deficiencies in this area and concluded that there is a need to explore the appropriateness of a legislative proposal on the transfer of proceedings. The EU Strategy to tackle organised crime 2021–2025 mentions the transfer of criminal proceedings as an issue for further action and a legislative initiative was announced in the Commission's Work Programme for 2022. A public consultation was launched and the legislative proposal was scheduled for the third quarter of 2022. After these first steps, on 5 April 2023 the Commission presented a Proposal for a Regulation on the transfer of proceedings in criminal matters,[50] including specific grounds for jurisdiction; criteria under which a transfer of criminal proceedings can be requested; certain rights for suspects and accused persons as well as for victims; a procedure for requesting a transfer; time limits for taking the decision on the request as well as an exhaustive list of grounds for refusing a transfer. In July 2023, the Swedish Presidency tabled an initiative on behalf of 16 EU MSs, and the proposal was submitted to the ordinary legislative procedure.[51] In March 2024, the European Parliament and the Council provisionally agreed on the proposed Regulation, maintaining most of the elements of the Commission proposal.[52] On 5 November 2024, the Council adopted the European Parliament's first reading position, by all EU MS but two abstentions.[53]

In the absence of a specific EU instrument, MSs have been using a variety of legal bases for this purpose, resulting in different conditions and procedures to allow the transfer of proceedings. The Council of Europe Convention on the Transfer of Proceedings in Criminal Matters of 15 May 1972 (hereafter 'CoE Convention No 73') is recognised as a useful instrument for the transfer of proceedings between Contracting States, despite its uneven ratification rate among EU MSs,[54] and may constitute a worthy frame of reference in other cases.

[50] European Commission, 'Proposal for a Regulation of the European Parliament and of the Council on the transfer of proceedings in criminal matters' COM(2023) 185 final (April 2023).

[51] The first reading at the European Parliament took place on 23 April 2024, available at https://eur-lex.europa.eu/procedure/EN/2023_93?&sortOrder=desc.

[52] See https://commission.europa.eu/law/cross-border-cases/judicial-cooperation/types-judicial-cooperation/transfer-criminal-proceedings_en.

[53] See https://data.consilium.europa.eu/doc/document/ST-15221-2024-REV-1/EN/pdf.

[54] To date (January 2025), this Convention has been ratified by 13 of the 27 EU MSs (Austria, Bulgaria, Cyprus, Czech Republic, Denmark, Estonia, Latvia, Lithuania, Netherlands, Romania, Slovakia, Spain and Sweden, although many of them introduced reserves particularly in relation to infractions which are considered as administrative sanctions, according to their own laws. Eight other EU MS have signed but not ratified it (Belgium, Croatia, Greece, Hungary, Italy, Luxembourg, Portugal and Slovenia), available at www.coe.int/en/web/conventions/full-list?module=treaty-detail&treatynum=073.

Eurojust's joint recommendations for transfer of proceedings are based on Article 4(2)(b) of the EJR.[55] Based on its casework experience, Eurojust published a report on the transfer of proceedings in the EU[56] in January 2023, which underlines that the current fragmented legal framework leads to difficulties and legal obstacles in the procedures.

In Eurojust's view, a new EU instrument laying down common criteria and procedures for transferring proceedings to another MS would serve to improve the current situation in terms of legal certainty, effectiveness and efficiency (see section IV).

The interests of victims are often considered by the national authorities and Eurojust when deciding which State is best placed to prosecute a concrete case, even if the victims have no right to participate in the transfer of proceedings under the applicable national legislation. This factor is particularly important in relation to certain types of crime, such as human trafficking.[57]

Significant differences exist between national laws in relation to the procedural guarantees granted to suspects and victims in the context of a transfer of proceedings, both in terms of the subjects involved and the extent of their involvement.[58]

Sometimes the consultation of the suspect on the transfer of proceedings risks endangering the victim. In a case supported by Eurojust, MS A initiated criminal proceedings into an incident of domestic violence that occurred on its territory while the suspect and the victim were on holiday. As both the suspect and victim immediately returned to their home country, MS B, and there were elements suggesting that other episodes of domestic violence had already occurred there, transferring the proceedings to MS B was considered, as it was better placed to prosecute these facts in their entirety. However, informing the suspect of the request to transfer the proceedings, as required

[55] Under the Eurojust Decision (n 9), they were based on Art 6(1)(a)(ii).

[56] Eurojust, 'Report on the Transfer of Proceedings in the European Union' (January 2023), available at www.eurojust.europa.eu/publication/eurojust-report-transfer-proceedings-european-union. Prior to this Report, in January 2015 Eurojust held a strategic seminar on this matter, co-organised with the Latvian presidency, available at www.eurojust.europa.eu/publication/report-strategic-seminar-conflicts-jurisdiction-transfer-proceedings-and-ne-bis-idem.

[57] Eurojust Report 2023, ibid, with further references. For instance, in a MS, where the victim of the offence is a national of that MS, a transfer of proceedings cannot be requested without the consent of the victim, unless the victim has already been able to obtain compensation. Second, in that same MS, a transfer cannot take place if a freezing order targeting the proceeds of crime was issued, unless the authorities are satisfied that the receiving MS has adequate legislation in place that would allow the recovery of those illicit assets (Eurojust Report 2023 (n 57) p 6).

[58] With regard to the parties involved, a whole range of situations can be observed in the MS: from no possibility of involvement of either the suspect or the victim in most MSs, to the involvement of only the victim or the suspect, to the possibility of involvement of both categories of subjects. Furthermore, in MSs where the involvement of the victim and/or the suspect is provided for, it may take place at different stages, ensuring a greater or lesser degree of participation. In most of these MSs, suspects and/or victims are already involved before a decision on the transfer is taken: they must be consulted before a request for transfer is sent to the other MS and they can express their views on the transfer. In most cases, their opinion is not binding on the part of the authorities, but is simply taken into account when the transfer decision is taken. However, there are only a few MSs where the victim's consent is required for the transfer, with some limited exceptions (eg where it is not possible to obtain the consent). In some other MSs, the involvement of victims and/or suspects is ensured only at a later stage, with a right to be informed of the transfer, which is sometimes (but not always) coupled with the possibility of appealing against it. In some cases, the consultation of the suspect may also pose a risk to the victim, which is why alternative solutions to the transfer of proceedings are sought. See section 2.2.4. of the Eurojust Report 2023 (n 57), s 2.2.4.

by the national law of MS A, could have put the victim at risk, as it was not possible to also request the enforcement of a protection measure by MS B. Based on a spontaneous exchange of information, MS B was able to initiate its own parallel investigation to take measures to protect the victim.[59]

As far as the substantive conditions are concerned, few MSs have a *de minimis* rule discouraging the transfer of proceedings for minor and less serious offences.[60] With regard to victims, it should be noted that, even in those MSs where they are not involved in the procedure at all, their interests are often taken into account when deciding on the transfer of proceedings.

There are also many differences in the legal remedies available to suspects and/or victims against a decision to transfer the proceedings abroad. In the vast majority of the MSs, no legal remedies are provided, even if national law provides for their consultation in the transfer procedure.[61] As an example of how Eurojust protects the interests of the victims in cross-border cases with implications at EU-level, mention should be made to a specific case where Eurojust requested to concentrate the proceedings in a single MS. The scope and severity of the case had repercussions at EU level, but the criminal action taken on a country-by-country basis would have gone unnoticed by the national authorities. The case was triggered by information provided by the European Anti-Fraud Office (OLAF)[62] to Eurojust concerning an organised crime group involved in the large-scale production, distribution and sale of counterfeit washing powder. The case was opened as a College case[63] because it required a coordinated European response to avoid the risk of uncoordinated parallel investigations and possible (negative) conflicts of jurisdiction, while the criminal activity involved affected a significant number of victims located in many MSs.

C. Competing EAWs

When giving priority to a EAW over another, the rights of the victims can be impacted by the fact that, if priority is given to a EAW other than the one on 'their case', there would be delays in the proceedings affecting them. Factors such as the severity of the

[59] See Eurojust Report 2023 (n 57), case 16: Consultation of the suspect on the transfer of proceedings risks endangering the victim, p 23.

[60] Furthermore, in one MS, national legislation contains a clear rule not allowing transfer of proceedings against its own nationals. Nevertheless, competent courts sometimes adopt a flexible interpretation of that provision, considering that surrender of own nationals to other MS is now possible under the European Arrest Warrant (EAW) system and, therefore in some cases allow the transfer of proceedings against own nationals. Another MS adopts a rigid interpretation of the territoriality principle which, combined with a strict principle of legality of prosecutions, does not allow the transfer of proceedings if that MS would have jurisdiction over the crime that was committed, even in part, on its territory, regardless of additional considerations concerning other relevant factors such as the availability of the evidence, the location of the suspect and the interests of the victims (Eurojust Report 2023 (n 57) p 6).

[61] On the other hand, in some MSs, legal remedies are available either only to the suspect or the victim, or else to both, regardless of whether consulting them during the proceedings was foreseen or not. In one MS, legal remedies are available only if the transfer concerns a criminal proceeding that has already reached the trial stage (Eurojust Report 2023 (n 57) p 7).

[62] The European Anti-Fraud Office, set up by the 1999/352/EC, ECSC, Euratom, Commission Decision establishing the European Anti-fraud Office (OLAF) (28 April 1999). Cooperation in this case was based on Article 26 (4) Eurojust Decision (n 9).

[63] Under Eurojust Decision (n 9) Art 7 (1)(b).

crime or the number of victims would be taken into account when weighting competing EAWs.

Eurojust's advice on competing EAWs pursuant to a request under Article 16(2) of the Framework Decision 2002/584/JHA of 13 June 2002 on the European Arrest Warrant and Surrender Procedures between MSs (hereafter 'EAW FWD').

Eurojust published Guidelines for Deciding on Competing EAWs in its Annual Report 2004[64] (hereafter in this section: 'the Guidelines'), which were revised in 2019, in light of the 2017 European Commission Handbook on how to issue and execute a EAW. The Guidelines provide non-binding advice to the national competent authorities on how to decide on competing requests for surrender/extradition. Eurojust regularly refers to these Guidelines when providing guidance to national authorities on this matter.[65]

The revised Guidelines extend the scope of the original ones by including scenarios not only for Article 16(1) EAW FWD but also for its Article 16(3).[66] Moreover, these revised Guidelines further develop the factors to be taken into account in the decision-making process. They also address coordination and follow-up measures that may be relevant before and after the executing authority decides which of the requests it will execute. In the scenario of deciding which jurisdiction should prosecute first, it is important that the competent authorities involved also consider the possibility of a subsequent surrender or transfer of proceedings.

The Commission Handbook does not include the interest of the victim among the main factors to be taken into consideration. However, the list is not exhaustive. Furthermore, there are no strict rules as to which of these factors should be prioritised and the executing authority could consider a number of elements, including the interest of the victims, as recommended by the Eurojust Guidelines.

In one case, when weighting two conflicting EAWs, the following considerations were taken into account: the proceedings in country A would have had a direct impact on one individually identified victim, whilst the proceedings in country B, concerning the same suspects as in country A, aimed at dismantling the whole organised criminal group (OCG) and therefore would have had a wider impact on potential victims. Although the victims of the latter offences were 'yet to be determined', the fact that the material seized during the joint action (organised by Eurojust through a coordination centre) was estimated to be 10 per cent of the material used by the OCG in one year, led to the assumption that the OCG was targeting a high number of victims. On this basis, Eurojust advised, in a joint recommendation, that the EAW issued by country B (where the procedure concerned a larger number of potential victims) should be given priority.

[64] Eurojust Annual Report 2004 82–88, available at www.eurojust.europa.eu/sites/default/files/assets/annual-report-2004-en.pdf. See also: Eurojust Annual Report 2014, 53–55 available at www.eurojust.europa.eu/publication/eurojust-annual-report-2014.

[65] Guidelines for Deciding on Competing Requests for Surrender and Extradition. Revised 2019. ISBN: 978-92-9490-313-6. Eurojust's expertise in this field was gathered in its 2021 'Report on Eurojust's Casework in the Field of the European Arrest Warrant' (2021), available at www.eurojust.europa.eu/publication/report-eurojusts-casework-field-european-arrest-warrant-july-2021. The Agency keeps abreast of the case law of the CJEU by analysing the relevant judgments that Eurojust publishes in biannual reports. The latest report, published in October 2023, included references to 77 adjudicated cases, plus eight other pending cases.

[66] This Art 16(3) provides an identical solution where an EAW competes with an extradition request for the same person.

D. European Investigation Orders

Despite being one of the most recent mutual recognition instruments in the EU, the European Investigation Order (EIO)[67] has, in a few years, become a cornerstone of judicial cooperation in criminal matters and experience has demonstrated its relevance to the protection of victims. Today, the EIO has replaced the Convention of 29 May 2000 on Mutual Assistance in Criminal Matters between the MSs of the EU and its Protocol, as well as the now obsolete Council Framework Decision 2003/577/JHA of 22 July 2003 on the execution in the European Union of orders freezing property or evidence, and the now repealed Council Framework Decision 2008/978/JHA of 18 December 2008 on the European Evidence Warrant for the purpose of obtaining objects, documents and data for use in proceedings in criminal matters.

From a practical point of view, the EIO thus constitutes one single instrument based on the principles of mutual trust and mutual recognition, replacing the fragmentary and insufficient previous legal tools. Creating a single comprehensive framework for obtaining evidence in cases with a cross-border dimension, allows not only for the request of a specific measure but also commits the authorities of the executing EU MS to take all the necessary measures at their disposal to investigate the crime.[68] Nevethteless, the EIO excludes some investigative measures, that are regulated by other specific legal instruments, such as information on criminal records or search and seizures.

Where victims have been heard in the executing State, solutions can be found with the help of Eurojust to ensure that their statements are admissible in the issuing State without the need for them to be heard again abroad[69] (thus avoiding secondary victimisation). In this respect, Eurojust promotes the use of *video conferencing* and *video recording* in the execution of an EIO when dealing with victims, thus sparing them the further trauma of being exposed to their aggressors and/or of being subjected to repeated witness interviews in different jurisdictions.

Eurojust also encourages the use of video conferencing to facilitate cooperation with third countries as permitted by Article 18(18) (mutual legal assistance) and Article 24(2) (protection of witnesses) of the UN Convention against Transnational Organised Crime.[70] This Convention is supplemented by the Protocol to Prevent, Suppress and Punish Trafficking in Persons, Especially Women and Children, and by the Protocol against the Smuggling of Migrants by Land, Sea and Air, which allow the

[67] The EIO was set up by Directive 2014/41/EU of the Europea Parliament and the Council of 3 April 2014 regarding the European Investigation Order in criminal matters [2014] L130/1.

[68] For further information, see L Bachmaier Winter, 'La Orden Europea de Investigación y el principio de proporcionalidad' ('European Investigation Order and the Principle of Proportionality') (2011) 25 *Revista General del Derecho Europeo*, as well as its extensive bibliography. See also M.ª I González Cano (Dir.): *Orden Europea de Investigación y prueba transfronteriza en la Unión Europea (European Investigation Order and Transnational Evidence in the European Union)* (Tirant lo Blanch, 2019), and the article therein of C Arangüena Fanego, *Orden Europea de Investigación: aspectos generales del nuevo instrumento de obtención de prueba penal* (*European Investigation Order: General Overview of the New Instrument for Obtaining Evidence in Criminal Matters*) 297–326.

[69] Eurojust Report 2023 (n 57) 24 with further references.

[70] United National Convention against Transnational Organised Crime and the Protocols Thereto, adopted by General Assembly Resolution 55/25 of 15 November 2000, available at www.unodc.org/unodc/en/organized-crime/intro/UNTOC.html.

use of video conferencing and other audio-visual transmission in cases of trafficking of human beings and migrant smuggling respectively (Article 1 of each Protocol).

Eurojust assists national authorities in preventing secondary victimisation of vulnerable victims during the criminal proceedings. In some cases, Eurojust has helped to ensure that interviews with children can be recorded and transcribed for presentation at trial, thus avoiding the need for children to be called and subjected to further trauma.

To illustrate the above, a recommendation to use video conferencing was used in a case of sexual offences committed within the jurisdiction of both the executing State and the issuing State. At the time the EIO was issued, the victims were living on the territory of the executing State. The particularities of the case related to the young age of the victims, justifying a specific hearing procedure with the support of the psychologist from the child protection agency. All formalities and procedures indicated by the issuing authority were respected by the executing authority to minimise the impact on the victims.[71]

In another case, the victim triggered the issuance of an EIO, facilitated by Eurojust, from Spain to Italy for the hearing of the trial of the victims/witnesses of a terrorist attack in 2017 in Barcelona via video conference. The main particularity is that the EIO was issued at the request of the victim's lawyer. This case illustrates how an EIO can serve to promote victims' rights. The solution found in this case is of particular interest as the EIO Directive[72] does not explicitly provide for the possibility for victims to request the issuance of an EIO from the competent authorities, but only for the defence (Article 1(3) EIO Directive). The exercise of the victims' rights to be heard in cross-border proceedings was greatly facilitated by the proactive initiative of the victim's representative during trial and the broad interpretation of the EIO Directive's provisions by the competent authorities.[73]

E. European Protection Order (EPO)

The origin of Directive 2011/99/EU (hereafter 'the EPO Directive')[74] lies in the need to ensure the free movement of victims within the EU by avoiding a scenario in which the protection measures enjoyed by victims in one EU MS cease to apply simply because the victim travels, looks for work or goes on holiday in another MS. The premise was that the EPO would grant victims with a level of protection identical or equivalent to the protection that they enjoyed in the MS that adopted the protection measures. The initiative was launched in 2010 by 12 EU MSs under the Spanish Presidency of the EU.

The EPO is essentially an instrument of mutual recognition of judicial decisions in criminal matters. Therefore, practitioners should also consider Regulation 606/2013 on the mutual recognition of protection measures in civil matters,[75] and the VRD.

[71] See Eurojust Report on Eurojust's Casework on Victims' Rights (n 44) 14.

[72] EIO Directive (n 68).

[73] ibid 15.

[74] Directive 2011/99/EU, of the European Parliament and the Council of 13 December 2011, on the European Protection Order ('EPO Directive') [2011] OJ L338/2.

[75] Regulation (EU) No 606/2013 of the European Parliament and of the Council of 12 June 2013 on mutual recognition of protection measures in civil matters [2013] OJ L181/4.

The protection of victims is one of the rights included in the VRD,[76] the Anti-Trafficking Directive and in Directive 2011/93/EU on combating the sexual abuse, sexual exploitation of children and child pornography, which address the specific needs of victims of these particular crimes. Article 13 of the Council of Europe Convention on the Prevention of Terrorism[77] and Article 52 of the Istanbul Convention (Council of Europe Convention on preventing and combating violence against women and domestic violence)[78] also provide for measures to protect victims.

Based on the definition of the EPO Directive in Article 2(1), the requirements for issuing an EPO are: first, that a person is in danger in a MS; second, that there is a protection measure or a set of protection measures issued by a judicial or equivalent authority of that State for that person; and third, that a victim or person in danger moves from his or her country of origin to another EU MS. In relation to the specific protection measures envisaged, Article 5 of the EPO Directive requires that there is an existing national protection measure in force in that EU country that imposes one or more of the following bans or restrictions on the person causing danger to the protected person: 1) a ban on entering certain places or defined areas where the protected person lives or visits; 2) a ban or a restriction on contact with the protected person in any form, including by phone, electronic or ordinary mail, fax or any other means; and 3) a ban or restriction on approaching the protected person closer than a specified distance.

The EPO is designed to cover all victims of all crimes. The need to identify the person causing danger suggests that this instrument is most useful in cases involving a close relationship between the offender and the victim. This would explain why the use of the EPO is mainly associated with cases of domestic violence.

However, the level of implementation of this Directive is not what the legislator expected. A general lack of knowledge on the part of both victims and professionals responsible for their protection has been identified as one of the main obstacles for its full implementation. In April 2024, Eurojust organised a symposium on victims' rights in Europe under the auspices of the Belgium Presidency of the EU,[79] aiming at stepping up its efforts to assist victims of crime and to work on ways to more effectively integrate victims' rights into every step of judicial cooperation processes by national authorities. During the symposium, in an attempt to bring awareness among the members of the judiciary, Eurojust and the European Institute for Gender Equality (EIGE) presented the preliminary findings of their joint assessment on the implementation of the EPO. This is presented in section IV.

[76] In accordance with the VRD (n 8) Recital 9, '[v]ictims of crime should be protected from secondary and repeat victimisation, from intimidation and from retaliation, should receive appropriate support to facilitate their recovery and should be provided with sufficient access to justice'. Consequently, Chapter 4 of the VRD (Arts 18 to 24) is devoted to victims' right to protection.

[77] CETS No 196 from 16.5.2007. This CoE Convention No 196 has been ratified by all the EU MSs, apart from Greece and Ireland, and it has also been signed and ratified by the EU itself. See www.coe.int/en/web/conventions/full-list?module=treaty-detail&treatynum=196.

[78] CETS No 210 available at www.coe.int/en/web/istanbul-convention. This CoE Convention has been signed and ratified to by the EU and also by most EU MSs.

[79] Eurojust, 'Eurojust Focuses on More Attention for Victims' Rights in Cross-Border Judicial Cooperation', available at www.eurojust.europa.eu/news/eurojust-focuses-more-attention-victims-rights-cross-border-judicial-cooperation.

IV. Challenges and Prospects

As analysed above, the challenges faced by the judiciary in safeguarding victims' rights in cross-border cases can take different forms. In addition, many authors have pointed out that the first challenge is to define who a victim is,[80] as there is no uniform definition at EU level, and what can be defined as 'a victim's legitimate interest', as different victims may have very different interests, ranging from which jurisdiction offers greater participation in criminal proceedings to where they can expect better compensation or have easier access to compensation.

A. Challenges Arising from Eurojust Casework

The challenges of implementing victims' rights at national level are exacerbated when a case has a cross-border element. This is the case, for example, when the crime has been committed in one MS and affects victims of different nationalities, or when the crime has been committed in more than one MS. In such situations, practitioners face several difficulties, which have been identified in the report on Eurojust's casework on victims' rights.[81] This sub-section focuses only on the most fundamental difficulties: those related to the identification of the victims, which have a direct impact on their right to information and compensation.

The mere *identification* of the victims can be made more complicated by a number of factors. Eurojust's casework shows that, in cross-border cases, the different stages of the parallel investigations may have an impact on the determination of the status of a particular person. For example, in a human trafficking case, the same person was considered to be a victim by the investigation in country A, which was less advanced than the investigation in country B. The latter found that the person had, in the meantime, acquired responsibilities in the activities of the organised crime group and therefore qualified as a suspect. In other cases, such as investment fraud, it can be difficult to get a full picture of the victims because not all of them will report to the police. Victims may not necessarily be aware that they have been defrauded, especially when organised crime groups mix legitimate and fraudulent activities. Some criminal activities affect a large number of victims, particularly in cyber-enabled crimes such as investment fraud, where criminals use attractive schemes to lure their victims. In such cases, victims can number in the thousands and be located in different jurisdictions, including outside the EU. Such cases pose operational challenges to ensure an exhaustive list of the victims.

Once identified, another prerequisite for victims to be able to assert their rights is to receive *information on their rights*. During the investigation of a terrorism case at Eurojust, a number of difficulties were identified in this respect, such as the lack of knowledge of the language of the country where the attack took place – which proved

[80] In this respect, see M Simonato, 'What Role for Crime Victims in the Forum Choice?' in K Ligeti, J Vervaele and A Klip (directors), *Preventing and Resolving Conflicts of Jurisdiction in EU Criminal Law* (Oxford University Press and European Law Institute, 2018).

[81] Eurojust Casework on Victims' Rights Report (n 45).

to be a challenge throughout the proceedings – or the lack of knowledge of the foreign legal system, the available victims' rights, legal (and other) aid and representation, which also applies beyond the investigation stage.

Challenges may also arise when it comes to *compensation and restitution*, as illustrated by Eurojust's casework. For example, in cases involving many victims located in different jurisdictions, the question arises as to how to avoid a 'first come, first served' effect when dealing with so many victims. In this regard, Eurojust casework advocates the need to establish a coordinated approach and methodology for the return of criminal assets seized and confiscated for the purpose of restitution based on EU and non-EU legal instruments.

Other difficulties associated with the restitution of illicit gains from fraudulent schemes have been highlighted in the context of the Regulation on mutual recognition of freezing orders and confiscation orders.[82] For example, even if the authorities in charge of the money-laundering case are willing to enforce the restitution, there may be issues when it becomes apparent that other victims have sent money to the same bank account, but the amount seized is insufficient to compensate all the victims because of subsequent debit movements, while there are no other pending requests for restitution.[83]

As far as compensation is concerned, in some MSs the difficulty of assessing the exact amount of loss may hinder the granting of fair and appropriate compensation to the rights holders/victims. This is particularly problematic in the area of audiovisual piracy, where it is usually handled by confiscating the money made from the sale of pirated material for the benefit of the confiscating State. However, this does not compensate the rights holders/victims unless they, in turn, seek compensation from the confiscating State through a separate civil procedure, which can be lengthy and cumbersome.

The report on 'Strengthening Victims' Rights: From Compensation to Reparation'[84] of March 2019 elaborates on the shortcomings identified at that time and makes a number of recommendations. From the point of view of judicial cooperation, the report highlights the lack of cooperation between MSs on compensation. The report mentioned above also supports the findings of the Eurojust report when it highlights the 'dramatically low number of cross-border cases' where Member States concerned cooperate in order to compensate the damages encountered by victims.[85]

[82] Regulation (EU) 2018/1805 of the European Parliament and of the Council of 14 November 2018 on the mutual recognition of freezing orders and confiscation orders [2018] L303/1.

[83] This raised several questions for practitioners: (i) Should the restitution be enforced without giving other victims the opportunity to pursue their claims in other jurisdictions? (ii) What actions should be taken to inform national authorities of the existence of the frozen bank account and the possible existence of other victims in their jurisdiction (in particular through spontaneous exchanges of information)? (iii) Can victims be considered affected persons, in the sense of the provision of Art 2(10) of Regulation 2018/1805, ibid, if the enforcement of a restitution order in its entirety in favour of one victim may affect, at least in part, the possibility for other victims to obtain restitution? The Commission clarified that, for the purposes of interpreting Regulation 2018/1805 (n 78), victims should not be considered as 'affected persons' within the meaning of Art 2(10). This notion is particularly important in the context of Art 32 (obligation to inform affected persons) and Art 33 (legal remedies against the recognition and execution of freezing and confiscation orders).

[84] European Commission: Directorate-General for Justice and Consumers and J Milquet, 'Strengthening Victims' Rights – From Compensation to Reparation – For a New EU Victims' Rights Strategy 2020–2025' (Publications Office, 2019), available at https://data.europa.eu/doi/10.2838/37801.

[85] ibid 26.

The VRD is unlikely to alleviate the current obstacles. State compensation does not fall within its scope. Meanwhile, the content, scope and eligibility conditions of the rights to both compensation from the offender and restitution of the confiscated property that it confers are left to the discretion of the national legislator.

A revision of Directive 2004/80/EC on State compensation may be necessary in the coming years. This would require a thorough and comprehensive mapping of existing compensation schemes. The current revision process of the VRD could be seen as an opportunity to explore complementarities and synergies between State compensation and offender compensation.

Eurojust noted the lack of uniform rules on compensation across the EU for victims of terrorism (eg under a specific compensation scheme for victims of terrorism or under the general compensation scheme for victims of crime) or the fact that the principle of full compensation is not applied in all States.

Fraud cases are often referred to Eurojust because the vast majority of them have a cross-border element. Such crimes typically involve a large number of victims located in different countries. It is therefore essential to identify as many victims as possible and to coordinate compensation between different national jurisdictions. Eurojust has published 'Guidelines on How to Prosecute Investment Fraud'.[86] The Guidelines provide best practices for dealing with large numbers of victims, such as categorising victims to help practitioners manage such complex cases. The Guidelines also suggest that, where appropriate, victims share legal counsel to avoid the need for all victims to be heard separately, thus facilitating the implementation of the right to participate in legal proceedings.

Eurojust's casework shows that, when a victim may be eligible for compensation, its obtention is not always effective. For example, in a number of cases, the bank accounts of the offenders or suspects are empty at the time of seizure and confiscation. In some jurisdictions, even under Regulation 2018/1805, it is not possible to freeze money/assets for the purpose of restitution or compensation of victims in a cross-border case. In practice, this matter can be addressed by lifting the freezing order and issuing a civil order in the context of civil proceedings conducted in relation to the criminal proceedings.

Eurojust helps create templates for practitioners to identify, support and compensate victims (as was the case for the Barcelona and Cambrils terrorist attacks). As mentioned above, in this case, Eurojust helped the Spanish authorities to prepare and disseminate across Europe a specially designed template informing victims of their rights. The template was specifically designed to be understood by victims and their relatives and helped them to identify their procedural rights to assistance and compensation. It may be worth recalling that Eurojust does not provide information to the victims directly but assists the national judicial authorities in providing that information to the victims.

Finally, national judicial authorities have become aware of the additional difficulties that may arise for the protection of the rights of victims in certain complex cases with a cross-border dimension. This was recently illustrated in a case of cyber-enabled

[86] Eurojust, 'Eurojust Guidelines on How to Prosecute Investment Fraud' (February 2021).

fraud, where the need to ensure that German victims were not deprived of their right to compensation was one of the main reasons for the Preliminary Ruling of March 2023[87] (see section III.B).

B. Opportunities Arising from the European Commission's Proposal to Amend the VRD

The VRD is an instrument for harmonising criminal law. It applies horizontally to all victims of crime, regardless of victims' nationality or residence status. However, the current version of the VRD touches only marginally on judicial cooperation as such. Only one Article specifically refers to 'the rights of victims in another Member State'.[88] The challenges associated with the continuum of protection of victims' rights in cross-border cases are largely unaddressed. For example, the right to information about the case in the proceedings in MS A, where the victim resides, might be affected by virtue of the transfer of proceedings in MS B. The latter might indeed not always inform the victim, when he/she has expressed this request, for example when a final judgment is issued or to notify the victim about the release from custody of the offender.

Following a thorough evaluation,[89] the Commission has drafted a proposal to amend the VRD. The proposed amendments relate to five main victims' rights: access to information; improved support and protection; improved participation in criminal proceedings; and facilitated access to compensation.[90]

Eurojust contributed to the evaluation through a special interview and a detailed report published in February 2022.[91] The report identifies challenges and best practices to overcome them.

During the revision process, Eurojust advocated the recognition and strengthening of its operational role in the protection of victims' rights. The aim of the suggested amendment is to promote the referral of information to Eurojust in cases where victims'

[87] *Generalstaatsanwaltschaft Bamberg* (n 46).

[88] VRD (n 8) Art 17.

[89] Following the evaluations of the improvement of this VRD carried out on 11 May 2020 (Report from the Commission to the European Parliament and the Council on the implementation of Directive 2012/29/EU of the European Parliament and of the Council of 25 October 2012 establishing minimum standards on the rights, support and protection of victims of crime and replacing Council Framework Decision 2001/220/JHA, COM(2020) 188 final) and on 28 June 2022 (Commission Staff Working Document Evaluation of Directive 2012/29/EU of the European Parliament and of the Council of 25 October 2012 establishing minimum standards on the rights, support, and protection of victims of crime, and replacing Council Framework Decision 2001/220/JHA. Brussels, 28.6.2022, SWD (2022) 179 final), in which the EU noted that, in some MSs, progress towards guaranteeing victims' rights in practice remains very slow. The EC launched a reform initiative on 12 July 2023 aimed at strengthening victims' rights.

[90] The EU agency for Fundamental Rights (FRA) and the European Parliament had also published comprehensive reports on the implementation of crime victims' rights in the EU (See the 'Report on the Implementation of Directive 2012/29/EU Establishing Minimum Standards on the Rights, Support and Protection of Victims of Crime' (LIBE Commission of the European Parliament, May 2018). The FRA has repeatedly highlighted the gaps in the implementation of the VRD in its annual reports (in particular since the 216th report) and has published reports on the subject: 'Victims of Crime in the EU: The Extent and Nature of Support for Victims', in 2014, and 'Underpinning Victims' Rights. Support Services, Reporting and Protection', in 2023.

[91] See Eurojust Casework on Victims' Rights Report (n 45).

rights are at stake in the context of judicial cooperation. This information may, where appropriate, be shared by national judicial authorities with Eurojust based on Article 21 of the EJR.

If adopted, the amendment will encourage MSs to refer to Eurojust cases where victims' rights are identified as warranting specific coordination at judicial level.[92] Eurojust's role as an auxiliary to national authorities in facilitating judicial cooperation will help foster early cooperation and coordination between the countries and actors involved as part of the obligation to respect victims' rights.

Other parts of the Commission proposal could have an impact on judicial cooperation.

This is the case, for example, with the obligation to ensure that victims can report crimes using information and communication technologies (Article 5(a)(1)). This could lead to an increase in reporting by victims residing or located in a MS other than the one where the crime was committed or where the investigation was initiated. This in turn could lead to an increase in parallel proceedings and thus to the risk of conflicts of jurisdiction. In such cases, a referral to Eurojust could remedy this situation.

Other amendments aim to further strengthen victims' rights. This is the case, for example, with the right to compensation. This proposal could have implications in the field of judicial cooperation, as the proposed amendment would oblige MSs to pay the compensation due from the offender to the victim in advance, immediately after the judgment, and then seek reimbursement of the compensation from the offender. While this proposal would give victims the certainty that they will be compensated, it could have a significant financial impact for MSs.

C. The European Commission's Proposal on the Transfer of Proceedings

As indicated in the Eurojust Report on the Transfer of Proceedings in the European Union, the transfer of proceedings to another MS has far-reaching consequences for victims, both in terms of their procedural rights to which they may be entitled during the criminal proceedings and in terms of the substantive criminal law applicable to the offence.

The proposal is extremely welcome from a judicial cooperation perspective.

With respect to victims specifically, one of the novelties of the draft is the general obligation to inform certain victims, and the suspect, of the intention to transfer proceedings (Article 7(4)). Despite some exceptions, this obligation could be problematic as it could make the procedure excessively cumbersome in practice. This could be particularly acute in investment fraud cases, for example, which typically involve many victims. As mentioned previously, in some cases, notably in a case of domestic violence, consulting the suspect before issuing a request for transfer may also lead to a potential

[92] The amendments put forward by the Commission in July 2023 acknowledge Eurojust's role in a new para 4 under Art 17: 'Member States shall ensure that the competent authorities may request assistance from Eurojust and transmit to Eurojust the information aimed at facilitating cooperation with the competent authorities of other Member States in cross-border cases'.

risk for the victim.[93] Moreover, the granting of this right may in turn imply the granting of a right to an effective remedy, for example to complain about a lack of information, which could increase the risk of significantly delaying the proceedings.

A possible solution could be to provide for prior consultation of the victim and, for that matter, of the suspect, not as an obligation but only as a possibility, where appropriate, depending on the circumstances of the case, for instance taking into account the stage of the proceedings.

D. An Improved Mechanism for the Full Implementation of the EPO?

A study conducted by the European Parliamentary Research Service (EPRS)[94] in September 2017 found that the EPO Directive[95] has not delivered the expected results. The comparative study on criminal procedural laws across the EU, published in August 2018 at the request of the European Parliament's Civil Liberties, Justice and Home Affairs (LIBE) Committee, reached a similar conclusion.[96] A report from the Commission to the European Parliament and the Council of 13 December 2011 on the implementation of the EPO[97] concluded that the national implementing provisions received from all 26 MSs bound by the Directive[98] seem to be satisfactory overall, but the practical application of the Directive shows that it has not yet reached its full potential.

According to the information available to the Commission and released in its report in 2020, only 37 EPOs were issued and only 15 were executed in the period 2015–2018.

Major obstacles to the full implementation of this instrument have been identified. The EPRS and EC reports highlight the wide variety of national approaches to protection measures. For example, in a number of MSs, these types of measure are mainly the responsibility of civil or even administrative authorities. A general lack of knowledge on the part of both victims and professionals responsible for their protection is also mentioned. According to the EPRS report, 'a recent EP study reveals that victims still lack awareness of their rights, and information on how they could exercise them is scarcely available'.[99]

[93] See in this chapter section III.B.

[94] European Parliamentary Research Service, 'European Protection Order Directive 2011/99/EU, European Implementation Assessment', PE 603.272 (September 2017).

[95] EPO Directive (n 75).

[96] E Sellier and A Weyembergh, 'Criminal Procedural Laws across the European Union – A Comparative Analysis of Selected Main Differences and the Impact they have over the Development of EU Legislation' (2018) PE 604.977, available at www.europarl.europa.eu/RegData/etudes/STUD/2018/604977/IPOL_STU(2018)604977_EN.pdf.

[97] COM(2020)187final, available at https://eur-lex.europa.eu/legal-content/EN/TXT/?uri=COM%3A2020%3A187%3AFIN.

[98] Indeed, in post-Brexit Europe, the Directive is binding for 25 MSs, as Denmark and Ireland have excluded themselves.

[99] Regarding the scope, prerequisites and practical application of the EPO, see the following: V Mitsilegas, *EU Criminal Law after Lisbon: Rights, Trust and the Transformation of Justice in Europe* (Hart Publishing, 2016); G Vernimmen-Van Tiggelen, L Surano, and A Weyembergh (eds), *The Future of Mutual Recognition in Criminal Matters in the European Union* (Presses Universitaires de Bruxelles, 2009); S van der Aa and J Ouwerkerk, 'The European Protection Order: No Time to Waste or a Waste of Time?' (2011) 18 *European*

The application of the measures provided for in the EPO Directive may also overlap with those provided for in other instruments.[100] This is notably the case for the measures provided in the Framework Decision 2008/947/JHA on probation measures and alternative sanctions, or a decision on supervision measures within the meaning of Article 4 of Framework Decision 2009/829/JHA.

Against this background, the European Commission has demonstrated its commitment to improving this situation: the Commission is promoting, notably through financial support, the effective application of national protection orders by raising awareness and stressing the need to train practitioners on the issue of the availability of the EPO.[101]

During the symposium on victims' rights organised by Eurojust under the auspices of the Belgium Presidency of the EU in April 2024, Eurojust and EIGE presented the preliminary findings of their joint assessment on the implementation of the EPO. One of the main findings is that while an instrument at EU level aimed at protecting victims is necessary, the EPO is under used. The under use of the EPO is mainly due to the lack of awareness of this instrument by the judiciary and support services.

V. Conclusions

Taking victims' interests into consideration, particularly when facilitating the execution of judicial cooperation instruments, has always been an integral part of Eurojust's activities since its inception. This broad experience, the essence of which we have tried to summarise in these pages, shows the value of including the victims' rights perspective when designing investigation and prosecution strategies to tackle cross-border crime.

By bringing together prosecutors and judges, Eurojust can contribute to a greater convergence and coherence of national efforts in this area, thereby helping to ensure that the fundamental right to an effective judicial remedy is observed and not hindered by the cross-border nature of the case.

Eurojust is committed to supporting these efforts by including the dimension of victims' rights more systematically in the support that it provides to national judicial authorities, particularly in coordination meetings and JITs. Indeed, through its casework experience, Eurojust is in a unique position to promote victims' rights. This applies in particular to the prevention and resolution of conflicts of jurisdiction. Eurojust can also

Journal of Crime, Criminal Law and Criminal Justice; S van der Aa, J Niemi, L Sosa, A Ferreira and A Baldry, *Mapping the Legislation and Assessing the Impact of Protection Orders in the European Member States* (Wolf Legal Publishers, 2015); T Freixes and L Román (eds), *Protection of the Gender-Based Violence Victims in the European Union, Preliminary study of the Directive 2011/99/EU on the European Protection Order* (Universitat Autònoma de Barcelona Servei de Publications, 2015).

[100] See in particular, Framework Decision 2009/829/JHA on supervision measures as an alternative to provisional detention and Framework Decision 2008/947/JHA on probation measures and alternatives to detention.

[101] To raise awareness among the practitioners and assist in an already complex legal framework, some MSs have issued Guides directed at their members of the judiciary on how to issue and execute an EPO. This is the case, for example, in Spain, where the Spanish General Council of the Judiciary published a Guide and templates (last reviewed in November 2021).

boost cooperation among national authorities and find concrete solutions to enhance victims' procedural rights, such as the right to compensation, throughout the EU.

Eurojust can and must play a pivotal role in minimising the risks associated with the cross-border dimension of cases by ensuring timely and efficient coordination between the various countries and actors involved to safeguard victims' rights. Eurojust is in a unique position to facilitate the exchange of information on victims to identify, rescue and protect them.

In the context of the revision of the VRD, the new wording of Article 17 in the Commission proposal recognises and further enhances Eurojust's role in this field within the EU legal framework. The facilitating role of Eurojust in relation to the promotion, protection and implementation of victims' rights could be further enhanced in the next EU Strategy on Victims' Rights. In addition, avenues for reflection could be explored. This could be done, for example by addressing the gaps that exist in relation to compensation to victims of cross-border crimes.

7

Council of Europe Instruments and the Case Law of the ECtHR on Victims' Rights: What Influence on EU Law?

LORENA BACHMAIER WINTER

I. Introduction

Recognition of the rights of victims of crime has evolved exponentially since the 1960s, both at the international[1] as well as at the national level – a development that has been especially significant in Europe over the last three decades. The criminal procedure, which had been characterised by the dominance and quasi-monopoly of the interests of the State for the last two centuries, has increasingly moved towards being a more victim-oriented procedure.[2]

With the exception of some legal systems, such as the Spanish one, which has considered the victim as another player in the criminal procedure for more than a century,[3] in most European countries the victim either did not have any say in the criminal procedure or played a secondary role, for example as a civil actor. Usually, the victim was involved in the criminal prosecution only as a witness of the facts.[4] But, over time, the

[1] For an overview on the international recognition of the victims' rights, see MC Bassiouni, 'International Recognition of Victims' Rights' (2006) 6(2) *Human Rights Law Review* 203–79; J Doak, *Victim's Rights, Human Rights and Criminal Justice: Reconceiving the Role of Third Parties* (Hart Publishing, 2008).

[2] See *Khlyustov v Russia* App no 28975/05 (ECtHR, 11 July 2013) para 103. Further on the victim's rights under Art 6 European Convention on Human Righs (ECHR), see 'CoE Guide on Article 6 of the European Convention on Human Rights. Right to a Fair Trial' (criminal limb) (2022) 8, available at https://ks.echr.coe.int/documents/d/echr-ks/guide_art_6_criminal_eng. On the different meanings of the concept of victim in international as well as in national law, see eg, M de Hoyos Sánchez, *El ejercicio de la acción penal por las víctimas* (Thomson-Aranzadi, 2016) 19–44.

[3] On the position and rights of the victim as full accusing party in the Spanish criminal procedure, see L Bachmaier and A del Moral, *Criminal Law in Spain*, 3rd edn (Kluwer Law International, 2020) 233 ff. For a comprehensive analysis of the victims' rights in the Spanish justice system, although as of 2012, see MP Martín Ríos, *Víctima y justicia penal* (Atelier Barcelona, 2012); JL Gómez Colomer, *Estatuto Jurídico de la Víctima del Delito*, 2nd edn (Thomson-Aranzadi, 2015).

[4] My own perspective, coming from a system where the participation of the victim in the criminal proceedings has been seen as an 'of course' right since the 19th century, tends to see this involvement as something natural and logical. However, as the vast scholarly literature shows, this is a very much debated

victim has been increasingly understood in terms of harm, in the sense that the harmed person needs also to be protected within the criminal procedure, and 'there is a far greater recognition now of the need for perpetrators to be held accountable to victims and that victims need to be embedded in the pre-trial, trial and post-trial processes'.[5]

This new approach to victims' rights, as is well known, is partly due to the studies on victimology, which have called for a more relevant role of the victim both as parties in the criminal proceedings and in general in enhancing the protection of the victims by providing more comprehensive support for their physical as well as their emotional needs.[6] There are numerous studies on the rights of crime victims, covering almost every aspect of victims' rights: from the very concept of the victim, their status in the proceedings, their legitimacy, the scope of their rights, etc. Considerable progress has been made in this field, starting from the possibility for the victim to participate in the criminal procedure and moving towards recognising a number of rights that revolve around three concepts: information, support and protection. At the same time, these rights, which were initially linked to the criminal procedure, have also evolved beyond the criminal procedure and on many occasions irrespective of it.

My aim here is not to analyse each of the legal instruments that have been adopted in the European Union on victims' rights, but only to address a very specific aspect of this topic,[7] namely the impact of the work of the Council of Europe (CoE) on the development of European Union (EU) law in the field of victims' rights. To this end, I will start with a brief overview of the main CoE Recommendations dealing with victims' rights (section II) and identify the main case law of the European Court of Human Rights (ECtHR) (section III). The next step is to reflect on the impact of ECtHR case law on EU law and to what extent there has been mutual interaction between the EU and CoE instruments (section IV). Finally, I will try to assess the outcome of this interaction, pointing out some of the pending issues (section V).

I will not discuss here the different meanings of the concept of victim, and for the purposes of this study I will assume the definition adopted by the CoE in Recommendation (2023)2.[8] This definition differs slightly from that included in the

issue, especially in the common law systems. See, eg, A Ashworth, 'Victim Impact Statements and Sentencing' (1993) *Criminal Law Review* 498–509; D Garland, 'The Culture of High Crime Societies' (2000) 40(3) *British Journal of Criminology* 357.

[5] As expressed by A Amatrudo and L William Blake, 'Victims, Victimology and Human Rights' in *Human Rights and the Criminal Justice System* (Routledge, 2015) 101.

[6] On this evolution see, eg, A Crawford and J Goodey (eds), *Integrating a Victim Perspective within Criminal Justice* (Ashgate Publishing, 2000). For a brief overview of the victims' rights in the US justice system, see P Sattler, 'The Crime Victims' Rights Act: Rhetoric or Reality?' (2020) 1(1) *Greenwich Social Work Review* 50–58, available at www.researchgate.net/publication/343778826_The_Crime_Victims'_Rights_Act_Rhetoric_or_Reality.

[7] This study is based on the oral presentation during the ECLAN Annual Conference held in Brussels on 18 April 2023. I thank the organisers for the invitation to participate in this discussion forum and take this opportunity to congratulate them for what was a very interesting conference, with the participation of all the sectors involved.

[8] Council of Europe (CoE), Recommendation CM/Rec(2023)2 of the Committee of Ministers to member States on rights, services and support for victims of crime adopted by the Committee of Ministers on 15 March 2023, available at https://rm.coe.int/cm-rec-2023-2e-eng-recommendation-trafficking/1680ab4922. Article 1:

> '"victim" means:
>
> 1. a natural person who has suffered harm, including physical, mental, emotional or economic harm, directly caused by a criminal offense;

CoE Recommendation CM/Rec(2006)8,[9] narrowing the victim to those who have suffered 'direct' harm, and specifying that family members can only be considered as 'victims' in cases of death directly caused by the criminal offence. Importantly, the ECtHR's own case law has recognised that a person may not claim to be a victim of a violation of the rights under Article 6 European Convention on Human Rights (ECHR) which occurred in the course of proceedings in which the applicant was acquitted, or which were discontinued.

II. Brief Overview of the Council of Europe Instruments on Rights, Support and Protection of Victims of Crime

When it comes to the rights of victims of a criminal offence, the first thing to note is that the ECHR does not make any specific reference to victims' rights. Nevertheless, there is an abundance of ECtHR case law on the protection of victims and their rights in criminal proceedings, especially under the right to a fair trial of Article 6 ECHR.

In addition to ECtHR case law, the Council of Europe has produced numerous documents, mainly recommendations that over time have defined the status of the victims of crime and their rights, both within criminal proceedings and outside the procedural setting. Initially there were isolated references to the position and rights of victims in documents, which did not aim to establish a comprehensive framework on the rights of victims of a criminal offence.

Thus, CoE Recommendation No R (83) 7 'On participation of the public in crime policy',[10] which deals with the need to involve and encourage the participation of the general public in crime prevention and control policies, already includes a specific section on the need to take victims into account when designing such policies. Specifically, it establishes that the Council of Europe's Member States should promote a framework for protection and assistance to victims of crime.[11] Section III.D lists a series of measures that should define a crime policy taking into account the victim's interests,[12] including specific measures on the treatment of victims by the police; the need to establish victim assistance services encompassing material and psychological assistance; facilitating compensation of damages by the offender, and by the State in the absence of compensation by the offender; or advocating the establishment of an efficient system of legal aid for victims so that they may have access to justice in all

2. family members of a person whose death was directly caused by a criminal offense and who have suffered harm as a result of that person's death;'.

[9] CoE, Recommendation CM/Rec(2006)8 on assistance to crime victims adopted by the Committee of Ministers on 14 June 2006, available at https://rm.coe.int/16805afa5c.

[10] CoE, Recommendation No R (83) 7 on participation of the public in crime policy adopted by the Committee of Ministers on 23 June 1983.

[11] ibid, '*Considering* that a crime policy directed towards the prevention of crime, the promotion of alternatives to custodial sentences, the social reintegration of offenders and the provision of assistance to victims should be followed and developed in the Council of Europe's member states;'.

[12] ibid, paras 25 to 32.

circumstances. This was a first step in recognising the need to provide comprehensive support to victims of crime, albeit this instrument did not yet define victims' rights.

Shortly thereafter, CoE Recommendation No R (85) 11 'On the position of the victim in the framework of criminal law and procedure'[13] already recognised that 'it must be a fundamental function of criminal justice to meet the needs and to safeguard the interests of the victim', stating also that, on many occasions, rather than protecting the victims, the criminal proceedings had contributed to their revictimisation. This recommendation sets precise guidelines to be followed by the CoE Member States on the treatment of the victims at all stages of proceedings, from police to trial, and enforcement (compensation), including rights to information, right to protection and also right to be heard regarding the decision not to prosecute or close a case. Two years later, the CoE Recommendation No R (87) 21 on assistance to victims and the prevention of victimisation[14] promotes further measures to protect the victims of crimes 'considering that in many cases the intervention of the criminal justice system is not sufficient, alone, to make good the harm and disturbance occasioned by the offence'. In particular, it recommends that CoE Member States raise awareness about the needs of victims of crime, carry out research on the matter of victims' protection, expand the support to the assistance services for victims and it further includes a list of further measures and rights that should be granted to the victims. It also extends those rights to the families of the victims and underlines the importance of urgently adopting measures for vulnerable victims. Its paragraph 4 recommends that States ensure that victims and their families, especially those who are most vulnerable, receive broad assistance during the criminal process, with due respect to the defence.[15]

The action of the CoE has steadily continued in the direction of recognising and extending rights for the victims of crimes,[16] mainly in the form of the most complete recommendations, namely CM/Rec(2006)8 on assistance to crime victims,[17] which is

[13] CoE Recommendation No R (85) 11 on the position of the victim in the framework of criminal law and procedure adopted by the Committee of Ministers on 28 June 1985, available at https://rm.coe.int/16804dccae.

[14] CoE Recommendation No R (87) 21 on assistance to victims and the prevention of victimisation adopted by the Committee of Ministers on 17 September 1987, available at https://apav.pt/apav_v3/images/pdf/recom_CE_1987.pdf.

[15] ibid. The measures to be adopted by the Member States as listed under para 4 are:

'– emergency help to meet immediate needs, including protection against retaliation by the offender; continuing medical, psychological, social and material help;
– advice to prevent further victimisation;
– information on the victim's rights;
– assistance during the criminal process, with due respect to the defence;
– assistance in obtaining effective reparation of the damage from the offender, payments from insurance companies or any other agency and, when possible, compensation by the State'.

[16] Recommendations on the protection of the victims' rights are also included in Rec(2000)19 on the role of public prosecution in the criminal justice system, adopted by the Committee of Ministers on 6 October 2000, underscoring again the right of identified victims to be able to challenge decisions of public prosecutors not to prosecute. Relevant provisions on victims' protection are also included in the following CoE Conventions: On Preventing and Combating Violence against Women and Domestic Violence adopted on 7 April 2011 (CETS No 210, 2011); On the Compensation of Victims of Violent Crimes (CETS No 116, 1983); On the Prevention of Terrorism (CETS No 196, 2005); and On Action against Trafficking in Human Beings (CETS No 197, 2005) (this list is not exhaustive).

[17] CM/Rec(2006)8 (n 9).

an update of the previous Rec(87)21, with the addition of an appendix specifying many of the aspects included in previous recommendations. For example, the right of the victim to receive assistance has been recognised from the outset. However, each of the following recommendations have clarified what this assistance should consist of and, therefore, what type of obligations it implies for the States, extending the coverage – not only to the victim but also to the family members – and extending the type of benefits and services that should be made available to the victims in an easily accessible way and for free.

Clear progress can be seen in the instruments of the CoE, starting from a general acknowledgement of the victim and their needs, towards achieving the effective assistance and support for victims of crime in all spheres: procedural and extra-procedural measures; support and assistance by police, the judiciary and social services bodies; extending the support beyond material compensation to health issues, both physical and psychological. Ensuring the effective protection of victims not only involves raising awareness of their needs and rights but also demands extensive training for professionals. This is crucial to enable victims to receive the necessary protection and support and empowers them to make informed decisions regarding actions related to criminal proceedings. Significant progress has also been made on the compensation scheme: from the vague statement that victims should be compensated, to the obligation of the State to provide for such compensation for every victim of violent crime.[18]

The long and continuous effort of all stakeholders has led to the adoption, in 2023, of the most comprehensive CoE Recommendation up to now on rights, services and support for victims of crime, the CM/Rec(2023)2.[19]

This Recommendation follows a more holistic approach to victims' rights in seeking to further develop and expand victims' rights and services beyond the context of the criminal procedure by not only promoting victims' rights in the context of criminal proceedings, but also before and after. The victims' rights are thus not linked to the position of the victim in the criminal procedure and are not subject to the 'identification, apprehension, prosecution or conviction of the perpetrator of the criminal offence',[20] but only 'on the filing of a formal complaint by the victim or the familial relationship between the victim and offender'.[21] Furthermore, access to services to support a victim shall be granted 'irrespective of the filing of a formal complaint'.[22]

All in all, this Recommendation seeks to improve the effective protection of the rights already recognised in previous instruments, clarifying their scope and the elements to consider making proper assessments of the needs of the victims. It specifically encourages the States to make use of the information technology to seek the protection and support of the victims of crimes, including the functioning of free telephone help lines and websites for victims.[23]

[18] See CM/Rec(2006)8 (n 9) para 8.
[19] CM/Rec(2023)2 (n 8).
[20] ibid Art 2.5.
[21] ibid.
[22] ibid Art 19.3.
[23] ibid Arts 3 and 19.

Does this Recommendation represent a new shift in the recognition of rights, measures to protect and support victims? In general, the answer should be no, as it responds to the need for updated and more detailed guidance on the development and practical implementation of victims' rights previously recognised, as, for instance, the right to be informed, the right to be heard, the right to an interpreter and translator, or the right to compensation. The provisions regarding legal aid remain, however, almost unchanged, referring to the national law in determining when it should be granted when the interests of justice so require.

Also relevant is the specific recommendation on improving coordination between the different agencies and authorities involved as well as cooperation in cases of cross-border victims.[24]

III. ECtHR Case Law

Victims' rights have been primarily outlined under Article 6 ECHR. However, the Court has also recognised that States have a number of positive obligations to protect individuals from violations of the Convention.[25] These positive obligations can be put into three categories: the first is *the duty to enact criminal laws* that criminalise certain behaviours.[26] The second category is *the duty to undertake preventive operative measures* to protect individuals. And the third category deals with *the duty to investigate* cases of a potential violation, connected to the obligation of an effective prosecution.[27] The impact of the 'positive obligations' doctrine to the protection of victims of crime, with the exception of the duty to conduct an effective investigation and prosecution,[28] is limited mainly to the position of individuals *before* becoming victims.

Regarding the obligation to adopt adequate criminal legislation to protect individuals from crime, and in some specific cases where the victim had not been adequately 'protected' by criminal law, the ECtHR has found violations under Articles 2, 3 or 8 of the ECHR.

[24] ibid Art 19.9.

[25] See generally, J-F Akandji-Kombe, 'Positive Obligations under the European Convention on Human Rights. A Guide to the Implementation of the European Convention on Human Rights' (CoE, 2007), available at https://rm.coe.int/168007ff4d; A Mowbray, *The Development of Positive Obligations under de European Convention of Human Rights by the European Court of Human Rights* (Hart Publishing, 2004) 10 ff.

[26] See *Osman v the United Kingdom* App no 23452/94 (ECtHR, 28 October 1998) para 115. Further see B Emmerson, A Ashworth, and A Macdonald, *Human Rights and Criminal Justice*, 2nd edn (Sweet & Maxwell, 2007) 741.

[27] The effectiveness of an investigation is not based on the number of measures taken, but the quality and adequacy of the measures adopted. The number of reports made, witnesses questioned, or other investigative measures taken is only indicative, but crucial is that the conclusions are based on thorough, objective and impartial analysis of all relevant elements, see *Anguelova v Bulgaria* App no 38361/97 (ECtHR, 13 June 1999) para 144; and *Pankov v Bulgaria* App no 12773/03 (ECtHR, 7 October 2010) para 51.

[28] The duty to conduct an effective investigation is even more stringent in cases where the victim is under custody or in military service, with the burden of proof being on the State that the adequate protection measures to prevent ill-treatment or death were in place. See, eg, *Muradyan v Armenia* App no 11275/07 (ECtHR, 24 November 2016) para 135. In the same sense, *Mikheyev v Russia* App no 77617/01 (ECtHR, 26 January 2006) para 108; and *Virabyan v Armenia* App no 40094/05 (ECtHR, 2 October 2012) para 162.

Thus, for example, in the case *X and Y v The Netherlands* of 1986, the Court found that Dutch criminal law does not offer adequate legal protection in general against the sexual assault of women and in particular of mentally handicapped persons over the age of 16, finding that this had violated Article 8 ECHR.[29] Behind this approach is the idea that civil law is not enough to grant adequate protection of the rights and freedoms under the Convention and that the States should implement the adequate criminal provisions to ensure an effective deterrence effect. Although very interesting, this substantive aspect of the protection of the victims, which plays a role mainly at the preventive level, cannot be said to have had a decisive influence on European law. It may have served to raise awareness of the need to enact adequate laws at the national level to grant protection through criminal law to certain vulnerable persons, especially child victims of sexual crimes or persons who have a diminished mental capacity. In any case, I thought it appropriate to point out this substantive aspect here, before focusing on the rights of persons who have been victims of crime.

With regard to the duty to investigate a crime, which is linked to the involvement of the victim in the criminal investigation, it should be noted that, in a case where the State's inaction has prevented the prosecution of certain crimes because of the statute of limitations, the Court has also found breach of the ECHR infringing its positive obligation in granting protection of the rights under the Convention.[30]

In this context it is interesting to refer to the case of *Romeo Castaño v Belgium*,[31] in which the ECtHR considered Belgium's refusal to execute a Spanish European Arrest Warrant (EAW) as a violation of its obligation to cooperate under the procedural aspect of Article 2 ECHR. The Court first underlines that the obligation to cooperate can only be an obligation of means, not one of result, but that it requires the States concerned to 'take whatever reasonable steps they can to cooperate with each other, exhausting in good faith the possibilities available to them under the applicable international instruments on mutual legal assistance and cooperation in criminal matters'.[32]

And quoting its prior case of *Güzelyurtlu and Others*, the Court states:

> In cases where an effective investigation into an unlawful killing which occurred within the jurisdiction of one Contracting State requires the involvement of more than one Contracting State, the Court finds that the Convention's special character as a collective enforcement treaty entails in principle an obligation on the part of the States concerned to cooperate effectively with each other in order to elucidate the circumstances of the killing and to bring the perpetrators to justice.[33]

In the current case, the Court found that the examination carried out by the Belgian courts, regarding the allegation that the conditions of detention in Spain entailed a risk

[29] See *X and Y v The Netherlands* App no 8978/80 (ECtHR, 26 March 1986). This approach has also been used in a case involving acts of torture by the police, where the Court held that Art 3 of the Convention was violated because the criminal law did not adequately criminalise and respond to such acts. See *Hristovi v Bulgaria* App no 42697/05 (ECtHR, 11 October 2011); *Myumyun v Bulgaria* App no 67258/13 (ECtHR, 3 November 2015).

[30] See, eg, *Sandra Janković v Croatia* App no 38478/05 (ECtHR, 5 March 2009).

[31] *Romeo Castaño v Belgium* App no 8351/17 (ECtHR, 9 July 2019).

[32] ibid para 81.

[33] *Güzelyurtlu and Others v Cyprus and Turkey* [GC] App no 36925/07 (ECtHR, 29 January 2019).

of violation of Article 3 ECHR, 'was not sufficiently thorough for it to find that the ground they relied on in refusing to surrender N.J.E., to the detriment of the applicants' rights, had a sufficient factual basis'.[34] The Court found that Article 2 ECHR (procedural aspect) had been infringed, due to the lack of sufficient factual basis for the refusal to surrender the requested person. In this way, the obligation to cooperate is linked to the positive obligation to investigate a crime and thus, to the obligation of protecting the victim's rights, in this precise case related to a crime of murder.

A. The Rights of the Victim as a Civil Party in the Criminal Proceedings

ECtHR law has certainly played a crucial role in recognising the right of the victims to participate in the criminal proceedings against their offenders under the right to access to justice, albeit almost always in connection with their position as a civil party in the criminal proceedings. As a civil party, their role in the criminal proceedings, as the ECtHR itself has stated, 'cannot be regarded as either the opponent – or for that matter necessarily the ally – of the prosecution, their roles and objectives being clearly different'.[35]

The right to participate in the procedure is not limited to being able to intervene in the prosecution or the trial stage but can apply to any of the phases of the criminal proceedings. Within the pre-trial stage, the first thing to be clarified is whether the victim has a right to have the criminal investigation launched and carried out. The right to have criminal proceedings initiated and the case investigated when the victim files a criminal complaint is not expressly recognised in the case law of the ECtHR.[36] Nor is there any right under the Convention for the victim to join the criminal proceedings as a civil party.[37] However, if such a possibility is provided under national law, an undue restriction of this right would be against the right to access to justice granted under Article 6 ECHR.[38] Notwithstanding this, the ECtHR has recognised that there is a duty to carry out an effective investigation whenever there is an allegation of a violation of Articles 2, 3, 4 or 5 of the Convention, and this means that the victim might trigger this obligation *vis-à-vis* the State authorities.

With regard to the involvement of victims in the pre-trial stage, in certain cases the Court has also recognised that relatives of the victims – specifically in cases dealing with

[34] *Romeo Castaño v Belgium* (n 31) para 90.

[35] *Berger v France* App no 48221/99 (ECtHR, 3 December 2002) para 38.

[36] See, eg, *Helmers v Sweden* App no 11826/85 (ECtHR, 29 October 1991); *Perez v France* [GC] App no 47287/99 (ECtHR, 12 February 2004).

[37] See *Ernst and Others v Belgium* App no 33400/96 (ECtHR, 15 July 2003), originated in a case for violation of professional secrecy of a judge, where he argued that the privilege of jurisdiction and the consequence that he could not file a civil suit in the criminal proceedings, entailed a discrimination with regard to other victims. The Court stated that this legal difference did not entail any breach of Article 14 ECHR, to the extent that the applicant, 'regardless of the attitude of the public prosecutor, retained the right to bring an action for civil liability against the Belgian State' (para 82).

[38] See *Ligue du Monde Islamique and Organisation Islamiquie Mondiale du Secours Islamique v France* App no 36497/05 (ECtHR, 15 January 2009), where a legal person was not admitted as a civil party in a criminal procedure on the basis of a mere formality which was interpreted in an unreasonable way.

infringements of Articles 2 or 3 ECHR – should be informed about the progress of the investigation[39] unless there is a justified reason to limit such access to the victim, as for example, the need to protect the privacy of other parties, security reasons or when the interests of justice justify it.

The Court has also found a breach of Article 6 ECHR, in a criminal case of perjury connected to a case of a sexual assault where neither the victim nor her lawyer were given the chance to question the witness before the case was dropped.[40] In another case, where the victim was not allowed to request for evidence to be immediately produced during the pre-trial stage, with the risk of such evidence disappearing, the Court also found a violation of the Convention.[41] However, this does not mean that the victim acting as a civil party in the criminal proceedings has a right for any evidence that he/she requests to be produced as this depends on the assessment of the adequacy, necessity and appropriateness of the production of the requested evidence.[42]

A further judgment that shows how the victim is granted rights during an investigation is *Poltoratskiy v Ukraine*, a case of alleged violation of Article 3 ECHR for the bad conditions of the detention and ill-treatment against the inmate who had been sentenced to life imprisonment. In this case, the Court found violation of the Convention for lack of effective investigation to the alleged ill-treatment and the parents of the applicant – who filed the complaint as representatives – had not been given enough reasons for the dismissal of the case.[43]

In *Bouyid v Belgium*,[44] the applicants filed a complaint as civil parties in criminal proceedings against police officers for having used violence against them. In this case of alleged ill-treatment, the Court found violation of Article 3 of the Convention for lack of effective investigation – the investigation was mainly based on interviews of the officers suspected, carried out by other police officers. In addition, the Court took into account that the victims had not been able to confront the accused police officers during the pre-trial stage: the investigating judge 'failed to hold, or arrange for, a face-to-face confrontation between the police officers in question and the applicants, or to interview or order an interview of the physicians who had drawn up the medical certificates produced by the applicants'.[45]

The victim, acting as a civil party in the criminal procedure, should be granted access to the prosecution file[46] although this access can be limited and subject to restrictions based on the protection of other rights and the interests of justice as assessed by the relevant judicial authority.[47] The right to be heard is also granted to the civil

[39] See eg, *McKerr v United Kingdom* App no 28883/95 (ECtHR, 4 May 2001); *Menet v France* App no 39553/02 (ECtHR, 14 June 2005); *Mocanu and Others v Romania* [GC] App no 10865/09 (ECtHR, 17 September 2014).

[40] *M C v Bulgaria* App no 39272/98 (ECtHR, 4 December 2003).

[41] See *Sottani v Italy* App no 26775/02 (ECtHR, 24 February 2005).

[42] See *Lacerda Gouveia and Others v Portugal* App no 11868/07 (ECtHR, 1 March 2011), although in this case the Court found that the refusal to produce the evidence requested by the victim had not been arbitrary or unreasonable, thus finding no violation of the Convention on this ground.

[43] *Poltoratskiy v Ukraine* App no 38812/97 (ECtHR, 29 April 2003).

[44] *Bouyid v Belgium* App no 23380/09 (ECtHR, 28 September 2009).

[45] ibid para 128.

[46] See *Forum Maritime SA v Romania* App no 63610/00 (ECtHR, 4 October 2007).

[47] See *Menet v France* (n 39) para 47 ff.

party under Article 6(1) ECHR, as recognised, among others, in *Perez v France*.[48] The Court has not set out a right to be heard with regard to the entering of a plea agreement with the defendant, although when this affects the right to an effective investigation, the rights of the victim might be infringed. However, in the decision in the case of *Nikolov v Bulgaria*,[49] the Court did not find a violation of the Convention because the victim who had joined the criminal proceedings as a civil party could not object to the plea agreement reached by the prosecution and the defendant. In such a case, the Court took into account that the victim was not prejudiced and could still institute civil proceedings against the offender.

As regards the right to appeal to the Court of Cassation, in a case against France,[50] the ECtHR has stated that 'civil parties should not have an unlimited right to appeal to the Court of Cassation against judgments discontinuing the proceedings', accepting the legal restriction on filing such an appeal in cassation when the public prosecutor does not appeal the judgment. As stated by McBride when describing the rights of victims as civil parties,

> although there is no explicit ruling of the European Court that requires the establishment of a right of appeal against a decision not to prosecute someone, the rulings (of the Court) all point to the need for effective judicial control – in which the rights under Article 6(1) of the European Convention are respected – over such a decision.[51]

The Court has also dealt with cases where the civil party had been precluded from claiming from the offender the compensation of damages within the criminal proceedings, because the proceedings had been discontinued or time barred.[52] In the case of *Kamenova v Bulgaria*, the issue before the Court was whether, despite the fact that the applicant retained the right to seek compensation in the civil courts, the criminal court's decision not to examine her civil claim once the criminal proceedings had been discontinued under the statute of limitations had infringed her right of access to a court competent to hear civil claims. The applicant's daughter had been killed in a road accident, but differently from other victims, the applicant did not file the civil claim in the criminal proceedings at the very beginning – as required by the national law. Once she tried to do it – when the case was remitted again to first instance – the civil claim was

[48] *Perez v France* (n 36), a case where a mother accused her sons of assault against her, and she claimed that the proceedings had not been fair, because in deciding the Cassation Court had not provided a detailed answer to each argument presented by her as civil party. In this case the Court held that 'the right of the parties to the trial to submit any observations that they consider relevant to their case' and that such right can only be seen 'to be effective if the observations are actually "heard", that is duly considered by the trial court', but finally found that there had been no violation of Art 6(1) ECHR, because such right does not mean that the party has a right to a detailed answer to each of the allegations of the parties (ibid paras 80–84). See also, the inadmissibility decision in *McCourt v United Kingdom* App no 20433/92 (ECtHR, 2 December 1993).

[49] *Nikolov v Bulgaria* App no 39672/03 (ECtHR, 28 September 2010).

[50] See *Berger v France* (n 35) para 35.

[51] See the report of J McBride, 'The Case Law of the European Court of Human Rights on Victims' Rights in Criminal Proceedings', prepared within the European Union and the Council of Europe joint project 'Application of the European Convention on Human Rights and Harmonisation of National Legislation and Judicial Practice in Line with European Standards in Georgia' (2015–2018) 17, available at https://rm.coe.int/council-of-europe-georgia-european-court-of-human-rights-case-study-vi/16807823c4.

[52] See, eg, *Kamenova v Bulgaria* App no 62784/09 (ECtHR, 12 July 2018); *Atanasova v Bulgaria* App no 72001/01 (ECtHR, 2 October 2008); or *Anagnostopoulos v Greece* App no 54589/00 (ECtHR, 3 April 2003).

first admitted, but then rejected by way of appeal. The criminal proceedings experienced huge delays, for the appellate court remitted the case again to the lower instance because of procedural infringements. After the criminal case was sentenced, the applicant filed the civil claim before the civil courts to see it refused for being already time barred. The ECtHR does not find a violation of Article 6 ECHR in this case for it considers that 'the applicant failed to make use of the indisputable possibilities to have her claim duly examined'.[53] The approach of the Court is very formalistic, and it is no surprise that the judgment includes several dissenting opinions, which consider that there has indeed been a violation of the Convention.[54]

While in general the ECtHR has considered the possibility to file a civil claim after discontinuing the criminal proceedings as a factor capable of counterbalancing the impossibility to be compensated within the criminal proceedings, in the case of *Atanasova v Bulgaria*, the Court found violation of the right to access to Court, despite the existing possibility to claim before the civil courts for damages. This case is also a road traffic offence entailing physical injuries, where the victim brought her claim for damages in the criminal proceedings. Due to the huge delays (from 1994 to 2002) the criminal proceedings were discontinued for being time barred. Although the applicant could file the claim before the civil courts, the Court found in this case that the victim had a legitimate expectation to be compensated in the criminal proceedings, and that this was not possible due to the negligent delays in handling the criminal proceedings, amounted to a violation of the right to access to court. Obliging the victim to bring a civil action for compensation years after the accident had taken place, was considered by the Court as being against Article 6 ECHR.

B. The Protection of the Victims within the Criminal Proceedings

The victims, like any other persons, are entitled to have their rights recognised under the Convention protected. Their participation in criminal proceedings may entail risks to their physical integrity and to their own lives, in addition to the possibility of being subjected to secondary victimisation. ECtHR case law has addressed the protection of the victim, mainly when called to testify in the proceedings, in so far as such rights are compatible with the fair trial rights of the defendant.[55] Among those measures that have been recognised for the victim as witness, but could also be adopted with regard to other witnesses who might be at risk, are *inter alia*: the hearing of the witness in camera[56] or without being seen by the public and/or the defendant;[57] keeping the identity of the victim confidential to the defendant;[58] limiting the access to the court record and or prosecution file;[59] or restricting the possibility of the defendant to put questions to the

[53] See *Kamenova v Bulgaria*, ibid para 54.

[54] See the dissenting opinion to the judgment by judges Grozev, Mits and Hüseynov.

[55] *Doorson v Netherlands* App no 20524/92 (ECtHR, 26 March 1996) para 70.

[56] *B and P v United Kingdom* App no 36337/97 (ECtHR, 24 April 2001).

[57] *Crook and National Union of Journalists v United Kingdom* App no 11552/85 (ECtHR, 15 July 1988); *Accardi v Italy* App no 30598/02 (ECtHR, 20 January 2005).

[58] *Doorson v Netherlands* (n 55).

[59] *Z v Finland* App no 22009/93 (ECtHR, 25 February 1997).

victim and providing for the cross-examination to be carried out to protect the victim.[60] In particular, in criminal proceedings concerning sexual offences, the Court has held that Article 6(3)(d) ECHR cannot be interpreted as requiring in all cases that questions be put directly by the accused or the defence counsel through cross-examination or by other means.[61]

In the context of victim protection and the validity of plea agreements in the criminal proceeding, the case of *VCL and AN v the United Kingdom* is of interest.[62] This case pertains to drug-related offences, where the defendants pleaded guilty to the charges. At the same time, the accused persons were themselves victims of human trafficking. The Court found that the guilty pleas were not made 'in full awareness of the facts', first because they themselves were in a vulnerable position, and second because the waiver of rights by the applicants would have run counter to the important public interest of combating human trafficking and protecting its victims.

IV. The Impact of ECtHR Case Law upon EU Law

In view of ECtHR case law, its impact on the development of EU law in relation to the rights of victims of criminal offences might be questioned.

It is clear that ECtHR case law does not contain a systematic definition of the rights of victims when acting in criminal proceedings. However, several rights can be identified from its decisions, such as the right to be informed, the right to request evidence to be produced, or the right to be actively involved in the proceedings if this is required for an effective investigation. Furthermore, following the Court's case law, the civil party has the right to be heard, also with regard to the dismissal or discontinuance of the criminal case, and has the right to have access to court when claiming for compensation. The Court has addressed the rights of the victim when acting as a civil party to the proceedings primarily from the perspective of the right to have access to justice under Article 6(1) ECHR. This means that, rather than defining intrinsic rights to the victim under the Convention, the usual analysis is based primarily on the position the national law grants to the victim as a civil party. In this vein, the Court has stated that, when the national law provides for the civil party to intervene in the proceedings, any restriction on their possibilities to act must be justified given that arbitrary or irrational limitations would run counter to Article 6 ECHR.

In terms of measures to protect the victims of crime, ECtHR case law has marked a clear line towards the protection of victims as witnesses in criminal proceedings, especially in the case of minor victims and victims of sexual crimes. While the ECtHR has always held that the protection of the witness and victims has to be counterbalanced with the rights of the defence – and in particular the right to cross-examination – the

[60] *Oyston v United Kingdom* App no 42011/98 (ECtHR, 22 January 2002); *Y v Slovenia* App no 41107/10 (ECtHR, 28 May 2015); also *RB v Estonia* App no 22597/16 (ECtHR, 22 June 2021).

[61] *SN v Sweden* App no 342/09 (ECtHR, 2 July 2002) para 52; *WS v Poland* App no 21508/02 (ECtHR, 19 June 2007) para 55.

[62] *VCL and AN v the United Kingdom* App nos 77587/12 and 74603/12 (ECtHR, 16 February 2021).

fact is that the Court has not found violation of the Convention when needed measures to protect the victims were adopted even when this entailed some restriction of the rights of the defence. Thus, in general, the definition of victims' rights by the ECtHR is mainly linked to the rights under Article 6 ECHR, and mainly focused on their involvement as a civil party or witness, and its case law – as it could not be otherwise – is not the place to elaborate a comprehensive and holistic list of measures to protect victims. This does not mean, of course, that its impact has not been relevant in drafting the rights of victims in EU law, only that such impact should be seen in conjunction with the role that the CoE Recommendations have played in recognising the victims' rights.

Having a look at the EU Directives on the protection of victims' rights,[63] it is manifest that ECtHR case law is reflected in them. Clearly, the rights recognised in EU Directive 2012/29/EU establishing minimum standards on the rights, support and protection of victims of crime (hereinafter 'the Victims' Rights Directive') had already been outlined in specific judgments and decisions of the ECtHR, among others, the rights recognised in Articles 10 (right to be heard), 11 (rights with respect to the decision not to prosecute), 12 (rights in the context of restorative justice),[64] 16 (right to compensation from the offender), 18 (right to protection) or 19 (right to avoid contact between victim and offender).

However, as an international court adjudicating *ex post* on possible violations of the rights recognised in the ECHR, its role in advancing the recognition of victims' rights, while relevant, is also limited in many occasions by the national law applicable to the particular case. In judging whether national law is in conformity with the Convention, the ECtHR can only apply the test of reasonableness, proportionality and absence of arbitrariness. But it cannot create or configure new victims' rights or procedural rights for the civil party beyond what is permitted by the doctrine on the positive obligation of States to grant protection of the rights recognised in the Convention. Thus, for example, in its case law it has not established the right for the victims' compensation to take place in any case in the criminal proceedings or for the victim to be compensated in any case for the damages caused by the criminal act by the State, in case the offender is insolvent. This has recently been recognised both in the CoE CM/Rec(2023)2 and in the Proposal for the revision of the Victims' Rights Directive of 12 July 2023, where it is already set out that the victim not only has the right to obtain compensation from the offender

[63] The main instrument of EU law on victims' rights is Directive 2012/29/EU of the European Parliament and of the Council of 25 October 2012 establishing minimum standards on the rights, support and protection of victims of crime, and replacing Council Framework Decision 2001/220/JHA [2012] OJ L315/57. However, many other Directives contain specific provisions for the protection and support of the victims of crime. See, eg, Directive 2011/36/EU of the European Parliament and of the Council of 5 April 2011 on preventing and combating trafficking in human beings and protecting its victims, and replacing Council Framework Decision 2002/629/JHA [2011] OJ L101/1 (Arts 11 to 17); Directive 2011/93/EU of the European Parliament and of the Council of 13 December 2011 on combating the sexual abuse and sexual exploitation of children and child pornography and replacing Council Framework Decision 2004/68/JHA [2011] OJ L335/1 (Arts 19 and 20); Council Directive 2004/80/EC of 29 April 2004 relating to compensation to crime victims; or Directive (EU) 2017/541 of the European Parliament and of the Council of 15 March 2017 on combating terrorism and replacing Council Framework Decision 2002/475/JHA and amending Council Decision 2005/671/JHA [2004] OJ L261/15 (Arts 24, 25 and 26).

[64] On the issue of victims and restorative justice, see the comprehensive study of H Strang, *Repair or Revenge: Victims and Restorative Justice* (Oxford Clarendon Press, 2002).

within the criminal proceedings but also to get such compensation directly from the State, which can then claim this from the offender.[65]

At the same time that the ECtHR was outlining certain rights of victims in criminal proceedings, with the limitations implied in deciding on a specific case, the action of the CoE by way of the Recommendations on victims' rights has also continued advancing towards the protection of victims of crimes. Both have served as a guide and driving force to the national legislator of the Member States of the CoE. However, there is also an influence of the EU Directives upon the CoE Recommendations. In short, the mutual influence between CoE instruments and EU law is undeniable. Both institutions have so far been moving forward in the same direction – although not completely aligned – in expanding the rights and protection of victims of crime. For example, looking at Article 19 CoE CM/Rec(2023)2 (right to victim support), this provision is almost identical to Articles 8 and 9 of the Victims' Rights Directive. And the other way round, the CoE Recommendation provision on right to State compensation included in the CoE CM/Rec(2023)2, goes beyond the right provided under Article 16 of the Victims' Rights Directive, although the intial text of the proposed revision of the said Directive also reflects the content of the CoE CM/Rec(2023)2 in this aspect. However, it is uncertain whether the right to compensation as envisaged in the EU Directive Proposal of July 2023 will be kept as a right of the victims, since along the discussions at the European Council, this right as it was conceived in the proposed text, has been watered down to an extent that it has disappeared. In fact, while the proposed Article 16 included the right of the victim, not only to be compensated of the damages, but the right that this compensation was granted within the criminal procedure, the last available version of the text under discussion has deleted this provision. The same applies to the right to be compensated directly by the State, which has also been eliminated in the last available text.[66]

If we take as an example the rules on 'individual assessment' of the needs of the victims, which is regulated under Article 22 of the Victims' Rights Directive – and is

[65] See Article 13 Rec(2023)2 and Proposal for a Directive of the European Parliament and of the Council amending Directive 2012/29/EU establishing minimum standards on the rights, support and protection of victims of crime, and replacing Council Framework Decision 2001/220/JHA SWD(2023) 246 final, Art 16. The text of the Proposal for a Directive amending Directive 2012/29/EU of 12 July 2023, provided to amend Article 16 of the Directive including following provision on compensation of damages for the victims:

[66] The text of the Proposal for a Directive amending Directive 2012/29/EU of 12 July 2023, provided to amend Article 16 of the Directive including following provision on compensation of damages for the victims:

> '1. Member States shall ensure that, in the course of the criminal proceedings, victims are entitled to obtain a decision on compensation by the offender, within a reasonable time.';
>
> (b) paragraph 2 is replaced by the following:
>
> '2. Member States shall ensure that their competent authorities pay directly to the victim the adjudicated compensation without undue delay. The competent authorities shall be subrogated to the right of the victim in relation to the offender for the amount of the adjudicated compensation.'

This amendment has been struck out in the last available version of the text, which is currently under the legislative procedure. See the document of the Council of the European Union, done in Brussels, 14 June 2024 (11260/24, JAI 1055 COPEN 320 DROIPEN 179).

This is to be criticised by the main organisations active in the field of protecting victims rights, as for example, 'Victim Support Europe' in its 'Joint Statement in Reaction to the Council Position on the Victims' Rights Directive Revision' published on 4 July 2024, available at: https://victim-support.eu/news/joint-statement-in-reaction-to-the-council-position-on-the-victims-rights-directive-revision/.

later included almost in the same sense in Article 4 of the CoE Recommendation of 2023 – the symmetry and interaction is also clearly visible. The Proposal for the revision of the Victims' Rights Directive further specifies what the previous provisions had already established, although underlining that the individual assessment of the victims' needs does not only aim to provide protection, but also support. In improving the prior rules, the proposed amendments to Article 22 of the Victims' Rights Directive adds other elements to consider in making the individual assessment, such as the relationship of the victim with the offender and the characteristics and risks emanating from the offender. This represents a slight improvement by comparison with the CoE Rec (2023)2 and seeks to ensure that the individual assessment is correctly done in every legal system. In this realm, it is also interesting to see how both CoE and EU law instruments are aligned. For example, when regulating the individual assessment, Article 22 of the Victims' Rights Directive of 2012 establishes that it should be done in a 'timely' way. Later, the CM/Rec(2023)2 provides that it should be carried out 'from the first appropriate moment' that the victim comes into contact with the justice authorities. And finally, the proposed revision of the Victims' Rights Directive of July 2023, suggests revising Article 22 to include that the timely assessment 'shall be initiated upon the first contact of the victim with the competent authorities, and shall last as long as necessary depending on the specific needs of each victim'.[67] This interaction and alignment are not only logical, but also very beneficial.

It would be an interesting but perhaps not very useful exercise to continue comparing each of the CoE Recommendations with the content of the different EU Directives on the status of victims in criminal proceedings to see on which points they are aligned or not. The above examples show that there is a certain symmetry although EU Directives logically include a more precise regulation of each of these rights. In sum, the EU Directives include more precise provisions for the States in implementing the rights of the victims of crime, while the latest CoE CM/Rec(2023)2 follows a broader approach, beyond the scope of the criminal proceedings. As it reads in its preamble, the holistic approach is pursued 'beyond and irrespective of the criminal proceedings',[68] with the purpose of achieving a cultural change, so that the justice systems are designed precisely to give support to the victims' needs. Of course, the CoE Recommendation might follow a broader approach, since unlike the EU Directives, it is not legally binding, but is only soft law.

V. Conclusions

ECtHR case law has undoubtedly marked the content of the CoE Recommendations and both have influenced the shaping of EU law. From the ECtHR judgment in the *Doorson* case where the Court explicitly mentioned the interests of the victims and

[67] See Proposal for a Directive, ibid, Art 10b.

[68] CM/Rec(2023)2 (n 8): 'Supporting a more holistic approach to victim rights in seeking to further develop and expand victim rights and services beyond the context of the criminal procedure by not only promoting victim rights in the context of criminal proceedings, but also before, after or irrespective of such proceedings;'.

witnesses in relation to their testimonies in the criminal procedure, to the proposed revision of the Victims' Rights Directive of 2023, the mutual influence between CoE and EU law is visible. Initially the CoE has been a forerunner in promoting the rights of the victims in the criminal proceedings through its case law as well through its soft law, setting the tone for what later has been regulated in the EU Directives. But later, the Victims' Rights Directive of 2012 represented a clear advancement when compared to the rights recognised by the Court and by the CoE Recommendations.

It can be said that there is an interaction between the CoE and EU where sometimes the CoE's action has been ahead and at other times the EU has been setting the pace towards more protection and more support for the victims. All in all this interaction has been very fruitful for the advancement of victims' rights, specifically in the criminal procedure. At this point it can be affirmed that EU law has gone much further than the case law of the ECtHR in ensuring an adequate support system for the victims of crime. This progress is also manifest regarding the rules on individual assessment for adopting the needed protection and support measures. These aspects could only be pointed out in a generic way by the ECtHR, by establishing the need for granting protection to the victims against violation of the rights recognised in the ECHR.

In terms of recognising rights for the victims of crimes, it is clear that there has been considerable progress and that the justice systems are slowly adapting to the 'cultural change', which means that the criminal procedure needs to provide all safeguards for the defendant, but also needs to ensure the protection of the victim.[69] Despite this formidable progress in the regulation of victims' rights, the current challenge is to ensure the adequate implementation of such rules and this requires commitment by the Member States, investment and training.[70] An adequate monitoring of the measures adopted by the Member States is foreseen to seek the objective of professional and adequate support for victims of crime.

There are still issues that might be subject to further improvement. As in other areas of justice, the provision of legal aid is still subject to national law and is only to be provided when 'the interests of justice so require'. This broad concept obviously does not cover all situations for the victim to be granted access to justice. No advancement is seen in this area, as the wording of the Directives and Recommendations have remained unchanged in recent decades. It is precisely in those legal systems where the prosecution is only triggered when the victim presses charges and files a criminal complaint and the legal aid is only provided when the legal assistance is mandatory that there is still much room for improvement in the protection of the victim's rights. This could be considered

[69] The adjustment, however, is slow. It is really disappointing that, for example, the EU Commission opened infringement proceedings against nine EU Member States for not having completely transposed Directive 2012/29/EU on the rights, support and protection of victims of crime, in 2019. See T Wahl, 'Victims' Rights Directive: Commission Initiates Infringement Proceedings Against Nine Member States' (*Eucrim*, 2019), available at https://eucrim.eu/news/victims-rights-directive-commission-initiates-infringement-proceedings-against-nine-member-states/.

[70] With regard to the practical implementation and its deficits, the empirical study of A ten Boom, 'How Do Victims With the Need for Protection Judge Their Experiences With the Police in the Netherlands?' (2021) 3 *Erasmus Law Review* 121–33, available at www.erasmuslawreview.nl/tijdschrift/ELR/2021/3/ELR-D-21-00017, reflecting the perception of the victims when reporting a crime to the police in the Netherlands, is highly interesting, showing that much more needs to be done in implementing victims' rights.

a pending issue, which needs to be tackled if the rights already recognised are to be implemented effectively.

Finally, there is also the question of the scope of the protection of victims of crime. The first step, which was to allow the victim to participate in the criminal proceedings, can be said to have been accomplished, pending the issue of legal aid. The time where the victim had no say in the criminal proceedings, could not act, was not informed and was neither heard nor protected, seems, fortunately, to be over. However, there is still the challenge to define what the rights of victims of crime outside the criminal proceedings are. The right to be protected and the right to be supported have been recognised regardless of the position or participation of the victim in the criminal proceedings. But the question goes further, since CM/Rec(2023)2 speaks of rights 'irrespective of a criminal procedure'. Does this mean that the rights of victims are to be granted even if no criminal proceedings have been instituted? Could this mean that, for example, victims of war crimes, where there is no pending criminal procedure in a certain country, could claim to be granted the rights recognised under EU law? If the rights are granted to persons who have suffered a harm caused 'directly' by a crime, how can the condition of being a victim who has suffered a direct harm, be established if not by way of a criminal procedure? Could a new approach be taken and support and protection be granted to persons who are manifestly suffering harm caused by war crimes even if such crimes have not yet triggered any criminal procedure? If this were to be the case, current EU law is clearly not sufficient, nor is the proposed update of the Victims' Rights Directive as envisaged in the Proposal adopted in July 2023.

The protection of and support for victims of warfare also raises questions[71] because, although they are suffering huge harms, they generally would not fall within the definition of victim either under the EU Directive or the CoE Recommendations given that their harm would possibly not be considered as 'directly' caused by the crime.

As for now, it can only be welcomed that, thanks to ECtHR case law and the actions of the CoE and the EU, the much needed cultural change towards the adequate protection of the victims of crime is taking place.

[71] As expressed by D Kauzlarich, 'Victimization and Supranational Criminology' in A Smeulers and R Haveman (eds), *Supranational Criminology: Towards a Criminology of International Crimes* (Intersentia, 2008) 439: 'families are divided, people turn up missing, buildings and homes are destroyed, and the basic needs for proper nutrition, clean water and working sewers cannot be met, etc.'. On the needs of war victims, see also the empirical study of A ten Boom and KF Kuijpers, 'Victims' Needs as Basic Human Needs' (2012) 18(2) *International Review of Victimology* 155–79.

8

Victim Participation in International Criminal Trials: A Way Forward?

VAIOS KOUTROULIS AND MARIE-LAURENCE HÉBERT-DOLBEC

I. Introduction

Any development in EU law relating to victims and their place in criminal proceedings cannot operate in a vacuum. Victims' participation in criminal proceedings and the rights recognised to them in connection with such participation have been the object of continuous evolution in international criminal law, creating a context that cannot be ignored by any actor or stakeholder involved with the issue of victims' rights.

These developments have taken place on two levels. On the one hand, victims' rights have explicitly been recognised and applied in the context of proceedings before international and internationalised jurisdictions. The centerpiece of this edifice is, of course, the International Criminal Court (ICC). The ICC was famously the first international criminal jurisdiction whose Statute acknowledged victims – in their own right and not just as witnesses – and provided a place for them in the proceedings.[1] The central provision dedicated to victims in the ICC Statute – Article 68 on 'protection of victims and witnesses and their participation in the proceedings'[2] – was enough to turn the tide. Since the adoption of the Statute, victims have become impossible to ignore in international criminal proceedings. This is reflected in the statutes of the international and internationalised criminal jurisdictions established after the ICC, all of which have specific provisions concerning victims.[3] Naturally, victims' rights in international proceedings

[1] For the place of victims in the proceedings of international tribunals before the ICC, see M-L Hébert-Dolbec, *La place des victimes dans la justice internationale pénale* (PhD Thesis, Université libre de Bruxelles, 2021).

[2] Rome Statute of the International Criminal Court (Rome, 17 July 1998) (hereinafter 'Rome Statute' or 'ICC Statute').

[3] See, eg, Statute of the Special Tribunal for Lebanon, S/RES/1757, 2007, Arts 17 and 25; The Extraordinary Chambers in the Courts of Cambodia, Internal Rules (Rev 10) as revised on 27 October 2022, rr 12, 12*bis*, 12*ter*, 23, 23*bis*, 23*ter*, 23*quater*, and 23*quinquies*; Statute of the Extraordinary African Chambers within the courts of Senegal created to prosecute international crimes committed in Chad between 7 June 1982 and 1 December 1990, Arts 14 and 27; Law No 05/L-053 on Specialist Chambers and Specialist Prosecutor's Office, 3 August 2015, Arts 22–23; Loi n°18-010 portant règlement de la procedure et de la prevue devant la cour pénale spéciale de la République centrafricaine, 2 July 2018, Art 6.

are not necessarily fully transposable to domestic proceedings. It is, however, essential to be aware of the relevant provisions since they form part of the context which will be part of any regime regulating victims and their rights in criminal proceedings.

On the other hand, international criminal law conventions – that are not explicitly dedicated to the creation of an international or internationalised tribunal – establish rights for victims that are directed to national criminal proceedings. Here again, this is an evolution that has taken place in the last decades. Indeed, early conventions establishing international crimes, like, for example, the 1970 Convention for the Suppression of Unlawful Seizure of Aircraft,[4] the 1971 Convention for the Suppression of Unlawful Acts Against the Safety of Civil Aviation,[5] the 1979 International Convention Against the Taking of Hostages,[6] the 1988 Convention for the Suppression of Unlawful Acts Against the Safety of Maritime Navigation,[7] the 1994 Convention on the Safety of United Nations and Associated Personnel,[8] or the 1997 International Convention for the Suppression of Terrorist Bombings,[9] do not contain any specific provisions on victims. This trend has been reversed in more recent conventions, presumably under the influence of Article 68 of the ICC Statute. For example, the 2000 United Nations Convention Against Transnational Organized Crime (UNTOC),[10] the 2003 United Nations Convention Against Corruption (UNCAC),[11] or the 2010 International Convention for the Protection of All Persons from Enforced Disappearances,[12] all contain provisions relating to the protection of victims and witnesses. The Draft Articles on Prevention and Punishment of Crimes Against Humanity adopted in 2019 by the International Law Commission (Draft Articles on Crimes Against Humanity),[13] as well as the Convention on International Cooperation in the Investigation and Prosecution of the Crime of Genocide, Crimes against Humanity, War Crimes and other International Crimes, adopted in Ljubljana on 26 May 2023, opened for signature at The Hague on 14 February 2024 (hereafter: Ljubljana – The Hague Convention),[14] confirm that it is very difficult today to ignore the issues and needs related to the participation of victims in the proceedings when drafting a convention relating to international criminal law.

As it has been developed in other contributions to this edited volume, at the EU level, the key instrument with respect to victims' rights is Directive 2012/29/EU,

[4] Convention for the Suppression of Unlawful Seizure of Aircraft (The Hague, 16 December 1970).

[5] Convention for the Suppression of Unlawful Acts Against the Safety of Civil Aviation (Montreal, 23 September 1971).

[6] International Convention Against the Taking of Hostages (New York, 17 December 1979).

[7] Convention for the Suppression of Unlawful Acts Against the Safety of Maritime Navigation (Rome, 10 March 1988).

[8] Convention on the Safety of United Nations and Associated Personnel (New York, 9 December 1994).

[9] International Convention for the Suppression of Terrorist Bombings (New York, 15 December 1997).

[10] United Nations Convention Against Transnational Organized Crime (New York, 15 November 2000).

[11] United Nations Convention Against Corruption (New York, 31 October 2003) Arts 32–33.

[12] International Convention for the Protection of All Persons from Enforced Disappearances (New York, 23 December 2010) Arts 12 and 24.

[13] Draft Articles on the Prevention and Punishment of Crimes Against Humanity ('Draft Articles on Crimes Against Humanity'), 2019, *ILC Report 2019*, A/74/10, art 12.

[14] Ljubljana – The Hague Convention on International Cooperation in the Investigation and Prosecution of the Crime of Genocide, Crimes against Humanity, War Crimes and other International Crimes (Ljubljana/The Hague, 26 May 2023), available at www.gov.si/assets/ministrstva/MZEZ/projekti/MLA-pobuda/The-Ljubljana-The-Hague-MLA-Convention.pdf (hereinafter 'Ljubljana – The Hague Convention').

establishing minimum standards on the rights, support and protection of victims of crime (hereafter: the Victims' Rights Directive).[15] Furthermore, specific rules have been adopted for victims of particular crimes such as human trafficking,[16] child victims of sexual exploitation and child pornography,[17] and terrorism.[18] Following an evaluation of the Victims' Rights Directive in 2022, the need to revise its text in view of strengthening victims' rights became apparent.[19] After conducting an open public consultation on 12 July 2023, the European Commission proposed a series of amendments (hereafter: 2023 Commission Proposal).[20]

Given this ongoing amendment procedure, this chapter aims to give an overview of the place and rights awarded in international law to victims in criminal proceedings relating to the most serious international crimes. The international law instruments that were mentioned above concern criminal proceedings relating to the commission of international crimes before either national or international, internationalised and hybrid tribunals. This chapter will primarily focus on international criminal proceedings, particularly those conducted at the ICC, as they have led to a significant practice concerning the role of victims in proceedings related to the most serious international crimes. However, it is equally important to keep in mind the rules on victims, which are set down in international criminal law conventions and have been considered appropriate for national criminal proceedings.

The objective of this overview is to establish some points of convergence and divergence between international criminal law and EU law on the treatment of victims, in order to identify potential lessons learned and elements that could be useful to consider in view of the revision of the Victims' Rights Directive. It should however be pointed out from the outset that this comparison has its limits. As indicated above, at

[15] Directive 2012/29/EU of the European Parliament and of the Council of 25 October 2012 establishing minimum standards on the rights, support and protection of victims of crime, and replacing Council Framework Decision 2001/220/JHA (Victims' Rights Directive) [2012] OJ L315/57. See in this volume the contribution by C Chioni-Chouman, 'Victims' Rights in the EU: Boosting the Recognition and Participation of Victims in Criminal Proceedings' in chapter 2.

[16] See Directive 2011/36/EU of the European Parliament and of the Council of 5 April 2011 on preventing and combating trafficking in human beings and protecting its victims, and replacing Council Framework Decision 2002/629/JHA [2011] OJ L101/1; Directive (EU) 2024/1712 of the European Parliament and of the Council of 13 June 2024 amending Directive 2011/36/EU on preventing and combating trafficking in human beings and protecting its victims [2024] OJ L2024/1712.

[17] Directive 2011/93/EU of the European Parliament and of the Council of 13 December 2011 on combating the sexual abuse and sexual exploitation of children and child pornography, and replacing Council Framework Decision 2004/68/JHA [2011] OJ L335/1; European Commission, Proposal for a Directive of the European Parliament and of the Council on combating the sexual abuse and sexual exploitation of children and child sexual abuse material and replacing Council Framework Decision 2004/68/JHA (recast), COM(2024) 60 final.

[18] Directive (EU) 2017/541 of the European Parliament and of the Council of 15 March 2017 on combating terrorism and replacing Council Framework Decision 2002/475/JHA and amending Council Decision 2005/671/JHA [2017] OJ L88/6.

[19] European Commission, 'Evaluation of Directive 2012/29/EU of the European Parliament and of the Council of 25 October 2012 establishing minimum standards on the rights, support and protection of victims of crime, and replacing Council Framework Decision 2001/220/JHA', Commission Staff Working Document, SWD(2022) 179 final, available at https://eur-lex.europa.eu/legal-content/EN/TXT/PDF/?uri=CELEX:52022SC0179.

[20] European Commission, Proposal for a Directive of the European Parliament and of the Council amending Directive 2012/29/EU establishing minimum standards on the rights, support and protection of victims of crime, and replacing Council Framework Decision 2001/220/JHA (2023 Commission Proposal), COM(2023) 424 final, available at https://eur-lex.europa.eu/legal-content/EN/TXT/?uri=CELEX%3A52023PC0424.

the international level, the protection of victims has developed with respect to both national and international criminal proceedings. International criminal proceedings, more specifically the ones before the ICC on which this contribution draws heavily, are subject to the conditions which (de)limit the exercise of jurisdiction of the ICC: the international character of the Court implies that its jurisdiction is inherently extraterritorial and subject to limitations relating, for example, to the nature of the crime (only the most serious international crimes fall under the jurisdiction of the Court: the crime of genocide, crimes against humanity, war crimes and the crime of aggression). On the other hand, the Victims' Rights Directive deals only with proceedings at a national level and, although it also covers the abovementioned international crimes, it is by no means limited to them. The Directive thus applies to all victims in criminal proceedings conducted at a national level to ensure they are granted a minimum level of protection. Therefore, contrary to the rules applicable within the ICC, the Directive was primarily designed to apply to intra-EU situations, its extraterritorial dimension being the exception rather than the rule.

With these elements in mind, the comparison between the rights and protection of victims in EU law and international criminal proceedings will be organised around two main axes. First, we will analyse the elements relating to the scope of application of victims' rights in criminal proceedings (section II). We will then proceed to an examination of the substantive aspects of victim participation in such proceedings (section III).

II. Scope of Application of Victims' Rights

This first section will focus on the scope of application of victims' rights. It is in this respect that the differences between the inherently extraterritorial ICC proceedings and the national, primarily intra-EU, proceedings to which the Victims' Rights Directive applies become more apparent. As explained above, we will compare what is set down in the relevant international law instruments with the scope of application of the Victims' Rights Directive and suggested amendments, focusing on three main questions relating to the scope of application of the Directive: what are the crimes covered by the Directive? (section II.A) What are the criminal proceedings to which the Directive applies? (section II.B) Finally, and undoubtedly most importantly, which victims fall under the scope of the Directive? (section II.C).

A. Which Crimes?

Using international criminal proceedings as a starting point, this question will be examined from the perspective of the material (i) and territorial (ii) scope of jurisdiction exercised by the relevant tribunals, particularly the ICC.

i. Material Scope of Jurisdiction

The establishment of international, internationalised or hybrid tribunals has always been associated with the clear determination of the crimes over which such tribunals would have jurisdiction. These crimes were explicitly mentioned in the statutes of the relevant judicial institutions thus (de)limiting their material scope of jurisdiction. Hence, for example, the International Criminal Tribunals for the Former Yugoslavia and Rwanda (respectively 'the ICTY' and the 'ICTR') had jurisdiction only over war crimes, the crime of genocide and crimes against humanity (respectively Articles 2–5 of the ICTY Statute and 2–4 of the ICTR Statute), while the ICC's jurisdiction covers all these crimes but includes the crime of aggression as well (Articles 5–8bis of the ICC Statute).

More generally, the concepts of 'core international crimes' or the 'most serious international crimes' are often used by international institutions, EU networks such as the so-called 'Genocide Network', and scholars in order to refer to a limited number of crimes which are considered of particular gravity in international criminal law: war crimes, crimes against humanity, the crime of genocide, usually also complemented by the crime of aggression.[21] Since these concepts are not legal terms, they may also encompass other crimes which are provided for in international criminal law instruments, like, for example, enforced disappearances or torture. The characteristic all these crimes are reputed to have in common is that they protect universally shared legal values and thus are 'of concern to the international community as a whole'.[22]

Probably the most essential common specificity of core international crimes is that they usually involve a large number of victims, among others, due to the nature of the crimes in question. For instance, by 2022, more than 10,000 victims of atrocities have been recognised as such before the ICC for participation, while, the ICC Trust Fund for Victims has provided physical, psychological and socio-economic support to more than 450,000 victims through its assistance programmes.[23] If we turn to concrete cases, in the case against Bosco Ntaganda, 2,121 victims participated in the trial proceedings.[24]

[21] See among many C Damgaard, *Individual Criminal Responsibility for Core International Crimes* (Springer, 2008); C Schwöbel-Patel, 'The Core Crimes of International Criminal law' in K Jon Heller et al (eds), *The Oxford Handbook of International Criminal Law* (Oxford University Press, 2020); SD Murphy, Special Rapporteur, 'First Report on Crimes against Humanity' UN Doc A/CN.4/680 (*Yearbook of the International Law Commission*, 17 February 2015) vol II, part one, 228; UN General Assembly, Resolution 71/248, adopted on 21 December 2016, 'International, Impartial and Independent Mechanism to Assist in the Investigation and Prosecution of Persons Responsible for the Most Serious Crimes under International Law Committed in the Syrian Arab Republic since March 2011', UN Doc A/RES/71/248, 11 January 2017; Eurojust, European Network for Investigation and Prosecution of Genocide, Crimes against Humanity and War Crimes, '20 Years On: Main Developments in the Fight against Impunity for Core International Crimes in the EU' (The Hague, May 2022), available at www.eurojust.europa.eu/sites/default/files/assets/developments-in-the-fight-against-impunity-for-core-international-crimes-in-the-eu.pdf; Eurojust, 'Conclusions of the 35th Meeting of the Network for Investigation and Prosecution of Genocide, Crimes against Humanity and War Crimes' (The Hague, 16–14 April 2024), available at www.eurojust.europa.eu/sites/default/files/assets/genocide-network-conclusions-35th-meeting-apr-2024.pdf; Statement by ICC Prosecutor, Karim AA Khan QC, 'Office of the Prosecutor Joins National Authorities in Joint Investigation Team on International Crimes Committed in Ukraine' (25 April 2022), available at www.icc-cpi.int/news/statement-icc-prosecutor-karim-aa-khan-qc-office-prosecutor-joins-national-authorities-joint.

[22] See the first preambular Recital of Ljubljana – The Hague Convention (n 14) 6: 'Recalling that the international crimes to which this Convention applies are among the most serious crimes of concern to the international community as a whole'. As the reference to 'other international crimes' in its title suggests, the crimes which may come under the scope of application of the Convention include the crime of aggression, torture and enforced disappearances, see Arts 2§2 and 6, pp 8 and 14 respectively.

[23] United Nations, 'ICC at 20: Five Things you should know about the International Criminal Court' (27 June 2022), available at https://news.un.org/en/story/2022/06/1121282.

[24] ICC, *Prosecutor v Bosco Ntaganda*, Reparations Order, Trial Chamber VI, ICC-01/04-02/06, 8 March 2021, para 22.

In its order for reparations delivered on 28 February 2024 in the case against Dominique Ongwen, Trial Chamber IX underlined that '4,096 victims were authorised to participate in the proceedings pursuant to Article 68(3) of the Statute', while it is estimated 'that there would be approximately 49,772 potential beneficiaries of reparations'.[25] These numbers make clear that the ICC had to deal with the effects that a mass number of victims would have on the trial and criminal proceedings in general.

As mentioned above, the Victims' Rights Directive is a horizontal instrument applying to victims of all national criminal proceedings. Consequently, and in stark contradiction to the practice of international criminal jurisdictions, it does not specify the crimes to which it applies. Indeed, according to Recital 13 of the Preamble:

> This Directive applies in relation to criminal offences committed in the Union and to criminal proceedings that take place in the Union. *It confers rights on victims of extra-territorial offences only in relation to criminal proceedings that take place in the Union.* Complaints made to competent authorities outside the Union, such as embassies, do not trigger the obligations set out in this Directive (emphasis added).[26]

This Recital confirms that there is no limit based on the nature or type of crime. In other words, the Directive applies to more than just 'core international crimes'. The notion of 'core international crimes' is used in the 2023 Commission Proposal to amend the Directive. The term comes up in preambular Recital 7, Article 1(4)(b) (on the availability of targeted and integrated support services) and Article 1(10)(d) (on individual assessment of victims), but it remains undefined.[27] The 2023 Proposal lacks any recommendations for altering the Directive's Preamble; thus, no amendments are proposed for Recital 13, as mentioned above. In other words, the Directive's general scope of application is not – and, given the horizontal nature of the instrument, will probably continue not to be – limited to core international crimes, regardless of how this term may be defined. Nevertheless, if the notion of 'core international crimes' is inserted in the Directive, it would be helpful to clearly state which crimes are covered by it, especially if this concept is likely to influence the application of certain provisions of the Directive.

ii. Territorial Scope of Jurisdiction

The inherently extraterritorial character of international criminal institutions implies that the territorial aspect of their jurisdiction has to be determined with precision, and the ICC is probably the best illustration of the importance of this aspect of jurisdiction. According to Article 12§ 2 of the ICC Statute, the Court may exercise its jurisdiction over crimes which have either been committed in the territory of a State party to the Statute or which have been committed by a national of a State party to the Statute.[28]

[25] ICC, *Prosecutor v Dominic Ongwen*, Reparations Order, Trial Chamber IX, ICC-02/04-01/15, 28 February 2024, para 577 (hereinafter 'Ongwen Reparations Order').

[26] Victims' Rights Directive (n 15) 58.

[27] 2023 Commission Proposal (n 20) 23, 28, 30.

[28] Rome Statute (n 2) Art 12(2).

The Court's jurisdiction is thus conditioned by the territory of the commission of the crime and the nationality of the presumed author.

The interpretation of the term 'territory' has given rise to significant jurisprudential developments within the ICC, which deserve to be highlighted. With respect to the facts related to the treatment of the Rohingya population by the Government of Myanmar, the ICC Office of the Prosecutor was faced with a significant limitation in the ICC jurisdiction: in view of the conditions set out in Article 12§2 of the ICC Statute, since Myanmar is not a party to the ICC Statute, and given that there is no UN Security Council resolution adopted under Chapter VII of the UN Charter referring the situation to the ICC,[29] it would appear that this situation lies outside of the reach of the ICC jurisdiction. Nevertheless, the Office of the Prosecutor identified certain crimes which could be considered as having been partially committed in the territory of Bangladesh, which is party to the ICC Statute.[30] The Pre-Trial Chamber agreed with this analysis and confirmed that the ICC did have jurisdiction over those crimes.[31] One example is the crime of deportation whose *actus reus* takes place by definition in the territory of two States: the one from whose territory the civilians are forced to flee (in this case, Myanmar) and the other in whose territory the civilians are forced to end up (in this case, Bangladesh). Another example is the crime against humanity of other inhumane acts consisting of the violation of the Rohingyas' right to return to Myanmar. Here again, with respect to the Rohingyas found in Bangladesh that Myanmar refuses to allow to come back, by definition, at least part of the *actus reus* of the crime is committed outside the territory of Myanmar.

The issue of territoriality does not arise in the same way under the Victims' Rights Directive. The text of Recital 13 provides that the Directive 'applies in relation to criminal offences committed in the Union *and* to criminal proceedings that take place in the Union'. The Recital mentions both the territory of the commission of the offence and the existence of criminal proceedings in the Union as relevant for determining the scope of application of the Directive. The word 'and' in Recital 13 should be read as being disjunctive, and thus, the two elements (territory of the commission of the offence and existence of criminal proceedings in the Union) are not cumulative.

In reality, it is the existence of criminal proceedings in the Union which is the key condition for the application of the Directive, irrespective of whether the crime has taken place in the Union (even partly if the terms 'in the Union' are interpreted in a similar way to the interpretation followed by the ICC case law[32]) or outside it. This interpretation is confirmed by the second paragraph of Recital 13, according to which the Directive: 'confers rights on victims of extra-territorial offences only in relation to

[29] ibid Art 13(b).

[30] ICC, *Situation in the People's Republic of Bangladesh / Republic of the Union of Myanmar*, Request for authorization, of an investigation pursuant to article 15, Office of the Prosecutor, ICC-01/19-7, 4 July 2019.

[31] ICC, *Situation in the People's Republic of Bangladesh / Republic of the Union of Myanmar*, Decision Pursuant to Article 15 of the Rome Statute on the Authorization of an Investigation into the Situation in the People's Republic of Bangladesh / Republic of the Union of Myanmar, Pre-Trial Chamber III, ICC-01/19-27, 14 November 2019.

[32] ibid para 61: cases where 'at least part of the conduct (*i.e.* the *actus reus* of the crime) … take[s] place in the territory of a State'.

criminal proceedings that take place in the Union'.[33] It is also the interpretation that best fulfils the objective of the Directive as provided for in Article 1:

> 1. The purpose of this Directive is to ensure that victims of crime receive appropriate information, support and protection and are able to participate in criminal proceedings.
>
> Member States shall ensure that victims are recognized and treated in a respectful, sensitive, tailored, professional and non-discriminatory manner, in all contact with victim support or restorative justice services or a competent authority, operating within the context of criminal proceedings.[34]

This is linked to the European Union's ambition of 'maintaining and developing an area of freedom, security and justice', the strengthening of 'the rights and protection of victims, in particular in criminal proceedings', and the improvement of 'legislation and practical support measures for the protection of victims, with particular attention paid to, support for and recognition of, all victims'.[35] This means that the Directive will cover cases where the criminal jurisdiction of a State is exercised by virtue of some version of universal jurisdiction. By universal jurisdiction, we refer to the jurisdiction exercised by the tribunals of a State 'over persons for extraterritorial events where neither the victims nor the alleged offenders are nationals of the forum State and no harm was allegedly caused to the forum State's own national interests'.[36] Naturally, the Directive remains silent on the question of the establishment of universal jurisdiction as such. Whether and to what extent a Member State will establish the jurisdiction of its courts and tribunals over events occurring abroad remains a sovereign prerogative and depends on the conventional and customary norms binding on the State concerned. However, if a Member State chooses to establish such jurisdiction, then the relevant proceedings do fall under the scope of application of the Directive.

B. Which Criminal Proceedings?

The question of the definition of criminal proceedings does not arise in the same way under international criminal law and the Victims' Rights Directive.

From the point of view of international criminal law, the existence of specific jurisdictions (and statutes and rules of procedure and evidence applicable to such jurisdictions) offers the necessary delimitation as to the proceedings to which the rights of victims apply in each case.

Things are different in the context of the Victims' Rights Directive. Here, the notion of 'criminal proceedings' is conceived rather broadly. Indeed, according to preambular Recital 22, these proceedings start from the moment a complaint is made:

[33] Victims' Rights Directive (n 15) 58.

[34] ibid 65. Along similar lines, further reinforcing the extraterritorial reach of the Directive, Recital 10 of the Directive states that 'Member States should take the necessary measures to ensure that the rights set out in this Directive are not made conditional on the victim's residence status in their territory or on the victim's citizenship or nationality'.

[35] ibid Recitals 1, 4 and 2 respectively.

[36] International Law Commission, 'The Obligation to Extradite or Prosecute (*aut dedere aut judicare*)' (Yearbook of the International Law Commission. 2014) Vol II, part two, para 18 (reference omitted).

> The moment when a complaint is made should, for the purposes of this Directive, be considered as falling within the context of the criminal proceedings. This should also include situations where authorities initiate criminal proceedings *ex officio* as a result of a criminal offence suffered by a victim.[37]

This approach does not change in the 2023 Commission Proposal, which refers to 'criminal proceeding', 'criminal proceedings', or 'criminal procedure',[38] and does not amend the definition of the proceedings as such.

It is also worth noting that the Directive does not lose sight of alternative processes of dealing with the effects of criminal offences pertaining to 'restorative justice', which is defined by the Directive as 'any process whereby the victim and the offender are enabled, if they freely consent, to participate actively in the resolution of matters arising from the criminal offence, through the help of an impartial third party'.[39] The inclusion in the Directive of restorative justice processes and relating rights and safeguards for the victims further broadens the material scope of application of the Directive.[40] This usefully complements and reinforces the wide range of rights recognised in the Directive.

After having examined the scope of the Directive's application in terms of the crimes and criminal proceedings involved, we will explore the notion of victims, which is central to the Directive's application.

C. Which Victims?

Article 2§1. of the Victims' Rights Directive defines victims in the following way:

> a) 'victim' means:
>
> i. a natural person who has suffered harm, including physical, mental or emotional harm or economic loss which was directly caused by a criminal offence;
>
> ii. family members of a person whose death was directly caused by a criminal offence and who have suffered harm as a result of that person's death.[41]

Family members are defined in the Directive as 'the spouse, the person who is living with the victim in a committed intimate relationship, in a joint household and on a stable and continuous basis, the relatives in direct line, the siblings and the dependants of the victims'.[42]

Comparing the definition of victims under the Victims' Rights Directive to what exists in international criminal law is no easy task since it is not easy to identify a universally accepted and applied definition of victims. The starting point of any effort

[37] ibid 59.

[38] See 2023 Commission Proposal (n 20) (preambular para 9 of the proposed directive amending the 2012 Directive), 29 (proposal to amend Arts 16 and 17 of the 2012 Directive), and 32 (proposal to insert new Art 26a(1)(c)).

[39] Victims' Rights Directive (n 15) Art 2§1(d).

[40] See, eg ibid Art 4§1(j), Art 12 (right to safeguards in the context of restorative justice services), and Art 25§4.

[41] ibid Art 2§1(a).

[42] ibid Art 2§1(b).

to delineate the notion of victim in international law is undoubtedly the definition included in the UN Declaration of Basic Principles of Justice for Victims of Crime and Abuse of Power (hereinafter '1985 UN Declaration'), adopted on 29 November 1985 by the UN General Assembly:

> 1. 'Victims' means persons who, individually or collectively, have suffered harm, including physical or mental injury, emotional suffering, economic loss or substantial impairment of their fundamental rights, through acts or omissions that are in violation of criminal laws operative within Member States, including those laws proscribing criminal abuse of power.
> 2. A person may be considered a victim, under this Declaration, regardless of whether the perpetrator is identified, apprehended, prosecuted or convicted and regardless of the familial relationship between the perpetrator and the victim. The term 'victim' also includes, where appropriate, the immediate family or dependants of the direct victim and persons who have suffered harm in intervening to assist victims in distress or prevent victimization.[43]

In international criminal law more specifically, as it has already been explained above, the adoption of the ICC Statute represents a turning point for protecting victims. In this respect, although it does contain an article bearing on the protection of victims and witnesses and their participation in the proceedings of the ICC (Article 68), the Rome Statute does not define who can be considered a 'victim' before the ICC.[44] The definition is provided in the Rules of Procedure and Evidence adopted in 2002. Rule 85 defines victims as including both natural and – to a limited extent – legal persons:

> (a) 'Victims' means natural persons who have suffered harm as a result of the commission of any crime within the jurisdiction of the Court;
> (b) Victims may include organizations or institutions that have sustained direct harm to any of their property which is dedicated to religion, education, art or science or charitable purposes, and to their historic monuments, hospitals and other places and objects for humanitarian purposes.[45]

Leaving aside the specific issue of legal persons, to which we will return later, the definition of the natural persons who can be considered victims of a crime has been taken up to a large extent by other international or internationalised jurisdictions created after the ICC, like for example the Special Tribunal for Lebanon,[46] the Extraordinary Chambers in the Courts of Cambodia,[47] or the Extraordinary African Chambers.[48] It is equally important that the definition of Rule 85 was also reproduced as such in Article 81 of Ljubljana – The Hague Convention.[49] The Article states that the definition is adopted

[43] UN General Assembly, A/RES/40/34, 29 November 1985 (1985 UN Declaration) paras 1–2.

[44] Rome Statute (n 2) 129–30.

[45] ICC Rules of Procedure and Evidence (ICC RPE) (New York, 3–10 September 2002) rule 85.

[46] Special Tribunal for Lebanon Statute, S/RES/1757 (30 May 2007) Art 25(1): 'The Special Tribunal may identify victims who have suffered harm as a result of the commission of crimes by an accused convicted by the Tribunal.'

[47] Extraordinary Chambers in the Courts of Cambodia, Internal Rules (12 June 2007), Glossary, 72: 'a natural person or legal entity that has suffered harm as a result of the commission of any crime within the jurisdiction of the ECCC.'

[48] Statute of the Extraordinary African Chambers within the Senegalese judicial system for the prosecution of international crimes committed on the territory of the Republic of Chad during the period from 7 June 1982 to 1 December 1990 (22 August 2012) Art 14.

[49] Ljubljana – The Hague Convention (n 14) 53.

'[w]ithout prejudice to broader definitions under domestic law', thereby clearly indicating that this definition was considered the lowest threshold below which States cannot fall.

Other international criminal law instruments contain definitions of victims, which are more closely tailored to the relevant crimes. For example, the International Convention for the Protection of All Persons from Enforced Disappearance defines a victim as 'the disappeared person and any individual who has suffered as the direct result of an enforced disappearance'.[50] Similarly, the Convention on Cluster Munitions defines victims as

> all persons who have been killed or suffered physical or psychological injury, economic loss, social marginalisation or substantial impairment of the realisation of their rights caused by the use of cluster munitions. They include persons directly impacted by cluster munitions as well as their affected families and communities.[51]

The articles adopted by the UN International Law Commission on the prevention and punishment of crimes against humanity do not include a definition of the term 'victim'. The commentary on Article 12 states the following:

> Most treaties that address the rights of victims within national law do not define the term 'victim', allowing States instead to apply their existing law and practice, provided that it is consistent with their obligations under international law. At the same time, practice associated with those treaties and under customary international law provides guidance as to how the term should be viewed.[52]

The Draft Articles on Crimes Against Humanity point to the definitions of victims in international criminal courts and tribunals as rules where 'guidance may exist'.[53] It also considers that human rights instruments are relevant for defining the term victim and refers to the several definitions of regional instruments before concluding that '[u]nder all such treaties, the term "victim" is not construed narrowly or in a discriminatory manner'.[54] In this respect, for example, the Committee against Torture, in its General Comment No 3, defines victims as follows:

> Victims are persons who have individually or collectively suffered harm, including physical or mental injury, emotional suffering, economic loss or substantial impairment of their fundamental rights, through acts or omissions that constitute violations of the Convention. A person should be considered a victim regardless of whether the perpetrator of the violation is identified, apprehended, prosecuted or convicted, and regardless of any familial or other relationship between the perpetrator and the victim. The term 'victim' also includes affected immediate family or dependants of the victim as well as persons who have suffered harm in intervening to assist victims or to prevent victimization. The term 'survivors' may, in some cases, be preferred by persons who have suffered harm. The Committee uses the legal term 'victims' without prejudice to other terms which may be preferable in specific contexts.[55]

[50] International Convention for the Protection of All Persons from Enforced Disappearances (n 12) Art 24(1).

[51] Convention on Cluster Munitions (Dublin, 30 May 2008) Art 2§1.

[52] Draft Articles on Crimes Against Humanity (n 13) commentary to Article 12, para 3.

[53] ibid para 6.

[54] ibid para 5.

[55] Committee against Torture, *General Comment No. 3 (2012): Implementation of Article 14 by States Parties* (UNCAT General Comment No 3), CAT/C/GC/3, 13 December 2012, para 3.

The primary conclusion derived from the discussion above is that international criminal law appears susceptible to an expansive interpretation of the concept of victims.

Concerning legal entities, the definition in the ICC Rules of Procedure and Evidence makes it clear that they can be considered as victims for the purposes of the proceedings before the ICC. Such entities

> may include, inter alia, non-governmental, charitable and non-profit organisations, statutory bodies including government departments, public schools, hospitals, private education institutes (primary and secondary schools or training colleges), companies, telecommunication firms, institutions that benefit members of the community (such as cooperative and building societies, or bodies that deal with micro finance) and other partnerships.[56]

As an example, in the case against Al Mahdi, the accused was found guilty of the war crime of having destroyed religious and historic buildings in Timbuktu – nine mausoleums and one mosque – which were protected as a significant part of the cultural heritage of Timbuktu and of Mali and were, all except one, listed as UNESCO World Heritage Sites. In this context, the ICC has recognised that both the Malian State and the international community represented by UNESCO were victims of the crime and awarded them a symbolic reparation of one euro.[57]

Comparing these definitions to Article 2§1 of the Victims' Rights Directive,[58] one significant aspect in which the definition of victims within the Directive seems restrictive is the exclusion of legal persons from being classified as victims. As noted above, before the ICC, legal persons can be recognised as victims in the specific case of a crime that has caused harm to historic monuments, hospitals, and property dedicated to religion, education, art, science, or charitable purposes.[59]

For natural persons, to correctly circumscribe the scope of the definition as understood in the context of proceedings before the ICC, one must focus on some of the key parts of the definition, like the requisite harm (i), the causal link required between the harm and the offence (ii) as well as the way the term 'family' is construed (iii).

i. Definition of Harm

The Victims' Rights Directive does not define what harm the offence must have inflicted on an individual for them to be considered a victim. Article 2§1(a) simply enumerates the most common types of harm: 'physical, mental or emotional harm or economic loss'.[60] As the phrasing of the text clearly indicates ('including …'), these are just examples of harm; in other words, the list is an indicative one. It is thus possible for persons having suffered other types of harm to be considered victims under the Directive.

In the words of the abovementioned 1985 Declaration of Basic Principles of Justice for Victims of Crime and Abuse of Power and General Comment No 3 of the Committee

56 ICC, *Prosecutor v Thomas Lubanga Dyilo*, Order for Reparations (amended), Appeals Chamber, ICC-01/04-01/06-3129-AnxA, 3 March 2015, para 8; ICC, *Prosecutor v Ahmad Al Faqi Al Mahdi*, Reparations Order, Trial Chamber VIII, ICC-01/12-01/15, 17 August 2017, para 41.

57 ICC, *Prosecutor v Ahmad Al Faqi Al Mahdi*, ibid paras 106–107.

58 Victims' Rights Directive (n 15) Art 2§1(a).

59 ICC RPE (n 45) rule 85(b).

60 Victims' Rights Directive (n 15) Art 2§1(a).

against Torture, persons having suffered a 'substantial impairment of their fundamental rights' are considered as victims. This is in line with Article 8 of the 1948 Universal Declaration of Human Rights, which stipulates that '[e]veryone has the right to an effective remedy by the competent national tribunals for acts violating the fundamental rights granted to him by the constitution or by law'.[61] Very early in its case law, the ICC looked to the 1985 Basic Principles for Victims for guidance concerning the interpretation of the harm required for someone to qualify as a victim under Rule 85 of the Rules of Procedure and Evidence of the Court:

> The Rome Statute framework does not provide a definition of the concept of harm under Rule 85 of the Rules. However, in accordance with Principle 8 of the Basic principles, a victim may suffer, either individually or collectively, from harm in a variety of different ways such as physical or mental injury, emotional suffering, economic loss or substantial impairment of his or her fundamental rights. This principle provides appropriate guidance.[62]

More recently, the ICC Appeals Chamber recalled

> that the 'concept of "harm", while not defined in the Statute or the Rules of Procedure and Evidence, denotes "hurt, injury and damage"' and that it 'may be material, physical and psychological'. (…) '[M]aterial harm' includes 'lost earnings and the opportunity to work; loss of, or damage to, property; unpaid wages or salaries; other forms of interference with an individual's ability to work; and the loss of savings.[63]

In its 2024 reparations order in the *Ongwen* case, the Trial Chamber identified five types of harm. The relevant excerpt sums up the ICC case law relating to the way these types of harm are defined by the Court, and it would therefore be useful to reproduce it *in extenso*:

> The Chamber notes that physical harm encompasses physical and bodily injury, impairment of the body, pain, and illness. The Chamber emphasises that 'the concept of physical harm is not restricted to the infliction of a physical or bodily injury', and notes that 'hurt, pain or suffering otherwise not caused by a bodily injury can also amount to physical harm'. Moral harm may include psychological harm or trauma, mental pain and anguish, emotional distress, psychosocial harm, and loss of life plan. Material harm refers to loss of or damage to property, loss of earnings, opportunity to work, reduced standard of living and socio-economic opportunities, and loss of schooling and vocational training. Community harm is that suffered by persons as members of a group, family and or community. Lastly, transgenerational harm relates to the phenomenon in which traumatised parents set in motion an intergenerational cycle of dysfunction, handing-down trauma to their children, who themselves did not directly experience the atrocities their parents endured, affecting their children's emotional behaviour, attachment, and well-being as a result.[64]

[61] Universal Declaration of Human Rights (New York, 10 December 1948).

[62] ICC, *Prosecutor v Thomas Lubanga Dyilo*, Decision on victims' participation, Pre-Trial Chamber I, ICC-01/04-01/06, 18 January 2008, para 92.

[63] ICC, *Prosecutor v Bosco Ntaganda*, Judgment on the appeals against the decision of the Trial Chamber VI of 8 March 2021 entitled 'Reparations Order', Appeals Chamber, ICC-01/04-02/06-2782, 12 September 2022, para 703 (citing the Lubanga Order for Reparations (amended); references omitted) (hereinafter 'Ntaganda Appeal judgment on Reparations').

[64] ICC, Ongwen Reparations Order (n 25) para 168.

The ICC has thus adopted a broad enough understanding of harm to recognise the harm suffered by persons as members of a group or a community (community harm) as well as by children of individuals who have themselves suffered trauma due to the commission of an international crime (transgenerational harm).

Examples of community harm include the loss of access to health care and schooling due to the destruction of community property such as schools and hospitals, or the loss of the ability to engage in religious practices due to the destruction of churches.[65] Similarly, in the *Ongwen* case, the pillaging and destruction of livestock resulted in the attacked communities being impaired in carrying out traditional rituals and customs (bridewealth was traditionally paid with livestock and goats were used during traditional rituals to heal health conditions and to bury deceased persons).[66] Preventing these communities 'from engaging in and performing traditional rituals and customs that are important to them' was recognised by the ICC Trial Chamber as constituting community harm.[67]

As for transgenerational harm, after an initially somewhat cautious approach,[68] the ICC has accepted the 'existence of the phenomenon of transgenerational harm'.[69] In the words of the Trial Chamber in the *Ongwen* Reparations Order, 'children of victims of unimaginable atrocities may also experience personal suffering even if they did not personally experience the atrocities that caused their parents' trauma'.[70] Not only children born out of sexual and gender-based crimes but also, more generally, children of direct victims have been found to have suffered transgenerational harm.[71]

ii. Causal Link between the Harm and the Offence

According to the Victims' Rights Directive, the harm must have been 'directly caused by' a criminal offence. The broad or narrow interpretation of this causal link will have a direct (pun intended) impact on the Directive's scope of application.

[65] ibid para 387.

[66] ibid paras 393–98.

[67] ibid para 398.

[68] ICC, Ntaganda Appeal judgment on Reparations (n 63) para 494–95; the Appeals Chamber reversed the finding of the Trial Chamber relating to transgenerational harm:

> 'the Trial Chamber is directed to consider the issue of scientific certainty as to the concept of transgenerational harm and whether it is appropriate to award reparations therefore at this Court and, if so, what the evidentiary requirements are for an applicant to establish that type of harm. (…)
>
> In sum, the Appeals Chamber considers it appropriate for the Trial Chamber to consider whether it needs to address such issues as: the matter of the basis for the concept of transgenerational harm; the evidence needed to establish it; what the evidentiary requirements are for an applicant to prove this type of harm; the need, if any, for a psychological examination of applicants and parents; the need, if any, to exercise caution in assessing applications based on transgenerational harm; whether Mr Ntaganda is liable to repair such harm in the specific context of the crimes of which he has been convicted and taking into consideration the impact, if any, that the protracted armed conflict in the DRC may have as to the possibility of establishing that the trauma associated with transgenerational harm was caused by Mr Ntaganda.'

[69] ICC, *Prosecutor v Bosco Ntaganda*, Addendum to the Reparations Order of 8 March 2021, Trial Chamber II, ICC-01/04-02/06-2659, 14 July 2023, para 175.

[70] Ongwen Reparations Order (n 25) para 207.

[71] ibid para 413.

Concerning the required causal link between the harm and the offence, it is interesting to note that, as it has already been mentioned, the definition of victims enshrined in Rule 85 of the Rules of Procedure and Evidence does not require the harm to be a 'direct' one, except for the specific case of legal persons.[72] Indeed, for natural persons, the ICC has focused on the necessity for the harm to be personal, not direct: 'the notion of victim necessarily implies the existence of personal harm but does not necessarily imply the existence of direct harm.'[73] This led to the recognition by the Court of categories of persons considered as 'indirect victims'. Thus, to identify the beneficiaries of reparations, the ICC has determined that the following categories fall under the concept of 'indirect victims':

i. the family members of direct victims;
ii. anyone who attempted to prevent the commission of one or more of the crimes under consideration;
iii. individuals who suffered harm when helping or intervening on behalf of direct victims; and
iv. other persons who suffered personal harm as a result of these offences.[74]

These victims

> must establish that, as a result of their relationship with the direct victim, the loss, injury, or damage suffered by the latter gives rise to harm to them. It follows that the harm suffered by indirect victims must arise out of the harm suffered by the direct victims, brought about by the commission of the crimes charged.[75]

Moreover, the categories of direct and indirect victims are not mutually exclusive. For example, 'children born out of rape and sexual slavery may qualify as direct victims, as the harm they suffered is a direct result of the commission of the crimes of rape and sexual slavery'.[76] However, 'although children born out of rape are considered direct victims, they may have also suffered transgenerational harm as indirect victims'.[77]

In its case law, the ICC has 'adopt[ed] the "but/for" standard of causation as to the relationship between the crimes and the harm'.[78] According to the Court's established jurisprudence, 'it is required that the crimes for which a person was convicted were the "proximate cause" of the harm for which reparations are sought', meaning that it must be 'assess[ed], *inter alia*, whether it was reasonably foreseeable that the acts and conduct underlying the conviction would cause the resulting harm'.[79]

[72] See ICC RPE (n 45) and relevant text: on the one hand, 'natural persons who have *suffered harm* as a result of' the crime and, on the other, 'organizations or institutions that have *sustained direct harm* to any of their property' (emphasis added).

[73] ICC, *Prosecutor v Lubanga*, Judgment on the appeals Chamber of The Prosecutor and The Defence against Trial Chamber I's Decision on Victims' Participation of 18 January 2008, Appeals Chamber, ICC-01/04-01/06-1432, 11 July 2008, paras 32, 38; ICC, Ntaganda Appeal judgment on Reparations (n 63) para 650.

[74] ICC, *Prosecutor v Lubanga*, Order for Reparations (amended) (n 56) para 6(b); ICC, Ntaganda Appeal judgment on Reparations, ibid para 619.

[75] ICC, *Prosecutor v Lubanga*, Redacted version of 'Decision on "indirect victims"', Trial Chamber I, ICC-01/04-01/06-1813, 8 April 2009, para 49; ICC, Ntaganda Appeal judgment on Reparations, ibid para 617.

[76] ICC, Ntaganda Appeal judgment on Reparations, ibid para 652.

[77] ICC, Ntaganda Reparations Order (n 24), para 182.

[78] Ongwen Reparations Order (n 25) para 419.

[79] ibid para 420.

iii. Definition of Family

With respect to the definition of the term 'family', the jurisprudence of the ICC explains that

> due regard ought to be given to the applicable social and familial structures in the affected communities, subscribing to the understanding that, broadly, in the African continent, (…) the concept of family goes beyond the strict frame of a couple and their children, to include their father and mother, brothers and sisters, and other relatives.[80]

Within the framework of the ICC, in view of the existence of the category of indirect victims,

> it is not relevant whether the family member is close or distant to the direct victim in the abstract, as long as the indirect victim can demonstrate to have suffered personal harm as a result of the commission of the crime against the direct victim.[81]

As previously noted, the Victims' Rights Directive not only explicitly includes family members among the victims it covers but also contains a definition of the term family, which is sufficiently broad[82] to accommodate how family is defined before the ICC.

This general overview of the way the notion of victims has been defined in international criminal law and applied more concretely before the ICC illustrates the importance of the personal scope of application of the 2012 Directive. It is important to be conscious of this practice in order to avoid a narrow interpretation of the notion of victims, which would leave substantial categories of individuals without the benefit of the rights enshrined in the Directive. We will turn to these rights in the next part of this chapter.

III. Substantive Aspects of Victim Participation in Criminal Proceedings

The adoption of the Rome Statute constituted a pivotal shift in the treatment of victims within the realm of international criminal justice: it introduced a framework where victims could, to some extent, be acknowledged and granted specific rights within the proceedings of international criminal tribunals.

This heralded a paradigm shift, as it recognised the previously marginalised role of victims in the pursuit of justice for international crimes. Previously, for example, before the tribunals for the former Yugoslavia and Rwanda, victims – and a very limited number of them – could be protected by international criminal institutions or heard there only in their capacity as witnesses.[83]

[80] ibid para 131 (references omitted).

[81] ibid para 132.

[82] Victims' Rights Directive (n 15) Art 2§1(b).

[83] On the protection and treatment of victims who acted as witnesses before the international criminal tribunals for Former Yugoslavia and Rwanda, see M Bachrach, 'The Protection and Rights of Victims under International Criminal Law' (2000) 34(1) *International Lawyer (ABA)* 7; L Bonnet, 'La protection des témoins par

Victims appearing before the ICC and international or hybrid tribunals established thereafter are entitled to specific rights that are also recognised by international criminal law instruments. These rights are mainly based on the 1985 Declaration, often referred to as the Magna Carta of victims' rights by legal scholars.[84] They can be categorised into three main groups: the right to protection and support, the right to participate in judicial proceedings, and the right to receive reparations for the harm they have suffered.

At the European level, the Victims' Rights Directive provides a detailed and comprehensive range of rights for victims. As is the case under international criminal law, victims are not only entitled to protection and support but also have the right to participate in legal proceedings and seek reparation for the harm they have suffered. In addition to these fundamental rights, other rights are often advocated for, including the right to be recognised and treated with respect, the right to receive information about the legal process and their case, the right to privacy, and the right to file a complaint to ensure their grievances are addressed. These additional rights have been considered crucial for ensuring that victims are adequately supported and have their dignity and well-being respected throughout the justice process.

The disparities between the two regimes are especially pronounced in the definition and implementation of victims' rights. This is due to their divergent scope and context, as well as the varying nature of the crimes they address and the judicial frameworks within which they operate. As a result, the EU system provides a significantly more detailed and comprehensive outline of victims' rights compared to the other regime. The ICC practice, however, offers precious input as to dealing with mass crimes prosecuted in extraterritorial contexts.

In this part of the chapter, we will delve into the substantive aspects of victims' rights in criminal proceedings. As previously mentioned, we will conduct a comparison of the scope of application of the Victims' Rights Directive and the suggested amendment with the provisions outlined in relevant international law instruments. This comparison will primarily focus on three fundamental categories of rights that are shared by both regimes: the right to file a complaint or launch proceedings (section III.A), the right to protection and support (section III.B), the right to participation (section III.C), and the right to reparation (section III.D).

A. Right to File a Complaint or Launch Proceedings

The Victims' Rights Directive and international criminal law embody distinct approaches to the victim's part in the initiation of criminal proceedings, each shaped by its unique legal and operational context.

le Tribunal pénal international pour l'ex-Yougoslavie' (2019) 05 *Droits fondamentaux*, available at www.crdh.fr/wp-content/uploads/la_protection_des_temoins_par_le_tpiy.pdf; Å Rydberg, 'Case Analysis: The Protection of the Interests of Witnesses – The ICTY in Comparison to the Future ICC' (1999) 12(2) *Leiden Journal of International Law* 455; MB Dembour and E Haslam, 'Silencing Hearings? Victim-Witnesses at War Crimes Trials' (2004) 15(1) *European Journal of International Law* 151.

[84] 1985 UN Declaration (n 43).

On the one hand, the Directive emphasises the critical role of crime reporting in the criminal justice process, recognising it as the initial step that triggers most domestic criminal proceedings. The Directive outlines several provisions aimed at encouraging victims to report crimes, facilitating their access to justice, and ensuring that their reports are handled with the utmost sensitivity and professionalism. The importance given to crime reporting is underlined right from the Preamble:

> In order to encourage and facilitate reporting of crimes and to allow victims to break the cycle of repeat victimization, it is essential that reliable support services are available to victims and that competent authorities are prepared to respond to victims' reports in a respectful, sensitive, professional and non-discriminatory manner. This could increase victims' confidence in the criminal justice systems of Member States and reduce the number of unreported crimes. Practitioners who are likely to receive complaints from victims with regard to criminal offences should be appropriately trained to facilitate reporting of crimes, and measures should be put in place to enable third-party reporting, including by civil society organisations. It should be possible to make use of communication technology, such as e-mail, video recordings or online electronic forms for making complaints.[85]

The Directive consequently highlights the importance of reliable support services for victims and the need for authorities to respond to reports in a respectful, sensitive, and non-discriminatory manner. The provision emphasises that proper training for practitioners, the possibility of third-party reporting (eg by civil society organisations), and the use of communication technologies for submitting complaints can significantly increase victims' confidence in the justice system and reduce the number of unreported crimes.

The 2023 Commission Proposal to revise the Victims' Rights Directive aims to further strengthen these provisions, with the sixth preambular Recital stressing the importance of improving crime reporting across the EU to combat impunity, avoid repeat victimisation, and ensure safer societies.[86] Notably, the Proposal includes specific provisions to protect vulnerable victims, such as irregular migrants, children, and those in detention, ensuring they can report crimes in safe and confidential environments.[87] Article 5a of the Proposal states that:

> 1. Member States shall ensure that victims can report criminal offences to the competent authorities through easily accessible, user friendly information and communication technologies. Such possibility shall include submission of evidence where feasible.
> 2. Member States shall take the necessary measures to encourage any person who knows about or suspects, in good faith, that criminal offences have been committed, or that further acts of violence are to be expected, to report this to the competent authorities.
> 3. Member States shall ensure that victims can effectively report crimes committed in detention facilities. Detention facilities shall include in addition to jails, detention centres and holding cells for suspects and accused, specialized detention facilities for applicants of international protection and pre-removal centres, and accommodation centres where applicants and beneficiaries of international protection are located.

[85] Victims' Rights Directive (n 15) para 63.
[86] 2023 Commission Proposal (n 20) Recital 6.
[87] ibid Art 5a.

4. Where children report criminal offences, Member States shall ensure the reporting procedures are safe, confidential, designed and accessible in a child-friendly manner and use language in accordance with their age and maturity.
5. Member States shall ensure that the competent authorities coming in contact with a victim reporting crimes are prohibited from transferring personal data pertaining to the residence status of the victim to competent migration authorities, at least until completion of the first individual assessment referred to in Article 22.

This proposal hence introduces a dedicated provision on crime reporting, mandating that Member States ensure victims can report crimes through accessible and user-friendly information and communication technologies. It also encourages the reporting of crimes by third parties and mandates protection for victims in detention facilities and children, ensuring their safety and privacy during the reporting process. Crucially, it prohibits the transfer of personal data concerning the residence status of victims to migration authorities during the initial stages of reporting, thus reducing the fear of deportation among irregular migrants. Therefore, the proposed amendments to the Victims' Rights Directive appear to pave the way for elevating minimum standards in relation to crime reporting, with the ultimate goal of facilitating the filing of direct complaints before the domestic courts.

On the other hand, the Rome Statute, which governs the ICC, does not provide a formal mechanism for victims to file complaints directly with the Court or its Office of the Prosecutor (OTP). The Rome Statute allows the Prosecutor to initiate investigations based on information about crimes within the Court's jurisdiction, but victims and their relatives cannot directly trigger the Court's jurisdiction. Instead, victims can submit 'communications' to the Prosecutor, which may prompt the initiation of an investigation *proprio motu* (on the Prosecutor's own initiative).[88]

The ICC Appeals Chamber has clarified that while victims can participate in pre-trial proceedings, they do not have the right to initiate proceedings under Article 15 of the Statute. In the *Situation in Afghanistan*, the ICC Appeals Chamber held that while '[v]ictims may participate in the proceedings before the pre-trial chamber, pursuant to Article 15(3) of the Statute', they 'do not have the right to trigger proceedings under article 15 [as] this right is reserved for the Prosecutor'.[89]

Another approach was envisaged during the negotiation of the Statute:

> There was broad support for the principle of victims having a role at this stage of the Court's consideration of admissibility questions, because of the inclusion of provisions to that effect in articles 15 and 19 of the Statute. However, the degree and nature of that participation generated lengthy discussions. On the one hand, there were delegations that believed that victims should participate as full parties in proceedings at this stage, including the right to request the hearing, to receive communications from all parties, and to appeal a decision not to authorize an investigation. [...] Other delegations believed that allowing this degree of participation was contrary to the intent of article 15, which was to ensure expeditious consideration of the

[88] Rome Statute (n 2) Art 15(3).

[89] ICC, *Situation in the Islamic Republic of Afghanistan*, Reasons for the Appeals Chamber's oral decision dismissing as inadmissible the victims' appeals against the decision rejecting the authorization of an investigation into the situation in Afghanistan, Appeals Chamber, ICC-02/17-137, 4 March 2020, para 12 citing Transcript of hearing, 5 December 2019, ICC-02/17-T-002-ENG, p 3, line 2 to p 4, line 3.

> Prosecutor's request for authorization of an investigation. Moreover, some delegations argued that if victims were permitted to play an extensive role in article proceedings, then for reasons of fairness and balance, States should be given equal rights and opportunities to make representations and participate in article 15 hearings. In the end, this argument was not pursued since it was acknowledged that the right of victims to make representations at this stage was set out in the Statute, whereas no such right existed for States.[90]

The degree and nature of victim participation in these early stages have, therefore, been the subject of significant debate, with some delegations advocating for full participation rights for victims, including the right to request hearings and appeal decisions.[91] However, concerns about the expeditiousness of proceedings and the balance between victims' and states' rights ultimately limited the extent of victims' involvement.

Despite the lack of a formal complaint mechanism, the OTP has established an online portal where victims and other parties can submit information about alleged crimes. Victims, especially in recent investigations, are encouraged to provide information through this system. For instance, in the Ukrainian situation,

> At the current investigation stage, victims can communicate with the Court in a number of ways:
>
> Any individual, group or State can send information to the Office of the Prosecutor regarding any alleged crimes in the Ukraine Situation falling under the jurisdiction of the Court. Persons with such information, including affected communities of the situation, can communicate to the Office of the Prosecutor any relevant information for the purposes of the investigation on the following dedicated portal.
>
> […].[92]

Similar opportunities are now publicised for all other situations.[93] While this system allows victims to provide relevant information, it does not obligate the Prosecutor to launch an investigation or even review the submitted information.

As stated before, international criminal law conventions are intended to apply in domestic criminal proceedings, which could explain why they give greater weight to crime reporting and victim complaints, similar to the approaches adopted in the European system.

For instance, Article 12 of the Draft Articles on Crimes Against Humanity provides:

> 1. Each State shall take the necessary measures to ensure that:
>   a. Any person who alleges that acts constituting crimes against humanity have been or are being committed has the right to complain to the competent authorities.

[90] JT Holmes, 'Jurisdiction and Admissibility' in R Lee (ed), *The ICC: Elements of Crimes and Rules of Procedure and Evidence* (Transnational, 2001) 332–33.

[91] Draft Statute for an International Criminal Court, Report of the International Law Commission on its Forty-Sixth Session, 2 May-22 July 1994, UN GAOR, 49th sees., Supp. No. 10, UN Doc A/49/10, 1994, § 117. See W Schabas and G Pecorella, 'Article 13. Exercise of Jurisdiction' in K Ambos (ed), *Rome Statute of the International Criminal Court: Article by Article Commentary*, 4th edn (Beck/Nomos/Hart, 2022) para 6.

[92] ICC, Information for victims: Ukraine, available at www.icc-cpi.int/victims/ukraine.

[93] See, eg, ICC, Information for victims: State of Palestine, available at www.icc-cpi.int/victims/state-palestine; ICC, Information for victims: Situation in the Bolivarian Republic of Venezuela I, available at www.icc-cpi.int/victims/situation-bolivarian-republic-venezuela-i; ICC, Information for victims: Republic of the Philippines, available at www.icc-cpi.int/victims/republic-philippines; ICC, Information for victims: Bangladesh/Myanmar, available at www.icc-cpi.int/victims/bangladesh-myanmar.

Similarly, the Ljubljana – The Hague Convention provides specifically for a 'Right to complain' in its Article 12:

> 1. Each State Party shall take the necessary measures to ensure that any person who alleges that crimes to which State Party applies this Convention in accordance with article 2 have been or are being committed has the right to complain to its competent authorities.
> 2. State Parties shall undertake to examine any received complaints, promptly and impartially, in accordance with their domestic law and, where appropriate, relevant domestic policies.

The differences in approaches to crime reporting can be attributed to the distinct contexts in which these legal frameworks operate. The Victims' Rights Directive – like to some extent the international criminal law conventions – focuses on domestic criminal proceedings within the EU, where the immediate and accessible reporting of crimes is essential to the functioning of national justice systems. The Directive thus places a strong emphasis on encouraging and facilitating crime reporting, particularly for vulnerable groups such as irregular migrants and children.

In contrast, the Rome Statute deals with crimes of a far broader scope and often involves a large number of victims across multiple jurisdictions. The ICC's extraterritorial mandate and the scale of the crimes within its jurisdiction present significant challenges for a crime reporting mechanism comparable to that prescribed by the Victims' Rights Directive or any domestic criminal system.

That being said, EU States could find themselves in the same position to some extent. The 2023 Commission Proposal to revise the 2012 Victims' Rights Directive, which emphasises ensuring that crime reporting is not contingent on victims' residence status,[94] is particularly relevant when considering crimes under the jurisdiction of the ICC. Victims located outside the territory of the State where proceedings are held, especially in cases involving extraterritorial jurisdiction, face additional challenges in accessing justice. The Commission's approach to protecting the rights of non-resident victims could inform improvements in international law, particularly regarding the facilitation of crime reporting and victim participation in transnational contexts.

The Victims' Rights Directive and the Rome Statute represent two different approaches to crime reporting in criminal proceedings, shaped by their respective legal and operational contexts. While the 2012 Directive provides a detailed and accessible framework for crime reporting within the EU, the Rome Statute's approach reflects the complexities of international criminal justice. As the EU continues to refine its victim protection framework, the experiences and lessons learned from international criminal law could offer valuable insights for enhancing victim participation in cases involving transnational crimes and large numbers of victims.

B. Right to Protection

Victims involved in any criminal justice system are susceptible to intimidation and retaliation, along with their families, as a result of their involvement in criminal proceedings.

[94] 2023 Commission Proposal (n 20) Arts 5a, paras 3 and 5; Art 8(6).

Both domestic and international criminal justice systems traditionally offer safeguards for victims who are crucial as witnesses in prosecutions.

The 2012 Directive represents a significant advancement in the protection and support of crime victims within Member States, offering a detailed and comprehensive framework to ensure their safety, dignity, and well-being throughout the criminal justice process. The Directive outlines key rights designed to protect victims and their families from further harm, such as secondary victimisation, intimidation, and retaliation, as well as to safeguard their dignity during criminal proceedings.

Article 18 of the Directive establishes the right to protection for victims and their families, mandating that Member States implement measures to protect them from secondary and repeat victimisation, emotional or psychological harm, and threats to their dignity during questioning and testimony. Article 19 further emphasises the right to avoid contact between the victim and the offender, while Article 20 focuses on protecting victims during criminal investigations. The Directive also includes the right to privacy (Article 21) and provides special protection measures for victims with specific needs, particularly those who have been victims of severe crimes, or crimes committed with bias or discriminatory motives (Articles 22–24).

In addition to protection rights, the Directive ensures that victims have access to necessary support services. Article 4(a) establishes the right to information regarding available support, including medical, psychological, and alternative accommodation services. Articles 8 and 9 further detail the right to access victim support services, ensuring that victims receive the assistance they need.

The 2023 Commission Proposal to revise the 2012 Victims' Rights Directive goes further. Article 3a suggests establishing an accessible, free and confidential victims' helpline in each Member State. These helplines would provide not only information but also emotional support and referrals to specialised services. More importantly, the 2023 Commission Proposal would establish a burden on the Member States to

> ensure that victims are contacted by the relevant general or specialised support services if the individual assessment referred to in Article 22 demonstrates the need for support and the victim consents to be contacted by support services or if the victim requests support.[95]

The amendments suggested to Article 9, and the introduction of new provisions (9a, 10a, and 10b) aim to strengthen the support framework for victims, ensuring that specialised, integrated, and accessible services are available, particularly for those with specific needs, including children.

International criminal law also provides a framework for the protection of victims. Every convention provides some right to protection for victims, witnesses, and their families. While the EU Directive offers a comprehensive and detailed protection framework, international criminal law, through instruments like the International Law Commission's 2019 Draft Articles on Crimes Against Humanity, provides similar protections, though they may be less explicitly detailed in their wording. For example, Article 12(1)(b) guarantees the right to protection for complainants, victims, witnesses, and their relatives, safeguarding them from ill-treatment or intimidation due to their

[95] ibid Art 8.

participation in criminal proceedings. The accompanying commentary expands on these protections, emphasising the inclusion of psychological well-being, dignity, and privacy within the scope of protection. The commentary also outlines specific protective measures, such as the use of electronic means to present evidence, in-camera proceedings, and the relocation of victims and witnesses, all while maintaining a balance with the rights of the accused. The Ljubljana – The Hague Convention also mandates protection for victims, witnesses, experts, and other participants in legal proceedings (Article 82). It specifies that these protections should include measures against retaliation or intimidation, such as relocating victims, limiting disclosure of their identities, and using technology to ensure their safety and privacy during testimony. Again, these protections are to be balanced with the defendant's right to due process.

This is in line with the extensive practice developed by the ICTY and the ICTR regarding the protection of victims and witnesses that led to a uniform and effective methodology of protection.[96] Their law and practice prepared the terrain for the insertion of more detailed provisions on victims' protection before the ICC.[97] This right to protection is principally provided in Article 68, paragraphs 1, 2, 4 and 5 of the Rome Statute:

> 1. The Court shall take appropriate measures to protect the safety, physical and psychological well-being, dignity and privacy of victims and witnesses. In so doing, the Court shall have regard to all relevant factors, including age, gender as defined in Article 7, paragraph 3, and health, and the nature of the crime, in particular, but not limited to, where the crime involves sexual or gender violence or violence against the children. The Prosecutor shall take such measures particularly during the investigation and prosecution of such crimes. These measures shall not be prejudicial to or inconsistent with the rights of the accused and a fair and impartial trial.
> 2. As an exception to the principle of public hearings provided for in Article 67, the Chambers of the Court may, to protect victims and witnesses or an accused, conduct any part of the proceedings in camera or allow the presentation of evidence by electronic or other special means. In particular, such measures shall be implemented in the case of a victim of sexual violence or a child who is a victim or a witness, unless otherwise ordered by the Court, having regard to all the circumstances, particularly the views of the victim or witness.
>
> […]
>
> 4. The Victims and Witnesses Unit may advise the Prosecutor and the Court on appropriate protective measures, security arrangements, counselling and assistance as referred to in Article 43, paragraph 6.

[96] See V Morris and MP Scharf, *The International Criminal Tribunal for Rwanda* (Transnational Publishers, 1998) 136: 'Two witnesses who testified before the Rwanda Tribunal in the *Jean-Paul Akayesu case* and the *Obed Ruzindana case*, were also killed'. See also the Second Annual Report of the ICTR covering the period from 1 July 1996 to 30 June 1997, UN Doc A/52/582-s/1997/868, 6 June 1997, para 51.

[97] The ICTY and the ICTR Statutes both contain in Article 22 and 21 the same provision: 'The International Tribunal shall provide in its rules of procedure and evidence for the protection of victims and witnesses. Such protection measures shall include, but shall not be limited to, the conduct of *in camera* proceedings and the protection of the victim's identity.' Rule 75 of both Tribunals' Rules of Procedure and Evidence provides specification, including concealing identities, using pseudonyms, altering voices, or holding closed sessions, can be requested by the prosecution, defence, the witness or victim themselves, or initiated by the Tribunal. The rule also requires the Tribunal to balance these protective measures with the rights of the accused to a fair and public trial. Protective measures must not undermine the fairness of the proceedings.

5. Where the disclosure of evidence or information pursuant to this Statute may lead to the grave endangerment of the security of a witness or his or her family, the Prosecutor may, for the purposes of any proceedings conducted prior to the commencement of the trial, withhold such evidence or information and instead submit a summary thereof. Such measures shall be exercised in a manner which is not prejudicial to or inconsistent with the rights of the accused and a fair and impartial trial.

Moreover, Rule 86 of the Rules of Procedure and Evidence states as a general principle that:

> A Chamber in making any direction or order, and other organs of the Court in performing their functions under the Statute or the Rules, shall take into account the needs of all victims and witnesses in accordance with article 68, in particular, children, elderly persons, persons with disabilities and victims of sexual or gender violence.

The ICC practice interpreted Article 68 as affording a non-derogable right to protection to victims and witnesses and, inversely, an obligation on all organs of the Court – including the Prosecutor[98] – at all stages of the proceedings,[99] to protect the life, dignity, and well-being of victims and witnesses.[100]

[98] Specific provisions impose obligations to the Prosecution with respect to victims. Article 54(1)(b) of the Rome Statute (n 2) asks of them and their Office to '[t]ake appropriate measures to ensure the effective investigation and prosecution of crimes within the jurisdiction of the Court, and in doing so, respect the interests and personal circumstances of victims and witnesses, including age, gender as defined in article 7, Paragraph 3, and health, and take into account the nature of the crime, in particular where it involves sexual violence, gender violence or violence against children'.

[99] In the Burundi situation, when authorising the Prosecutor to open an investigation, Pre-Trial Chamber III specified that the Prosecutor should ensure the protection of victims even before the opening of the investigation: 'the Chamber finds it imperative to clarify that, contrary to the Prosecutor's argument, meaningful steps to protect victims and (potential) witnesses may already be undertaken under Article 68(1) of the Statute prior to the authorization of an investigation by a Pre-Trial Chamber pursuant to Article 15 of the Statute. Article 68(1) of the Statute provides in the relevant part that the Prosecutor "shall take such measures particularly during the investigation and prosecution" of crimes within the jurisdiction of the Court. The use of "particularly" indicates that such measures are not confined to the investigation and prosecution stages and may, therefore, also be applied at the preliminary examination stage. Indeed, pursuant to Article 15(2) of the Statute, the Prosecutor may receive written or oral testimony at the seat of the Court at this stage and may even, under rule 47 of the Rules, request the Pre-Trial Chamber to take measures as may be necessary to ensure the efficiency and integrity of the proceedings. In such circumstances, the Prosecutor, or the Pre Trial Chamber acting under rule 47 of the Rules and Article 57(3)(c) of the Statute, would be required to take measures to protect the safety and well-being of those witnesses. Further, the fact that States Parties are not obliged to cooperate with the Court prior to the initiation of an investigation does not prevent the Prosecutor from seeking their voluntary cooperation in the implementation of protective measures. The same would apply to States not Parties to the Statute and non-State entities. Therefore, measures [...] could be implemented before a Pre-Trial Chamber decides on an Article 15 request. Nevertheless, the steps that the Prosecutor can take are subject to consultation with and the cooperation of the VWU, taking into consideration its unique mandate pursuant to Article 43(6) of the Statute and rules 17 to 19 of the Rules.' ICC, *Situation in the Republic of Burundi*, Public Redacted Version of 'Decision Pursuant to Article 15 of the Rome Statute on the Authorization of an Investigation into the Situation in the Republic of Burundi', ICC-01/17-X-9-US-Exp, 25 October 2017, Pre-Trial Chamber III, ICC-01/17-9-Red, 9 November 2017, para 15.

[100] ICC, *Situation in the Democratic Republic of the Congo*, Decision on Protective Measures Requested by Applicants 01/04-1/dp to 01/04-6/dp, Pre-Trial Chamber I, ICC-01/04-73, 21 July 2005, 3; *Prosecutor v Bemba*, Second Redacted version of 'Decision on "Prosecution's Information to Trial Chamber III on issues involving witness CAR-OTP-PPPP-0169"' (ICC-01/05-01/08-3138-Conf-Red) and 'Defence Urgent Submissions on the 5 August Letter (ICC-01/05-01/08-3139-Conf)' of 2 October 2014, Trial Chamber III, ICC-01/05-01/08-3154-Red2, 11 December 2014.

The ICC Chambers have ordered a wide range of protective measures throughout the years, going from *in camera* hearings to reinstallation. In some cases, when it was considered the only available means to comply with the obligation of protection victims and witnesses were able to testify anonymously.[101] Some measures become mandatory when requested by minors or victims of sexual violence.[102]

A comparative analysis of the Victims' Rights Directive and international criminal law instruments reveals that while the EU Directive provides a more detailed articulation of victims' rights, the substance of these rights is largely mirrored in international law. However, the specificity of the Victims' Rights Directive, which enshrines these rights in detailed provisions, contrasts with the often inferred or broadly stated rights in international criminal law, such as those within the Draft Articles on Crimes against Humanity or the Ljubljana – The Hague Convention.

The question of whether victims of core international crimes should be considered as entitled to specific protection is particularly relevant.[103] Core international crimes, by their nature – often involving severe, transnational violations – create unique vulnerabilities for victims, especially when they or their families are located in foreign territories where they may lack adequate protection from local authorities. This issue is crucial, as victims' willingness to participate in proceedings can be significantly undermined by fears of retaliation or intimidation. Therefore, the experiences and lessons learned from implementing victims' protection in proceedings before the ICC could be instrumental in refining international protections, particularly for cases with transnational dimensions.

In light of the complex and hazardous contexts in which core international crimes are perpetrated, it is imperative to acknowledge victims of such crimes as a vulnerable group deserving of comprehensive protective measures. Given the renewed prominence of universal jurisdiction and transnational prosecution, it is incumbent upon Member States of the European Union to be mindful of this imperative.

C. Right to Participation

Victims' participation in criminal proceedings is crucial to an effective access to justice. As such, the Victims' Rights Directive recognises victims' right to be heard and present evidence during (domestic) criminal proceedings.[104] It is a widespread practice for victims to participate in domestic proceedings, particularly within continental justice

[101] ICC, *Prosecutor v Lubanga*, Judgment on the Prosecutor's appeal against the decision of Pre-Trial Chamber I entitled 'Decision Establishing General Principles Governing Applications to Restrict Disclosure pursuant to Rule 81(2) and (4) of the Rules of Procedure and Evidence', Appeals Chamber, ICC-01/04-01/06-568, 13 October 2006; *Prosecutor v Lubanga*, Decision on Protective Measures requested by Applicants 01/04-1/dp to 01/04-6/dp, Pre-Trial Chamber I, ICC-01/04-73, 21 July 2005.

[102] ICC, *Prosecutor v Bemba*, Public Redacted Version of Decision on the modalities of the presentation of additional evidence pursuant to Articles 64(6)(b) and (d) and 69(3) of the Rome Statute, Trial Chamber III, ICC-01/05-01/08-3157-Red, 8 October 2014.

[103] 2023 Commission Proposal (n 20) Art 9, para 3(b). Proposed Art 9, para 3(b) appears to imply this concept of vulnerability: 'targeted and integrated support, including trauma support and counselling, for victims with specific needs, such as victims [....] of core international crimes'.

[104] Victims' Rights Directive (n 15) para 42.

systems. The inclusion of certain rights to participation within the Directive was therefore normal. However, the extent of victims' involvement and the specific form of their participation remain guided by national law and can differ from one State to another.

The 2023 Commission Proposal to revise the Victims' Rights Directive aims to further enhance victims' participation in criminal proceedings. Its authors underlined in its preamble that '[f]or victims to sense that justice is done and to be able to defend their interest, it is important that they are present and able to actively participate in the criminal proceedings.'[105] This involves introducing a new Article 10a that guarantees the right to receive assistance in court. Additionally, Article 10b proposes establishing the right for victims to challenge decisions made during court proceedings that affect them directly.

The Rome Statute is often celebrated for its groundbreaking inclusion of victims' rights, particularly the right to participate in criminal proceedings. Traditionally, in international criminal justice systems rooted in common law traditions, victims were largely confined to the role of witnesses, with little opportunity to influence the proceedings beyond their testimony. The Rome Statute marked a significant departure from this model by explicitly providing victims with a role that extends beyond oral testimony, allowing them to present their views and concerns during various stages of the trial. This innovation reflects a broader commitment to ensuring that victims' voices are heard within the justice process, aligning with contemporary principles of restorative justice.

Article 68(3) of the Rome Statute encapsulates this right to participation,[106] stating:

> Where the personal interests of the victims are affected, the Court shall permit their views and concerns to be presented and considered at stages of the proceedings determined to be appropriate by the Court and in a manner which is not prejudicial to or inconsistent with the rights of the accused and a fair and impartial trial. Such views and concerns may be presented by the legal representatives of the victims where the Court considers it appropriate, in accordance with the Rules of Procedure and Evidence.

This provision, though broad and somewhat equivocal, draws inspiration from the UN Declaration of Basic Principles of Justice for Victims of Crime and Abuse of Power of 1985.[107] Paragraph 6(b) of the Declaration similarly advocates for the inclusion of victims' views and concerns at appropriate stages of proceedings, ensuring that their involvement does not prejudice the rights of the accused and is consistent with the relevant national legal frameworks. This language, designed for flexible implementation across diverse legal systems, has since been incorporated into various international legal instruments. For instance, Article 25(3) of the UN Convention against Transnational

[105] 2023 Commission Proposal (n 20) preambular recital 9.

[106] Other provisions relate to victims' participation in the proceedings. Art 15(3) provides for a conditioned right to make representations before the Court prior to the beginning of an investigation. Article 19(3) provides the unconditioned right to submit observations 'in proceedings with respect to jurisdiction or admissibility'. See for instance ICC, *Prosecutor v Lubanga*, Decision on the Applications for Participation in the Proceedings of a/0001/06, a/0002/06 and a/0003/06 in the case of the Prosecutor v. Thomas Lubanga Dyilo and of the investigation in the Democratic Republic of the Congo, Pre-Trial Chamber I, ICC-01/04-01/06-228, 28 July 2006. Article 75 (3) provides for the right for victims to be heard before decisions on reparations and the right to intervene on appeals concerning reparations' orders.

[107] 1985 UN Declaration (n 43) para 6(b).

Organized Crime,[108] and Article 12(2) of the Draft Articles on Prevention and Punishment of Crimes Against Humanity echo this principle,[109] mandating that victims' perspectives be considered during criminal proceedings, provided such consideration does not infringe on the rights of the defence.

In the initial stages of the ICC proceedings, the judges deliberated the fact that Article 68(3) of the Rome Statute placed an obligation upon them:

> With regard to Article 68(3), the Chamber considers that it imposes an obligation on the Court vis-à-vis victims. The use of the present tense in the French version of the text ('la Cour permet') makes it quite clear that the victims' guaranteed right of access to the Court entails a positive obligation for the Court to enable them to exercise that right concretely and effectively. It follows that the Chamber has a dual obligation: on the one hand, to allow victims to present their views and concerns, and, on the other, to examine them.[110]

Despite the promising framework established by the Rome Statute, the actual implementation of victims' participation in ICC trials has been more limited. In practice, victim participation is in almost all cases channelled through legal representatives,[111] who may represent large groups of victims,[112] potentially diluting the individual voices within the collective representation. The ICC's Rules of Procedure and Evidence offer some guidance on the role of these legal representatives, allowing them to participate in hearings and question witnesses, though the Court retains the discretion to restrict their participation to written submissions.[113] In practice, the victims are kept out of the courtroom and cannot access the documentation produced during and around the proceedings.[114] Consequently, the participation of victims has become increasingly peripheral in the trials conducted before the ICC, with only a small number of victims being heard directly by the Court.[115]

While the peripheral role of victims in ICC proceedings raises important questions about the effectiveness of the right to participation as envisioned by the Rome Statute, its experience highlights the complexity of implementing meaningful victim participation, especially in cases involving a large number of victims or in situations where victims are represented collectively or any situation featuring extraterritorial aspects. As the international community continues to refine the mechanisms

[108] UN Convention against Transnational Organized Crime (n 10).

[109] Draft Articles on Crimes Against Humanity (n 13) commentary to Art 12, para 3.

[110] ICC, *Prosecutor v Lubanga*, Decision on the Applications for Participation in the Proceedings of VPRS 1, VPRS 2, VPRS 3, VPRS 4, VPRS 5 and VPRS 6, Pre-Trial Chamber I, ICC-01/04-101, 17 January 2006, para 71.

[111] Outside of the wording of Art 68(3), the possibility of legal representation is set in Rules 90 and 91 of the ICC RPE (n 45).

[112] For instance, in the *Bemba* case, 5,229 victims were represented by a sole legal representative. ICC, *Prosecutor v Bemba*, Fifth Decision on Victims' Issues Concerning Common Legal Representation of Victims, Pre-Trial Chamber III, ICC-01/05-01/08-322, 16 December 2008, para 7.

[113] See, eg, ICC, *Prosecutor v Katanga and Ngudjolo*, Decision on the Set of Procedural Rights Attached to Procedural Status of Victim at the Pre-Trial Stage of the Case, Pre-Trial Chamber I, ICC-01/04-01/07-474, 15 May 2008, para 43.

[114] ICC, *Prosecutor v Bemba*, Corrigendum to Decision on the participation of victims and on 86 applications by victims to participate in the proceedings, Trial Chamber III, ICC-01/05-01/08-807-Corr, 14 July 2010, para 47; *Prosecutor v Banda*, Decision on the participation of victims in the trial proceedings, Trial Chamber IV, ICC-02/05-03/09-545, 20 March 2014, para 39.

[115] See Hébert-Dolbec (n 1).

for victim participation in criminal proceedings, the lessons learned from the ICC's practices could inform future developments in both international and European legal frameworks, ensuring that victims' rights are upheld without compromising the fairness and impartiality of trials.

D. Right to Reparation

The European Union's approach to victims' rights, as articulated in the Victims' Rights Directive, reflects a comprehensive view of reparation. Article 16 of the Directive ensures that victims have the right to a decision on compensation from offenders during criminal proceedings. This provision aligns with the broader international legal trend of ensuring that victims are not merely entitled to seek reparation but are guaranteed a mechanism to obtain it. Additionally, Article 15 of the Directive grants victims the right to the return of their property, directly addressing the need for restitution as a key element of reparation.

The noteworthy suggestion within the 2023 Commission Proposal concerning reparation primarily relates to the allocation of compensation payment. The Commission's amendment to Article 16, paragraph 2, aims:

> to make it mandatory for Member States to pay compensation due from the offender upfront to the victim immediately after judgment and then seek the reimbursement of the compensation from the offender.

This will simplify the process of compensating victims and is consistent with recent developments in international criminal law.

In international criminal law, the discourse on victims' right to reparation has been centered on two pivotal issues: the existence of a right to obtain reparation versus merely to seek reparation and the range of reparation forms encompassed by such a right. The International Law Commission, in its 2019 Draft Articles on Crimes Against Humanity, embraced an expansive interpretation of these issues. The Draft Articles on Crimes Against Humanity recognised that victims possess a right to obtain reparation, thereby affirming that this right is not limited to seeking redress but extends to ensuring that victims receive reparations for material and moral damages.[116] This recognition encompasses a broad spectrum of reparation forms, including restitution, compensation, satisfaction, rehabilitation, cessation, and guarantees of non-repetition.[117] As sources of this right to obtain reparation, the commentary to the draft article refers to the right to an effective remedy under human rights law (the 1948 Universal Declaration of Human Rights, the 1966 International Covenant on Civil and Political Rights and 'some regional human rights treaties') as well as to Article 14 of the 1984 UN Convention against Torture and Article 24 of the 2006 International Convention on Enforced Disappearance.[118]

[116] Draft Articles on Crimes Against Humanity (n 13) commentary to Art 12, para 3.
[117] ibid.
[118] ibid para 17.

Restitution and compensation, as specific forms of reparation, are given particular emphasis within international legal frameworks. Restitution aims to restore the victim to the original situation before the crime occurred, while compensation provides monetary reparation for damages that cannot be undone by restitution alone. The Draft Articles on Crimes Against Humanity, as well as other legal instruments such as the Rome Statute, reinforce the importance of these two forms of reparation. Article 75 of the Rome Statute underscores the Court's responsibility to establish principles regarding reparations, including restitution, compensation, and rehabilitation. It further highlights the potential for reparations to include measures that are symbolic, preventive, or transformative, thus broadening the understanding of how justice can be served.

Although the draft of the Ljubljana – The Hague Convention, which served as the basis for the negotiations, provided for the right to *seek* reparation,[119] in the final text adopted at the Ljubljana Conference, the phrasing was changed into the more open-ended 'right to reparation',[120] which indicates that at least some of the participants considered that a mere right to seek reparation was insufficient. Moreover, Article 83§ 3 of the Convention provides for the possibility of obtaining reparation in a State different from the one which convicted the person accused of international crimes:

> Each State Party shall, to the extent provided for in its domestic law and if so requested, give effect to a judgment or order in criminal proceedings, issued in accordance with the domestic law of the requesting State Party, to provide restitution, compensation or rehabilitation to victims of crimes to which it applies this Convention.[121]

The ICC's jurisprudence further illustrates the application of these principles. In the Al Mahdi case, for example, the Court ordered a range of reparations, including individual reparations for those directly affected by the destruction of cultural heritage, collective reparations through the rehabilitation of destroyed sites, and symbolic reparations such as memorials and commemoration.[122] The Court also held the convicted individual financially liable, determining the scope of their responsibility for reparations, as seen in the Ntaganda case, where a $30 million reparations order was issued.[123] In practice, however, direct reparations to victims remain more modest and symbolic. The reparation order is delivered against the culprit, who is generally indigent.[124] As a consequence, the ICC's reparations framework is supported by the Trust Fund for Victims, an independent fund established by the Rome Statute.[125] This Fund plays

[119] Draft Convention on International Cooperation in the Investigation and Prosecution of the Crime of Genocide, Crimes against Humanity, War Crimes and other International Crimes (version 30/11/2022), MLA/2, 8 May 2023, Art 75(1), available at www.gov.si/assets/ministrstva/MZEZ/projekti/MLA-pobuda/20221130-ENG-MLA-DRAFT-CONVENTION-CLEAN.pdf.

[120] Ljubljana – The Hague Convention (n 14) Art 83(1).

[121] ibid Art 83(3).

[122] ICC, *Prosecutor v Ahmad Al Faqi Al Mahdi*, (n 56).

[123] ICC, Ntaganda Reparations Order (n 24); ICC, Ntaganda Appeal judgment on Reparations (n 65).

[124] ICC, *Prosecutor v Lubanga*, Judgment on the appeals against the 'Decision establishing the principles and procedures to be applied to reparations' of 7 August 2019 with amended order for reparations (Annex A) and public annexes I and 2, Appeals Chamber, ICC-01/04-01/06-3129, 3 March 2015, para 65. See also *Prosecutor v Katanga*, Order for Reparations pursuant to Article 75 of the Statute, Trial Chamber II, ICC-01/04-01/07-3729-tENG, 27 March 2017, para 31.

[125] Rome Statute (n 2) Art 79. See also Regulations of the Trust Fund for Victims, ICC-ASP/4/Res.3 (3 December 2005) Art 56; ICC RPE (n 45) r 98(5).

a crucial role in implementing reparations orders and providing assistance to victims beyond the confines of specific cases, ensuring that even when convicted individuals are indigent, victims can still receive the reparations they are entitled to. The Fund is mainly financed by the voluntary contributions of States Parties.[126] Its resources are therefore limited. Therefore, when the Fund is financing reparations, some kind of collective or institutional reparations are favoured. Indeed, the Court decided that victims do not have an internationally recognised right to have their individual claim for reparation examined by a judicial body.[127]

The evolving framework of international criminal law, as well as regional instruments like the Victims' Rights Directive, have increasingly recognised and operationalised victims' rights to obtain reparation. This shift from a right to seek to a right to obtain reparation reflects a growing commitment to ensuring that justice for victims includes tangible, meaningful redress for the harms they have suffered. The main distinction resides once again in the nature of the crimes international criminal proceedings have to deal with. If the Victims' Rights Directive entrenches an individual right to reparation, this may prove impossible to implement in the context of mass crimes. As for the other categories of rights discussed above, EU Member States are not immune to similar situations in prosecution guided by extraterritorial or universal jurisdiction.

IV. Conclusions

The involvement of victims in international criminal trials has undergone significant development, indicating an increasing acknowledgement of their rights and roles within the judicial process. Starting from the establishment of the ICC and extending to the ratification of various international conventions, there exists a discernible tendency towards incorporating victims' viewpoints into both international and national criminal proceedings. The ICC's pioneering step of incorporating victims not only as witnesses but also as active participants has established a paradigm that has been mirrored in other international and hybrid tribunals.

This illustrates the crucial nature of prioritising the needs and rights of victims throughout all phases of criminal proceedings, particularly in instances involving the most severe international core crimes. While the scope and implementation of victims' rights may differ between international and domestic contexts, the fundamental principle remains steadfast: victims must be duly acknowledged, assisted, and shielded throughout the judicial process.

In amending the Victims' Rights Directive, the European Union must draw insights from international practices to ensure that it not only meets, but exceeds the standards for victim participation, protection and reparation. While the implementation of victim rights in international criminal proceedings shows a sometimes underwhelming yet ongoing progression, it offers a framework that can inform and enhance the EU's approach. Ultimately, it can contribute to the establishment of a fairer and more

[126] Regulations of the Trust Fund for Victims, ibid Art 21.
[127] ICC, *Prosecutor v Lubanga* (n 124) paras 155–56.

comprehensive legal system, one that effectively acknowledges and addresses the suffering of a specific category of especially vulnerable victims: victims of core international crimes. With the recent migratory movements to Europe and growing interest in some form of universal, or at least extraterritorial, jurisdiction (particularly in relation to the conflicts in Ukraine, Palestine or Syria, amongst others), several EU Member States are or will be confronted with massive numbers of victims in a single proceeding. Drawing insights from the successes and pitfalls of international criminal law practice can be invaluable in this context.

PART III

Selected National Perspectives on Victims' Rights across the EU: Major Trends and EU Law Impact

9

Victims' Rights in Belgian Law: Significant Progress Due to the Influence of EU Law but Still Gaps to be Filled

MARYSE ALIÉ AND CLÉMENTINE SAMRI

I. Introduction

After building on the rights of suspects, Belgian legislation has gradually turned towards the rights of victims following a number of high-profile cases (including the Marc Dutroux serial killer and rapist case), the Brussels bombing attacks and the increased attention to women victims of violence. Belgium has theoretically transposed three European directives concerning victims' rights, namely Directive 2012/29 EU of 25 October 2012 establishing minimum standards on the rights, support and protection of victims of crime (hereafter Directive 2012/29/EU);[1] Directive 2011/99 EU of 13 December 2011 on the European protection order (hereinafter Directive 2011/99 EU);[2] and Directive 2004/80/EC relating to compensation to crime victims.[3] However, in practice, there are some gaps and, surprisingly despite the long existence of EU directives, the process of transposing EU laws into national laws is still ongoing. This contribution aims to examine the notion of victim (section II), the place of victims in criminal proceedings (section III), the existing protection measures (section IV) and the means to compensate the injured parties (section IV) in the Belgian criminal system.[4]

II. Definition of Victim

In order to provide a useful basis for the considerations developed in the remainder of this contribution, we should first look at the concept of victim in Belgian law, the way

[1] Directive 2012/29/EU of the European Parliament and of the Council of 25 October 2012 establishing minimum standards on the rights, support and protection of victims of crime, and replacing Council Framework Decision 2001/220/JHA (Victims' Rights Directive) [2012] OJ L315/57.

[2] Directive 2011/99/EU of the European Parliament and of the Council on the European protection order [2011] OJ L338/2.

[3] Council Directive 2004/80/EC of 29 April 2004 relating to compensation to crime victims (Compensation Directive) [2004] OJ L261/15.

[4] Due to the limits imposed on the length of this contribution, we will not deal with the specificities of proceedings against internees and minors, nor those in the field of traffic offences.

in which it is – or is not – defined and the way in which it complies with applicable EU law.

A. A Fragmented Definition

Despite its central importance, the notion of victim is still not uniformly defined in Belgian law.[5] At first glance, it seems contradictory given that, since the 1970s, victims' rights in criminal law have been increasingly asserted, partially in line with developments in European and international legislation.[6] This lack of a coordinated definition is partly due to the fact that the *Code pénal* (hereinafter CP) and the *Code d'instruction criminelle* (hereinafter CICr) were originally dedicated to the prosecution and punishment of authors of offences.[7] Victims were not intended to be considered.[8] The institutional structure and the fragmentation of competences between the federal State and the federate entities may well explain the discrepancies in the definition of the notion of victim.[9] The absence of harmonisation is not purely theoretical since the scope of victims' rights may vary depending on the stage of the proceeding and the legal instrument that can be mobilised.[10]

Belgian criminal law contains no definition of the notion of victim as such, either at the investigation stage or at the trial stage.[11] Among the broader definitions that can be found in the existing instruments, Article 3 of the *Titre préliminaire du Code de procedure pénale* (hereinafter TPCPP) states that compensation action for damage caused by a criminal offence belongs to those who have suffered the damage. This definition does not exclude indirect victims and does not explain which kind of damages are included.

The prerogatives available to victims vary depending on their status: plaintiff, injured party or civil party.[12] As a civil party, the victim plays an active role in the criminal proceedings and holds the most comprehensive set of rights. This status allows the victim to claim reparation without having to initiate a proceeding, for instance before a civil court. It can be acquired at different procedural stages.[13] Conversely, plaintiff status confers far fewer rights (no access to the case file, no right to request investigative measures). The status of injured party is an intermediate one: it must be declared to the police or judicial authorities and gives access to the prerogatives stated in

[5] O Michiels and G Falque, *Principes de procédure pénale* (Larcier, 2023) 99.

[6] A Masset and G Falque, 'Victime – Le droit des victimes' (2020) 941 *Postal Memorialis* 6. See also G Falque, 'La victime dans le débat pénal' (2018) *Droit pénal et procédure pénale* 17.

[7] A Jacobs and D Chichoyan, 'Évolution du statut des parties au procès pénal. Du Code d'instruction criminelle au projet de Code de procédure pénale' in H Bosly, G Demanet, J Messine and B Michel (dir), *Cent ans de publication de droit pénal et de criminologie* (La Charte, 2007) 124.

[8] Falque (n 6) 19.

[9] K Decramer and L Gyselaers, 'La victime dans la procédure pénale belge : victime de son succès ?' in G Giudicelli-Delage and C Lazergues (eds), *La victime sur la scène pénale en Europe* (Presses Universitaires de France, 2008) 65.

[10] M Venturoli, 'La directive 2012/29/UE : dernière étape du processus de construction d'un « droit européen des victimes de la criminalité' in A Bailleux, M-A Beernaert, D Bernard (dir), *Fondements et objectifs des incriminations et des peines en droit international européen* (Anthemis, 2013) 669.

[11] Falque (n 6) 241.

[12] ibid 21. Michiels and Falque (n 5) 99.

[13] CICr, Art 63 and 67.

Article 5*bis* of the TPCPP. However, the differences between the rights of injured parties and civil parties are gradually disappearing. The new Article *21quater* in the CICr, recently introduced by Article 54 and 55 of the *loi du loi du 27 mars 2024 portant dispositions en matière de digitalisation de la justice et dispositions diverses Ibis*, allows an injured party who has made a statement pursuant to Article 5*bis* of the TPCPP to request the Public Prosecutor to carry out an additional act of information (including the right of appeal in case of refusal).[14]

Aside from the rights conferred by the CICr, Article 17 of the *Code judiciaire* – applicable to the admissibility of a claim for compensation before a criminal jurisdiction – provides that the action can only be admitted if the plaintiff bears capacity and interest to file it. A victim's interest in bringing a civil action relates to the event in which he/she has suffered damage as a result of a criminal offence.[15] Reference can also be made to the definition given to the notion of victim in non-legally binding domestic legal instruments,[16] as the internal circulars from the College of Prosecutors to Appeal Courts.[17] The Circular on the reception of victims in the Prosecutor's Office and courts specifies, for instance, that the notion of victim covers 'a natural person who has suffered harm, including physical or mental injury, emotional suffering or material loss, directly caused by acts or omissions that contravene criminal legislation'.[18]

In addition, as mentioned above, the Belgian institutional framework also influences the understanding of the notion of victim: the competence to assist victims is shared between the State and the different federate entities, more precisely the Communities. This reality is reflected in various definitions of the victim depending on the instruments consulted from one level of power to another. In order to ensure smooth operation in practice, a Memorandum of Understanding was concluded on 5 June 2009 and, recently, a new cooperation agreement has been adopted; both texts define the notion of victim by referring to the person who directly suffered from an injury but also including close relatives.[19]

At the stage of enforcement of sentences, the applicable legislation specifies which persons may be considered as victims, without defining the concept itself.[20] There are three categories of persons who may request to be informed and/or heard by the sentence enforcement judge during the examination of release applications: a) the natural person whose civil action is declared admissible and well-founded; b) a person who

[14] *cf* Art 54–55 de la loi du 27 mars 2024 portant dispositions en matière de digitalisation de la justice et dispositions diverses I*bis*, *M.B.*, 29 March 2024.

[15] A Verheylesonne, *Manuel de l'action civile – L'action en réparation du dommage causé par l'infraction pénale* (Wolters Kluwer, 2021) 43.

[16] Falque (n 6) 21.

[17] ibid.

[18] Circulaire commune du ministre de la justice et du Collège des procureurs généraux près les cours d'appel relative à l'accueil des victimes au sein des parquets et des tribunaux, *No.16/2012*, 12 Novembre 2012, 11–12.

[19] Art 1 du Protocole d'accord entre l'État, la Communauté française et la Région wallonne en matière d'assistance aux victimes, *M.B.*, 15 juillet 2009 ; Art. 1, 1° et 2° de la loi du 28 mars 2024 portant assentiment à l'Accord de coopération entre l'Etat fédéral, la Communauté française, la Communauté flamande, la Commission communautaire française et la Commission communautaire commune en matière d'assistance aux victimes pour la Région bilingue de Bruxelles-Capitale, *M.B.*, 22 avril 2024.

[20] Art 2, 6° de la loi du 17 mai 2006 relative au statut juridique externe des personnes condamnées à une peine privative de liberté et aux droits reconnus à la victime dans le cadre des modalités d'exécution de la peine, *M.B.*, 15 juin 2006.

was a minor, a prolonged minor or a prohibited minor at the time of the acts and for whom the legal representative has not lodged a civil claim; c) a natural person who was unable to bring a civil action due to material impossibility or vulnerability.[21] For these two latest categories, the competent court is required to determine the existence of a direct and legitimate interest.[22]

B. Coherence of Belgian Legislation and Practice with European Standards

Article 2 of Directive 2012/29/EU defines the victim as including the person who has suffered harm, including mental or emotional harm or economic loss, which was directly caused by a criminal offence, but also the family members of a person whose death was directly caused by a criminal offence and who have suffered harm as a result of that person's death. Despite the absence of a uniform definition of the victim in Belgian legislation, it is interesting to note that both practice[23] and certain legal instruments applicable to victims' rights include the close relatives and family members of the direct victim. However, it should be remembered that Article 1 of Directive 2012/29/EU states that its aim is to ensure that victims of crime receive appropriate information, support and protection and are able to participate in criminal proceedings. In these circumstances, the adoption of a unified definition would better contribute to inform victims and protect their rights. Otherwise, there is a risk that litigants will not be able to determine whether or not they can define themselves as victims and claim the benefit of certain prerogatives in this capacity.

III. The Place of the Victim in Criminal Proceedings

Historically, as mentioned, criminal legislation prioritised the targeting of prosecution and punishment of authors of offences. It was not until the 1970s, with the contribution of victimology, that victims were gradually taken into consideration and given an active procedural role.[24] The legislative changes towards recognition of a greater role for victims did not necessarily result from the implementation of national obligations under European law. In fact, high-profile cases (including the Dutroux case in 1996) have prompted the legislature to gradually enshrine victims' procedural rights, such as the right of access to the case file at the investigation stage, the possibility of requesting

[21] ibid.

[22] ibid.

[23] See a.o. the judgment of the Court de Cassation of 26 March 1997: 'As soon as a person can claim to have been personally harmed by the offence, he or she can claim compensation and bring a civil action, i.e. by anyone who can prove that he or she may have been the victim of the offence to his or her person, property or honour' (P.970249, *Pas.*, 1997, 163). See also Cass., 26 October 2011, P111199F; Cass., 22 June 2016, P150001F. See also M-A Beernaert, HD Bosly and D Vandermeersch, *Droit de la procédure pénale*, Tome II (La Charte, 2021) 2258.

[24] Falque (n 6) 1.

that the investigating judge takes on additional duties, and so on. These dramatic events significantly contributed to the momentum towards recognising greater rights for victims. It is undeniable, however, that European legislation has contributed to strengthening victims' rights and has had a significant impact on Belgian law. The aim of this section is not to draw up a complete catalogue of victims' procedural rights in Belgian legislation, but to draw the reader's attention to a number of key advances and remaining gaps.

A. Main Added Value of EU Legislation

i. *Interpretation and Translation*

EU law has had a decisive influence on the recognition of victims' rights to interpretation and translation: Directive 2012/29/EU led to the adoption of the Belgian Act of 28 October 2016.[25] In addition to Articles 31 and 32 of the *loi du 15 juin 1935 concernant l'emploi des langues en matière judiciaire*, the text reinforces the victims right to interpretation at the investigation stage[26] and the courts hearings' stage,[27] as well as the right to request a translation of information relating to the trial conduct, and of the summary or relevant extracts of a judgment in order to enable the civil party to effectively exercise its rights.[28] Translation may also be requested, subject to compliance with strict conditions, for documents in the criminal case file; however this is limited to passages that are essential to the effective exercise of the rights of the party concerned.[29]

In addition, the Act of 28 October 2016 exempts the certificate for lodging a complaint from the obligation to translate it, which can be considered problematic in terms of conformity with Article 5.3 of Directive 2012/29/EU. The TPCPP does not regulate the procedure for issuing such a certificate: it is regulated by a circular from the College of Prosecutors at the Appeal Courts, which does not provide any right to translation (apart from the fact that the document can be issued in one of the three national languages).[30] After a complaint has been lodged, Article 3*bis* of the TPCPP provides for an injured party's declaration form. This is an essential document as it enables the victim to be informed of the action taken on the basis of their complaint by the Prosecutor's Office (dismissal of the case, direct summons to appear in court, etc). Even if this statement is intended for the Prosecutor's Office, the victim must fill it in: unless they are assisted by an interpreter, it will be impossible for them to complete this document, which only exists in the three national languages. It would therefore make sense to fill this legislative gap.

[25] For an analysis, see A Baldovin, 'Le renforcement du droit à l'assistance linguistique dans le cadre des procédures pénales' (2017) 4 *Rev. dr. pén.* 215–55.

[26] CICr, Art 47*bis*.

[27] ibid Art 152*bis*, 211, 282 et 283; Art 23*bis* al. 4 de la loi du 15 juin 1935 concernant l'emploi des langues en matière judiciaire, *M.B.*, 22 juin 1935.

[28] ibid Art 164 § 1er, 189, 211.

[29] Art 22 de la loi du 15 juin 1935.

[30] This issue is addressed by the COL5/2009, revised version 24.06.2021.

ii. Information on Detention and Release of Convicted Persons

Certain provisions of Directive 2012/29/EU were transposed into a Belgian law at a later stage. The most recent example concerns the transposition of Article 6(5) and (6) of the Directive concerning victims' rights to receive information about their case. On 2 March 2023, the legislature adopted a text amending the *loi sur la detention préventive* with a view to creating a right to information for victims of a crime or offence that threatens or harms their physical and/or psychological integrity or that of a third party that they represent,[31] in particular victims registered as injured parties or as civil parties. When a prison sentence is being served, the legislation requires any victim who so wishes to be kept informed of how the sentence is being served and to be invited to be heard by the competent sentence enforcement court (sentence enforcement judge or sentence enforcement court, depending on the length of the sentence handed down) in the event of an application for release.[32] This jurisdiction may subject the sentenced person to specific individualised conditions if these are necessary in order to limit the risk of re-offending or if these are necessary in the interests of the victim.[33] However, the victim's procedural rights are limited: there is no access to the case file and the victim is only heard by the court in the absence of the convicted person without taking part in the debates.

Until recently, there was no information communicated to victims about the provisional release of a suspect at the investigation stage. The Act of 2 March 2023 fills this legal vacuum and the investigating judge's clerk is now required to notify the victims concerned within 24 hours of the decision taken (the issue or release of an arrest warrant; the execution of pre-trial detention under electronic surveillance; the decision to release; and any conditions imposed on the released suspect that affect the victim – prohibition on contact, prohibition on frequenting certain places or regions, etc).[34] The only exception relates to a risk of harming the suspect.[35]

B. Remaining Gaps

Besides the deficiencies that we mentioned in the previous paragraphs, we have to point out some weaknesses and efforts to be made to better guarantee and strengthen victims' rights regarding the discontinuation of proceedings and the complaint for international crimes.

[31] Loi du 2 mars 2023 modifiant la loi du 20 juillet 1990 relative à la détention préventive en vue de créer un droit à l'information pour les victimes, *M.B.* 14 avril 2023, entry into force: 1 April 2024.

[32] For prison sentences of less than three years, see Art 34, §1er, al.2, 35 § 1er al. 2 et 3, et 44 § 2, al. 2 et 5 and for sentences of more than three years, see Art 52 § 1, al. 2 et 5 and 53 al. 2 et 3 de la loi du 17 mai 2006 relative au statut juridique externe des personnes condamnées à une peine privative de liberté et aux droits reconnus à la victime dans le cadre des modalités d'exécution de la peine. See also, M-A. Beernaert, *Manuel de droit pénitentiaire*, 4th edn (Anthemis, 2023) 64–70.

[33] ibid, Art 40 and 56.

[34] Art 38*ter*, al. 2 nouveau de la loi du 20 juillet 1990.

[35] ibid, Art 38*ter*, al. 3.

i. No Review of Decisions to Discontinue Proceedings

The Prosecutor decides whether or not to prosecute.[36] Two major concerns emerge. On the one hand, the Prosecutor is not required to provide a detailed justification of their decision: citing the reason is deemed sufficient (eg absence of an offence, statute of limitations on public action, limited social repercussions, minimal harm, research capacity too low, lack of priority, etc). For victims, many situations in which it has been decided not to prosecute lead to misunderstanding and secondary victimisation, which is contrary to the objectives of Directive 2012/29/EU.[37] On the other hand, even in the same situation, the outcome of a complaint may vary depending on the magistrate in charge of the case or the suspect concerned. For instance, a victim will have a better chance of having their complaint dealt with if the targeted suspect has a criminal record. Various authors have also criticised the vagueness of the law, which creates legal uncertainty for those liable to prosecution.[38]

Decisions to discontinue proceedings are not subject to appeal, which appears contrary to the intent of Article 11 of Directive 2012/29/EU despite the room for manoeuvre left to the Member States. The victim may provide additional information or may request that the decision to close the case be reconsidered, but this is an informal procedure that is not enshrined in any legal text, as suggested by Article 11(2) of Directive 2012/29/EU. In the absence of a positive response from the Prosecutor's Office, the victim may file a complaint to an investigating judge or summon the suspect directly to appear before the criminal court but this option only applies to misdemeanours.[39]

ii. Access to Justice for Victims of International Crimes

With regard to international crimes (war crimes, crimes against humanity and genocide), the principle of extraterritorial jurisdiction based on passive personality (victim) is governed by Article 10, 1°bis of the TPCPP. Only the Federal Prosecutor can initiate proceedings but the victim must be a person who, at the time of the crime, was a Belgian national or a recognised refugee in Belgium and has had their habitual residence there for a person who, for at least three years, has been residing effectively, habitually and legally residing in Belgium. This provision does not distinguish between direct and indirect victims and therefore does not exclude the indirect victim as a plaintiff.

In an isolated decision, the Court of Cassation interpreted the scope of the Act restrictively: '[…] the residence condition referred to in Article 10, 1°*bis*, of the TPCPP must be met, not by the plaintiff, but by the person against whom a serious violation of international humanitarian Act has been committed'.[40] This limitation still applies

[36] CICr, Art 28*quater*.

[37] See Victims' Rights Directive (n 1) Recitals 9 and 26.

[38] C Guillain and M Alie, 'La légalité en procédure pénale: mutations contemporaines d'une exigence constitutionnelle' in L Detroux, M El Berhoumi, B Lombaert (dir), *La légalité: un principe de la démocratie belge en péril ?* (Larcier, 2019) 115–16; P Traest, G Vermeulen, W De Bondt, T Gombeer, S Raats and L van Puyenbroeck, *Scénarios pour une nouvelle procédure pénale belge. Etude pratique des problèmes rencontrés* (Maklu, 2015) 64.

[39] However, if it is unsuccessful in its action, it may have to bear the legal costs and fees of the opposing party's Actyer.

[40] Cass.,17 décembre 2003, N° P.03.1517.F.

today. For example, the Brussels Court of Appeal declared inadmissible the complaint of Mrs X seeking justice for the murder of her brother in the Eastern Democratic Republic of Congo as a war crime and crime against humanity, stating that: 'in this case, Mrs [X] is of Belgian nationality but there is nothing to indicate that she personally was a direct victim of the alleged acts'.[41] It is noteworthy that, although the case involves a crime committed outside the territory of the EU Member States, Directive 2012/29/EU confers rights on victims of extraterritorial offences in relation to criminal proceedings that take place in the Union.[42] The abovementioned restriction therefore seems to contradict the definition of victim as set out in Article 2(1)(a)(ii) of Directive 2012/29/EU, which encompasses the relatives of the deceased person. In this context, it would make no sense not to consider as victims, for instance, the children or parents of direct (murdered) victims of war crimes.

To clarify the conformity of this interpretation, the Brussels Court of Appeal has recently referred to the European Court of Justice (ECJ)[43] with two specific questions which target the notion of victims of international core crimes. These questions are worded as follows:

1. Must Article 2, 1, a, i of Directive 2012/29/EU of the European Parliament and of the Council of 25 October 2012 establishing minimum standards on the rights, support and protection of crime victims and replacing Council Framework Decision 2001/220/JHA, be interpreted as including, in the concept of 'victims', and as giving access to the rights defined by the Directive, close family members of a person who, in the context of a serious violation of international humanitarian law, has been subjected to enforced disappearance or torture, taking into account the International Convention for the Protection of All Persons from Enforced Disappearance and the United Nations Convention against Torture?
2. Must Article 2(1)(a)(i) of Directive 2012/29/EU of 25 October 2012 be interpreted as including, in the concept of 'victims', and as giving access to the rights defined by the Directive, family members who have suffered mental or emotional harm or material loss directly caused by a serious violation of international humanitarian law that has primarily targeted a close family member?[44]

Additionally, victims of international crimes have no means of appeal against the inadmissibility of their complaint. When the Federal Prosecutor considers that the complaint is inadmissible, he will draw up an indictment to this effect and the Indictments Division of the Appeal Court will hear the case, excluding the victims, before confirming or rejecting the admissibility of the complaint. The Constitutional Court took a positive stance on the legality of this provision[45] but, since its decision, EU law, and in particular Directive 2012/29/EU, has imposed new obligations. A question remains: whether combining Article 47 of the European Charter of Fundamental Rights and Recital 22 (even if not binding) and Article 10 of Directive 2012/29/EU, could or not

[41] Appeal Chamber, Indictments Division, judgment 2022/4596, 2 November 2022.
[42] See Victims' Rights Directive (n 1) Preamble, Recital 13.
[43] ECJ, Case C-239/24 (no official data is available at this stage).
[44] Ch. mise en acc. (Bruxelles), 12 décembre 2023, inédit.
[45] C.C. Decision 62/2005, 23 March 2005 and Decision 21/2008, 21 February 2008.

lead to the victims' right to be heard by the Court when reviewing the inadmissibility of a complaint for international crimes?

IV. Protection Measures

Chapter four of Directive 2012/29/EU deals with victims' protection and the recognition of special needs. After briefly listing existing protection measures in the Belgian system, which is unfortunately lagging behind, we will examine their compliance with standards set out in Directive 2012/29/EU[46] and efforts which remain to be undertaken.

A. Existing Framework for Protection Measures

i. Protective Measures Available Independently of Legal Proceedings

Independently of the judge's intervention, the police and the Prosecutor have gradually developed methods for assessing risk and caring for victims within the framework of internal decisions and circulars. For the sake of brevity and relevance, two measures will be specifically mentioned below.[47]

a. The Act of 15 May 2012 on Temporary Residence Bans in Cases of Domestic Violence

The Act of 15 May 2012,[48] as amended by the Act of 5 May 2019,[49] establishes the possibility of a temporary residence ban in cases of domestic violence.[50] This mechanism aims at preventing and limiting the escalation of violence.[51] The ban, which lasts for a

[46] We should also refer to Directive 2011/99/EU on the European protection order, which allows victims of violence to continue to enjoy protection from offenders when they move to another EU country. This instrument has been transposed in the Belgian system through the loi du 9 avril 2017 relative à la décision de protection européenne, *M.B.*, 18 May 2017. However no data is available for analysis.

[47] In addition to these measures, the Belgian Act also provides for mechanisms in the civil and administrative Act. See A van Vossole, *Mapping the Legislation and Assessing the Impact of Protection Orders in the European Member States (POEMS)*, available on Belgium.pdf (poems-project.com). Reference may also be made to the possibility for victims to request that their address not be communicated to third parties (Art 11 de l'Arrêté royal du 16 juillet 1992 relatif à la communication des informations contenues dans les registres de la population et dans le registre des étrangers, *M.B.*, 15 August 1992).

[48] Loi du 15 mai 2012 relative à l'interdiction temporaire de résidence en cas de violence domestique, *M.B.*, 1er octobre 2012.

[49] Loi du 5 mai 2019 portant des dispositions diverses en matière pénale et en matière de cultes, et modifiant la loi du 28 mai 2002 relative à l'euthanasie et le Code pénal social, *M.B.*, 24 mai 2019.

[50] The application of this Act is set out in a joint circular, *cf* Circulaire du 20 décembre 2012, n° COL18/212 du ministre de la Justice, du ministre de l'Intérieur et du Collège des procureurs généraux, relative à l'interdiction temporaire de résidence en cas de violence domestique.

[51] C Philips, 'Interdiction temporaire de résidence en cas de violence domestique' (2019) *Bulletin juridique et social* 15. See also Michiels and Falque (n 5) 201; D Chichoyan, 'L'interdiction temporaire de résidence en cas de violence domestique' (2013) *Revue belge de droit pénal et de criminologie* 799–818; HD Bosly and V Bosly, 'L'interdiction temporaire de résidence en cas de violence domestique' in N Dandoy et al (dir), *Individu, Famille et Etat: Réflexions sur le sens du droit de la personne, de la famille et de son patrimoine*, 1st edn (Larcier, 2022) 455–70.

maximum of 14 days, may be imposed by the Prosecutor when a serious and immediate threat to the safety of an inhabitant exists. The person subject to the temporary restraining order is required to leave the premises immediately and is prevented from returning or coming into contact with residents, on pain of criminal sanction.[52] The legal conditions and duration of the ban (up to three months) are supervised by the Family Court.[53]

b. The Mobile Harassment Alarm or 'Stalking Alarm'

The mobile harassment alarm is an application integrated into the emergency services application and combines a portable alarm button linked by Bluetooth to the protected person's smartphone.[54] This measure can be requested by the victim, for example when a complaint is filed, or when the police intervenes; in certain cases, it can also be requested by the police, the Prosecutor or a third party.[55] The granting of this protection measure depends solely on the Prosecutor, after examining the circumstances of the case.[56] If the decision is positive, the protection measure is taken for a period of nine months and can be extended for a further period of the same length if an alert is received or if new facts are reported or observed.[57] This mechanism, introduced by a circular from the executive, is only applicable in certain parts of the country, but should be extended to the whole country in the future.

ii. Protective Measures During Legal Proceedings

There is no legal framework to protect the victim at the investigating stage. However, the judge can take the victim's interests into account:[58] the release of a suspect can take place under certain conditions, including a ban on contact with the victim or approaching certain places.[59]

Another issue arises as to whether victims who do not wish to reveal their identity or their details are given the opportunity to do so. Concerning the identity, the legislation does not provide any positive answer but, informally, the police could hide certain details while registering a complaint (the victim's address for instance). During the hearing and in the sentence, anonymity has also been granted to some police officers who were victims of a terrorist attack, but this is an isolated case.[60]

[52] Loi du 15 juin 2012 tendant à réprimer le non-respect de l'interdiction temporaire de résidence en cas de violence domestique et modifiant les articles 594 et 627 du Code judiciaire, *M.B.*, 1er octobre 2012.

[53] Art 4 de la loi du 15 mai 2012 and Art 572*bis*, 11° du Code judiciaire.

[54] Circulaire COL 03/2023 commune du Ministre de la Justice, du Ministre de l'Intérieur, du Secrétaire d'État à l'égalité des genres et du Collège des Procureurs généraux visant à encadrer le déploiement national de l'alarme mobile harcèlement ('stalking alarm') 4.

[55] ibid 9–10.

[56] ibid 11.

[57] ibid 19.

[58] Falque (n 6) 132.

[59] Art 35 de la loi du 20 juillet 1990 relative à la détention préventive, *M.B.*, 14 août 1990.

[60] Tribunal de première instance francophone de Bruxelles (90e ch., corr.), 23 avril 2018, (2019), *Revue belge de droit pénal et de criminologie*, p 173–187; A De Brouwer, 'Partie civile: mon nom est Personne' (2019) *Revue belge de droit pénal et de criminologie*, p 194–202.

Belgian law provides for various protection measures for witnesses during the investigation and at the trial stages.[61] They can even benefit from enhanced protection measures extending to their family members.[62] These measures are granted by a Witness Protection Commission and range from police patrols to the installation of alarms, rehousing and, in exceptional circumstances, a change of identity.[63] Witnesses under protection have the option to appear remotely, by videoconference for instance.[64] No such measure exists for victims unless they have a witness status.[65]

The investigating judge may restrict access to certain documents of the case file if this presents a danger to individuals or seriously infringes their privacy. However, in accordance with the rights of the defence, the identity of the civil party is never kept confidential during the proceedings.[66] The same does not apply to the protection of the victim's identity outside the proceedings, particularly in the press or on television. In the case of certain offences, such as sexual offences or human trafficking, the disclosure of the victim's identity is, unless authorised in writing by the victim, the Prosecutor or the investigating judge, punishable by law.[67]

During the trial itself, courthouses do not provide an entrance or waiting area separate from that in which the other parties to the trial, including the defendant, will be held. Nor are courtrooms designed to limit contact between victims and defendants.[68] Gradually, the Code of Criminal Procedure (CCP) developed provisions relating to the adjustments that could be made for vulnerable adults (audio-visual recording, hearing by specially trained personnel, production of the recording instead of personal appearance, etc).[69] However, practice shows that the notion of 'vulnerable adult' is interpreted restrictively and therefore only applies to a small percentage of victims.[70]

In practice, since no measures are actually in place during the hearings and given the layout of the courtrooms, some victims are reluctant to attend the hearing. Although the presiding judge will always ensure they are respected and safe in the courtroom, they very often choose to be represented by their counsel[71] instead of facing the perpetrator and/or his relatives, both in the courtroom and outside, in or around the court building.

iii. Protective Measures Available at the Sentencing and Enforcement Stages

Victims play no role in criminal sentencing.[72] However, judicial authorities may take their interests into account. For instance, in the event of a probative sentence, the

[61] CICr, Art 75*bis*, 86*bis*, 86*ter*, 294, 296. See HD Bosly, 'La protection de l'identité des policiers' (2019) *Revue de droit pénal et de criminologie* 734.

[62] CICr, Art 102–11.

[63] ibid Art 103–11. See also Finnin (n 60) 39 and Bosly (n 61) 734.

[64] CICr, Art 158*bis*.

[65] Finnin (n 60) 40.

[66] ibid.

[67] CP, Art 417/63 and Art 433*quinquies*. See also Falque (n 6) 101.

[68] Finnin (n 60) 41.

[69] CICr, Art 95-101 and Art 311.

[70] Finnin (n 60) 42.

[71] CICr, Art 152, 185 and 277.

[72] Falque (n 6) 55. See also Michiels and Falque (n 5) 538.

judge may impose certain conditions relating to a ban on contact with or frequentation of certain places.[73] Some criminal provisions relating to sexual offences or trafficking in human beings also explicitly provide for the possibility of the judge imposing a ban on living, residing or being in certain specified areas, as well as a ban on contact with individually designated persons.[74] This may change in the future, as the draft reform of the CP provides for a more general prohibition of place or contact.[75]

At the sentence enforcement stage and, as explained above, the competent jurisdiction will be able to hear the civil parties who so request about the arrangements and conditions that can be imposed during the probative period after the release of the condemned person.[76]

B. Influence of European Law and Remaining Gaps

The Belgian legal landscape continues to evolve towards greater recognition of victims' rights due to the influence of EU law. This is exemplified by the adoption of new legislation transposing Directive 2012/29/EU, which, although broadly applicable to all victims of crime, has significant potential to improve the rights of certain vulnerable victims with specific needs. As a key step in this direction, Article 15 of the Act of 13 July 2023 on preventing and combating feminicide, gender-based homicide and violence[77] establishes a right to be heard in a suitable room, to receive information, including information about the application of existing protection measures.[78] These measures include, in particular, the temporary ban on residence and the 'stalking alarm' mentioned above.[79]

The Act of 13 July 2023 was adopted far too long after Directive 2012/29/EU. The improvement in favour of victims appears to be consistent with the assessment made of the implementation of Directive 2012/29/EU.[80] The Belgian legal landscape therefore seems to meet several of the 'minimum standards' set out in the fourth chapter of Directive 2012/29/EU and to be pursuing a process of reflection with a view to achieving these protection objectives.

[73] *cf* Art 9-12 de la loi du 19 juin 1964 concernant la suspension, le sursis et la probation, *M.B.*, 17 juillet 1964. See Falque (n 6) 56.

[74] CP, Art 417/58 and Art 433*novies*. On this subject, see C-E Clesse, *La traite des êtres humains* (Larcier, 2013).

[75] Ch. des Rep., *Projet de loi (I) introduisant le Livre Ier du Code pénal – Projet de loi (II) en vue d'insérer une mesure de sûreté pour la protection de la société*, Doc 55 3374/001 et 55 3375/001, 198.

[76] Arts 10, 13, 14, 17, 19, 20/2, 46, 58, 71, 74, 78, 95, 95/1, 95/7, 95/14, 95/16 de la loi du 17 mai 2006. See also Michiels and Falque (n 5) 715.

[77] Art 2 de la loi du 13 juillet 2023 sur la prévention et la lutte contre les féminicides, les homicides fondés sur le genre et les violences, *M.B.*, 31 août 2023.

[78] S Wattier, 'La nouvelle loi sur la prévention des féminicides: quelle avancée dans la lutte contre les violences de genre' (2023) 6960 *Journal des tribunaux* 662.

[79] Art 15 de la loi du 13 juillet 2023.

[80] European Commission, 'Commission Staff Working Document – Evaluation of Directive 2012/29/EU of the European Parliament and of the Council of 25 October 2012 establishing minimum standards on the rights, support and protection of victims of crime, and replacing Council Framework Decision 2001/220/JHA' SWD(2022) 180 final, 3.

Alongside the influence of that Directive, other instruments of European law are likely to exert an influence on Belgian practice. By an Act of 9 April 2017 on the European Protection Order, Belgium transposed Directive 2011/99/EU of the European Parliament and of the Council of 13 December 2011.[81] The aim of this text is to enable victims of crime who have obtained protection measures in an EU State to continue to benefit from similar protection in their destination State, within the EU.[82] In civil matters, a similar mechanism is provided for by Regulation 606/2013 of the European Parliament and of the Council of 12 June 2013 on the mutual recognition of protection measures in civil matters.[83]

Despite the changes introduced, efforts are still required to ensure that Belgian legislation complies with the European framework. Three criticisms can be made in the context of this contribution.

i. Inadequacy and Risks Associated with Available Protection Measures

As Belgian legislation currently stands, there is no mechanism similar to an injunction or protection order.[84] We have referred to the mechanism provided for in the Act of 15 September 2012 and the probation arrangements that may accompany sentences or cases in which perpetrators are released. To ensure better protection for victims, it would be desirable to make it possible for victims to request a judge to order injunctive or protective measures, independently of any ongoing criminal proceedings.[85] According to some authors,[86] these mechanisms could be inspired by the Act in force in Spain and provide for the possibility of effective monitoring of the perpetrator's compliance with the aforementioned measures, in particular through the wearing of an electronic bracelet.

Deployment of the 'stalking alarm' may prove promising in the future, but care must be taken to avoid placing a disproportionate burden of responsibility on victims, by placing the assurance of their protection solely on their shoulders and on their compliant use of the system.

ii. Inadequate Protection for Victims at the Investigation and Trial Stages

As explained above, the Belgian legal system currently provides no genuine measures to protect the identity or even the anonymity of victims in legal proceedings. Nor is access to court buildings and the layout of courtrooms adapted to avoid contact between victims and perpetrators. This situation does not comply with the minimum

[81] Directive 2011/99/EU of the Parliament and of the Council of 13 December 2011 on the European protection order, [2011] OJ L338/2.

[82] Beernaert, Bosly and Vandermeersch (n 23) 2258.

[83] Regulation (EU) No 606/2013 of the European Parliament and of the Council of 12 June 2013 on mutual recognition of protection measures in civil matters [2013] OJ L181/4.

[84] A François, 'Les violences domestiques en matière pénale: entre obligations internationales, politique criminelle et réalités de terrain' (2022) 2 *Revue de droit pénal et de criminologie* 124.

[85] ibid.

[86] ibid.

standards set out in the fourth chapter of Directive 2012/29/EU and, more specifically, in Article 19, whereas the provisions on the protection of the identity and anonymity of witnesses could be a source of inspiration for legislative change. Nor does the current legislation appear to comply with Article 20 of Directive 2012/29/EU since, as we have seen, the vulnerability of the victim, which conditions access to certain measures such as video recordings, is assessed restrictively and cannot be guaranteed on a systematic basis.[87]

This restrictive assessment of the vulnerability of victims and, consequently, of their special procedural needs within the meaning of Article 22 of Directive 2012/29/EU, is questionable. This issue is given greater attention in the new Proposal for a Directive of the European Parliament and of the Council amending Directive 2012/29/EU.[88]

The European institutions have concluded that the implementation of Directive 2012/29/EU is not fully satisfactory, partly due to the lack of clarity and precision with which certain rights are formulated and the considerable room for manoeuvre left to the Member States.[89] As a result, the victims' right to protection is not sufficiently consolidated. This observation is confirmed in practice and contributes to secondary victimisation of victims.[90] In line with what other authors have already suggested, the above-mentioned Article 158*bis* of the CCP could, for instance, be amended to allow vulnerable victims to express their views by videoconference or closed-circuit television during the main hearing in order to avoid direct contact with the accused.[91] The practice of the International Criminal Court in terms of victim protection and participation in trials could also serve as guidelines.[92]

Other measures also appear to be feasible at no great cost, such as legislating for better protection of victims' data. As explained above, the rights of the defence are opposed to the anonymity of civil parties, but other data, such as their address, could remain confidential. As the Act currently stands, it is possible for victims to elect domicile at their counsel's office, but the adoption of a legal basis, comparable to Article 75*ter* of the CICr,[93] which would systematise the anonymity of this type of data, seems reasonably conceivable.

iii. Pitfalls Associated with Cross-Border Situations

The effectiveness of Directive 2011/99/EU on the European protection order is dependent on the availability of protection measures and, in the specific case of gender-based

[87] Finnin (n 60) 40.

[88] European Commission, Proposal for a Directive of the European Parliament and of the Council amending Directive 2012/29/EU establishing minimum standards on the rights, support and protection of victims of crime, and replacing Council Framework Decision 2001/220/JHA, COM(2023) 424 final, 12 July 2023.

[89] ibid 22.

[90] Finnin (n 60) 40.

[91] François (n 84) 134.

[92] Rome Statute of the International Criminal Court (Rome, 17 July 1998) Art 68. *cf* P Massidda and C Walter, 'Article 68' in J Fernandez, X Pacreau et M Ubeda-Saillard (dir), *Statut de Rome de la Cour pénale internationale – Commentaire article par article* (Editions Pedone, 2019) 1869.

[93] This provision enshrines the possibility of indicating the business address or elected domicile instead of the home or private residence for persons who, in the course of their professional activities, are responsible for establishing and investigating an offence or who, in the course of the application of the law, become aware of the circumstances in which the offence was committed, and who, in this capacity, are heard as witnesses. See Bosly (n 58) 730.

and intra-family violence, anti-violence measures put in place in the various Member States.[94] In Belgium, the lack of human and financial resources to implement protection measures and victims' lack of information about their rights remain issues. Shortcomings at national level are an additional barrier to dealing with cross-border situations. According to the statistics of the Prosecutor's Office for 2018, the number of cases of domestic violence in Belgium amount to 41,861. Only 169 were subjected to a temporary restraining order, which corresponds to 0.40 per cent of cases. These figures show that the mechanism is poorly applied, which is obviously alarming.[95] Some grassroots associations denounce the lack of training for staff responsible for implementing these procedures and the poor assessment of the risks involved.[96] How could the protection be efficient at transnational level when it does not function smoothly at international level?

The preparatory work for the Act of 9 April 2017 suggests that protection measures in Belgian law correspond to the protection measures referred to in the Act on pre-trial detention, the Act on suspended sentences, the Act on the execution of sentences or the Act on internment, ie legislative measures provided for by the judiciary (see above).[97] In these circumstances, questions may arise as to the applicability of certain measures provided for, not by law, but by instruments such as circulars adopted by the executive. This comment is echoed in the criticisms expressed by the Legislation Section of the Belgian Council of State regarding the Act of 13 July 2023. The Council notes that several of the rights enshrined in this Act are set out in circulars. However, these instruments do not constitute normative acts creating rights: rather, they are tools enabling the minister concerned to give instructions to their administration, the scope of which is certainly important but limited to the hierarchical relationship which it forms part of.[98]

In addition, a significant concern emerges regarding the awareness of the very existence of this possibility: in view of the figures available on the implementation of certain protection measures under Belgian law and the serious problems raised by the lack of human and financial resources, can we reasonably anticipate that victims who have obtained protection measures in another EU Member State can rely on their implementation in Belgium? Conversely, does this mean that a victim who has obtained protection measures under Belgian law via a police zone or a Prosecutor's Office will not be able to enforce them outside Belgium?

V. Compensation to Victims of Crime

In case of a criminal conviction, the court will rule at the same time on any civil claims.[99] The victim does not therefore necessarily have to bring the case before a civil court, even

[94] D Porcheron, 'Le principe de reconnaissance mutuelle au service des victimes de violence' (2016) 2 *Revue critique de droit international privé* 283.

[95] François (n 84) 129–30.

[96] GREVIO, *Rapport d'évaluation de référence – Belgique*, 21 September 2020, 67, available at https://rm.coe.int/rapport-du-grevio-sur-la-belgique-/16809f9a2b.

[97] Beernaert, Bosly and Vandermeersch (n 23) 2259.

[98] Ch. des Rep, 'Projet de loi sur la prévention et la lutte contre les féminicides, les homicides fondés sur le genre et les violences qui les précèdent', Doc 55 3400/001, 97.

[99] TPCPP, Art 4, al 1. It should be noted that Art 27 of the revised Penal Code, which will come into force on 28 April 2026, defines the objectives of the sentence, one of which relates to victims, since the sentence must promote the restoration of social equilibrium and repair the damage caused by the offence.

if this is possible. The claim for compensation may even be lodged after the criminal trial, since the judge is obliged to reserve judgment on the civil interests in the absence of a civil party or when the case is not ready for compensation exam.[100] In this case, the victim can submit a simple request, free of charge, to have the case brought back before the criminal court.[101] The successful submission of a claim for compensation is therefore highly dependent on access to adequate information, which is a debate that goes beyond the scope of our contribution.[102] In this section, we will examine the possibility of restitution, the assistance that can be provided to victims, and the system of cooperation to facilitate access to State compensation within the EU and its impact on victim compensation.

A. Existing Framework for the Compensation of Victims

i. *Confiscation and Restitution*

Where the seized property belongs to the victim, it is automatically returned to him or her. In cases where restitution is not possible, reparation may also be made by equivalent means (allocation of a sum of money corresponding to the value of the property lost, etc).[103] This mechanism is not linked to the implementation of Directive 2012/29/EU but to the transposition of Directive 2014/42/EU of the European Parliament and of the Council of 3 April 2014 on the freezing and confiscation of instrumentalities and proceeds of crime in the EU.[104] If the assets in question were seized during the preliminary investigation, it will be sufficient to transfer them or their financial equivalent to the victim. Otherwise, the victim will be dependent on the steps taken to enforce the confiscation, the convicted offender's cooperation and any insolvency. Finally, under Article 121 of the CICr, bail deposit for the provisional release of an accused person may be used to reimburse civil damages.[105]

Until now, the Act has only partially regulated the order of priority for the enforcement of pecuniary penalties in criminal judgments.[106] Article 69 of the new CP[107] provides that the interests of victims will take precedence, since restitution and damages will come first. It should also be noted that Article 67 of the same text specifies that the

[100] TPCPP, Art 4, al. 2.
[101] ibid Art 4 al. 3.
[102] Among the criticism, we may point out the fact that a copy of the judgment is not systematically transmitted to victims and no information to guide them on reparation enforcement is provided.
[103] CP, Art 43*bis*, al. 3. For more information, see F Lugents, 'Recherche, saisie et confiscation des avantages patrimoniaux tirés de l'infraction – Sanction de l'auteur et indemnisation de la victime dans une approche patrimoniale de la délinquance' in N Colette-Basecqz and F George (dir), *Responsabilité civile et responsabilité pénale, regards pratiques* (Coll. Unité de droit des obligations de l'Unamur, Anthémis, 2021) 586 et ss. See also F Lugentz and D Vandermeersch, 'Saisie et confiscation en matière pénale', *Répertoire pratique du droit belge* (Bruylant, 2017) 76–78; Verheylesonne (n 15) 247 et ss.
[104] Ch. Repr., Projet de loi modifiant diverses dispositions du droit pénal, de la procédure pénale et du droit judiciaire, 6 novembre 2017, Doc 542753/001, 14–15.
[105] Verheylesonne (n 15) 263–64.
[106] CP, Art 49.
[107] Loi du 29 février 2024 introduisant le livre Ier du Code pénal, *M.B.*, 8 avril 2024.

rights of the victim, who was not yet a civil party at the time of confiscation, will be safeguarded.

ii. Reparation

a. Financial Assistance for Victims of Violence

If the perpetrator has not been identified or is insolvent, there is a State compensation fund dedicated to victims managed by the 'Commission d'aide aux victimes d'actes intentionnels de violence – Commission for assistance to victims of intentional acts of violence' (hereinafter Commission).[108] This administrative body was created to implement the European Convention on the Compensation of Victims of Violent Crimes of 24 November 1983.[109] Unintentional acts of violence and crimes and offences that do not constitute violence against the person are excluded. The Commission's role is not to endorse the full compensation payment but to provide assistance (between €500 and €125,000).[110] In addition, the assistance intervenes in a subsidiary way to the perpetrator, the civilly liable party, or even the insurance company if the victim benefits from it.[111] The deadline to file a request before the Commission is three years from the final decision (dismissal of the case, criminal judgment or civil judgment).[112]

b. Financial Assistance for Victims of Terrorist Attacks

The Commission includes a specialised Terrorism Division,[113] which is competent if the crime has been labelled as a terrorist act by Royal Decree.[114] This recognition can be problematic as certain acts have been condemned by the Judiciary as terrorist but have not been recognised as such by Royal Decree.[115] The acts giving rise to compensation

[108] Loi du 1er août 1985 portant des mesures fiscales et autres, *M.B.*, 6 août 1985.

[109] Projet de loi du 7 mai 1985 portant des mesures fiscales et autres, Exposé des motifs, Doc. parl., Sénat, 1984–1985, no 873/1, 17. For a comprehensive analysis, *cf* A Cataldo and C Devillers, 'La Commission pour l'aide financière aux victimes d'actes intentionnels de violence: limites et réalités pratiques' in Colette-Basecqz and George (n 103) 333–89.

[110] Art 33 § 2 de la loi du 1er août 1985.

[111] ibid Art 31*bis*.

[112] ibid.

[113] A section on victims of terrorism has been created by the 1st August 1985 Act while amended by the Loi du 1er avril 2007 relative à l'assurance contre les dommages causés par le terrorisme, *M.B.*, 15 mai 2007. See also, Loi du 15 janvier 2019 modifiant la loi du 1er août 1985 portant des mesures fiscales et autres en ce qui concerne l'aide aux victimes du terrorisme, *M.B.*, 8 février 2019.

[114] ibid, Art 42*bis*.

[115] See for instance: Bruxelles (chambre correctionnelle 90), judgment, 23 avril 2018. It concerns the attempted terrorist assassination of police officers committed by Salah Abdeslam and Sofien Ayari on 15 March 2016, Dries Street in Forest, Brussels. For eight years, the authorities refused to recognised this attack as a terrorist crime, although, on 23 April 2018, a criminal chamber did recognise it as such. The Brussels' Cour of Assizes in its trial of the Brussels terrorist attacks did not sentence Abdeslam and Ayari but referred to the sentences handed down in the judgment of 23 April 2018 (See: Assises, Sentencing Judgment, 15 septembre 2023). In view of this new legal finding, the attempted murders in the rue du Dries have eventually been recognised as terrorist acts: Arrêté royal du 14 avril 2024 portant reconnaissance d'un acte en tant qu'actes de terrorisme au sens de l'article 42*bis* de la loi du 1er août 1985, M.B., 24 avril 2024.

may have been committed abroad, on European soil or in a third country[116] provided that the victim is Belgian or has their main residence in Belgium.[117]

In this case, a simplified procedure exists: the victim of a terrorist act does not need to present an enforceable judgment to obtain assistance, nor does he or she even need to have filed a complaint or brought a civil action before a Court. According to Art 42*quinquies*, § 1er, 2° of 1st August 1985 as revised by the 1st September Act, application for assistance must be introduced within three years of the Royal Decree.[118] As the lawyer Valérie Gérard pointed out: '[…] the expiry of the time limit, as set out in Article 42*quinquies*, undermines victims' rights and discriminates against victims of any type of intentional act of violence'.[119] On this point, the Constitutional Court found a violation of Articles 10 and 11 of the Constitution, in conjunction with Article 6 of the European Convention for the Protection of Human Rights and Fundamental Freedoms (ECHR).[120] To date, Article 42 *quinquies*, §1, 2° has been amended and the deadline to apply has been extended to five years.[121] The scope of the assistance is larger than for other crimes in terms of rights and deadlines.[122] Eventually, victims of terrorism are entitled to full legal remedy,[123] unlike the victims of other acts of violence, who only benefit from legal review by the Council of State.[124]

iii. System of Cooperation to Facilitate Access to State Compensation

On 13 January 2006, Belgium adopted an Act to transpose Council Directive 2004/80/EC of 29 April 2004 relating to compensation to crime victims, which establishes a cooperation system to facilitate access to State compensation in cross-border situations.[125] Under Article 40 of the said Belgian Act, where an act is committed on the territory of another EU Member State and the plaintiff is habitually resident in Belgium, they may apply to the Commission, which will assist them in obtaining compensation from the competent authority. And *vice versa*, Article 40*bis* provides that, when the intentional act was committed on Belgian territory and the victim is habitually resident in another EU Member State, they may send their claim via the authority specially designated by that State, using a standard form drawn up by the European Commission.

[116] Cataldo and Devillers (n 106) 368–69.

[117] Art 42*quinquies*, § 1er, 1° de la loi du 1er aout 1985.

[118] ibid, Art 42*quinquies*, § 1er, 2°.

[119] V Gerard, *Victimes d'attentats en Belgique: aides et indemnisations, Analyse juridique et critique* (Anthemis, 2023) 197.

[120] C.C., arrêt n°91/2022, 30 juin 2022.

[121] Art 53 de la Loi du 18 janvier 2024 visant à rendre la justice plus humaine, plus rapide et plus ferme III, *M.B.*, 26 janvier 2024.

[122] *cf* a.o. Art. 42*sexies* and 42*septies* de la loi du 1er aout 1985.

[123] ibid Art 42*undecies*.

[124] ibid Art 42*quater* § 2.

[125] *M.B.*, 31 janvier 2006.

B. Steps Needed for Improved Victim Compensation

i. Ineffectiveness of Compensation from the Offender

Enforcing the compensation awarded by the court is particularly difficult due, for instance, to the need to use a bailiff and the high costs involved. The victim is too often left without any help. Even when a condemned person applies for their anticipated release before the sentence enforcement judge, they only have to demonstrate an effort to compensate the victim:[126] a few hundred euros is sufficient to prove such an effort. In the end, the victim is better protected under a penal transaction[127] or a mediation procedure and measures[128] rather than after a formal trial. Indeed these 'alternative means' require the victim to be compensated before they can be implemented.

As for referral to the victim support commission, this is subject to a burden of proof far too heavy for victims (proof of the legal proceeding and its outcome, judgment enforcement, solvency of perpetrator, etc). This burden on the victim inevitably leads to secondary victimisation, although prohibited by Directive 2012/29/EU.

ii. Victim Support Commission: Barriers to Cross-Border Implementation

Measuring the effectiveness of Directive 2004/80/EC is difficult and complex in the absence of systematic data and case Act publication. The single report available, which covers the 2006–2009 period, shows that 32 applications were lodged on the basis of Articles 40 and 40bis of the 1st August 1985 Act.[129] According to Olivier Lauwers, Chief Secretary and Head of the Commission's Terrorism Division, the Commission continues to receive requests, but these remain marginal.[130] Is this linked to the small number of events concerned or rather to the lack of communication of useful information to victims?[131] We believe the latter to be the case. It should also be noted that, after the 2016 Brussels terrorist attacks, little use was made of Article 40*bis* as contacts were made by the Commission Secretary directly with victims or via embassies or through lawyers who submitted requests for assistance directly to the Commission. In practice, the procedure is far too complex and the final outcome in terms of financial compensation uncertain.

Olivier Lauwers shared a number of crucial points of attention to move forward with an efficient victims' support mechanism for handling cross-border compensation claims:[132]

1. Deadlines to submit a request for assistance to the competent national authority vary from one country to another.

[126] Articles 28 and 47 de la loi du 17 mai 2006.
[127] CICr, Art 216*bis* § 4 CCI.
[128] ibid Art 216*ter* § 1er, al. 1er.
[129] Commission d'aide aux victimes, Rapport d'activités 2005–2009, 2009, available at https://justice.belgium.be/sites/default/files/downloads/aide_victimes_rapport_2005-2009.pdf.
[130] Interview conducted on 1 December 2023.
[131] ibid.
[132] ibid.

2. There is a procedure for transferring claims / documents between EU countries, but it is still necessary for the competent officials to be pro-active in establishing contacts and finding out about the procedural elements of the other European countries concerned regarding the conditions for access to compensation.
3. In Belgium, the Commission accepts processing documents in French, Dutch, German and English, but this is not the case for other counterparts limited to their national language and possibly one more language.
4. The type of compensation is not harmonised between EU countries (existence or not of emergency aid; simple aid versus compensation for the entire loss, etc).
5. The extent of compensation varies from one country to another. In Belgium, non-material damage is one of the items to be compensated, which is not the case in other European countries: the differences in compensation are therefore enormous and harmful to victims, as it is essential that psychological suffering is taken into consideration.

One of the aims of the proposed revision of Directive 2012/29/EU is to simplify access to compensation from the offender in all situations, including national and cross-border situations.[133] Olivier Lauwers rightly suggests that a body be set up to give practical effect to victims' rights, namely a European Commissioner for Victims or a joint coordinating body composed of practitioners.

VI. Conclusion

Strengthening victims' rights is primarily a political choice. More than theoretical reflections and dogmatic debates, victims need a precise framework that enables them to be effectively considered at all stages of the proceedings. First of all, Belgium should adopt a comprehensive definition of the notion of victim. Qualitative and easy to understand information should be developed and distributed to victims more effectively. The national legislator should move forward with the adoption of specific protection measures for victims, including for the most vulnerable ones. Regarding compensation, the proposed revision of Directive 2012/29/EU calls for the State to be obliged to pay the offender's compensation to victims in due time following the judgment on compensation, with a possibility for the State to recover it from the offender subsequently.[134] Without necessarily going that far, compensation for victims, regardless of the type of offence committed (including non-violent or non-intentional offences), should be better guaranteed (eg through the *ex officio* commissioning of a bailiff, obligation imposed on the convicted offender as part of the enforcement of their criminal sentence, etc).

[133] Proposal for a Directive of the European Parliament and of the Council amending Directive 2012/29/EU (n 88) 3.
[134] ibid 10.

10

Victim Rights in the Netherlands: Unconditional Compliance or Pursuing the National Agenda?

SUZAN VAN DER AA

I. Introduction

The extent to which international and European Union (EU) obligations are transposed or implemented into national criminal law and practice can be theoretically framed with the help of three different 'worlds of compliance', that represent different archetypical implementation styles.[1] Countries belonging to the first category – the 'world of law observance' – are prone to implement EU commitments in their national legal systems in a timely and correct fashion, even if these commitments are not in line with national policies. The second category consists of 'world of domestic politics' countries, which are only characterised by non-compliance if national interests collide with the aspiration to comply with EU requirements. It means that timely and correct transposition ensues when there is no conflict of interests, but in the case of conflicting domestic concerns, EU rules are more likely to be disobeyed. The final category involves the 'world of transposition neglect', where national standards are generally viewed as superior and non-compliance with EU standards is commonplace. If EU rules are transposed into the national legal system, this is often the result of external pressure, but even then, compliance is sometimes limited to the 'law on paper' without correct implementation in practice.

Based on an assessment of the implementation of EU social policy in the different EU Member States, Falkner and Treib identified the Netherlands as belonging to the 'world of domestic politics'.[2] It is interesting to see whether this classification also holds true when it comes to EU obligations in the context of victim rights in criminal proceedings. In order to do this, the chapter will start with a description of the Dutch

[1] See, eg, G Falkner and O Treib, 'Three Worlds of Compliance or Four? The EU-15 Compared to New Member States' (2008) (46) 2 *Journal of Common Market Studies* 293–313.

[2] ibid 297.

legal definition of 'victim' (section II), followed by a summary account of the Dutch legal framework on victim rights and an assessment of the extent to which this framework complies with different EU instruments in the field of victim rights, such as the Victims' Rights Directive, the Compensation Directive, the European Protection Order Directive and Court of Justice of the European Union (CJEU) case law (sections III to VI).[3] The chapter concludes with an evaluation of whether EU obligations in the field of victim rights have been fully complied with in the Netherlands or whether some of them were trumped by conflicting domestic concerns. I will further hypothesise what the current Dutch victim policy in combination with the 'world of domestic politics' approach might mean for the implementation of future EU endeavours in this field (section VII).

II. Delineating the Different Roles of the Victim

The Dutch definition of 'victim' within criminal law can be found in Article 51a(1) of the Code of Criminal Procedure (*Wetboek van Strafvordering*, hereafter: CCP). The direct victim is 'the person who has suffered from property or other damage as a direct result of a punishable act', but legal persons (Art 51a(1)(a)(2°) CCP) and family members of the person who died as a direct consequence of the criminal act are also included (Art 51a(2) CCP). 'Family members' are further defined as 'the spouse, registered partner or other life companion of the victim; first line blood relatives, sideline relatives up to and including the fourth degree, and the dependants of the victim'.[4] The inclusion of 'dependants of the victim' was a later extension of the Dutch definition in order to bring the Dutch law up to par with the Victims' Rights Directive.[5]

Somewhat confusing, however, is the fact that not all provisions containing victim rights are using the victim definition stipulated in Article 51a CCP. Sometimes older concepts and definitions, such as 'aggrieved party' (*benadeelde partij*) or 'directly interested party' (*rechtstreeks belanghebbende*) are used instead, for example in the case of the right to join the criminal case with a civil claim for compensation or the right to request for a judicial review. A victim can also take part in criminal proceedings as a witness.

[3] Directive 2012/29/EU of the European Parliament and of the Council of 25 October 2012 establishing minimum standards on the rights, support and protection of victims of crime, and replacing Council Framework Decision 2001/220/JHA (the 'Victims' Rights Directive') [2012] OJ 315/57; Council Directive 2004/80/EC of 29 April 2004 relating to compensation to crime victims (the 'Compensation Directive') [2004] OJ L261/15; Directive 2011/99/EU of the European Parliament and of the Council of 13 December 2011 on the European Protection Order (the 'European Protection Order Directive') [2011] OJ L338/2.

[4] In terms of 'sideline' relatives, the Dutch definition is more inclusive than the Victims' Rights Directive, in the sense that the Dutch definition also includes cousins, uncles and aunts, while the Victims' Rights Directive only includes siblings.

[5] *Kamerstukken II* 2014/15, 34236, 3, 11, available at https://zoek.officielebekendmakingen.nl/kst-34236-3.html?idp=https%3A%2F%2Fengine.surfconext.nl%2Fauthentication%2Fidp%2Fmetadata. The Dutch definition is slightly different from the one articulated in the Victims' Rights Directive, but this was merely done to align the criminal law definition with the one used in Dutch civil law (Article 6:95 Dutch Civil Code). It was explicitly not meant as a means to introduce a definition with a narrower scope than the one in the Victims' Rights Directive (*Kamerstukken II* 2014/15, 34236, 3, 12, available at https://zoek.officielebekendmakingen.nl/kst-34236-3.html?idp=https%3A%2F%2Fengine.surfconext.nl%2Fauthentication%2Fidp%2Fmetadata).

It is important to realise that the scope of these alternative concepts and victim roles can differ from the victim definition in Article 51a CCP.

It is furthermore important to note that victims are 'participants' (*deelnemer*) to the Dutch criminal procedure, not 'parties' (*partij*). This means that in contrast to certain other jurisdictions, the notion of private or auxiliary prosecution is foreign to the Dutch legal system. The victim is only considered a party to the 'adhesion procedure', when the victim joins the criminal proceedings with his civil claim for compensation as the 'aggrieved party'.

III. The Place of the Victim in Criminal Proceedings

Since the 1980s, victim rights in Dutch criminal proceedings have gradually extended and gained strength, even resulting in the implementation of a special section in the Dutch CCP exclusively dedicated to crime victims (section IIIA CCP). In addition to the procedural rights contained in this section, relevant rights are also found elsewhere in the CCP – for instance the right to apply for a judicial review of the decision not to prosecute (Art 12 CCP) or the right to report a crime to the police (Art 161 CCP) – but these rights are typically based on other roles than that of 'victim' per se, such as that of 'directly interested party' or witness. Next to provisions in the CCP, victim rights are furthermore established in other laws or elaborated upon in lower order decrees and regulations.

The Victims' Rights Directive had a direct impact on the further development of the legal victim rights framework in the Netherlands. Although the legislator asserted that most of the minimum standards had already been introduced in the Dutch criminal law system prior to the coming into force of the Victims' Rights Directive, some of its provisions necessitated further extension of existing rights or even the introduction of new rights.[6] Below is a brief overview of some of the most important victim rights in the Netherlands.[7]

A. Right to Proper Treatment

The dedicated victim section in the CCP begins with stipulating the victim's right to 'proper treatment'. Its generic redaction makes this more of an instruction norm for the criminal justice authorities, rather than an enforceable right, but it is considered of great symbolic value nonetheless.[8] It entails treatment that prevents secondary victimisation

[6] See the explanatory memorandum of the Dutch Act for the implementation of Directive 2012/29/EU (*Kamerstukken II*, 34236, 2014-15, nr 3 (MvT).

[7] For readers interested in a more detailed account of the Dutch legal and policy framework regarding victims, see the edited volume by J van Doorn, J Brands, MJJ Kunst, ER Muller, A Pemberton and L van Reemst (eds), *Slachtoffers: Onderzoek, beleid en praktijk* (Wolters Kluwer, 2023) (in Dutch).

[8] See also AK Bosma and MS Groenhuijsen, 'Slachtofferrechten en –participatie in het strafproces', in van Doorn, et al, ibid 453–67 on 478.

because of the victim's participation in criminal proceedings.[9] During the pre-trial phase proper treatment is the public Prosecutor's responsibility (Art 51aa(1) CCP), while the presiding judge has to ensure the proper treatment of victims during trial (Art 288a CCP). Article 9 of the Victims of Crime Decree provides further guidance on what exactly constitutes 'proper treatment'.[10] In this Decree it is, for instance, prescribed that interviews of victims are conducted without unjustified delay after the complaint was made, that the number of interviews of victims is kept to a minimum, and that interviews are carried out only when strictly necessary for criminal investigation purposes. These and other 'proper treatment' provisions clearly demonstrate the direct influence of the Victims' Rights Directive on the Dutch criminal justice system.[11]

B. Right to Information

The right to information consists of a detailed framework of rights scattered over the CCP, two Regulations and a binding Guideline for the Public Prosecution Service.[12] These provisions meticulously prescribe which criminal justice authority is responsible for the provisions of what type of information at each stage of the criminal procedure. In conformity with the Victims' Rights Directive, a distinction is made between generic information rights (Art 51ab CCP and the Regulation on the provision of generic information to victims) and case-specific information rights (Art 51ac CCP and the Regulation on the provision of case-specific information to victims). Victims are not obliged to receive information: a wish not to be informed will be respected.[13] Importantly, the right to information exists even when no suspect has been identified or when the victim has not filed a complaint.

Next to information on all the aspects prescribed by the Victims' Rights Directive, victims involved in Dutch criminal proceedings also have additional information rights that exceed the minimum EU standards, for instance regarding the right of victims to access the case file (Art 51b CCP).[14] Victims of serious crimes are even invited to a private meeting with the public prosecutor prior to the trial (*slachtoffergesprek*), during which the victim can be informed of the case and the sentence that the prosecutor intends to request of the court.[15] Victims are furthermore allowed to request the public prosecutor to add information to the case file that they deem relevant for the criminal case or their claim for compensation (Art 51b(2) CCP).

[9] AL Melai, MS Groenhuijsen e.a., Wetboek van Strafvordering, Art 51a Sv, aant. 6.

[10] Besluit slachtoffers van strafbare feiten (besluit van 24 augustus 2016, *Stb.* 2016, 310, laatstelijk gewijzigd bij besluit van 21 april 2022, *Stb.* 2022, 180, i.w.tr. op 1 juli 2022).

[11] See Art 20 of the Victims' Rights Directive where these exact circumstances surrounding victim interviews are also described.

[12] Articles 51ab, 51ac and 51b CCP, in combination with provisions from the Victims of Crime Decree; the Regulation on the provision of generic information to victims; the Regulation on the provision of case-specific information to victims; and the PPS Victim Rights Guideline (Besluit slachtoffers van strafbare feiten, *Stb.* 2016, 310; Regeling algemene informatievoorziening slachtoffers, *Stcrt.* 2017, 18951; Regeling verstrekken zaaksinformatie aan slachtoffers, *Stcrt.* 2017, 18999; Aanwijzing slachtofferrechten (2021A003).

[13] See, eg, Regeling algemene informatievoorziening, but also the PPS Victim Rights Guideline under 2.4.

[14] The public prosecutor can only deny the victim access to the case file or a transcript of the case file upon authorisation of an examining judge (Art 51b(4) CCP).

[15] Article 5.6 *Aanwijzing slachtofferrechten.*

C. Right to Translation and Interpretation

The right to translation and interpretation during criminal proceedings is laid down in Articles 51c(5), 51ca, and 51d CCP. Victims with difficulties understanding the Dutch language, but also speech and hearing impaired victims can request free interpretation and translation assistance in their contacts with criminal justice authorities and Victim Support Netherlands. Translation of various pieces of case-specific information can be requested, such as information regarding the dismissal of the case; the summons of the suspect; an out-of-court settlement; the nature of the criminal charge; the place, date and time of the trial; the final verdict; and whether an appeal was lodged (Article 51ca jo 51ac CCP). A victim can furthermore request for the translation or interpretation of parts of the case file that she 'deems relevant for the execution of his rights' (Art 51ca(3) CCP). It is important to note that – in accordance with Article 7(7) of the Victims' Rights Directive – the right to translation and interpretation is strengthened by a right to review: if the victim's request for translation or interpretation is rejected by the public prosecutor, she has the right to have this rejection reviewed within 14 days by an examining judge (Art 51ca(6) CCP).[16] A translator can also be arranged at the trial stage, even when the victim is only there as a spectator. In practice, the Netherlands has a relatively advanced system that allows for easy access to translators, inter alia with the help of the 'translator phone', but every now and then, it can take a little longer to find a suitable translator. It is safe to conclude that the minimum standards of Article 7 of the Victims' Rights Directive related to translation and interpretation have been transposed into Dutch national law, while the Netherlands has even extended translation rights to the execution phase.[17]

D. Right to Legal Aid and Representation

Victims also have the right to legal aid and representation by a victim lawyer, a legal representative, and/or another person of the victim's choice (Art 51c CCP).[18] Although victims already had the right to legal aid and representation prior to the Victims' Rights Directive, this right was only applicable in the trial stage. As a consequence of the Victims' Rights Directive, this right was extended to the investigation stage, so nowadays the right to legal aid and representation applies throughout the criminal procedure. Legal aid and representation can, for instance, consist of a third person (or multiple persons) being present during victim interviews;[19] in person helping the victim gain access to information; or in person helping the victim claim compensation. Victims

[16] If the request is made during trial, the court is responsible for this decision. If the request is denied at that stage, no review procedure is available (Art 51ca(5) jo 51ca(7) CCP).

[17] *Wetsvoorstel herziening tenuitvoerlegging strafrechtelijke beslissingen* (USB) (*Kamerstukken II* 2014/15, 34086, nr.2).

[18] Legal aid is provided when the victim is being accompanied by another person, while legal representation is provided when this third person acts on behalf of the victim in his absence (*Kamerstukken II*, 34236, 2014-15, nr 3 (MvT), 15).

[19] Persons can, however, be barred from being present, eg, when this person is suspected of having committed a crime against the victim.

of serious sexual or violent crimes have the right to free legal aid from a specialised victim lawyer.[20]

E. Right to Make a Victim Personal Statement

A highly controversial right that goes beyond the minimum standards prescribed by the Victims' Rights Directive is the right to make a Victim Personal Statement (*spreekrecht*). Originally, this right was restricted to victims making a statement on the impact that the crime had on the victim's life, but its scope was expanded in 2016 so that victims could also narrate on the facts of the crime, the guilt of the suspect, the manner in which they have experienced the criminal procedure, or even the sentence they deem appropriate.[21] The purpose of the Victim Personal Statement is fourfold: helping the victim to begin his emotional recovery; informing the court and the suspect regarding the impact of the crime on the victim; reducing the risk of recidivism; and improving the visibility and the position of victims in criminal proceedings. The Dutch Supreme Court ruled that an oral Victim Personal Statement cannot be used to prove the indictment,[22] but it can influence the sentencing in that it can 'accentuate the impression that was already established' based on the case file and discussions during trial.[23]

In order not to overburden the criminal justice system, this right is reserved for victims of serious crimes carrying a maximum statutory penalty of eight years imprisonment or more, or serious crimes with a lower statutory penalty enlisted in Article 51e(1) CCP. Victim Personal Statements can be made in writing (Article 51b(2) CCP) or orally during the trial (Article 51e CCP). Victims of 12 years and older are allowed to make a Victim Personal Statement, but younger victims 'who are considered capable of reasonably assessing their interests in this regard' can also qualify (Article 51e(5)CCP). If the direct victim is deceased as a result of the crime, or if the direct victim cannot express himself (eg, a comatose victim or a victim below 12 years of age), relatives are allowed to make a Victim Personal Statement instead. In case more than three relatives have expressed a desire to make an oral statement during trial, and they cannot come to an agreement themselves, the presiding judge decides which three relatives are allowed to speak (Article 51e(4) CCP).

F. Restorative Justice

The Dutch criminal justice system facilitates various forms of restorative justice, such as victim-offender meetings in the execution phase, or restorative justice during criminal

[20] All lawyers involved in victim aid and representation have to follow a specialisation course in order to guarantee the quality of their assistance.

[21] Wet van 14 april 2016 tot wijziging van het Wetboek van Strafvordering ter aanvulling van het spreekrecht van slachtoffers en nabestaanden in het strafproces en wijziging van de Wet schadefonds geweldsmisdrijven ter uitbreiding van de mogelijkheid van uitkering aan nabestaanden, *Staatsblad* 2016, 160.

[22] Hoge Raad 11 oktober 2011, ECLI:NL:HR:2011:BR2359. This is different for written Victim Personal Statements.

[23] Hoge Raad 6 maart 2012, ECLI:NL:HR:2012:BR1149; Hoge Raad 8 juli 2014, ECLI:NL:HR:2014:1695.

proceedings, but the term 'mediation' is exclusively used for conversations between victim and offender, mediated by an independent third party, that lead to agreements that are legally relevant, such as agreements on the payment of compensation. The police need to inform the victim and suspect of restorative justice options, the public prosecution service needs to stimulate mediation between victim and suspect (Article 51h(3) CCP), and the criminal courts can take the result of a successful mediation into account in their sentencing decisions (Article 51h(2) CCP). Despite these stipulations, research demonstrated that the Dutch criminal justice system has not widely implemented mediation or other forms of restorative justice just yet: mediation is initiated in less than one per cent of the criminal (court) cases.[24]

G. Victim Support Netherlands

Victims in the Netherlands can make use of a wide variety of private and public, specialist and generic victim support services.[25] The largest and best known organisation for providing these services is Victim Support Netherlands (*Slachtofferhulp Nederland*). Since its establishment in 1984, Victim Support Netherlands has grown into an organisation with nationwide coverage. Its paid staff and volunteers not only support victims of crimes, but also help victims of traffic accidents, disasters and calamities deal with the aftermath of these events. Their services include, inter alia, emotional support, support during criminal proceedings and support with filing a claim for compensation.[26] In addition to providing generic assistance, Victim Support Netherlands also offers specialised support to certain categories of victims.[27] It furthermore employs specialised legal experts and case managers for victims of serious (sexual) violence. One of the features that make Victim Support Netherlands successful is their cooperation with the police and their proactive outreach to victims: the police actively inquire with victims whether they object to Victim Support Netherlands receiving their contact details. If the victim does not object, Victim Support Netherlands will receive this information and contact the victim within two work days to assess whether they need help. This practice alleviates the burden of the victim of having to initiate this contact himself, resulting in a higher number of victims making use of the services of Victim Support Netherlands.

H. Cross-Border Victims

The predicaments of cross-border victimisation was an important factor of why the EU deemed it necessary to create legislation in this field in the first place. In the Netherlands,

[24] C van der Wilt, 'Tien jaar mediation in de strafrechtelijke jurisprudentie' (2021) 21(2) *Tijdschrift voor Herstelrecht* 8–28.

[25] Providing a detailed account of all the different victim support services, such as the various specialised centres for victims of sexual violence and the centres for victims of domestic violence and child abuse, is not possible within the confines of this chapter. For more information on the Dutch victim support landscape, see ER Muller, 'Slachtofferbeleid: Inhoud en organisaties' in van Doorn et al (n 7) 453–67.

[26] For more information, see the website of Victim Support Netherlands, available at www.slachtofferhulp.nl.

[27] This pertains to victims of sexual violence, traffic accidents or cases involving missing persons.

the abovementioned rights and support services are accessible to cross-border victims as well as victims of crimes without a cross-border dimension, but in addition, cross-border victims can make use of special rights geared towards their special needs. If Dutch residents are victimised in another EU Member State, they are allowed – in conformity with Article 17 of the Victims' Rights Directive – to file a complaint with the Dutch police if they were *unable* to do so in the country where the criminal offence happened or – in the case of a serious offence – if they were *unwilling* to file a complaint abroad.[28] They can also apply to Victim Support Netherlands for socio-psychological support.

Vice versa, when residents of other EU Member States are victimised in the Netherlands, they can sometimes make use of videoconferencing facilities. For victims who are resident abroad, this saves them the burden of having to travel back to the Netherlands to give (further) evidence, but it is the criminal justice authorities who decide on the question of whether videoconferencing is allowed. In conformity with Article 17(1) of the Victims' Rights Directive, Article 78a of the Dutch Criminal Code and Article 131a CCP allow for the hearing, interrogating, or questioning of persons with the help of a direct audio and video connection between the persons involved.[29] There is currently a legislative proposal pending which aims to extend the option of videoconferencing to victims who wish to attend the trial digitally as a spectator or who wish to make a Victim Personal Statement through videoconferencing.[30] Cross-border victims can furthermore benefit from the state compensation scheme, which will be discussed in section IV.B.

IV. Compensation of Crime Victims

A. Compensation by the Offender in Criminal Proceedings

The Netherlands has a sophisticated adhesion procedure through which victims can have their civil claim for compensation dealt with within criminal proceedings (Article 51f, 51g, 361 CCP). An important advantage of having a criminal court adjudicate on the civil claim simultaneous with the criminal case is that it saves an extra procedure before a civil court, thereby alleviating the overburdened justice system and victims alike. In addition, victims avoid the risk of having to pay civil court fees and – very importantly – the burden of execution lies with a public service: the awarded claim for compensation is typically strengthened by a 'compensation order' (Article 36f CCP) which makes the Central Judicial Collection Agency (*Centraal Justitieel Incassobureau*) responsible for retrieving the money from the offender instead of the victim. In cases involving serious violent and sexual crimes, payment of compensation is even guaranteed

[28] This right was not transposed into Dutch law, but was included as an instruction norm in the Victim Guidelines of the Public Prosecution Service (OM Aanwijzing Slachtofferrechten (2021 A003).

[29] Videoconferencing can also be used for Dutch residents who are victimised as a protection measure to avoid direct contact with the defendant during trial (Art 12 Besluit slachtoffers van strafbare feiten).

[30] See the Arts 1.11.3–1.11.5 of the bill 'Wetsvoorstel tot vaststelling van het nieuwe Wetboek van Strafvordering (ambtelijke versie juli 2020)' and its explanatory memorandum (Memorie van toelichting nieuwe Wetboek van Strafvordering (Ambtelijke Versie, Juli 2020) 218).

by the State if the offender has not fully paid the awarded sum within eight months after the final verdict.[31] This is called the 'advance payment scheme' (*voorschotregeling*).[32] The advance payment scheme does not require the victim to initiate another procedure, but automatically comes into force if the Central Judicial Collection Agency has not received full payment by the offender eight months after a final verdict.

However, the above only applies if the court awards the victim's claim for compensation. The situation is different if the claim is (partially) rejected or if the claim is deemed 'inadmissible'. This latter decision is made if the court considers that a substantive assessment of the claim would place an 'undue burden' (*onevenredige belasting*) on the criminal proceedings. In that scenario, victims can in theory still resort to a civil court, but in practice it means they are left empty-handed, because research has demonstrated that this option is not very popular as an alternative.[33]

B. State Compensation

When victims are targeted by an unknown offender or when the damage incurred as a result of the crime is not covered by their insurance, there is only one way to retrieve part of the damages: via the Dutch Violent Offences Compensation Fund (*Schadefonds Geweldsmisdrijven*).[34] This state-funded Compensation Fund was founded in 1976 – before the coming into force of the Council of Europe's European Convention on the Compensation of Victims of Violent Crimes (ETS, No 116) and the EU Council Directive 2004/80/EC of 29 April 2004 relating to compensation to crime victims (the 'Compensation Directive') – and it aims to provide victims of violent crimes with at least partial compensation for their material and immaterial damages up to a maximum of €35,000. The compensation is based on fixed amounts, subdivided into six categories, relative to the estimated seriousness of the injuries suffered by the victim, the consequences and the circumstances of the crime.[35] In other words, instead of making an individual assessment of the exact damage suffered by each individual victim, victims falling within a certain category receive the same fixed amount of compensation. This allows for relatively quick proceedings and it aligns with the rationale of only providing a *contribution* towards the damage. In that sense, compensations provided by the Compensation Fund are meant as an expression of societal solidarity with victims of serious crimes,[36] not as a means to provide complete reparation of material and

[31] In cases involving serious violent and sexual crimes, victims receive full payment of the awarded damages via the advance payment scheme. In other cases, the advance payment is limited to a maximum of €5,000.

[32] Art 6:4:2(7) CCP; Art 4:14(2) Besluit tenuitvoerlegging strafrechtelijke beslissingen. Victims of other crimes also receive an advance payment, but only up to a maximum of €5,000.

[33] RSB Kool, MR Hebly, DP van Uhm and L Orvini, *Schadeverhaal na een strafbaar feit via de kantonrechter. Een verkennend onderzoek* (WODC Den Haag, 2014).

[34] See *Wet Schadefondsgeweldsmisdrijven* and *Besluit schadefondsgeweldsmisdrijven* for the legal basis of the Dutch Compensation Fund. Even victims with known offenders can resort to the Dutch Compensation Fund to have immediate damages recovered.

[35] The fixed payments of the six categories amount to €1,000, €2,500, €5,000, €10,000, €20,000 or €35,000. See Beleidsbundel Schadefonds Geweldsmisdrijven (1 November 2022) 22.

[36] M Huibers, M Kunst and S van Wingerden, 'De beslispraktijk van het Schadefonds Geweldsmisdrijven: een kwalitatieve studie naar de beoordeling van verzoeken tot tegemoetkoming' (2019) 40(1) *Recht der Werkelijkheid* 50–70.

non-material loss suffered by the victim. In 2022, over 10,000 victims applied for payment from the Compensation Fund, while almost 7,000 applications were granted with an average compensation of 3,883 euros.[37]

The following eligibility criteria apply:

1. The victim has to be a natural person who suffered serious physical or psychological damage as a result of an intentional violent crime. Surviving relatives of victims who died as a result of an intentional violent crime or a crime of negligence are also eligible; and so are relatives of victims with severe and permanent injuries as a result of an intentional violent crime.
2. The crime must have occurred on Dutch territory (including the Caribbean part of the Kingdom), on board of a Dutch airplane or Dutch vessel. Aligning with the EU prohibition of discrimination, having the Dutch nationality is *not* a requirement for eligibility.
3. It is not required to prove the crime (beyond reasonable doubt), but the crime victimisation needs to be 'plausible'. Reporting the crime to the police can help establish this plausibility.
4. An application for compensation must be filed within a period of ten years after the violent crime was committed or after the direct victim's death.

As a result of EU Directive 2004/80/EC of 29 April 2004 relating to compensation to crime victims, Dutch residents who were victimised in another EU Member State are also eligible to apply with their claim to the Dutch Violent Offences Compensation Fund. After receiving the application, the Dutch Fund will then transmit this application to the Compensation Fund of the Member State in which the crime was committed. This latter Fund is responsible for payment of compensation to the victim. The Dutch Fund will only transfer the application and provide continuous support for the applicant in the further communication with this foreign Fund.

V. Available Protection Measures

A. Individual Assessment

Whether a victim needs certain protection measures within criminal proceedings is evaluated with the help of an individual assessment (Article 51aa(3)(b) CCP). This assessment was introduced as a result of the Victims' Rights Directive and, as of June 2018, all victims who come into personal contact with the police are assessed on their individual protection needs.[38] Based on an introductory conversation, in combination with information from judicial data systems and a list of indicators, the police officer tries to establish whether this particular victim runs a higher risk of secondary and

[37] See Annual Report (Schadefonds Geweldsmisdrijven, Jaarverslag 2022).

[38] See Besluit slachtoffers van strafbare feiten (*Stb*. 2016, 310) for more information regarding the individual assessment.

repeat victimisation, intimidation and retaliation, and tries to assess which special protection measures could reduce this risk.

B. Protection Measures

The protection measures that can be imposed as a result of the individual assessment are diverse and cover all phases of the criminal procedure. Some of these measures are only available to a limited extent and under strict conditions (eg, anonymity). If the assessment leads to the implementation of protection measures, this needs to be recorded in the case file and communicated to the public prosecution service and Victim Support Netherlands. What follows is a non-exhaustive list of protection measures that can result from the individual assessment.[39]

Protection measures in the investigation phase:

1. Leaving out the address of the victim in the complaint (*domiciliekeuze*).
2. Replacing the name, birth date, and address of the victim with a number in the complaint (*aangifte op nummer*) or (partially) anonymous complaints.
3. Victim interviews by specially trained police officers.
4. Interviews in special (eg, child-friendly) interrogation rooms.
5. Taking down the complaint at the victim's home.
6. Presence of a victim advocate or other person during the interview.
7. An audio or audiovisual registration of the interview.
8. Arresting the suspect.
9. Location or no contact protection order.
10. A temporary barring order (from the home).
11. A mobile (Aware) alarm system.
12. Temporarily relocating the victim to a victim shelter.
13. Various measures to secure the victim and/or his home.
14. (Guided) referral to police, public prosecution service or victim support services.
15. Involvement of child protection services or support services specialised in domestic violence.
16. Involvement of a specialised 'family detective'.
17. Dedicated work protocols (eg, domestic violence, stalking).
18. Mediation.

Protection measures in the prosecution phase:

1. (Partially) anonymous testimony before the investigative judge or in court.
2. Anonymity of witnesses and witness protection programmes.
3. Trials in camera.
4. Location or no contact protection orders.
5. Imposing conditional measures for the protection of victims.

[39] This is based on the document 'Lijst beschermingsmaatregelen met toelichting' from Victim Support Netherlands.

6. Securing the victim (after police analysis).
7. Involving a case-manager from the public prosecution service.
8. Mediation.

Protection measures during trial:

1. Separate waiting rooms for victims.
2. Prevention of eye contact between victim and defendant, eg, through the use of screens or videoconferencing.
3. Victim interviews without the victim being present, eg, through videoconferencing.
4. Trials in camera.

In addition to the protection measures during criminal proceedings, various protection measures can also be imposed as part of the sentence or in the execution phase.

C. Protection Orders

One way in which victims can be protected against their offenders is with the help of protection orders. A common example is a protection order which prohibits the offender to enter a certain area – eg, the neighbourhood where the victim lives – or to contact the victim. The Dutch criminal justice system has a myriad of criminal law provisions on which protection orders can be based.[40] A study from 2011 found no less than 14 legal provisions within criminal (procedural) law that can form the basis of a protection order, and relevant provisions are available at all stages of the criminal procedure.[41] These provisions differ in terms of application requirements, consequences of violating the order, maximum duration, etc. Most often protection orders within the criminal procedure are imposed as a condition to a conditional suspension of pre-trial detention (*bijzondere voorwaarde bij de schorsing van de voorlopige hechtenis*; Article 80 CCP), a conditional suspension of the sentence (*bijzondere voorwaarde bij een voorwaardelijke straf*; Article 14c section 2 CCP), or a conditional release from prison (*bijzondere voorwaarde bij een voorwaardelijke invrijheidstelling*; former Article 15a section 2 CCP).[42]

For victims involved in cross-border cases, the European Protection Order Directive[43] could be of relevance. This Directive was transposed into Dutch legislation in 2015.[44] In accordance with the European Protection Order Directive, Dutch public

[40] In addition, there are also protection measures available in civil and administrative law.

[41] For an overview of these provisions, see S van der Aa, K Lens, F Klerx, A Bosma and M van den Bosch, *Aard, omvang en handhaving van beschermingsbevelen in Nederland. Deel 1: Wettelijk kader en handhaving* (INTERVICT, 2011) 26. In the meantime, however, some of these provisions have changed or disappeared again, eg, as a consequence of the new system of conditional release from prison (see the new Art 6:2: 11(3) CCP).

[42] S van der Aa, F Klerx, M Bosmans, A Bosma and M van den Bosch, *Aard, omvang en handhaving van beschermingsbevelen in Nederland. Deel 2: Aard en omvang* (INTERVICT, 2011).

[43] European Protection Order Directive (n 3).

[44] Wet tot implementatie van richtlijn 2011/99/EU van 13 december 2011 betreffende het Europees beschermingsbevel, available at https://eur-lex.europa.eu/LexUriServ/LexUriServ.do?uri=OJ:L:2011:338:0002:0018:nl:PDF (*PbEU* L 338, available at https://eur-lex.europa.eu/legal-content/NL/AUTO/?uri=uriserv:OJ.L_.2011.338.01.0002.01.NLD) (*Stb* 2014) 40.

prosecutors can now issue and execute protection measures to or from another EU Member State. This only applies to prohibitions from entering certain localities, places or areas; prohibitions of contact; and prohibitions on approaching the protected person closer than a prescribed distance. Other protection measures cannot be converted into a European Protection Order. In 2011 a case file analysis was performed, to predict the frequency with which European Protection Orders would have to be issued once the law transposing the Directive would come into effect. This study yielded little evidence for a cross-border dimension in the large majority of criminal cases in which a national protection order was imposed. The victims and suspects generally had a Dutch nationality and address, and other indicators of cross-border elements were also practically absent. Furthermore, if cross-border elements were present in a case, these often related to non-EU countries. As a consequence the study hypothesised that there would be only very few requests for a criminal European Protection Order coming from the Netherlands and this hypothesis was substantiated in practice: to date there are no reports of the Netherlands ever having issued or executed a European Protection Order.[45]

VI. Possible Impact of CJEU Case Law

A final question to explore is whether CJEU case law has had an impact on victim rights within the Dutch criminal law system. Although the CJEU has ruled several judgments that are important to the interpretation of victim rights under the EU *acquis*, none of these judgments give rise to substantial concerns regarding the implementation of the EU body of victim rights and obligations within Dutch criminal procedure.[46]

A possible exception might be the CJEU judgment in *Presidenza del Consiglio dei Ministri v BV* (C-129/19) of 16 July 2020 which first clarified that Article 12(2) of Council Directive 2004/80/EC of 29 April 2004 relating to compensation to crime victims 'imposes the obligation on each Member State to provide for a scheme of compensation covering all victims of violent intentional crime committed on their territory and not only those victims that are in a cross-border situation'. While this clarification was of little relevance to the Netherlands – the Dutch Violent Offences

[45] This conclusion was based on a desk search of open internet sources; no authorities were contacted to verify the conclusion. However, support for this conclusion can be drawn from the fact that in the period 2015–2018 only 37 European Protection Orders had been issued across the EU Member States (Report from the Commission to the European Parliament and the Council on the implementation of Directive 2011/99/EU of the European Parliament and of the Council of 13 December 2011 on the European protection order (COM(2020) 187 final). This suggests that even if European Protection Orders were issued or recognised by the Netherlands, their numbers are not high. This outcome was also hypothesised in S van der Aa, 'National Report The Netherlands' as part of the overarching POEMS project, available at http://poems-project.com/wp-content/uploads/2015/02/Netherlands.pdf.

[46] See, for instance, Jaarbericht 2019 Procesvertegenwoordiging Hof van Justitie van de EU, 52-53 (annex to *Kamerstukken II*, 2019-2020, 35300-V nr. 74), where the Dutch Ministry of Foreign Affairs concluded that the judgment of the CJEU in *Gambino and Hyka* (C-38/18) (Italy) of 29 July 2019 – on the Victim Rights Directive and the re-examination of victims – is in line with the Dutch point of view.

Compensation Fund provides state compensation to all victims of serious intentional crimes of violence on Dutch territory, regardless of the residence status of the victim or the cross-border dimension of the case – this might not be true for the second question where the CJEU elaborated on the meaning of a 'fair and appropriate' compensation within the context of Article 12(2) of Directive 2004/80.[47] While the CJEU acknowledged that the Member States have discretion as to how to arrange for the determination of such compensation (consideration 58), and that full compensation of material and non-material loss is not necessarily required (consideration 60), it also specified certain criteria for the assessment of whether the compensation offered by the State is 'fair and appropriate'. These criteria entail that compensation must not be 'purely symbolic or manifestly insufficient having regard to the seriousness of the consequences' of the crime (consideration 63), but must compensate 'to an appropriate extent, the suffering to which those victims have been exposed' (consideration 64). Compensation schemes based on fixed rates are not prohibited, as long as the fixed amounts are 'capable of being varied in accordance with the nature of the violence suffered' (consideration 65), and 'the compensation scale is sufficiently detailed so as to avoid the possibility that, having regard to the circumstances of a particular case, the fixed rate of compensation provided for a specific type of violence proves to be manifestly insufficient' (consideration 66). Taking into account that sexual violence 'is likely to give rise to the most serious consequences of violent intentional crime' (consideration 67), the Italian fixed amount of €4,800 to a victim of sexual violence did not appear, at first sight, 'fair and appropriate compensation' according to the CJEU.

In placing those criteria next to the manner in which the Dutch Violent Offences Compensation Fund operates, Lindenbergh 'cautiously' concludes that the Dutch scheme provides a 'fair and appropriate compensation'.[48] He, however, also points out that the indicated compensation for cases of sexual violence in the Netherlands would amount to €5,000, which is very similar to the €4,800 that the CJEU weighed and found wanting in the case of *Presidenza del Consiglio dei Ministri v BV*. But since the Dutch scheme allows for more differentiation and higher amounts of compensation if a sexual violence victim is, for instance, diagnosed with serious psychological damage, while the Italian system provided a single amount across the board, he reckons that the Dutch system might pass the test. Nonetheless, the fact that the maximum compensation of €35,000 does not come close to the actual damages in some very serious cases, the fact that this amount has not been indexed for years, but also the fact that surrounding countries allow for much higher maximum payments, makes Lindenbergh question whether the Dutch State compensation scheme is in fact fully compliant with Article 12(2) of Directive 2004/80.[49]

[47] See also case note of Lindenbergh (HvJ EG 16 juli 2020, C-129/19, ECLI:EU:C:2020:566, NJ 2020/424 m.nt. SD Lindenbergh (Presidenza del Consiglio dei Ministri tegen BV).

[48] See also case note HvJ EG 16 juli 2020, C-129/19, ECLI:EU:C:2020:566, NJ 2020/424 m.nt. S.D. Lindenbergh (Presidenza del Consiglio dei Ministri tegen BV).

[49] Possibly, the maximum payments for various categories will be increased in the future.

VII. Conclusion

It is safe to conclude that, by and large, the EU victim instruments have successfully been transposed into Dutch national law by now. In some respects, the Dutch framework on victim rights even exceeds the minimum standards contained in EU legislation, for instance by allowing victims of serious crimes to make a Victim Personal Statement, by providing an advance payment of compensation eight months after the final verdict, or by extending the application of various victim rights to the execution phase.

However, the Dutch have not always been that receptive of EU initiatives in this context. For instance, when the European Commission evaluated the implementation of Council Framework Decision 2001/220/JHA on the standing of victims in criminal proceedings,[50] it concluded that the Netherlands had not transposed all rights contained in that instrument. Some argue that the fact that the transposal was not always satisfactory or timely, had to do with other factors, such as unrealistic deadlines in the EU Framework Decision or the mistaken belief that the Dutch framework of victim rights was already in compliance with EU obligations.

Since the EU victim agenda largely aligns with domestic political aspirations to improve the standing of victims in criminal proceedings, these deficiencies have been remedied in the meantime. Although there are some provisions where there is still some discussion on the question of whether the Dutch are actually in full compliance with EU obligations,[51] most obligations are observed, making the qualification of the Netherlands as belonging to the 'world of domestic politics' adequate, also in the context of victim rights.

If we look to the future, it is good to keep this basic stance of the Netherlands in mind when developing new victim rights and predicting the extent to which new proposals may prove contentious or make implementation difficult. Recently, the European Commission published a proposal for a new Directive amending the Victims' Rights Directive.[52] On 6 October 2023, the Minister of Foreign Affairs wrote a letter to the Chair of Parliament in which she shared a primary reaction of the Government to this proposal and, again, this document provides testimony of the Dutch adherence to the 'world of domestic politics', for while the Government supports the vision of the Commission regarding the improvement of certain victim rights, the Government is not in favour of other proposed rights, in particular those that are not in line with the existing Dutch victim policy (2022–2025),[53] or those that could potentially affect the foundations of Dutch criminal procedure. During the past decade, many new victim

[50] Report from the Commission pursuant to Article 18 of the Council Framework Decision of 15 March 2001 on the standing of victims in criminal proceedings (2001/220/JHA), COM(2009) 166.

[51] See, for instance, the discussion on the Victim Injuries Compensation Fund in para 6. Another example pertains to the fact that victims are not allowed to call witnesses to the stand or to question them. Some authors argued that this would be in disregard of Article 3 Council Framework Decision 2001/220/JHA (WvSv, AL Melai/MS Groenhuijsen e.a., Artikel 51b Sv, aant. 6).

[52] Proposal for a Directive of the European Parliament and of the Council amending Directive 2012/29/EU establishing minimum standards on the rights, support and protection of victims of crime, and replacing Council Framework Decision 2001/220/JHA (COM(2023) 424 final.

[53] This new policy is expressed in the Meerjarenagenda Slachtofferbeleid 2022–2025.

rights were introduced into Dutch legislation. While some new rights might be introduced still, the current political focus is on improving the execution of rights that are already in place, and this focus also applies to victim instruments in the EU context. According to the letter: 'the execution in practice of existing guidelines and legislation takes priority'.[54] So there seems to be a certain reluctance towards accepting additional laws and regulations in this respect, and this reluctance might hinder the introduction of far-reaching new rights, such as the Commission's proposal to oblige Member States to pay compensation due from the offender up front (new Article 16(2)). Although the Dutch advance payment scheme may have inspired the Commission's proposal, it is more limited than the one proposed by the Commission. In the Dutch scheme, the advance payment is only awarded eight months after the verdict becomes final – if the offender has not paid the compensation in the meantime – whereas the Commission proposes to pay the upfront compensation *immediately* after the judgment. In addition, the Dutch scheme has limited the upfront payments in cases other than serious violent and sexual crimes to a maximum of €5,000. Such limitation is not foreseen in the Commission's proposal either and could potentially be very costly. The proposal to introduce a right to remedies (Article 26d) is even more controversial. According to the Government, introduction of a generic right to remedy means victims would increasingly assume the role of 'parties' to the proceedings, while they are currently positioned as 'participants' in Dutch criminal procedure (see section II). It is feared that making such substantial changes to the role of one of the participants, could infringe upon the position of the public prosecution service, the suspect, and the judiciary and create an unbalance in the criminal justice system. Because of the potentially serious impact on the foundations of Dutch criminal procedural law, the Government would prefer to leave the decision-making on how to safeguard the effectuation of victim rights on the national level. Now that the European agenda seems to collide with Dutch victim policy, a fierce negotiation trajectory is to be expected.

[54] Brief van de minister van Buitenlandse Zaken Aan de Voorzitter van de Tweede Kamer der Staten-Generaal Den Haag, 6 Oktober 2023 (*Kamerstukken II*, 2022-2023, 22 112, nr. 3799).

11

Victims' Rights in Romania: The Gap between the Adoption of Legal Texts and their Effective Implementation

DIANA IONESCU

I. Introduction

As an EU Member State since 2007, Romania had to transpose the European legislation and ensure its practical application. This contribution aims to review this process in the area of EU law on crime victims' rights. In this framework, Directive 2012/29/EU establishing minimum standards on the rights, support and protection of victims of crime ('Victims' Rights Directive' or 'Directive 2012/29'),[1] Directive 2004/80/EC relating to compensation to crime victims ('Compensation Directive'),[2] Directive 2011/99/EU on the European Protection Order ('EPO Directive')[3] and Regulation (EU) No 606/2013 on mutual recognition of protection measures in civil matters[4] will be taken into consideration.

As documented, EU intervention concerning victims' rights has taken place in 'a landscape of considerable legal diversity'.[5] This research will analyse Romania's position and assess the EU intervention's added value and effectiveness. To achieve this goal, it focuses on legislation and its application, using case law and empirical data reflecting the real-life impact of legal texts. In this light, section II will assess the Romanian perspective on victims of crime, the victims' definition, and their role in criminal proceedings.

[1] Directive 2012/29/EU of the European Parliament and of the Council of 25 October 2012 establishing minimum standards on the rights, support and protection of victims of crime, and replacing Council Framework Decision 2001/220/JHA (Victims' Rights Directive) [2012] OJ L315.

[2] Council Directive 2004/80/EC of 29 April 2004 relating to compensation to crime victims (Compensation Directive) [2004] OJ L261/15.

[3] Directive 2011/99/EU of the European Parliament and of the Council of 13 December 2011 on the European Protection Order (EPO Directive) [2011] OJ L338.

[4] Regulation (EU) No 606/2013 of the European Parliament and of the Council of 12 June 2013 on mutual recognition of protection measures in civil matters [2013] OJ L181.

[5] V Mitsilegas, *EU Criminal Law after Lisbon. Rights, Trust, and the Transformation of Europe* (Hart Publishing, 2016) 186.

The right to information, participatory rights, victims' compensation, and protection measures will be analysed in sections III, IV and V. The training of practitioners will be assessed in section VI. The research findings will support policy proposals regarding victims' rights at the EU and domestic levels. These claims are presented in section VII.

II. Background

A. The Domestic Perspective on Victims' Participation in Criminal Proceedings

Romania has had a centralised Government since its formation in the mid-nineteenth century. The strong nation-state and the State-centered model of criminal justice, as presented by Albin Dearing,[6] are the foundational approaches to domestic criminal justice.

Considering the categories advanced by Mirjan Damaška, these approaches includes understanding criminal justice as 'a policy-implementing process of hierarchical officialdom'.[7] On one hand, crime is understood as a violation of the State's policies, and criminal justice as a vehicle for implementing these policies. On the other hand, criminal justice is dominated by the exclusivity of officials over the proceedings and the deterrence of private procedural involvement. These two perspectives significantly affect the victims' role in criminal proceedings, the exercise of their participatory rights, and the understanding of victims as vulnerable individuals.

i. The Victims' Role in Criminal Proceedings

Romania adopted its first Code of Criminal Procedure (CCP) in the mid-nineteenth century under French influence.[8] The civil party system was, therefore, adopted. The harmed person could claim offender compensation by initiating a civil action. On the other hand, the prosecutor was the State official with the right to initiate and exercise criminal action (ie, the right to prosecute). However, these two actions were not completely separated. When prosecutors dismissed a case, the civil parties could initiate civil and criminal action by submitting the case to the investigative judge or the court. This was strongly inspired from the French system.[9] The 1936 CCP maintained this approach.[10]

Since 1938, authoritarian governments have strengthened public prosecutors' powers, a trend especially noticeable during the communist dictatorship. During this

[6] A Dearing, *Justice for Victims of Crime. Human Dignity as the Foundation of Criminal Justice in Europe* (Springer, 2017) 3–9, 299.

[7] M Damaška, *The Faces of Justice and State Authority. A Comparative Approach to the Legal Process* (Yale Univesity Press, 1986) 182–86.

[8] Code of Criminal Procedure (CCP) [1864] Romanian Official Journal (ROJ) No 230, 2.12.1864.

[9] French CCP, Art 1(2).

[10] CCP [1936] ROJ No 66, 19.3.1936.

period, the legal position of the civil party was maintained, while the civil party's right to initiate criminal action was repealed. The 1968 CCP[11] also granted the victims the legal status of injured party,[12] a status not provided in the previous CCPs. The injured parties had participative rights in the criminal action, aiming to support the prosecutors' powers to investigate and prosecute. However, in contrast with the rights of the civil parties under the French influence, the injured parties had no right to initiate criminal action when prosecutors dismissed the case; they were not even entitled to judicial review against the prosecutors' decision to dismiss a case.

The 1968 CCP granted the victims the right to initiate criminal action but on a track separated from the prosecutor's power to prosecute. Offences were divided into two categories, namely offences in respect of which the criminal action was exercised by the prosecutors (with no right of the victims to initiate criminal action or to exercise judicial review in case of dismissal) and offences in respect of which criminal action was exercised only by the injured parties (and not by the prosecutors). The second category was limited to petty offences such as assault, threats, insults, and trespass.[13] No pretrial investigation was needed, and the victims acted as private prosecutors during the trial.

After the fall of communism, the legal status of injured party and civil party have been preserved. In 1997, the Constitutional Court granted victims the right to judicial review of the prosecutor's decision to dismiss a case.[14] Starting in the 2000s, the emerging normative trend was to limit the role of the victim in the criminal action. The status of private prosecutor was repealed in 2006. Moreover, the 2014 CCP[15] introduced a distinction between parties and other participants involved in criminal proceedings. The parties are the persons who exercise a judicial action or against whom such action is exercised.[16] Because the prosecutors had exclusivity over criminal action, the victims' role was downgraded from injured party to injured person, a legal position in the 'main procedural participants' category.[17]

In Romania, an injured person is someone who has suffered a physical, material, or moral injury due to an offence.[18] The CCP definition refers to both natural and legal persons. When criminal proceedings are initiated *ex officio* or by complaint, the victims receive *de jure* this status.[19] Victims do not have to apply for the legal position of injured person; however, they can waive it. In such cases, subject to their discretion, the judicial authorities can examine the victim as a witness.[20]

The 2014 CCP preserves the role of the civil party. It is limited to civil action, with the civil party having no power to initiate a criminal action when the prosecutors deny it. The injured person must submit a civil claim to receive the civil party status. A victim

[11] CCP [1968] ROJ No 145, 12.11.1968.

[12] ibid Art 24(1).

[13] ibid Art 279 (1)(1), Art 282.

[14] Constitutional Court, Decision No 486/1997, ROJ No 105, 6.3.1998.

[15] Law No 135/2010 on the CCP [2010] ROJ No 486, 15.7.2010. The Code entered into force on 1 February 2014 and will be identified as the 2014 CCP.

[16] 2014 CCP Art 32(1).

[17] ibid Art 33(1).

[18] ibid Art 79.

[19] ibid Art 79.

[20] ibid Art 81(2).

can be an injured person and a civil party simultaneously.[21] If the victim died because of the offence, the successors could claim damages for the harm produced by the victim's death. The compensation claim can be submitted during investigations or at the beginning of the trial. If the injured persons do not want to submit a compensation claim in criminal proceedings, they can initiate litigation at a civil court.

The 2014 CCP acknowledged that parties can have more procedural rights than the main procedural participants.[22] The underlying reason for this approach was a domestic trend focused on the efficiency of criminal proceedings.[23] The Romanian Government did not claim the duty to protect victims' rights – the 'individualization of security'[24] – to justify strengthening State power. On the contrary, the 2014 CCP claimed efficiency as an argument to limit the role of the victims and their participatory rights in criminal proceedings.

After the 2014 CCP came into effect, the Constitutional Court balanced out this trend. It increased the participatory rights of the injured persons by conferring several rights that were initially denied by the CCP, such as the right to participate in the preliminary chamber,[25] the right to participate in the court validation of the prosecutor–defendant plea agreement, and the right to submit an appeal against the judgment validating such agreement.[26]

Despite the increase in participatory rights, their exercise is dependent on prosecutors' exclusivity on the right to initiate and exercise criminal action. In a judicial system dominated by the responsibilities of State officials, the private involvement of victims is not appreciated as support for prosecution or as an exercise of procedural rights. On the contrary, it is seen as meddling in the efficient performance of official responsibilities.[27] This was the approach of the 2014 CCP. From this perspective, as a mindset, the judicial authorities often disregard the victims' rights.

When the Victims' Rights Directive had to be transposed, most of its participatory rights were already regulated in the domestic legislation. Some components of the right to information (eg, information about the release of the offender remanded in custody or sentenced, information in the case of victims resident in a Member State other than the one in which the offence was committed), the right to reimbursement of expenses, the measures to encourage the offenders to pay compensation to the victim, and the reasonable delay for the judgment awarding civil damages represent the added value of the Directive in relation to the existing Romanian legislation.

The definition of the victim as provided for by Article 2 of the Victims' Rights Directive was transposed *verbatim* in Law No 211/2004 on Measures to Ensure the

[21] ibid Art 85(2).

[22] ibid Art 33(2).

[23] For an analysis of the 2014 CCP's efficiency objective, see D Nițu and D Ionescu, 'Romanian Criminal Procedure at a Crossroads: Legacies of the Past and Current Challenges' in É Sellier and A Weyembergh (eds), *Criminal Procedures and Cross-Border Cooperation in the EU Area of Criminal Justice. Together but Apart?* (Éditions de l'Université de Bruxelles, 2020) 208–11.

[24] Mitsilegas (n 5) 207.

[25] Constitutional Court, Decision No 641/2014 [2014] ROJ No 887, 5.12.2014.

[26] Constitutional Court, Decision No 235/2015 [2015] ROJ No 364, 26.5.2015.

[27] Damaška (n 7) 186.

Protection of Crime Victims ('Victims Law').[28] The only particular feature is that the definition of family members was limited to second-degree relatives in a direct line. The exercise of the rights conferred by Romanian Victims Law is not subject to filing a criminal complaint.[29] However, the participatory rights, as provided by the CCP, depend on victims having a role in criminal proceedings, namely being injured persons or civil parties (ie, participating victims, not witnesses).

ii. The Victim as a Vulnerable Individual

Legislation addressing the victims' vulnerability was introduced in Romania only recently. Because criminal justice is a matter between the State and the offender, it does not express concerns about the resulting trauma that victims endure. In this light, domestic legislation did not address support services and State compensation until the EU accession process.

Additionally, domestic laws failed to consider the potential negative impact of criminal proceedings on the victims. The general approach was that State officials, as legal professionals, carry out their responsibilities in the State's interest and for the benefit of society, including victims. Under this approach, domestic legislation did not assess the idea that criminal proceedings can hurt the victim, resulting in the risk of secondary victimisation.

Directive 2012/29 added significant value in this regard by obligating Member States to adopt measures aimed at addressing the vulnerability of victims, thus significantly enhancing the level of protection afforded by Romanian Law. On the other hand, since, by tradition, in Romania, vulnerability was not considered a critical issue, transposition was completed only under pressure from infringement procedures.

B. General Overview of the Transposition Process

Romania adopted a particular statute on victims' rights in the EU accession process. Law No 211/2004 provided the victims' right to information and specific rights of victims of violent intentional offences (eg, the right to access psychological support accorded by the Probation Services, the right to legal aid, and the right to access State compensation). At that moment, the law's Explanatory Memorandum referred to the former Framework Decision on the Standing of Victims (since then replaced by the Victims' Rights Directive)[30] and the Compensation Directive's draft.

When adopting Law No 211/2004, the CCP already regulated the victims' role in criminal proceedings, their participatory rights, and the procedural steps for questioning and testifying. Thus, the Romanian legislative framework contained two statutes regulating the status and rights of victims in criminal proceedings.

[28] Law No 211/2004 on Measures to Ensure the Protection of Crime Victims [2004] ROJ No 505, 4.6.2004, Art 3^4 (1)(a), introduced by GEO No 24/2019 [2004] ROJ No 274, 10.4.2019.

[29] ibid Art 3^1(1).

[30] Council Framework Decision of 15 March 2001 on the standing of victims in criminal proceedings [2001] OJ L82/1.

In this normative framework, some provisions of the Victims' Rights Directive have been transposed and incorporated in Law No 211/2004, and others have been integrated in the CCP. For instance, Articles 23 and 24 on the protection measures have been included in the CCP, Article 22 on the individual assessment and Articles 8 and 9 on the support services in Law No 211/2004. Sometimes, even the same provision was transposed in a fragmented manner. For instance, Article 4 of the Victims' Rights Directive was transposed by means of both amendments to the CCP (eg, the right to be informed about the offender's release) and to the Law No 211/2004 (eg, the right to be informed about the legal aid and State compensation). Since, in practice, the main focus of judicial authorities is on the CCP, the legal rules provided by Law No 211/2004 are considered as marginal and without real importance. This approach significantly affects the effective implementation of victims' rights in Romania, at least for the ones regulated in Law No 211/2004, such as the right to legal aid and State compensation.

Some legal texts of EU law have been transposed in a unitary manner (ie, through a single statute) and in a smooth legislative process. In 2007, the Compensation Directive was transposed by amending Law No 211/2004.[31] In 2016, Law No 151/2016[32] transposed the EPO Directive, and Law No 206/2016[33] regulated some measures to implement the Civil Regulation. Both laws have not been further amended. On the contrary, other legal texts have been transposed mainly under the pressure of infringement procedures. For instance, many provisions of the Victims' Rights Directive were transposed after the deadline, under the pressure of infringement procedures and by the Government through emergency ordinances (ie GEO No 18/2016[34] and GEO No 24/2019).[35]

Since Romania has no law reform bodies, the Ministry of Justice (MJ) is the main legislative initiator. As an executive agency, it is mainly tributary to the policy-implementing model focused on the State officials' control. Furthermore, victims' rights have never been a central topic in the Government's political discourse surrounding the criminal justice system. Therefore, the Romanian Ministry of Justice was less determined to initiate paradigm shifts in the sector of victims' rights. This approach also influenced the Romanian transposition process.

III. Victims' Right to Information and Participatory Rights

Although the right to receive information about their rights is not a victims' participatory right in a strict sense, it is a critical factor in claiming both participatory and compensatory rights. The right to information, the right to legal assistance, and the right to interpretation and translation are 'super-rights' that functionally precede not only the victim's right to 'participate in the criminal justice system', which serves as an important

[31] GEO No 113/2007 amending Law No 211/2004 [2007] ROJ No 729, 26.10.2007.
[32] Law No 151/2016 regarding the European Protection Order [2016] ROJ No 545, 20.7.2016.
[33] Law No 206/2016 on measures needed to apply European regulations [2016] ROJ No 898, 9.11.2016.
[34] GEO No 18/2016 amending the Criminal Code (CC) and CCP [2016] ROJ No 389, 23.5.2016.
[35] GEO No 24/2019 amending Law No 211/2004 [2019] ROJ 274, 10.04.2019.

symbolic form of compensation for the crime, but also the right to 'monetary compensation' from both the offender and the Member State.[36]

From this perspective, this section outlines the right to receive information alongside participatory rights and their transposition in Romania.

A. Victims' Right to Receive Information about their Rights

Traditionally, in Romania, the CCP provides the procedural steps for questioning participating victims (ie, injured persons or civil parties). At the beginning of the first questioning, the investigative authorities must inform them about the right to legal assistance and, in cases of mandatory assistance, the right to an appointed lawyer, the right to mediation, the right to present evidence, to submit claims and closing remarks, the right to be informed about the state of the proceedings and to submit a civil claim, and the duty to appear before the judicial authorities when summoned.[37]

Since it entered into force, the Victims Law has provided other duties to inform. From their first contact with the victims, the investigative authorities must inform them about the right to psychological support, the authority where they can file a complaint, the requirements and the procedural steps to access legal aid and State compensation, and the protection measures for witnesses.[38]

In 2019, Article 4 of Directive 2012/29 was transposed by amending the CCP and Law No 211/2004. The duty to inform about the offender's release was transposed into the CCP.[39] The duty to inform about the support services, the specific rights of residents in another Member State,[40] and the requirement of simple and accessible language[41] were introduced in the Victims Law. The duty to take into account the personal characteristics of victims when informing them about their rights, as provided by Article 2(2) of the Victims' Rights Directive,[42] and information on the reimbursement of expenses have, however, not been transposed.

The case law studied at the court archive[43] revealed that in two of the eight cases, the investigative authorities informed the injured persons about their rights based on both CCP and Law No 211/2004. In both cases, the information contained *verbatim* the legal texts without any explanation. Furthermore, the content was not tailored to the case. For

[36] L Lupária and J Della Torre, 'Victims of Crime in the Area of Freedom, Security and Justice' in S Iglesias Sánchez and M González Pascual (eds), *Fundamentals Rights in the EU Area of Freedom, Security and Justice* (Cambridge University Press, 2021) 329.

[37] 2014 CCP, Art 111(1)(a)-(e).

[38] Law No 211/2004 (n 28) Art 4(1) (a)-(g) (3).

[39] 2014 CCP, Art 111(5), introduced by GEO No 18/2016.

[40] Law No 211/2004 (n 28) Art 4 (1)(a)(k), introduced by GEO No 24/2019 (n 28).

[41] ibid Art 4(2), amended by GEO No 24/2019 (n 28).

[42] See also Victims' Rights Directive (n 1) Preamble, Recital 21.

[43] To obtain data about the application of the legislation, eight finally decided cases regarding violent intentional offences have been studied at the archives of Cluj-Napoca courts. The cases were selected randomly. The District Court has been asked and allowed access to three cases regarding domestic violence and one concerning a robbery. A request regarding two case files concerning sexual offences has been denied (District Court Cluj-Napoca, Document No P27/2023, 21.9.2023). The Tribunal has been asked and allowed access to three cases regarding attempted murder and one concerning human trafficking.

instance, the right to access mediation was communicated in both cases, even if one case concerned attempted murder and mediation was not applicable. In the other six cases, the information concerned only the rights provided by CCP.

According to the online survey,[44] out of 21 lawyers who provided legal assistance to crime victims, two reported that the information contained the rights provided by Law No 211/2004. The remaining 19 lawyers said that only information provided by CCP had been communicated.

The enforcement of the investigative authorities' duties is essential for effectively implementing the victims' right to information. In the published case law,[45] there is only one case in which a participating victim submitted a motion to the judge for failure to comply with the information duty provided by Victims Law. The object of the case was attempted murder. The judge declared:

> [t]he fact that the judicial authority did not inform the civil parties about the possibility of getting in touch with the service for victims' support, with such departments and social care providers, does not represent a nullity, and Law No 211/2004 does not provide a sanction in such case.[46]

This case may provide evidence of some features of the Romanian implementation of victims' rights. A first one is the low level of victims' active participation. While the lack of information based on Victims Law is commonplace, only one victim submitted a motion asking the judge to find a law violation. Secondly, legal assistance has a vital role. In this case, the victim has been assisted by a lawyer. Thirdly, since the judge did not attach a remedy to the rights provided by Victims Law, this might suggest that the mindset of the judicial system is still attached to the CCP and the traditional approach of criminal justice focused only on the State and the offender.

Beyond the minimum standard of Directive 2012/29, Law No 211/2004 provides two more duties regarding the right to receive information.

First, it requires the investigative authorities to present the victims with a written form containing all the rights provided by Article 4(1) of the same law.[47] This form resembles the Letter of Rights regulated by Directive 2012/13.[48] Following a request for public information,[49] the Prosecutors' Office attached to the High Court of Cassation and Justice (POHCCJ) shared that the standardised form for communicating victims'

[44] To collect data on lawyers' perspectives on victims' rights, an online questionnaire was distributed to lawyers from Cluj Bar. It received 33 answers, 15 from trainee lawyers and 18 from lawyers in total capacity. Although the sample is not representative, the findings will be presented because, so far, they are the only source presenting these perspectives.

[45] In Romania, the case law is published in a database named ReJust, managed by the Superior Council of the Magistracy. ReJust is available at https://rejust.ro.

[46] Bucharest Tribunal, Preliminary Chamber Judgment, 9.7.2021, ReJust No d3552g2d, available at www.rejust.ro/juris/d3552g2d.

[47] Law No 211/2004 (n 28) Art 4(3), amended by Law No 255/2013 [2013] ROJ No 515, 14.8.2013.

[48] Directive 2012/13/EU of the European Parliament and of the Council of 22 May 2012 on the right to information in criminal proceedings [2012] OJ L142/1, Art 4.

[49] To obtain data about the application of the legislation, based on Law No 544/2001 on free access to public information [2001] ROJ No 663, 23.10.2001, requests have been submitted to all Romanian courts, to the Ministry of Justice, to the Prosecutors' Office attached to the High Court of Cassation and Justice (POHCCJ), and to other institutions or agencies that have responsibilities in the area of victims' rights.

rights has been implemented from 1 January 2024.[50] The form has seven pages and contains the applicable legal texts except those regulating the right to State compensation for moral damages.

Secondly, since 1 January 2005, Law No 211/2004 imposed the duty of the Ministry of Justice and the Ministry of Internal Affairs to establish a free-of-charge telephone line dedicated to victims.[51] Its role was to inform the victims of their rights and to notify the police if it appeared from the conversation that the victims were in danger. Following a request for public information, the Ministry of Justice communicated that this telephone line had not yet been established.[52]

The POHCCJ website contains informative materials for the victims.[53] It is an example of proactive dissemination of information. The material is written only in Romanian, but it is easy to find, and the language is accessible. The Ministry of Justice website also contains such material, but it isn't easy to find, and its language is technical.[54]

B. Right to be Heard and to Provide Evidence

In Romania, the victims' interview is rather an investigative power than a right. In the same framework, the evidence presentation stage during the trial includes *de jure* the victims' interrogation. The victims are compulsorily summoned to their investigation interview or trial interrogation under a penalty of up to 5,000 ron (ie, €1,000). Participating victims are not required to take an oath or tell the truth. Only when the victims are examined as witnesses do they give statements under oath. The participating victims can submit motions regarding evidence during the investigation and trial. The case files studied at the courts' archive indicate that victims exercise this right only when they have legal assistance.

In line with Article 20(a) of the Victims' Rights Directive, the CCP requires that injured persons be interviewed promptly following their criminal complaint.[55] In the investigation stage, the injured persons can be examined during an adversarial hearing before a judge to prevent their further examination during trial.[56]

C. Right to Review the Decision not to Prosecute

In cases where prosecutors dismiss a case, the victims have the right to judicial review by the preliminary chamber judges.[57] When the dismissal is based on a lack of public interest, the prosecutors must submit this decision to the preliminary chamber judge

[50] POHCCJ, Document No 279/VIII-3/2024, 2.2.2024.
[51] Law No 211/2004 (n 28) Art 5.
[52] MJ, Document No 50580/2023, 22.9.2023.
[53] The material can be found at www.mpublic.ro/sites/default/files/DOC/victimeinfractiuni/drepturi_victime.html#/.
[54] The material can be found at www.just.ro/drepturile-victimelor-infractiunilor/.
[55] 2014 CCP, Art 111(9).
[56] ibid Art 308.
[57] ibid Art 341.

for confirmation. Therefore, since the judge's intervention is mandatory *ope legis*, the victims do not have the right to initiate a judicial review.

When the appeal against the dismissal decision is granted, the judge can order prosecutors to continue investigations or to prosecute. Because the Romanian judicial system has the prosecutors' monopoly over the criminal action at its heart, in practice, the judges refer mainly to the duty to continue investigations. When prosecutors decide to prosecute but do not submit the case to trial (eg, due to the statute of limitations), judges can admit the victims' review and order the beginning of the trial. However, such cases are sporadic. The ReJust platform does not even have criteria to find them. In legal terms, in such a situation, the victims are not qualified as private prosecutors and do not have the power to compel the prosecutor to endorse the prosecution. In practice, however, victims can act as private prosecutors by exercising their procedural rights. When judges do not confirm the dismissal decision based on the lack of public interest, the prosecutors must continue the investigation.

The data regarding the practical application of the right to review indicate that in 2022, from 536,556 cases solved by police or prosecutors, in 428,785 cases, prosecutors ordered a case dismissal, and in 57,592 cases, a dismissal based on lack of public interest. The victims submitted 8,068 appeals against the dismissal (1.88 per cent). From these, 1,716 reviews have been admitted (21 per cent).[58] The data indicates that the victims do not often claim this right. However, when the right to judicial review is claimed, in one-fifth of cases, the judges decided that the prosecutor's decision was wrong and that more investigations were needed. There are no data on the prosecutors' decisions after completing the investigations. Regarding dismissal based on lack of public interest, the ReJust database indicates that judges denied the confirmation in 1.1 per cent of cases. This is a high level of judicial confirmation.

D. Right to Safeguards in Restorative Justice

The domestic approach is reluctant to allow third parties outside the State officials to influence criminal proceedings. Considering the forms of restorative justice indicated in the Victims' Rights Directive,[59] namely victim-offender mediation, family group conferencing, and sentencing circles, Romania has adopted only mediation.

In the EU accession process, Law No 192/2006 introduced mediation for a limited list of offences such as assault with less than 90 days of medical care, theft between family members, and trespass.[60] Prosecutors cannot divert a case to mediation for other offences.

The regulation of victim safeguards and the judicial authorities' duty to facilitate referral to restorative justice services are direct outcomes of Article 12 of the Victims' Rights Directive. The safeguards were transposed in 2018[61] and 2019.[62] However, the

[58] POHCCJ, 'Activity Report for 2022', 167, available at www.mpublic.ro/sites/default/files/PDF/raport_activitate_2022.pdf.

[59] Victims' Rights Directive (n 1) Preamble, Recital 46.

[60] Law No 192/2006 on mediation [2006] ROJ No 441, 22.5.2006, Art 67(2).

[61] Law No 97/2018 concerning some protection measures for victims [2018] ROJ No 376, 2.5.2018.

[62] GEO No 24/2019 (n 28).

duty to facilitate referrals has not been transposed in Romanian legislation or practical guides.

Following a request for public information, the POHCCJ shared that 160 mediation agreements were concluded in 2021, 128 in 2022,[63] and 159 in 2017.[64] In 2022, 58 cases were solved through mediation, 98 in 2021, and 113 in 2017. The data indicate a low level of practical criminal mediation, and, as for the cases solved through this form of restorative justice, the trend is going downwards. This is due to several factors, such as the lack of a referral system, lack of awareness about mediation, and lack of public aid for mediation fees.

E. Right to Legal Aid

Law No 211/2004 was the first statute to recognise the victims' right to legal aid.[65] Under this law, legal aid is not awarded *ex officio* but only at the victim's request. No financial means assessment is required when the case concerns a violent intentional offence. In other cases, this assessment is required. The commission with jurisdiction over such requests sits within the tribunals and consists of two judges. It also has jurisdiction over State compensation.

Legal aid is provided for criminal proceedings and for the enforcement of criminal judgments awarding civil damages. For these two proceedings, the value of legal aid was at most two minimum gross salaries. Starting in November 2024, the value of legal aid is at most five minimum gross salaries (18,500 ron or €3,700). This amendment was brought by Law No 272/2024,[66] a legislative initiative of several members of the Parliament (not the Ministry of Justice) aimed at improving victims' access to legal aid and State compensation.

The legal aid is paid by public funds managed by the Ministry of Justice. The financial aid may cover the fee of a privately retained lawyer or a lawyer appointed by the Bar.

Since the Ministry of Justice lacks statistical data on legal aid provided by Law No 211/2004,[67] such information has been obtained from the judicial authorities responsible for deciding on victims' requests. The data shared by all 42 tribunals shows that between January 2005 and September 2023, 245 requests for legal aid had been submitted by the victims. From these, 116 requests have been granted. The data suggests that victims do not often claim their right to legal aid under Law No 211/2004. This is due to several factors. First, the legal requirement to file a criminal complaint within 60 days from the offence commission. In November, Law No 272/2024 repealed this requirement. Secondly, the nonfulfillment of the information duties results in the victim's lack of awareness of this right. As previously indicated,[68] only recently have the investigative authorities started to use a written form containing the rights provided by

[63] POHCCJ, Document No 963/VIII-3/2023, 26.9.2023.
[64] POHCCJ, Document No 42/2018, 1.2.2018.
[65] Law No 211/2004 (n 28) Art 14-20.
[66] Law No 272/2024 on the amendment of Law No 211/2004 (n 28), [2024] ROJ No 1103, 5.11.2024.
[67] MJ, Document No 56580/2023, 22.9.2023.
[68] See section III.A on right to information above.

Law No 211/2004. The online survey revealed that only 11 out of 33 lawyers knew of the victims' right to legal aid under this law. The data may suggest that lawyers are less involved in supporting victims claiming their right to legal aid. Several factors might contribute to this reality, such as the lack of continuous training and the low fee value compared to the lengthy duration of criminal proceedings. It remains to be seen whether the recent increase in the value of legal aid will affect lawyers' decisions to provide legal assistance to victims on the basis of Victims Law.

The 2014 CCP provided that legal assistance is mandatory when the participating victims are minors or persons lacking legal capacity.[69] Such assistance is also mandatory for victims of human trafficking.[70] In other cases, legal aid for adult victims is granted when judicial authorities appreciate, based on their discretion, that victims' legal assistance is necessary.[71] As a result of a public debate that will be presented below,[72] from 1 January 2024, mandatory legal assistance has been extended to victims of domestic violence and sexual offences.[73]

In cases of mandatory legal assistance, the victims may be assisted by a privately retained lawyer (whose fees are paid by the victims) or by an appointed one (whose fees are paid from public funds). The Bar will appoint a lawyer only if the victims do not have a privately retained one. No assessment of financial means is required. In the majority of cases involving mandatory legal assistance, the lawyers are appointed. For instance, in all three cases with child victims that have been studied at the court archive, the legal assistance was exercised by such lawyers.

The fees for appointed lawyers are paid from public funds managed by the Ministry of Justice. The flat fee value is 510 ron for each stage of criminal proceedings.[74] This means 1530 ron (ie, €300) for the whole proceeding. This value is lower than the one provided by the Victims Law.

F. Right to Reimbursement of Expenses

The witnesses, experts, and interpreters can receive reimbursement of their expenses from public funds.[75] On the contrary, the participating victims may access reimbursement only from the offenders and only when the courts deliver a guilty verdict and award civil damages or when the prosecutors decide dismissal because of a lack of public interest.[76] As previously indicated,[77] in practice, the victims are not informed about the right to reimbursement of expenses.

[69] 2014 CCP Art 93(4).
[70] Law No 678/2001 on human trafficking [2001] ROJ No 783, 11.12.2001, Art 44(1).
[71] 2014 CCP, Art 93(5).
[72] See section V.B. on protection measures in criminal proceedings below.
[73] Law No 217/2023 amending CC and CCP [2023] ROJ 634, 11.07.2023.
[74] Agreement between MJ, POHCCJ and Romanian Bar Association, 8.2.2024, Art 5(1)(g).
[75] 2014 CCP, Art 272(1).
[76] ibid Art 276(1).
[77] See section III.A. on the right to information above.

G. Rights of Victims Resident in Another Member State

The provisions of the Victims' Rights Directive regarding victims resident in another Member State have been transposed in a fragmented manner, either in Law No 211/2004 or in the CCP. When the victims are residents in another Member State, Law No 211/2004 provides the duty of the investigative authorities to inform them about the right to make a complaint in the country of residence and about the mechanism of cooperation that can be used.[78]

When the victims are Romanian citizens and file a complaint about an offence committed in another Member State, the CCP provides that the investigative authorities have to receive the complaint and send it to the competent authorities.[79] The duty to send the complaint without delay, as Article 17(3) provides, has not been transposed.

IV. Compensation

A. Compensation by the Offender

To access offender compensation, the victims must submit a civil claim. It is exempted from court fees[80] and is governed by civil law rules.[81] When the victims are minors or persons lacking legal capacity, the claim is submitted by the prosecutors in their name.[82] Joining the civil claim to the criminal proceedings has practical advantages for victims (eg, a single trial and use of evidence obtained by the prosecutors).

This research included a review of the 20 most recent cases of conviction for attempted murder in the Bucharest Tribunal, as published on the ReJust database. Out of 20 cases, civil claims were filed in 10 and granted in six. Among these six cases, the victims had legal assistance in four; in one case, the victim had no legal assistance; in another, the prosecutor exercised the civil action. The data indicates that only a minority of victims had successfully claimed the right to access offender compensation in criminal proceedings. This is mainly because the exercise of this right is dependent on legal assistance. In addition, the prosecutor's involvement does not always ensure success. In a case studied at the Cluj Tribunal, the civil claim for two child victims of attempted murder should have been submitted by the prosecutor. Because the claim was introduced after the legal deadline, the court denied its granting.[83]

Confiscated assets cannot be returned directly to the victims as compensation. In 2022, the National Crime Prevention Mechanism was established.[84] Its resources are confiscated money or money from capitalising confiscated goods. Of the funds the

[78] Law No 211/2004 (n 28) Art 4(1)(k), amended by GEO No 24/2019 (n 28).
[79] 2014 CCP, Art 289 (10).
[80] ibid Art 20(8).
[81] ibid Art 19(5).
[82] ibid Art 19(3).
[83] Cluj Tribunal, Case No 3151/117/2021, Judgment No 104/2022, 29.4.2022.
[84] Law No 318/2015 regarding the National Agency for the Management of Seized Assets [2015] ROJ No 961, 24.12.2015, Art 37^1 -37^{13}, introduced by Law No 230/2022 [2022] ROJ No 734, 19.7.2022.

Mechanism collects, 15 per cent are directed to the State compensation budget managed by the Ministry of Justice. This is the legal track for using confiscation for victims' compensation.

Where damages may be remedied in the criminal proceedings by returning property, restitution is ordered by the judicial authorities without the requirement of a civil claim.[85] Restitution is not required without delay, as Article 15 of Directive 2012/29 provides.

In Romania, the principle of reasonable time governs the whole criminal proceeding.[86] There is no particular requirement for the civil claim. On the contrary, if the court examination of civil action causes a violation of the reasonable time principle for the criminal action, the court can order their separation.[87] In this case, the procedural framework remains the same, namely criminal proceedings, but the criminal court will examine the civil claim only after deciding on the criminal action. In this scenario, the criminal court may decide on the civil action after devoting a reasonable amount of time primarily to solving the criminal action. This may raise a question of conformity with Article 16(1) of Directive 2012/29, which provides the victims' right to obtain, in the criminal proceedings, a decision on compensation by the offender within a reasonable time.

Furthermore, no measures are in place to motivate offenders to compensate victims. It is up to the courts' discretion to consider the offender's stance on civil damages during sentencing (eg, an agreement with the civil party may be appreciated as a mitigating factor). This may also raise a question of conformity with Article 16(2) of the Directive.

B. State Compensation

During the EU accession process, the victim's right to State compensation was introduced for the first time in Romanian legislation by Law No 211/2004.[88] At that moment, the law reflected the minimum standard required by the Council of Europe Convention on the Compensation of Victims of Crime.[89] Thus, only Romanian citizens or permanent residents who were victims of violent intentional offences had the right to claim compensation from the State and only for material damages. Compensation for damage to the victim's property was limited to 10 gross minimum salaries.

In 2007, the right to State compensation was extended to citizens of other Member States.[90] The Ministry of Justice was designated the assistance authority and the Bucharest Tribunal the competent court. The fact that the website of the Ministry of Justice does not contain information on the right to access State compensation in cross-border cases seems to contradict the duty provided by Law No 211/2004.[91]

[85] 2014 CCP, Art 255(1).
[86] ibid Art 8.
[87] ibid Art 26(1).
[88] Law No 211/2004 (n 28) Art 21-34.
[89] Council of Europe, Convention on the Compensation of Victims of Crime [1983].
[90] Law No 211/2004 (n 28) Art 34^1-34^{13}, introduced by GEO No 113/2007 [2007] ROJ No 729, 26.10.2007.
[91] ibid Art 34^8.

Jurisdiction to decide on State compensation belongs to a commission composed of two judges within the tribunals. Starting with November 2024, these judges have to be members of the tribunals' criminal division. The victim must submit a written request. There are no user-friendly forms or digital services for submitting such requests. Filing a criminal complaint within 60 days after the offence commission was a requirement for granting State compensation. This requirement was repealed in November 2024. The victims can request an advance of compensation up to 10 times the gross minimum wage.

In 2022, significant amendments have been brought to the object of State compensation. The Explanatory Memorandum of the draft law referred to the recommendations of the Council of Europe regarding human trafficking[92] and Court of Justice of the European Union (CJEU) case law.[93] First, compensation has been extended to moral damages. The Memorandum indicates that the CJEU *BV* judgment[94] was the main reason for introducing this amendment. Secondly, the limit for material damages to property has been repealed. Thirdly, it was provided that in case of an emergency, the victims could ask for the advance as a voucher for essential products with an upper limit of five gross minimum salaries (ie, 18,500 ron or €3,700). The amendments were introduced in Law No 318/2015 regarding the National Agency for the Management of Seized Assets.[95] The Victims Law has not been amended accordingly, producing much confusion. Currently, the written forms used by prosecutors and police officers to inform victims of their rights mention only the right to access State compensation for material damage. The voucher system is yet to be implemented in practice. The requirements for accessing State compensation, as provided by Law No 211/2004, have not been amended at that moment.

There is inconsistency in the case law regarding the calculation of the amount of compensation awarded for moral damages. In a case regarding a rape offence, the Compensation Commission from Iaşi Tribunal has taken into consideration the moral damages awarded by the final judgment convicting the offender and granted €40,000 of State compensation.[96] In another case regarding a murder offence, the Compensation Commission from Constanţa Tribunal decided that compensation for moral damages has to be limited to the maximum previously applicable to material damages to property, namely 10 gross minimum salaries.[97] Both judgments are final.

Since the Ministry of Justice lacks statistical data on State compensation,[98] such information has been obtained from tribunals, the judicial authorities responsible for

[92] Council of Europe, Group of Experts on Action against Trafficking in Human Beings, 'Evaluation Report. Romania. Third Evaluation Round' (2021), available at rm.coe.int/evaluation-report-on-the-implementation-of-the-council-of-europe-conve/1680a2b0f8; Committee of the Parties to the Council of Europe Convention on Action against Trafficking in Human Beings, 'Recommendation CP/Rec(2021)05 on the implementation of the Council of Europe Convention on Action against Trafficking in Human Beings by Romania', 4.6.2021, available at rm.coe.int/recommendation-cp-rec-2021-05-on-the-implementation-of-the-council-of-/1680a2bc3e.

[93] Case C-129/19 *Presidenza del Consiglio dei Ministri v BV* ECLI:EU:C:2020:566, 16.7.2020.

[94] ibid paras 60–69.

[95] Law No 318/2015 (n 84), Art. 37^{14} (1)(2) -37^{15}(1).

[96] Iaşi Tribunal, Judgment No 2266/2022, 28.09.2022, ReJust No eee5g6g6d, available at www.rejust.ro/juris/eee5g6g6d.

[97] Constanţa Tribunal, Judgment No 2374/2023, 21.08.2023, ReJust No 9852g48e3, available at www.rejust.ro/juris/9852g48e3.

[98] MJ, Document No 56580/2023 (n 67).

deciding on victims' requests. The data shared by all 42 tribunals indicate that from January 2005 to September 2023 victims of violent intentional crimes submitted 314 requests for State compensation. From these, 89 requests have been granted. The most considerable damages were awarded for the loss of maintenance for child victims due to the murder of a parent. Ten requests have been submitted to Bucharest Tribunal in cross-border cases. From these, two have been awarded. The total value of public funds victims accessed in this period was 2,298,503 ron (ie, €459,700). This includes State compensation, advance compensation, and legal aid, as provided by Law No 211/2004. The data shared by tribunals could not be separated to reflect only State compensation.

The data indicate that the capacity of victims to access State compensation is low. Over almost 19 years, nine tribunals have not received requests on this issue. Several factors might contribute to this reality. First, the legal requirement to file a complaint within 60 days from the offence commission. In this framework, the trust victims have in the criminal justice system, and its influence on reporting is relevant. Secondly, the victims' lack of awareness mainly because of the investigative authorities' nonfulfillment of the duty to information. Thirdly, the dependence on legal assistance. Moreover, even when legal assistance is available, our evidence so far shows that out of 33 lawyers surveyed, only 13 reported knowledge of State compensation. The data indicate that most lawyers are unaware of this victims' right and this is due mainly to the lack of continuous training.

In November 2024, the Victims Law was significantly amended by Law No 272/2024,[99] especially in the area of legal aid and State compensation. Regarding compensation, it repealed the requirement that criminal proceedings must be commenced due to the victim's criminal complaint submitted within 60 days after the offence commission. Currently, the victims can access State compensation even if they did not report the offence to the police or prosecutors. Second, it repealed the requirement that the offender has no financial resources to pay victims damages. Victims now have the right to access State compensation directly without proving previously that the offender lacks financial resources. Law No 272/2024 has also added the victim's right to access State compensation for moral damages to the Victims Law, thereby enhancing the clarity of the legislation.

V. Protection Measures

A. Victims' Individual Assessment

In 2016, seeking to avoid the transposition of the measures aimed at offering a support service tailored to the victims' needs, as provided under Articles 8 and 9 of the Victims' Rights Directive, the Government decided that the victims indicated in Article 22(3) of the Directive (eg, victims of terrorism, human trafficking, sexual violence) are presumed vulnerable.[100] Thus, these victims may benefit from protection measures without a prior

[99] Law No 272/2024 (n 66).
[100] 2014 CCP, Art 113 (2), introduced by GEO No 18/2016.

individual assessment recommending them. The CCP did not provide for an individual evaluation with specific criteria, as provided by the Directive.

In 2019, under the pressure of infringement procedures, the Government decided to transpose Articles 8 and 9 of the Directive. At that moment, in Romania, there were in place specific support services for child victims, domestic violence victims, and human trafficking victims. Because the General Directorates for Social Assistance and Child Protection (GDSACP) managed the first two, generic support services have also been established within them. They also received the power to conclude the individual assessments.[101] The GDSACPs are local-level social care units headquartered in the county capital and each Bucharest sector. The generic support services must have at least one social care worker, one psychologist, and one legal adviser.

The victim's referral mechanism from the investigative authorities to the support services was regulated in 2021 through a ministerial order.[102] No amendments have been introduced in the CCP. As a result, in practice, the investigative authorities assess the requirements of the protection measures without seeking prior evaluation from the support services. Thus, all the measures provided by Articles 20, 23, and 24 of the Directive, as transposed into the CCP, are ordered by the judicial authorities based on their own assessment.

The available data shows that only a small number of victims have received support from the services established in 2019. Law No 211/2004 provides the GDSACP's duty to collect data on victim referrals and to report them to the Ministry of Justice each semester.[103] However, the Ministry of Justice shared that only GDSAPC Argeş (a county in Romania with a population of around 600,000 inhabitants) reported such data.[104] The data from Argeş county indicates that, during the first semester of 2023, 29 victims were referred to GDSACP. Out of the 29, 25 were child victims and four adult victims. The data shared by the European Commission indicates that Romania reported that 1,739 victims received support from generic support services in 2020.[105]

B. Right to Protection of Victims During Criminal Proceedings

In Romania, the victim's protection was traditionally assessed by considering the offenders' behaviour and, consequently, by ordering pre-trial detention or criminal restrictive orders. As a novelty, the 2014 CCP introduced the rights of victims having the role of participating victims or witnesses to benefit from the witnesses' protection measures.[106] These measures ensure the transposition of Article 23(3) of Directive 2012/29. There are no publicly accessible data on their practical application.

[101] Law No 211/2004 (n 28) Art 3^1-3^{12}, introduced by GEO No 24/2019 (n 28).
[102] Order of the Ministry of Labour, the Ministry of Internal Affairs, and the Ministry of Justice No 173/65/3.042/C/2021 [2021] ROJ No 587, 12.2.2021.
[103] Law No 211/2004 (n 28) Art 3^9 (11).
[104] MJ, Document No 50580/2023 (n 52).
[105] EC, Document No (2023) 7957135, 22.11.2023.
[106] 2014 CCP, Art 113(1).

In 2016, the protection measures provided by Articles 20, 23(2) and 24 of the Victims' Rights Directive were transposed.[107] As previously indicated,[108] several categories of victims have been presumed vulnerable in 2016, and the individual evaluation was introduced in 2019. The protection measures can be applied to victims presumed vulnerable and to other victims with specific needs, as identified on a case-by-case basis.

In 2016, in Romania, there were no structures in place to ensure the victims' examination in specific premises and no devices to ensure the recording of child victims' interviews. In 2014, only two child-friendly interview rooms were put in place at the GDSACP Cluj and Craiova with financial support from the French Embassy and non-governmental organisations (NGO). Starting in 2022, other child-friendly premises have been set up with Norway funding (50 premises within the courts and 29 within the prosecutors' offices). In June 2023, an interview room for child victims and adult victims of human trafficking was established within the Directorate for the Investigation of Organised Crime and Terrorism in Bucharest.

Out of the eight cases studied at the court archive, only in one case, regarding the attempted murder of two child victims aged eight and six, did the prosecutor order protection measures. As a result, a psychologist interviewed the victims in the specific premise within GDSAPC Cluj. No prior individual assessment has been concluded; the measure has been decided by the prosecutor only by considering the victims' age. In another case regarding domestic violence, the child victim was only 11 months old and she was not interviewed. The other six cases dealt with domestic violence (two cases, each one with one adult victim), robbery (one case with two child victims), attempted murder (two cases, each one with one adult victim), and human trafficking (one case with two adult victims). In these cases, the prosecutors ordered no protection measures, even if the victims were presumed vulnerable due to the offence's nature or age.

In 2020, the European Court of Human Rights (ECtHR) case law against Romania on sexual offences[109] drove a public debate on victims' rights, including the protection measures. As a result, the Superior Council of the Magistracy (SCM) decided to carry out a study about how sexual offences with child victims were investigated and adjudicated in Romania in the years 2014–2020.

The report was presented in 2021.[110] Some of the conclusions can be summarised as follows. As a rule, the child victims have had legal assistance as part of the legal aid. The report identified only several interviews conducted without a lawyer being present. The assistance of a privately retained lawyer was a scarce exception. The interviews of child victims have been undertaken at the police stations or prosecutors' offices without any reference to specific premises. No interviews with child victims have been recorded at the police stations, but they were recorded at the prosecutors' offices. Child victims were repeatedly reinterviewed during the investigation and trial. There were no separate areas for child victims and offenders within the premises where criminal proceedings were

[107] ibid Art 111(6)(7)(8), Art 113 (2), as amended by GEO No 18/2016.

[108] See section V.A. on individual assessment above.

[109] *MGC v Romania* App no 61495/11 (ECtHR, 15 March 2016); *IC v Romania* App no 36934/08 (ECtHR, 24 June 2016); *CAS and CS v Romania* App no 26692/05 (ECtHR, 20 March 2012).

[110] Romanian Judicial Inspectorate, 'Report on the Investigation and Adjudication of Cases regarding Sexual Offences with Child Victims' (2021), approved by SCM Decision No 127/2021, available at www.inspectiajudiciara.ro/search-pace?search=victime%20minore&page=1.

conducted. There were no teams with an integrated and multidisciplinary approach that could offer support to child victims. There were no guides regarding the child victims' interviews.

The public presentation of the report had several consequences. First, POHCCJ has drawn up a guide regarding the investigation of rape with child victims.[111] Secondly, several members of Parliament (not the Ministry of Justice) presented draft legislation to amend the Criminal Code (CC) and CCP, resulting in two laws being adopted.

Law No 51/2023[112] transposed Article 24(1)(b) of Directive 2012/29. The interviewing of child victims under 14 years has to occur in the presence of their legal representative and a psychologist.[113] When the representative has legal status in the proceedings or when he/they may influence the child victim's statement, the judicial authorities must nominate another representative.[114]

Law No 217/2023[115] amended the definition of rape by raising the age of victims' consent to 16 years.[116] Considering Directive 2012/29, it also amended the rules applicable to victims with specific needs. First, it added a protective measure, namely the interview through video conference from the shelter where the victim is located.[117] Secondly, it mandated judicial authorities to order at least one protection measure for victims with specific needs, whereas previously, it was at their discretion.[118] The requirement to protect the sound administration of justice and the rights of the defence has been maintained. The victims have the right to renounce to these measures. Thirdly, in cases of domestic violence and sexual assault, as well as in other instances in which the investigative authority deems it necessary, the interview of the victims must be conducted by a police officer of the same sex as the victim.[119] Previously, this was done at the victim's request. If this is not possible, the interview may be carried out by a person who is not of the same sex as the victim, but the victim's lawyer and the psychologist must agree. Fourth, the audiovisual recording of the child victims' interviews has become mandatory. When this is not possible, an audio recording is required. The recording shall be presented during the trial, and the court may order the interrogation of the child victims only in thoroughly justified cases.[120]

C. Right to Avoid Contact between Victim and Offender

Starting 1 June 2018, the newly built court premises must provide separate waiting rooms for victims. Starting 1 January 2019, different waiting areas for victims must be

[111] POHCCJ, 'Theoretical and Practical Guide on the Rape Offence. An Approach Focused on Child Victims' (2022), available at www.mpublic.ro/sites/default/files/PDF/indrumar.pdf.

[112] Law No 51/2023 amending the CCP [2023] ROJ No 186, 6.3.2023.

[113] 2014 CCP, Art 111 (8^1), introduced by Law No 51/2023.

[114] ibid Art 111 (8^2), introduced by Law No 51/2023.

[115] Law No 217/2023 amending the CC and the CCP (n 72). Law No 217/2023 entered into force on 1 January 2024.

[116] CC, Art 218^1, introduced by Law No 217/2023.

[117] 2014 CCP) Art 111 (6)(d), introduced by Law No 217/2023.

[118] ibid Art 111(6), amended by Law No 217/2023.

[119] ibid Art 111(7), amended by Law No 217/2023.

[120] ibid Art 509(8), introduced by Law No 217/2023.

established within court premises.[121] These measures still need to be implemented at the national level.

D. Right to Protection of Privacy

During the trial hearing, as a general rule, the court may reject questions when they are not relevant.[122] The protection measure provided by Article 23(3)(c) of Directive 2012/29, namely the duty to avoid unnecessary questioning concerning the victim's private life not related to the criminal offence, has not been transposed.

As previously indicated,[123] accessibility of court judgments is ensured by the online platform ReJust. Civil and criminal judgments are always made public in an anonymised form.[124] This includes the names of judges, prosecutors, lawyers, defendants, any other parties, and witnesses. Therefore, both civil and criminal judgments never disclose the victim's name. Additionally, the criminal judgments delivered in cases concerning, for instance, sexual offences, child pornography, and ill-treatment of children are never made public.[125] Searching ReJust by case number or by judgment number is impossible. Thus, even if the parties' names are presented on the online database concerning all the civil and criminal cases tried in Romanian courts,[126] the judgment delivered in a specific case cannot be identified on ReJust.

Under Superior Council of Magistracy rules,[127] journalists cannot film or take photos inside the courtroom, but the judges can grant such requests except for closed hearings. Law No 504/2002 rules that providers of audiovisual media services must protect children's rights.[128] When children under the age of 14 are victims of sexual abuse, the dissemination of any information that could lead to their identification is prohibited.[129] Where such children are over 14, the publication of images or information is subject to the agreement of minors and the written agreement of their legal representatives.[130]

E. Protection of Victims in Cross-Border Cases

i. Criminal Protection Orders

Law No 151/2016 outlines the criminal protection measures that can justify the issuance of an European Protection Order (EPO) if the victims request it.[131] These measures

[121] Law No 211/2004 (n 28) Art 35^1, introduced by Law No 97/2018 (n 61).
[122] 2014 CCP, Art 380(3).
[123] See section III.A. above.
[124] Superior Council of Magistracy, Decision no 998/2022, 17.3.2022, Art 5(3).
[125] ibid Art 5(1).
[126] The online platform can be found at https://portal.just.ro/.
[127] Superior Council of Magistracy, Decision No 197/2019, 17.9.2019.
[128] Law No 504/2002 on audio and audiovisual media services [2002] ROJ 534, 22.7.2002.
[129] Council of Audiovisual, Decision No 220/2011 on the Code Regarding Audiovisual Content [2011] ROJ No 174, 11.3.2011, Art 4(1).
[130] ibid Art 4(2).
[131] Law No 151/2016 (n 32) Art 4(1).

cover all crimes.[132] Civil protection orders may be applied in cases of domestic violence and, starting with 31 August 2024, in all cases of violence and harassment.

During criminal proceedings, the protection orders can take the form of judicial control, which includes the offenders' obligation to keep their distance from the victims and avoid communicating with them or their families.[133] House arrest may include the duty not to communicate with the victims or their families.[134] As part of the final judgments, a restraining order may be imposed when the courts decide to defer the application of a criminal penalty,[135] decide to apply it as an ancillary penalty alongside the main penalty that is imprisonment or fine,[136] decide the conditional release from prison[137] or when the court decides the sentencing of minors.[138]

When Romania is the executing State, the competent authority to recognise an EPO is the tribunal in whose jurisdiction the protected person wishes to move.[139] All the refusal grounds have been transposed as optional.[140] Recognising the EPO, the tribunal may order one or more of the following measures: a prohibition from entering certain localities or places, a prohibition of contact with the protected persons or their family members, or a ban on approaching the residence, the workplace, or the school of the protected persons.[141] Law No 151/2016 does not specify the legal nature of these measures.

Since no data on EPOs were available, the data collection for this research included filing requests for public information. The Ministry of Justice[142] and the POHCCJ[143] indicated that they have no data on the application of the EPO Directive. The European Commission communicated that Romania did not provide data under Article 22 of the EPO Directive.[144]

Out of 234 courts, 230 responded by September 2023. One court of appeals and three district courts did not reply. Based on the information received, no EPO has been issued by a Romanian court. When Romania was the executing State, the data communicated by all 42 tribunals indicated that four tribunals received six requests for recognising an EPO issued in another Member State. All of them have been admitted.

Romania has a high level of labour migration in the EU, with an essential part of the work being seasonal. Therefore, the EPO could be a valuable instrument for guaranteeing the continuance of the victim's protection within the EU. The data indicate, however, that no Romanian courts issued an EPO. This may result from victims not claiming

[132] For an analysis of criminal protection orders, see Nițu and Ionescu (n 23) 238–40, 245–47.
[133] 2014 CCP, Art 215(1)(d).
[134] ibid Art 221(2)(b).
[135] Law No 286/2009 on the Criminal Code [2009] ROJ No 510, 24.7.2009, Art 85(2)(e).
[136] ibid Art 66(1)(n).
[137] ibid Art 101 (2)(c).
[138] ibid Art 21 (1)(d).
[139] Law No 151/2016 (n 32) Art 3(2).
[140] ibid Art 14 (1)(a)-(i).
[141] ibid Art 13 (5).
[142] MJ, Document No 56580/2023 (n 67).
[143] POHCCJ, Document No 885/VIII/2023, 31.8.2023.
[144] EC, Document No (2023) 7571115, 8.11.2023.

their right to benefit from such measures. The data could also confirm the arguments made in the literature regarding the lack of impact of the EPO Directive.[145]

ii. Civil Protection Orders

In 2011, the lack of efficiency of criminal restrictive orders in cases of domestic violence sparked a public debate. As a result, in 2012, the civil division of district courts received competence to issue civil restrictive orders based on Law No 217/2003.[146] The orders can last up to 12 months.[147] Electronic surveillance started to be applied in 2022 in Bucharest and three counties. Its application on the whole territory of Romania is set up for 2025. When there is a need for immediate protection, the victims can ask the police officers to order an interim order that lasts up to five days.[148] Violating the protection or temporary protection orders constitutes a criminal offence.[149]

When Romania is the issuing State, the civil court may issue the certificate provided by Article 5 of Regulation No 606/2013 at the victims' request. When Romania is the executing State, the protection measure is directly enforceable by the police. The protected person can ask the civil division of the district court to order an adjustment of the protection measure.

The data collection process included requests for public information regarding the civil restrictive orders in cross-border cases. The Ministry of Justice communicated that it has no data on this issue.[150] Out of 177 district courts, 174 shared an answer. Based on the information received, no certificate was issued, and no adjustment had been ordered by September 2023. The Ministry of Internal Affairs should have shared data on executing civil measures ordered in another Member State, but it did not.[151]

VI. Training of Practitioners

The Victims' Rights Directive provides training of practitioners as a critical factor for ensuring its applicability.[152] In Romania, Law No 211/2004 provides the duty of the authorities managing human resources within the criminal justice system and support services to ensure training on victims' rights.[153] This duty has been in force since 1 January 2005. The practical implementation of this provision was left to non-legislative measures.

Following a request for public information, the National Institute of Magistracy, the public institution providing initial and continuous training for judges and prosecutors,

[145] S van der Aa and J Ouwerkerk, 'The European Protection Order: No Time to Waste or a Waste of Time?' (2011) 19 *European Journal of Crime, Criminal Law and Criminal Justice* 267–87, 280.
[146] Law No 217/2003 on domestic violence [2012] ROJ No 365, 30.5.2012, Art 23–35, introduced by Law No 25/2012 [2012] ROJ No 165, 13.3.2012. Law No 217/2003 has been republished, [2020] ROJ No 948, 15.10.2020.
[147] ibid Art 39, amended by Law No 240/2023, [2023] ROJ No 669, 20.7.2023.
[148] ibid Art 31, amended by Law No 174/2018, [2018] ROJ No 618, 18.7.2018.
[149] ibid Art 47.
[150] MJ, Document No 56580/2023 (n 67).
[151] General Police Inspectorate, Document No 26374/2023, 11.09.2023.
[152] Victims' Rights Directive (n 1), Art 25.
[153] Law No 211/2004 (n 28) Art 2(1).

communicated that victims' rights, as provided for under EU law, are part of the continuous training within the courses regarding human trafficking. Eight workshops were organised from 2018 through to August 2023, with 61 judges and 63 prosecutors in attendance.[154] The POHCCJ Reports of Activities for 2018–2022 did not indicate specific victims' rights training. Four out of seven centres of the Institute for Initial and Continuous Training for Lawyers submitted an answer and communicated that no training on victims' rights had been organised. One answer indicated that the Bar partnered a NGO conference on the subject. Three out of 33 surveyed lawyers indicated that they had participated in training on victims' rights and from these three lawyers one indicated that NGOs and the Council of Europe organised the training. Overall, the data on professional training suggests that there is significant room for improvement.

In Romania, training primarily focuses on legal texts, emphasising the CCP, while other statutes are considered less critical. Training on EU law is not as prevalent as ECtHR case law. Guides and recommendations are still uncommon. As previously indicated,[155] only in 2022 did POHCCJ provide a guide on the investigation of sexual offences with child victims. No additional guidelines or best practices regarding victims have been elaborated. In these circumstances, the support of experts from countries with experience in victims' rights or from EU agencies, such as the Fundamental Rights Agency, may be needed.

VII. Conclusions

At the EU level, the key points of the Strategy for Victims' Rights 2020–2025[156] can positively affect Romania if implemented. In this framework, the need for empirical data has to be emphasised. Data are essential to analyse the EU Directives' implementation and improve public policies; the legal texts, as the main proof of transposition, can be misleading.

Several findings related to the implementation of victims' rights in Romania suggest that more harmonisation is needed. First, low access to State compensation seems to be mainly the result of restrictive domestic requirements, which hinder the effectiveness of this right, including in cross-border cases. From this perspective, amending the Compensation Directive would positively affect victims' right to State compensation in Romania. However, it is important to note that Law No 272/2024 recently repealed the most restrictive domestic requirements.

Secondly, the Romanian approach to criminal justice suggests that the lack of a prosecutorial role for victims influences the exercise of their participatory rights. Consolidated patterns regarding the dominant role of public prosecutors can marginalise victims, contrary to the spirit of Directive 2012/29. Even if the victims' role in criminal proceedings is left to the Member States' autonomy, a minimum harmonisation might be worth considering regarding the right to review the prosecutors' decision

[154] National Institute of Magistracy, Document No 487/2023, 30.8.2023.

[155] See section V.B. on protection measures above.

[156] EC, Communication from the Commission to the European Parliament, the Council, the European Economic and Social Committee and the Committee of the Regions, EU Strategy on victims' rights (2020-2025), COM(2020) 258 final, available at eur-lex.europa.eu/legal-content/EN/ALL/?uri=CELEX:52020DC0258.

to dismiss a case. However, the European Commission's Proposal amending the Victims' Rights Directive[157] does not address this issue.

If adopted, this Proposal's most important positive effect in Romania will be the consolidation of victims' right to obtain compensation during criminal proceedings. This is due to the newly introduced duty of the State to pay the compensation in due time following the final judgment, with the possibility for the State to recuperate it later from the offender. This new approach to civil action will be a game-changer in Romania, effectively implementing the victims' right to obtain compensation.

At the domestic level, the implication of several stakeholders is necessary.

First, the Ministry of Justice must be appropriately involved in supporting victims and must fulfill its legal duties. In this sense, it has to establish a telephone line for victims, duty in force since 2005, and to make public on its website information on State compensation in cross-border cases, duty in force since 2007. It also has to enforce the duty of GDSACPs to report data regarding the victims' access to generic support services. Since State compensation and legal aid budgets are in its jurisdiction, the Ministry must have specific data on these issues. Without data, the Ministry of Justice, the main legislative initiator in Romania, cannot provide solid public policies or draft legislation on victims' rights.

Secondly, at the normative level, the requirements and the procedural steps for accessing State compensation need amendments. The relationship between the investigation *ex officio* and the requirement for victims to file a complaint within 60 days from the offence commission must be clarified. As already indicated, Law No 272/2024 clarified this issue by repealing the requirement that victims have to file a criminal report to access State compensation. Several amendments regarding reimbursing expenses, the reasonable delay of judgment on civil claims, and measures to encourage offenders to compensate the victims are still needed.

Thirdly, at the practical level, judicial authorities and lawyers have to give the appropriate importance to victims' rights. Since rights without remedies cannot be effective, judges must enforce victims' rights and determine the investigative authorities to properly exercise their duty to provide information, support, and protection to the victims. In this framework, training judges, prosecutors, police officers, and lawyers is vital. As a training component, guides and good practices could be critical factors in addressing the implementation challenges. Mutual training activities with NGOs could also enhance the judicial authorities' support for victims' rights.

As the Council stated in 2019, Member States must ensure the complete and correct transposition and effective implementation of EU law on victims' rights.[158] Five years later, Romania still has a long way to cover from legal texts to implementation. The process of turning statutes into best practice appears to be a challenging journey ahead. Romania, as an EU Member State lacking tradition in protecting victims' rights, needs further EU support in this process.

[157] EC, Proposal for a Directive of the European Parliament and of the Council amending Directive 2012/29/EU establishing minimum standards on the rights, support and protection of victims of crime, and replacing Council Framework Decision 2001/220/JHA, COM/2023/424 final.

[158] Council of the EU, Conclusions on Victims' Rights, available at www.consilium.europa.eu/en/meetings/jha/2019/12/02-03/.

12

The Status of the Victim in Latvian Criminal Procedure Law – When the Most Urgent Thing is to Strengthen Active Participation with Effective Protection

KRISTĪNE STRADA-ROZENBERGA AND ĀRIJA MEIKALIŠA

I. Introduction

In Latvia, the victim of a criminal offence has long since been assigned an important role in criminal proceedings. Untypically for most European countries, the victim has been granted the status of an autonomous participant in criminal proceedings for decades, with the scope of rights changing over time. Currently, the victim's criminal procedural status is regulated by the country's Criminal Procedure Law[1] which entered into force on 1 October 2005. Until then, for more than 50 years, the status of the victim had been defined in the Criminal Procedure Code of the Latvian SSR of 1961[2] which was renamed the Latvian Criminal Procedure Code in 1991.[3]

The victim has been known as a distinct participant in criminal proceedings since 1961 and this is still the case today. Over time, however, there have been changes, of greater or lesser significance, to many elements of the victim's legal status. The following are examples of such changes. In 1998, the Criminal Procedure Law was amended,[4] providing that a legal person could also be recognised as a victim. In 2010, the

[1] Criminal Procedure Law of Latvia 2005. Consolidated version available at https://likumi.lv/ta/en/en/id/107820.

[2] Criminal Procedure Code of Latvia SSR 1961. Consolidated version available at https://likumi.lv/ta/id/90971-latvijas-kriminalprocesa-kodekss.

[3] Amendments to the Criminal Procedure Code of Latvia SSR of 22 August 1991 (entered into force on 22 August 1991).

[4] Amendments to the Criminal Procedure Code of Latvia of 14 October 1998 (entered into force on 1 April 1999).

possibility for the victim to maintain the accusation was excluded.[5] And, in 2016, a specially protected status of the victim was introduced,[6] etc.

This chapter mainly focuses on the current legal regulation of the victim's status in Latvian law, occasionally also pointing to past events that characterise particularly significant turning points in the victim's legal status. It starts with a general presentation of the legal framework applicable to victims, in which the understanding of the concept of the victim, the acquisition of the status of a distinct participant in the proceedings, as well as a general description of the role of the victim in criminal proceedings, are examined. This is followed by a description of the victim's rights and obligations as well as the protection measures available under Latvian law. The review concludes with a description of the victim's right to receive compensation.

II. Overview of the Legal Framework Applicable to Victims under Latvian Law

The criminal procedural status of the victim in Latvia used to be included in the codified legal norms regulating criminal proceedings – until the restoration of independence in 1990 – in the Criminal Procedure Code, then – in the Criminal Procedure Law. The scope of the victim's rights and obligations has been reviewed in recent decades, with major or minor adjustments being introduced occasionally. The basis for making the amendments has been trends defined by the national legal policy, as well as other circumstances, among which the adoption of basic EU instruments, such as the Framework Decision on the standing of victims in criminal proceedings and several directives of both sectoral and horizontal scope, which directly or indirectly affect the status of the victim in criminal proceedings. Four Directives, the transposition of which resulted in significant changes to the criminal procedural status of the victim in Latvia are noteworthy: 1) Directive 2011/36/EU on preventing and combating trafficking in human beings and protecting its victims,[7] which was transposed into the Criminal Procedure Law in 2013,[8] 2) Directive 2011/92/EU on combating the sexual abuse and sexual exploitation of children and child pornography,[9] which was transposed into the Criminal Procedure Law in 2014,[10] 3) Directive 2011/99/EU on the European Protection Order,[11]

[5] Amendments to the Criminal Procedure Law of 21 October 2010 (entered into force on 1 January 2011).

[6] Amendments to the Criminal Procedure Law of 18 February 2016 (entered into force on 23 March 2016).

[7] Directive 2011/36/EU of the European Parliament and of the Council of 5 April 2011 on preventing and combating trafficking in human beings and protecting its victims, and replacing Council Framework Decision 2002/629/JHA [2011] OJ L101/1.

[8] Amendments to the Criminal Procedure Law of 12 December 2012 (entered into force on 1 April 2013) and Amendments to the Criminal Procedure Law of 23 May 2013 (entered into force on 10 October 2013).

[9] Directive 2011/92/EU of the European Parliament and of the Council of 13 December 2011 on combating the sexual abuse and sexual exploitation of children and child pornography, and replacing Council Framework Decision 2004/68/JHA [2011] OJ L335/1.

[10] Amendments to the Criminal Procedure Law of 29 May 2014 (entered into force on 25 June 2014).

[11] Directive 2011/99/EU of the European Parliament and of the Council of 13 December 2011 on the European Protection Order [2011] OJ L338/2.

which was transposed into the Criminal Procedure Law in 2015,[12] and 4) Directive 2012/29/EU establishing minimum standards on the rights, support and protection of victims of crime[13] (the 'Victims' Rights Directive'), which was transposed into the Criminal Procedure Law in 2016.[14] It is the latter Directive that has had the most significant impact, although, as acknowledged in theory, overall, the European Union's (EU) efforts to ensure that criminal justice systems recognise a more important role for victims in criminal proceedings have not had a major impact since the victim had already been granted relatively extensive powers in Latvia. The greatest impact may have been in so-called non-procedural protection and the creation of a special legal regime for specially protected groups of victims.[15]

It is important to point out that, although the procedural status of the victim has not fundamentally changed in recent decades in terms of formal rights and obligations, it can be generally recognised that the view of the victims and respect for their interests has changed fundamentally in Latvia. Basically, this can be explained by the revised purpose of the criminal proceedings and the inclusion of the victim's rights therein. The prevailing opinion in Soviet law, which, due to certain circumstances, was also widespread in the Latvian criminal law theory and criminal law regulatory framework in the second half of the last century, essentially, linked the purpose and tasks of the criminal proceedings to punishing the guilty person.[16] The leading doctrinal studies recognised that, in addition to legal punishment, it was important to reinforce the soviet legal order in general and to promote the education of citizens. Respecting the interests of specific victims was not emphasised.[17] At the end of the last century and at the beginning of this century, other trends appeared: in the Criminal Procedure Law of 2005, indications already appear that the purpose of the criminal procedure is linked to 'fair settlement of criminal legal relations'.[18] In the explanations of 'fair settlement', in theory, next to other achievable results, the protection of the victim's interests is also indicated.[19]

In providing a general description of the victim's status in modern Latvia, it should be pointed out initially that the use of the term 'victim' in Latvia is by no means uniform. This concept can be understood in at least two ways – 1) a person who has actually suffered from a criminal offence, and 2) a victim in the procedural

[12] Amendments to the Criminal Procedure Law of 1 January 2015 (entered into force on 25 February 2015).

[13] Directive 2012/29/EU of the European Parliament and of the Council of 25 October 2012 establishing minimum standards on the rights, support and protection of victims of crime, and replacing Council Framework Decision 2001/220/JHA ('Victims' Rights Directive') [2012] OJ L315/57.

[14] Amendments to the Criminal Procedure Law of 18 February 2016 (entered into force on 9 March 2016).

[15] More detailed insight into the impact of the EU directives on the regulation on the victim's status can be found in: Ā Meikališa, 'Victims in Criminal Procedure: A Review of Latvian Criminal Procedure Norms through the Prism of Minimal EU Standards' (2014) 4 *Journal of the University of Latvia. Law* (6) 4–19, Ā Meikališa and K Strada-Rozenberga, 'Impact of Directives of European Parliament and of Council on Development of Latvian Criminal Procedure Law: General Overview and Procedural Protection of Victims with Specific Protection Needs' (2019) 41 *Journal of the University of Latvia. Law* (12) 41–57.

[16] Criminal Procedure Code of Latvia 1961, Art 2.

[17] See, eg, A Liede, *Latvijas PSR kriminālprocess un tiesu pierādījumi* (Zvaigzne, 1970) 9–13.

[18] Criminal Procedure Law 2005, Art 1.

[19] eg K Strada-Rozenberga, '1.panta komentārs' in Ā Meikališa and K Strada-Rozenberga (ed), *Kriminālprocesa likuma komentāri A daļa* (Latvijas Vēstnesis, 2019) 25; A Judins 'Fiziskā persona kā cietušais Latvijas kriminālprocesā' (2023) 7 *Jurista vārds* 29(1295) 7.

sense – a participant in criminal proceedings with an autonomous legal status. If the first one includes, for example, the right to report a criminal offence, to complain about the decision not to start criminal proceedings, as well as to receive a certain type of protection, then only the second one is characterised by the typical criminal procedural rights, such as the right to submit complaints, requests, applications in criminal proceedings, participate in court hearings, having an active status, including to speak in court debates, where it is possible to express an opinion on the punishment to be applied to the accused, apply for compensation and deal with other issues affecting the victim's interests.

The provisions of the Criminal Procedure Law, essentially, apply to the victim as a discrete participant in the criminal proceedings, although some separate norms apply to everyone who has suffered from a criminal offence, regardless of whether or not the person has been recognised as a victim. Thus, the term 'victim' in the Criminal Procedure Law is applied only to a participant in criminal proceedings with an autonomous criminal procedural status. In the Criminal Procedure Law, all participants in the proceedings are divided into four groups – the officials who conduct criminal proceedings, persons who provide defence, victims and the representatives thereof, as well as other persons involved in criminal proceedings. Criminal procedural provisions regarding the rights, duties and protection of a victim of a criminal offence are mainly regulated in Chapter 6 of the Criminal Procedure Law, although certain aspects are to be found in other provisions of the Criminal Procedure Law.[20]

Latvian procedural criminal law includes several provisions providing for the criteria to be met to obtain victim status in criminal proceedings. It is envisaged that a victim in criminal proceedings may be a natural person or a legal person to whom harm was inflicted by a criminal offence,[21] that is, a moral injury, physical suffering, or a material loss (Article 95(1)). At the same time '[a] victim in criminal proceedings may not be a person to whom moral injury was caused as to a representative of a specific group or part of society' (Article 95(2)). As to the situations where the victim of a criminal offence has died, it is determined that 'If a person dies, one of the members of the immediate family of the deceased may be the victim in criminal proceedings'.

Thus, in Latvia, the following persons have the right to be recognised as a victim:

1. a natural or legal person who has been harmed by the criminal offence,
    a. which may take the form of moral injury and/or physical suffering and/or property loss,
        i. the moral harm has not been inflicted as to a representative of a certain group or part of society;
2. one of the relatives of the natural person, if the person who meets the abovementioned characteristics has died.

[20] This refers to the victim's rights, obligations regarding a specific issue, such as receiving compensation, or a specific action at specific stages of the criminal process.

[21] In Latvia, the term 'criminal offence' is used to describe all offences for which liability is provided for in the Criminal Law ('Criminal Law 1998'). According to Article 7 of the Criminal Law, all criminal offences are divided into misdemeanours and crimes, while crimes are divided into less serious, serious, and especially serious crimes.

It is interesting to note that, in relation to subjects who can enjoy the status of a victim in criminal proceedings, Latvia has adopted a relatively broad view: 1) not only natural persons but also legal entities may be victims, 2) as regards relatives of the deceased, in Latvia, they can be recognised as victims regardless of the cause of death, ie also in cases where the death of the victim did not occur due to a criminal offence, but due to other causes. In addition, even though the law uses the phrase 'one of the relatives of the deceased', the jurisprudence has confirmed that several relatives of the deceased can also be recognised as victims in this situation.[22] Thus, Latvian laws include a wider range of potential 'victims' than the Victims' Rights Directive stipulates in Article 2(1). The fact that even legal entities under public law, such as ministries, various public service institutions, etc, can also be recognised as victims – autonomous participants in criminal proceedings – could be considered as a specificity of Latvian law.

To obtain the status of the victim as a participant in the criminal proceedings with all the rights of an active participant in the process, the person must be recognised as such by a special decision of an official. Detailed regulation on how a person is recognised as a victim is provided in Article 96 of the Criminal Procedure Law. A person can be recognised as a victim only if the person wants it. If a person does not want to be recognised as a victim, such a decision cannot be made. There is only one exception to this: 'If a person, due to physical or mental deficiencies, is not able to express will to be a victim by themself, the person shall be recognised as a victim without their consent.'

Thus, we see one of the most important rights of a victim of a crime guaranteed in Latvia, and that is the right to be recognised as a victim in criminal proceedings, alongside the right not to be recognised as such. The decision depends on how active a role a person wants to play in the criminal proceedings because, as already indicated, only a victim of a criminal offence who has been recognised as a victim by a special decision of an official has the opportunity to become actively involved and influence the proceedings, within the limits of their legal powers. Respecting the will of a person to be recognised or not as a victim is an innovation in Latvia since 2005. Before that, the Criminal Procedure Code did not provide for the respect of a person's will – anyone whom the officials had reason to believe had suffered from a criminal offence was recognised as a victim, regardless of their will and position. In 2014, a study conducted by one of the authors confirmed that the absolute majority of victims decided to accept the status of a victim in criminal proceedings.[23]

As already indicated, for a person to be granted the status of a victim actively participating in the criminal proceedings, they must be officially recognised as a victim, if that is their wish. Answering the question that could reasonably arise here – what should be done if that is not their wish? It should be stated that the status of a victim cannot be granted against the person's will (except for the specified individual cases related to the person's own inability to grasp their situation and fully protect themselves). This affects the scope of rights and obligations for the specific person but does not significantly affect the existence and course of the criminal proceedings, as the principles

[22] Decisions of the Supreme Court of Latvia 18 December 2013, Case 11370050809 (SKK-0514-13); 12 February 2015, Case 11390017712 (SKK-0018-15).

[23] K Strada-Rozenberga, 'Victims and their Criminal Procedure Status in Law Enforcement Practices in Latvia' (2014) 51(6) *Journal of the University of Latvia. Law* 87.

of mandatory criminal proceedings and public prosecution are recognised in Latvia. A person's refusal to be a victim does not mean that they will not be involved in the proceedings at all. If information needs to be obtained from them, then the person will participate in the proceedings as a witness, ie, as a participant in criminal proceedings with the sole procedural role of testifying.

Concluding this section, one cannot fail to mention one of the most significant, in our opinion, perhaps the most significant, changes in Latvian criminal procedural norms regarding the victim, which are directly related to the transposition of EU norms. When the Victims' Rights Directive was transposed into the Criminal Procedure Law, a new category of victim requiring specific protection was included in Latvian criminal procedural law (called 'specially protected victim').[24] An official can grant this status to a wide range of persons – ie to victims of criminal offences directly referred to in the norm (a minor, a person who has suffered from a criminal offence directed against the morality or sexual inviolability of a person, or from human trafficking, a person who has suffered from a criminal offence related to violence or threat of violence and committed by a member of the family, etc), and everyone, 'who, due to the harm inflicted as a result of a criminal offence, is particularly vulnerable and is not protected from repeated threat, intimidation, or revenge, shall be recognised as a specially protected victim' (Criminal Procedure Law, Article 96–1). Granting such a special status to the victim does not increase the role or importance in the criminal process, but is related to the granting of additional respect and protection, which we will consider a little later.

III. Victim in Criminal Proceedings – Passive Observer or Active Participant? The Status of the Victim in Criminal Proceedings

As previously said, a person recognised as a victim has the status of an active participant in criminal proceedings. At the same time, it cannot be said that the victim is the central participant in the criminal proceedings – the role is limited and possibilities to influence the course of the proceedings are quite restricted.

At the level of basic principles, it is established in Latvia that 'Criminal proceedings shall be conducted in the interests of society regardless of the will of the person upon whom the harm was inflicted'.[25]

Currently, in Latvia, all criminal proceedings are characterised by a pre-trial stage, in which the investigation is basically carried out by investigators, which are independent and whose activities are monitored by prosecutors (in exceptional cases – by prosecutors themselves), and prosecution by prosecutors. The role of the victim during the criminal proceedings includes the right to report the offence that has occurred, submit evidence, including being a source of evidence themselves, appeal against rulings, etc, but they are not responsible for prosecutions.

[24] This type of victim was included in the Criminal Procedure Law in 2016 (Amendments to the Criminal Procedure Law of 18 February 2016 (entered into force on 23 March 2016).

[25] Criminal Procedure Law 2005, Art 6.

It should be noted that, in the relatively recent past, there was a radically different solution. Before 2005, when the Law on Criminal Procedure came into force and during the first years of its operation in Latvia, the so-called private prosecution in criminal proceedings was applicable. In this case, the victim played a central role in the criminal proceedings because they were given the right to act as the private prosecutor. This type of private prosecution could be carried out only with respect to less severe/minor offences (intentional minor bodily harm, denigration and defamation). The criminal proceedings in these cases were characterised by the following features – the absence of the pre-trial stage (the victim filed a complaint directly to court), the prosecution was not conducted by the prosecutor, as in all other criminal cases, but by the victim or victim's representative.[26] Given the problems identified in practice in this type of criminal proceedings (insufficient protection for the victim, at the same time, the possible excessive infringement of the legal interests of the accused, difficulties in ensuring the fulfilment of legal requirements, etc), a large-scale study, commissioned by the Ministry of Justice, was conducted, identifying the existing problems and possible solutions.[27] These potential solutions included either maintaining private action by modifying the rules governing it or abandoning private action. In 2010, the Latvian legislator chose the second option; hence, since 1 January 2011, private prosecution is no longer recognised in Latvia.[28] Offences, for which private prosecution was available, have either decriminalised over time or are being publicly prosecuted.

At the same time, it should be emphasised that there are criminal offences for which the existence of criminal proceedings depends directly on the victim. Article (2) of the Criminal Procedure Law refers to 10 types of criminal offences for which criminal proceedings can be initiated and carried out only if the victim's application has been received.[29] This includes, for example, theft of up to one minimum monthly salary (currently €620), minor bodily injury, excluding domestic violence, etc. For these offences, criminal proceedings are initiated only if the victim so wishes (except if the victims are unable to assess the situation due to physical or mental deficiencies, then criminal proceedings can be initiated without their request). The conduct of the criminal proceedings may be interrupted by the withdrawal of the application by the victim if it happens during the investigation in the pre-trial criminal proceedings, as well as by settlement during the entire process.[30] Thus, it can be recognised that, under Latvian law, the victim has been granted decisive influence in criminal proceedings for offences of a certain type. The range of offences for which the victim is given greater powers has evolved significantly over time, sometimes in a restrictive sense, sometimes in an extensive sense. Thus, for example, in the initial version of the Criminal Procedure Law, such a procedure was also provided for rape without qualifying circumstances, but in 2016 such a possibility was deleted.[31] Currently, the theory of criminal procedure in Latvia

[26] ibid Arts 7(3), 44, c 58 (not in force since 1 January 2011).

[27] K Strada-Rozenberga, 'Cietušo tiesību realizācija privātās apsūdzības lietās – krimināltiesiskais regulējums, prakse, problēmas, risinājumi' (2008), available at www.tm.gov.lv/sites/tm/files/2020-01/Documents/lv_documents_petijumi_cietuso_tiesibu_realizacija_petijuma_atskaite.doc.

[28] Amendments to the Criminal Procedure Law of Latvia of 21 October, 2010 (entered into force on 1 January, 2011).

[29] For a more detailed review, see Strada-Rozenberga (n 19) 40–43.

[30] Criminal Procedure Law, Art 377(11).

[31] The range of offences has been changed seven times since the Criminal Procedure Law came into force.

recognises that criminal procedures, the existence of which depends on the will of the victim, are an expression of the principle of opportunity (prosecutorial discretion), which, substantially, are well received; however, at the same time frequent criticism is heard, related to the lack of clear criteria and consistency, as well as the excessive influence of private interests on the public sphere of law.[32]

If a person who has suffered a criminal offence wants to actively protect their interests, the primary legal interest of the victim is the initiation of criminal proceedings. Therefore, the commencement and proper legal conduct of criminal proceedings represent one of the primary rights and procedural guarantees of the victim. This right is respected by the State, with the mediation of its officials, involved in criminal proceedings, ensuring timely initiation and effective course of the criminal proceedings. At the national level, there is a special law – the Law on Compensation for Harm Caused in Criminal Proceedings and Administrative Offence Proceedings,[33] according to which the victim can receive compensation from the State in a situation where a criminal offence has not been properly and effectively investigated.[34]

Description of the rights and obligations of the victim in the framework of existing criminal proceedings reveals that the victim's criminal procedural rights is determined to primarily ensure the personal goal of the victim's participation – financial or non-financial satisfaction for the final result of the criminal process, while the duties of the victim are intended for the broader interests of the criminal justice system. Thus, for example, the right to receive information or to appeal decisions is primarily related to the realisation of the interests of an individual victim, while their duty to testify is linked to the broader interest of criminal justice in establishing the truth.

At the beginning of the review of the victim's rights, it is indicated that the right to receive compensation for the damage caused by a criminal offence is recognised as one of the basic rights of the victim, which is discussed in more detail in the next section. Likewise, the right to information, an interpreter, legal assistance, filing complaints, as well as other rights typical of the so-called active or interested participant in the proceedings have been defined as the victim's basic rights. Also, the right of the victim to conclude a settlement with the perpetrator of the criminal offence is recognised. The Criminal Procedure Law also includes a more detailed list of rights regarding the rights of the victim at specific stages of the criminal procedure.[35]

Earlier in the text, we indicated that the legal regulation of victim status was influenced by EU norms. At the same time, we also pointed out that in the field of rights established in legal norms, the impact of EU law is not significant and is mostly related to the right to protection, but less so to the so-called right to participate in criminal

[32] Ā Meikalisa and K Strada-Rozenberga, 'The Victim – A Passive Observer or an Active Participant in Criminal Proceedings. General Observations Following From the Assessment of Latvia's Experience' in G Mesko, A Sotlar and JR Greene (ed), *Criminal Justice and Security – Contemporary Criminal Justice Practice and Research Conference Proceedings* (Ljubljana, 2013) 247–48.

[33] Law on Compensation for Harm Caused in Criminal Proceedings and Administrative Offence Proceedings 2017.

[34] For the State's responsibility in case of violation of the victim's rights in Latvia, see in detail: K Strada-Rozenberga and D Gurevičs, 'Victim of Crime and the State's Liability for the Result of Criminal Proceedings' (2023) 60 *Journal of the University of Latvia Law 16* 60–70.

[35] Criminal Procedure Law 2005, Arts 98–101.

proceedings. Paying a little more attention to this, it can be pointed out that such typical participation rights, including the right to compensation, the right to submit complaints about officials' criminal procedural decisions, the right to get acquainted with case materials, the right to present evidence, the right to be informed about the progress of the process and final decisions, the right to participate in court, including in the examination of evidence and speaking in debates, etc, have been recognised by victims in Latvia for decades. Thus, their existence cannot be linked to the EU's efforts to expand the role of the victim in criminal proceedings. The EU's efforts had a much more significant impact on the so-called protection rights.

It is essential that the principle of voluntariness is observed in exercising the rights of the victim – ie, the victim themself chooses whether to exercise rights or not and to what extent. Consequently, it is essential to distinguish between the rights and obligations of the victim in criminal proceedings. Coercive measures against the victims cannot be applied to make them exercise their rights, but can be applied if they do not fulfill their obligations. As a striking example, in principle, the victim's participation in the court session in Latvia is a right, while giving testimony is an obligation (except against themselves and their relatives). Therefore, if the victims did not arrive at the court session when they were summoned to testify, these are grounds for finding that they failed to fulfil their duty, and conveyance by force may be applied. On the other hand, if the participation in the court session is not related to testifying, then the victim's non-appearance is not a ground for their conveyance by force or other adverse consequences.

The exercise by the victims of certain of their rights can significantly affect the course of criminal proceedings. Settlement can be mentioned as a striking example in this respect. According to Latvian law, if a settlement has been reached between the victim and the suspect or the accused and the damage caused by the offence has been compensated, this may be the basis for mandatory termination of criminal proceedings (if the offence belongs to the type of criminal offences for which criminal proceedings can only be initiated if the victim so wishes) or for possible termination of criminal proceedings in the case of other criminal offences or less serious crimes. In the latter case, additional conditions must be met, for example criminal proceedings against the suspect or the accused for committing an intentional crime on the basis of a settlement must not have been terminated within the previous year.[36]

As for every participant in proceedings, there are also responsibilities alongside the rights and protection. In criminal proceedings, they are not numerous and are quite general. For example, the obligation to arrive at the time and place indicated by an official authorised to conduct criminal proceedings and to participate in investigative activities, and an obligation to immediately notify, in writing, the postal or electronic address for the receipt of their consignments (Criminal Procedure Law, Article 103).

As regards victims as a source of evidence, they do not enjoy any special privileges. In testifying, the victim has the same rights and obligations as the witness. The main thing is that the victims are obliged to testify (they can only refuse to testify against themselves and their relatives), they are also criminally liable if knowingly providing

[36] Criminal Procedure Law 2005, Arts 377, 379(1), Criminal Law 1998, Art 58(2).

false testimony.[37] In some instances, the conduct of investigative activities provides for specific arrangements to take into account the protection needs and interest of the victim. Thus, for example, Article 51(4) of the Criminal Procedure Law provides that 'The interrogation of a victim is conducted as soon as possible. The number of interrogations is as small as possible. The interrogation of a victim shall be performed, as much as possible, by the same person'. Additional procedural guarantees in the performance of investigative activities are established for victims who need additional protection. For example,

> Interrogation of such person who has been recognised as a victim of violence committed by a person upon whom the victim is dependent financially or otherwise, a victim of human trafficking, or a criminal offence directed against morality or sexual inviolability of the person, shall be conducted by a performer of an investigative action of the same gender. The above-mentioned condition need not be complied with if the victim themself or victim representative agrees thereto. If the victim of a criminal offence directed against morality or sexual inviolability of a person and the person who has the right to defence is of the same gender and if it is requested by the victim or representative, the interrogation shall be performed by a performer of an investigative action of the opposite gender.[38]

The participation of the victims in the criminal proceedings can undeniably be in their interest, ie by actively participating, they can to a greater or lesser extent ensure the achievement of the goals for which they chose to actively participate in the process. However, the victim may also be harmed during the criminal proceedings (a phenomenon which is commonly referred to as 'secondary and repeat victimisation'), which should be avoided as much as possible.

Damage to victims (moral suffering, the remembering of what happened, unpleasant feelings when seeing the offender, etc) may be caused due to participation in criminal proceedings. For this reason, involving the victim in the process should be empathetic, understanding the risks and mitigating them as much as possible. Norms, which can generally be called 'attitude' norms, are a certain novelty in the Criminal Procedure Law, the inclusion of which has largely taken place by transposing EU norms. Thus, for example, when transposing the Victims' Rights Directive, the Criminal Procedure Law was supplemented with several direct instructions such as:

> In performing the procedural actions, communication between the victim and victim's immediate family with the person who has the right to defence shall be avoided as much as possible, unless such communication is necessary for achieving the objectives of criminal proceedings.[39]

Further, 'The interrogation of a victim is conducted as soon as possible. The number of interrogations is as small as possible. The interrogation of a victim shall be performed, as much as possible, by the same person.' (Criminal Procedure Law Article 151(4) etc).

In addition to the harm that may result from unprofessional involvement in criminal proceedings, it cannot be ruled out that damage to the victim can also be caused by

[37] Criminal Procedure Law 2005, Art 98(2), Criminal Law 1998, Arts 300, 302, 303.

[38] Criminal Procedure Law 2005 Art 151–1(2). A special procedure is provided for the prosecution of minors (Criminal Procedure Law 2005 Arts 152, 153).

[39] ibid Art 139(7).

other persons involved in criminal proceedings or even by those not directly involved in criminal proceedings (for example, suspects or accused persons, other victims, their acquaintances or relatives). At the level of the basic principles of criminal procedure, the State's duty to protect the victim from threats that could arise due to participation in criminal proceedings is established by a special principle – 'Protection of a Person and Property in the Case of a Threat' (Criminal Procedure Law Article 24). Pursuant to this Article, the State is obliged to respond to the threat that the victim or any other participant in the proceedings has been subject to due to participation in criminal proceedings, by taking one of the following measures:

1. to initiate other criminal proceedings for the investigation of the threat;
2. to select a corresponding security measure for the person in the interest of whom the threat has taken place;
3. to institute determination of special procedural protection for the person who is being threatened;
4. to assign law enforcement institutions with the task of protecting the person or property, as well as protecting the immediate family of such person.

The aforementioned measures apply to situations where the victim is endangered due to participation in the proceedings. On the other hand, threats that could potentially be directed against the victim for reasons other than participation in the criminal proceedings (for example, repeated victimisation in the case of domestic violence) are dealt with both by criminal procedural means, such as applying appropriate security measures to the suspect and the accused (prohibition of approaching, contacting, etc), as well as non-criminal procedural means (for example, when the police make a restraining order or when the court makes a decision on temporary protection against violence in a civil procedural order).[40]

According to the principle of equality, equal treatment is ensured to all victims, regardless of their age, gender or characteristics. However, in certain cases, some victims enjoy additional rights or additional protection. For example, the status of a specially protected victim gives the victim additional procedural rights, such as, for example, to 'participate in procedural activities, with a permission of the person directing the proceedings, together with the trusted person' (Criminal Procedure Law, Article 96–1(5)), 'request and receive information regarding release or escape of such arrested or convicted person from a place of imprisonment or a place of temporary detention who has inflicted harm on them, if there is a threat to the victim and there is no risk of harm to the arrested or convicted person' (Criminal Procedure Law, Article 96–1(6)), they are subject to special interrogation requirements (Criminal Procedure Law, Article 151–1). Certain procedural guarantees are also granted to minors. For example, such victims are provided with mandatory legal assistance (Criminal Procedure Law, Article 108(5)), special features of interrogation (Criminal Procedure Law, Articles 152, 153), etc.

[40] Civil Procedure Law 1998, Art 2; Law On Police 1991, Arts 12, 12-1; Regulation of Cabinet of Ministers No 161 Procedures for the Prevention of Threats of Violence and Ensuring of Temporary Protection against Violence 2014.

To conclude the review of the victim's rights, obligations and protection in Latvia, some current trends should be highlighted. In recent years, the tendency to apply various simplified forms of criminal proceedings has increased significantly in Latvia, mainly focusing on out-of-court models for resolving criminal litigation. According to the data published by the General Prosecutor's Office, the use of out-of-court models is increasing every year and, in 2022, more people were found guilty of certain types of offences (for example, theft of up to one minimum monthly salary, etc) and punished out-of-court rather than in judicial proceedings.[41] This undoubtedly raises the question – to what extent does the simplification of criminal proceedings meet the interests of the victim? From a formal point of view, the protection of financial interests seems to be more or less ensured, as both the settlement process and the application of the prosecutor's penal order are possible only if the damage caused has been compensated for or a specific agreement has been reached to cover it.[42] However, in our opinion, the interest of the victim's participation in the criminal proceedings should not be reduced only to the possibility of receiving compensation but should be viewed more broadly. Respecting other interests (the interest that the accused receives a punishment appropriate to the offence, etc) in the case of the application of the simplified forms of criminal proceedings is at risk because the laws of Latvia do not envisage the victim's decisive influence on the exact form that the criminal proceedings take. In this situation, since hearing the victim's point of view is mandatory, but respecting it is not (whether it is taken into consideration or not depends upon examination of the specific circumstances),[43] high expectations are placed on the competence and professionalism of officials.

IV. Compensation for Victims

The right to receive compensation for damage caused by a criminal offence is recognised as one of the basic principles of the criminal procedure in Article 22 of the Criminal Procedure Law. Detailed rules regarding the application, justification, amount, allocation of compensation and other issues can be found in Chapter 26 of the Criminal Procedure Law. It is important to point out that these criminal procedural norms regulate the compensation paid to the victim by the perpetrator of the criminal offence (if the offender is a minor, this includes the parents or persons who replace them). The Criminal Procedure Law does not regulate compensation from the State. A study conducted in 2014 confirmed that the possibility of receiving compensation was one of the most important reasons why victims wished to participate in criminal proceedings, as well as the fact that, if a victim received compensation during the proceedings, it was less likely that they would be actively involved in further proceedings.[44] Although more

[41] Latvijas Republikas Ģenerālprokurora ziņojums par 2022.gadā paveikto un 20223.gada darbības prioritātēm, available at prokuratura.lv/media/Normativie_akti/generalprokurora_zinojums_2022_01_03.pdf.

[42] Criminal Procedure Law 2005, Arts 420(5), 433(1), 437.

[43] ibid Arts 420(5), 421, 422, 436, 437.

[44] Strada-Rozenberga (n 23) 87.

recent studies have not been conducted in Latvia, general observations would allow us to assume that the situation has not changed significantly.

According to the Criminal Procedure Law, compensation can only be paid in monetary terms. Compensation by the offender in the meaning of the Criminal Procedure Law does not include other types of compensation (for example, elimination of damage by one's own work or return of other goods). Likewise, compensation is considered to be an element of a fair solution to criminal legal dispute. The amount of compensation is determined either by agreement between the parties involved or by the decision of an official (the court or the prosecutor). When determining this, the officials take into account both the financial situation of the persons involved, the damage caused by the specific offence and other circumstances. If the victims are dissatisfied with the amount of compensation awarded to them in the criminal proceedings, they can file a claim for additional compensation in the civil procedure.

The State's compensation to the victim is granted in a special administrative procedure regulated by a special law – 'On State Compensation to Victims'.[45] This law was adopted in 2006 for the purpose of transposing the 2004/80/EC Compensation Directive.[46] This law establishes the procedure by which victims can receive compensation from the State if they are victims of a criminal offence.[47] However, not all victims can receive compensation under this law. Several prerequisites must be met:

1. the criminal offence must be intentional, so those victims who suffered a criminal offence committed due to negligence do not receive compensation;
2. damage caused must reach a certain degree of severity: '1) the person has died; 2) severe or moderate bodily injuries have been caused to the victim; 3) the morality or sexual inviolability of the person has been violated; 4) the victim is a victim of trafficking in human beings; 5) the victim has been infected with human immunodeficiency virus, Hepatitis B or C'(Law on Compensation, Articles 1 and 3(4));

A special procedure is applied to situations where the victim suffered from a criminal offence in road traffic:

> The victim has no right to receive the State compensation if the criminal offence was directed against the traffic safety and the victim has the right to insurance compensation in accordance with the laws and regulations regarding the compulsory civil liability insurance of owners of motor vehicles.[48]

Thus, obviously, compensation from the State can be requested only for some criminal offences – those in which a natural person's life, health, sexual integrity, etc are threatened – and also if the offence was intentional. In addition, it should be noted that not all victims use the opportunity to receive this compensation.

> Comparative data show that less than 20 per cent of victims take advantage of this mechanism. Thus, it may be assumed that that under-use of the State compensation mechanism is

[45] Law On State Compensation to Victims, 2006.

[46] Council Directive 2004/80/EC of 29 April 2004 relating to compensation to crime victims [2004] OJ L261/15.

[47] A brief review of the procedure can be found at https://e-justice.europa.eu/491/EN/if_my_claim_is_to_be_considered_in_this_country?LATVIA&member=1.

[48] Law On State Compensation to Victims 2006 Art 2(3).

> that victims are not sufficiently informed about it in all cases or the person is informed but for some reasons does not want to use the offered service; therefore, it is likely that the goal of providing an accessible support service to all crime victims in the sense of the Victims Directive is not fully achieved.[49]

The amount of the State compensation (Law on Compensation, Article 7) cannot be recognised as particularly large – currently, its maximum amount is set at five minimum monthly wages[50] determined in the Republic of Latvia, which in 2024 is €700. Thus, the maximum amount of compensation in 2024 is €3,500.[51] The maximum amount of compensation is granted only if the death of a person has occurred as a result of a criminal offence, in other cases, it is smaller – for example,

> if severe bodily injuries have been caused to the victim or the criminal offence has been classified as rape or sexual violence, or the morality or sexual inviolability of the minor victim has been violated, or the victim is a victim of trafficking in human beings – in the amount of 90%.

Or further, 'if a minor victim has suffered moderate bodily injuries or the minor victim has been infected with human immunodeficiency virus, hepatitis B or C – in the amount of 70%'. Practice shows that the maximum amounts of compensation are paid out very rarely. Thus, for example, in the period 2014–2022, these maximum amounts were granted only five times per year. In 2023, there were five such cases by the middle of the year.[52]

It is very important to mention that unlike most Member States, the State compensation mechanism is not intended to apply only when the victim is unable to obtain compensation from the offender. More precisely – a victim is not obliged to seek first compensation from the offender in order to be granted State compensation. From this point of view, these two types of compensation are not interrelated. However, it cannot be said that there is no connection between them at all.

The question of the interrelationship between compensation paid by the State and the compensation by the offender is intriguing. This has, in certain theoretical studies in Latvia, prompted the question – what is the nature and purpose of the compensation paid by the State? According to the Law on Compensation '[i]f a victim has received compensation from the offender or another person on theirs or them behalf, the amount of the State compensation shall be reduced according to the compensation already received' (Article 7-1(1)). The Criminal Procedure Law, however, does not say anything about how compensation from the accused should be determined if the victim has already received compensation from the State. Jurisprudence provides an answer to this question – the amount of compensation to be recovered from a person can be reduced by the amount received as compensation from the State.[53] At the same

[49] A Turlaja, 'Valsts kompensācija cietušajiem: iestāžu sadarbība, kompensācijas apmērs un informatīvais atbalsts' (2023) 32 *Jurista Vārds* 29 (1295) 36.

[50] It should be noted that this amount was determined only this year. Previously, it was up to four or even up to three minimum monthly salaries.

[51] For comparison, the average salary in Latvia in the second quarter of 2023 was €1,525, see stat.gov.lv/lv/statistikas-temas/darbs/alga?themes=2386#tabulas.

[52] Turlaja (n 49) 35.

[53] Decisions of the Supreme Court of Latvia 2 September 2020, SKK-200/2020; 12 February 2015, case 11390017712 (SKK-0018-15).

time, in theoretical literature, we find different opinions about what the actual purpose of the compensation paid by the State is. Some have expressed the view that it represents 'State support for victims of serious crimes', serving as 'an additional guarantee for individuals against whom a serious crime has been committed'.[54] It is also suggested that this support is not merely supplementary, but 'ensures prompt compensation, as swiftly as possible, as a result of a criminal offence, mitigating the adverse consequences of the damage caused'.[55] Theoretical discussion about this can be continued, however, we are more inclined to support the opinion that the State-paid compensation is not an 'additional' protective measure but rather an opportunity to receive at least partial compensation for damage in a faster and easier way. An additional argument supporting this view can also be found in the fact that the money paid out by the State as State compensation is later recovered from the person found guilty of committing a criminal offence (Law on Compensation, Article 21).

To conclude this section, it is important to mention that compensation in criminal proceedings is a mechanism to 'compensate' for the damage, including property damage. In addition, there is another instrument for the prevention of consequences which has affected interests in the case of crimes against property. It is applicable when the specific property that had been criminally obtained from the victim has been found during the proceedings. In such a case, the rights of the victim are ensured by returning this property, which can happen either at the end of the proceedings or during the proceedings.[56]

V. Conclusions and General Remarks

The victim has long since been known in Latvia as a potentially active 'player' in criminal proceedings with the status of an autonomous participant in the criminal proceedings and the ability to influence the existence, progress and outcome of the criminal proceedings. Although the victim's active role in the course of criminal proceedings has long since been foreseen in Latvia, at the turn of the century the view on the importance of respecting the victim's interests changed. To a large extent, this has happened due to the transition from the findings of the Soviet school of law to an approach characteristic of Western Europe, primarily in terms of the goal and tasks of criminal proceedings. If, in the second half of the last century, the goal of the criminal proceedings was basically linked to punishing the perpetrator of the criminal offence and ensuring general legality, then the beginning of this century is characterised by the 'fair settlement of criminal legal relations' as the goal of criminal proceedings. The latter is unconceivable without properly ensuring the interests of the victim. This should mark a change in legal thinking not so much from the point of view of the formal rights and obligations of the victim but from the understanding of the role of the victim in criminal proceedings.

[54] D Gurēvičs, 'Cietušā loma krimināltiesisko attiecību taisnīgā noregulējumā' in *Latvijas Republikas Satversmei – 100. Latvijas Universitātes 80. starptautiskās zinātniskās konferences krājums* (Riga, LU akadēmiskais apgāds, 2022) 257–58.

[55] Turlaja (n 49) 33.

[56] Criminal Procedure Law 2005 c 27.

Currently, Latvian criminal procedural law defines the victim as a distinct participant in criminal proceedings who has sufficiently broad powers, even without taking the central role in criminal proceedings. However, there is an essential prerequisite for this – the victim's own wish. The status of a victim is completely voluntary and the decision on whether to obtain it or not and, consequently, to obtain the 'privileges' that this status gives is a free choice of each victim.

Modernisation in the victim's legal protection, largely influenced by the EU's efforts, is associated with greater concern for the victim's well-being and safety, as well as the introduction of a specially protected group of victims. Formally, in the field of procedural rights (eg the right to participate in the proceedings, to provide evidence, to speak about the sentence imposed on the accused, to receive legal assistance, etc), the last decade has not brought any significant changes, as such rights have long since been known in the law. Thus, changes are related more to attitude and empathy than to formal legal regulation. Consequently, there is a reason to draw a similar conclusion about whether or not Latvia has fully complied with EU norms regarding victim participation in criminal proceedings and protection. In our opinion, Latvian procedural legal norms fully comply with EU texts. At the same time, there is potential for a more systematic, comprehensive and effective implementation of the protection and support for victims in practice. This is largely due to the insufficiency of resources (both money and highly professional employees, etc), which prevents allocating them in sufficient quantity for all objective needs.

One of the most important interests of victims of criminal offences has always been receiving compensation. It is also sufficiently regulated in the legal norms of Latvia, both by providing for the victim's right to receive compensation from the perpetrator of the crime and – in some cases – from the State. However, the financial circumstances of the perpetrators, coupled with the limited State compensation amounts, often result in the receipt of compensation falling short of real and adequate levels, remaining below expectations.

Certain risks related to the protection of the victim's interests can also be seen in the overall modernisation trends of the criminal procedure. An ever-increasing tendency to solve criminal legal issues outside the court, as well as other ways of simplifying proceedings, which are associated with less openness and public accessibility of proceedings, to a certain extent, threaten not only the full respect for public interests but also the interests of specific victims.

These and other relevant aspects allow us to recognise that the victims and respect for their interests in criminal proceedings is not a subject that we can consider as being exhausted and the related problems solved. It is not expected that the issue will lose its relevance in the future either. Likewise, considerations should focus primarily on how to prevent situations where a person suffers from a criminal offence (being aware that these attempts will never be fully successful) and researching the best ways to improve the status of a victim in criminal proceedings should not be discontinued.

13

Impact of EU Law Instruments Regarding Victims' Rights on Lithuania's Criminal Procedure

GINTARAS ŠVEDAS

I. Introduction

Traditionally, victims' rights are associated with the principle of human dignity, which implies that the State has an obligation to provide a legal framework ensuring that a person has effective mechanisms to achieve restoration of his/her violated rights. From the victim's perspective, restoration of the victim's violated dignity is an essential requirement of fair criminal procedure. Article 47 of the Charter of Fundamental Rights of the European Union[1] declares that: '[E]veryone whose rights and freedoms guaranteed by the law of the Union are violated has the right to an effective remedy before a tribunal in compliance with the conditions laid down in this Article'.

Corresponding provisions are set out in Article 13 of the Convention for the Protection of Human Rights and Fundamental Freedoms,[2] which states that: '[E]veryone whose rights and freedoms as set forth in this Convention are violated shall have an effective remedy before a national authority notwithstanding that the violation has been committed by persons acting in an official capacity'.

Also Article 30 of the Constitution of the Republic of Lithuania,[3] which declares that: '[A] person whose constitutional rights or freedoms are violated shall have the right to apply to a court. Compensation for material and moral damage inflicted upon a person shall be established by law'.

Moreover, the Constitutional Court of Lithuania has emphasised that it is necessary to seek to achieve a situation in which the protection of the rights of the persons who suffered from crimes and the rights of the persons who committed crimes are not unreasonably restricted. The legal regulation of criminal procedure should not create

[1] Charter of Fundamental Rights of the European Union [2012] OJ C326/02.

[2] Convention for the Protection of Human Rights and Fundamental Freedoms (1950) UNTS 2889.

[3] Lietuvos Respublikos Konstitucija (1992) *Valstybės žinios* 33–1014.

any pre-conditions for delaying the investigation of crimes or the consideration of criminal cases, and should not create any pre-conditions for those participating in the criminal procedure to abuse their procedural and other rights.[4] This decision highlighted an element of 'fairness' – the right to effective remedy, which, inter alia, must create the basis of justice for victims.

In 1985, the Council of Europe[5] adopted Recommendation R 85(11) on the position of the victim in the framework of criminal law and procedure.[6] In this Recommendation, victims' interests, such as access to information about the ongoing criminal case, expression of an opinion regarding prosecution and conviction of the offender, legal representation and aid, obtaining compensation for the suffered harm, etc, were emphasised.[7] Also in 1985, the United Nations adopted another significant international legal act on the rights of victims – the UN Declaration of Basic Principles of Justice for Victims of Crime and Abuse of Power.[8] This UN Declaration is sometimes referred to as the 'Magna Carta' of victims' rights given that it consolidates the main principles of the victim's rights in the course of criminal proceedings, formulates the essence of the victim's role in the proceedings, etc. It should be noted that the provisions of the aforementioned non-binding legal acts were taken into account when preparing Lithuania's new Code of Criminal Procedure[9] (henceforth referred to as CCP), which was adopted in 2002 and came into force on 1 May 2003.[10]

Meanwhile, transposition of the requirements of EU legal acts, for example the former Council Framework Decision 2001/220/JHA on the standing of victims in criminal proceedings[11] (henceforth referred to as Framework Decision 2001/220/JHA), which obliged EU Member States to ensure the victim's 'real and appropriate role in its criminal legal system' was already mandatory for Lithuania. Framework Decision 2001/220/JHA encouraged EU Member States to boost the victim's role in the proceedings by guaranteeing certain participatory rights such as the right to be heard and to supply evidence, the right to information about the case in understandable language, the right to representation and legal aid, the right to mediation, etc.

In 2012, Framework Decision 2001/220/JHA was replaced by Directive 2012/29/EU establishing minimum standards on the rights, support and protection of victims of

[4] Constitutional Court of Lithuania decision of 16 January 2006 'On private accusations and the right of the person, against whom the institution of a criminal case is refused, to lodge a complaint against the decison of the prosecutor'.

[5] About the development of the position of the victim at the European level, see J Casey, 'Terra incognita: Victim Participation Rights, Sexual Offending and Brexit' (2022) 13 *New Journal of European Criminal Law* 420–38.

[6] Recommendation Council of Europe Recommendation (85) 11 on the Position of the Victim in the Framework of Criminal Justice and Procedure (1985).

[7] MEI Brienen and EH Hoegen, *Victims of Crime on 22 European Criminal Justice Systems. In: The Implementation of Recommendation (85) 11 of the Council of Europe on the Position of the Victim in the Framework of Criminal Justice and Procedure* (Wolf Legal Productions, 2000) 12–22.

[8] UN Declaration of Basic Principles of Justice for Victims of Crime and Abuse of Power (1985) A/RES/40/34.

[9] Baudžiamojo proceso kodeksas (2002) *Valstybės žinios* 37–1341.

[10] MJ Lehmkuhl, 'The Value of Legal Provisions for an Adequate Treatment of Victims of Crime: Does the Victims' Rights Directive of the European Union Set a New Benchmark?' in J Joseph and S Jergenson (eds), *An International Perspective on Contemporary Developments in Victimology* (Springer, 2020) 181.

[11] Council Framework Decision (EU) 2001/220/JHA of 15 March 2001 on the standing of victims in criminal proceedings [2001] OJ L82/1.

crime,[12] (henceforth referred to as Directive 2012/29/EU). This Directive aims to amend and expand the provisions of Framework Decision 2001/220/JHA. As rightly observed in the doctrine of criminal procedure, the Directive required EU Member States to enact and implement a broad range of victims' rights. These rights seek to ensure that varying degrees of participation are achieved: from what have been called service rights, such as the right to passively receive information, to active participation. Irrespective of the degree of direct involvement of the victim in the criminal justice system, the common denominator of all these rights is that they are designed to acknowledge victims.[13]

In 2022, the European Commission published an evaluation of Directive 2012/29/EU (henceforth referred to as Evaluation of Directive 2012/29/EU), in which it admitted, *inter alia*, that 'the lack of a clear legal concept for the status of a victim in criminal proceedings potentially raises practical issues for the achievement of the directive's objectives'. The European Commission's evaluation clearly recognises that the variety of viewpoints on the victim's status in criminal proceedings creates obstacles to the harmonisation of the victims' rights among the EU Member States.[14] Taking into account the conclusions made in the evaluation, the European Commission announced that a possible revision of Directive 2012/29/EU is required in order to strengthen standards of justice for victims of crime.[15] Such a position of the European Commission also requires re-evaluation of the Lithuanian system of victim status and its peculiarities.

The main objective of this chapter is to assess the significance of EU directives related to the rights of victims for the definition and status of the victim in the Lithuanian criminal justice system. This chapter will be divided into four main sections dealing respectively with the definition of victim, the place of the victim in criminal procedure, compensation for victims of violent crimes and protection measures available for victims in Lithuania and conclusions.

II. Definition of the Victim in Lithuania's Criminal Justice System

Lithuania's criminal justice system, which consists of several distinct independent branches of law (criminal law, criminal procedure, execution of punishment), uses terms such as 'victim', 'injured person', 'person harmed by criminal act', 'person who has suffered as a result of a crime', 'victim of a violent crime', 'victim of domestic violence'.

[12] Directive 2012/29/EU of the European Parliament and of the Council of 25 October 2012 establishing minimum standards on the rights, support and protection of victims of crime, and replacing Council Framework Decision 2001/220/JHA [2012] OJ L315/57.

[13] AK Bosma, MS Groenhuijsen and M de Vries, 'Victims' Participation Rights in the Post-Sentencing Phase: The Netherlands in Comparative Perspective' 2021 (12) *New Journal of European Criminal Law* 129–30.

[14] Evaluation of Directive 2012/29/EU of the European Parliament and of the Council of 25 October 2012 establishing minimum standards on the rights, support and protection of victims of crime, and replacing Council Framework Decision 2001/220/ JHA available at https://ec.europa.eu/info/law/better-regulation/have-your-say/initiatives/12727-Supporting-crime-victims-evaluation-of-the-Victims-Rights-Directive_en.

[15] 'Revision of the victims' rights *acquis*. In "A New Push for European Democracy" (modified 2022-10-22). available at www.europarl.europa.eu/legislative-train/theme-a-new-push-for-european-democracy/file-revision-of-the-victims-rights-acquis?sid=6301.

Although all these terms describe a person who is a victim of a criminal act, they have significant differences. There is no doubt that the main (general) definition of the victim in the criminal procedure is provided in Lithuania's CCP. This definition was directly influenced by the former Council Framework Decision 2001/220/JHA, according to which: '[V]ictim shall mean a natural person who has suffered harm, including physical or mental injury, emotional suffering or economic loss, directly caused by acts or omissions that are in violation of the criminal law of a Member State'.

It should be noted that this definition underwent significant changes in Lithuania in 2015, 2020 and 2023, which were related, *inter alia*, to the proper implementation of the requirements of Directive 2012/29/EU, and the United Nations International Convention for the Protection of all Persons from Enforced Disappearance.[16] Currently, Article 28 of the CCP states that:

> [T]he victim is a natural person who suffered physical, material or moral damage as a result of a criminal act, or a family member or close relative of a natural person who died or was subjected to enforced disappearance as a result of a criminal act, who suffered physical, material or non-material damage as a result of the death or enforced disappearance of that person.

Article 38 of the CCP provides that the family members (of a natural person who died or was subjected to enforced disappearance as a result of criminal act) shall be:

> [T]he parents (adoptive parents), children (adopted children), brothers, sisters and their spouses residing together with that person, the spouse of the person or the person with whom the person is cohabiting without registering a marriage or the person with whom that person agreed to enter into marriage in accordance with the procedure laid down by the Civil Code of Lithuania, as well as the parents and dependants of the spouse or former spouses.

Meanwhile, Article 248 of the Criminal Code of Lithuania[17] (henceforth referred to as CC) states that close relatives (of a natural person who died or was subjected to enforced disappearance as a result of a criminal act) shall be: '[P]arents (adoptive parents), children (adopted children), brothers, sisters, grand-parents and grand-children'.

A natural person shall be recognised as a victim by the decision of a pre-trial investigator or a prosecutor or by a court ruling. A decision or ruling on the recognition of a person as a victim is adopted, after determining that there are grounds to recognise the person as a victim. Thus, the pre-trial investigator or prosecutor (during the pre-trial investigation) must resolve the issue of recognition as a victim as soon as possible from the beginning of the pre-trial investigation, even if a request to recognise him as a victim has not been received, but there must be enough data in the pre-trial.[18]

Furthermore, in criminal law, the legislator uses the term of 'injured person', which is broader than the definition of 'victim'. Explaining the differences between these terms, the Supreme Court of Lithuania emphasised that the term 'injured person' is used in the title of Article 38 of the CC. The definition of 'injured person' is not provided in the CC. From the aforementioned Article of the CC, it can be seen that the injured person

[16] UN International Convention for the Protection of All Persons from Enforced Disappearance (2010) No 48088.

[17] Baudžiamasis kodeksas (2001) *Valstybės žinios* 89–2741.

[18] Ruling of the Supreme Court of Lithuania Case No 2K-252-654/2023.

may be the victim or representative of a legal person or State institution. According to Article 28 of the CCP, only a natural person is recognised as a victim to whom a criminal act has caused physical, material or moral damage.[19] In another case, the Supreme Court of Lithuania pointed out that the legislator in the CCP also uses the term 'injured person' (or 'person harmed by criminal act'), which cannot be identified with the victim; it can be not only a natural person, but also a legal person who can acquire the status of a civil plaintiff during the pre-trial investigation.[20]

In addition, two other laws provide for a definition of specific categories of victims. First, the Law on Protection against Domestic Violence[21] provides for the concept of a victim of domestic violence, which means: '[A] person against whom domestic violence has been used, also a child who has become a witness of domestic violence and (or) lives in an environment exposed to violence'.

Secondly, the Law on Compensation for Damage Caused by Violent Crimes[22] (henceforth referred to as Law on Compensation) provides the definition of the victim of violent crime, which means:

> [A] citizen of the Republic of Lithuania, a citizen of another EU Member State or his/her family member, another person who legally resides in the Republic of Lithuania or another EU Member State, or in the cases specified in the international treaties of the Republic of Lithuania, another person to whom a violent crime has been committed, or the spouse, partner, child, adopted child, father, mother, adoptive parent, stepmother, dependent of a person whose life was taken by a violent crime, if they meet the above-mentioned criteria.

The Supreme Administrative Court of Lithuania separated the definitions of 'victim of a violent crime' and 'victim'. The Court noted that, when defining the subject entitled to compensation for damages, the legislator uses the definition of 'victim of a violent crime', therefore the definition of the 'victim' enshrined in Article 28 of the CCP cannot be equated with the definition of a victim of a violent crime enshrined in the Law on Compensation. Interpreting the term 'victim of a violent crime' by teleological (purpose of the legal norm), linguistic and systematic methods of legal interpretation, the panel of judges concludes that these are the persons to whom a violent crime was directed. Therefore, the definitions of victim of a violent crime and victim (in criminal proceedings) do not match given that the definition of victim enshrined in Article 28 of the CCP is broader.[23]

So far, Lithuanian doctrine on criminal procedure has not paid much attention to the analysis of the concept of the victim, of his/her rights and obligations. The Lithuanian doctrine on criminal procedure emphasises that only a natural person can be recognised as a victim.[24] Meanwhile, a legal person who has suffered from a criminal act may be

[19] Ruling of the Supreme Court of Lithuania Case No 2K-P-464/2005.

[20] Ruling of the Supreme Court of Lithuania Case N. 2K-565/2014.

[21] Apsaugos nuo smurto artimoje aplinkoje įstatymas (2011) *Valstybės žinios* 72–3475.

[22] Smurtiniais nusikaltimais padarytos žalos kompensavimo įstatymo Nr. X-296 pakeitimo įstatymas (2019) TAR, 858.

[23] Ruling of the Supreme Administrative Court of Lithuania Case No. A-492-1285/2012.

[24] G Goda, M Kazlauskas, P Kuconis and G Švedas, *Lietuvos Respublikos baudžiamojo proceso kodekso komentaras. I-IV dalys (1-220 straipsniai)* (Teisinės informacijos centras, 2003) 62.

recognised only as a civil plaintiff in the criminal procedure. Every natural person can be recognised as a victim, regardless of their age, gender, citizenship, nationality, physical and mental health status, or other circumstances.[25] A person acquires victim status only if there is a factual and legal basis. The factual basis consists of physical, material or moral damage caused by the criminal act, and the legal basis – decision of the pre-trial investigator or prosecutor, also court ruling to recognise a person as a victim.

In Lithuanian doctrine on criminal procedure in 2002, there was a proposal to expand the concept of a victim by providing that the victim

> shall be a natural or legal person about which sufficient data is available to confirm that, as a result of criminal activities, he/she has suffered physical, material or moral damages, as well as a result of preparation or attempt to commit a crime or there has been a great probability that the damage will occur.[26]

On the other hand, such a proposal was not discussed (or even mentioned) by scholars and supported by legislators.

In Lithuanian doctrine on criminal procedure, the delay in recognising a person as a victim was also criticised because it prevents timely exercise of procedural rights and protection legitimate interests. It is completely understandable that the sooner a person becomes an active participant in criminal process relations as a victim, the sooner he/she will be able to use the granted procedural rights of a victim.[27] On the other hand, in 2010, according to the data of the General Prosecutor's Office, this problem was no longer so acute: persons who have suffered from criminal acts are usually immediately recognised as victims at the beginning of the pre-trial investigation, after the first interview. Although it is also noted that in some criminal cases, eg due to severe health impairment, murder, etc (for subjective and objective reasons) persons are recognised as victims only after several months after the crime.[28]

Lithuanian doctrine on criminal procedure also provides such examples of the jurisprudence of the Supreme Court of Lithuania, when a person was recognised as a victim and actively used the victim's rights in the criminal process but, at the end of the process, a decision was made that the person could not be recognised as a victim because there were no grounds for criminal proceedings, and an attempt was made to use criminal justice to resolve a civil legal dispute.[29]

[25] Recital 9 of the Preamble of Directive 2012/29/EU (n 12) provides a wider (comprehensive) list of possible grounds for discrimination: … victims of crime should be recognised and treated … without discrimination of any kind based on any ground such as race, colour, ethnic or social origin, genetic features, language, religion or belief, political or any other opinion, membership of a national minority, property, birth, disability, age, gender, gender expression, gender identity, sexual orientation, residence status or health; G Goda, M Kazlauskas and P Kuconis, *Baudžiamojo proceso teisė* (Registrų centras, 2011) 87.

[26] P Ancelis, S Juzukonis, 'Nukentėjusiojo sąvoka Lietuvos ir kitų valstybių baudžiamajame procese' 2002(35) *Jurisprudencija* 105–106, 107.

[27] P Ancelis, *Nukentėjusiojo apklausos parengtinio tyrimo metu svarbiausi procesiniai praktiniai, psichologiniai aspektai. Teisiniai medicininiai smurto aspektai* (Lietuvos teisės universitetas, 2002) 104.

[28] R Ažubalytė, 'Nukentėjusio nuo nusikalstamos veikos asmens teisė kreiptis į teismą kaip teisminės gynybos realizavimo baudžiamajame procese prielaida' 2010(4) *Jurisprudencija* 231–32.

[29] Rulings of the Supreme Court of Lithuania Cases No. 2K-7-251/2013, 2K-7-262/2013; G Goda, *Vertybiniai prioritetai baudžiamajame procese* (Registrų centras, 2014) 180.

III. The Place of the Victim in Criminal Proceedings and its Compatibility with Directive 2012/29/EU

In order to understand the place of the victim in criminal proceedings according to Lithuanian law, there is a need to understand that victims' rights are regulated differently in Lithuanian law compared to the provisions of Directive 2012/29/EU. Victims' rights in Lithuania are regulated in general and are not classified (as it is done in Directive 2012/29/EU) into rights concerning: (a) information and support, (b) participation in criminal proceedings, and (c) protection of victims. Moreover, victims' rights in Lithuania are regulated in laws of different branches, for example, rights concerning information are provided not only in the CCP, but also in the Code of Punishment Execution[30] (henceforth referred to as CPE), rights concerning protection of victims are set out not only in the CCP, but also in the Civil Code of Lithuania,[31] Law on Protection against Domestic Violence, etc. It is noteworthy that even the CCP victims' rights regulation is not consistent (systematic) and clear enough, because, for example, Article 28 of the CCP, which is dedicated to the definition and status of the victim, does not provide a detailed and exhaustive list of the victims' rights during a criminal procedure. In addition (as it was mentioned in section II), the CCP uses different and not always systematic terms of a person who has suffered from the crime (for example, 'victim', 'injured person', 'person harmed by criminal act', etc), which also hinders the determination of their real procedural rights, as well as the scope of these rights.

In Lithuania, the participating rights of the victim are regulated by Article 28 of the CCP, which specifies that:

> [A] victim and his/her representative shall have the right: to be informed of the state of criminal proceedings concerning him/her; to give testimony; to submit requests; to file motions for challenge; to participate in the assessment of his/her special protection needs; to have access to the case file during a pre-trial investigation and in court; to participate in the hearing of the case in court; to appeal against the actions of a pre-trial investigator, a prosecutor, a pre-trial investigation judge and a court, also to appeal against a court judgment or a ruling; to deliver a closing speech. The victim shall also have the right to refuse to be informed of the status of the criminal proceedings concerning him/her, unless such refusal would prejudice the rights of a suspect or an accused person.

Moreover, Article 45 of the CCP states that:

> [E]very person who suffered from the crime shall have the right to request that the perpetrator of the criminal act be identified and justly punished, to be paid compensation for the damage caused by the criminal act and, in the cases provided for by law, also compensation from the Crime Victims Fund, also receive State-guaranteed legal aid free of charge.

Some authors indicate that this provision of the CCP '... determined the state's positive obligation to lead criminal proceedings to resolution not just in the interest of society but for the sake of the victim as an individual'.[32] It should be noted that the list of

[30] Bausmių vykdymo kodeksas (2022) *Valstybės žinios*, 73-3084.
[31] Civilinis kodeksas (2000) *Valstybės žinios*, 74-2262.
[32] See D Gurevičs, 'Victim's Paradigm in European Union Criminal Law' 2023(127) *Teisė* 132.

victims' participating rights presented in the aforementioned Articles of the CCP is not exhaustive since other Articles of the CCP also provide separate rights. The following participating rights of the victim can be mentioned:

a) the right to have a legal representative who may participate in proceedings and defend the interests of the victim (if they are minors or have been recognised as legally incapable) (Articles 53, 54 of the CCP);
b) the right to have an authorised representative (a person who provides legal assistance to the victim and defends their rights and legitimate interests) (Articles 55, 56 of the CCP);
c) the right to be accompanied by a person of his/her own choosing during criminal proceedings (Article 56(1) of the CCP);
d) the right to reimbursement of costs of proceedings (money paid to victim to cover the expenses of their travel to and residence at the place to which they are summonsed) (Articles 103, 104 of the CCP);
e) the right to return the objects or valuables found and seized in the course of proceedings belonging to a victim (Article 108 of the CCP);
f) the right to file a civil claim (if a victim suffered damage as a result of a criminal act) in criminal proceedings against a suspect or an accused person or against the persons who are materially liable for acts of the suspect or the accused person (Articles 109–117 of the CCP);
g) the right to request the questioning to be conducted by a person of the same sex in cases concerning criminal acts against an individual's freedom of sexual self-determination and inviolability, cases of domestic violence, trafficking in human beings, profiting from another person's prostitution, etc (Article 185 of the CCP);
h) the right for a victim who is a minor to be questioned in the premises adapted for questioning children, usually not more than once and with the presence of a psychologist. In the cases when, during the pre-trial investigation, it is necessary to repeat the questioning of the minor victim, he/she shall usually be questioned by the same person (Article 186 of the CCP);
i) the right to file a complaint or a motion regarding the criminal act in the victim's native language or in another language that he/she speaks or the right of access to the services of an interpreter when filing an oral complaint (if the person who suffered from the criminal act or his/her representative do not speak Lithuanian) (Article 8 of the CCP);
j) the right to hear the case in closed court (*inter alia*, in the cases where minors are recognised as victims, the cases where the aim is to prevent the publication of information about the private life of parties to proceedings or where this is necessary to ensure the victim's special protection needs, also when questioning a victim in cases in which anonymity is applied) (Article 9 of the CCP).

In addition, the Law on State-Guaranteed Legal Aid[33] foresees the victim's right to State-guaranteed legal aid during criminal proceedings. According to this law, certain categories of victims (eg victims of terrorist acts, trafficking in human beings, children

[33] Valstybės garantuojamos teisinės pagalbos įstatymas (2000) *Valstybės žinios* 30-827.

who are victims of crimes against human health, liberty, etc) in criminal cases where the participation of an authorised representative has been recognised as necessary, shall be eligible for legal aid (including representation in court).

Furthermore, the CPE also provides victims' rights to information. Article 96 of the CPE states that:

> [I]f the victim wishes to be informed about the future release of the convicted person or his/her escape from the institution of deprivation of liberty, it must inform the victim about it. The victim is also notified of the protective measures established in legal acts, which may be applied to him/her, and the procedure for granting these measures.

It should be noted that significant victims' rights are provided by the CC, according to which the position of victim is important for: (1) release from criminal liability, (2) imposition of the punishment, and (3) suspension of the execution of punishment or release from the execution of punishment.[34] For example, the victim's consent to reconcile with the offender (which is basically a victim's right) is a mandatory condition for the release from criminal liability upon reconciliation between the offender and the victim. Article 38 of the CC sets out that:

> [A] person who commits a misdemeanour, a negligent crime or a minor or less serious intentional crime may be released by a court from criminal liability where: (1) he has confessed to commission of the criminal act, and (2) voluntarily compensated for or eliminated the damage incurred to a natural or legal person or agreed on the compensation for or elimination of this damage, and (3) *reconciles with the victim* [emphasis added] or a representative of a legal person or a State institution, and (4) there is a basis for believing that he/she will not commit new criminal acts.

In addition, taking into account the jurisprudence of the Supreme Court of Lithuania[35] in connection with the victim's opinion, which the Court must listen to, but does not have to fully take into account, is also important in cases of release from criminal liability due to minor relevance of a crime (Article 37 of the CC), release from criminal liability on bail (Article 40 of the CC), release from criminal liability of a minor from criminal liability (Article 93 of the CC), suspension of the execution of punishment (Articles 75 and 92 of the CC), etc.

It is noteworthy that, even in the case of sentencing, the courts must listen to the victim's opinion since the Supreme Court of Lithuania has indicated that the punishment is fair when the interests of both the perpetrator and the victim are assessed when it is imposed and when none of them is given priority.[36] Lithuanian doctrine on criminal law stated that these examples of release from criminal liability provided for in the criminal law only have certain elements of restorative justice.[37] Meanwhile, the jurisprudence of the Supreme Court of Lithuania shows only a tendency to give the victim more of a role in the determination of criminal liability of the offender.

[34] G Švedas, *Criminal Law in Lithuania* (Wolters Kluwer, 2022) 146–90.

[35] See Rulings of the Supreme Court of Lithuania Cases No. 2K-231-489/2020, 2K-36-788/2021, 2K-54-976/2023.

[36] See Rulings of the Supreme Court of Lithuania Cases No. 2K-7-5-895/2018, 2K-198-303/2022.

[37] I Michailovič, S Bikelis, A Čepas, M Dobrynina, R Simaitis, D Šneideris, L Ūselė and J Venckevičienė, *Atkuriamojo teisingumo perspektyvos Lietuvoje* (Lietuvos teisės institutas, 2014) 206–17.

Moreover, in Lithuanian doctrine on criminal procedure, it is also emphasised that the victim not only has rights, but also must fulfil his/her duties: (a) must testify on oath and will be held responsible for committing any perjury as a witness; (b) the summonsed must appear before the pre-trial investigator, prosecutor, pre-trial investigation judge or court; (c) must not interfere with investigation actions of criminal procedure and follow the order of proceedings.[38]

Most often, Lithuanian doctrine on criminal procedure draws attention to the problematic aspects of the implementation of certain victims' rights. For example, assessing the application of victims' rights in national practice, the doctrine has emphasised that

> the victim (and defendant) must be informed of the decision to dispose of the case in an alternative way and agree (or object) with the chosen modality, also of the right to appeal against prosecutorial decision to the superior prosecutor or the court.[39]

Moreover, the State's duty 'to settle the question on timely rendering of the legal aid guaranteed by the State to the victims' is also emphasised.[40]

Lithuanian doctrine on criminal procedure has noted that national legal provisions concerning the legal possibilities to defend the rights of the victim are, in general (without mentioning concrete rights), fully compatible with the requirements of Directive 2012/29/EU.[41] However, the Reasoned opinion of the European Commission in infringement procedure no 2016/0109 showed that the existing legal regulation in Lithuania did not fully comply with the requirements set forth in Directive 2012/29/EU. First, the Commission evaluation drew attention to the fact that the national criminal process establishes too narrow a definition of 'family members', which does not include 'the dependants of the victim' provided for in Directive 2012/29/EU. Second, the Commission indicated that the 'wish of victims as to whether or not to receive information, as well as the right to change their minds shall bind the competent authority' was not accurately implemented into the national CCP. Third, the analysis also noted that the national criminal process did not provide for the victim's right to submit a reasoned request to consider a document as essential during the criminal process and to demand that it be translated into the language he/she understands.

Finally, in the Explanatory Memorandum concerning the Proposal for a directive of the European Parliament and of the Council amending Directive 2012/29/EU,[42] the European Commission drew attention to the fact that, in Lithuania, 'victims do not have adequate legal remedies to challenge decisions that concern them directly' and highlighted that free psychological support for victims (where the individual assessment shows a need for it) is not always available; also proposed to establish a victim's right to assistance in court, which should ensure more effective participation in criminal proceedings by victims. Thus, the aforementioned aspects allow us to state that

[38] Goda, Kazlauskas and Kuconis (n 25) 88–89.

[39] R Ažubalytė 'Nukentėjusiojo teisėtų interesų ir teisių realizavimas baigiant ikiteisminį tyrimą' 2005 (70) *Jurisprudencija* 125.

[40] Ažubalytė (n 28) 243.

[41] Goda (n 29) 183–84, 197.

[42] Proposal for a directive of the European Parliament and of the Council amending Directive 2012/29/EU establishing minimum standards on the rights, support and protection of victims of crime, and replacing Council Framework Decision 2001/220/JHA 12.7.2023 COM(2023) 424 final 2023/0250 (COD) 15–17.

the regulation of the victims' rights in Lithuanian criminal procedure is not yet fully compatible with the requirements of the EU law and that it will undoubtedly have to be improved in the near future.

Therefore, in the opinion of the author of this chapter, Directive 2012/29/EU undoubtedly provided additional value because such victims' rights as the right to be accompanied by a person of his/her own choosing during criminal proceedings, the right to participate in the assessment of his/her special protection needs and their protection, the right to file a complaint or a motion regarding the criminal act in the victim's native language or in another language that he/she speaks or the right of access to the services of an interpreter when filing an oral complaint in the national criminal procedure, etc were introduced into national criminal procedure as a result of the Directive's requirements. On the other hand, the list of the victims' rights in Lithuania's criminal procedure will have to be supplemented with such rights as the right to adequate legal remedies to challenge decisions that concern them directly, the right to free psychological support (where the individual assessment of the victim shows a need for it), the right to assistance in court, etc.

IV. Compensation for Victims of Crime: The Impact and Added Value of Directive 2004/80/EC

For the purpose of implementing Council Directive 2004/80/EC of 29 April 2004 relating to compensation to crime victims[43] (henceforth referred to as Directive 2004/80/EC) on 30 June 2005, Lithuania's Parliament adopted a special legal act – Law on Compensation. It should be noted that this law in Lithuania provided the legal basis for the establishment of a system of compensation by the State for victims who suffered damage from violent crimes. Before the adoption of Directive 2004/80/EC, Lithuania's legal system did not provide for a mechanism for State compensation for victims of crime and compensation for the damage caused by any crime was exclusively the responsibility of the perpetrator (or the person responsible for his/her behaviour). Thus, the Law on Compensation provides compensation (including advance compensation) for material and non-material damage caused by violent crimes; differentiated amounts of compensation for separate categories of violent crimes; establishes implementation of the Crime Victims Fund programme; regulates cooperation with other EU Member States in paying compensation for damage caused by violent crimes in cross-border situations, etc.

The Law on Compensation provides three necessary conditions for compensation for damage by the State:

1) the violent crime was committed on the territory of the Republic of Lithuania or on a ship or aircraft with the flag or insignia of the State of Lithuania;
2) damage caused by a violent crime awarded by the court was not compensated;

[43] Council Directive (EU) 2004/80/EC of 29 April 2004 Relating to Compensation to Crime Victims [2004] OJ L261/15.

3) the request for compensation for the damage caused by a violent crime awarded by the court was submitted no later than 10 years after the court decision came into force.

The requirement that the damage caused by a violent crime was not compensated means that the person responsible for the damage did not voluntarily compensate the damage awarded by the court and there were no objective opportunities to forcibly recover the compensation. Damage caused by violent crime is compensated by the State from the Crime Victims Fund programme, whose funds consist of: 1) State budget allocations; 2) payments from the penal measure – Contribution to the Crime Victims Fund; 3) funds recovered from the offender; and 4) other funds. It should be noted that the Law on Compensation does not regulate compensation for damages caused by violent crimes from the perpetrators. The practice of applying the Law on Compensation (according to the statistics of the Ministry of Justice)[44] shows that, in 2018–2021, 1016 decisions were made regarding the compensation of damage caused by violent crimes, of which 757 were positive and 259 were negative.

The establishment in 2005 and development of this new system in Lithuania underwent several legal reforms in 2008, 2019 and 2022.[45] During these reforms, the concept of violent crime was expanded and all acts with the characteristics of a crime, which intentionally took a person's life or intentionally caused serious or minor damage to their health, are considered violent crimes (regardless of the severity of the crime); the definition of the victim of violent crime was revised; the amounts of compensation from the Crime Victims Fund programme were increased; the list of injured persons who are entitled to compensation in the event of the death of a victim was clarified, etc.

Most of these fundamental changes were determined by reasons,[46] which stem from the search for greater legal certainty and consistency between the instruments for protecting victims' rights under Lithuanian law. For example, jurisprudence of the Supreme Administrative Court of Lithuania revealed that the definitions of injured person and victim (in criminal proceedings) did not correspond; the definition of a victim enshrined in Article 28 of the CCP is broader than that enshrined in the Law on Compensation;[47] the definition of a violent crime is not entirely accurate.[48]

Meanwhile, the EU Court of Justice held that Directive 2004/80 must be interpreted as imposing on each EU Member State the obligation to establish a compensation scheme covering all victims of violent intentional crime committed on its territory and

[44] Activity reports of the Ministry of Justice of Lithuania for 2018, 2019, 2020 and 2021, available at https://tm.lrv.lt/uploads/tm/documents/files/TM%202018%20metu%20veiklos%20ataskaita%20viesinimas(1).pdf; https://tm.lrv.lt/uploads/tm/documents/files/TM%202019%20metu%20veiklos%20ataskaita.pdf;; https://tm.lrv.lt/uploads/tm/documents/files/TM_2020%20m_%20_veiklos%20ataskaita_final.pdf; https://tm.lrv.lt/uploads/tm/documents/files/dokumentai/Administracinė%20informacija/Veiklos%20ataskaitos/TM%202021%20m%20veiklos%20ataskaita.pdf.

[45] Smurtiniais nusikaltimais padarytos žalos kompensavimo įstatymo pakeitimo įstatymas Nr. X-1848 (2008). *Valstybės žinios* 137-5387; Smurtiniais nusikaltimais padarytos žalos kompensavimo įstatymo Nr. X-296 pakeitimo įstatymas (2019) TAR, 858; Smurtiniais nusikaltimais padarytos žalos kompensavimo įstatymo Nr. X-296 2, 6, 7, 8, 10, 11 ir 14 straipsnių pakeitimo įstatymas (2022) TAR, 27302.

[46] It should be noted that Lithuanian doctrine on criminal procedure did not examine or discuss these aspects.

[47] Ruling of the Supreme Administrative Court of Lithuania Case No. A-492-1285/2012.

[48] Ruling of the Supreme Administrative Court of Lithuania Case No. A-502-2360/2013.

not just victims in cross-border situations. In this respect, the Court requires the amount of compensation to be 'fair and appropriate' while leaving EU Member States a margin of discretion in interpreting this concept.[49] It should be noted that this Court decision has not yet had any impact on the regulation of the Lithuanian system of compensation to victims of violent crime. Finally, the Reasoned opinion of the European Commission in infringement procedure no 2016/0109 showed that the existing legal regulation in Lithuania did not fully comply with the requirements set forth in Directive 2012/29/EU, for example, the national criminal procedure establishes too narrow a definition of 'family members', which does not include 'the dependants of the victim', etc.

Also worth mentioning is the decision of the Constitutional Court of Lithuania regarding the application, in which the applicant, who has received only partial repayment of the pecuniary and non-pecuniary damage awarded to him/her from the perpetrator, complained that, based on the provisions of the Law on Compensation, the Ministry of Justice refused to compensate the remaining unpaid part of awarded material and non-material damage caused by a violent crime.[50] The Constitutional Court of Lithuania refuses to accept the application as admissible because the applicant

> has not exhausted all the means of defence of his/her constitutional rights or freedoms established by law, and if he/she is no longer able to exhaust them, a person according to the Constitution … does not have the right to apply to the Constitutional Court.

Reflecting the diversity of existing legal systems across the EU, Lithuanian law does not provide for the possibility of returning confiscated property to the victims as a form of compensation because, according to the CC, the confiscation of property and extended confiscation of property means a: '[C]ompulsory and uncompensated taking *into the ownership of a State* [emphasis added] of any form of property subject to confiscation and held by the offender or other persons'.

It should be noted that, in Lithuanian doctrine on criminal law, it was proposed that all proceeds from criminal fines and property confiscation be transferred to the Crime Victims Fund, but such a proposal did not receive the support of the legislator.[51]

On the other hand, the CC provides for penal measure – a Contribution to the Fund for Victims of Violent Crime. Article 71 of the CC provides that:

> [A] court may order payment of a contribution in the amount from 10 up to 250 the basic amounts of punishments and penalties[52] (henceforth referred to as BAPP) for adults and from 3 up to 25 BAPP for juveniles to the Crime Victims Fund. The minimum and maximum amount of the payment of a contribution to the Crime Victims Fund for a legal entity shall be from 100 up to 2000 BAPP.

Finally, it can be concluded that Directive 2004/80/EC had a major impact on Lithuania's legal system as it led to and was the legal basis for the establishment of the material and

[49] C-129/19 *Consiglio dei Ministri v BV* [16 July 2020] ECLI:EU:C 220:566, paras 42, 43, 58–61.

[50] Constitutional Court of Lithuania decision No. KT2-A-S2/2022 [2022] 'Regarding refusal to consider application No. 1A-139/2021'.

[51] G Šulija *Baudos bausmė ir jos skyrimas. Daktaro disertacija, socialiniai mokslai, teisė (01S)* (Vilniaus universitetas, 2005) 53.

[52] From 1 January 2018, the basic amount of punishments and penalties is equal to €50 (Lietuvos Respublikos Vyriausybės nutarimas, 2017).

non-material damage compensation by the State for the system for victims of violent crime in Lithuania.

V. Available Protection Measures in Lithuania's Legal System

Victims' protection rights are regulated by several general and special laws – these are the Civil Code, the CCP, the CC, the Law on Protection of the Participants of the Criminal Proceedings and Criminal Intelligence, Officials of Justice and Law Enforcement Institutions Against Criminal Influence[53] (henceforth referred to as Law on Protection) and the Law on Protection against Domestic Violence. The victims' protection measures provided for in these laws can be classified according to several criteria:

- according to the time of their application, it can be divided into measures applied: (a) before prosecution; (b) during prosecution; and (c) in post-sentencing (punishment execution) period;
- according to its purpose, it can be divided into: (a) preventive measures; (b) provisional and other special measures of procedural nature in criminal procedure; and (c) penal measures of criminal nature;
- according to the status of the person targeted by the measure, it can be divided into: (a) suspected, accused or sentenced person(s); (b) victims and (or) their family members.

Moreover, all protection measures available under Lithuanian law are of a criminal (including procedural), civil or administrative nature. It should be mentioned that, in Lithuania, the legal regulation of the application of protection measures is not sufficiently consistent and systematic because all these measures may be applied simultaneously and independently of each other.

Protection measures of a civil nature are provided in the Civil Code, Article 3.65 of which provides that: '[H]aving regard to the interests of the spouses' children as well as the interests of one of the spouses, the court may make orders for provisional protection measures pending the outcome of the divorce case'.

The court may make the following orders for provisional protection measures, *inter alia*: (1) to order one of the spouses to live separately; (2) to order one of the spouses to refrain from impeding access for the other spouse to certain property; (3) to prohibit one of the spouses from having contact with his/her minor children or visiting certain places; (4) other measures deemed necessary by the court. It should be noted that the possibilities of applying protection measures of a civil nature are limited in terms of time and persons, because they can be applied only during the divorce case and only to one of the spouses.

[53] Baudžiamojo proceso ir kriminalinės žvalgybos dalyvių, teisingumo ir teisėsaugos institucijų pareigūnų apsaugos nuo nusikalstamo poveikio įstatymas (2008) *Valstybės žinios* 63-2380.

A new version of the Law on Protection against Domestic Violence, which came into force on 1 July 2023, provides for the possibility to apply a special preventive measure of an administrative nature – an order for protection against domestic violence, which may be applied even before prosecution. Article 8 of this Law states that:

> [I]f there is a sufficient risk that domestic violence may be used, a protection against domestic violence order may be issued to those who pose a risk of domestic violence. For a period of 15 days from the moment of issuing a protection against domestic violence order, a person who poses a risk of domestic violence is obliged to: (1) temporarily move out of the place of residence, if he/she lives with a person at risk of domestic violence, regardless of who owns the home; (2) not to visit the residence of a person at risk of domestic violence, regardless of whether the person at risk of domestic violence lives there or not together with the person who poses a risk of domestic violence; (3) not to approach the person at risk of domestic violence and adult persons living with him/her and (or) children living in an environment where the risk of domestic violence has been created within the distance specified in the protection against violence order; (4) not to communicate, not to seek connections with a person at risk of domestic violence and adult persons and (or) children living with him/her.

It should be noted that, under the new procedure, 5,468 protection against domestic violence orders were issued during the first three months (July–September 2023).

During a pre-trial investigation, according to Articles 36(2) and 186(1) of the CCP, a pre-trial investigator or a prosecutor shall, not later than during the first questioning of a victim, perform an assessment of the victim's special protection needs, regarding access to the measures in order to protect the victim from mental trauma, criminal influence or other negative consequences.

The CCP provides a provisional measure – the obligation to reside separately from a victim and (or) prohibition to approach the victim closer than a prescribed distance. According to Article 132(1) of the CCP:

> [A] suspect may be placed under the obligation to reside separately from a victim and (or) prohibition to approach the victim closer than a prescribed distance where there are reasonable grounds for believing that he will attempt to unlawfully influence the victim or will commit new criminal acts against the victim or persons residing together with him/her.

When imposing this provisional measure, the suspect may also be placed under the obligation not to communicate and seek contact with the victim and persons residing with him/her, also not to visit certain places which the victim or persons residing with him/her visit. The victim shall remain in the dwelling where the suspect and the victim previously permanently resided. This provisional measure shall, at a prosecutor's request, be imposed by a ruling of the pre-trial investigation judge.

Article 198 of the CCP provides the victim's right to request a prosecutor or pre-trial investigator to apply anonymity to him/her. Moreover, a prosecutor or pre-trial investigator may apply anonymity of his/her own motion. Anonymity may be applied to a victim where: (1) there is an identified danger to the life, health, liberty or property of the victim or his/her family members or close persons, also service, business or other legitimate interests; (2) the testimony of the victim is material in criminal proceedings; and (3) the victim participates in proceedings related to a grave, serious or less serious crime. Lithuanian doctrine on criminal procedure stated that the victim's anonymity can be applied only in exceptional cases, when there is no other possibility to protect the victim from the threats he/she faces.[54] Moreover, Article 199(1) of the CCP provides for the possibility of also applying partial anonymity, when there are grounds for anonymity or where there is evidence that the disclosure of certain data on a victim may have negative consequences for the rights and legitimate interests of the victim, his/her family members or close relatives. In these cases, the prosecutor or a pre-trial investigator shall determine the extent of classification of the data by a decision to apply partial anonymity. Classification may be applied to the forename and surname of the witness or the victim, their date of birth, personal number, address of the place of residence, profession, place of work or study, kinship, also other data on the victim (except for data on the relationship of the victim with the suspect). In Lithuanian doctrine on criminal procedure, granting anonymity to the victim is considered only as a theoretical possibility, because it is practically impossible to bring a criminal charge without specifying the victim.[55]

The Law on Protection provides protection measures of a procedural nature that can be applied to the victim, his/her family members or close persons before prosecution, during prosecution and in the post-sentencing (punishment execution) period. Protection measures against criminal influence may be applied if, during the criminal intelligence or pre-trial investigation, or during the trial of criminal cases for grave, serious and some less serious crimes, or after the completion of the criminal intelligence or prosecution, verified data have been obtained showing that: (1) the life or health of individuals is in real danger; and (or) (2) personal property may be destroyed or damaged. One or more of the following protection measures may be applied: (1) physical protection of the person and his/her property; (2) temporary transfer of the person to a safe place; (3) establishment of a special regime according to which data about a person are provided from State and other registers and information systems; (4) change of a person's place of residence, work or education; (5) change of personal identity and biography data; (6) plastic surgery that changes a person's appearance; (7) issuance of a firearm, special measures to a person; (8) financial support.

Certain victims' protection measures, which can be applied by the judgment or other final decision of the court in the determination of criminal liability, are provided by the CC. Lithuania's doctrine on criminal law classifies some penal measures as measures intended for the protection of victim's rights.[56] For example, Article 72(1) of the CC provides for a penal measure – obligation to reside separately from the victim and (or) prohibition to approach the victim closer than a prescribed distance, which the court may impose where this is necessary with a view to protecting the legitimate interests of the victim. Upon imposition of this penal measure, the offender shall be prohibited from communicating and seeking contact with the victim and visiting the indicated places at which the victim is usually present. Moreover, Article 72(4) of the CC sets out that the obligation to notify a change of place of residence or departure from the place of residence is imposed by the court in cases where the person has committed some kind of sexual crime (eg rape, sexual assault, etc). This penal measure means that a person

[54] Goda, Kazlauskas and Kuconis (n 25) 331.
[55] Goda (n 29) 182.
[56] Švedas (n 34) 160–67.

who intends to change his/her place of residence or to leave the place of residence for more than seven days must notify the police before the change or leave no later than three days after leaving. This penal measure may be imposed from one up to five years.

Finally, Article 72(2) of the CC provides for a penal measure – obligation to participate in violence correction programmes, which the court may impose on a person who has committed criminal acts in respect of a close relative or family member.

The requirements of Directive 2011/99/EU of the European Parliament and of the Council of 13 December 2011 on the European Protection Order (henceforth referred to as EPO)[57] did not raise serious issues and were transposed into national law by adopting certain amendments and changes to the CCP[58] and the Law on Mutual Recognition and Enforcement of Decisions of the EU Member States in Criminal Cases.[59] The essential requirements of the aforementioned Directive were transposed in the Law on Mutual Recognition and Enforcement of Decisions of EU Member States in Criminal Cases, which was supplemented with two new chapters regulating the recognition and enforcement of EPOs in Lithuania, as well as the transfer of EPOs issued by Lithuania to another EU Member State.

Moreover, the requirements of Regulation (EU) No 606/2013 of the European Parliament and of the Council of 12 June 2013 on mutual recognition of protection measures in civil matters[60] did not raise serious issues and were transposed into national law by adopting amendments to the Law on the Implementation of EU and International Legal Acts Regulating Civil Procedure.[61] This Law was supplemented by a new chapter regulating the recognition and enforcement of protection measures in civil matters in Lithuania, as well as the transfer of protection measures in civil matters issued by Lithuania to another EU Member State.

Similarly, the Regulation (EU) No 606/2013 on mutual recognition of protection measures in civil matters and Directive 2011/99/EU on the EPO did not raise serious issues during implementation into the national legal system and application, since Lithuania has already had experience in cooperating with other (Baltic) countries in this area. For example, since 2001, the Agreement of the Government of the Republic of Lithuania, the Government of the Republic of Estonia and the Government of the Republic of Latvia on cooperation in the protection of witnesses and victims,[62] which is currently in force, already provided such forms of cooperation between Baltic States in the protection of witnesses and victims as (a) recognition and enforcement of the decision of the requesting Party on protection of the person being valid in the territory of

[57] Directive 2011/99/EU of the European Parliament and of the Council of 13 December 2011 on the European Protection Order [2011] OJ L338/2.

[58] Baudžiamojo proceso kodekso 120, 121, 126, 132(1), 139 straipsnių ir priedo pakeitimo įstatymas (2015) TAR, 7564.

[59] Įstatymo 'Dėl ES valstybių narių sprendimų baudžiamosiose bylose tarpusavio pripažinimo ir vykdymo' Nr. XII-1322 1, 2, 40 straipsnių ir priedo pakeitimo ir Įstatymo papildymo naujais VIII ir IX skyriais įstatymas (2015) TAR, 7408.

[60] Regulation (EU) No 606/2013 of the European Parliament and of the Council of 12 June 2013 on mutual recognition of protection measures in civil matters [2013] OJ L181/4.

[61] Civilinį procesą reglamentuojančių ES ir tarptautinės teisės aktų įgyvendinimo įstatymo Nr. X-1809 papildymo devintuoju-4 skirsniu ir Įstatymo priedo pakeitimo įstatymas (2014) TAR, 20541.

[62] Lietuvos Respublikos Vyriausybės, Estijos Respublikos Vyriausybės ir Latvijos Respublikos Vyriausybės sutartis dėl bendradarbiavimo vykdant liudytojų ir nukentėjusiųjų apsaugą, (2001) *Valstybės žinios*, 49-1705.

the receiving Party; (b) summoning protected persons to the court and interrogation, observing the necessary confidentiality and taking the necessary interrogation protection measures; (c) temporarily or permanently transferring protected persons to the territory of the receiving Party without revealing their personal identity and, if necessary, ensuring the protection or monitoring of their location, etc.

VI. Conclusions

Summarising this chapter, the following essential conclusions can be drawn:

1. Directive 2012/29/EU on victims' rights gave additional value to Lithuania's criminal procedure, as it expanded the definition of victim, and provided for new victims' rights within the criminal procedure and the post-sentencing (punishment execution) stage. However, the regulation of the victims' rights in Lithuania's criminal procedure is not yet fully compatible with the requirements of EU law. Therefore, the list of victims' rights will have to be supplemented with such rights as the right to adequate legal remedies to challenge decisions that concern them directly, the right to free psychological support and the right to assistance in court.
2. Directive 2004/80/EC on compensation had a major impact on the national legal system, since it led to and was the legal basis for the establishment of the material and non-material damage compensation by the State for the system for victims of violent crime in Lithuania.
3. Meanwhile, Regulation (EU) No 606/2013 on mutual recognition of protection measures in civil matters and Directive 2011/99/EU on the EPO did not raise serious issues during implementation into the national legal system and did not have a major impact on the national legal system because Lithuania already had experience in cooperation in the protection of witnesses and victims.

14

The Protection of Victims of Crime in the Italian Criminal Justice System

VALERIA SCALIA

I. Preliminary Remarks

The present contribution aims at briefly outlining the legal framework concerning the rights of victims of crime and their protection in all stages of criminal proceedings set out in the Italian criminal justice system.[1] The exam of such legal framework will be conducted taking account of the relevant European Union (EU) legislation (namely, EU Directive 2012/29[2]) and of the case law of the EU Court of Justice and national courts. Such goal will be pursued trying to give a perspective capable to reconcile the need of protecting victims, especially those deemed as vulnerable, and the other valuable competing interests, such as the fundamental rights and safeguards to be recognised to suspect, accused, convicted and detained people respectively in criminal investigation, in criminal trial, and while they are serving the sentence in prison, according to the principle of proportionality and the presumption of innocence.

The analysis will start from the definition of 'victim', which was introduced in the Italian legal system in 2022 within a more comprehensive reform concerning restorative justice. Investigating the scope of such definition and the needs of coordination with the traditional definitions provided for in criminal procedure law and criminal substantive law will facilitate the understanding of the Italian legal system in this matter.

Special attention will be devoted to the Italian legislation addressing vulnerable victims, both at a substantive and procedural level. The definition of vulnerable victims and the scope of individual assessment concerning their specific needs will also be addressed, in order to evaluate the alignment with Directive 2012/29. In this respect, the contribution will give an overview on the national legal framework aimed at protecting victims of violence against women and domestic violence. The transposition of EU

[1] The present contribution was drafted within the activities of the Research Project *Recover* GA no 101091375 JUST-2022-JCOO – Co-funded by the Justice Programme of the European Union 2021–2027.

[2] Directive 2012/29/EU of the European Parliament and of the Council of 25 October 2012 establishing minimum standards on the rights, support and protection of victims of crime, and replacing Council Framework Decision 2001/220/JHA [2012] OJ L315/57–73.

Directive 2011/99/EU, on the European Protection Order,[3] into the Italian criminal justice system will be specifically addressed.

This contribution will also examine the measures set out in the national legal system to allow victims to have access to justice and to fully participate in criminal proceedings and those provided for to protect victims from secondary and repeat victimisation, from intimidation and from retaliation in all stages of criminal proceedings, according to Directive 2012/29 (protection *from* criminal proceedings and protection *in* criminal proceedings).

The last part of this work intends to outline the Italian legal provisions providing for restitution and compensation to victims, highlighting shortcomings and critical issues.

II. The Definition of 'Victim': One-Size-Fits-All Definition or the Beginning of an Incoherent Legislation?

There was no specific definition of 'victim' in the Italian legal system until Legislative Decree No 150 of 10th October 2022 entered into force.

Under substantive criminal law, the wording used by the Italian Criminal Code (ICC) [Chapter IV of Heading IV of the First Book] is *injured person* ('persona offesa'), even if there is no explanation or definition about this concept, since the provisions set out under this Heading basically deal with issues pertaining to criminal procedure law (Arts 121–130).[4]

According to criminal law scholars, the holder of the legal interest protected by criminal law provisions and affected by a criminal offence is to be defined as the *passive subject* ('soggetto passivo') of the criminal offence. The *passive subject* has the right to report the crime committed affecting his/her legal interest.[5] In this respect, it is of the utmost importance to identify the specific legal interest protected by criminal law provisions. Such an operation is not always easy to carry out, especially where offences affecting more than one interest or collective and immaterial interests are at stake or where the offence concretely affected several persons, among whom it might be difficult to distinguish between *passive subjects* and *damaged person* harmed by the criminal offence, who suffered damage for which compensation is likely to be awarded, according to civil law ('danneggiato').

Injured person and *damaged subjects* often overlap. In some circumstances, however, there is no coincidence among them. For instance, in cases of murder or manslaughter, the *injured person* is the person, who was directly deprived of their life (*direct victim*), closer relatives (eg parents, sons and daughters, siblings) are to be identified as the persons who suffered damage, as a consequence of the crime (*indirect victims*).

[3] Directive 2011/99/EU of the European Parliament and of the Council of 13 December 2011 on the European protection order [2011] OJ L338/2–18.

[4] See C Mazzucato, 'Capo IV – Della persona offesa dal reato. Nota introduttiva' in G Forti, S Riondato, S Seminara, *Commentario breve al Codice Penale*, 7th edn (Wolters Kluwer, 2024) 555 ff.

[5] See the wide analysis conducted by M Venturoli, 'La vittima nel sistema penale dall'oblio al protagonismo?' (Jovene ed, 2015); T Rafaraci, 'La tutela della vittima nel sistema penale delle garanzie' (2010) *Criminalia* (2010) 258–59.

By contrast, the Italian Criminal Procedure Code (ICPC) provides a broader notion of *injured person*, since it always comprises closer relatives of the person who died as a consequence of the crime (Art 90, para 3). Legal entities may be *injured persons* and stand as civil parties in the criminal trial under certain conditions (see for further details section III).

A distinction has been drawn between the powers and rights of the *injured person* during the pre-trial stage (ie reporting, rights to be informed, possibility to request public prosecutor to undertake investigative activities or to suggest gathering evidence) and those concerning the trial, where the *injured person* may become a party, since the Italian legal system is grounded on the principle of separation between criminal and civil action, according to the most recent Constitutional Court case law.[6] As a consequence, the *injured person* is not a necessary party of a criminal trial. In this respect, if the *injured person* becomes a party of the criminal trial through the relevant specific procedure provided for by legislation ('costituzione di parte civile', see Arts 76–79), they hold a personal interest in ascertaining the criminal liability of the accused, that is accessory and adheres to that of public prosecutor (no private action is provided on behalf of the *injured person*, even where the prosecution concerning a criminal offence depends on the victim's report ['procedibilità a querela']). The *injured person*, as a party of the criminal trial, holds rights and powers of promoting and stimulating the public prosecution's action, for example in identifying and gathering evidence. At the same time, they hold an interest to be compensated for the economic and moral harm suffered as a result of the crime committed or to obtain restitution (see section VII).

As a distinct status, the *damaged person* ('danneggiato') brings only civil claims into the criminal trial. This is because the damages eligible for compensation may not align with the legal interest protected by the criminal offence. For instance, in certain offences related to public administration, such as bribery offences, competitors in a public tender may suffer damages due to a corrupt agreement, despite the primary legal interest affected by the criminal offence being the impartiality and the sound management of public administration.

The different positions of such subjects are more identifiable during the investigations, where the role of *injured person* is prominent, whereas they tend to disappear during the trial, since both (*injured* and *damaged person*) may bring a civil claim within the criminal trial, standing as a civil party. For the purpose of this chapter, we will basically use the term 'victim' as also referring to 'injured person', unless a distinction between 'injured person' and 'damaged person' is necessary to clarify the relevant different regimes applicable to them.

A. Definition of Victim Embedded in the Restorative Justice Legal Framework (Legislative Decree No 150/2022)

The legal framework outlined in the previous paragraph has been significantly developed after the entry into force of Legislative Decree No. 150 of 10 October 2022, which

[6] See, for instance, decisions 4 November 2020, No 249/2 and 23 September 2021, No 203.

introduced a comprehensive regulation concerning restorative justice in the Italian legal system (Arts 42–67),[7] widely inspired by relevant European and international legal instruments.

According to the most widely held opinion among legal scholars, the newly adopted restorative justice system (RJS) complements the traditional criminal justice system, since the new legislation provides some rules in the ICC, ICPC, prison law and proceedings relating to minors, that align the criminal justice system with RJS, with respect to times and procedures of access to (Art 129-bis ICPC, Art 15-bis, Law No 354/1975, Art 1-bis, Legislative Decree No 121 of 2nd October 2018) and effects of RJS' outcomes on criminal proceedings.[8] It is worth noting that such a new piece of legislation (Legislative Decree No 150/2022) has provided, for the first time in the Italian legal system, a broad definition of 'victim' in Art 42, para 1 (b). Pursuant to such provision, the notion of victim of crime has to be conceived as embedding both the natural person, who has suffered any kind of harm or economic loss, which was directly caused by a criminal offence, and the relatives of the person who died as a direct consequence of the commission of a criminal offence, who suffered harm as a result of such person's death, as Art 2(1)(a) of EU Directive 2012/29 also provides. The definition of 'family members' is provided for in (d) of the said provision, as including the following persons: the spouse, the partner of a recognised same-sex relationship,[9] the person who is living with the victim in a committed intimate relationship based on reciprocal moral and material assistance, in a joint household, on a stable and continuous basis,[10] the relatives in direct line, the siblings, the dependants of the victim or of the person identified as the offender.

It should be noted that the scope of this definition of victim is expressly limited to the application of the legislation on restorative justice programmes.

The entry into force of such a new piece of legislation and the provision of the definition of victim, thus seems as if it has not changed rules concerning the existing

[7] On the terminological issues relating to the definition of 'restorative justice' and its translation into different languages pertaining to different legal traditions, see G Mannozzi, 'Traduzione e interpretazione giuridica nel multilinguismo europeo: il caso paradigmatico del termine «giustizia riparativa» e delle sue origini storico-giuridiche e linguistiche' (2015) *Rivista italiana di diritto e procedura penale* 137–53; L Parlato, 'Verso un dialogo tra giustizia riparativa e penale? Bisognerà «mediare»' (4 July 2022) *Giustizia Insieme*, available at www.giustiziainsieme.it.

[8] V Patanè, 'Il modello di giustizia riparativa introdotto dal d.lgs. n. 150/2022' in G Di Chiara-V. Patanè-F. Siracusano (eds), Siracusano-Galati-Tranchina-Zappalà, *Diritto processuale penale* (Milan, 2023); G Mannozzi, 'La giustizia riparativa: brevi note su contesto, disciplina ed effetti trasformativi' (2023) *Rivista Italiana di Diritto e Procedura Penale* 649 ff; G Di Paolo, 'La giustizia riparativa: esperienze oltre confine' (2023) *Cassazione Penale* 3850 ff; E Mattevi, 'La giustizia riparativa: disciplina organica e nuove intersezioni con il sistema penale' in D Castronuvo, M Donini, EM Mancuso and G Varraso, *Riforma Cartabia. La nuova giustizia penale* (Wolters Kluwer, 2023) 233 ff; L Parlato, 'La giustizia riparativa: i nuovi e molteplici incroci con il rito penale' in ibid 267 ff; F Parisi, 'Giustizia riparativa e sistema penale nel decreto legislativo 10 ottobre 2022, n. 150. Parte I. "Disciplina organica" e aspetti di diritto sostanziale'(27 February 2023) *Sistema penale*; P Maggio, 'Giustizia riparativa e sistema penale nel decreto legislativo 10 ottobre 2022, n. 150. Parte II. "Disciplina organica" e aspetti di diritto processuale' (2023) *Sistema penale*; G De Francesco, 'Rieducazione, giustizia riparativa, logiche premiali: appunti minimi per un confronto' in C Piergallini et al (eds), *Studi in onore di Carlo Enrico Paliero* (Giuffrè Francis Lefbvre, 2022) Vol I, 361; R Bartoli, 'Giustizia vindicatoria, giustizia riparativa, costituzionalismo' in ibid 527.

[9] Pursuant to Art 1, para 2, of Law No 76 of 20 May 2016: two adult same-sex persons set up a 'unione civile' by an official declaration in front of a civil servant, representing the State, and two witnesses.

[10] Pursuant to Art 1, para 36, ibid: two adult persons who are neither married, nor joint in a 'unione civile', who are not family members or in-laws.

terminology within the criminal justice system, which continues to apply to criminal proceedings. In this respect, an overlapping or duplication of obligations – especially those concerning the victim's right to be informed – is likely to arise. A more coherent and coordinated regulation concerning the victim should be adopted by the Italian legislature. Currently, the legislation is quite fragmented in different normative texts, such as the Criminal Code, the Criminal Procedure Code, the new legislation relating to RJS and other provisions concerning specific types of victims. Nevertheless, the introduction of RSJ in the national legal system can be conceived as the beginning of a new pathway in considering the role of the victim, whose needs to be recognised and listened to (even special needs in the case of vulnerable victims) become prominent within restorative justice programmes.[11]

III. The Possibility to Extend the Definition of Victim to Legal Entities: National Perspective and the EU Perspective

The definition of victim set out in Directive 2012/29/EU does not include legal entities. The Court of Justice of the EU confirmed such an interpretation in some judgments concerning the former Framework Decision 2001/220/JHA of 15 March 2001 on the standing of victims in criminal proceedings and Directive 2004/80/EC relating to compensation to crime victims.[12] The new Proposal aimed at amending the Directive 2012/29 (Proposal) does not provide any change concerning the definition of victim outlined by Art 2(1)(a).[13] A different perspective has been expressed by Recital 45 of Regulation 2018/1805/EU, on the mutual recognition of freezing orders and confiscation orders,[14] stating that 'The notion of "victim" is to be interpreted in accordance with the law of the issuing State, which should also be able to provide that a legal person could be a victim for the purpose of this Regulation'. Recently, Art 3(1)(8) of Directive (EU) 2024/1260 on asset recovery and confiscation[15] provides for a definition of victim, which recalls Art 2(1)(a) of Directive 2012/29, but also adds 'legal person, as defined in national law, that has suffered harm or economic loss as a direct result of any of the offences within the scope of Directive'.

[11] See Parisi (n 8); E Venafro, 'Giustizia riparativa e sistema penale alla luce della riforma Cartabia' *Legislazione penale* (21 December 2023) 19.

[12] Council Directive 2004/80/EC of 29 April 2004, relating to compensation to crime victims [2004] OJ L261/15–18. CJEU, 28 June 2007, C-467/05, *Giovanni Dell'Orto* EU:C:2007:395. See in this respect A Nisco, 'Persona giuridica "vittima" di reato ed interpretazione conforme al diritto comunitario' (2008) *Cassazione penale* 2, 784 ff; C Mazzucato, 'Victims of Corporate Violence in the European Union: Challenges for Criminal Justice and Potentials for European Policy' in G Forti, C Mazzucato, A Visconti and S Giavazzi, *Victims and Corporations. Legal Challenges and Empirical Findings* (Milan, 2018) 53. See also CJEU, 21 October 2010, C-205/09, *Emil Eredics, Mária Vassné Sápi* [2010] OJ C 346/14.

[13] Proposal for a Directive of the European Parliament and of the Council amending Directive 2012/29/EU establishing minimum standards on the rights, support and protection of victims of crime, and replacing Council Framework Decision 2001/220/JHA, Brussels, 12.7.2023, COM(2023) 424 final.

[14] Regulation (EU) 2018/1805 of the European Parliament and of the Council of 14 November 2018 on the mutual recognition of freezing orders and confiscation orders [2018] OJ L303/1–38.

[15] Directive (EU) 2024/1260 of the European Parliament and of the Council of 24 April 2024 on asset recovery and confiscation [2024] OJ L2024/1260.

Taking account of the worldwide evolution of the society, the increased role of legal entities in all sectors, the process of (social and legal) *accountability* of legal entities and corporations for the prevention of crimes likely to derive from the development of their activities, a general extension of the EU's harmonised notion of 'victim' to legal entities would be desirable. In this respect, the recent adoption of Directive 2024/1260 would appear as a first step in such a direction.

In the Italian legal system, *injured person* or *damaged person* by crime may also include a legal entity, regardless of their juridical status and their private or public nature (ie political party, association, corporation, public administration, non-governmental organisations). In this respect, Art 337 ICPC, para 3, expressly provides the right to report by the legal representative of entities, associations or legal persons, requiring the specific indication of the source of legal representation.[16] Sometimes, special legislation grants associations and entities (such as associations representing disabled people;[17] associations and foundations against usury;[18] the Minister of Environment and Protection of territory and sea acting for compensation;[19] public entities protecting labour safety[20]) the right to civil party standing.

In the realm of restorative justice, Art 42 (1)(b), of Legislative Decree No 150/2022 states an extension of the rights and faculties attributed to natural persons by the Decree to legal entities that have suffered harm and economic loss as a consequence of crime. Therefore, legal entities can take part in restorative justice programmes and benefit from them, according to the same rules applicable to natural persons.

IV. Vulnerable Victims

In the Italian legal system, Art 90-*quater* ICPC, transposing Directive 2012/29, states that the

> vulnerability may derive from age, physical or mental illness, type of criminal offence committed, specific modalities and circumstances of conduct. Furthermore, it may stem from violence perpetrated against people or racial hatred. It can also be inferred if the crime may be referred to organised crime, terrorism, trafficking in human beings, or it was committed to discriminate the victim, or the victim is emotionally, psychologically or economically dependent.

[16] According to legal scholars, where the *injured person* is a corporation, a distinction should be operated by *internal* and *external* criminal offences. In the first situation (*internal criminal offences*), committed by CEOs and top-level managers or controllers, the decision to report would be up to shareholders and partners. Whereas, in the other scenario (*external criminal offences*), the decision to report would be up to CEOs. Some other differences in identifying persons responsible for reporting could depend on the nature of legal persons and the type of criminal offence committed. See, in this respect, C Mazzucato, 'Art 120' in Forti, Riondato and Seminara (n 4) 574.

[17] See Art 36, para 2, Law No 104 of 5th February 1992.

[18] See Art 10, Law No 108 of 7th March 1996.

[19] See Art 311, Legislative Decree No 152 of 3rd April 2006.

[20] See Art 61, para 1, Legislative Decree No 81 of 9th April 2008. Paragraph 2 provides for the faculty of union organisations and associations of victims' relatives to intervene in the criminal proceedings, according to Arts 91 ff ICPC.

On the one hand, the Italian legislature has introduced Art 90-*quater*, providing a general definition of the condition of particular vulnerability; on the other hand, some provisions of the ICPC have been modified to make the national criminal justice system consistent with Arts 23 and 24 of Directive 2012/29, which already provide special measures for carrying interviews (for example, as a witness in a criminal trial or at an earlier stage during the investigation) with victims deemed as vulnerable, according to the individual assessment provided for in Art 22, and child victims. This approach might result in a lack of protection for victims apparently falling outside the characteristics and situations listed in Art 90-*quater* ICPC, even when they would need in fact protective measures.[21] However, in order to overcome such concerns, an interpretation consistent with the rationale of Art 22 of Directive 2012/29 must ensure a flexible, individualised case-by-case approach in determining the specific protection needs of victims.[22] To better corroborate the proposed interpretation, some legal scholars make a distinction among the characteristics and situations listed in Art 90-*quater*. Actually, it would be possible to distinguish between 'general parameters', aimed at *diagnosing* the condition of vulnerability, and 'evaluation criteria', having an additional demonstrative potential, not excluding the autonomous significance of the former.

As for the competent authorities in charge of individual assessment, some legal scholars pointed out that the wording of Art 90-*quater* would be excessively vague in identifying such competent authorities responsible for carrying out the individual assessment and the timing of its execution. It has been further argued that the individual assessment concerning vulnerability should be conducted by bodies equipped with specific training rather than only by law enforcement authorities. In this respect, new Directive (EU) 2024/1385, on combating violence against women and domestic violence,[23] in addition to the requirements of Art 22 of Directive 2012/29, at least for cases of sexual violence and domestic violence, require Member States to identify at the earliest possible stage a victim's specific protection needs by means of an individual assessment, where appropriate in collaboration with all relevant competent authorities depending on the stage of the proceedings, and relevant support services, such as victim protection centres, specialised services, social services, healthcare professionals, shelters, specialist support services and other relevant stakeholders (see Art 16).

In conclusion, the general vagueness of the provision has raised several concerns, even because the rule omits to indicate the modalities and the nature of the assessment, which are often better identified in protocols and guidelines addressed to authorities and bodies likely to get in touch with victims.[24] In this respect, at a legislative level, a

[21] T Alesci, 'Art 90-quater' in A Giarda and G Spangher (eds), *Codice di procedura penale commentato* (Wolters Kluwer, 2023) 1340 ff.

[22] See S Quattrocolo, 'Vulnerabilità e *indidividual assessment*: l'evoluzione dei parametri di individuazione' in M Bargis and H Belluta (eds), *Vittime di reato e sistema penale. La ricerca di nuovi equilibri* (Giappichelli, 2017) 316; L Vispo, 'La riscoperta del ruolo della persona offesa nel sistema processualpenalistico italiano: prime riflessioni a margine del d.lgs. 212/2015' (2016) *Legislazione penale*.

[23] See Directive (EU) 2024/1385 of the European Parliament and of the Council of 14 May 2024 on combating violence against women and domestic violence [2024] OJ L2024/1385.

[24] See, eg, the 2023 National Referral Mechanism for the identification, assistance and protection of victims of human trafficking and/or severe exploitation (2023 NRM), Italian Department of Equal Opportunities, December 2023, drafted according to OSCE National Referral Mechanism. See, also, with respect to violence against women, the National Guidelines addressed to National Health Service relating to the social and

more precise definition of this provision has been deemed desirable by some commentators, even with the goal of harmonising the mentioned guidelines and protocols, making them more effective.[25]

Besides the general definition of vulnerability embedded in Art 90-*quater* ICPC and other relevant provisions set out in the same Code, the Italian legal system provides specific sets of rules aimed at ensuring protection and rights for special categories of victims with specific needs.[26] Some legal scholars have expressed concerns that this could lead to the creation of several sectors of criminal law characterised by a victim-centred approach. Such fragmentation may result in a detrimental impact on the equality principle, because of different regimes relating to level of sanctions, statute of limitations, times and modalities of reporting, application of preventive (administrative and judicial) measures interfering with the enjoyment of fundamental rights of individuals (see the next section in this respect). From a point of view focused on criminal policy, this panoply of criminal sub-systems might generate, as specific *types of victims* (or *super-victims*, as some scholars named them[27]), so many *types of offenders* (*Tätertyp*), resulting in the establishment of a *Täterstrafrecht*.[28] Such remarks are not meant to deny or minimise victims' protection needs, especially vulnerable ones. However, they offer a warning about the risk that boosting the protection of victims may result in an excessive sacrifice of the most fundamental principles governing criminal policy, depending on the modalities chosen by the legislature to pursue such an objective. Striking a fair balance between the need to protect vulnerable victims and the need to comply with principles governing criminal policy and fundamental rights of suspects and accused persons, is really crucial. Preventing an exploitation of the protection of victims to legitimate and justify law and order policies or unreasonable increases of the levels of sanctions or the creation of unjustifiably rigorous legal regimes should be considered a priority by the legislature.[29]

medical assistance to victims of violence against women, adopted in 2016, pursuant to Law No 208 of the 28th December 2015.

[25] See, in this respect, the remarks of the Italian Parliamentary Commission of Enquiry on the phenomenon of feminicide in its 2022 report (121–22). The text of the report adopted on 8th November 2022 is available in Italian at www.senato.it.

[26] See the remarks on terminology of R Parizot, 'Notazioni comparate' in L Luparia (ed), 'Lo Statuto europeo delle vittime di reato. Modelli di tutela tra diritto dell'Unione e buone pratiche nazionali' (Wolters Kluwer, 2015) 287.

[27] See S Allegrezza-S Martelli, 'Vittime di violenza domestica e sistema penale italiano', in Luparia, ibid 209.

[28] F Cingari, 'Vittime del reato e diritto penale' in Piergallini et al (n 8) 11.

[29] Venturoli (n 5) 138 ff; ID, 'La vulnerabilità della vittima di reato quale categoria "a geometria variabile" del diritto penale' in B Varraso, 'Le vittime vulnerabili. Introduzione al focus' (2018) *Rivista italiana di medicina legale e del diritto in campo sanitario*2, 555 ff. In relation to EU legal provisions concerning vulnerable victims, see C Amalfitano, *La vittima vulnerabile nel diritto internazionale e dell'Unione europea* in ibid, 525 ss; S Allegrezza, 'Il ruolo della vittima nella direttiva 2012/29/UE', in Luparia (n 26) 3 ff; M Gialuz, 'La protezione della vittima tra Corte EDU e Corte di Giustizia, in ibid, 20 ff; GM Vagliasindi, 'Protecting Vulnerable Victims and Beyond: The Duty of Consistent Interpretation in Criminal Matters in Italy after Pupino' in V Mitsilegas, A Di Martino and L Mancano, *The Court of Justice and European Criminal Law: Leading Cases in a Contextual Analysis* (Hart Publishing, 2021) 83 ff.

V. Gender-Based Violence and Domestic Violence: Balancing Victims' Protection and Punitive Excesses

Victims of gender-based violence and domestic violence are considered particularly vulnerable and, as such, deserving of specific protective measures.

Since the introduction of Law No 7 of 9th January 2006,[30] and of Law Decree No 11 of 23th February 2009, converted in Law No 38 of 23th April 2009,[31] a set of legal provisions aimed at preventing, respectively, female genital mutilation and stalking have been provided in the Italian legal system. Beside preventive measures requiring the setting up of awareness-raising campaigns and specific interventions of education in schools and universities and of training concerning healthcare professionals and school-teachers, they provide as criminal offences, respectively, female genital mutilation (Art 583-*bis* ICC), and stalking (Art 612-*bis* ICC). Law No 38 of 23th April 2009 set out at the same time a special administrative procedure ('ammonimento'), that allows the victim, before reporting, to request a formal warning to be addressed to the person identified by the victim by public security authorities ('questore'). It also provided for some aggravating circumstances applicable to the criminal offence of murder, implying the application of life sentence, where the perpetrator had previously committed the criminal offences of ill-treatment (Art 572 ICC), permanent face disfigurement (Art 583-*quinquies* ICC), child prostitution (Art 600-*bis* ICC) and child pornography (Art 600-*ter* ICC), sexual violence and group sexual violence (Art 609-*bis* and Art 609-*octies* ICC), child sexual abuse (Art 609-*quater* ICC) or stalking (Art 576, para 1, No 5 and 5.1, ICC).[32]

Moreover, Law Decree No 93 of 14th August 2013, converted in Law No 119 of 15th October 2009, provided an increase of penalties relating to criminal offences falling in the category of gender-based violence and domestic violence, also making it more difficult for the victim to withdraw the report. It extended the mentioned administrative procedure of 'ammonimento' to domestic violence, making it applicable by the public security authorities, regardless of a request of the victim.

Law No 69 of 19th July 2019 introduced new criminal offences punishing coercion and induction to marriage (Art 558-*bis* ICC), non-consensual sharing of intimate material (Art 612-*ter* ICC), violation of obligations and prohibitions imposed through the precautionary measures, provided for in Arts 282-*bis* and 282-*ter* ICPC (Art 387-*bis* ICC), permanent face disfigurement (Art 583-*quinquies* ICC). It further increased penalties concerning the mentioned offences and stressed the importance of specific programmes of rehabilitation devoted to perpetrators both with respect to forms of probation and during the serving of the sentence, as a condition for accessing parole and other kinds of measures alternative to prison. Such legislation also stated the duty incumbent on the Government to adopt a National Action Plan on violence against women and domestic violence at least every three years, with the aim to prevent, raise awareness about the phenomenon, provide support and assistance to the victims, identify

[30] G.U. n. 14, 18 January 2006.
[31] G.U. n. 95, 24 April 2009.
[32] The list of the criminal offences provided for in this rule has been updated by different legislation.

training programmes for professionals and rehabilitation and support programmes for offenders, gather data and information about the characteristics of the phenomenon, promote positive policies and activities to foster gender equality and contrast gender stereotypes about the social role of men and women (see Art 39 of Directive 2024/1385).

In relation to strategies concerning investigation and prosecution, Law No 69/2019, Laws No 122 of 15 September 2023,[33] and No 168 of 24 November 2023,[34] aim to create a fast track for investigation and criminal proceedings concerning crimes related to the criminological area of gender-based and domestic violence (see, eg, Arts 347, para 3, 362, para 1-*ter*, 370, para 2-*bis*, ICPC). Considering the criminological features of such phenomena, which often result in a rapid escalation of violence, and according to Art 15 of Directive 2024/1385 and to Arts 49 and 50 of the Council of Europe Convention,[35] the legislator has imposed very tight and strict timelines for the initiation of investigations by police to gather the necessary elements to clarify the circumstances and identify the offender, and to acquire information from the victim by the public prosecutor. Compliance with these deadlines must be monitored by judicial offices and, in case of non-compliance, the general prosecutor at the Court of Appeal may revoke the assignment, with a reasoned order, taking it over directly or assigning it to another magistrate of the office. The introduction of such provisions has been criticised. A first criticism deals with the lack of adequate financial resources to set suitable training programmes for police officers and the judiciary with respect to these crimes and to reorganise judicial offices to ensure their rapid and effective activation.[36]

A. Protection Measures: Emergency Barring Orders, Restraining Orders, Protection Orders and the European Protection Order

Besides the normative changes already described above, the legal framework concerning the protection of victims in this field has been progressively enriched by the provision of two precautionary measures to prevent repeat victimisation (first introduced by Law No 154 of 4th April 2001, together with correspondent measures applicable by civil judge pursuant to Arts 342-*bis* and 342-*ter* of the ICC and Art 736-*bis* of the ICPC). The standard required to apply such measures seems to be the existence of serious circumstantial evidence concerning a crime committed in the family context or in the context of a relationship.

By applying the first measure provided for in Art 282-*bis* ICPC, the competent judicial authority orders the accused to vacate the family house immediately, not to return to it, not to enter it without judicial authorisation (the authorisation may provide specific visit modalities). Where there are protection needs concerning the physical integrity of the victim or their relatives, the judicial authority may also prescribe that the accused

[33] GU n. 216, 15 September 2023.

[34] GU n. 275, 24 November 2023.

[35] 35-bis Council of Europe Convention on preventing and combating violence against women and domestic violence, Istanbul, 11/05/2011, CETS No 210 entered into force on 1 August 2014.

[36] See in this respect A Marandola, 'Codice rosso rafforzato' (2023) *Diritto penale e processo* 11, 1428 ff; F Menditto, 'Indagini in materia di "codice rosso": un aggiornamento delle linee guida della procura di Tivoli alla luce delle novità della l. 122/2023' (29 September 2023) 5 ff, available at www.sistemapenale.it.

does not approach places where the victim usually lives (such as, workplace, domicile of family or relatives), unless it is necessary for reasons concerning the job of the accused, identifying the relevant modalities (for example, specific distances) and imposing more clear-cut limits. The procedure concerning the assessment of the existence of precautionary needs has been recently speeded up in relation to a list of criminal offences, basically falling within the category of gender-based and domestic violence,[37] with the objective of giving priority to a quick assessment of the outcome of the investigation in order to protect the victim.[38]

The second measure aims at preventing the accused from approaching specific places the victim usually visits or to keep a specific distance from such places or from the victim,[39] even using the electronic tag (Art 282-*ter* ICPC). Where there are further needs for protection, the same order may be issued by judicial authority in relation to places usually visited by the victim's relatives or cohabitants or by people with whom the victim has a relationship or to identify specific distances to be maintained from such people. The judicial authority may also prohibit any form of communication between the accused and the victim. The prescriptions may be adjusted by judicial authority, taking account of the work and residence needs of the accused.

The violation of obligations and prohibitions imposed by the above-mentioned measures and by the order issued pursuant to Art 384-*bis* ICPC represents a criminal offence punished with imprisonment from six months up to three years (Art 387-*bis* ICC). On the one hand, these measures are conceived as flexible as possible, to allow the judicial authority to effectively pursue the goals of protection of victims.[40] On the other hand, however, such flexibility may be seen as a *vulnus* in terms of lack of clarity and precision of legal provisions, in so doing attributing broad discretionary powers to the judicial authority.

Pursuant to Directive 2011/99, establishing the European Protection Order, the protection measures[41] provided to victims in one Member State may be recognised in other Member States where the victim has moved to or is going to move to, even temporarily. This important judicial cooperation tool, based on mutual recognition of judicial protection measures,[42] has been transposed into the Italian legal system by Legislative

[37] Many recent provisions, concerning different types of measures or special faster procedures in relation to gender-based and domestic violence, embody a list of criminal offences, that often differ, creating risks of lack of coordination among them and shortcomings in their application.

[38] See, in this respect, L Algeri, 'Tempi rapidi per l'adozione delle misure cautelari a protezione delle vittime' (2024) *Diritto penale e processo* 2, 172–80.

[39] Recently the Italian Supreme Court has stated that where the judicial authority decides to order the accused to keep a distance, it only needs to indicate the specific distance. By contrast, where the judicial authority decides to order the accused both the prohibition to get close to places where the victim lives or visits, and the obligation to keep a distance, it needs to identify the specific places for which the order operates. See Corte di Cassazione, SS.UU., 29-04-2021, n. 39005.

[40] See in this respect Cassazione penale, sec. V, 20-02-2023, n. 7228, in G Lattanzi, 'Codice di procedura penale annotato con la giurisprudenza' (Giuffrè, 2023) 1008.

[41] For the definition of 'protection measure', see Art 2(1), n. 2, of Directive 2011/99 and Art 2(1), lett. b, of the Legislative Decree, No 9/2015.

[42] V Mitsilegas, 'The Symbiotic Relationship Between Mutual Trust and Fundamental Rights in Europe's Area of Criminal Justice' (2015) *New Journal of European Criminal Law* 4, 457; R Sicurella, 'Introduction. Fostering a European Criminal Law Culture: in Trust We Trust' in R Sicurella et al (eds), *General Principles for a Common Criminal Law Framework in the EU* (Giuffrè, 2017) XVII.

Decree No 9 of 11th February 2015.[43] According to Art 5, such an order may be issued by the judicial authority that ordered the mentioned measures provided for in Arts 282-*bis* and 282-*ter* ICPC, upon a request of the victim, who declares that they are visiting or reside in a different Member State or expresses their will to move to another Member State to visit it or to reside there. Where the judicial authority rejects the request, refusing to issue the order, the victim, their defence lawyer and the general public prosecutor at the Appeal Court have access to a judicial remedy before the Supreme Court ('ricorso per cassazione').Where the order has been issued, the judicial authority sends it without delay to the Minister of Justice, who transmits it (adequately translated) to the competent authority of the executing Member State. The same Minister also informs the competent authority of the executing Member State about any change, revocation, prorogation, annulment or substitution concerning the measures or the order. Where the executing Italian judicial authority has to recognise the foreign order, it issues one of the two measures, provided for in Arts 282-*bis* and 282-*ter* ICPC, ensuring that the prescriptions imposed correspond to those required by the protection order coming from the issuing State. The order may not be recognised where one of the grounds of refusal provided for in Art 8 exists.

Legal doctrine has raised some concerns about such legislation. In summary, such concerns relate to the following shortcomings: i) an alleged defect in complying with the adversarial principle within the proceedings before the Court of Appeal; ii) the provision of a further ground of refusal not listed in those outlined by Directive 2011/99/EU; iii) the significant involvement of a political authority in a mutual recognition mechanism, that should work among judicial authorities; iv) the compulsory declaration of the reason of the visit by the victim in their request to obtain the protection order; v) the limitation of the territorial scope to the EU (especially in cases concerning the international removal of children). Such shortcomings could, on the one hand, hamper a smooth functioning of the mutual recognition mechanism, jeopardising the victim's protection; on the other hand, they could also negatively affect the protection of fundamental rights and procedural safeguards of the persons involved in the proceedings.[44]

VI. Rights of the Victims, Access to Justice and Participation of Victims in Criminal Proceedings

The victim's interests in criminal proceedings basically consist of: i) the identification and prosecution of the perpetrator, which may coexist with the will to initiate a restorative justice programme; ii) the prevention of repeat and secondary victimisation; iii) the compensation of economic loss and physical and psychological harm suffered as a result of the commission of the criminal offence, when they stand as a civil party in a criminal trial.[45]

[43] GU n. 44, 23 February 2015.

[44] See, in this respect, A Sivier, 'Art 282-bis and Art 282-ter' in Giarda and Spangher (n 21) 212–13; F Ruggeri, 'Ordine di protezione europeo e legislazione italiana di attuazione: un'analisi e qualche perplessità' (2015) *Processo penale e giustizia* 99.

[45] See B Romanelli, 'La vittima e l'azione civile da reato nel processo penale' in Castronuovo,Donini, Mancuso and Varraso (n 8) 527.

In the following sub-sections, the legal provisions adopted to transpose EU Directive 2012/29 into the Italian legal system will be examined, with specific respect to rights to information, right to legal assistance, rights to protection during criminal investigation and criminal trial and right to safeguards in the context of restorative justice services.

A. The Transposition of Directive 2012/29 into the Italian Legal System. A New Pathway for the Protection of Victims

Directive 2012/29 has been transposed into the Italian legal system by Legislative Decree No 212 of 15th December 2015,[46] which modified some provisions and introduced new ones in the ICPC.[47]

Art 90 ICPC, sets out rights and powers of the victim.[48] Generally speaking, besides powers and rights expressly recognised by specific legal provisions, the victim may produce notes at every stage of criminal proceedings and show evidence, except for the trial before the Supreme Court. Legislative Decree No 150/2022 has recently amended Art 90 ICPC, introducing a new para 1-*bis*, stating that the victim has the power to declare or elect domicile. In line with the principles aimed at a greater 'sustainable' digitalisation of criminal proceedings,[49] the victim may also indicate a certified email address or other qualified certified electronic delivery service.[50]

i. Rights to Information of the Victim

In order to transpose Arts 4 to 6 of Directive 2012/29 related to the provision of information and support, Art 90-*bis* ICPC grants victims the right to be informed about their rights and powers and to obtain information aimed at accessing justice and participating in criminal proceedings and in restorative justice programmes. Such a rule, firstly introduced by Legislative Decree No 212/2015, has been subsequently amended by Law No 103/2017, Law No 69/2019, and most recently by Legislative Decree No 150/2022. Pursuant to Art 90-*bis*, therefore, the victim is provided with information in a language that they understand from the first contact with the competent authority, regarding how to report the crime, the role they assume during investigations and trial, the right to know the date and location of the trial and the charges, and, if they decide to stand as a civil party in a criminal trial, the right to receive notification of the judgment, even in a short form. Information must be provided to victims about the possibility that they have access to restorative justice programmes. Specific duties of information refer to

[46] GU n. 3, 05 January 2016.

[47] G Illuminati, 'La vittima come testimone' in Luparia (n 26) 63–80; G Todaro, 'Il sistema italiano di tutela della vittima del reato: analisi e prospettive' in ibid, 99–114; M Caianiello, 'Notazioni comparate' in ibid, 183–90; H Belluta, 'Eppur si muove. La tutela delle vittime particolarmente vulnerabili nel processo penale italiano' in ibid, 257–70; L Luparia and R Parizot, 'Quali buone prassi in materia di protezione delle vittime?' in ibid 337–46.

[48] Alesci (n 21) 1318.

[49] The objective of digitalisation of criminal proceedings has been one of the main objectives pursued by the last comprehensive reform of the Italian criminal justice system. See B Galgani, '… *Along came* il processo penale telematico. Le disposizioni generali sugli atti' in Castronuovo, Donini, Mancuso and Varraso (n 8) 397.

[50] On digital domicile and notifications, see F Nicolicchia, 'Domicilio digitale e notificazioni' in ibid 429 ff.

the modalities concerning the exercise of the right to interpretation and translation of procedural documents. In this respect, pursuant to Art 143-bis ICPC, transposing Art 7 of Directive 2012/29, victims have the right to an interpreter and a translator in criminal proceedings.

Even according to Art 282-*quater* ICPC, victims must be informed about the possibility to request protective measures that may be ordered in their favour, even when they reside in an EU Member State different from that where the crime was committed. The victims also have the right to be informed about services or organisations that can provide support and assistance.

According to some legal scholars, the list of rights to information provided for in Art 90-*bis* would be inadequate to pursue the goals of victims' protection pursued by Directive 2012/29, due to the vagueness and complex language of the provisions. It would represent a kind of formal bureaucratic transposition of the Directive, that would not take into sufficient account the need to individualise the information depending on different types and needs of actual victims.[51] Moreover, Art 90-*bis* does not expressly provide any nullity sanction for the violation of the information duties listed therein. The lack of a specific procedural sanction may render the provision less efficacious.[52] Similar issues have been identified in relation to Article 90-ter ICPC, which provide a set of rules concerning the duty to inform the victim about the release and escape of the person remanded in custody, prosecuted or sentenced.[53] Analogous duties are provided in relation to coercive measures ordered according to Arts 282-bis, 282-ter, and decisions to release and cease the custodial security measure for criminal offences committed with violence against the person,[54] basically concerning gender-based violence and domestic violence (Art 299 ICPC, as modified by Law 168/2023[55]). Even in this case, procedural sanctions are not provided for non-compliance with the prescribed obligations. However, according to established jurisprudence, the victims, who have not received the prescribed information and notifications, would be entitled to lodge a claim before the Supreme Court.[56] In these provisions, the vague wording 'criminal proceedings relating to criminal offences perpetrated by violence against the person' does not refer to specific rules, in doing so giving rise to many issues in terms of interpretation.[57]

[51] See in this respect Alesci (n 20) 1336; M Bouchard, 'Prime osservazioni al decreto legislativo sulle vittime di reato' (2016) *Questione Giustizia*; Vispo (n 21).

[52] See Alesci (n 21) 1339–40.

[53] See recently in this respect Corte di Cassazione, sec. I, 09-06-2022, n. 31630.

[54] See, in this respect, Cassazione penale, SS.UU. 10959/2016, which widely interpreted the wording 'violence against person'. For some remarks on this judgment, see MC Amoroso, 'La nozione di delitti commessi con violenza alla persona: il primo passo delle Sezioni Unite verso un lungo viaggio' (2016) *Cassazione Penale* 10, 3714B; G Schena, 'Il concetto progressivo di violenza alla persona e tutela informativa della persona offesa' (2017) *Cassazione Penale* 4, 1523; C Minnella, 'Per le Sezioni Unite la persona offesa va sempre avvisata della richiesta di archiviazione' (2016) *Diritto & Giustizia* 14, 88.

[55] The new legislation extends the duties of information without delay in favour of the victim in relation to all pre-trial precautionary measures ordered against the offender. See on this reform, A Marandola, 'I nuovi presidi a tutela della vittima: rimedi pre-cautelari, cautelari e obblighi informativi (2022) *Diritto penale e processo* 2, 191–92.

[56] See Corte di Cassazione, sec. VI, 09-02-2016, n. 6864, W.J.B; Corte di Cassazione, sec. VI, 23.07.2015, n. 35613.

[57] See Corte di Cassazione, SS.UU., 30.09.2021, *Gallo*; Corte di Cassazione, SS.UU., 28.09.2022, n. 36754. See also K La Regina, 'Art 408' in Giarda and Spangher (n 21) Vol II, 2732.

ii. Right to Legal Assistance

Art 13 of Directive 2012/29 requires Member States to provide victims participating in criminal proceedings with access to State-funded legal aid under the conditions and the procedures set out in national legislation.

The legal framework existing in the Italian legal system to comply with this obligation has been progressively modified. Since 2013, Art 101, para 1, ICPC,[58] provides a specific obligation to inform the victim about their power to appoint a defence lawyer to exercise their rights and powers. Such an obligation is incumbent on the police and the public prosecutor when they acquire the *notitia criminis*. However, there is no proper sanction in case of violation of such a rule. Therefore, a lack of effectiveness may affect the application of this provision. The same provision sets out a further obligation to inform the victims about the possibility to have access to State-funded legal aid. Pursuant to Arts 74, para 1, and 75, of Presidential Decree No 115 of 30th May 2002, State-funded legal assistance concern any civil, criminal and administrative judicial proceedings, including proceedings for the execution of compensation orders, and covers court expenses and taxes (in so doing, complying with Art 13 of Directive 2012/29). In this respect, income requirements are listed in Art 76. According to Art 76, para 2, victims of some criminal offences basically concerning gender-based violence, domestic violence, child sexual abuse, and child victims of trafficking, enslavement and servitude, child prostitution and pornography, child grooming, may have access to State-funded legal aid, regardless of income requirements mentioned in para 1 of Art 76. However, some shortcomings, especially concerning the availability of funds and the management of administrative organisation, often hinder the smooth functioning of this mechanism.[59]

iii. Right to Protection of the Victims During Criminal Investigation and Criminal Trial

Some provisions in the Italian criminal justice system ensure the protection of the victims from secondary and repeat victimisation, intimidation and retaliation during criminal investigation and criminal trial, in order to transpose the obligations stemming from the rules set out in Chapter 4 of Directive 2012/29, especially Arts 18–24 (see also Art 12 of Directive 2011/36/EU,[60] Art 20 of Directive 2011/93/EU[61]). The rights provided under these provisions are conceived as protective means for the victims,

[58] See M Violante, 'Art 101 in Giarda and Spangher (n 21) 1416–18.

[59] See, in this respect, for example, the last evaluation report on Italy of the Group of Experts on Action against Trafficking in Human Beings (GRETA) focused on access to justice and effective remedies for victims of trafficking in human beings, published on 23rd February 2024, which also encourages Bar Associations to offer specialised training to lawyers assisting and representing victims of trafficking (18).

[60] Directive 2011/36/EU of the European Parliament and of the Council of 5 April 2011 on preventing and combating trafficking in human beings and protecting its victims, and replacing Council Framework Decision 2002/629/JHA [2011] OJ L101/1.

[61] Directive 2011/93/EU of the European Parliament and of the Council of 13 December 2011 on combating the sexual abuse and sexual exploitation of children and child pornography, and replacing Council Framework Decision 2004/68/JHA [2011] OJ L335/1.

especially for the vulnerable ones. However, they need to be interpreted and applied in a manner consistent with the right to defence and the right to the equality of arms (adversarial principle), as it is expressly stated in Arts 18, 20 and 23 of Directive 2012/29 (Art 6 of the European Convention on Human Rights (ECHR) and Art 48 EU Charter of Fundamental Rights). The need to strike a fair balance between the victim's need for protection and the full enjoyment of the right to defence by the person under investigation has also been taken into account by the Italian legislature, ensuring an early disclosure by the public prosecutor (concerning all investigative actions carried out), according to Art 393, para 2-*bis*, ICPC.

During the criminal investigation, where the police and the public prosecutor acquire information and statements ('sommarie informazioni') by minors or adults deemed as vulnerable persons, in proceedings relating to alleged criminal offences basically concerning domestic violence, sexual violence, enslavement and servitude, trafficking in human beings, sexual child abuse, child prostitution and pornography, child grooming, stalking, the support of a psychologist or psychiatrist, appointed by the public prosecutor, is required.[62] The police and the public prosecutor also ensure that the vulnerable victim does not have any contact with the person under investigation and that they do not repeat the same declarations several times, unless this is necessary for investigation (Arts 351 and 362 ICPC).

Pursuant to Art 392 ICPC, that regulates forms and requirements of early acquisition of evidence during the investigation or the preliminary hearing ('incidente probatorio'), in the proceedings basically concerning the abovementioned criminal offences, the public prosecutor, even upon the request of the victim or the person under investigation, has the possibility to request an early acquisition of the testimony of a minor, an adult or, in any case, a vulnerable person, even beyond the cases in which it would be regularly permitted.[63] In such proceedings, where the early acquisition is ordered by a judge and a minor is involved as a witness, the hearing may be performed at a different place, such as specialised social premises or the house of the person interested in the acquisition of evidence. Statements must be wholly videotaped or audiotaped, unless this is technically impossible. The same modalities may be requested by the parties where an adult who is deemed to be particularly vulnerable must be heard.

Specific modalities for carrying out the examination of vulnerable victims are provided by the Italian legal system to protect their dignity, their right to private life, and the reliability of the statements during criminal trial. Generally speaking, in some prescribed circumstances, the judge may decide to restrict access to the public and to the press,[64] for the whole or a part of the trial, in cases concerning the examination of

[62] See also in this respect the wording of Art 609-decies ICC, that ensures psychological and emotional assistance to minors, who are alleged victims of the criminal offences provided for in the mentioned provisions, during all stages of criminal proceedings.

[63] See in this respect Court of Justice of European Union, Grand Chamber, 16.06.2005, Case C-105/03, *Pupino* EU:C:2005:386, where the Court stated that Art 392 had to be interpreted consistently with EU law, and in particular with the Framework Decision 2001/220/JHA, then repealed by Directive 2012/29. See also ECtHR, sec. 4, 12.06.2018, application n. 14000/12, *TK v Lithuania*; ECtHR, sec. 4, 28.09.2010, application n. 40156/07, *AS v Finland*.

[64] We intentionally use the same wording of Art 6 ECHR, that mentions expressly the press, apart from the public, to stress the importance of the role of press in informing people about topics of public interest, but, at the same time, the necessity to ensure a fair and serene representation of the facts under trial.

a minor. However, in proceedings concerning the criminal offences relating to enslavement and servitude, child prostitution and pornography, trafficking in human beings, sexual violence, the public and the press are always excluded by the judge where the victim is a minor. Otherwise, the public and the press have access to the trial, unless the victim requests their exclusion. In such proceedings, questions about the victim's private life or sexuality are not allowed, unless they are strictly necessary to reconstruct the events (Art 472 ICPC), in accordance with Art 21 of Directive 2012/29 and Art 20 of Directive 2024/1385.[65] Additionally, during the criminal trial, some special modalities to carry out interviews with minors and adults deemed as particularly vulnerable are provided by Art 498 ICPC, according to Arts 23 and 24 of Directive 2012/29 (see also Directive 2011/36, Art 15).[66] As for minors, the interview is carried out by the court's President (even supported by a minor's relative or a psychologist) who questions the minors about the queries proposed by the parties, unless the ordinary examination procedure is deemed adequate to safeguard the interests of minors and the reliability of the testimony.

iv. Right to Safeguards in the Context of Restorative Justice Services

As already mentioned in section II.A of this chapter, Legislative Decree No 150/2022 introduced restorative justice in the Italian criminal justice system. It is nonetheless worth questioning whether this new legislation meets the transposition requirements of Art 12 of Directive 2012/29, concerning the right of victims to safeguards in the context of restorative justice services.

Fundamental safeguards to protect the rights of parties and ensure the fairness of the restorative process are established by Italian law.[67] In particular, the parties have the right to consult with legal counsel concerning the restorative justice programmes and, where necessary, have access to translation and/or interpretation. The rights of children must be specifically addressed and the process must ensure the achievement of the child's best interest, taking account of their personality and needs and assuring the participation of professionals who have specific competences and are adequately trained (Art 46 of the Legislative Decree).

Before agreeing to participate in a restorative process, the parties must be fully informed, in a timely manner, of all possibilities to participate in the programmes and their rights, the nature of the process and the possible consequences of their decision (Arts 47 and 48). Their consent is required and they are free to withdraw from the process at any point. Special advice and assistance are provided for children and the mentally disabled to support them in forming a valid and informed consent. The participation of the person indicated as offender in the restorative justice process, the

See M Chiavario, 'Art 6' in S Bartole, B Conforti and G Raimondi (eds), *Commentario alla Convenzione europea per la tutela dei diritti dell'uomo e delle libertà fondamentali* (Padua, 2001) 201.

[65] See in this respect the recent ECtHR's decision on the case *JL c Italie*, Requête n. 5671/16, 27 mai 2021, §§ 136–142, that convicted Italy for a violation of the positive obligation stemming from Art 8 ECHR to protect private life.

[66] See S Corbetta, 'Art. 498' in Giarda and Spangher (n 21) Vol III, 359 ff.

[67] See in this respect Chapter II – Section I of the Legislative Decree No 150/2022.

statements and all information gathered during the process cannot be used as evidence in criminal proceedings or during the serving of the sentence, according to the principle of the presumption of innocence, and the confidentiality of proceedings must be protected (Arts 50, 51, 52). Lack of participation in the programme, interruption in terms of participation and failure to reach an agreement must not be used against the person identified as offender in subsequent criminal justice proceedings (Art 58). By contrast, the restorative outcome may be assessed by the judicial authority in different ways. As we have already mentioned, the Italian legislature introduced a model of restorative justice that complements the criminal justice system (Art 129-bis ICPC), outlining informative mechanisms in favour of parties during the criminal proceedings (pre-charge, charge and post-charge stage, trial and sentencing[68]) or the serving of the sentence in prison by the convicted person.

VII. Compensation and Restitutions to Victims of Crime

According to Arts 15 and 16 of Directive 2012/29, victims have the right to the return of property and to compensation from the offender, which can be decided in criminal proceedings or in other legal proceedings. Moreover, Directive 2004/80 sets up a system to facilitate access to compensation to victims of crimes in cross-border situations, which should operate on the basis of Member States' schemes on compensation to victims of violent intentional crime, committed in their respective territories. This requires a more detailed examination of whether Italian law meets the requirements of EU law as interpreted by the CJEU on this matter.

Art 185 ICC states that the commission of any criminal offence gives rise to an obligation to restitutions, according to the relevant civil legislation. Such rule also specifies that economic loss and harm suffered by the victim as a direct consequence of the commission of a criminal offence must be compensated by the offender or by the person legally liable for her conduct (for example, parents, employers, insurance companies, newspaper editors). Restitutions and compensations are to be considered as civil consequences of crime. Such obligations thus pursue reintegrative and compensative goals. A causal link between the commission of the crime and the harmful (civil) consequences must be established, even if the most recent jurisprudence recognises the existence of such a link with respect to consequences not directly and immediately connected to the commission of the criminal offence or only presumably linked to it.[69]

In order to save the property of the perpetrator to guarantee civil obligations stemming from the commission of the crime, upon request of the civil party, the judge may

[68] Important changes have been consequently adopted to coordinate such rules with those provided for in the ICPC. In this respect, Arts 90-bis, lett p-bis and pter, and 90-bis.1, relating to information, respectively, to *injured person* and victim (according to the definition set forth in Art 42, Legislative Decree No 150/2022); Art 129-bis (lastly modified by Legislative Decree No 31 of 19th March 2024), regulating the tasks of competent judicial authority, depending on the stage of criminal proceedings (Art 45-ter of Enforcement Rules attached to ICPC ['Disposizioni di attuazione']), concerning the access of parties to restorative justice programmes and their beginning.

[69] See Cassazione penale, n. 32899/2021; Cassazione penale, n. 28216/2020; Cassazione penale, n. 6380/2017.

order a conservative freezing of the property of the accused or of the person legally responsible (basically, in this kind of seizure the freezing of third-party property – different for the abovementioned persons legally responsible – is not allowed), where there are reasonable grounds to believe that such assets can be disbursed (*periculum in mora*), pursuant to Arts 316–320 ICPC.[70] However, in order to strike a fair balance between the competing interests at stake (ie the right to property and the presumption of innocence and the right to compensation for victims of crime), the freezing should not be ordered where the alleged perpetrator is likely to be acquitted.[71]

Arts 29 and 30 of Regulation 2018/1805 on the mutual recognition of freezing and confiscation orders are devoted to the restitution of frozen property to victims. In particular, Art 29, para 2, requires that, where a property has been frozen, it is restituted as soon as possible to the victim under specific conditions. A similar provision is provided in Art 30 with respect to a decision to restitute confiscated property or money. It may happen that executing authorities, receiving European freezing orders, which only contain a request to freeze assets for the purpose of victim compensation, may not execute it, because – according to the scope of the Regulation, pursuant to Art 2(1)(1) – the 'freezing order' is defined as a decision issued or validated by an issuing authority in order to prevent the destruction, transformation, removal, transfer or disposal of property *with a view to the confiscation* (emphasis added). They would need, thus, to contact issuing authorities and discuss the possibility to adjust the order identifying the confiscation of property as the objective of the freezing.[72] In this respect, it has been stressed that a better clarification of the valid legal basis on which freezing orders can be issued and executed to seize property to be returned to victims or to compensate them would be desirable, even with the involvement of Eurojust. It has been also proposed to undertake a legislative reform of the Regulation aimed at extending its scope to freezing orders pursued to compensate victims.[73]

The recently adopted Directive 2024/1260 on asset recovery and confiscation states in Recital 25 that, in the context of criminal proceedings, property can also be frozen with a view to its possible subsequent restitution or to safeguard compensation for damage caused by criminal offence. Moreover, the general definition of freezing, as 'the temporary prohibition of the transfer, destruction, conversion, disposal or movement of property or temporarily assuming custody or control of property', provided for in Art 3(1)(5), no longer refers to the objective of confiscation. Although an amendment of the Regulation is the option, that best fits the rule of law, an interpretation of national legislation consistent with the rules provided for in Directive 2024/1260 might overcome some shortcomings relating to the mutual recognition of freezing orders aimed at compensating victims, not expressly referring to the objective of confiscation, as long

[70] See M Scoletta, 'Il risarcimento del danno da reato nel sistema italiano a fronte dei vincoli europei' in Luparia (n 26) 308.

[71] See, in this respect, R Belfiore, *Il sequestro preventivo. Tra esigenze impeditive e strumentalità alla confisca* (Torino, 2019) 53, and bibliography and case law quoted.

[72] See, in this respect, Project RECOVER, Mutual recognition of freezing and confiscation orders between efficiency and the rule of law, coordinated by Prof AM Maugeri and involving academics, practitioners and representatives of EU and national institutions, 2022–2024. All information and deliverables about the project are available at www.recover.lex.unict.it.

[73] See outcomes and documents of the project available at ibid. See, in particular, Reform Proposal n 10, available at https://recover.lex.unict.it/wp-content/uploads/2024/12/Pagine-da-handbook-completo-21.pdf.

as the safeguards and fundamental rights of the suspect/accused are ensured and the freezing is ordered by a judicial authority in a judicial proceeding, as provided for in Arts 316–320 ICPC in the Italian legal system.

A. The Transposition of Directive 2004/80: Right to Compensation in Cross-Border Cases

After a judgment of the Court of Justice declaring Italy non-compliant with the requirements of Art 12 of Directive 2004/80, following proceedings initiated in 2014,[74] the Italian legislature adopted Law No 122 of 7th July 2016,[75] with the aim of transposing Directive 2004/80. Arts 11–16 of Law No 122/2016 apply to victims of: intentional criminal offences committed by violence against the person; exploitation of irregular workers (Art 603-bis ICC); mafia-type crimes; extortion and usury. Some conditions are required by Art 12 to claim for compensation by victims. The amount of compensation is fixed in accordance with the scale laid down by the Ministerial Decree, adopted pursuant to Art 11(3), within the limits of the budget allocated.

In fact, Italian legislation has only partially transposed the requirements set out in Directive 2004/80. It lists several access conditions to compensation (Art 12), which are not provided for in the Directive. It refers to intentional criminal offences committed by violence against the person,[76] in so doing using a wording narrower than that provided for in the Directive (ie 'violent intentional crime'). As some recent decisions of the CJEU showed, the compensation mechanism established by the Italian legislature does not ensure a fair and appropriate level of compensation to crime victims in many situations.[77]

Besides Law No 122/2016, many special legislative provisions regulate forms of compensation concerning the following specific categories of crime victims: victims of terrorism and organised crime;[78] victims of usury and extortion;[79] police officers, public servants disabled in the line of duty and their families, even in case of the killing of their relatives;[80] minors of a parent murdered by the spouse, even separated or divorced, by partners or former partners;[81] victims of war crimes and crimes against humanity committed in Italy or against an Italian citizen by Nazis between 1 September 1939 and 8 May 1945.[82]

[74] See CJEU, 11 October 2016 Grand Chamber, C-601/14 [2016] OJ C 462/2.

[75] GU n. 158, 08 July 2016.

[76] Moreover, we have already mentioned the interpretative issues which have arisen regarding this expression in the Italian jurisprudence (see n 6).

[77] See CJEU, 16 July 2020, C-129/19. See also the Opinion of Advocate General Richard de la Tour delivered on 8 May 2024 in the Case C-126/23 [Burdene]), point 47. See in this respect in this volume the contribution by Łazowski, 'The Flood that Never Came: Case Law of the Court of Justice on the Victims' Rights *Acquis*' in chapter 4.

[78] See Law No 302 of 20 October 1990.

[79] See Law No 108 of 7 March 1996, providing financial support to obtain mortgages with favourable interest conditions by entrepreneurs or professionals, and Law No 44 of 23 February 1999, providing a public contribution to cover economic losses.

[80] See, Law No 266 of 23 December 2005 and Decree No 243 of the President of the Italian Republic of 7 July 2006.

[81] Law No 4 of 11 January 2018.

[82] Legislative Decree No 36/2022.

The legal framework in this field is too fragmented and confusing, poor resources are allocated to finance the funds for compensation and the compensation schemes often pursue repressive/punitive goals instead of solidarity-based assistance, as in other countries.[83] A more comprehensive and coherent legal framework would be highly desirable, with the aim being to ratify the 1983 Council of Europe Convention on the Compensation of Victims of Violent Crimes,[84] and to set up a national mechanism for compensation to crime victims that is based on solidarity and provided with adequate resources and means.

The amendment of Art 16, para 2 of Directive 2012/29, proposed by the Proposal to revise the Victims' Rights Directive, would oblige Member States to ensure that their competent authorities pay directly to the victim the adjudicated compensation without undue delay, allowing then the same authorities to subrogate to the right of the victim in relation to the offender for the amount of the adjudicated compensation. Such a mechanism would guarantee prompt compensation to victims, without burdening them with the failure by the State to allocate adequate financial resources. It would also ensure a full compensation of harm suffered by the victims as a result of the crime committed.

[83] See in this respect the GRETA report (n 58) that stressed some shortcomings in the implementation of the obligations stemming from the Council of Europe Convention on Action against Trafficking in Human Beings Warsaw, 16/05/2005, CETS No 197, concerning effective information to victims and mechanisms of compensation.

[84] Strasbourg, 24 November 1983. European Treaty Series – No 116. Italy has not ratified the Convention yet. There have been some recent legislative proposals, that have promoted the ratification of the Convention, such as Legislative Proposal No 530, presented on 18 April 2018 by Roberta Mura.

15

An Evaluation of the Impact of the EU Victims' Rights Directive on the Scope of Victims' Rights in Ireland

GERARD CONWAY

I. Introduction

The EU Victims' Rights Directive[1] ('the Directive', 'Victims' Rights Directive' or 'VR Directive') is perhaps the most significant cross-border legal instrument concerning the right of victims in the criminal justice process; it is certainly the most significant from the point of view of Irish law. As well as extending the range of substantive rights of victims, the Directive significantly expands the scope of protection in national systems; a key principle it contains, reflecting the free movement principle of European Union (EU) law, is that the rights and protections it contains should not be made conditional upon residence.[2] The Victims' Rights Directive takes a global approach and applies to all types of crime victim. This chapter focuses on the implementation of the Victims' Rights Directive in Irish law from the point of view of criminal procedure and the pre-existing framework of Irish law relating to the standing and rights of victims of crime. It has not been possible in the timeframe to carry out direct research with victims of their actual experience of the criminal justice process. From the point of view of victims, the implementation of the law is not just confined to the question of acquittal or conviction of the accused, but encompasses their experience of the procedure from the beginning of being a victim through to acquittal or sentencing. Only some of this can be assessed through the standard of legal and doctrinal sources of criminal procedure and existing evaluations of implementation of the VR Directive.[3]

[1] Directive 2012/29/EU of the European Parliament and of the Council of 25 October 2012 establishing minimum standards on the rights, support and protection of victims of crime, and replacing Council Framework Decision 2001/220/JHA [2012] OJ L315/57.

[2] ibid, Recital 10.

[3] Criminological research on the victim's experience of the criminal justice process in Ireland has been undertaken: see S Kilcommins and L Moffett, 'The Inclusion and Juridification of Victims on the Island of Ireland' in D Healy, C Hamilton, Y Daly, and M Butler (eds), *Routledge Handbook of Irish Criminology* (UL repository version, 2016) 10–11. Official government surveys of crime tend to concentrate on the incidence of crime, rather than the experience of victims of the criminal justice system, see www.cso.ie/en/statistics/crimeandjustice/. In 1999, the Irish Government published a Victims' Charter, but this was and remains a non legally binding consolidation of principles and resources for victims.

Ireland is a common law country heavily influenced by the United Kingdom (UK) due to having been within the UK until 1922. It has not been influenced, or has been influenced very little, by the continental legal tradition. However, the constitutional framework in Ireland under the Constitution of 1937 reflects a mixture of a UK-style parliamentary government and a United States (US)-inspired system of constitutional review. In criminal law and procedure, Ireland is very close to the UK legal approach. It is an adversarial system, with relatively few inquisitorial elements.[4] As with the UK, it has dispensed with grand juries; it has established a central prosecution authority in recent decades; there is a clear division of powers between the police and the prosecutor;[5] juries retain an important symbolic role even though as with the UK, they are only used in indictable cases.[6] From a comparative perspective, Ireland is the only exclusively common law jurisdiction in the EU; as the discussion below seeks to illustrate, case law is important for understanding the range and potential of Irish transposition of the Directive. Ireland has chosen to cautiously participate in European cooperation measures in criminal justice to date, and along with the UK, negotiated a Protocol to the Lisbon Treaty providing for the possibility to opt out of measures across the Area of Freedom, Security and Justice, including criminal justice.[7] A major reason for this approach is the difference in criminal procedure across common law and civil law traditions (for example, concerning suspects' rights and the law of evidence) and a consequent concern that harmonisation measures or a broad acceptance of mutual recognition could encroach upon accepted principles of Irish criminal procedure.

II. Overview of the Evolution of the Role of Victims of Crime in Irish Law

Relative to the status of victim as prosecutor earlier in the evolution of criminal procedure in Ireland, in more recent decades the victim has had a more marginal role.[8] Similarly to the UK, in the nineteenth and twentieth centuries, the State through firstly the police and later the emergence of centralised public prosecutors normally became the prosecutor of crime in court; public prosecution became the norm and private prosecution the exception, to the point where now private prosecution can be considered a way of notifying the public prosecutor of a prosecutable case.[9] Routinely, victims appear as witnesses for the prosecution, often as the principal witness. In Ireland, as in other common law jurisdictions, the rule against hearsay applies particularly in criminal procedure and requires that witnesses in general (subject to some exceptions) must give evidence in person in court

[4] Extradition proceedings are an exception.

[5] See, eg, A FSH Alhajri, 'Separation of Powers in the Kuwaiti Criminal Justice System: A Case Study' (2018) 4(2) *European Journal of Interdisciplinary Studies* 59–79.

[6] Ireland, as with the UK, distinguishes between trials on indictment (before a jury, usually) and summary trials. Ireland instituted a Special Criminal Court to try offences that would otherwise be tried before a jury by instead a panel of three judges. This was done to respond to the challenges of the political violence of the Troubles in Northern Ireland. The jurisdiction of the Special Criminal Court was extended to cover certain other kinds of offences deemed unsuitable for ordinary jury trial.

[7] Protocol on the UK and Ireland.

[8] See generally S Leahy and E Spain, 'Exploring the Impact of the Victims' Directive on Service Provision for Victims of Crime in Ireland' (2017) 68(4) *Northern Ireland Legal Quarterly* 519–38.

[9] *Kelly & Anor v District Judge Ann Ryan* [2013] IEHC 321, para 20 (per Hogan J in the High Court).

and cannot do so through prior sworn testimony given in a police interview (such out-of-court statements are not admissible as evidence in a criminal trial).[10] Private prosecutions are now restricted by legislation in that trials on indictment are automatically taken over by the Office of the Director of Public Prosecutions (DPP),[11] who also has the authority to withdraw prosecutions by entering a *nolle prosequi* (although this may not prevent a subsequent prosecution).[12] Outside of this, victims have no particular status as a party to a criminal trial in Ireland, unlike in continental jurisdictions such as France or Sweden. Victims have also been traditionally excluded from influencing sentencing, although now they may give evidence of the effects of the crime on them as part of the sentencing process (which in Ireland is generally separate to the trial).[13] Regarding sentencing, Geoghegan J in the Supreme Court summarised their position as follows.

> Under the provision of s.5 of the Criminal Justice Act, 1993, a sentencing court is obliged to take into account any effect (whether long term or otherwise) of the offence on the victim. The section permits evidence to be given by or on behalf of the victim in this regard. From time to time victims in that situation express views as to sentence such as for instance 'he should be locked up for life'. It has never been the practice in this jurisdiction for the victims of an offence to be permitted to express views in that sense as to what a proper sentence might be. In the opinion of the court, s.5 makes no change in that regard. While a victim or a relative of a victim or a relative of an accused would not be entitled to express an opinion in court as to what was an appropriate sentence, they are always entitled to put forward an *ad misericordiam* plea [ie a plea in favour of mercy].[14]

The overall approach of the Irish courts is that while a forgiving attitude by a victim can be one factor in determining sentence, it can never be determinative because a crime is a wrong against society and not just against the victim.[15]

III. An Analysis of the Victims' Rights Directive and its Transposition in Irish Law

As noted in Recital 11, the Victims' Rights Directive lays down minimum rules and Member States may extend the rights set out in the Directive in order to provide a higher level of protection. The main transposition measure in Irish law is the Criminal Justice (Victims of Crime) Act 2017 (hereafter 'CJ(VC)A 2017'), but a range of other Irish statutes and case law are also important to understand the scope of Irish compliance to date. Given the general wording of some of the provisions of the Victims' Rights Directive, and reflecting the character of directives as a type of legal instrument in EU law, more or less discretion may be left to national authorities as to how to achieve its purposes or objectives. In Table 15.1, an

[10] See generally, Law Reform Commission, *Hearsay in Civil and Criminal Cases* (LRC CP 60 – 2010).

[11] Criminal Justice (Administration) Act 1924, s 9; Criminal Procedure Act 1967 (as amended), ss 4–4A. See *Kelly & Anor* (n 9) paras 10–22.

[12] Office of the DPP, *Guidelines for Prosecutors*, 5th edn (2019) para 4.32.

[13] Criminal Justice (Victims of Crime) Act 2017 (No 28 of 2017) ('CJ (VC)A 2017'), s 31. Previously under the Criminal Justice Act 1993, s 5, victim impact evidence could be given in certain sexual offence cases and cases involving violence to a person.

[14] *DPP v R O'D* [2000] 4 IR 361, at 363 (approved by O'Malley J in *DPP v Duffy* [2023] IESC 1 para 29).

[15] *The People (DPP) v WD* [2008] 1 IR 308, per Charleton J cited by O'Malley J in *Duffy* (n 14) para 28.

Table 15.1 A Summary of the Implementation of the Victims' Rights Directive into Irish Law

Victims' Rights Directive Article	Victims' Rights Directive Content	Corresponding Provisions in Irish Law	Extent of Implementation in Irish Law: Including Different or Additional or Further Content of Irish Law
Article 1	Objectives: 'The purpose of this Directive is to ensure that victims of crime receive appropriate information, support and protection and are able to participate in criminal proceedings' – Para 2 refers to the child's best interests.	– CJ(VC)A 2017 s 7(1)(g) regarding information on first contact for any particular measures, procedures or arrangements which are available to a victim who is a child – CJ(VC)A 2017 s 7(1)(g) provides for a presumption of protection for children, best interests assessment – CJ(VC)A 2017 s 18 provides for appropriate persons to accompany child to court.	Article 1 implemented in Irish law; a more specific provision on children than the VR Directive is contained in CJ(VC)A 2017 is s 2(3) (presumption of child if uncertain).
Article 2	Definitions: – Definition of 'victim', natural person who has suffered harm, extending to family members of deceased crime victims – Family includes 'intimate connection' – Art 2(c) defines child as below 18.	– Similar definition in s 1 of the CJ(VC)A 2017, family includes 'sufficiently close connection' – Art 2(2) of VR Directive reflected in CJ(VC)A 2017 s 3 on nomination of family members – CJ (VA)A 2017 defines child in same way (below 18 years) (s 2(1)).	Irish law had not previously included a general definition of victims of crime.
Article 3	Right to understand and be understood.	Reflected in CJ(VC)A 2017 s 7(1)(d).	– This is a long-standing principle of Irish constitutional law pre-dating the Directive (see below on Article 7) – Not expressed as a substantive right in CJ(VC)A2017, but reflected in various provisions procedurally, esp s 8(5) on translation and s 22(1) on simple and accessible language.

Article 4	Right to receive information from the first contact with a competent authority.	– Closely reflected in CJ(VC)A 2017 s 7 – The CJ(VC)A 2017 provides for: ~ special measures for children (s 7(1)(g))[1] ~ victim to specify how information to be provided (s 7(3)).	Article 4 is implemented in Irish law. The range of information included seems uncertain, eg to what extent does it apply to protection orders?[2] This point applies both to Irish implementing law and EU law.
Article 5	Rights of victim in making a complaint (making of complaint in writing, linguistic assistance and translation).	Closely reflected in CJ(VC)A 2017 ss 12–13.	In implementing Article 5, the C(VC)A 2017 creates a right for victims to receive a written acknowledgement of a complaint to the Gardaí, which was not previously set out in this way in legislation.[3]
Article 6	Right to receive information about their case.	Detailed provisions in CJ(VC)A 2017, ss 7–8.	– The CJ(VC)A 2017 provides for a legislative framework for the right of victims to information – Compared to the VR Directive, notably more broadly worded exceptions on providing information are set out in CJ(VC)A 2017 s 11 relating to interference with the investigation of an alleged offence, prejudice to ongoing or future criminal proceedings in respect of an alleged offence, endangerment of the personal safety of any person, or endangerment of the security of the State; however, these probably can be interpreted to fall within the scope of Art 6(6).[4]

(continued)

[1] *cf* Victims' Rights Directive Art 1(2).

[2] A Ryan, *The Adoption of EU Measures in Ireland for the Rights of Victim: Not Quite the Full Package* (Centre for Criminal Justice University of Limerick, n.d.).

[3] *cf* Garda Síochána Act 2005 s 7.

[4] The European Parliament Research Service (EPRS) gives Ireland as an example of detailed implementation: EPRS, *The Victims' Rights Directive 2012/29/EU European Implementation Assessment* (2017) ('EPRS (2017a)') 54. For further discussion, including of a lack of consistency in previous Garda practice on providing information, see S Leahy and E Spain, 'Exploring the Impact of the Victims' Directive on Service Provision for Victims of Crime in Ireland' (2017) 68(4) *Northern Ireland Legal Quarterly* 527, 521–27; Law Reform Commission, *Consultation Paper: Compensating Victims of Crime* (LRC CP 67 – 2022) paras 2.13–2.16.

Table 15.1 ***(Continued)***

Victims' Rights Directive Article	Victims' Rights Directive Content	Corresponding Provisions in Irish Law	Extent of Implementation in Irish Law: Including Different or Additional or Further Content of Irish Law
Article 7	Right to interpretation and translation.	– General provision in CJ(VC)A 2017 s 22; the police, the prosecutor or the courts shall make such arrangements as soon as practicable regarding interpretation and translation as are considered appropriate in the circumstances, or as directed by the court – CJ(VC)A 2017 s 24 reflects the requirement in the Victims' Rights Directive Art 7(7) for review of refusals to translate.	– Prior to the CJ(VC)A 2017, the right to an interpreter if necessary for an accused to understand criminal proceedings against him or her has long been recognised as an aspect of right to a fair trial now protected under the Constitution (Bunreacht na hÉireann) Art 38.1.[5]
Article 8	Right to access victim support services.	– Support services are referred to in CJ(VC)A 2017 s 7 on the right to information – Irish criminal justice agencies engage in victim support as a matter of administrative practice (Gardaí, Office of the Director of Public Prosecutions (DPP), Courts Service) – Non-governmental agencies play an important role also, chiefly Victim Support at court.	– CJ(VC)A 2017 mostly concerned with criminal procedure, rather than support services,[6] and Irish law does not have a corresponding general provision to Article 7.

[5] *State (Buchan) v Coyne* [1936] 70 ILTR 185, cited in J Hamilton, *Report: Fair Trial in Ireland*, CoCoSem (2008) 12 (Venice Commission, 2012) 6.

[6] Leahy and Spain (n 4) 527–29. The same authors note (ibid, 537), for example, that while s 7(9) of the CJ(VC)A 2017 provides that a member of the Garda Síochána or an officer of the Ombudsman Commission may arrange for the victim to be referred to a victim support service with their consent, the obligation is limited to these organisations and this is not reflective of Art 8 of the Victims' Rights Directive under which the obligation to facilitate referrals of victims to victim support services applies to both competent authorities and 'other relevant entities'.

Article 9	Support from victim support services, including, measures (eg interim accommodation for those in imminent risk) for particular victims.	– Victim support is referred to in CJ(VC)A 2017 s 7(1) on right to information – There is no dedicated or specific statutory right to housing or accommodation for crime victims as a category – Housing or accommodation are not referred to in the Victims' Charter – The Housing Acts 1966–2009 provide the legal basis for local authorities to make assessments of social housing, and this can be done to support victims of crime, although legislation does not express social housing as a right[7] – Various charities, which often receive government funding, provide housing for certain groups, eg victims of domestic violence[8] – The Gardaí have a Victims Liaison Office for coordinating and implementing policy on victims[9] – The Gardaí have recently established Garda Divisional Protective Support Units, to provide specialist investigators for victims of sexual crime, human trafficking and domestic abuse.	Ireland has not implemented Article 9 through legislation on housing or accommodation for victims of crime, making it more likely that this is not provided in a systematic way; for example, in September 2023, UN Special Rapporteurs called on the Irish Government to take urgent steps to ensure access to housing and assistance for victims of trafficking[10] – The current Programme for Government commits to implementing a plan for future refuge space.[11]

(continued)

[7] Department of Housing, Planning, Community & Local Government, *Policy and Procedural Guidance for Housing Authorities in Relation to Assisting Victims of Domestic Violence with Emergency and Long-Term Accommodation Needs* (2017) 4–9.
[8] A report from TUSLA – Child and Family Agency in 2022 found that there was an under-supply of accommodation for victims of domestic violence: *Review of the Provision of Accommodation for Victims of Domestic Violence* (February 2022) 31.
[9] See Garda Victim Liaison Office (GVLO), available at www.garda.ie/en/about-us/organised-serious-crime/garda-national-protective-services-bureau-gnpsb-/garda-victim-liaison-office-gvlo-/.
[10] United Nations Office of the High Commissioner, Press Release, 'UN Experts Urge Ireland to Strengthen Access to Housing and Assistance for Trafficking Victims (Special Rapporteurs Siobhán Mullally & Ashwini K.P.)' (11 September 2023).
[11] Department of Justice, *Supporting a Victim's Journey A Plan to Help Victims and Vulnerable Witnesses in Sexual Violence Cases* (October 2021) 6.

Table 15.1 ***(Continued)***

Victims' Rights Directive Article	Victims' Rights Directive Content	Corresponding Provisions in Irish Law	Extent of Implementation in Irish Law: Including Different or Additional or Further Content of Irish Law
Article 10	Right to be heard in criminal proceedings	– As a matter of routine, victims usually give evidence against an accused in open court – Victim impact evidence is provided for under CJ(VC)A 2017 s 7(1)(k) – CJ (VC)A 2017 s 19 provides for protection measures when a victim is giving evidence: exclusion of persons from court during evidence, judicial direction on questioning about private life, evidence by video link – Criminal Justice (Miscellaneous Provisions) Act s 55 provides for witness anonymity in certain circumstances, which could also apply to victims.	– Now implemented in Ireland[13] – The term 'criminal proceedings' used in Article 10 of the VR Directive would suggest procedure at trial, whereas CJ(VC)A 2017 s 10 regulates the taking of complaints/evidence by the Gardaí prior to a decision to go to trial.
Article 11	Right in the event of a decision not to prosecute – Mainly concerned with reviewing decisions not to prosecute – Art 11(3) seems to necessarily imply the giving of reasons for not prosecuting.	– The DPP in Ireland introduced a policy of giving reasons for non-prosecution for cases involving death in 2008, since extended to other categories of cases[12] – A procedure for reviews of decisions to not prosecute exists, as now mandated by CJ(VC)A 2017 s 10 – CJ(VC)A 2017 s 10(6) specifies that victims be notified of the outcome of reviews of decisions not to prosecute (although it does not actually state that reasons must be given).	– Prior to 2008, the DPP in Ireland had a strict policy of not giving reasons for not prosecuting, after which a policy was adopted of giving reasons in cases involving fatalities – An effect of the Victims' Rights Directive was that this policy was extended to all offences by administrative practice (it was not implemented through legislation).

[12] It was decided to slowly change the prior policy of not giving reasons in all cases, and cases involving deaths were chosen (it seems on grounds of their seriousness) in 2008 as the first category of cases where it was possible to give reasons without creating injustice: see Office of the DPP, *Report on the Prosecution Policy on the Giving of Reasons for Decisions* (2008) 25–28.

[13] See Department of Justice, *Review of Protections for Vulnerable Witnesses in the Invetsigation and Prosecution of Sexual Offences* ('O'Malley Report') (Department of Justice, 2020) 115.

Article 12	Right to safeguards in the context of restorative justice services.	Closely reflected in CJ(VC)A 2017 s 26, which established a framework of general rules for restorative justice.	Express legislative recognition of restorative justice is new in Ireland, an innovation resulting from implementation of the VR Directive.[16]
Article 13	Right to legal aid setting out that victims have the right to legal aid where they have the status of parties and that such rules shall be prescribed by law.	– Victims do not have the status of parties in Irish criminal procedure and are not generally entitled to legal aid – However, the Legal Aid Board provides legal advice to *potential victims* of human trafficking[14] and the complainants in certain sexual assault[15] cases	– Inapplicable to Ireland as victims do not have the status of parties in Irish law – The Legal Aid Board provides legal advice and aid to complainants in sexual offence cases,[17] under the Civil Legal Aid Act 1995 s 28(5A) (as amended)[18] and in certain other cases where a victim or complainant is entitled to legal representation for specifc purposes.[19]

(continued)

[14] The US State Department observed 'Services available from the government's Legal Aid Board were inadequate for victims' needs, as the board only provided information to potential victims referred by police but did not provide legal assistance or support to victims during investigations or trials. Two government-funded NGOs provided legal representation for labor trafficking victims in 2021': Office to Combat & Monitor Trafficking in Persons, *2022 Trafficking in Persons Report: Ireland*, available at www.state.gov/reports/2022-trafficking-in-persons-report/ireland/. The Legal Aid Board is under a statutory duty to provide legal advice to a person who is an alleged victim of a trafficking offence: s 26(3B) of the Civil Legal Aid Act 1995, as amended. The O'Malley Report (n 12) 137, recommended that further legislative provision be made for legal aid, including that s 26(3A) of the Civil Legal Aid Act 1995 should be amended so that the Legal Aid Board may provide free legal advice to victims of sexual offences (and not just in cases where a prosecution is being taken). The Department of Justice has committed to scope out and determine the extent of any legislative amendments required so that the Legal Aid Board can provide free legal advice to victims of sexual offences, not just in cases where a prosecution is being taken, but also regarding a wider range of sexual offences and allow for legal advice to be granted to a parent, guardian or other responsible adult in certain cases: Department of Justice, *Supporting a Victim's Journey* (n 11) 7.

[15] Civil Legal Aid Act 1995, s 26.

[16] However, without using the term restorative justice, legislation previously provided for measures that can be considered to fall within restorative justice; for example, the Children Act 2001 in ss 26–29 provides for mediation or dialogue between child offenders, the child's family, and victims, while s 78 provides for family conferences. Payments from offenders to victims under s 6 of the Criminal Justice Act 1993 might also be considered restorative measures. See generally, eg, I Marder and L Forde, 'Challenges in the Future of Restorative Youth Justice in Ireland: Minimising Intervention, Maximising Participation' (2023) 23(2) *Youth Justice* 201–25, esp 204–206.

[17] Legal Aid Board, 'Advice for Complainants in Rape & Certain Sexual Assault Cases', available at www.legalaidboard.ie/en/our-services/legal-aid-services/common-legal-problems/rape-and-sexual-assault/.

[18] For background on legal aid in criminal cases, see M Keenan, D Healy, G McLoughlin-Burke and K Keenan, *A Review of the Processing of Sexual Offences in Ireland: Stakeholder Experiences* (University College Dublin, 2023) 162–163.

[19] Civil Legal Aid Act 1995 as amended, s 28(5B-D).

Table 15.1 ***(Continued)***

Victims' Rights Directive Article	**Victims' Rights Directive Content**	**Corresponding Provisions in Irish Law**	**Extent of Implementation in Irish Law: Including Different or Additional or Further Content of Irish Law**
		– Some special cases exist, principally, regarding rape trials: victims have a right to separate legal representation under the Criminal Law (Rape) Act 1981 ss 3–4 during the hearing of an application to question a victim about other sexual experience, but a legal representative in this situation does not represent the victim during the cross-examination itself.[20]	
Article 14	Right to reimbursement of expenses.	Courts may and generally do order the payment of witnesses' expenses.[21]	– Article 14 has not been implemented expressly as Irish law does not recognise a *right* to expenses; in Irish law, victims are not generally treated differently to other witnesses, reflecting that they do not have the status of parties, but as with other witnesses will generally get expenses

[20] O'Malley Report (n 12) para 6.15; Office of the DPP, 'Victims of Crime', available at www.dppireland.ie/criminal-justice-system/victims-of-crime/. The O'Malley Report recommended that this representation be extended to the cross-examination of the victim about his or her sexual history, and the Department of Justice has committed to implementing this proposal: *Supporting a Victim's Journey* (n 11) 41.

[21] See, eg, District Court Rules, Order 36 rule 1 substituted by SI 496 of 2020, effective 10th November 2020.

			– Research indicates that in Ireland 'in case of financial hardship, victims might be entitled to receive an advance payment to cover the cost of their participation in the criminal proceedings, encouraging their active participation and mitigating the financial losses of victims who are already in a dire situation.'[23]
Article 15	Right to the return of property	– Proceeds of Crime Act 1996–2016 s 3(3) provides for an owner of property to apply to a court for the return of property when it has been subject to an interlocutory order not to be disposed of due to being the proceeds of crime – Garda Síochána Act 2005 s 82(2)(a)(i) provides that it is neglect of duty for a member of the Gardaí to properly account for any money or property received in his or her capacity as a member – The Gardaí (po without good and sufficient cause to fail or neglect lice) operate a scheme registering stolen property so that its owners can reclaim it.[22]	Ireland has not introduced new provisions to implement Art 15, but the substance of the Article is reflected in Irish law and practice.
Article 16	Right to decision on compensation from the offender in the course of criminal proceedings	– Criminal Justice Act 1993 s 6 permits a court of trial to order a convicted person to pay compensation to the victim.	– The European Parliament Research Service (EPRS) in its evaluation report on the implementation of the Victims' Rights Directive gives Ireland as an example of non-transposition of Art 16[24] – The issue of compensation to offenders is discussed in more detail below in section IV.

(continued)

[22] See Garda Síochána, 'Unclaimed Property', available at www.garda.ie/en/about-us/online-services/unclaimed-property/.

[23] VOCIARE, *Synthesis Report: Assessing the EU Victims' Rights Directive* (2019) 114.

[24] EPRS (2017a) (n 4) 58.

Table 15.1 ***(Continued)***

Victims' Rights Directive Article	Victims' Rights Directive Content	Corresponding Provisions in Irish Law	Extent of Implementation in Irish Law: Including Different or Additional or Further Content of Irish Law
Article 17	Rights of victims resident in another Member State to assistance to minimise the difficulties faced where the victim is a resident of a Member State other than that where the criminal offence was committed.	– CJ(VC)A 2017 s 7(1)(f) provides for victims to receive information on first contact on any particular measures, procedures or arrangements which are available to victims who are resident in a Member State other than where the alleged offence occurred – CJ(VC)A 2017 s 13 provides that where a victim from another Member State makes a complaint about an offence that has occurred in another Member State, unless the (Irish) State proposes to exercise jurisdiction, the Gardaí will arrange for the details of the complaint to be transmitted as soon as practicable to the competent authority of the territorial Member State – CJ(VC)A 2017 s 14(1)(a) provides for residents of other Member States to be able to make complaints – The Criminal Justice (Mutual Assistance) Act 2008 implements in Ireland the Convention on Mutual Assistance in Criminal Matters between the Member States of the European Union of 29 May 2000 regarding video and telephone evidence for court hearings (as referred to in VR Directive Art 17(1)(b)).	– Irish law gives effect to the content of Art 17 (through several different provisions of Irish law).

Article 18	Right to protection (against secondary and repeat victimisation).	– CJ(VC)A 2017 ss 15–16 provides for measures relating to the assessment of victims (either by Gardaí or the Ombudsman Commission) – CJ(VC)A 2017 s 17 sets out the protection measures that may be taken regarding interviews – CJ(VC)A 2017 s 21 relates to directions a court considers just and proper regarding any evidence to apply in cases where, inter alia, 'there is a need to protect a victim of the offence from secondary and repeat victimisation, intimidation or retaliation'[25] – CJ(VC)A 2017 s 26 provides for general rules for restorative justice – See above concerning Art 9, 12.	– One of the main and novel effects in Ireland of the VR Directive was to prompt explicit measures on secondary and repeat victimisation.[26]
Article 19	Right to avoid contact between victim and offender.	– CJ (VC)A 2017 ss 16–17 on application of protection measures and special measures during investigations, mainly concerning interviews – Under Criminal Evidence Act 1992, ss 13 and 16 respectively, for victims under 18, evidence can be given by live television link or by video-link – CJ(MP)A 2023 s 55 provides for anonymity of witnesses.	Indirectly implemented in Irish law.

(continued)

[25] See comment in O'Malley Report (n 12) 67. See also European Parliament, *The Victims' Rights Directive 2012/29/EU: European Implementation Assessment* (European Parliamentary Research Service PE611, 2017) 61.

[26] See, eg, comment in O'Malley Report (n 12) 5: 'Above all, we have been conscious of the need for measures to prevent repeat victimisation.'

Table 15.1 ***(Continued)***

Victims' Rights Directive Article	Victims' Rights Directive Content	Corresponding Provisions in Irish Law	Extent of Implementation in Irish Law: Including Different or Additional or Further Content of Irish Law
Article 20	Right to protection of victims during criminal investigations.	– CJ(VC)A 2017 s 14 provides for interviewing of victims, while CJ (VC) A 2017 s 15 provides for assessment of victims and protection measures for them – CJ(VC)A 2017 s 17 defines special measures that may be taken, while s 2 provides a non-exhaustive list of protection measures – CJ(VC)A 2017 s 30 amends the Criminal Evidence Act 1992 to provide for the screening of witnesses when they appear in court to give evidence.	– Overall implementation of Art 20 in Irish law is discussed further below in section V – The O'Malley Report gives the example of Irish law on evidence being given by intermediaries as an example of Irish criminal procedure[27] being 'very much to the fore'[28] – The definition of protection measures in CJ(VC)A 2017 s 2 is different to the Directive, eg in contrast to the Directive s 20(b), the CJ(VC)A 2017 does not require that the number of interviews of victims is kept to a minimum, though CJ(VA)A 2017 s 14(1)(c) may have a similar effect.
Article 21	Right to protection of privacy.	– CJ(VC)A 2017 s 20 provides that a court has a general power to exclude the public, if there is a need to protect a victim from secondary and repeat victimisation, intimidation or retaliation, and that it would not be contrary to the interests of justice to do so	Implemented in Irish law through specific provisions, mainly in CJ(VC)A 2017. The VR Directive has resulted in more procedural protection of the right to privacy in Irish law, which previously regulated particular types of cases only.[29]

[27] Criminal Evidence Act 1992 s 14, as amended.
[28] O'Malley Report (n 12) 99.
[29] Criminal Law (Rape) Act 1981 s 6 (as amended); Children Act 2001 s 252; Criminal Law (Human Trafficking) Act 2008 s 11.

		– CJ(VC)A 2017 s 21 provides for the restriction of questions in cross-examination at trial – CJ(MP)A 2023 s 55 provides for witness anonymity generally, which appears worded broadly enough so as to apply also to media reporting (eg s 55(1)).	
Article 22	Individual assessment of victims to identify specific protection needs.	CJ(VC)A 2017 s 15(2) closely reflects the wording of Art 22.	Clearly implemented in Irish law now in CJ(VC)A 2017 s 15, a legislative basis for individualised assessment is one of the main impacts of the VR Directive in Irish law.
Article 23	Right to protection of victims with specific protection needs during criminal proceedings.	CJ(VC)A 2017, Part 3, ss 12–26, sets out a wide range of protection measures during investigations and proceedings.	Overall, the Irish provisions closely reflect the elements of Art 23, especially CJ(VC)A 2017 ss 18–20. VR Directive Art 23(a)–(b) on avoiding visual contact between victims and offenders and witness evidence-giving outside of the courtroom are not mirrored in the CJ(VC)A 2017, but witnesses are permitted to give evidence outside of court (and outside the State) under Criminal Evidence Act 2013 s 13, and anonymity of witnesses under CJ(MP)A 2023 s 55 is an alternative procedure.
Article 24	Protection of child victims.	– CJ(VC)A 2017 s 18 provides for the accompaniment of children – Children are presumed to have protection needs under CJ(VC)A 2017 s 15(7) – Criminal Justice (Withholding of Information on Offences against Children and Vulnerable Persons) Act 2012 s 2 makes it an offence to withhold information from the Gardaí of one of a range of listed serious offences.	– The EPRS gives Ireland as an example of this protection being specified without reference to sub-articles of the Directive[30] – The permissibility of audio-visual live or recorded testimony from child victims had already been possible under Irish law (Criminal Evidence Act 1992 ss 13 and 16 respectively and Criminal Evidence Act 1993 s 5A).

(continued)

[30] EPRS (2017a) (n 4) 52

Table 15.1 ***(Continued)***

Victims' Rights Directive Article	**Victims' Rights Directive Content**	**Corresponding Provisions in Irish Law**	**Extent of Implementation in Irish Law: Including Different or Additional or Further Content of Irish Law**
Article 25	Training of practitioners.	– Training of officials is not in general subject to legislation specific to the criminal justice area[31] – CJ(VC)A 2017 s 17(2) provides that special protection measures for victims be carried out by those trained for that purpose – Victim Support at Court provides training for its volunteers[32] – The Gardaí, DPP[33] and Courts Service are responsible for training their own officials.	Provided for mostly by administrative practice.[35]
Article 26	Cooperation and coordination of services.	Since 2015, the heads of the main criminal justice agencies work together on a Criminal Justice Strategic Committee 'to strengthen and improve how we work together, with a particular focus in this first strategy on improving the experience of those who come into contact with the criminal justice system and how we communicate about the work we do'.[34]	One of the five pillars of the 2022–2024 Strategy of the Criminal Justice Strategic Committee is to improve user experience, and this includes embedding a victim-centred approach across the system.[36]

[31] Judicial Council Act 2019 s 7 provides that one of the functions of the Council, whose role extends to all levels of judges, is to promote and maintain the continuing education of judges.

[32] See V-SAC – Victim Support at Court, available at www.vsac.ie.

[33] See, eg, Office of the DPP, *Annual Report* (2021) 52.

[34] Criminal Justice Strategic Committee, *Criminal Justice Sectoral Strategy 2022–2024* 3.

[35] For background and the deliberate omission of training from the CJ(VC)A 2017, see M McDonald, *The Victims Directive and the Criminal Justice (Victims of Crime) Act 2017* (Irish Council for Civil Liberties, 2018) 37–39, noting a possible separation of powers issue with the legislature regulating judicial training.

[36] ibid 18.

overall summary is given of the implementation in Irish law of each of the Articles of the Directive. In the space available, it has not been possible to do this individually for all of the sub-divisions of each Article, but the overall extent to which a provision of the Directive has already been reflected in Irish law or has been implemented by the CJ(VC)A 2017 is indicated, with reference to the corresponding Irish legislation or other source of law. The Table covers all of the provisions of the Directive from Articles 1–26; it has not been possible to do this for every sub-provision of each Article, rather a broad outline is given.

Perhaps the main effect of the Victims' Rights Directive was to recognise victims as being bearers of rights.[16] The Directive established a different normative standpoint on criminal procedure in the context of the relative side-lining of victims in the development of adversarial process, especially through the lack of status of victims as parties to a trial, and the increasing role of the State through more powerful public prosecution. As reflected in Table 15.1, a good deal of the content of the Directive was at least to some extent already found in either Irish law or practice, at least in the last two–three decades, even if not systematically expressed in legislation as the rights of victims.

In its evaluation of the effects of the Victims' Rights Directive, the European Parliament Research Service (EPRS) observed concerning France that 'one of the directive's major impacts was the creation of a standardised individual assessment to determine the special needs of victims throughout the criminal procedure – this can be considered good practice'.[17] This can also be said of Ireland, which such individualisation is now required under s 15 of the CJ(VC)A 2017.[18] Other significant effects in Ireland concern in particular (i) the provision of information[19] and (ii) the impetus it gives to an awareness and targeting of secondary and repeat victimisation. One possible shortcoming of the implementation of the Directive in Ireland is that it may not fully address the information needs of victims throughout the entire criminal process, given that s 7 of the CJ(VC)A 2017 focuses on the initial making of a complaint.[20]

The Commission's 2023 Proposal to amend the Victim's Rights Directive[21] is evolutionary. It strengthens the existing mechanisms, rather than adding new ones. Perhaps the most significant change it would introduce is that the State should pay directly to the victim adjudicated compensation without undue delay and that the State would then be entitled to recover the payment from the offender.[22] Article 16 of the Directive would be amended to provide 'Member States shall ensure that, in the course of the criminal proceedings, victims are entitled to obtain a decision on compensation by the offender, within a reasonable time'. The general issue of compensation is considered in more detail in the next section.[23] Irish practice currently provides for an administrative

[16] Leahy and Spain (n 8) 520; Department of Justice, *Review of Protections for Vulnerable Witnesses in the Invetsigation and Prosecution of Sexual Offences* ('O'Malley Report') (Department of Justice, 2020) 23.

[17] EPRS, *European Protection Order Directive 2011/99/EU European Implementation Assessment* (2017) 83.

[18] However, research has identified that a single or standardised form has not always been used for this purpose in Ireland: See VOCIARE, *Synthesis Report: Assessing the EU Victims' Rights Directive* (2019) 155.

[19] O'Malley Report (n 16) 87.

[20] ibid.

[21] Proposal for a Directive of the European Parliament and of the Council amending Directive 2012/29/EU establishing minimum standards on the rights, support and protection of victims of crime, and replacing Council Framework Decision 2001/220/JHA, COM/2023/424 final.

[22] ibid, Art 10b amending Art 16 of the Victims' Rights Directive (n 1).

[23] For discussion regarding compensation and the Commission's 2023 Proposal, see the contribution in this volume by L O'Driscoll, 'Being 'Fair and Appropriate' to Victims of Violent Crime: Evaluating the Provision of State Compensation in the European Union' in chapter 5.

scheme of compensation from the State in some more serious criminal cases (and for an under-used power of a criminal court to order compensation *from the offender*), whereas the Commission Proposal would require compensation from the State to apply to all offences and to be decided during the criminal trial and not in a separate civil procedure. Another important development in the Commission Proposal is greater provision for vulnerable categories of victim,[24] including children[25] and victims of sexual violence and gender-based violence,[26] and persons with disabilities.[27] Current Irish law already reflects to a greater or lesser extent some of the proposed content of a amended Victims' Rights Directive, for example, concerning the provision of information to children,[28] aspects of crime reporting relating to children,[29] needs assessment for children,[30] and accommodation of the needs of persons with disabilities.[31]

IV. Compensation for Victims in Irish Law

A measure of redress can be provided for all types of crime through the payment of compensation. Ireland was in comparative terms a relatively early provider of compensation of victims of crime, although it did so not on the basis of a right established in legislation, but through a discretionary administrative scheme initiated in 1974.[32] As a result of this pre-existing Irish scheme, Irish practice was not significantly impacted by the first EU measures on compensation for crime victims, particularly as EU legislation was initially understood to only apply to cross-border situations. As more recently interpreted by the Court of Justice, EU law now requires the establishment of national compensation schemes for victims of intentional violent crime. This is done principally through Article 12(2) of Directive 2004/80 regarding compensation by the State, rather than by the offender.[33] The Court of Justice clarified in *Presidenza del Consiglio dei Ministri v BV*, in contrast to previous case law, that this provision *does apply* to purely internal situations and does not require cross-border elements (unlike the earlier Chapter 1 of that Directive on compensation from the State of residence to victims of intentional violence). Its interpretation in *BV* was based not only on the wording of that provision, but also its context and the objectives of the legislation of which it forms part.[34] However, this instrument applies to victims of intentional violent crime only.

[24] Commission Proposal (n 21) Art 1 inserting, *inter alia*, Article 9a).
[25] ibid, Art 1 inserting Arts 9a, 27a.
[26] ibid, Art 1 amending Art 9.
[27] ibid, Art 1 inserting Art 26c.
[28] CJ(VC)A 2017 (n 13) s 7.
[29] See the Criminal Justice (Withholding of Information on Offences against Children and Vulnerable Persons) Act 2012.
[30] CJ(VC)A 2017 (n 13) s 7(1)(g).
[31] ibid ss 15(2), 22(1).
[32] For more background and discussion, see O'Driscoll (n 23), including discussion of the recent High Court judgment in *Bowes & Brophy v Criminal Injuries Compensation Tribunal* [2022] IEHC 703 (particularly concerning time limits).
[33] Council Directive 2004/80/EC of 29 April 2004 relating to compensation to crime victims [2004] OJ L261/15.
[34] Case C-129/19 *Presidenza del Consiglio dei Ministri v BV* ECLI:EU:C:2020:566, paras 38–52. See also earlier Case C-601/14 *Commission and Council v Italian Republic* ECLI:EU:C:2016:759, judgment of 11th October 2016, para 49.

Irish practice on compensation has two main elements: (i) a non-statutory, administrative scheme to grant State compensation to victims of any crime (the CICS scheme, discussed in the next section, (ii) legislative provision for a criminal court of trial to make an order of compensation by a convicted person to a victim in s 6 of the Criminal Justice Act 1993. Article 12(2) of the Directive refers to 'national rules', without specifying the legal form these must take, ie the wording of Article 12(2) does not seem to require a statutory scheme.

A. The Criminal Injuries Compensation Scheme (CICS)

The rules of the CICS are set out on the Government portal, and it is administered through the Department of Justice. The CICS grants compensation under the terms of the Civil Liabilities Acts, ie the legal test for the payment of compensation is based on the existence of liability under the Civil Liabilities Acts. As a public administrative scheme, it is subject to judicial review. The Scheme covers compensation only for personal injuries received as a result of being a victim of a violent crime and does not provide for compensation in respect of stolen or damaged property. It mainly covers costs and loss of income.

1. Ireland was one of the first jurisdictions to establish such a scheme.[35] Following a ruling of the Court of Appeal in 2020,[36] a number of changes were made to the Scheme, although its basic framework remains the same.[37] The Scheme remains non-legislative. These changes are mainly as follows:The phrase '*ex gratia*' was removed as a description of the basis on which the State gave compensation,[38] but still without expressing that there is a right to compensation in that the Terms and Conditions state:

   > The Criminal Injuries Compensation Tribunal established under Paragraph 16 of the Scheme *may* pay compensation in accordance with this Scheme in respect of personal injury where the injury is directly attributable to a crime of violence, or, as provided for in Paragraph 4, to circumstances arising from the action of the victim in assisting or attempting to assist the prevention of crime or the saving of human life.

   A feature of the Irish scheme is that it does not require there first be a conviction, only that the offence have been subject to criminal proceedings or have been reported to the Gardaí as soon as possible but, except in circumstances determined by the Tribunal to justify exceptional treatment, not later than three months from its occurrence.[39] It is also meant to be user-friendly and not require legal

[35] Law Reform Commission, *Consultation Paper: Compensating Victims of Crime* (LRC CP 67 – 2022) para 1.31 et seq.

[36] *Doyle & Kelly v Criminal Injuries Tribunal, Minister for Justice & Equality, Ireland and the Attorney General* [2020] IECA 342.

[37] At the time of writing, the most recently published version of the Scheme dates from January 2024. The terms and conditions for the award of compensation are set out on the Department of Justice website: gov – Terms and conditions of the Criminal Injuries Compensation Scheme, available at www.gov.ie.

[38] Which O'Malley J referred to as noteworthy in *Duffy* (n 14) para 69.

[39] Terms and Conditions, paras 20, 22. In any case, the claim must be no later than two years from when the crime occurred: See also Department of Justice, 'gov – Criminal Injuries Compensation Scheme: Your questions answered', available at www.gov.ie/en/service/30dc8-criminal-injuries-compensation-scheme/.

representation.[40] It thus does not seem open to the criticisms made in the Milquet Report of some national compensation schemes in the EU involving procedural obstacles, although the same report also points out that the requirement in several Member States for offences to be first reported for compensation to be awarded excludes some of the most vulnerable victims such as children, undocumented migrants, homeless, and trafficked victims who are arguably the most in need of emergency compensation.[41]

2. Decisions started to be published online more systematically,[42] and this appears to have resulted from the finding in the Court of Appeal judgment in *Doyle v Kelly* that the previous practice by which decisions were sometimes published in annual reports that were not readily available online or publicly was not consistent with constitutional justice requiring consistency or non-arbitrariness.[43] This judgment identified both Irish constitutional law and EU law as the legal basis for requiring adequate information on prior decisions to be made available to contribute to ensuring consistency. Regarding EU law, Ní Raifeartaigh J in the Court of Appeal observed:

   > One of the effects of the [*BV*] decision must be that while the Irish Scheme was previously conceptualised in domestic legal terms as a mere non-statutory *ex gratia* scheme … it must now be seen as the means by which the State gives effect to its obligations under the Directive both as regards cross-border and purely domestic scenarios.[44]

   This suggests an element of obligation now applies to the granting of compensation. From the perspective of Irish constitutional law, the judgment observed:

   > It seems to me that, speaking at the most general level, some types of decision (or aspects of a decision) can truly be said to be responsive only to the particular personal circumstances of the individual affected by the decision, while other types of decision (or aspects of a decision) are ones which require some measure of consistency of approach. One way of testing which category a particular decision or aspect of decision falls into is perhaps to ask whether it would be unfair to treat equally-situated cases differently. … it would be unfair for two decision-makers to treat two individuals from the same country of origin differently (all other features of the two cases being equal) based on different views of the decision-makers as to the available facts about that country.[45]

It may be worth observing here that the reference to country of origin, although not in issue on the facts of the *Doyle v Kelly* case and which can thus be considered *obiter* (it is given as an example of consistency), can be differentiated from the specific provisions of the CICS and from the context of EU law given that the CICS only requires the crime to have occurred within the State,[46] rather than that the victim be of any particular nationality, and that EU law requires non-discrimination on grounds of nationality.

[40] ibid. In particular, see *Explanatory Notes (Non-Fatal Cases)*.

[41] European Commission, *Report of the Special Adviser, J. Milquet on Strengthening Victims' Rights: From Compensation to Reparation* (March 2019) 25.

[42] See 'Decisions by the Criminal Injuries Compensation Tribunal', available at www.gov.ie/en/collection/ae2c6-decisions-by-the-criminal-injuries-compensation-tribunal/.

[43] *Doyle & Kelly* (n 36) at para 162.

[44] ibid at para 81.

[45] ibid at para 157.

[46] See terms and conditions of the Criminal Injuries Compensation Scheme, paras 2–4, available at www.gov.ie/en/campaigns/criminal-injuries/?referrer=http://www.gov.ie/en/organisation/90ab1-criminal-injuries-compensation-scheme/.

The wording of the Terms and Conditions of the 2021 CICS states:

1. The Criminal Injuries Compensation Tribunal established under Paragraph 16 of the Scheme may pay compensation in accordance with this Scheme in respect of personal injury where the injury is directly attributable to a crime of violence, or, as provided for in Paragraph 4, to circumstances arising from the action of the victim in assisting or attempting to assist the prevention of crime or the saving of human life. …
2. The Tribunal will be entirely responsible for deciding in any particular case whether compensation is payable under the Scheme, and, if so, the amount. There will be no appeal against or review of a final decision of the Tribunal.[47]

As well as limiting the scheme to particular crimes, those in which injury results directly from violence, it also avoids using the language of entitlement, instead suggesting that decisions to grant compensation are essentially discretionary ('the Scheme may pay').[48] However, this observation needs to be qualified by reference to the recognition in *Doyle & Kelly*, quoted above, of the need for consistency in the judgments of the Criminal Injuries Compensation Tribunal. However, it may be wondered whether even with the requirement of consistency identified in *Doyle & Kelly*, the requirement in Article 12(2) of the Directive that national rules '*guarantee* fair and appropriate compensation' (emphasis added) to victims is fully reflected at least in the current wording of the non-statutory CICS; the language of Article 12(2) is clearly more mandatory than that of the CICS.

B. Compensation from the Offender under s 6 of the Criminal Justice Act 1993

The second possibility for victims of crime to receive compensation in Ireland is under s 6 of the Criminal Justice Act 1993. This provision is the closest in Irish law and practice[49] to Article 16 of the Victims' Rights Directive, which provides that Member States shall ensure that, in the course of criminal proceedings, victims are entitled to obtain a decision on compensation by the offender, within a reasonable time, except where national law provides for such a decision to be made in other legal proceedings.[50] The scope of Article 16 of the VR Directive seems somewhat open or uncertain on a number of points. First, it only refers to a 'decision' on compensation by the offender, without establishing a right as such;[51] literally interpreted, it might be thought to

[47] ibid, paras 1–2.

[48] One of the unsuccessful grounds of claim in *Doyle & Kelly* related to the lack of compensation for non-material losses, which the Court of Appeal indicated may need further clarification from the Court of Justice. *Doyle & Kelly* (n 36) para 129. See further the discussion in O'Driscoll (n 23) citing MW Murphy, 'The Right under EU Law to Compensation for Injuries Criminally Inflicted: the Implications of BV for Irish Law' (2021) 23(1) *Irish Journal of European Law* 219.

[49] Another avenue for victims of crime would be to sue for a remedy in tort law, eg some crimes have equivalent torts, which could entitle a person to damage, such as the tort of battery.

[50] Victims' Rights Directive (n 1) Art 16(1).

[51] One view is that the Victims' Rights Directive, ibid, Art 16 confers a right to information on the victim concerning the outcome of her claim for compensation rather than a right to compensation *per se*: See A Weyembergh and E Sellier, *Criminal Procedures and Cross-Border Cooperation in the EU Area of Criminal Justice. Together but Apart?* (de l'Université de Bruxelles, 2020) 401.

encompass national procedures that provide for a decision on compensation, including a refusal, so long as such a decision is done at a certain point in the proceedings. Second, the scope of the excepting clause at the end of Article 16(1) might be debated. It is stated that the obligation to enable victims to obtain a decision from offenders does not apply where national law provides for 'such a decision' to be made in other legal proceedings. It might be debated what 'such a decision' refers to, eg does the exception still require compensation to be made by the offender, or can 'such a decision' be broadly interpreted to include any decision on compensation, whether or not it is the offender who is paying (eg if the State were to pay). If the latter broader, while admittedly less likely interpretation (since 'such a decision' seems more plausibly to be a reference to 'a decision on compensation by the offender' and not just to any decision on compensation), were tenable, then a compensation scheme such as the CICS operated in Ireland might be thought to satisfy Article 16 at least as regards those cases to which the CICS applies. However, if Article 16 is interpreted as requiring national law to provide a legal basis for offenders to be ordered by the authority of the court of trial to pay compensation (though Article 16 does not set out what criteria are to apply), which appears to be how it is generally understood, then the non-statutory CICS in Ireland, whereby the Government pays compensation in certain cases only, by itself does not discharge the obligation to implement Article 16 of the Directive.

Section 6(1) of the Irish Criminal Justice 1993 Act provides that on conviction of any person of an offence, the court, instead of or in addition to dealing with him in any other way, may, unless it sees reason to the contrary, make an order, called a 'compensation order', requiring him to pay compensation in respect of any personal injury or loss resulting from that offence (or any other offence that is taken into consideration by the court in determining sentence) to any person who has suffered such injury or loss. The Irish Law Reform Commission observed:

> [7.3] Unlike in many American States where 'restitution' orders from offender to victim are mandatory, there is no such uniformity in the approach to compensation in the Irish sentencing system. Equally, there is no interaction between the Criminal Injuries Compensation Tribunal and the criminal court in which a related criminal prosecution takes place[52] (references omitted).

A central feature of s 6 of the 1993 Act is its discretionary nature; courts 'may' order the payment of compensation by the offender. This is qualified by the phrase 'unless it sees reason to the contrary', which suggests a general presumption in favour of the requiring of compensation orders, but as the above quote indicates, there is no particular consistency around this in the approach of the Irish courts; actual practice is that s 6 is not often or is only rarely applied by courts in Ireland.

Charleton J, concurring in the Supreme Court in *Duffy*, indicates both the limited impact that an offer of compensation should have on sentencing and the limited use of s 6 in judicial practice:

> Money may be a context but it can never be a determinative factor. It is one to be sceptically assessed and the overall duty to publicly do justice remains the core imperative. As to s 6

[52] Law Reform Commission (LRC CP 67 – 2022) 193–94.

> of the 1993 Act, none of the judges on the bench at this hearing or the practitioners could remember it being used in a case.[53]

In 1994, Carroll J in the High Court had rejected an argument that there was in Irish law any constitutional entitlement or right of a victim to compensation for criminal injury, holding that is was a matter of policy for the executive or Oireachtas [Parliament] to determine,[54] a view affirmed by Charleton J in *Duffy*.[55]

Interestingly, the Supreme Court in *Duffy* did not advert to the Victims' Directive as requiring any particular approach to interpreting Irish legislation, eg by invoking the Directive in favour of a broad reading of the CJ(VC)A 2017 through an application of the doctrine of indirect effect. A standard expression of the doctrine of indirect effect is the statement in *Pfeiffer v Deutsches Rotes Kreuz* that the principle requires the national court to do whatever lies within its jurisdiction, having regard to the whole body of rules of national law, to ensure that a directive is fully effective.[56] This formulation indicates a relatively wide-ranging and pro-active duty to maximise the effectiveness of a directive through sympathetic interpretation of national law, save that the CJEU has emphasised this duty does not require or warrant *contra legem* interpretation of national law.[57] Article 16 of the VR Directive, for example, could justify the Irish courts treating compensation orders under s 6 of the 1993 Act as routinely to be made or at least considered,[58] which the wording of the section itself suggests in any case.[59] Neither in judicial practice nor in legislation, nor formal administrative measures, therefore, does it appear that Ireland has taken particular steps to implement Article 16(2) of the VR Directive going beyond practice prior to the coming into effect of the Directive.

Ireland has not neglected the provision of compensation to victims of crime. However, it has not established a right to compensation, even though practice is coming closer to *de facto* recognising this at least regarding offences against the person. In so far as the EU Victims' Rights Directive requires Member States to treat compensation as a right, there is still scope for better Irish implementation. An obvious interim step would be a greater judicial resort to s 6 of the Criminal Justice Act 1993.

V. Available Protection Measures

Directive 2011/99/EU on the European Protection Order (EPO) in criminal matters[60] allows for the extension of the effects of a national protection order in one Member

[53] *Duffy* (n 14) para 21. Charleton J was a leading criminal law practitioner and academic before being appointed to the judiciary. Under s 6, the Court may order compensation whether or not the convicted person offers it, and this is procedurally distinct from situations where the convicted person offers to pay compensation: J O'Malley in *Duffy* (n 14) para 44.

[54] *AD v Ireland* [1994] IR 369.

[55] ibid para 22.

[56] Case 397/01 *Pfeiffer v Deutsches Rotes Kreuz* [2004] ECR I-8835.

[57] Case 105/03 *Criminal proceedings against Maria Pupino* [2005] ECR I-5285, para 47.

[58] In *The People (DPP) v Lyons* [2014] IECCA 27, Murray J noted that one reason for the infrequent use made of s 6 could be that many criminal accused were of limited means, see para 63.

[59] CJ(VC)A 2017 s 7(1) only refers to compensation in the context of providing information to victims about the CICS and s 6 of the 1993 Act.

[60] Directive 2011/99/EU of the European Parliament and of the Council of 13 December 2011 on the European protection order [2011] OJ L338/2.

State to another Member State by way of the principle of mutual recognition. Ireland has not opted into this Directive, as it is permitted to do under the Protocol to the Lisbon Treaty on the UK and Ireland. Ireland has a range of provisions for protective measures in its legislation as well as relevant common law principles. In general, these measures, reflecting the criminal justice context and that they may at least in some cases be considered part of the punishment of crime, are at the discretion of the sentencing court following conviction and are not accessible by application to court of the victim.

This Directive sets out rules allowing a judicial or equivalent authority in a Member State, in which a protection measure has been adopted with a view to protecting a person against a criminal act by another person which may endanger his life, physical or psychological integrity, dignity, personal liberty or sexual integrity, to issue a EPO enabling a competent authority in another Member State to continue the protection of the person in the territory of that other Member State, following criminal conduct, or alleged criminal conduct, in accordance with the national law of the issuing State.[61] A judicial or equivalent authority of the issuing State may issue a EPO only at the request of the protected person and after verifying that the protection measure meets the requirements set out in Article 5.[62] The requirements in Article 5 are that there be an existing national protection order containing: (a) a prohibition from entering certain localities, places or defined areas where the protected person resides or visits; or (b) a prohibition or regulation of contact, in any form, with the protected person, including by phone, electronic or ordinary mail, fax or any other means; or (c) a prohibition or regulation on approaching the protected person closer than a prescribed distance. The Member State that issued the original protective measure on foot of which it then adopts an EPO transmits the EPO to the executing Member State.[63]

The closest equivalent in Irish law to a restriction on movement in Article 5(a) is a restriction on movement order under s 101 of the Criminal Justice Act 2006. Section 101 provides that where a person aged 18 years or more is convicted of an offence specified in Schedule 3 and the court that convicts him or her of the offence considers that it is appropriate to impose a sentence of imprisonment for a term of three months or more, it may as an alternative make a restriction on movement order. The closest equivalent in Irish law of Article 5(b) and (c) is s 10(3) of the Non-Fatal Offences Against the Person Act 1997. Section 10(3) empowers a trial court to impose an order on a person convicted of harassment or stalking to not approach or communicate with a victim. Both these Irish legislative measures are expressed as an alternative type of punishment, ie they are penal and not civil in nature.

Section 26 of the Criminal Justice Act 2007 provides that on conviction of a person for a listed/scheduled offence, the court may provide in a protection of persons order that the offender is prohibited from engaging in any behaviour that, in the opinion of the court, would be likely to cause the victim of the offence concerned or any other person named in the order fear, distress or alarm or would be likely to amount to intimidation of any such person. Section 26 is more widely framed and allows for a greater range of

[61] ibid Art 1.
[62] ibid Art 6(2).
[63] ibid Art 8.

protective measures than envisaged in Article 5 of the EPO Directive. Section 26 is not expressed as an alternative to punishment, it appears to be more preventative in nature.

Another broadly based power in Irish law is that traditionally under the common law,[64] as later codified in s 54 of the Courts (Supplemental Provisions) Act 1961, a court in Ireland has the power to bind a person over to keep the peace, ie to be of good behaviour, on pain or penalty of a fine.[65] Although it has been described as preventative in nature,[66] and preventative penal measures, such as preventative detention, are *generally* not accepted in Irish law, the constitutionality of the power has been upheld on the basis of the interests of the common good and the proven previous outrageous behaviour or language of the person concerned so long as the person was not subject to commitment to pay an amount of money beyond their means or to other than a defined and limited committal to prison in default of payment.[67] Binding over to the peace at common law is not directed at the protection of victims in particular, it is more for the protection of the community in general.

Binding over to the peace is one of the measures in Irish law that could be considered to fall within the scope of Regulation 606/2013 on mutual recognition of protection measures in civil matters.[68] This Regulation established a certification process so that a civil protection order or measure issued in one Member State can be recognised in another Member State through a certificate without the need for further proceedings. The Regulation is directly applicable in Irish law and does not require implementing legislation. The scope of it extends to national law regulating how someone may contact or approach a protected person.[69] Apart from Irish law on 'binding over to keep the peace' outside of a conviction, other provisions in Irish law that fall within the scope of Regulation 606/2014 are found under the Domestic Violence Act 2018.

In summary, Irish law contains a range of protection or preventative orders, including a long-standing jurisdiction to bind someone to the peace, that are broader in scope than those provided for under EU law, but to date Ireland has chosen not to opt in to the EPO.

VI. Conclusions

As a result of the EU Victims' Rights Directive, Irish law has taken a more systematic approach to the recognition of the interests and rights of victims of crime. The CJ(VC)A 2017, enacted as a result of the Directive, is the first Irish legislation dedicated to crime victims. Its rationale, and that of the Directive, might be understood as ensuring that victims of crime are not subject to secondary and repeat victimisation in the criminal

[64] Discussed by O'Hanlon J in *Gregory v Judge Windle* [1994] 3 IR 613.

[65] See Law Reform Commission, *Consultation Paper on Prosecution Appeals from Unduly Lenient Sentences in the District Court* (33-2004) 30–32.

[66] *Gregory v Judge Windle* (n 64) at 619–20, citing, *inter alia*, *The People (Attorney General) v Callaghan* [1966] IR 501.

[67] *Gregory v Judge Windle* (n 64), ibid 623–24.

[68] Regulation (EU) No 606/2013 of the European Parliament and of the Council of 12 June 2013 on mutual recognition of protection measures in civil matters [2013] OJ L181/4.

[69] ibid Art 3(1).

justice process. The most obvious point on which Irish law could be seen as falling short of the Directive is the lack of recognition of a right to compensation, a matter regulated more indirectly in Ireland through a non-statutory and discretionary scheme of compensation from the State to victims of crime to the person and a discretionary and under-used power of a court of trial to order compensation be paid directly from offenders to victims of crime. The significance of the Directive and the Act should be seen in the context of the limited recognition of the interests and rights of victims in the common law, which has seen the emergence of powerful central public prosecutors, as well as an emphasis on defence rights in an adversarial process. An adversarial perspective does not naturally focus on the standing of victims. From that perspective, the EU Directive undoubtedly advances the cause of victims in Ireland.

PART IV

Key Challenges: Ensuring Coherence, Crisis Responses and Balancing Competing Interests

16

(Human Trafficking) Victims on the Margins of Protection: The (In)coherence of Sectoral Instruments?

AMY WEATHERBURN

I. Introduction

The concept of victimhood in criminal law is highly contextual as it depends upon the determination of the scope and scale of the phenomenon at hand and the extent to which judicial and police authorities officially recognise the harm and suffering of victim(s). The attribution of victimhood in the context of trafficking in human beings is highly illustrative of this conundrum and, as this chapter will demonstrate, has significant implications on the subsequent legal and political responses and the prospects of persons who have experienced exploitation from receiving assistance and support.[1] The specific focus of this chapter will be to highlight how European Union (EU) legal instruments that seek to protect victims of exploitation, in practice, places certain victims of human trafficking and (labour) exploitation on the margins of protection and consequently without access to remedy.

The most recent global estimates on modern slavery have calculated that on any day in 2021, 50 million people are held in forced labour or forced marriage. Of these, 27.6 million are held in forced labour globally, with 4.1 million people held in forced labour in Europe and Central Asia.[2] From a methodological and conceptual perspective,

[1] The academic debate has pertained most significantly to the 'ideal' trafficking victim focusing on gender eg, the victimhood of women and form of exploitation (eg sexual exploitation) and has subsequently excluded certain categories of victims (eg men, irregular migrants) from the mainstream criminal justice approach to tackling human trafficking: M Wijers, 'Purity, Victimhood and Agency: Fifteen years of the UN Trafficking Protocol' (2015) 4 *Anti-Trafficking Review* 56–79; A Forringer-Beal, 'Why the "Ideal Victim" Persists: Queering Representations of Victimhood in Human Trafficking Discourse' (2022) 19 *Anti-Trafficking Review* 87–102. The overarching emphasis on the ideal victim has also led to the exclusion of certain categories of workers from seeking remediation beyond criminal law, eg IK Thiemann, 'Beyond Victimhood and Beyond Employment? Exploring Avenues for Labour Law to Empower Women Trafficked into the Sex Industry' (2019) 48(2) *Industrial Law Journal* 199–22.

[2] International Labour Organisation, 'Global Estimates of Modern Slavery: Forced Labour and Forced Marriage' (Geneva, 2022).

the estimates of forced labour victims comprise human trafficking victims, including those who are, as yet, undetected by competent authorities.[3] Whilst academic debate pertaining to how global estimates of such a complex phenomenon have been compiled continues,[4] it is clear that these estimates are placed in stark relief when contrasted with the official national and European statistics on the detection and identification rates of human trafficking victims which are, in reality, much lower. Importantly, this trend is not only visible at an international level, but also regionally and nationally. The latest figures show that 53,800 victims were detected globally in 2020,[5] 7,155 victims were detected in 2021 in the EU 27 and (as an illustrative example), 67 per 100,0000 inhabitants victims registered in the Netherlands (notably the most number of victims proportionate to the population size, rather than the absolute number of victims).[6] Given the huge discrepancy between these figures, a key objective of this chapter will be to shine a light on victims who are included in the estimates but not officially detected and as such left on the margins of protection prescribed in both horizontal and sectoral legal instruments of the EU.

To add further to the complexity of the issue at hand, the United Nations for Drugs and Crime 2022 report on trafficking in human beings even identified a fall in the number of detected victims for the first time in 20 years. The justification for which was the impact of the Covid-19 pandemic on limiting opportunities and potentially pushed trafficking further underground, while constraining law enforcement capacities to target the crime.[7] The Covid-19 pandemic, whilst not the focus of this chapter, nevertheless contextualises the problematic at hand with a view to shaping future law and policy in a way that demonstrates that lessons have been learned from the short and long-term impact of the pandemic. It is on the basis of this reasoning, that the plight of migrant workers will be underscored. For instance, the Covid-19 pandemic highlighted the relevance of migrants working as arguably lower qualified 'essential workers' in the EU: with migrant workers amounting to an estimated average of 13 per cent of 'essential workers' in the EU.[8] Furthermore,

> migrants from non-EU countries are over-represented among 'essential workers', when compared to their share as part of the general migrant workforce. This over-representation

[3] International Labour Organisation, 'Methodology of the Global Estimates of Modern Slavery: Forced Labour and Forced Marriage' (Geneva, 2017) 10.

[4] See T Landman, 'Measuring Modern Slavery: Law, Human Rights, and New Forms of Data' (2020) *Human Rights Quarterly* 42, 303–31; On the concern relating to the use of Multiple Systems Estimation as a means of quantifying modern slavery, see O Binette and RC Steorts, 'On the Reliability of Multiple Systems Estimation for the Quantification of Modern Slavery' (2022) 185(2) *Journal of the Royal Statistical Society Series A: Statistics in Society* 640–76.

[5] United Nations Office on Drugs and Crime (UNODC), 'Global Report on Trafficking in Persons' (New York, 2022) (hereafter referred to as 'UNODC 2022 Global Report') 11.

[6] European Commission, Commission Staff Working Document Statistics and trends in trafficking in human being in the European Union in 2019–2020 Accompanying the document Report from the Commission to the European Parliament, the Council, the European Economic and Social Committee and the Committee of the Regions Report on the progress made in the fight against trafficking in human beings (Fourth Report), Brussels, 19.12.2022, SWD(2022) 429 final 1.

[7] UNODC 2022 Global Report (n 5) 13.

[8] F Fasani and J Mazza, 'Immigrant Key Workers: Their Contributions to Europe's COVID-19 Response' (European Commission – Joint Research Centre, 2020) 5.

stems mainly from their occupation as cleaners, in the construction and food processing sector, or as care and health workers.[9]

Importantly, the Covid-19 pandemic did not create but rather compounded the situation of migrant workers and, in the context of labour exploitation, it is important to underline that '[t]he share of migrants in the group of people in forced labour is much higher than the share of migrants in the overall labour force'.[10] Thus, a key point of assessment in this chapter will be to reconcile the challenges that victims of labour exploitation and forced labour encounter despite the fact that the legal and political responses – including those that are discussed in this chapter – often state that their purpose is to prevent exploitation and protect the rights of migrant workers.

In what follows, this chapter will, in section II, outline the existing protection measures for victims of exploitation that is considered to be severe enough to constitute a crime. First, in the context of human trafficking as provided for in Directive 2011/36/EU[11] (section II.A.) and second, for a very specific group namely workers in an irregular situation who have been intentionally subjected to 'particularly exploitative working conditions' in Directive 2009/52/EU on Employers' Sanctions[12] (section II.B.). In section III, the extent to which the rights of these victims of crime are effectively protected will be assessed by using key illustrative examples from practice and research to identify some of the limitations of these mechanisms. In section IV, the chapter will offer insights into the prospects for EU law and policy on the protection of victims' rights and state that victims' rights can only be guaranteed by adopting a holistic, multi-layered response that goes beyond a criminal law silo. It will be argued that the impact of exploitation in society not only hits at victims' rights under EU criminal law but also the development of EU policy in migration and asylum, and under the Social Europe Agenda and the imminent changes that are to be brought in relation to a just and sustainable economy.

II. Making the Inaccessible Accessible: EU Protection and Remedy Mechanisms for Victims of Labour Exploitation and Human Trafficking

Literature on migrant workers demonstrates that there is a gap between workplace rights violations and enforcement, particularly in relation to securing access to justice

9 L Rasche, 'The EU Talent Pool: An Opportunity for Skills-based Pathways to Protection' (Hertie School Jacques Delores Centre, 2021) 12.

10 International Labour Organisation, 'Global Estimates of Modern Slavery: Forced Labour and Forced Marriage' (Geneva, 2022) 34.

11 Directive 2011/36/EU of the European Parliament and of the Council of 5 April 2011 on preventing and combating trafficking in human beings and protecting its victims, and replacing Council Framwork Decision 2002/629/JHA ('Anti-Trafficking Directive') [2011] OJ L101/1.

12 Directive 2009/52/EC of the European Parliament and of the Council of 18 June 2009 providing for minimum standards on sanctions and measures against employers of illegally staying third-country nationals ('Employers' Sanctions Directive') [2009] OJ L168/24.

and effective remedies.[13] For instance, research in Europe reveals that significant barriers impede migrant workers' access to complaints mechanisms due to issues such as

> constraints that employers impose, victims' lack of awareness of their rights, and the fear of being returned to their countries of origin or losing their job – render victims of labour exploitation often unable or unwilling to come forward or report to the police.[14]

In addition to these challenges, migrant workers' '[…] lack of knowledge of the functioning of complaint mechanisms also prevents them from lodging a complaint'.[15] In what follows we will present the EU criminal law framework that 'establishes various remedies for victims of labour exploitation and human trafficking, including compensation funds and complaints mechanisms involving third parties' with a view to facilitating access to justice for migrant workers who have experienced exploitative labour practices.[16]

Two key European criminal law instruments prescribe the criminalisation of the exploitation of individuals: the Anti-Trafficking Directive 2011/36/EU criminalises trafficking in human beings and the Employers' Sanctions Directive 2009/52/EU requires Member States to criminalise the employment of illegally staying third-country nationals. Crucially, given the barriers to accessing justice mentioned above, particularly for exploited migrant workers, both of these instruments also include key protective measures for victims of human trafficking and for illegally staying third country nationals who have been subjected to 'particularly exploitative working conditions' with the aim of facilitating their access to remedy. In addition to the protective measures that these two sectoral Directives prescribe, it is important to underline that victims of exploitation are also entitled to the measures provided for in EU law under the horizontal rules that outline the rights of victims of crime[17] but, for the purposes of this chapter, are beyond the scope. Thus, the focus of this section will be to outline in more detail the specific protection mechanisms prescribed by the aforementioned two sectoral legislative instruments and to begin to identify some of the limitations that impacts on those who may have suffered harm but find themselves on the margin of protection and thus without effective access to justice.

[13] B Hastie, 'The Inaccessibility Of Justice For Migrant Workers: A Capabilities-Based Perspective' (2017) 34:2 *Windsor Yearbook Access Just* 20, 22; S Marsden, 'Migrant Workers, Rights, and the Rule of Law: Responding to the Justice Gap' (2019) *Dalhousie Law Journal* 42(1), 153–82; C Barnard, 'Enforcement of Employment Rights by Migrant Workers in the UK: The Case of EU-8 Nationals' in C Costello and M Freedland (eds), *Migrants at Work* (Oxford University Press, 2014); C Barnard and S Fraser Butlin, 'The Rule of Law and Access to the Courts for EU Migrants' (2020) 58 (6) *The Journal of Common Market Studies* 1621–34.

[14] European Union Agency for Fundamental Rights, 'Protecting Migrants in an Irregular Situation from Labour Exploitation – Role of the Employers' Sanctions Directive' (Publications Office of the European Union, 2021) 12.

[15] ibid. See further in European Union Agency for Fundamental Rights, 'Severe Labour Exploitation: Workers Moving within or into the European Union' (Publications Office of the European Union, 2015).

[16] C Methven O'Brien and A Weatherburn, 'Commission Proposal for a Regulation on Prohibiting Products Made with Forced Labour on the Union Market: The Issue of Remedies' (*Think Tank, European Parliament,* 2023) 2.

[17] Directive 2012/29/EU of the European Parliament and of the Council of 25 October 2012 establishing minimum standards on the rights, support and protection of victims of crime, and replacing Council Framework Decision 2001/220/JHA [2012] OJ L315/57–73; Council Directive 2004/80/EC of 29 April 2004 relating to compensation to crime victims [2004] OJ L261/15.

A further point of interest justifying the focus on these two Directives is that they are recognised as being complementary instruments that contribute to the policy aims pursued by the Union in tackling exploitation and reinforcing the protection of migrant workers' rights. Furthermore, the two instruments have, in the last two years, been singled out for review and evaluation with a view to strengthening their effectiveness and identifying areas of action for their future implementation.[18] As we will see, the results of these assessments have led to recommendations in both law and policy so as to guarantee a robust response to tackling trafficking in human beings and the exploitation of migrant workers on the European labour market.

A. Victims of Trafficking in Human Beings

The EU Anti-Trafficking Directive is the most prominent mechanism for defining common rules aimed at strengthening access to justice for victims of exploitation. The development of a victim-centered approach was a key driving force in the establishment of the Anti-Trafficking Directive that replaced Framework Decision 2002/629/JHA on combating trafficking in human beings, with a view to mirroring the growing international and regional consensus for a victim-centered approach that provides for support, assistance and protection.[19] This shift is reflected in the provisions of the Anti-Trafficking Directive that entitle victims of trafficking in human beings to support and assistance before, during and for an appropriate period of time after the conclusion of criminal proceedings (Article 11(1)). The support and assistance should begin as soon as there is a 'reasonable-grounds indication for believing that the person might have been subjected to human trafficking' (Article 11(2)) and should not be conditional on the victim's willingness to cooperate with authorities in the criminal investigation, prosecution or trial (Article 11(3)).

Assistance and support measures shall include at least standards of living capable of ensuring victims' subsistence through measures such as the provision of appropriate and safe accommodation and material assistance, as well as necessary medical treatment including psychological assistance, counselling and information, and translation and interpretation services where appropriate (Article 11(5)).

Protection measures for victims of human trafficking include access to legal counselling and legal representation (Article 12(2)), an individual risk assessment (Article 12(3)) and, in recognition of the particularly egregious nature of the crime,

[18] European Commission, Communication from the Commission to the European Parliament, the Council, the European Economic and Social Committee and the Committee of the Regions on the EU Strategy on Combatting Trafficking in Human Beings 2021-2025, Brussels, 14.4.2021 COM(2021) 171 final, 4; European Commission, Communication from the Commission to the European Parliament, the Council, the European Economic and Social Committee and the Committee of the Regions on a New Pact on Migration and Asylum, Brussels, 23.9.2020 COM(2020) 609 final 17.

[19] See Preamble of Council of Europe Convention on Action against Trafficking in Human Beings. Warsaw, 16.V.2005 and Guideline 6 of the Office of the High Commissioner for Human Rights, 'Recommended Principles and Guidelines on Human Rights and Human Trafficking' (2002). Text presented to the Economic and Social Council as an addendum to the report of the United Nations High Commissioner for Human Rights (E/2002/68/Add. 1).

specific treatment aimed at preventing secondary victimisation by avoiding, as far as possible and in accordance with the grounds defined by national law as well as with rules of judicial discretion, practice or guidance, the following: (a) unnecessary repetition of interviews during investigation, prosecution or trial; (b) visual contact between victims and defendants including during the giving of evidence such as interviews and cross-examination, by appropriate means including the use of appropriate communication technologies; (c) the giving of evidence in open court; and (d) unnecessary questioning concerning the victim's private life (Article 12(4)).

A key feature of anti-trafficking victim support and assistance mechanisms for potential victims of human trafficking with an irregular migration status is the inclusion of a reflection and recovery period. In accordance with Article 6 of Council Directive 2004/81/EC, third country nationals will be granted temporary residence for the duration of a reflection and recovery period with a view to 'allowing them to recover and escape the influence of the perpetrators of the offences so that they can take an informed decision as to whether to cooperate with the competent authorities'.[20] Implementation monitoring of the Directive has revealed that there has been inconsistent application of the recovery and reflection periods,[21] which is crucial for victims' to realise that they are in a place of safety and can be supported without having to rely upon their exploiters.

The 2022 Evaluation of the Directive (announced in the EU Strategy on Combating Trafficking in Human Beings[22]) conducted by the European Commission considered that, despite the fact that the Directive had been effective and had created a common framework for Member States to fight against trafficking in human beings, the Member States' implementation of Directive 2011/36/EU was nevertheless not consistent regarding a number of measures that have victim protection and access to justice at their core: namely, the protection of victims in criminal procedures; the non-punishment of victims; the assistance to victims, including vulnerable groups; and the provisions regarding compensation. In conclusion, the evaluation argued that these shortcomings impeded the full achievement of the Directive's objectives concerning 'prevention, prosecution, assistance of victims and monitoring'.[23]

The identification and protection of (potential) human trafficking victims have been identified as a challenge and have subsequently been acknowledged

[20] Notably the granting of a reflection and recovery period and the conditions of residence of the victims of trafficking in human beings in the territory of the Member States is not dealt with by the Anti-Trafficking Directive (save for a brief cross-reference to the relevant legal instrument in Art 11(6)) but by a separate Directive that prescribes the conditions for issuing a residence permit to third-country nationals who are victims of trafficking or illegal immigration: Council Directive 2004/81/EC of 29 April 2004 on the residence permit issued to third-country nationals who are victims of trafficking in human beings or who have been the subject of an action to facilitate illegal immigration, who cooperate with the competent authorities [2004] OJ L261/19–23.

[21] European Commission, Report from the Commission to the European Parliament and the Council Third report on the progress made in the fight against trafficking in human beings (2020) as required under Article 20 of Directive 2011/36/EU on preventing and combating trafficking in human beings and protecting its victims {SWD(2020) 226 final}, Brussels, 20.10.2020, COM(2020) 661 final, 14–15.

[22] European Commission, Communication from the Commission to the European Parliament, the Council, the European Economic and Social Committee and the Committee of the Regions on the EU Strategy on Combatting Trafficking in Human Beings 2021- 2025, Brussels, 14.4.2021 COM(2021) 171 final 4.

[23] European Parliament Research Service, 'Preventing and Combating Trafficking in Human Beings' (2023), Briefing 14-06-2023.

in key EU policy documents both more broadly in relation to the Security Union Strategy of 2020 and specifically targeted counter trafficking approaches.[24] Indeed, the Implementation Report and Evaluation of the Anti-Trafficking Directive highlighted that the victim-centred approach that was a key driving force of the Directive's design had not materialised and thus needed further strengthening and reinforcing. In particular a key deficiency was the insufficient early identification of victims despite the obligation imposed on Member States to establish a mechanism for this purpose.[25]

The 2024 revision of the Anti-Trafficking Directive seeks to address these deficiencies with a number of changes that modify (Article 2(3)) or introduce new criminal offences (Article 18(a)), establish mandatory support and assistance mechanisms (Article 11(4)) and strength anti-trafficking governance structures and data collection with a view to seeking further harmonisation (Article 19(a-b)).[26] The current chapter will highlight one of these that seeks to address the need to improve early identification and referral practices of Member States, both at the national and cross-border level. The key change is the formalisation of national referral mechanisms, with a requirement for them to be established by laws, regulations or administrative provisions. This revision goes some way to reconciling the current patchwork of practices across Member States and move towards a harmonisation of structures and practices on referring victims to appropriate assistance and support systems. This will be further enhanced by the creation of National Focal Points that will be responsible for identifying competent services and for coordinating the referral of victims at the national and EU level.[27]

During the revision process of the anti-trafficking rules, all legislative institutions acknowledged the increased attention paid to victims of trafficking in human beings with a clear emphasis on victims in the political messaging that identified the complex and diverse profile of human trafficking victims and the need for support and assistance measures to be tailored to their needs.[28] However, a note of caution must be

[24] European Commission, Communication from the Commission to the European Parliament, the European Council, the Council, the European Economic and Social Committee and the Committee of the Regions on the EU Security Union Strategy, Brussels, 24.7.2020 COM(2020) 605 final, 18; European Commission, Communication from the Commission to the European Parliament, the Council, the European Economic and Social Committee and the Committee of the Regions on the EU Strategy on Combatting Trafficking in Human Beings 2021-2025, Brussels, 14.4.2021 COM(2021) 171 final.

[25] European Commission, Commission Staff Working Document Evaluation of the Proposal for a Directive of the European Parliament and of the Council amending Directive 2011/36/EU on preventing and combating trafficking in human beings and protecting its victims, Brussels, 19.12.2022 SWD(2022) 427 final 32–33.

[26] Directive 2024/1712 of the European Parliament and of the Council of 13 June 2024 amending Directive 2011/36/EU on preventing and combating trafficking in human beings and protecting its victims [2024] OJ L2024/1712.

[27] European Commission, Proposal for a Directive of the European Parliament and of the Council amending Directive 2011/36/EU on preventing and combating trafficking in human beings and protecting its victims Brussels, 19.12.2022 COM(2022) 732 final 2022/0426 (COD), 6–7, 10 and 14.

[28] Council of the European Union, Proposal for a Directive of the European Parliament and of the Council amending Directive 2011/36/EU on preventing and combating trafficking in human beings and protecting its victims – General approach, 17 May 2023; European Parliament, Report on the proposal for a directive of the European Parliament and of the Council amending Directive 2011/36/EU on preventing and combating trafficking in human beings and protecting its victims (COM(2022)0732 – C9-0431/2022 – 2022/0426(COD)), 10 October 2023.

raised when considering these victim-focused perspectives against amendments to the other provisions of the Anti-Trafficking Directive. Indeed, the effectiveness of a 'victim-centred approach' must be mindful of the contradictory effect that some of the other provisions can engender. This is particularly the case in the context of sexual exploitation, where the introduction of a new criminal offence in Article 18(a) criminalising the knowing use of services of victims of human trafficking can in fact lead to potential victims of exploitation being less willing to engage with authorities and an overall erosion of victim's rights.[29] In particular, since the emphasis would be on prosecuting the user of sexual services and not on investigating the circumstances as a human trafficking case, that would then lead to the obligation to offer victim status and the whole range of above-mentioned specific rights to which they are entitled by virtue of the Anti-Trafficking Directive.[30]

B. Victims of Particularly Exploitative Working Conditions

A second EU sectoral legislative instrument that is of pertinence for the protection of migrant victims, is the Employers' Sanctions Directive 2009/52/EU that provides for sanctions and measures against employers of illegally staying third-country nationals.[31]

The primary objective of the Directive is to tackle irregular migration, as reflected in Article 3 that requires Member States to 'prohibit the illegal employment of illegally staying third-country nationals'. Article 9 of the Directive further requires Member States to ensure that any infringement of the prohibition constitutes a criminal offence when committed intentionally in circumstances where: (a) the infringement continues or is persistently repeated; (b) the infringement is in respect of the simultaneous employment of a significant number of illegally staying third-country nationals; (c) the infringement is accompanied by particularly exploitative working conditions; (d) the infringement is committed by an employer who, while not having been charged with or convicted of an offence established pursuant to Framework Decision 2002/629/JHA, uses work or services exacted from an illegally staying third-country national with the knowledge that he or she is a victim of trafficking in human beings; (e) the infringement relates to the illegal employment of a minor. For the purposes of this chapter, the criminalisation in Article 9(1)(c) of employers who subject workers in an irregular situation to 'particularly exploitative working conditions' will be a key focus of the subsequent analysis, as crucially, it provides victims of labour exploitation an alternative avenue of accessing the protection measures and entitlements that are granted to victims of crime in Europe.

The second feature of the Employers' Sanctions Directive that is of pertinence are the provisions that seek to protect workers' rights and facilitate their access to justice. Article 6 stipulates that workers in an irregular situation are entitled to recuperate

[29] La Strada International, 'The Impact of Criminalising the "Knowing Use" on Human Trafficking La Strada International' (Policy Paper, 2022) 12.

[30] ibid.

[31] Employers' Sanctions Directive (n 12).

outstanding wages, taxes and social security contributions and that Member States must implement mechanisms that facilitate the receipt of back pay, and, crucially, including for those who may no longer be physically present on the territory of the EU Member State where they suffered exploitative working conditions and have returned (Article 6(4)). Another measure that grants access to justice is the requirement, under Article 13(1), on Member States to provide for a complaint mechanism, that can be accessed directly or through third parties designated by Member States such as trade unions or other associations or other competent authorities designated by the Member States. A crucial complementary feature that is essential for guaranteeing that workers in an irregular situation can benefit from these administrative mechanisms is the requirement to grant temporary residence permits to third-country nationals who are involved in proceedings (Article 13(4)), including, an extension of the duration of these until the third-country national has received any back payment of his or her remuneration (Article 6(4)).

However, monitoring of the implementation of these provisions have revealed the lack of effective implementation by Member States of these mechanisms that are specifically designed to facilitate access to justice for workers in an irregular situation.[32] Academic research and literature clearly underscore the necessity for specific mechanisms that are dedicated to facilitating the access to justice for irregular migrant workers.[33] Unfortunately, the aspirations outlined in the Employers' Sanctions Directive have not been achieved in a national context. Indeed, the Commission's monitoring of the implementation of the Directive revealed that

> [V]ery few member States explicitly transposed the right of illegally employed migrants to make a claim against their employer for any outstanding remuneration, including once the worker has been returned to his or her country of origin. Most member States merely refer to general provisions concerning the right to bring a case before civil or labour courts.[34]

The lack of implementation by Member States merely exacerbates the barriers they face and gives *carte blanche* to employers who exploit their vulnerable status and fail to respect their labour and social rights by underpaying their wages and making them work in exploitative conditions.

The lack of willingness of Member States to recognise the specific vulnerability of migrant workers with an irregular status and to go beyond the general provisions that already exist in their national legal frameworks, fails to allow for a meaningful engagement with the mechanisms in place. Unfortunately, the possibility to recognise a migrant worker with an irregular status as a party to proceedings or to have access to additional support, often provided for by third party organisations such as trade unions have not been satisfactorily realised in the national implementation of the Directive's

[32] European Union Agency for Fundamental Rights (n 14) 10–12.

[33] ibid. On complaints mechanisms see also Platform for International Cooperation on Undocumented Migrants (PICUM), 'Undocumented Migrant Workers: Guidelines for Developing an Effective Complaints Mechanism in Cases of Labour Exploitation or Abuse' (Brussels, 2017).

[34] European Commission, Communication from the Commission to the European Parliament and the Council on the application of Directive 2009/52/ EC of 18 June 2009 providing for minimum standards on sanctions and measures against employers of illegally staying third country nationals, COM(2014) 286 final, Brussels, 25 May 2014, 7. References from original omitted.

provision for complaints mechanism.[35] These deficiencies fail to recognise the significance and prevalence of the multiple dependencies that many exploited migrant workers have on their employers. A dependent status is often due to their irregular migration status but also due to language barriers and a lack of financial means further entrenches their isolation and lack of opportunity to reach out to and engage with formal legal channels.[36] Thus, whilst the necessity to establish a complaint mechanism is a best practice, it is also imperative to permit the opportunity for third party organisations to make a complaint on behalf of third country nationals in an irregular situation. The assistance and support of third-party organisations, such as trade unions, are critical for achieving meaningful redress. Their expertise and knowledge of the avenues for remedy are deemed essential to guarantee a successful outcome.[37]

III. Assessment of the Legal Framework in Practice: Failing to Protect Migrant Worker Victims

Reflecting on the material scope of the existing legal framework, we must now assess to what extent it is fit for purpose, and – despite the recent review of their implementation – determine which aspects may require (further) attention. In what follows, we posit that the EU must strive for a coherent mechanism that maximises the possibility for all victims of exploitation, regardless of migration status, to be guaranteed their rights and access to justice and remedy, in compliance with Article 47 of the EU Charter of Fundamental Rights. A key starting point, that will be further illustrated in this section with reference to a case in practice, is that not all individuals who are subject to exploitation may be formally identified as victims of human trafficking, instead they will essentially fall through the gaps. Unfortunately, the design of the two instruments analysed in section II have limitations in this regard and as such the protective mechanisms they prescribe are not inclusive of all individuals who experience exploitation in the workplace.

The design of the Anti-Trafficking Directive, in some instances, fails to capture those who are entitled to have access to remedy but will not benefit from the support and assistance measures described above as they will not be formally identified as victims of trafficking. One reason for this lack of formal identification can be due to an assessment of the situation by authorities that leads to a decision not to prosecute and to discontinue the criminal investigation for human trafficking. Research in Belgium and the Netherlands has highlighted that such a decision will, in most cases, lead to a loss of human trafficking victim status and the associated rights and support. Instead,

[35] European Union Agency for Fundamental Rights (n 14) 12.

[36] On dependency in the context of human trafficking for the purpose of labour exploitation, see A Weatherburn, *Labour Exploitation in Human Trafficking Law* (Intersentia, 2021) 211–18. For financial dependency of migrant workers, see A Weatherburn and A Toft, 'Managing the Risks of Being a Victim of Severe Labour Exploitation: Findings from a Research Project Exploring the Views of Experts in the UK' (2016) 45(2) *Industrial Law Journal* 257–62.

[37] I Wintermayr and A Weatherburn, *Access to Protection and Remedy for Victims of Human Trafficking for the Purpose of Labour Exploitation in Belgium and the Netherlands* (ILO, 2021) 104–11.

in some instances, cases will be prosecuted for alternative criminal offences that do not place such an emphasis on the centrality of the victim in the proceedings and their entitlements to remedy such as compensation.[38] A lack of access to protection and support measures under the anti-trafficking framework can also be the result of the victims' response to their situation and their decision not to cooperate with authorities. Academic research and literature have recognised that many potential victims are hesitant to agree to cooperate with proceedings for fear of reprisals from their exploiters and due to a 'victim's lack of self-identification of their own victimhood that can lead to a refusal of potential victims to enter the procedures under the National Referral Mechanism'.[39]

From the perspective of the Employers' Sanctions Directive, a key limitation of the scope of the protective measures is that they are only extended to third country nationals with an irregular situation. Migrant workers who are regularly residing and working in an EU Member State or EU citizens who exercise their right to freedom of movement, do not have the same level of attention when it comes to mechanisms to guarantee their access to remedy in the case of labour and social rights violations. Furthermore, the complexity of labour exploitation and the discrepancy in the judicial understanding as to where the threshold at which poor working conditions are deemed to amount to criminal behaviour means that there are those who are not considered as victims of crime and therefore left with significantly less protection in terms of securing their rights, access to justice and compensating any harm.[40] The Borealis case in Antwerp, Belgium in the summer of 2022 has highlighted the limitations of the current approach to protecting victims of labour exploitation. The following example puts into perspective the challenges that practitioners can face when dealing with a large-scale case of alleged human trafficking, illegal working and social fraud.

Borealis, a chemical producing company, began the construction of a propane dehydrogenation plant in Kallo, Belgium in 2019. Borealis sub-contracted the engineering and construction to firms who then used subsidiaries to recruit the workforce, with as many as 1,500 sub-contracted workers on site at any one time. In July 2022, Belgian inspection services identified alleged social fraud practices and possible human trafficking cases amongst the workers, with a range of nationalities including Filipinos, Turks, Bengalis and Ukrainians. Allegations arose, particularly in the media, of exploitation, non-payment of wages, lack of social security and poor housing conditions. Workers were required to work extremely long hours, six days a week for a monthly salary of €650. Crucially to the focus of this chapter, the migration status of the third country national workers was in no way harmonised leading to a diversity across the workforce in terms of their right to work and/or reside in Belgium: some workers were Posted Workers, some were Single Permit Holders, and some were undocumented and thus working informally.

In accordance with Belgian law, and as stipulated in the EU Anti-Trafficking Directive, as soon as there was a suspicion of human trafficking, a large group of workers

[38] ibid 57.
[39] ibid 32.
[40] ibid 64–65.

were granted human trafficking victim status which entitles them to enhanced protection, support and assistance.[41] By August 2022, 174 workers were confirmed as possible victims of trafficking; with 55 officially granted human trafficking victim status following an inspection on the construction site. It was at this point that serious concerns were raised about the capacity for specialised human trafficking victim support services to guarantee the material support and assistance that these victims are entitled to.[42] By September, 138 victims were officially recognised as human trafficking victims and others had their provisional victim status revoked or had not been recognised as human trafficking victims. In addition, in response to the alleged social fraud and exploitative working conditions, the Flemish Government revoked 500 work permits that were connected to three sub-contracting businesses.[43] A further action that was taken in response to the large-scale fraud on the construction site was by Borealis itself, who terminated the contracts with the sub-contractors, meaning that more than 1,000 workers were unable to continue working on the Borealis site.

The impact on the workers of these two punitive actions aimed at the sub-contracting companies was significant. Not only were many workers left without any support or assistance via the Belgian National Referral Mechanism, but they were also immediately required to stop working and thus were left unemployed. The loss of employment can have severe impact on migrant workers, and in the absence of appropriate support mechanisms, can increase their risk of falling into irregularity and being (re)-exploited.[44]

In addition to the financial implications of their loss of employment, the individuals also had concerns related to their private and family life. Their accommodation had been provided by their employer and thus the loss of employment not only impacted their working conditions but also their living conditions since that had been provided by their employer.[45] This is increasingly a common arrangement for migrant workers who are offered both a job and accommodation by the employer and/or labour intermediary.[46] Indeed, where excessive deductions for sub-standard accommodation are made from migrant workers' pay, this can amount to an indicator

[41] Circular of 23 December 2016 relating to the implementation of a multidisciplinary cooperation concerning victims of human trafficking and/or certain aggravated forms of human smuggling (Circulaire relative à la mise en oeuvre d'une coopération multidisciplinaire concernant les victimes de la traite des êtres humains et/ou certaines formes aggravées de trafic des êtres humains), Belgian Official Gazette, 10 March 2017 and EU Anti-Trafficking Directive (n 11).

[42] Borealis, 'About the Kallo Case: Update on Alleged Human Trafficking Practices by (Sub)contractor at Propane Dehydrogenation Construction Site in Kallo, Belgium' (23 January 2023), available at www.borealis-group.com/news/about-the-kallo-case.

[43] VRT, 'Les ouvriers de Borealis victimes de traite d'êtres humains continuent à manifester à Anvers' (10 septembre 2022), available at www.vrt.be/vrtnws/fr/2022/09/10/les-ouvriers-de-borealis-victimes-de-traite-detre-humains-contin/; VRT, 'Traite des êtres humains sur un chantier d'Anvers: la Flandre retire 500 permis de travail à trois entreprises' (8 septembre 2022), available at www.vrt.be/vrtnws/fr/2022/09/08/traite-des-etres-humains-sur-un-chantier-danvers-la-flandre-re/.

[44] Borealis (n 42).

[45] Docwerkers Qatar in Belgium – Modern Slavery in the Port of Antwerp, available at www.docwerkers.be/en/projects/qatar-in-belgium/.

[46] See for instance emphasis on provision of accommodation in agricultural sector in Scotland and the pilot of a seasonal workers tied visa: Scottish Government, 'Seasonal Migrant Workers in Scottish Agriculture' (2023) 32–33.

of forced labour.[47] The loss of employment leads to a loss of accommodation, with the potential of leaving them destitute as they have no financial means for finding alternative accommodation on the private rental market.[48] The inability to continue working, even for such a low salary, means that the financial precarity of these workers is further exacerbated as they may already have accrued significant debts at the point of recruitment and/or be supporting family in their country of origin via remittances.[49] The precarity of migrant workers and thus their risk to secondary exploitation is further heightened.

The loss of employment is particularly critical for those migrant workers' whose status is tied to employment with a specific employer (and even in some cases in a specific sector). The implementation of the EU Single Permit Directive in Belgium requires single permit holders to be sponsored by an employer. If they wish to leave their employer, and or find themselves unemployed, they have a 90-day window to seek alternative employment and apply for a new single permit. The latter condition means that, in practice, it is nigh on impossible to find a new job with an employer who is willing to commit to the single permit application procedure, within the time limit.[50] Encouragingly, an extension to this period to 180 days for workers whose employers have violated their labour and social obligations has been announced but is not yet in force.[51] This type of measure is to be welcomed as facilitating the possibility to change employers and seek alternative employment is important for all workers, regardless of their migration status. This is due to the fact that in such circumstances they often have a high level of dependence on their employer not only for work but, as we have seen above, on the provision of accommodation, etc. The level of control over their personal life heightens their precarity and vulnerability to exploitation.[52]

Of those who were granted human trafficking victim status, the most significant distinction was that they are nevertheless those who were working without the right to work or reside in Belgium. Whilst it is certain that the undocumented status of these workers heightens their vulnerability to exploitation, the Borealis case demonstrates that even regularly residing third country nationals are not immune to exploitative working and living conditions. And what's more they are also suffering the same effects of the exploitative working conditions: eg, non-payment of wages, accruing significant debt to come and work in Belgium, long working hours, lack of guarantees in case of sickness and absence, etc. It is therefore necessary for measures to be taken to ensure that protective measures are implemented that seek to facilitate the access to justice

[47] Focus on Labour Exploitation (FLEX), 'Assessment of the Risks of Human Trafficking for Forced Labour on the UK Seasonal Workers Pilot' (2021) 45–50.

[48] A Weatherburn, E Herman Kruithof and C Vanroelen, 'Labour Migration in Flanders and the Use of the Single Permit to Address Labour Market Shortages: The Lived Experiences of Single Permit Holders Working in Medium Skilled Bottleneck Professions' (2022) 1 *VUB Interface Demography Working Paper*.

[49] Focus on Labour Exploitation (FLEX), 'The Risks of Exploitation in Temporary Migration Programmes (2019) 24–25.

[50] A Weatherburn, 'The Lived Experiences of Migrants in the EU with a Single Permit' (ULB Equality Law Clinic, 2023).

[51] Nicole de Moor (CD&V), Interministeriële Conferentie pakt misbruik en uitbuiting bij arbeidsmigratie aan, 7 July 2023, available at www.nicoledm.be/nieuws/interministeriele-conferentie-pakt-misbruik-en-uitbuiting-bij-arbeidsmigratie-aan/.

[52] Weatherburn, Herman Kruithof and Vanroelen (n 48); Wintermayr and Weatherburn (n 37).

for all migrant workers, as the Borealis case has demonstrated that those who are on the margins of protection are left without a safety net. Such a situation leads to a paradox whereby in the absence of minimal procedural safeguards such as the opportunity to seek alternative employment, or the granting of a temporary residence permit that would mitigate the risk of falling into irregularity, these individuals are in fact placed in a position where they find themselves to be at a heightened risk of further exploitation. The risk of leaving these victims of exploitation without any protection further contributes to the reticence that already exists amongst migrant workers and those who are experiencing exploitation in their working conditions to make themselves known to the authorities and make a complaint. Instead, the dissuasive effect will further entrench migrant workers' acceptance of sub-standard working and living conditions, allowing a tolerance of exploitation to germinate across society.

IV. The Prospects for Victims on the Margins of Protection

The preceding sections in this chapter have given insight into the current protection mechanisms that seek to facilitate access to justice for victims of exploitation and the limitations that situate some victims of exploitation on the margins of protection. Consideration of the implications of the Borealis case highlighted the complexities that confront authorities when dealing with a diverse and fragmented migrant labour force. It nevertheless must be at the heart of future discussion of labour migration law and policy across the EU, given that the reliance on migrant labour is only set to increase in the immediate future as an inherent part of the response to a shrinking working population.[53] This will require a coherent response to ensure that workers' rights are guaranteed, including their entitlement to access to justice and remedy. The following outlines a number of considerations for the future protection of victims' rights that reflects on the future direction of EU law and policy by adopting a three-pronged approach: current EU criminal law, going beyond EU criminal law and going beyond the EU.

An EU criminal law response to labour exploitation that seeks to place an emphasis on victims' rights by facilitating their access to justice through (horizontal and) sectoral protection mechanisms must be transposed in a timely manner by Member States. This will ensure that the minimum legal standards prescribed in EU law are coherent and effective in practice across all Member States. This is particularly important in the context of migrant workers, where short-term mobility is a more common feature and they may have worked (and experienced exploitation or violations of their rights) in more than one EU Member State. The historic slow engagement by Member States with the transposition of these instruments, in the first instance, suggests that Member States

[53] European Commission, Communication from the Commission to the European Parliament, the Council, the European Economic and Social Committee and the Committee of the Regions attracting skills and talent to the EU, Brussels, 27.4.2022 COM(2022) 657 final.

will need to demonstrate political will to reform their national law and policy framework in a timely manner. In seeking an effective criminal justice response, Member States must also readily engage with a common feature that applies to both instruments discussed in sections II and III: the right to be granted temporary residence for the duration of proceedings. Unfortunately, as it stands, this right to temporary residence emerges as a limitation to effective protection for many migrant workers who have encountered labour exploitation but are denied the possibility to remain on the territory of the EU with the primary objective of having the opportunity to pursue proceedings with a view to recuperating compensation or back pay of outstanding remuneration. To truly contribute to access to justice, temporary residence permits should be granted with realistic conditions that guarantee the subsistence of the individual, whether that be through financial assistance or access to the labour market. Finally, it is imperative that such permits are not conditional on cooperation with authorities in (any kind of) proceedings. One final consideration follows on from the conditionality of access to protection mechanisms provided for by EU criminal law instruments and underpins the need to place the victim at the centre of proceedings: victims must have support when seeking access to remedy, not just through criminal proceedings but also where alternative avenues of remedy are pursued.[54] The role of third party organisations, in offering insights into the functioning of remedial mechanisms based on their expertise, should not be overlooked and given a prominent position when designing protection mechanisms. The measures introduced in both Directives assessed in this chapter have acknowledged the need for the involvement of civil society and other specialised victim support organisations. However, it is imperative that the continued monitoring of the implementation of these measures guarantees that these mechanisms are formally established in national law and policy so as to have the mandate to make a real impact on the ground.

For victims on the margin of protection, the substantive and procedural limitations of the criminal justice response to labour exploitation need to be acknowledged and steps must be taken to move beyond criminal law when providing for access to remedy. Complementary developments in EU law could and should play a crucial role in the future design of victims' access to remedy. For instance, the emphasis on the European pillar of social rights and the (upcoming) introduction of key legislative instruments such as the Directive on Adequate Minimum Wages and the Transparent and Predictable Working Conditions Directive[55] and the Just and Sustainable Economy legislation such as the Corporate Sustainability Due Diligence Directive that will impose mandatory obligations on companies to account for the human rights and environmental impact of business activities throughout the whole supply chain. The overlap between business and human rights was acknowledged in the Commission's Proposal for the revised anti-trafficking rules with a recommendation for the Anti-Trafficking Directive to introduce mandatory sanctioning of legal persons that has until now been voluntary for Member States.[56] Whilst this particular

[54] I Wintermayr and A Weatherburn (n 37) 74–75, 79.

[55] Directive (EU) 2019/1152 of the European Parliament and of the Council of 20 June 2019 on transparent and predictable working conditions in the European Union [2019] OJ L186/105–121.

[56] European Commission Proposal (n 27) 13.

recommendation was not included in the final iteration of the 2024 Directive, such innovative considerations of how the imposition of such sanctions could be used for the benefit of victims' access to remedy are to be welcomed and further explored. Notwithstanding, the sanctioning of legal persons under the EU Anti-Trafficking legislation would have territorial limitations as its application would remain intra-EU, thus it is also necessary to consider the global reach of EU businesses, citizens, and consider the role of Member States and authorities to tackle exploitation beyond the borders of the EU.

The Borealis case, for instance, is a clear example of the need for mandatory due diligence. Notably, however, the economic activities of Borealis were, in this example, firmly grounded on European territory; whereas the wider implications of global supply chains and the negative human rights impact on workers in third countries should be carefully considered in the implementation and execution of EU due diligence legislation. For instance, the proposed Regulation on the prohibition of goods made with forced labour on the internal market of the EU will ban products after an investigation confirms that forced labour has been used at any point in the production. The Commission's proposal for the Regulation evoked its complementarity with the Anti-Trafficking Directive and the Employers' Sanctions Directive as a means of guaranteeing victims' rights.[57] However, this guarantee is limited in scope to victims of forced labour that occurs in supply chains within the EU, and does not extend to circumstances of forced labour that take place beyond EU-territory but the products are to be placed or made available on the EU market.[58] As a result, there is a gap in the Proposal in relation to the entitlement to access to justice and remedy for those who were involved in the production process, the workers, who are subsequently victims of forced labour and as such entitled to remedy, compensation, and a guarantee of non-recurrence. The consequence of the proposed Regulation's extra-territorial reach indeed renders things legally complicated, however, international and regional law guarantees the rights of victims of human rights abuses to remedy and thus should not be ignored by any efforts to address business related human rights violations. Encouragingly, the legislative process has moved beyond the silence of the initial proposal, on matters relating to remediation. However, the final text of the Regulation adopted by the Parliament that, at the time of writing, awaits formal approval by the Council, is disappointingly light on remediation obligations with, *inter alia* a requirement for the Commission to make available 'guidance for economic operators on best practices for bringing to an end and remediating different types of forced labour' (Article 11) and an assessment of 'the need for a specific mechanism to address and remediate forced labour [...]' (Article 38(4)).[59]

[57] European Commission, Proposal for a Regulation of the European Parliament and of the Council on prohibiting products made with forced labour on the Union market, Brussels, 14.9.2022 COM(2022) 453 final 2022/0269 (COD).

[58] ibid 2; Methven, O'Brien and Weatherburn (n 16) 2.

[59] European Parliament, Legislative resolution of 23 April 2024 on the proposal for a regulation of the European Parliament and of the Council on prohibiting products made with forced labour on the Union market (COM(2022)0453 – C9-0307/2022 – 2022/0269(COD)), 23 April 2024.

V. Conclusions

The introduction to this chapter raised the issue that the way in which victimhood is categorised can have significant impact on the direction in which law and policy is developed which in turn determines the recognition (or not) of the rights of victims of crime. The sectoral approach in EU criminal law underlines the recognition that victims of exploitation require additional attention when seeking access to remedy. However, as we have seen in the current chapter, there are nevertheless limitations and much depends upon identification as a victim that falls within the scope of the sectoral instruments. Trafficking in human beings, for instance, is one key area wherein the early identification of victims is hampered by several substantive and procedural obstacles that then can impact on the full enjoyment of the specific rights that trafficking victims are entitled to. Similarly, when dealing with migrant workers with an irregular status, the lack of willingness for Member States to recognise the need for specific protection measures significantly hampers their access to remedy. As a result, a large number of victims remain on the margins of protection.

17

Do Victims' Rights and Defendants' Rights Really have to be Equal?

KRISTĪNE STRADA-ROZENBERGA

I. Introduction

At the moment when a criminal offence is committed, two distinct 'roles' are created – that of the perpetrator and of the victim, each with their predominantly divergent interests, including legal ones. Currently, when public officials launch criminal proceedings with respect to the offence, the circle of protected interests expands even more, with the public interest being represented by the Public Prosecutor's Office. The co-existence and, sometimes, collision of different interests is a matter that can be justifiably recognised as being the central one in the theory, legal regulation and practice of criminal procedure.

Admittedly, the possibly asymmetric protection of victims' and defendants' rights in criminal procedures is a sufficiently provocative topic. Readers can read a lot in this volume about the need to protect the victims and their interests and relatively little, if at all, about the offender. Given the topic of this book, the reason for this is clear and justified. However, it is essential that victims' rights are dealt with in conjunction with the rights of the defendants in order to maintain a fair and balanced criminal justice system.

In this chapter, I have focused on those issues, which, to my mind, are made relevant by the topic that was initially assigned, 'Victims' rights and defendants' rights in criminal proceedings: Asymmetric protection?', *inter alia*, whether the victim and the defendant are in comparable positions, whether their rights should be equal and whether, in searching for the symmetry of criminal procedural interests, only the interests of the victim and the defendant matter. The relevance of these aspects is inevitably linked to a systemic view of the interests of the victim, defendant and society, as well as general insight into the victim's role in criminal proceedings. There is no general consensus on these issues set out in the jurisprudence.

The chapter has been written from an academic point of view. We all know that scholars, contrary to, for example, judges, prosecutors, etc, like to raise questions and not always provide precise answers, given that they are convinced that their main task is to provoke discussions and encourage thinking and analysis. Such a somewhat evasive position should not always be tolerated. However, this time, using the opportunity to address, in writing, an audience which is presumably interested in finding pathways towards solutions to problems that are far from simple, this is precisely my intention – to be slightly provocative, hopefully thought-provoking, without providing precise answers or suggestions but rather raising some controversial questions.

This chapter begins by exploring whether the rights of the victim and the defendant are truly unequal and, if so, whether this asymmetry deserves attention. It then examines the criminal process, as a system characterised by the coexistence of various interests, including those of the victim, the defendant and society at large. Following this, the role and position of the victim in the criminal process are analysed. The chapter concludes with a discussion on the coexistence of public and private interests in criminal proceedings, the resulting challenges for the defence and the public, and final general conclusions.

II. Asymmetry in the Protection of Victims' and Defendants' Rights? Some Noteworthy Questions

In order to set the terms of the discussion that will follow, it is important to make a few conceptual clarifications concerning the word 'asymmetric'. While I assume that we all know what asymmetric means, in order to offer as much clarity as possible from the outset in discussions of matters that are anything but simple, I have included some publicly available definitions here. According to the *Cambridge Dictionary*, asymmetry is the condition of not being equal or equally available between two people or groups.[1] The *Oxford Dictionary* tells us that asymmetric means not equal, for example, in the way each side or part behaves.[2] Similarly, the *Collins Dictionary* provides the following definition: 'not symmetrical; lacking symmetry; misproportioned'.[3] Thus, from the dictionary definitions, we can say that asymmetric is equivalent to lacking equality and that it can be applied to the law as well.

Thus, in the context of the topic being discussed, the issue of whether the rights of victims and defendants are not equal and/or equally protected should be put front and centre. Can disproportionality be discerned in ensuring the interests of the victim and defendant? One can only subscribe to the observation, stated in the academic literature, that, for a long time, lawyers have focused on the necessary conditions for creating and maintaining equity between the parties involved in a criminal trial.[4] However, this does not mean at all that this issue has been examined predominantly in the context of ensuring the interests of defendants and victims. It can be admitted that examination of equality between defendants/defence lawyers and the prosecutor prevails in the

[1] See the meaning of 'asymmetry' in English, available at https://dictionary.cambridge.org/dictionary/english/asymmetry.

[2] See the definition of 'asymmetric *adjective*' from the *Oxford Learner's Dictionary*, available at www.oxfordlearnersdictionaries.com/definition/english/asymmetric?q=asymmetric.

[3] See 'asymmetric' in British English, available at www.collinsdictionary.com/dictionary/english/asymmetric.

[4] J Barbot and N Dodier, 'Rethinking the Role of Victims in Criminal Prosecution. Lawyers' Normative Repertoire in France and the United States' (2014) 64(3) *Revue française de science politique* 30.

legal doctrine.[5] And, while it is so, there are no grounds for considering that the issue of equity of rights of the victim and the defendant is not worth examining. Even without delving deeper into the catalogue of the rights of victims and of defendants, every reader understands that the procedural rights that have been granted to the defendant and the victim in criminal proceedings are not the same. This finding leads us to the first provocative question: *Is this really a problem at all and/or an issue that we should be focusing on? When answering this, it seems reasonable to focus on the following question: Do victims' rights and defendants' rights really have to be equal?*

Other questions can help us find an answer to the last one, for example:

Do victims and the accused (suspects, etc) have comparable standings? Or do they have the same (comparable) reasons and goals for participation in criminal proceedings?

Are the victims and the accused really the [only] parties whose interests should be taken into account when looking for 'symmetry'?

In my opinion, all questions can be answered in the negative. Positive replies are also neither possible nor necessary, as demonstrated by slightly more elaborate answers to the previous questions.

Starting with the last question – Are the victims and the accused really the [only] parties whose interests should be taken into account when looking for 'symmetry'? The answer is obviously 'no'. We cannot forget that criminal law is and remains an area of public law where, regardless of how big a role the victim is granted in criminal proceedings, the offender's relationship with the State (serving as the representative of society's interests) is basically dealt with. It must be noted that, with such a statement, I am expressing my support for the traditional theories of criminal law.[6] At the same time, it cannot be denied that emphases are slightly changing in the light of restorative justice, which gives an increasingly greater role to the victim. However, irrespective of the role granted to the victim in criminal proceedings by different theories, the whole of society and the State also undeniably have certain interests in criminal proceedings. After all, a person is made criminally liable for an offence, which the State has declared as being criminally punishable, eg by deprivation of liberty, and the State is not only regulating the relationship between the victim and the offender but also aims to enforce liability in the public-legal area. Thus, at least one other 'party' appears here – the State or society. It can be concluded that criminal proceedings are characterised by the interests of at least three 'parties' – the victim, the accused and society (or the State). By the way, it should be mentioned that, in the academic literature, precisely because of the difficulties encountered in balancing all three interests, concerns are expressed regarding the victim's more active participation in court: '[i]t is hard for the judges when they have to weigh not just two interests – those of the defendant and of the public – but three'.[7]

Regarding the second question – Do victims and the accused (suspects, etc) have comparable standings? Or do they have the same (comparable) reasons and goals for

[5] ibid.

[6] K Braun, *Victim Participation Rights. Variation Across Criminal Justice Systems* (Springer International Publishing, 2019) 285.

[7] Y Baruma, 'Doubts on the Upsurge of the Victim's Role in Crime' in H Kaptein and M Malch (eds), *Crime, Victims and Justice; Essays on Principles and Practice* (Routledge, 2004) 9.

participation in criminal proceedings? The answer is self-evident – 'no'. To a large extent, it follows from the fact that the outcome of the criminal proceedings might be deeply personal both for the offender and the victim. However, basically, consequences that have to be 'endured' (to be found guilty of a criminal offence, penalty, obligation to pay compensation, etc) are incurred by the perpetrator of a criminal offence. Thus, the interest of the suspect or accused person should be linked to the existence of fair proceedings and the achievement of a fair outcome.

The victim's interest should, in turn, be linked to 'compensation' (in terms of the various meanings of this word) for the consequences of a past event, which can take various forms, including material compensation, a public statement that a socially unacceptable violation has been perpetrated against the victim, the feeling that the perpetrator received a just punishment, etc. In any case, the criminal process is not designed to create any negative consequences for the victim (this contribution does not examine situations where the victim's involvement in criminal proceedings leads to a risk of secondary victimisation or other negative effects).

It can therefore be recognised that differences in the very origins of their statuses, goals and reasons for participating, the impact of the possible outcome of criminal proceedings upon the person, etc, clearly point to an acknowledgement that the defendant and the victim are not in comparable positions.

All this leads to the conclusion that there is no need for or even the possibility of equality in terms of the rights of victims and defendants. Moreover, undeniably, 'similarity' in their rights should not be even sought because it is excluded by the differences in their statuses (likewise, we cannot examine similarity in the rights of the prosecution and the defence but only strive for equivalence).

Fully subscribing to the opinion that equality should not be sought but rather viewing this as an interplay of several actors looking for the 'legal Truth',[8] one could ask: maybe there is no reason to worry at all about potential imbalances between the rights of the victims and defendants because of the inherent difficulty in placing them in comparable situations? However, the answer is 'no' again. We can and should worry. The question is: what about? In the following section, I propose to focus on whether the rights of victims and defendants 'coexist' within a united system and whether there is a foreseeable conflict of protected interests and, if so, how to deal with it, etc.

III. 'Coexistence' of the Interest of the Victims, Defendants and Society within One Criminal Procedural System

The finding that the rights of the defendants and the victims are not similar or even not equivalent (which follows objectively from substantial differences in their statuses) raises the question as to whether their interests could potentially conflict. This prompts further inquiry into whether legal regulations on them can evolve independently, in isolation and without interconnection. Examining the victims' and defendants' rights

[8] Barbot and Dodier (n 4) 32.

from a systemic perspective, one cannot but notice that a systemic perspective has either been lacking or has been inadequately addressed. As Klip noted in 2015, '[T]here is no visible attempt to bring the two and their interests in line with each other',[9] and there is no reason to argue that, as things stand, the situation has radically improved.

Schematically, the interconnection between the defendant's and the victim's rights can become problematic in two hypotheses: 1) the scope of defendants' rights granted by law is too broad and offensive to the legal interests of the victims (as well as society); and 2) the scope of victims' rights granted by the law is too broad and potentially harmful to the legal interests of the offender.

Hypothesis 1) – the scope of defendants' rights granted by law is too broad and detrimental to the legal interests of the victims. Despite the intuitive awareness that such cases exist, particular examples cannot be found immediately. Some examples do come to mind. As defendants' rights that are overly damaging to the victim's legal interests, one could mention the right of the defendants' legal team to interrogate persons, whose testimonies are used to substantiate the charges, and the victim's (in particular – a victim in need of special protection) interest in not being too involved in the criminal proceedings. It is hard to find many other suitable examples. I cannot really imagine any right that the defendants could be deprived of, while still ensuring its right to a fair trial. Of course, it needs to be mentioned that the very existence of rights must be distinguished from their abuse, which can hurt the victim as well as society, and therefore should not be allowed in practice.

Hypothesis 2) – the scope of victims' rights granted by law is too broad and/or harmful to the legal interests of the offender – in general, this might seem strange and unusual at first. In our daily life, as well as in studies focusing on victims' rights, we are not particularly required to look at the issue from that point of view, except, perhaps, if we are defence attorneys. Until recently, most national legal systems were rather perceived as neglecting the role of the victim in their criminal justice systems. However, we must admit that, from an outsider's perspective, such situations cannot be completely ruled out. To clarify, perhaps it is not the victims' rights themselves that threaten the accused but rather their abuse. As a vivid example, we can mention disproportionate demands made by the victim to the offender as a prerequisite for not contacting the police, withdrawing their application, settling or otherwise influencing the outcome of the process in favour of the offender. It is worth mentioning that the growing role of the victim as a possible threat to the interests of the accused has not gone unnoticed in the academic literature. Thus, for example, Barbot and Dodier have cited authors who acknowledge the existence of such a risk. They quote, for example, Levy, who described the victims as 'new masters', who are 'even more blind, irrational and threatening than their predecessors'.[10] Henrion admits that 'victims are essentially a weapon for the prosecution',[11] while Salas indicates that 'civil parties constitute a second

[9] A Klip, 'On Victim's Rights and its Impact on the Rights of the Accused' (2015) 23(3) *European Journal of Crime, Criminal Law and Criminal Justice* 177.

[10] T Lévy, *Éloge de la barbarie judiciaire* (Odile Jacob, 2004) quoted in Barbot and Dodier (n 4) 31.

[11] H Henrion, 'La loi du 15 juin 2000 assure-t-elle l'équilibre nécessaire entre les droits et devoirs de l'État, de la personne mise en cause et de la victime?' (2002)24 *Archives de politique criminelle* 81–121 (111) quoted in Barbot and Dodier (n 4) 31.

prosecution team, and that the new powers they have been granted can seem excessive, especially with regard to sentencing'.[12]

However, it is not sufficient to examine the mutual impact of the defendant's and the victim's rights, illustrated only by examples. In this regard, two important directions of examination should be outlined. First, it might be sufficient to ensure only the mutual alignment and non-contradiction of the victim's and defendant's rights to recognise the general fairness of the criminal proceedings. Secondly, looking at the rights of the defendant and the victim, only ensuring the mutual alignment and non-contradiction of the victim's and defendant's rights might not ensure that the rights granted to them are sufficient to protect legal interests and needs. Examination of a deeper meaning is inevitably required in the framework of this book and this chapter, in this case – what the overarching legal goal for the victim's participation in criminal proceedings is. This is the only way to draw the conclusion as to whether they should be granted rights and what rights they should be granted and how conflicts of interests, if they arise, should be dealt with.

IV. The Victim's Role and Position in Criminal Proceedings

Defining the victims' role and the scope of their rights in criminal proceedings is difficult and controversial. This is so despite the fact that this role should be defined first in order to build a coherent criminal procedural system with balanced protection for the interests of the defendants, victims and society. Whilst fully aware of the breadth and complexity of this theme, I will venture, in this chapter, to outline only some possible directions for the discussion.

'Forgotten man', 'forgotten party' are words that have been used to describe the victim in the second half of the last century.[13] 'Victim as forgotten man' is how the US criminologist McDonald described the situation of victims of crime […]. McDonald's stance was later endorsed by Weigend in 1989 in his work 'Deliktsopfer und Straferfahren'.[14]

Currently, it must be recognised that, 'it is no longer true that victims can be considered forgotten persons in most Western justice systems, at least not in legal and political discourse and academic scholarship'.[15]

Undeniably, recent decades have featured considerable efforts to re-examine the victim's role in criminal proceedings. As stated expressively by Doak, 'in recent years, the phenomenon of victims' rights has been catapulted to the forefront of policymaking

[12] D Salas, 'Les enfants d'Orphée. Anciennes et nouvelles victimes' in R Verdier (ed), *Vengeance. Le face à face victime/agresseur* (Autrement, 2004) 209–21 quoted in Barbot and Dodier (n 4) 31.

[13] J Wemmers, 'Where do they Belong? Giving Victims a Place in the Criminal Justice Process' (2009) 20(4) *Criminal Law forum* 395.

[14] C Safferling, The Role of the Victim in the Criminal Process – A Paradigm Shift in National German and International Law? (2011) 11(2) *International Criminal Law Review* 183.

[15] Braun (n 6) 269.

on both domestic and international platforms'.[16] Noting a similar trend, Braun highlights that, 'in political discourse, the term "victim" has become so influential and powerful that some now call it a magical term'.[17] Moreover, the changes occurring in various legal systems are swift and substantial, which leads to the assumption that they will also bring about changes to the criminal procedural system: 'Regardless of the differences between legal traditions, the reassessment of the role of victims in criminal cases has been seen by many observers as a factor that is likely to bring about a serious reconfiguration of the justice system'.[18]

The growing participation of victims in criminal proceedings and the recognition of the importance of their role 'has provoked, and continues to provoke, a number of disputes among jurists. Some are highly sceptical of, and even at times opposed to, this evolution, while others have become fervent supporters'.[19] As described exhaustively by Barbot and Dodier in their publication, the assessments of participation by individual victims and victims' associations in criminal proceedings have differed. It has been positive – underscoring that: 1) without the victim's lawyers, society would not learn about what had happened to the victim; 2) the victim's active participation allows judges to examine the case more adequately; and 3) the victim's presence in criminal proceedings is helpful, in particular in large-scale cases, where otherwise the prosecutor would have to be alone. However, the broader and more active participation of victims in criminal proceedings has often been met with strong resistance, sometimes likened to a new form of political trial.[20]

Irrespective of the generally recognised growing role of the victim and resulting predictions expressed about the need to review the entire criminal justice system, one still has to recognise that the victim's position in criminal proceedings is much vaguer, more uncertain, lacking uniform perception, compared to the position of the defendant. It is confirmed by differences of a general nature in the legal regulation pertaining to the defendant and the victim.

First, unlike the rights of the defendant, for which the scope does not differ much in democratic states, major differences are still found in the victim's participation in criminal proceedings:

> Comparison of model justice systems demonstrates that it is primarily victims who face unequal procedural treatment. For defendants, it makes very little difference whether they are tried in Brisbane or Paris, London or Frankfurt, Chicago or Stockholm: in principle their procedural standing remains the same. For victims, however, the location of a trial can have a significant effect on their representation.[21]

[16] J Doak, *Victims' Rights, Human Rights and Criminal Justice. Reconceiving the Role of Third Parties* (Hart Publishing, 2008) 1.

[17] Braun (n 6) 285.

[18] Barbot and Dodier (n 4) 29–30.

[19] ibid.

[20] ibid.

[21] M Kilchling, 'Price for Victim Participation Rights' in Braun (n 6) xi. Such an assessment could be objected to a certain extent, because national divergences persist when it comes to procedural rights of the defence, which can be clearly seen in the practice of the European Court of Human Rights. We have also witnessed differences as an obstacle to effective cros-border cooperation. However, on a generalised level, one can agree with what Kilchling wrote, because the role and position of the defence is mostly clear, while the situation for the victims is significantly different.

To a large extent, this could be linked to the position (or lack thereof) of each State and its criminal procedural law on stabilising the victim's role in criminal proceedings.

The second issue, which seems even more important, is the definition of 'the meaning' of the criminal procedural rights of the defendant and the victim. The rights of the defendant are clearly related to the overarching aim – ensuring the right to a fair trial, while the 'meaning' of ensuring the victim's rights remains undefined.[22] Other scholars also emphasise that the scope of rights can be understood only by understanding the meaning of participation.[23]

The question arises – why, notwithstanding the need to protect the victim, which has been put to the fore for decades, the problems with 'the meaning' of the criminal procedural rights of the victim still persist. It seems that the answer should be sought in the question itself. The lack of definition of the general goal of the victim's participation in the criminal process is conditioned by the lack of a precise definition of the victim's role in the criminal process. The magical properties of the word 'victim' highlighted by Braun have not led to it being researched to the extent and level that would ensure at least some uniformity.

It does not go unnoticed that considerable attention is paid to the research of the victim's status from the perspective of international criminal law, whereas national and European Union (EU) law perspectives are lagging behind.[24] A study conducted in 2023 identifies a comparatively low level of research activity related to victim participation in criminal proceedings – studies were conducted:

> mostly on the North American continent (45%, number of studies = 26), with all of them focused on the United States alone. The next most common continent of focus was Europe with 13 studies (22%), 5 of which focused on the Netherlands, 3 on the United Kingdom, and 2 on Norway. The majority of studies (88%) focused on victim participation in domestic criminal justice, defined as nation-state jurisdiction.[25]

Although the authors did not have access to all studies of victims conducted in Europe and that had not been the aim of their research, there are no grounds for considering that some of the findings could not be attributed to the research into victim participation in criminal proceedings in general: 'Victim participation itself is clearly important but there is less agreement on what it is, and little on what it looks like for victims in criminal justice'.[26]

> Too often, the literature wields victim participation as a rhetorical device that has no solid base and shifts without explanation. Our review, nonetheless, highlights the wide range of situations and procedures in which victims do participate in criminal justice. This diversity illustrates that, while researchers are looking at different things in different contexts, they are often categorised as similar.[27]

[22] Klip (n 9) 187–89.
[23] S Zappala, 'The Rights of Victims v. the Rights of the Accused' (2010) 8(1) *Journal of International Criminal Justice* 155.
[24] Braun (n 6) viii.
[25] RL Holder and E Englezos, 'Victim Participation in Criminal Justice: A Quantitative Systematic and Critical Literature Review' (2023) 30 (1) *International Review of Victimology* 8.
[26] ibid 4.
[27] ibid 16.

The academic literature indicates that the lack of a theoretical and philosophical basis, as well as the lack of a clear strategy, hinders the consistent development of victim participation rights.[28] I cannot disagree with that. The diversity of opinions about the substance and objectives of criminal law itself has led to a diversity of opinion about the place of the victim within the criminal justice system. The differences may be examined in the light of various criminal law theories,[29] as well as highlighting the place of restorative justice, which, undeniably, is linked to the view on the essence of criminal law.[30] Restorative justice basically recognises the victim's important role; however, views can be found in theory that, if it is carried out under the 'criminal justice umbrella', it may be basically offender-oriented.[31] Likewise, proposals have been made to differentiate the victim's role, depending on the severity of the criminal offence committed.[32]

Although the majority of researchers can be included in either a 'pro-victim' or 'anti-victim' stream of thinking, contemporary doctrine can hardly be characterised as uniform:

> The complexity of the doctrinal space surrounding the issue of victims is due to the fact that these axes do not share the space in the same way. All jurists are not pro-victim or anti-victim along all the axes, though some of them may be. In order to elaborate a global position, each jurist must therefore structure and weigh his or her arguments along each axis.[33]

Pronounced polarisation of opinions is observed. Diversity within the 'pro-victim' stream itself is significant, as two sub-currents can be discerned – repressive and liberal: A 'repressive position brings together actors who have tried to expand the powers granted to victims and their representatives in the justice system while still defending an increase in repression', while, at the

> liberal end of the spectrum, in both the United States and France, we find actors who seek to improve the conditions of crime victims without necessarily increasing repressive measures. These actors prefer out-of-court mechanisms: improving compensation conditions, providing psychological support, and establishing mediation bodies.[34]

The inability to reach an agreement on the basics – the essence, goal and meaning of the victim participation in criminal proceedings and, consequently, his/her rights – is obvious. The lack of understanding of the meaning and purpose of exercising the victim's rights also raises a valid question regarding the consequences of disregarding these rights.[35]

All these are reasons for agreeing with Doak, who has recognised that

> the phrase 'victims' rights' has now entered into widespread usage among politicians, academics and the media. Unfortunately, the terminology tends to be deployed in an imprecise

[28] Braun (n 6) 285.

[29] ibid 271–72.

[30] H Kaptein and M Malch (ed), *Crime, Victims and Justice; Essays on Principles and Practice* (Routledge, 2004) vii–x.

[31] I Vanfraechem and D Bolivar, 'Restorative Justice and Victims of Crime' in I Vanfraechem, D Bolivar and I. Aersten, *Victims and Restorative Justice* (Routledge, 2015) 55–57.

[32] Baruma (n 7) 4–13.

[33] Barbot and Dodier (n 4) 43.

[34] Barbot and Dodier (n 4) 44.

[35] Klip (n 9) 187–89.

> manner. [D]iscussions around the idea of 'victims' rights' frequently produce more heat than light.[36]

The situation seems to be unclear but is there a way out of it? Obviously, there is no unified view in Europe on which dogmatic foundations criminal justice should be built and, consequently, what the role of the victim in it should be. Can it be remedied? I shall be pessimistic, taking the view which doubts that a consensus can be reached, at least in the near future.[37] This only means that the diversity of opinions will continue in theory, but, from a legal and political point of view, specific decisions will have to be made in this situation. Using the absence of unified doctrinal foundations as a pretext cannot be the grounds for refusing to ensure effective protection for the lawful interests of the participants in the proceedings. Moreover, undeniably, diversity and even contention in academic research and opinions *per se* are not bad and drive the development of science. However, the existence of different doctrinal views might urge the national legislator to make a clear and unambiguous law policy choice regarding the model selected as the foundation for the legal regulation. It is necessary to define clearly and comprehensively the purpose of various criminal procedural institutions, including the participation of victims and their rights, as well as to ensure internal alignment with and no contradiction with the legal protection system, which does not automatically exclude the possibility of legally protected interests colliding / clashing with each other.

V. The Coexistence of Public and Private Interests in the Criminal Proceedings and the Challenges it Creates

In criminal proceedings, where the protection of different interests should be ensured, situations where a conflict between these interests arises cannot be completely avoided. Although it should be admitted that, even if the occurrence of a conflict of interest cannot be excluded, it will not always arise. In the academic literature we see, at the same time, findings that 'it could easily lead to competition of interests between fair justice for the victim and a fair trial for the defendant',[38] 'a single issue policy pro-victim can be detrimental not only to the rights of the accused, but also to the efficiency and fairness of the proceedings as a whole',[39] '[i]t does not necessarily follow that the interests of victims and offenders will always conflict'.[40]

It would be cumbersome to enumerate all potential conflicts of protected interests that might arise in specific cases. The following could be mentioned, taking the Latvian national regulation as an example:

- different approaches to providing legal assistance (every accused person has the right to a lawyer paid for by the State, while not all victims have this right);

[36] Doak (n 16) 1.
[37] Braun (n 6) 286.
[38] Baruma (n 7) 9; Zappala (n 23) 162.
[39] Klip (n 9) 177–78.
[40] Doak (n 16) 247.

- the right to testify (remain silent) versus the duty to testify (while the accused has a general right to remain silent, the victims have the right not to testify about themselves and their relatives); and
- the right to examination of evidence versus the right not to be secondarily victimised (while the accused has the right to question the victim in court, it is probably in the best interest of the victim never to see the abuser again), etc.

One can agree, though, '[t]hat there are occasions when rights of victims and offenders will conflict, but this need not give rise to undue levels of concern'.[41] In case the interests clash, '[t]he better solution […] is to resolve conflicts of rights on a case-by-case basis using [a] principled rights-based framework'.[42] Since I side with those researchers who consider that the very essence of criminal procedure is the provision of criminal law solutions with respect to the defendant and, hence, recognising the primacy of the accused person's rights, I shall consent that

> any conflict between the rights of victims and the rights of defendants has to be the object of a delicate balancing [act] that must be carried out in the knowledge that the overarching purpose of criminal procedure is to reach a finding of guilt or innocence whilst protecting, at the highest level, the rights of those subjected to the proceedings (i.e. the suspect and the accused).[43]

Although all these issues deserve additional attention, in view of the general nature of this survey, this time I shall focus on *prima facie* contradictory interests and possible conflicts between them at a general level. And, even though many more cases of conflict of interest could be examined from this perspective, I have chosen to explore three of them: the need to protect victims in the criminal procedure versus the overuse of the criminal justice system; public versus private interests in criminal proceedings and the presumption of being a 'non-offender' versus the presumption of being a 'victim'.

Starting with the first one – the need to protect victims in the criminal procedure versus overuse of the criminal justice system. An offence that has been committed and has made someone a victim, of course, causes inconvenience, losses, emotions, etc to the person who has been harmed. It is only natural that support and protection are provided to this person. An important question, however, arises in such a case – should it always be protection belonging to the area of criminal justice? We see two opposing approaches when examining this issue – 'overuse of the criminal law system' and 'underuse of the criminal justice system'. While the first one sees risks in too intensive an 'operation' of the criminal justice system, both by criminalising offences and prosecuting them, as well as by punishing the offenders,[44] the other relates to an insufficient crackdown on criminals, which reduces the level of protection for victims.[45] Finding

[41] ibid.
[42] ibid 248.
[43] Zappala (n 23) 143–45.
[44] For more extensive research of this phenomenon, see PHPHMC van Kempen and M Jendly (eds), 'Overuse in Criminal Justice System. On Criminalisation, Prosecution and Imprisonment' (Intersentia, 2019).
[45] CL Ferguson, 'Actualizing Justice: Private Prosecution Regimes for Modern Social Movements' (2023) 56(4) *Columbia Journal of Law and Social Problems* 560–61.

a reasonable balance is not an easy task. Presumably, in this situation, the interests of society should be primary, not of specific people (where, supposedly, in the majority of cases, victims will wish to trigger criminal justice, severe penalties and large compensations, etc, whereas the offenders will wish for exactly the opposite).

For criminal law to be effective, it must be ensured that it is not overburdened. At the same time, it must ensure a fair process against violators and effective protection of victims. It is not simple at all. In order to initiate a discussion, a proposal may be made to consider effective protection of victims of less serious crimes without linking it to formal criminal proceedings. Thus, on the one hand, support, the possibility to receive compensation, etc would be ensured to victims and, on the other hand, to implement it, 'setting in motion' the rather unwieldy system of criminal proceedings would not be necessary.

Now I will discuss public and private interests in criminal proceedings. It is generally acknowledged that criminal law is a branch of public law. However, is it possible to have private interests (which, for the purposes of this chapter, refer to the interests of individual persons as opposed to the State/public interest) in a criminal procedure?

It is worth recalling that modern criminal law originates from tort law, where 'in the absence of a central State authority, the victim/offender conflict was historically conceptualised as a private matter outside the State's immediate interests'.[46] A significant turning point came in the Middle Ages when the view of criminal law as, basically, the way in which the State prosecutes a criminal, emerged.[47] Today, modern criminal law is generally perceived as having a predominant function in protecting the public interest and, consequently, as an area of public law. However, this does not provide grounds for excluding the existence of private interests from criminal proceedings and, likewise, protection thereof. See, eg, Recital 9 of Directive 2012/29/EU establishing minimum standards on the rights, support and protection of victims of crime (hereinafter the 'Victims' Rights Directive'),[48] which provides that 'crime is a wrong against society as well as a violation of the individual rights of victims'. Thus, if crime affects two types of interests, then two types of interests are also protected in the criminal proceedings for this crime. Likewise, undeniably, not only those who suffered from the criminal offence but also those who have committed it have protected interests. Thus, next to the interests of society and the victim, we also see a third set of protected interests – those that are characteristic of the defendant. And this is still not the end – other persons may become involved in criminal proceedings and criminal procedural decisions can be taken with respect to them (eg those whose property is confiscated within the framework of the so-called extended confiscation or whose premises are searched, etc). They also have their own private interests. Thus, undeniably, in the implementation of criminal proceedings, both public and private interests and protection of them are important. The only thing we need to understand is how public (characteristic of society as a whole) and private (characteristic of an individual

[46] Doak (n 16) 2.

[47] ibid 2–4.

[48] Directive 2012/29/EU of the European Parliament and of the Council of 25 October 2012 establishing minimum standards on the rights, support and protection of victims of crime, and replacing Council Framework Decision 2001/220/JHA ELI [2012] OJ L315/57, available at http://data.europa.eu/eli/dir/2012/29/oj.

person) can coexist within one common criminal justice system. At the same time, it needs to be understood that the prevalence of private interests is not characteristic of criminal procedure, rather – proportionate restriction of private interests (prohibition of arbitrary infringement) for the purpose of protecting public interests. In some cases, it cannot be established so clearly, leading to the valid question of how to strike a balance.

In the context of the coexistence of the victim's private rights and public interests, one way of looking at it is to see the interests of the victim as corresponding to the interests of the whole of society. It is undeniable that it is in the public interest to ensure the protection of victims, prevent repeated victimisation, etc. However, alignment between the interests of victims and the public interest will not always be apparent. For example, the inclusion of compensation paid by the perpetrator to the victim, which by its nature is a matter of private law (in the sense that it can be claimed and can remain unclaimed, a certain amount of it is defined through agreement, State institutions (society) have very limited possibilities to intervene in this, etc) in criminal proceedings clearly indicates that interests of a private law nature can also be ensured during criminal proceedings. The victim's opinion may be decisive in legal systems which provide for so-called private prosecution.[49] Thus, only this question remains open – which aspects of criminal proceedings need to be taken into account and to what extent do we make these aspects 'private'. I fully subscribe to Safferling's conclusion:

> If victim participation should lead to the privatisation of criminal proceedings, then the current procedural structure will be threatened. Not only would one be forced to reconsider the aims of the criminal process, but its very basis and purpose would be called into question.[50]

I believe that, in further strengthening the victim's role, ways for avoiding 'privatisation' of criminal proceedings should be sought, without leaving the solution to matters of public importance only at the discretion of private persons.

To illustrate my reflections I might ask – can the initiation of criminal proceedings be determined by the victim's private position? These reflections focus on the right of the victim to have a decisive influence on whether a criminal trial will take place or whether the person will be prosecuted, along with the resulting legal consequences. Specifically, I refer to criminal proceedings that can be initiated and continued only if the victim desires, a situation that is common in many European countries. There are clear benefits to this approach: it aligns with the trend towards simplifying criminal proceedings, supports efficiency considerations, and empowers the victim by giving them a decisive role in the process, etc. But there are also the negative ones – issues of public importance are left to the discretion of one or several private persons, criminal liability becomes dependent not upon the substance of the offences, but the

[49] Ferguson (n 45) 557–604; J Mujuzi, 'Victim Participation in the Criminal Justice System in the European Union through Private Prosecutions: Issues Emerging from the Jurisprudence of the European Court of Human Rights' (2016) 24(2-3) *European Journal of Crime, Criminal Law, and Criminal Justice* 107.

[50] C Safferling, 'The Role of the Victim in the Criminal Process – A Paradigm Shift in National German and International Law?' (2011) 11(2) *International Criminal Law Review* 186.

willingness/unwillingness and ability/disability of the involved subjects to reach an agreement, etc.[51]

In concluding my brief reflections on private interests in criminal proceedings, I remain convinced that the growing role of the victim should not be mandatorily linked to the re-examination of the very foundations of criminal procedure and, even more so, of criminal law as the means for protecting the interests of society and (at the same time) of the victim. The fairness of criminal law (both substantive and procedural) is and undeniably will be linked to respect for the victim's rights; however, within the limits defined by public interests. Thus, strengthening the protection of the victim is fully supported (within the criminal procedure and out of criminal proceedings). At the same time, the right to participation requires careful analysis to ensure that the victim's participation does not infringe on the accused's right to a fair trial, and secondly, the public interest in fair criminal law norms and ensuring the preventive role of criminal law.

I will now turn to the last point, namely the presumption of being a 'non-offender' or presumption of innocence versus the presumption of being a 'victim'. This is quite an interesting nuance, highlighted in recent literature,[52] *inter alia* pointing to the negative aspects that could be caused by calling someone a 'victim' prematurely. Without denying the existence of some controversial aspects, I support, however, the general view that it should not deter officials from granting the status of a victim to particular persons already during the proceedings, without waiting for the final legal ruling in the case on whether a crime has been committed and by whom. In fact, when we talk about victims in the course of criminal proceedings, we are talking about people who are presumed (but not proven) to have been victims of a crime. It is quite reasonable to apply the presumption that that person has suffered so that they can exercise their rights and be protected, as well as to ensure active participation in effective detection of the crime committed against that person. However, concluding from the fact that someone is considered a victim in the proceedings that there is also a [concrete] offender is not justified, as this would violate the latter's fundamental right to the presumption of innocence.

VI. Conclusions

As complex social and legal phenomena, a criminal offence and criminal proceedings are connected with the need to respect the interests of several subjects. Since, generally, there are two parties to a crime – the perpetrator and the victim, *prima facie*, the question of whether protection of their interests is provided equally seems valid. However, a deeper examination leads to the conclusion that the victim and the offender are not in comparable positions in the criminal proceedings – the prerequisites for

[51] For more detail, see A Meikalisa and K Strada-Rozenberga, 'The Victim – "A Passive Observer or an Active Participant". General Observations Following From the Assessment of Latvia's Experience' in G Mesko, A Sotlar and JR Greene (eds), *Criminal Justice and Security – Contemporary Criminal Justice Practice and Research Conference Proceedings* (University of Maribor, 2013) 255–56.

[52] Doak (n 16) 20–24; Klip (n 9) 186–89.

participation, the goals of participation, as well as the legally protected interests, etc, differ. This means that the inequality of their rights is not a relevant problem. However, we should be concerned about balancing the protection of the victims, the defendants and the public interest to ensure a fair result in terms of criminal justice.

Strengthening the 'participation rights' of the victim is currently not possible due to the lack of a unified theoretical and philosophical base, a clear strategy. The lack of consistent doctrinal perspective on the victim's role in criminal proceedings – stemming from the varied accepted models of such proceedings – should not be seen as a valid reason to deny improvements in victim protection and the legal framework governing their participation in criminal proceedings. This, however, requires a strict law policy choice, selecting the model of criminal proceedings as the basis for the legal regulation, which would be followed by consistent further activities to define, clearly and understandably, various criminal procedural institutions, including the purpose of victim participation and the victim's rights, as well as to ensure internal alignment with and no contradiction with the legal protection system and to ensure further actions that are internally aligned.

Situations where the interests of the defendants, victims and society collide with each other cannot be generally excluded. They can be solved in each specific situation by 'weighing and measuring' and finding the fairest solution for each situation. Subscribing to the so-called traditional theories of criminal law, I believe that it would be valid to recognise ensuring the right to a fair trial for the accused person as one of the most essential elements in 'weighing and measuring'.

Special attention should be paid to the trends of 'privatising' criminal proceedings by determining the prevalence of the victim's private interests in criminal proceedings. Public interests would be the appropriate grounds for setting limits in respecting the victim's private interests. In strengthening the victim's role, the approach to criminal law as, primarily, a tool for protecting public interests, should not be revised, at the same time ensuring the general function of criminal law in protecting society, as well as reinforcing its preventive nature.

18

Prospects of Increasing Victims' Rights in Criminal Proceedings: The Fault Lines in the EU Procedural Fairness Mode

LAURE BAUDRIHAYE-GÉRARD[1]

I. Introduction and Background

In its Proposal to strengthen the rights of victims published in July 2023,[2] the European Commission seeks to increase the participation of victims in criminal proceedings. It notes that currently, 'victims' participation in criminal proceedings is often difficult due to a lack of legal advice and guidance and differences in rules on victims' status in these procedures'[3] and sets as one of the specific objectives of the proposed revision 'more effective participation in criminal proceedings for victims'.[4]

This chapter seeks to contribute to the discussion by offering reflections based on experiences of the implementation of the European Union (EU) defence rights in Member States[5] and open a broader reflection on the wider criminal justice system in which defence and victim rights are given substance. Although the two sets of rights, defence rights on the one hand, and victims' rights on the other, are often branded against one another and analysed as conflicting,[6] the purpose here is not to pit one set

[1] Researcher, Faculty of Law and Criminology, Université Libre de Bruxelles. This chapter is based on the author's professional experience as Legal Director at Fair Trials Europe (2018–2023).

[2] Proposal of 12 July 2023 for a Directive of the European Parliament and of the Council amending Directive 2012/29/EU establishing minimum standards on the rights, support and protection of crime, and replacing Council Framework Decision 2001/220/JHA, COM(2023) 424 final ('Victims Rights Directive Revision Proposal').

[3] ibid 2.

[4] ibid 3.

[5] This chapter also includes experiences from the United Kingdom (UK), which are relevant for the purpose of this analysis to the extent that these illustrations date prior to the withdrawal of the UK from the EU or are indicative of broader trends across Europe.

[6] For instance, Klip argues that Directive 2012/29/EU of the European Paliament and of the Council of 25 October 2012 establishing minimum standards on the rights, support and protection of victims of crime, and replacing Council Framework Decision 2001/220/JHA [2012] OJ 315/57 makes the assumption that the victim is a victim of the accused: 'the question is whether this may not violate the presumption of innocence of the accused and affect the fairness of the proceedings as the accused will be confronted with an

of rights against the other or make the case for or against more defence rights or rights for victims. Instead, the reflections aim to extricate the discussion from what may be a reductive and artificial framework of analysis and understand the broader criminal justice system within which they operate.

After setting out a short overview of the EU law on defence rights, this chapter highlights the challenges that the procedural fairness model faces, in light of the shifting priorities of EU and national criminal justice systems towards efficiency and crime control.

A. Background on Defence Rights in EU Law

The right to a fair trial is an internationally recognised fundamental human right. As such, procedural rights aimed at ensuring fairness in criminal proceedings already existed in national legal systems and in the European Convention for the Protection of Human Rights (ECHR). However, as EU Member States started cooperating more closely in the field of criminal justice, in particular with the adoption of the European Arrest Warrant (EAW) Framework Decision in June 2002,[7] which involves particularly intrusive measures, enhancing mutual trust became part of the EU's political agenda. The Council, at the time of entry into force of the Lisbon Treaty, considered it necessary to create a common set of minimum EU standards for procedural safeguards in order to enhance mutual trust between European judicial authorities:

> mutual recognition presupposes that the competent authorities of the Member States trust the criminal justice systems of the other Member States. For the purpose of enhancing mutual trust within the European Union, it is important that, complementary to the Convention, there exist European Union standards for the protection of procedural rights which are properly implemented and applied in the Member States.[8]

In other words, mutual recognition could only function if judicial authorities were persuaded that the legal systems in other Member States offered equivalent safeguards.[9]

In order to strengthen EU judicial cooperation mechanisms, the EU initiated in 2009 the legislative process for the adoption of a suite of measures setting minimum standards for the procedural safeguards of suspects and accused persons in criminal proceedings, through the legislative programme known as the 'Stockholm Roadmap'.[10]

The EU adopted a total of six directives on procedural rights in criminal proceedings both pre-trial and at trial, based on Article 82(2) of the Treaty on the Functioning of the EU:

additional accuser on top of the prosecution. Nowhere in the Directive is it reflected that an alleged victim might not be (the) victim of the accused' in A Klip, 'On Victim's Rights and its Impact on the Rights of the Accused' (2015) 23 *European Journal of Crime, Criminal Law and Criminal Justice* 186–87.

[7] Council Framework Decision 2002/584/JHA of 13 June 2002 on the European arrest warrant and the surrender procedures between Member States [2002] OJ L190.

[8] Resolution of the Council of 30 November 2009 on a Roadmap for strengthening procedural rights of suspected or accused persons in criminal proceedings [2009] OJ C295/1, Recital 8.

[9] P Berthelet, 'Espace pénal et Sécurité intérieure, deux projets distincts de l'Union européenne aux dynamiques parallèles' (2017) 14 *Champ pénal* 8, available at https://journals.openedition.org/champpenal/9506.

[10] Resolution of the Council of 30 November 2009 on a Roadmap (n 8).

- Directive 2010/64/EU on the right to interpretation and translation in criminal proceedings,[11] which aims to provide a general right to interpretation and translation of documents from the moment persons are made aware by the competent authorities that they are suspected or accused of having committed a criminal offence until the conclusion of the proceedings; including a right to interpretation during consultations with lawyers.
- Directive 2012/13/EU on the right to information in criminal proceedings,[12] which notably includes the obligation that authorities provide a written letter of rights to people in case of arrest, as well as access to the case file where a person is detained, enabling a possible challenge of such detention.
- Directive 2013/48/EU on the right of access to a lawyer in criminal proceedings,[13] which is arguably the most progressive directive, in that it expressly grants the right for suspects or accused persons to consult with a lawyer before a police interrogation, and to having a lawyer present during the interrogation.
- Directive 2016/343/EU on the presumption of innocence and the right to be present at one's trial,[14] which was interpreted by the EU Court of Justice as pursuing 'minimal harmonisation',[15] and notably not regulating pre-trial detention which authorities may order when a person is still presumed innocent (ie before any finding of guilt).
- Directive 2016/800/EU on procedural safeguards for children who are suspects or accused persons in criminal proceedings,[16] covers a wide range of rights, including in relation to detention conditions.
- Directive 2016/1919/EU on legal aid for suspects and accused persons in criminal proceedings and for requested persons in European arrest warrant proceedings.[17] The purpose of this sixth directive is to ensure the effectiveness of the right of access to a lawyer enshrined in Directive 2013/48/EU, by making available the assistance of a lawyer funded by the Member States for suspects and accused persons under certain conditions (determined by national law) where the person cannot afford a lawyer.[18]

[11] Directive 2010/64/EU of the European Parliament and of the Council of 20 October 2010 on the right to interpretation and translation in criminal proceedings [2010] OJ L280/1.

[12] Directive 2012/13/EU of the European Parliament and of the Council of 22 May 2012 on the right to information in criminal proceedings [2012] OJ L142/1.

[13] Directive 2013/48/EU of the European Parliament and of the Council of 22 October 2013 on the right of access to a lawyer in criminal proceedings and in European arrest warrant proceedings, and on the right to have a third party informed upon deprivation of liberty and to communicate with third persons and with consular authorities while deprived of liberty [2013] OJ L294/1.

[14] Directive 2016/343/EU of the European Parliament and of the Council of 9 March 2016 on the strengthening of certain aspects of the presumption of innocence and of the right to be present at trial in criminal proceedings [2016] OJ L65/1.

[15] Case C-310/18 PPU *Emil Milev* [2018] ECLI:EU:C:2018:732, para 47.

[16] Directive 2016/800/EU of the European Parliament and of the Council of 11 May 2016 on procedural safeguards for children who are suspects or accused persons in criminal proceedings [2016] OJ L132/1.

[17] Directive 2016/1919/EU of the European Parliament and of the Council of 26 October 2016 on legal aid for suspects and accused persons in criminal proceedings and for requested persons in European arrest warrant proceedings [2016] OJ L297/1.

[18] ibid Recital 1.

The set of EU defence rights builds upon ECHR standards, which set a 'minimum' level of protection that EU law can expand upon, as specified in the Charter of Fundamental Rights of the EU.[19] Setting out defence rights in EU law also offers the prospect of heightened enforcement, with the European Commission's power to initiate infringement procedures against Member States who fail to implement the EU directives, and potentially pursue legal action before the Court of Justice of the EU (CJEU). To this suite of directives, it is necessary also to mention the Vulnerable Suspects Recommendation of 27 November 2013,[20] which, albeit non-binding for Member States, sets out specific procedural safeguards for vulnerable suspects.[21]

Whilst the original objective of this suite of measures is ensuring mutual trust between judicial authorities, the result is a set of directives binding national authorities, courts and tribunals in all criminal proceedings, including those which have no cross-border element. The EU defence rights model enshrines procedural fairness values and its potential appeared to be far-reaching.

The rights of victims are not mentioned in the defence rights directives.[22] Yet before the Stockholm Roadmap was adopted, the EU had already enacted legislation in relation to victims' rights, specifically the Council Framework Decision 2001/220/JHA of 15 March 2001 on the standing of victims in criminal proceedings. The instrument was subsequently replaced by Directive 2012/29/EU establishing minimum standards on the rights, support and protection of victims of crime (hereinafter 'Directive 2012/29/EU' or 'the Directive on Victims' Rights'). The Directive on Victims' Rights includes provisions in relation to the participation of victims in criminal proceedings. Specifically, it aims to ensure that 'victims of crime receive appropriate information, support and are able to participate in criminal proceedings'.[23] In this respect, Directive 2012/29/EU confirmed the choice made in Framework Decision 2001/220/JHA not to compel national governments to harmonise their legislation relating to the victim's role in criminal proceedings.[24] As a result, depending on the national legal system, this may include active participation, in the form of the right to be heard at trial; or it may be foreseen that the victim participate in a 'passive' way, by exercising the right to be present and observe the criminal trial.[25]

[19] Charter of Fundamental Rights of the European Union, Art 52(3), provides that: 'in so far as this Charter contains rights which correspond to rights guaranteed by the Convention for the Protection of Human Rights and Fundamental Freedoms, the meaning and scope of those rights shall be the same as those laid down by the said Convention. This provision shall not prevent Union law providing more extensive protection'.

[20] Commission Recommendation of 27 November 2013 on procedural safeguards for vulnerable persons suspected or accused in criminal proceedings [2013] OJ C378/02.

[21] In this context, vulnerability is restricted to age, mental or physical condition or disabilities (Recital 1).

[22] Only Recital 20 of Directive 2016/343/EU (n 14) requires authorities to abstain from the use of restraining measures in court or in public, unless required for case-specific reasons relating to 'the prevention of suspects or accused persons (…) from having contact with third persons, such as witnesses or victims'.

[23] Directive 2012/29/EU (n 6) Art 1(1).

[24] As can be inferred from Recital 20 of the Directive on Victims' Rights, ibid, Member States are free to determine whether victims should be accorded legal status as parties to proceedings, allowed to participate in proceedings or permitted to give evidence as a witness. This is notably reflected in the frequent use of cautious expressions such as 'if such a right exist in national law', 'in accordance with the role of the victim in the relevant criminal justice system' or 'in accordance with the procedural rules determined by national law'.

[25] Directive 2012/29/EU (n 6) Art 10 provides that: '1. Member States shall ensure that victims may be heard during criminal proceedings and may provide evidence. Where a child victim is to be heard, due account shall

In the Victims' Rights Directive Revision Proposal, the Commission seeks to increase the active participation of victims in criminal proceedings, by including two new provisions. First, a new Article 10a which would require Member States to take the necessary measures to establish assistance in court for victims 'to provide information and emotional support to victims'. Secondly, the right to challenge decisions taken during court proceedings which affect victims (Article 10b). Recital 9 of the Proposal states that: 'for victims to sense that justice is done and to be able to defend their interest, it is important that they are present and able to actively participate in the criminal proceedings'.

The two sets of rights – those of suspects and accused persons and those of victims – are seemingly developed in siloes,[26] and there is no guidance on their interaction in EU legislation: 'whilst it does recognise the relationship between the rights of the defence and the rights of the victim, it leaves quite some ambiguity as to which rights in the end prevail'.[27] Notwithstanding the fact that victims may be granted more or less extensive rights to participate in criminal proceedings in national legal systems, a study into the UK and French legal systems notes the predominance, in practice, of defence rights when they conflict with victims' rights:

> bolstered by the overarching standard of the right to a fair trial, systems tend to center on the rights of the accused. This means that when interests conflict – for example, the witness's desire not to testify in front of the accused, as against the accused's right to hear and challenge the evidence against her – it is the rights of the accused that will prevail, in order to respect the presumption of innocence and ensure a fair hearing.[28]

Such evidence can fuel calls for legislation that reinforces victims' rights in line with the rights of suspects and accused persons in order to even out this apparent imbalance.

Section II offers reflections from the implementation of defence rights that are aimed at informing the policy debate around increasing victims' rights of participation in criminal proceedings.

II. Reflections from the Practice of EU Defence Rights

Nearly 15 years since the adoption of the Stockholm Roadmap, and the affirmation of the procedural fairness model in EU law, there is widespread evidence of an implementation gap between EU law 'on books' and the practice of defence rights at the domestic level. The implementation gap can be seen as fault lines revealing the broader shifts in the objectives of criminal justice systems towards efficiency and punitiveness,

be taken of the child's age and maturity. 2. The procedural rules under which victims may be heard during criminal proceedings and may provide evidence shall be determined by national law'.

[26] The Explanatory Memorandum of the Proposal indicates that the Proposal has been assessed in light of the rights of 'offenders, suspects and accused persons' but does not provide any analysis (p 12).

[27] Klip (n 6) 185, using by way of example: 'Article 7, paragraph 6, deals with the issue that an oral summary or translate may be provided instead of a written translation on condition that such oral translation or summary does not prejudice the "fairness of the proceedings". This raises the question whether fairness to the victim or to the accused is meant here.'

[28] JS Hodgson, *The Metamorphosis of Criminal Justice, A Comparative Account* (Oxford University Press, 2020) 12–13.

conflicting with the values of procedural fairness (section II.A). The growth in the use of trial waiver systems (such as plea bargaining) and fast track proceedings across the EU, leading to an increasing number of offences being processed and punished without court proceedings, reveals the prioritisation on efficiency over the values of the procedural fairness model advanced by the EU (section II.B). The pursuit of 'crime control' objectives is also in tension with procedural fairness, and involves significant repercussions that affect people in contact with the criminal justice system, whether as 'suspects or accused persons' or as 'victims', that call for reflection well beyond new or reinforced individual rights (section II.C).

A. The Implementation Gap between the Law and Practice of the EU Defence Rights System: The Tension between Efficiency and Procedural Fairness

Member States have long been due to implement all six procedural rights directives, transposition deadlines having passed. However, there is empirical evidence that the EU law on defence rights faces significant implementation gaps, both in national law and in practice. The implementation reports published by the European Commission, assessing the extent to which Member States have taken the necessary measures to comply with the Stockholm Roadmap directives, reveal some of the challenges of translating law into practice. To date, the Commission published reports on the status of implementation of five of the six directives.[29] The Commission bases its analysis primarily on information provided by Member States through the notification of national measures transposing the relevant directives, studies by the European Union Agency for Fundamental Rights, as well as reports by civil society organisations. A common finding across the implementation reports is that the directives provide 'EU added value' by raising the level of protection of citizens involved in criminal proceedings, especially in some Member States where the EU procedural safeguards did not exist beforehand, but that the extent of the directives' impact on Member States varies according to the national criminal justice systems in place.

There is a certain tension between the harmonisation of procedural safeguards in criminal proceedings and the principle of national procedural autonomy, which provides that 'the detailed procedural rules applicable are a matter for the domestic legal order of each member State'.[30] As measures of implementation vary across Member States, the effectiveness of defence rights also varies across national legal systems. For example, in the most recent implementation report on Directive 2016/1919/EU on the right to legal aid, the Commission recognises that approaches to transposing the Directive varies between Member States:

> some Member States introduced specific legislative measures explicitly transposing the rights under the Directive alongside other legal or practical implementation measures. Other

[29] At the time of writing, the European Commission had not published an implementation report on Directive 2016/800/EU (n 16) on the rights of children in criminal proceedings.

[30] Case C-201/02 *The Queen, on the Application of Delena Wells v Secretary of State for Transport, Local Government and the Regions* EU:C:2004:12, para 67.

> Member States considered that their existing measures were already broadly in line with the Directive's requirements, and did not adopt any specific transposing measures.[31]

As a result of this disparity, the Commission identifies significant shortcomings:

> while the absence of dedicated transposing provisions is sometimes remedied at least to some extent by means of practical implementation measures and case law, this is not always the case. In a number of Member States (22), national provisions are thus insufficient to fully comply with certain key provisions of the Directive.[32]

The Commission can decide to initiate infringement proceedings pursuant to Article 258 of the Treaty on the Functioning of the European Union against Member States for failure to implement some of the elements of the directives. In the February 2024 infringement package, the European Commission referred Belgium and Luxembourg to the CJEU for not fully granting the right of access to a lawyer and communication upon arrest (having sent letters of formal notice to both countries in 2021). However, infringement proceedings remain the exception, the enforcement of EU law being decentralised and due to happen in the courts of the Member States by way of judicial review.[33] It is in national criminal proceedings that lawyers can seek to rely on EU law in their pleadings, and that courts make decisions on whether to apply EU law in the case at hand. It is on this 'frontline' that implementation happens, where EU law is 'in action'. In this respect, it is informative to turn to reports published by civil society organisations across Europe, which are based on consultations with criminal justice practitioners.

A consortium of organisations conducted a comprehensive empirical study of suspects' rights at the investigative stage of the criminal process in nine EU countries, focusing on the implementation of the relevant procedural safeguards enshrined in three of the directives in the context of police custody ('Inside Police Custody 2').[34] The most difficult area of implementation was in relation to access to a lawyer during police custody. Although the national legal systems of the studied countries provided for such a right, the research notes that 'effective exercise of the right of access to a lawyer is, in practice, limited by a range of factors'[35] such as the unavailability of legal aid, but also as a result of certain dissuasive police practices: 'the police use fears about the cost of having a lawyer to deter suspects from exercising their right'. Even when the right to a lawyer was exercised, the report questions its effectiveness, noting that: 'for a range of reasons, many lawyers in many of the countries, particularly legal aid

[31] Report from the Commission to the European Parliament and the Council on the implementation of Directive (EU) 2016/1919 of the European Parliament and of the Council of 26 October 2016 on legal aid for suspects and accused persons in criminal proceedings and for requested persons in European arrest warrant proceedings, 1 February 2023, COM(2023) 44 final, available at https://eur-lex.europa.eu/legal content/EN/TXT/HTML/?uri=CELEX:52023DC0044. According to Directive (EU) 2016/1919 (n 17) Art 12, Member States had to transpose the Directive into national law by 25 May 2019.

[32] ibid.

[33] Case C-64/16 *Associaçao Sindical dos Juízes Portugueses v Tribunal de Contas* ECLI:EU:C:2018:117, para 32.

[34] E Lloyd-Cape, 'Comparative Report, Inside Police Custody 2, An Empirical Study of Suspects' Rights at the Investigative Stage of the Criminal Process in Nine EU Sountries' (2018).

[35] ibid 53.

or ex officio lawyers, played a very limited, passive role'.[36] More generally, 'suspects were informed of their procedural rights in a formalistic manner that did not enable the suspect to understand them, or to make informed decisions about whether to exercise their procedural rights'.[37] The study concludes that a 'whole-system' approach is needed:

> whilst appropriate laws and regulations are a pre-condition for procedural rights to be effectively available, they are not sufficient. In order to ensure that procedural rights are routinely available for suspected and accused persons, a 'whole-system' approach is needed, which recognises the context in which procedural rights are to be implemented, and which makes connections between the various factors which determine whether they are effectively available.[38]

The difficulty to effectively access procedural rights even where available on paper was again noted in subsequent studies, for instance, by Fair Trials in 2019: 'even where Member States appear to have transposed all the provisions of the Directives into law, practical barriers persist and prevent the effective implementation of these safeguards'.[39] In 2023, civil society organisations sought to address the continuing gaps in implementation on access to information, access to a lawyer and access to legal aid, recognising that: 'even when appropriate legislative measures are taken to implement them, this does not mean that the requirements of the directives are adequately implemented in practice'.[40] In an article written by criminal defence lawyers from different EU countries, it is argued that 'the mission of achieving mutual trust has not been completed because partial distrust as an empirical phenomenon still clearly exists among EU Member States and judicial authorities'.[41] The authors explain the lack of mutual trust as resulting from the differences in regulation of procedural safeguards and the rights of the defence by Member States, and identify many areas for further EU legislative intervention, arguing that 'there is a long road ahead'.

But will more law reduce the gap between law and practice? The EU model of defence rights is widely considered to be insufficiently effective in practice. First, there are gaps in the EU normative system. By nature, the defence rights directives set out minimal standards and give Member States room to manoeuvre in the implementation of these standards. For instance, in a police interrogation, EU law stipulates that suspects and accused persons have a right for a lawyer to be present. But the law does not specify what role the lawyer should have: can they ask questions, can they participate? Or are they relegated to what has been described as the 'breathing lawyer

[36] ibid 54.

[37] ibid 58.

[38] ibid 58.

[39] Fair Trials, 'Where's my Lawyer?' (2019) 29, available at www.fairtrials.org/app/uploads/2019/10/Wheres-my-lawyer-making-legal-assistance-in-pre-trial-detention-effective.pdf.

[40] Ludwig Boltzmann Institute, 'From Law to Practice: Strengthening Procedural Rights in Police Custody (ProRPC)' (2023). available at https://gmr.lbg.ac.at/research/from-law-to-practice-strengthening-procedural-rights-in-police-custody-prorpc/?lang=en.

[41] V Costa Ramos, M Luchtman and G Munteanu, 'Improving Defence Rights, Including Available Remedies in and (or as a Consequence of) Cross-Border Criminal Proceeding' (2020) *EU Crim*, available at https://eucrim.eu/articles/improving-defence-rights/.

standard'?[42] Second, the disparities between the normative project and the observed practices are often explained by a lack of knowledge or familiarity with EU rules, or in certain cases, a resistance to using them. The many reports on the ineffectiveness of EU procedural rights recommend the training of prosecutors, judges and lawyers, and the European Commission finances a range of training programmes aimed at practitioners, to encourage the take-up of EU law at the domestic level.[43] Third, there are limitations to the sanction system. As noted above, to date, the Commission has only initiated a few infringement proceedings against Member States for failure to implement the directives, and none have reached a formal outcome in the form of a sanction. Moreoever at national level, courts do not appear inclined to sanction violations of the directives, as noted in a comparative study by Fair Trials which revealed how ineffective remedies are for violations of procedural safeguards by national courts.[44]

The existence of gaps between law and practice are a common observation,[45] and this type of 'gap analysis'[46] can be misguided. It is built upon the assumption that the law acts as a constraint over those who participate in its application, and therefore determines the conduct of practitioners.[47] But sociological studies, including in relation to criminal justice practitioners, reveal that a law or a policy should be understood as a series of propositions or resources for action, not as a sanctioned imperative.[48] Although the law may guide the behaviour of those involved in its implementation, it does not determine that behaviour: it is a tool within the toolbox of resources available to practitioners.[49] This means that there exists a 'social space' for the implementation of law, a space in which criminal justice actors can operate and make decisions as to whether and how EU law is mobilised in practice. That 'space' is telling to understand why there exists an implementation gap in relation to the EU defence rights directives, and relevant to informing future policy, including in respect of victims' procedural rights in criminal proceedings. Referring to the EU defence rights directives, Hodgson remarks that

> the success of these measures depends in part on countries' willingness to implement change, which in turn reflects the extent to which different procedural values are able to fit together. As with other criminal justice narratives and drivers of reform, the different ways in which processes of criminal justice seek to incorporate, adapt, or avoid these broader European

[42] A Soo, '(Effective) Remedies for a Violation of the Right to Counsel during Criminal Proceedings in the European Union: An Empirical Study' (2018) *Utrecht Law Review*, available at https://storage.googleapis.com/jnl-up-j-ulr-files/journals/1/articles/418/submission/proof/418-1-1122-2-10-20180209.pdf. The author concludes that: 'most of the Member States have adopted the "breathing lawyer" standard for the performance of counsel during proceedings'.

[43] For instance, the ongoing 'STARLIGHT' project which includes a criminal justice stream, funded by the Citizens, Equality, Rights, and Values (CERV) programme of the EU.

[44] Fair Trials, 'Unlawful Evidence in Europe's Courts: Principles, Practice and Remedies' (2021) available at www.fairtrials.org/app/uploads/2021/11/DREP-report.pdf.

[45] P Lascoumes and P Le Galès, *Sociologie de l'action publique* (Armand Colin, 2018) 28.

[46] Translated from French, 'sociologie des écarts'.

[47] D Kaminski, *Condamner: Une analyse des pratiques pénales* (Érès, 2015) 106.

[48] Lascoumes and Le Galès (n 45) 41.

[49] P Lascoumes, *Normes juridiques et mise en œuvre des politiques publiques* (1990) 40 *L'année sociologique* 43–71.

norms illuminate underlying process values and offer a dynamic perspective on the development of legal systems.[50]

What other elements, what other values guide the behaviour of criminal justice actors when deciding how and when to implement EU rules (or their national implementing legislation)? In her comparative research between the French and British legal systems, Hodgson concludes that:

> the criminal justice process has exhibited a fading preoccupation with the principles and values of a coherent procedural system, while demonstrating far greater concern with the efficient management of criminalisation. Efficiency is a key objective of contemporary criminal justice policy, alongside related concerns with austerity and cost-effectiveness, risk management, reductions in delay, and a more general productivity-driven managerialism'.[51]

It is necessary to grasp the adaptations made by criminal justice practitioners as a result of the tension between the requirements of a procedural fairness model and the efficiency objectives that drive criminal justice systems across Europe today. As is the case for procedural safeguards for suspects and accused persons, rights for victims to participate in criminal proceedings 'does require quite some efforts of the authorities in terms of logistics (informing victims, assisting victims, giving time to speak during the hearing), it may lead to more time-consuming trials'.[52] Where further procedural rights (for victims and for suspects and accused persons) increase workload, this creates a conflict for criminal justice practitioners on the 'frontline' (investigators, prosecutors, judges, in particular) who are drawn into prioritising efficiency and focusing on 'managerial preoccupations'.

The conflict in values between increasing rights for accused persons, victims on the one hand, and efficiency on the other hand, will inevitably lead to further adaptations of practices. For instance, empirical evidence collected in France reveals that efficiency targets are affecting sentencing decisions:

> managerial concerns have disrupted, beyond judicial practices, the meaning and nature of criminal responses, at least in the field of mid-level offences. In practice, a quantitative obsession tends to take precedence over the search for a qualitative adaptation of sentences, to the extent that the fact of a criminal justice response appears to be more important than the response itself.[53]

The prioritisation on efficiency has already led to major changes in the functioning of national criminal justice systems, and the place of procedural rights (for suspects, accused persons and victims) is increasingly unclear.

[50] JS Hodgson, *The Metamorphosis of Criminal Justice, A Comparative Account* (Oxford University Press, 2020) 4.

[51] ibid 72.

[52] Klip (n 6) 188.

[53] V Gautron, 'L'impact des préoccupations managériales sur l'administration locale de la justice pénale française' (2014) *Champ pénal* para 23, available at https://journals.openedition.org/champpenal/8715. Translated from: 'les préoccupations managériales ont bouleversé, au-delà des pratiques judiciaires, le sens et la nature des réponses pénales, du moins dans le champ délictuel. En réalité, une obsession quantitative tend à primer sur la recherche d'une adaptation qualitative des sanctions, au point que le fait de répondre semble parfois compter davantage que la réponse elle-même'.

B. Prioritising Efficiency Over Procedural Fairness: The Rise in Trial Waiver Systems in Europe

The shape of criminal justice proceedings is profoundly shifting.[54] In many parts of the world, Europe included, trials are being replaced by legal regimes that encourage suspects to admit guilt and waive their right to a full trial:

> in many member States of the Council of Europe and in States having observer or other status with the Council of Europe or the Assembly, regular criminal trials have gradually been replaced by different forms of trial waiver systems (also called plea bargaining, guilty pleas, abridged trials or summary procedures). In a number of countries, only a minority of criminal convictions are still based on regular trials.[55]

Criminal punishment is increasingly imposed without a trial, but instead through a trial waiver system or other alternative disposition systems that fall short of a trial. There are many different names for the varied practices falling under this definition including 'plea bargaining', 'guilty pleas', 'summary procedures', 'abbreviated trials' and 'penal orders', among others.[56] What these systems have in common is the agreement by the accused person to waive their full trial rights in exchange for a concession by criminal justice authorities.

Countries have justified the use of trial waiver systems as a means to clear long-standing case backlogs, which give rise to a risk of violating the right to a trial within a reasonable period of time. Trial waiver systems are seen as freeing up time for judges and prosecutors, and reducing public spending by avoiding lengthy trials. Reducing both cost and delay is 'one of the most pressing concerns' for domestic policy-makers.[57] Another reason commonly put forward as a justification for the introduction of trial waiver systems is to aid in the effective detection and prosecution of complex crime.[58] Moreover, trial waiver systems are presented as offering potential benefits to victims, by sparing victims the trauma of testifying, or being subjected to lengthy proceedings with uncertain conclusions.[59] The introduction of such systems is, in fact, rarely challenged or disputed. But what does this shift away from trials mean for the procedural fairness model?

The EU defence rights directives offer no guidance on procedural safeguards in a trial waiver setting. Three directives only envisage the possibility for suspects or accused persons to waive their procedural rights in general. In Directive 2016/343/EU on the presumption of innocence, the recitals indicate that individuals should be able to waive the right to be present at trial, expressly or tacitly, but unequivocally.[60] The directives on the right of access to a lawyer, and on the right to interpretation

[54] Hodgson (n 50).

[55] Parliamentary Assembly of the Council of Europe, Resolution 2, Resolution 2245 (2018), available at https://assembly.coe.int/nw/xml/XRef/Xref-XML2HTML-en.asp?fileid=25188&lang=en.

[56] Fair Trials, 'The Disappearing Trial' (2017), available at www.fairtrials.org/articles/publications/the-disappearing-trial/.

[57] Hodgson (n 50) 13.

[58] Fair Trials, 'The Disappearing Trial' (n 56) para 68.

[59] ibid para 72.

[60] Directive 2016/343/EU (n 14) Recital 35.

and translation, provide that anyone willing to waive a right protected under EU law must be provided with clear and sufficient information about the right and the possible consequences of waiving it.[61] The directives specify that waivers of procedural safeguards must be made 'voluntarily and unequivocally', but do not explicitly address the waiver of a full trial. The issue of plea bargaining was raised before the CJEU, specifically, in relation to the applicability of the right to the presumption of innocence in relation to plea-bargaining agreements. However, in the case *QR*,[62] the EU Court ruled that Directive 2016/343/EU did not govern the issue of consent by the co-accused to the conclusion of a plea-bargaining agreement and therefore failed to offer any guidance on the implications of EU law on plea bargaining arrangements. Procedural safeguards are, however, seen as essential to ensuring fairness in trial waiver settings in the jurisprudence of the European Court of Human Rights (ECtHR). The ECtHR has specified that a series of safeguards are necessary to ensure that an accused person has effectively consented to enter into such an agreement: (a) access to a lawyer; (b) understanding of the charges, waivers and the consequences of those waivers; (c) recording of the terms of the negotiation; and (d) independent judicial review with additional evidence supporting the conviction.[63] Moreover, decisions to waive the right to a trial must be taken 'in full awareness of the facts of the case and the legal consequences [of accepting the waiver]'.[64]

In practice, there is evidence of an erosion of procedural safeguards in trial waiver settings. In both the UK and France, the 'invocation of system efficiency in purely positive terms masks the more ideologically driven desire to remove due process safeguards that protect fundamental rights and which ensure some degree of equality of arms'.[65] A report by Fair Trials,[66] based on empirical findings in five different European countries,[67] reveals that accused persons are not routinely assisted by a lawyer when approached by prosecutors to negotiate a deal, despite the right to legal assistance being enshrined in EU law. Even where a lawyer is appointed, lawyers often do not have the resources and power (eg to make requests for certain investigations to be made) to be in a position to provide an effective defence during the negotiation with prosecuting authorities. Moreover, the report notes that accused persons and their lawyers often do not have timely and full access to case files to prepare their defence; and that they do not receive translations of essential documents. Although in theory 'the logic of a shift away from trial and toward earlier case disposition based on some agreed outcome is to have earlier and fuller discovery, rather than less',[68] another key area of concern is access

[61] Directive 2013/48/EU (n 13) Art 9(1)(a) and Recitals 39 and 55 on the right of access to a lawyer; Directive 2010/64/EU (n 11) Art 3(8) on the right to interpretation and translation.

[62] Case C-467/19 PPU *QR* 2019 ECLI:EU:C:2019:776, available at https://curia.europa.eu/juris/document/document.jsf?text=&docid=218181&pageIndex=0&doclang=EN&mode=lst&dir=&occ=first&part=1&cid=5205508.

[63] *Natsvlishvili and Togonidze v Georgia* App no 9043/05 (ECtHR, 29 April 2014), available at http://hudoc.echr.coe.int/eng?i=001-142672.

[64] ibid paras 91–92.

[65] Hodgson (n 50) 61.

[66] Fair Trials, 'Efficiency over Justice' (2022) available at www.fairtrials.org/articles/publications/efficiency-over-justice/.

[67] Albania, Cyprus, Hungary, Italy and Slovenia.

[68] Hodgson (n 50) 147.

to information, in particular to the case file, and its timing with respect to the accused person's decision to enter into a trial waiver agreement. The imbalance between the accused person and the prosecuting authorities, in a negotiation setting, is particularly stark in legal aid cases.

As the growth of trial waiver systems continues, progressively replacing full trials, the 'disappearance of the contested trial and the reduced opportunities for the defence to test the prosecution case shift the focus of fair trial rights such as equality of arms toward the pre-trial phase'.[69] This also has implications for a policy aimed at increasing the rights of participation of victims in criminal proceedings. In the context of trial waivers, the role of victims is also not addressed in the EU legal framework. The Directive on Victim Rights is based upon the assumption that proceedings will take place for the right to be heard to be exercised.[70] Article 11(5) of Directive 2012/29/EU refers to 'out-of-court settlements', which it assimilates to a decision not to prosecute, granting victims a right to review only where the settlement imposes a warning or an obligation on the person accused.[71] Any new EU model for enhancing the participation of victims in criminal proceedings will need to take account of the rise in plea-bargaining and other such trial waiver agreements, and determine what role, if any, the victim should have where a criminal trial does not take place.

The fault lines in the implementation of EU defence rights reveals not only the tension between efficiency objectives and procedural fairness values but also, more generally, the punitive turn in criminal justice systems across Europe: 'although presented in neutral and objective terms, these tools of management and accountability are ideologically driven, masking the increased punitiveness of criminal justice'.[72]

C. Prioritising Punitiveness Over Procedural Fairness: Unequal Fairness

Studies in criminology have long documented the 'punitive turn' in criminal justice systems across Europe and North America with increases in prison rates and the growth of preventive criminal law used to control people thought to be at risk of committing an offence.[73] The prioritisation of crime control means that criminal justice actors are focused on the processing of a high number of offenders and on obtaining a high conviction rate.[74] Crime control, in this sense, takes less the form of measures aimed at addressing presumed causes of crime (eg social housing, access to mental health support services), and is oriented towards the reinforcement of control and surveillance

[69] ibid 145–46.
[70] Klip (n 6) 181.
[71] Directive 2012/29/EU (n 6) Recital 45: 'A decision of the prosecutor resulting in an out-of-court settlement and thus ending criminal proceedings, excludes victims from the right to a review of a decision of the prosecutor not to prosecute, only if the settlement imposes a warning or an obligation.'
[72] Hodgson (n 50) 74.
[73] See, for instance, D Garland, *The Culture of Control* (Clarendon Press, 2001); L Wacquant, *Crafting the Neoliberal State: Workfare, Prisonfare, and Social Insecurity* (Sociological Forum, 2010); J Pratt, *Penal populism* (Routledge, 2007).
[74] Hodgson (n 50) 72.

measures over certain groups perceived to be more likely to commit offences. In other words, the 'crime control' model tends to focus on certain 'groups' perceived as dangerous,[75] resulting in disparate impacts. There has long been publicly available evidence of discrimination more widely in criminal justice systems in the EU, including in policing,[76] which has been recognised by the EU Parliament: 'whereas racism, discrimination and the excessive and lethal use of force by the police also exists within the EU'.[77] Where available, police and judicial statistics reveal the extent of overrepresentation of racialised people in the criminal justice system. In Belgium for instance, nearly half the prison population have a non-Belgian nationality: 'the probability of being detained rises sharply for those born outside Europe, regardless of whether or not the person has a residence in Belgium'.[78] As shown in a long-term empirical study in several French judicial districts,[79] people born abroad, unemployed people, unhoused people and people experiencing poverty are amongst the people most represented in pre-trial detention and incarcerated pursuant to prison sentences.

The pursuit of punitiveness conflicts with procedural fairness values. In France, Hodgson suggests that: 'the promotion of fairness as a procedural value was soon to be displaced by security and crime control concerns'.[80] It can be argued that this tension is revealed by evidence of unequal access to defence rights. In principle authorities are required to ensure that procedural safeguards are made available to all persons in contact with the criminal justice system, and that such safeguards are 'practical and effective', rather than 'theoretical or illusory'.[81] For example, interpretation services should not only be offered to people who do not speak the language of the proceedings, but the quality of the services provided must also be of a sufficient quality to ensure that the person can fully participate in the proceedings. In practice, there are indications of disparate accessibility to procedural rights,[82] based on responses to questionnaires

[75] P Mary, 'Pénalité et gestion des risques : vers une justice "actuarielle" en Europe ?' (2001) *Déviance et Société*, available at www.cairn.info/revue-deviance-et-societe-2001-1-page-33.htm.

[76] See, for instance, racism in policing documented by ENAR, available at www.enar-eu.org/policing-racialised-groups-briefing-paper/ and www.enar-eu.org/the-sharp-edge-of-violence-police-brutality-and-community-resistance-of-racialised-groups/; and by Equinox, available at www.equinox-eu.com/wp-content/uploads/2021/10/Equinox-Who-Protects-Us-from-the-Police.pdf. On racism in the criminal justice system more generally, see Fair Trials, 'Disparities and Discrimination in the European Union's Criminal Legal Systems' (2021); Fair Trials, 'Justice Denied: Roma in the Criminal Justice System' (2022); and Fair Trials, 'Racism in Europe's Law Enforcement and Criminal Justice Systems' (2022).

[77] European Parliament Resolution of 16 June 2020 on the anti-racism protests following the death of George Floyd (2020/2685(RSP)). See also: European Parliament Resolution of 10 November 2022 on racial justice, non-discrimination and anti-racism in the EU (2022/2005(INI) available at https://oeil.secure.europarl.europa.eu/oeil/popups/ficheprocedure.do?lang=en&reference=2022/2005(INI).

[78] D Burssens, C Tange and E Maes, 'A la recherche de déterminants du recours à la détention preventive et de sa durée' (2015) *Institut National de Criminalistique et de Criminologie*.

[79] V Gautron and J-N Retière, *La justice pénale est-elle discriminatoire ? Une étude empirique des pratiques décisionnelles dans cinq tribunaux correctionnels*, Colloque 'Discriminations: état de la recherche', Alliance de Recherche sur les Discriminations (ARDIS) (2013), Université Paris Est Marne-la-Vallée, France available at https://shs.hal.science/halshs-01075666. The research found that judges are not neutral to the personal characteristics of the person they are sentencing: 5.2% of people born outside of France are held in pre-trial detention, versus 1.8% of people born in France.

[80] Hodgson (n 50) 60.

[81] *Scordino v Italy (No 1)* App no 36813/9 (ECtHR, 29 March 2006) para 192.

[82] Based on data collected in Belgium, Bulgaria, Greece and Romania. Fair Trials, 'Equality Data in Criminal Justice' (2022), available at www.fairtrials.org/app/uploads/2022/10/FairTrials_EqualityDataReport_2022.pdf.

completed by people in prison who had been recently sentenced, on their experiences of their interactions with the criminal justice system pre-trial (including access to a lawyer, access to information about procedural rights and access to interpretation and translation services, where the arrested person did not speak the language of the proceedings). The study in Romania revealed that, in relation to access to information, only around 20 per cent of people who were assessed as not understanding Romanian were informed of their rights to interpretation and translation. The data collected also showed that people of racialised and ethnic groups were more likely to have been denied access to a lawyer, or received poor quality representation. In Greece, of the people who reported the absence of a lawyer during the first 24 hours of detention, 82 per cent identified as other than Greek. On access to interpretation and translation, in Bulgaria, more than half of respondents were not satisfied with the quality of oral and written interpretation. The report includes accounts of people who did not receive any translations, and further notes that 'the lack or poor quality of these services single handily make proceedings unfair'. Although the data from this study is incomplete, it echoes earlier findings.[83]

The prioritisation on punitiveness also has implications for people turning to the criminal justice system for redress. This is especially true in cases where the same person can be simultaneously classified as both a victim and a suspect, or may even transition from one status to the other during the course of the proceedings. The categorisation of a person as 'victim' or a 'suspect' is the result of a legal qualification, ie a decision, made by one or more criminal justice practitioners. In practice, the decision can be difficult and involves an inherently political choice, where boundaries between victim and suspect or accused are blurred. Through her empirical research, Koch has shown the difficulty in the decision-making process by police officers in the UK as to whether to treat a person as a victim of human trafficking or as a suspect of drug dealing, ultimately leading to further control of the persons concerned: 'policing the boundaries of genuine victimhood was thus a matter of delicate interpretation, one that opened the door for close monitoring and control of young people's lives'.[84] That qualification process, however, is only partially addressed in EU law in the field of human trafficking.[85] Klip argues, in relation to the Directive on Victims' Rights, that

> the decision to recognise somebody as a victim cannot be challenged, neither by the accused, nor by anyone else. (…) the status of the victim seems to be a once and forever decision and it is unclear which authority should take that decision.[86]

[83] For example, findings by the Council of Europe: European Commission Against Racism and Intolerance, ECRI Report on Bulgaria (Fourth Monitoring Cycle), Adopted on 20 June 2008, 26 CRI (2009) 2.

[84] IL Koch, 'From Criminals to Slaves. "Modern Slavery", Drug Trafficking, and the Cultural Politics of Victimhood in Postcolonial Britain' (2024) *Current Anthropology* available at www.journals.uchicago.edu/doi/epdf/10.1086/729537.

[85] Article 8, Directive 2011/36/EU of the European Parliament and of the Council of 5 April 2011 on preventing and combating trafficking in human beings and protecting its victims, and replacing Council Framework Decision 2002/629/JHA [2011] OJ L101/1: 'Member States shall, in accordance with the basic principles of their legal systems, take the necessary measures to ensure that competent national authorities are entitled not to prosecute or impose penalties on victims of trafficking in human beings for their involvement in criminal activities which they have been compelled to commit as a direct consequence of being subjected to any of the acts referred to in Article 2'.

[86] Klip (n 6) 187.

Equally, the decision to qualify a person as a suspect rather than a victim is difficult to challenge. Two recent cases illustrate the room for manoeuvre that exists for criminal justice actors in the selection of who qualifies for which status and, reveal the prevalence of the status of suspect or accused person, even though the person could also (or instead) be treated as a victim.

First, the case of a young British woman who was prosecuted, detained before her trial and sentenced for public mischief (false allegations) after she went to the police to report her rape in July 2019 when she was on holiday in Cyprus. During a six-hour interrogation, the police decided to switch her status from victim to suspect. She was charged with 'acts of public mischief' and was imprisoned for almost a month before she was released on bail. She could not leave Cyprus for another six months and was later sentenced at first instance. The six-hour police interrogation that led her to retract her original statement was conducted without a lawyer being present, despite the right to a lawyer applying 'to persons other than suspects or accused persons who, in the course of questioning by the police or by another law enforcement authority, become suspects or accused persons'.[87] It is on the basis of a violation of her right to a lawyer as a 'suspect' that the Supreme Court considered that the conviction was 'unjust and precarious' and acquitted her, but failed to address the question of the decision to deny her status as a victim. The case illustrates the well-documented failures of the criminal justice system in addressing gender-based violence, and the harm that the system can cause by prioritising punitiveness over care.[88]

In another case, UK authorities opted to prosecute undocumented children who had been found working on cannabis farms, despite indications that the children had been victims of human trafficking, and they agreed to enter guilty pleas. In *VCL and AN v the United Kingdom*, the ECtHR found that the UK had failed to fulfil its duty under Article 4 of the Convention to take operational measures to protect the applicants, either initially, as potential victims of trafficking, or subsequently, as persons recognised to be a victim of trafficking. The Court also turned to fair trial rights in this context, and considered whether, as a result of the violation of Article 4, the applicants had been denied their right to a fair trial pursuant to Article 6(1) of the Convention in so far as the particular vulnerability of the accused persons – children who had been victims of human trafficking – had been insufficiently taken into account by public authorities and courts when securing and overseeing plea deals.[89] In this case, the status of accused and victim could be cumulated, and the Court recognised that

> although victims of trafficking are not immune from prosecution, an individual's status as a victim of trafficking may affect whether there is sufficient evidence to prosecute and whether it is in the public interest to do so (…). Evidence concerning an accused's status as a victim of trafficking is therefore a 'fundamental aspect' of the defence which he or she should be able to secure without restriction.[90]

[87] Directive 2013/48/EU (n 13) Art 2(3).

[88] Fair Trials, 'How Criminal Justice Systems across Europe are Failing Women: Sarah's Case' (2022), available at www.fairtrials.org/app/uploads/2022/06/Sarah_case.pdf.

[89] *VCL and AN v the United Kingdom* App nos 77587/12 and 74603/12 (ECtHR, 16 February 2021), available at https://hudoc.echr.coe.int/eng#%7B%22itemid%22:[%22001-207927%22]%7D.

[90] ibid para 196.

The Court concluded that, in the context of Article 6 of the Convention, the lack of such an assessment prevented the applicants from securing evidence which may have constituted a fundamental aspect of their defence.

The challenges faced in the implementation of the procedural fairness model reveals the shift in criminal justice systems towards 'crime control'for people who come into contact with the criminal justice system, whether they are treated as a suspect or accused person, or as a victim. In fact, some argue that promoting the procedural fairness model might serve as a façade to further legitimise the control and punishment of certain people and groups: 'it is not just that procedural justice is a suboptimal type of reform; it is the type of reform that actively frustrates other reforms by dressing up policing with the perception of correctness and legitimacy'.[91] In the same way, the risk is that the EU policy on victims' rights will be co-opted to promote the punitive, 'tough on crime' agenda, and contribute towards detracting from the inherently discriminatory impacts that the 'crime control' model entails. As has been documented in Canada, legislative proposals made 'in the name of victims' are far from the complex realities faced by victims because they are almost exclusively oriented towards the imposition of a more punitive regime.[92] In Belgium, also, demands for more victim participation in the criminal process focused on the ability to obtain reparations eventually resulted instead in reforms oriented towards further punitiveness and crime control.[93] The punitive objective of victims' rights also emerges from the report of the EU Fundamental Rights Agency ('FRA') which argues that victims of 'violent crimes' should be recognised as 'persons wronged'[94] with 'full fair trial rights' in the proceedings against the 'offender'.[95] The EU FRA report reveals the common amalgam that is made between 'entitled to justice' and 'punishment of the offender' as the key purpose of enhanced victim participation in criminal proceedings.

To date, EU law did not specify the rationale behind a policy to enhance victims' rights to participate in criminal proceedings: 'the need for victims' rights is regarded as self-evident. (…) There is no explanation or rationale given for victims' rights, other than reference to the fact that it is one of its policies'.[96] This is problematic in two respects. First,

> it is relevant to raise the question what exactly the purpose of victims' rights in the context of a criminal trial is. Only if we know its purpose, it will be possible to match it with the other rights that are at stake in a criminal proceeding.[97]

Secondly, this leaves the door open for victims' rights to be instrumentalised in view of furthering punitive and efficiency considerations, rather than responding to the

[91] SE Fields, 'The Procedural Justice Industrial Complex' (2023) *Indiana Law Journal*.

[92] In this respect, the authors caution that only some victims or only some representatives of victims are recognised by law-makers: https://doi.org/10.4000/champpenal.14599.

[93] Mary (n 75).

[94] As opposed, for instance, to witness-victims as is the case in the national legal systems in several Member States.

[95] EU Fundamental Rights Agency, 'Victims' Rights as Standards of Criminal Justice, Justice for Victims of Violent Crime, Part I' (2019), available at https://fra.europa.eu/sites/default/files/fra_uploads/fra-2019-justice-for-victims-of-violent-crime-part-1-standards_en.pdf.

[96] Klip (n 6) 187.

[97] ibid.

complex needs that people have when they have suffered harm. In the Explanatory Memorandum for the Revision Proposal of the Victims' Rights Directive, the Commission indicates that the envisaged result is that 'victims' experiences with and trust in the criminal justice system will be improved. This will help their voices be heard, improve their testimonies, and improve their participation, which increases judicial effectiveness'.[98] This reveals a broader rationale behind the strengthening of victims' rights in criminal proceedings of reinforcing the criminal justice system itself, by increasing trust in the system and its effectiveness. In light of the trend towards prioritising efficiency, there is a need to foresee what potentially perverse effects[99] any procedural fairness reform may bring across the criminal justice system. For instance, will authorities be less willing to grant a person the status of 'victim' to avoid participation rights in the trial and resulting delays from potential challenges initiated by victims? Will the rights of victims at trial drive authorities to push for more plea-bargaining arrangements, to avoid the time and costs of involving victims in trial proceedings? Will the increase in 'judicial effectiveness' translate into further punitiveness, and if so, who does that serve?

III. Conclusions

Experiences of the implementation of the EU procedural safeguards system for suspects and accused persons calls for a reflection on the criminal justice system as a whole, beyond the narrow framing of the individual rights of victims or suspects and accused persons in criminal proceedings. It is tempting to believe that more participation of victims in criminal proceedings will benefit victims, just as reinforcing defence rights will prevent injustices for accused persons. But rights are only as powerful as is permitted by the legal system within which they operate, and that system prioritises efficiency and crime control over procedural fairness. In this context, victims' participation in criminal proceedings risks serving to legitimise punitive and discriminatory crime control.

Beyond the reflection on whether and how to reinforce the individual rights of people who come into contact with the criminal justice system, the discussion on strengthening the rights of victims offers an opportunity for the EU to engage in a broader reflection on the objectives pursued more generally through the growing body of EU criminal justice instruments. The procedural fairness model, as promoted in the EU defence rights directives, is in tension and inherently undermined by efficiency and crime control objectives. For some, we are even seeing the 'demise of procedural fairness'.[100] The contribution of EU criminal justice policy is equivocal in this respect. On the one hand, the EU defence rights directives seek to promote procedural fairness values, as does, to a more limited extent, the EU Directive on Victims' Rights

[98] Victims Rights Directive Revision Proposal (n 2) 17.

[99] For instance, the 'net-widening' effect of so-called alternatives to prison sentences, such as electronic monitoring, which, although intended to reduce the prison population, are used against people who would otherwise not have been incarcerated.

[100] Hodgson (n 50) 54.

which aims to encourage the participation of victims in criminal proceedings. But on the other hand, the EU has been focusing on an ever-expanding criminalisation and surveillance agenda (most recently, in respect of human smuggling)[101] and increasing policing powers,[102] with the EU agency for police cooperation, Europol, being afforded new powers and resources. The tension between the objectives of fairness, efficiency and crime control needs to be explicitly addressed, research duly considered and issues fully debated as part of the legislative process.

[101] European Commission 'package' on human smuggling, 28 November 2023.

[102] See, for instance, among other measures seeking to further expand the powers of Europol despite the 2022 extension of its mandate: Proposal for a Regulation of the European Parliament and of the Council on enhancing police cooperation in relation to the prevention, detection and investigation of migrant smuggling and trafficking in human beings, and on enhancing Europol's support to preventing and combating such crimes and amending Regulation (EU) 2016/794, 28 November 2023, COM/2023/754 final.

19

The Protection of Victims at EU Level: The Need for Cross-Border Cooperation and Coordination

ANIELLA FERENCZI

I. Introduction

Crime can affect victims in many ways, ranging from disturbance in several cases to trauma in more serious cases. In the European Union (EU)-level victims' rights policy, one of the most important concerns is to balance the rights of the victim and those of the defendant in the criminal proceeding. This balance can be realised only if victims are recognised and treated in a respectful, sensitive, tailored, professional and non-discriminatory manner, in all contacts with victim support or restorative justice services or a competent authority, operating within the context of criminal proceedings.

It shall be ensured that all crime victims, without any discrimination and regardless of where the crime took place, have access to their rights and, all stakeholders active in the field of victims' rights bear particular responsibility in taking measures, within the limit of their respective mandate, both individually and in collaboration for facilitating victims to rely on their rights.

Promoting victims' rights and facilitating access to them can be more challenging in cross-border cases. Cooperation on both the national and international stage has great potential when it comes to victims' access to their rights. In the context of cooperation and coordinaton at EU level, the benefits and added value can be manifested in multiple areas. Several good practices have already been established and a number of new methodologies applied in Member States' victim support systems, through the transposition of the related EU laws. The methodology used in the victim support structures of the different countries is, in positive terms, very diverse and constantly evolving. In this process, facilitating cooperation between professionals from different countries, fostering exchange of knowledge and collaborative reflection is essential. In addition, such cooperation and coordination mechanisms have the advantage of significantly boosting efficiency in terms of handling concrete cross-border cases. These benefits of cross-border cooperation are even more in the spotlight when answers have to be given to crisis situations with wide scope, such as the Covid-19 pandemic.

The present chapter aims to reveal the importance of the rights of cross-border victims, the relevance and aspects of cross-border cooperation and the role the European Network on Victims' Rights (ENVR) plays in this area, illustrated by some practical examples.

II. The Importance of EU-Level Coordination and Collaboration in Victim Support and Protection

Cross-border victims can face particular obstacles in exercising their rights, such as language barriers or a lack of knowledge regarding the applicable rules, competent authorities and the support available in another EU Member State. These cross-border challenges have served as a catalyst for many advancements in the field of victims' rights. Article 82 (2) of the Treaty on the Functioning of the European Union (TFEU) includes 'victims' rights' as an area of judicial cooperation where minimum standards may be adopted, thereby serving as an important basis for EU legislation of benefit to victims of crime. In that regard, the need to foster and strengthen cooperation and communication between EU Member States has long been recognised as crucial in supporting cross-border victims of crime. Consequently, the most relevant legal instruments in the field of general victim support and victims' rights are the Victims' Rights Directive (Directive 2012/29/EU)[1] and the Compensation Directive (Directive 2004/80/EC).[2] These accommodate the needs of cross-border victims and the necessary measures that Member States have to take in that regard. In particular, according to Article 26, para 1 of the Victims' Rights Directive:

> Member States shall take appropriate action to facilitate cooperation between Member States to improve the access of victims to the rights set out in this Directive and under national law. Such cooperation shall be aimed at least at: (a) the exchange of best practices; (b) consultation in individual cases; and (c) assistance to European networks working on matters directly relevant to victims' rights.

The need for cooperation is also highlighted in EU sectoral instruments[3] which refer to specific groups of (cross-border) victims. For example, the EU Counter-Terrorism Directive (2017/541/EU)[4] also emphasises that Member States should take appropriate action to facilitate cooperation with each other to ensure that victims resident in a

[1] Directive 2012/29/EU of the European Parliament and of the Council of 25 October 2012 establishing minimum standards on the rights, support and protection of victims of crime, and replacing Council Framework Decision 2001/220/JHA (Victims' Rights' Directive) [2012] OJ L315/57.

[2] Council Directive 2004/80/EC of 29 April 2004 relating to compensation to crime victims (Compensation Directive) [2004] OJ L261/15.

[3] *cf* Directive 2011/92/EU of the European Parliament and of the Council of 13 December 2011 on combating the sexual abuse and sexual exploitation of children and child pornography [2011] OJ L335/1; Directive 2011/36/EU of the EU Parliament and of the Council of 5 April 2011 on preventing and combating trafficking in human beings and protecting its victims [2011] OJ L101/1.

[4] Directive (EU) 2017/541 of the European Parliament and of the Council of 15 March 2017 on combating terrorism and replacing Council Framework Decision 2002/475/JHA and amending Council Decision 2005/671/JHA [2017] OJ L88/6.

Member State other than that where the attack occurred have access to information on their rights and are provided with the support that they need, in their home Member State and the Member State where the crime was perpetrated.

Furthermore, at a policy-oriented level, important EU initiatives[5] in recent years have been introduced to raise awareness, *inter alia*, of the needs of cross-border victims, to showcase achievements and shortcomings of cross-border cooperation and to suggest ways forward. Notably, in 2019, the Special Advisor to the former President of the European Commission, Jean-Claude Juncker, presented her report entitled 'Strengthening Victims' Rights: From Compensation to Reparation'.[6] The report includes distinctive findings on the situation of cross-border victims with regard to access to compensation, information and support. It also advocates closer cooperation in this field – between the Member States and at national level.

The EU Strategy on Victims' Rights (2020–2025),[7] which was published in June 2020, constitutes a milestone in efforts to strengthen the rights of and protection afforded to victims of crime in the EU. The Strategy's main objective is to ensure that all victims of all crime can fully rely on their rights[8] – no matter where in the EU or under what circumstances the crime took place. It identifies areas of improvement, *inter alia* in the area of cross-border cooperation. The strategy also seeks to find ways to give the existing legal instruments full effect. In that regard, specific actions are identified – at EU and national levels, as well as involving particular actors such as the ENVR.[9]

Lastly, with respect to specific categories of vulnerable victims, the EU Handbook on Victims of Terrorism[10] is a very valuable contribution to improving cross-border cooperation in providing support for victims in the aftermath of terrorist attacks. The Handbook provides an explanation of the relevant provisions applicable to the rights of victims of terrorism under EU law, combining it with Member States' good practices in implementing these EU rights.

In addition to the EU legal framework and policy initiatives, the Member States have – on various occasions[11] – reiterated the importance of strengthening cooperation and exchange of information in cases of cross-border crime. Ultimately, the Amsterdam Council Conclusions[12] in 2016 initially established the Informal European Network on Victims' Rights that led to the ENVR in its current form.

[5] *cf* recent EU Counter-Terrorism Programme of 9 December 2020.

[6] Report of the Special Adviser to the former President of the European Commission, Jean-Claude Juncker, 'Strengthening Victims' Rights: From Compensation to Reparation', 8629/19 (March 2019).

[7] EU Strategy on Victims' Rights (2020–2025), COM (2020) 258, 24 June 2020 (9178/20).

[8] Regarding the implementation status of the Victims' Rights' Directive (n 1) see Report of the Commission to the Parliament and the Council on the implementation of Directive 2012/29/EU of the European Parliament and of the Council of 25 October 2012 establishing minimum standards on the rights, support and protection of victims of crime, and replacing Council Framework Decision 2001/220/JHA.

[9] European Network on Victims' Rights, operated by the Association of the European Network on Victims' Rights, is a cooperation of Member States' public institutions responsible for victims' rights policy.

[10] EU Handbook on Victims of Terrorism, available at https://ec.europa.eu/info/sites/default/files/law/eu_handbook_on_victims_of_terrorism_2021_01_15_en.pdf.

[11] *cf* recent Council conclusions on victims' rights, 4 December 2019 (2019/C 422/05); Council conclusions on victims of terrorism, 4 June 2018 (9719/18).

[12] Amsterdam Conclusions available at https://data.consilium.europa.eu/doc/document/ST-9997-2016-INIT/en/.

III. The Mission of the ENVR

The ENVR was created to stimulate and aid the implementation of existing EU legislation on victims' rights, the improvement of the practical application of the transposed laws, and to suggest possible areas for developing the EU *acquis* in this field. Furthermore, its very purpose is to contribute to enhancing cooperation and coordination between the competent authorities in the Member States which can also result in the better practical management of cross-border cases.

Under the umbrella of the ENVR, the active cooperation and coordination is promoted between policy-makers and other experts working under the supervision of national public organs responsible for victims' rights, and covers three operational sections: the Generic Network, the EU Network of single contact points for compensation and the EU Network of single contact points for victims of terrorism. The mission of the ENVR (including all operational sections) is to serve as a hub of public experts engaged in mutual learning and in discussing practical issues with the overall objective of improving access to rights for all crime victims, including victims of cross-border cases.

The ENVR's contribution to the improvement of transnational cases is based on two pillars. Under the first pillar, the ENVR regularly organises various programmes for its experts to provide exclusive forums for building a common knowledge base and developing active cooperation between the experts. This can have positive impacts on the management of possible concrete cross-border cases as well. The second pillar is the actions of the ENVR as an organisation to add value to improve the situation of cross-border victims. Organisation level actions are mainly planned in annual working programmes, however ENVR remains open to take immediate action to respond to situations and emergencies arising from social needs related to victims' rights.

In the next section, some examples illustrate the actions undertaken by ENVR to improve the practical cooperation between different national professionals and to support victims in accessing their rights in cross-border cases.

IV. Actions for Improving Cross-Border Cooperation and Coordination in the Victims' Rights Area

A. Sharing Knowledge about Operating Support Services During the Covid-19 Pandemic

Active support and protection of victims of crime is always a high priority for the EU and its Member States, and in emergency situations this need is even more urgent. As the Covid-19 pandemic and the lockdowns affected plenty of aspects of our lives, the support and protection of crime victims became even more pressing during the crisis.

Member States had to adapt their support services to the constraints imposed by the confinement. They undertook the task of elaborating and implementing situation-specific support and protection services tailored to groups of vulnerable victims, in particular such as those affected by domestic violence, hate crime, and cybercrime.

Moreover, they had to adapt specific channels of communication. Additionally, they had to take measures quickly to find ways of communicating with victims and to ensure the continued operation of victim support services under these special circumstances. Notably, these measures were imperative for the enhanced protection of victims of domestic violence whose situation was aggravated due to isolation and social distancing measures imposed during lockdowns.

Beside the generic tools used by policy-makers, eg unified guidelines, more extended use of digital tools, the extension of opening hours, the availability of chat and helplines, psychology services via telephone on request, in some countries unique steps were made to communicate with victims, to prevent crime and to support, in particular, victims of domestic violence. Some examples of the specific measures for support and protection taken by national services included:

1. the implementation of a new tool for victims of domestic violence which allowed later court hearings to ensure that no facts and memories will be lost;
2. local services proactively contacting 'known' victims;
3. free mobile application for potential domestic violence victims, suitable for risk assessment, for storing a database of relevant support services, and with a function for recording pieces of evidence.

The involvement of civil society played a pivotal role in this context, particularly involving persons who, due to their interactions with the public, might be aware of instances of domestic violence. This included postal workers, delivery service persons, pharmacists, shop assistants who were identified as playing a key role in facilitating the reporting of cases. Several good practices were listed in this area, including for example: 1) establishing support service information desks in shopping malls and conducting awareness-raising campaigns for victims in supermarkets; 2) launching public awareness-raising campaigns (TV, radio), alerting perpetrators that preventing domestic abuse would continue to be a top priority within the civil and criminal justice system throughout the pandemic.

In this emergency situation, the role of the ENVR was to prepare a collection of the available policy measures and applicable practices of different countries, and to publish the full catalogue on its website[13] while also making it available on the e-Justice portal. The most important conclusion drawn from the national level information collected by ENVR, was that the measures regarding victim support services taken by Member States were timely, as these measures were taken shortly after the outbreak of the pandemic and they were incorporated into national Covid emergency schemes.

B. Operating the 'Find My Victim Support Service' Tool

The 'Find my victim support service' online tool[14] was developed in 2021 and is continuously managed by ENVR. It functions as a searchable database mapping both

[13] See ENCR website, available at www.envr.eu.
[14] ibid.

general and specific victim support services and their availabilities, operating in the Member States of the EU. The tool has multiple objectives: it enhances the effective practical cooperation between national authorities when handling cross-border cases. Additionally, with its public interface, the database serves as a valuable resource for victims/victim organisations, facilitating improved access to support services and functioning therefore as a victim-referral tool.

The database is available in a user-friendly version on the www.envr.eu website by computer, mobile phone and tablet.

The objective of the database is *not* giving detailed information on victims' rights either at national or at European level. The ENVR 'Find my victim support service' database aims to map the available national support services by classifying them according to their profile, such as generic services, support for child victims, support for victims of domestic violence, support for victims of terrorism, support for victims of human trafficking, support for victims of sexual abuse, victims of war crimes and compensation. The added value of the database lies in its simplicity, using only pertinent and updated contact information for the listed support services. Users can easily search the data by the location of the offence and by the type of crime in the above categories. The tool is available in 22 EU languages and in Ukrainian.

C. Developing the Operation Protocol for the SCPVOT

The Operational Protocol is a document developed by the EU Network of single contact points for victims of terrorism (SCPVOT), operating under the umbrella of the ENVR.

To ensure that SCPVOT functions not only as a platform for exchanging good practices but also as a practical mechanism capable of responding to the needs of victims in case of a cross-border attack, the Network prepared its own Operational Protocol. This Protocol defines the steps that national single contact points should follow in the event of a mass attack involving victims from more than one Member State. The Operational Protocol fully respects national particularities with regard to assistance, support, protection, and compensation for victims of terrorism (including cross-border victims). While respecting this principle, the Protocol outlines minimum standards, leaving single contact points the flexibility to provide higher levels of support beyond the standards recommended by the Protocol.

In cross-border cases, the single contact points are activated when two or more Member States are affected. The main task of SCPVOT is to gather information on available assistance, support, protection and compensation and subsequently relay this information to cross-border victims of terrorism. The Protocol also provides steps both for immediate, medium and long-term support for victims of terrorism. The application of the Operation Protocol is recommended for consideration by the Council Conclusions on improving support and recognition of victims of terrorism.[15]

[15] Council Conclusions on improving support and recognition of victims of terrorism, Council document 16336/23 of 4 December 2023.

D. Compensation for Victims' Rights: Introducing the Compensation Country Sheets

Another specialised network within the ENVR is the EU network of single contact points for compensation, which is primarily dedicated to the practical management of daily compensation cases. In order to support the practical work of the network, ENVR has developed and made available on its website[16] 'compensation country sheets'. These provide summaries of national compensation schemes and standardised contact information. The purpose of this tool is to facilitate seamless access for compensation professionals to up-to-date information about national schemes, thereby enhancing the efficiency of cross-border case management.

V. Conclusions

Victims have been given several rights in the EU via a solid set of EU laws that have been adopted in recent years, paying attention to cross-border victims and cross-border cooperation too. The relevance of cross-border cooperation is highlighted in several strategical documents as well, such as relevant Council Conclusions calling on stakeholders for action in order to improve the status of victims when accessing to their rights.

The EU Strategy for Victims' Rights (2021–2025) aims to ensure that all crime victims can fully rely on their rights, regardless of where the crime took place and the circumstances of it. One of the key priorities of the Strategy focuses on working together for victims' rights and for this end, has a set of clear actions for stakeholders in the area of cooperation and coordination. From a cross-border perspective, and with an outlook to the future, it is also essential to mention the ongoing Proposal of the European Commission for the amendment of the Victims' Rights Directive,[17] which contains a number of progressive provisions for enhancing victims' rights in general and in cross-border cases. These provisions, in terms of becoming part of the new legislation, can further improve the situation of cross-border victims.

In order to enable victims to gain access in practice to all rights ensured by legal instruments in the EU, their rights have to be promoted. Exchange of knowledge on methodology and exchange of information for individual case management are both activities that cannot do without cross-border cooperation. The relevance and credibility of the different formations for cross-border cooperation can be precisely achieved in this promotion.

[16] See ENVR website (n 13).

[17] Proposal for a Directive of the European Parliament and of the Council amending Directive 2012/29/EU establishing minimum standards on the rights, support and protection of victims of crime, and replacing Council Framework Decision 2001/220/JHA (COM(2023) 424 final.

PART V

Conclusion and Reflections

20

Transforming EU Victims' Laws into Reality for Victims: Developing a Strategic Framework for the Implementation of Victims' Rights

LEVENT ALTAN

In 2009, I was given an incredible opportunity. I was tasked with reviewing European Union (EU) legislation on victims' rights in order to draft a new law – one that would have the potential to benefit the 450 million citizens of the EU, as well as any visitors who were unfortunate enough to be the victim of a crime in one of the EU's Member States. I embarked on a journey, which is ongoing, to discover what victims of crime need and how to ensure that our laws and practices are successful in addressing those needs.

The history of the international order for victims' rights effectively dates back to the UN Declaration of Basic Principles of Justice for Victims of Crime and Abuse of Power, which was adopted in 1985. That Declaration was soon followed by a series of recommendations by the Council of Europe in the 1990s. It was only with the 2001 Framework Decision on the Standing of Victims in Criminal Proceedings (hereinafter, the Framework Decision)[1] that the EU obtained a broad legislative instrument covering all victims of crime.

For its time, the Framework Decision pushed the limits of what was possible for the EU to legislate on with regard to victims. It established a range of obligations for EU Member States, which broadly covered key priorities such as the respect and recognition of victims, information, support, protection from harm, protection of privacy, and situations where a person is a victim of a crime abroad. Despite these ambitions and some progress made in the course of the next decade, the Framework Decision had limited impact across the EU.

[1] Council Framework Decision 2001/220/JHA of 15 March 2001 on the standing of victims in criminal proceedings [2001] OJ L82/1.

Eight years later, I was fortunate enough to be seconded to the European Commission and was assigned the task of reviewing the Framework Decision and, if necessary, drafting a legislative proposal using the Article 82 legal base under the newly adopted Treaty on the Functioning of the European Union.

That review ultimately led to the adoption of the 2012 EU Directive on the Rights, Protection and Support of Victims of Crime (hereinafter, the Victims' Rights Directive).[2] Ten years later, I had the opportunity to assess its practical implementation as Executive Director of Victim Support Europe (VSE), the leading non-governmental organisation (NGO) in Europe advocating for the rights of all victims of crime.

The review that we carried out was through VSE's Project Vociare,[3] for which national reports in all Member States participating in the Directive (Denmark opted out) and a synthesis report were drafted. A follow-up to this project is currently underway – Benevict[4] – which is reviewing the most recent implementation data, developing a methodology for assessing implementation of rights through an index and developing a cost benefit analysis methodology for the establishment of support services.

Based on the report's findings, VSE developed a series of policy papers on a National Victim Support Framework,[5] on Safe Justice,[6] communicating with victims[7] and victim compensation.[8] Ultimately, ahead of the European Commission's Proposal for amendments to the 2012 Directive,[9] VSE also published its vision for the next Directive.[10]

Based on this work, I propose to briefly set out some of the main drivers for our policies – the problems that we have identified in the implementation of EU victims' laws over the last two decades, with a subsequent focus on the solutions that VSE has proposed. I won't provide lengthy references of the evidence for statements here as these are derived from the aforementioned reports.

[2] Directive 2012/29/EU of the European Parliament and of the Council of 25 October 2012 establishing minimum standards on the rights, support and protection of victims of crime, and replacing Council Framework Decision 2001/220/JHA (2012) OJ L315/57 (Victims' Rights Directive).

[3] See dedicated page on the Victim Support Europe website (VSE), available at https://victim-support.eu/what-we-do/our-projects/previous/prjct-vociare/.

[4] See dedicated page on the Victim Support Europe website (VSE), available at https://victim-support.eu/what-we-do/our-projects/ongoing/benevict/.

[5] Victim Support Europe, 'National Framework for Comprehensive Victim Support' (2022), available at https://victim-support.eu/wp-content/files_mf/1673427018NationalFrameworkforComprehensiveVictimSupportcompressed.pdf.

[6] Discussion paper, 'Safe Justice for Victims of Crime. Challenging How We Perceive Success in Justice. Moving Towards an Integrated, Victim-Sensitive System' (February 2023), available at https://victim-support.eu/wp-content/files_mf/1677284356SafeJusticeforvictimsofCrime_compressed1.pdf.

[7] 'Transforming How We Communicate with Victims. Moving Beyond Information Provision to a System of Communication' (December 2022), available at https://victim-support.eu/wp-content/files_mf/1681918001TransformingHowWeCommunicateWithVictims_compressed.pdf.

[8] Victim Support Europe, 'A Journey from Crime to Compensation. An Analysis of Victims' Access to Compensation in the EU' (2019), available at https://victim-support.eu/wp-content/files_mf/1574261567A_Journey_From_Crime_To_Compensation_2019.pdf.

[9] European Commission, Proposal for a Directive of the European Parliament and of the Council amending Directive 2012/29/EU establishing minimum standards on the rights, support and protection of victims of crime, and replacing Council Framework Decision 2001/220/JHA, COM(2023) 424 final.

[10] L Altan et al, 'Victims of Crime Model Provisions Paper. VSE's Vision for a Revised Victims' Rights Directive' (September 2023), available at https://victim-support.eu/wp-content/files_mf/1695887426VSEVictimsofCrimeModelProvisionsPaper_Final.pdf.

I. Key Challenges in Establishing Meaningful Change for Victims

A. Limits to EU Laws for Victims

When examining both the Framework Decision and the Victims' Rights Directive, implementation problems can be broadly divided into those that relate to the EU legislation itself and those that relate to the implementation methods pursued by Member States – with those two also being interrelated.

With respect to drafting legislation, we first have to recognise that EU legislative proposals are subject to impact assessments, which determine the necessity, feasibility, proportionality and subsidiarity aspects of any proposal. Those proposals must also conform to the legal basis for EU action. This means that, even if an action, right or obligation may make sense or be understood to be a best practice, it may not be appropriate to legislate on it at the EU level.

Even after having been moulded to fit these requirements, any proposal will be substantially changed as a result of the negotiating process between Member States in the EU Council and the European Parliament. Consequently, compromises are often evident in the drafting of the Framework Decision (FD) and Victims' Rights Directive (VRD), which tend to diminish the likelihood of achieving their objectives.

Firstly, language is used that limits the level of obligation imposed on Member States: this includes phrases such as:

- Member States may … – as opposed to shall. In other words, the action is optional;
- Member States shall make every effort to (Art 2 FD) – the end objective is not clearly articulated nor what actions are required to meet the obligation of 'every' effort;
- As far as possible (Art 5 FD);
- Seek to promote (Art 10 FD);
- Shall encourage (Art 14 FD);
- Support the progressive creation (Art 15 FD);
- Member States shall facilitate the referral of victims (Art 8(2) VRD).

As can be seen from the number of examples derived from the Framework Decision, the way that obligations were phrased changed significantly between the Framework Decision and the Victims' Rights Directive. In the latter case, all articles impose an obligation – 'Member States shall …' This overcame one identified challenge, which was that Member States considered a range of Articles of the Framework Decision to be optional.

It is perhaps opportune to note that such language from the Framework Decision is now being reintroduced by the Member States[11] in amendments to the Victims' Rights

[11] Council of the European Union, Proposal for a Directive of the European Parliament and of the Council amending Directive 2012/29/EU establishing minimum standards on the rights, support and protection of victims of crime, and replacing Council Framework Decision 2001/220/JHA – General approach, 10255/24 (2024).

Directive – a clear step backwards from the height of EU solidarity that we saw after the adoption of the Treaty on the Functioning of the European Union (TFEU).

Despite improvements in language in the Victims' Rights Directive, the nature of some obligations remains vague to the extent that it is easy to claim almost any action as sufficient to meet the obligation. In a similar vein, a range of obligations are either limited or are vague in terms of how the obligation should be implemented.

This is inevitable and necessary to some extent since EU directives provide the framework for what needs to be implemented whilst leaving the specific method of implementation to Member States. However, this has also become an important driver for a range of problems or inconsistencies in the way that rights are implemented by Member States.

Such language in the Victims' Rights Directive includes:

- Member States shall take appropriate measures – this leaves a wide margin of discretion as to what constitutes appropriate. The Directive doesn't set out how it can be determined if a measure is appropriate. The question to ask is if an end goal, eg to understand and be understood (Art 3), is not being achieved, would a measure still be deemed appropriate?
- Rights limited to victims based on their role in the relevant criminal justice system and status of parties to criminal proceedings – a number of rights, eg Art 6(2) – right to information – are limited to only those victims who have a role in the criminal proceedings, eg parties to proceedings. The impact of this limit is that, despite not having a designated role, victims who would still wish to benefit from the right cannot or may not benefit from the right.
- In accordance with the rules of judicial discretion, eg Art 7 – right to interpretation and translation – judicial discretion is a vague and undefined term which can leave victims without legal certainty about their rights.
- Without prejudice to the rights of the defence – similarly vague and arguably not always appropriate (see below on the question of balancing two competing fundamental rights).
- Upon request – it is well understood that where the onus is put on victims to request a right, they are less likely to seek the right compared with when the right is offered to them.
- May provide and may be heard – optional language.
- Member States shall afford the possibility of reimbursement – the notion of possibility is extremely broad and can be interpreted such that the right is largely inaccessible.
- Unless required for the purposes of criminal proceedings – this leaves broad scope without any limiting rules on what may be deemed as required. It is therefore open to abuse.

As can be seen, a range of language limits obligations on Member States. Phrases such as 'may', 'as far as possible', 'shall seek to promote', etc largely leave Articles as optional, reducing the likelihood of their implementation.

Other language may be vague or provide exceptions or limitations to obligations. For example, with respect to the right to be understood and to understand, the requirement is that Member States shall take appropriate measures, but there is little guidance on what those measures should be and little in terms of obligations to follow those rules.

Similarly, a number of rights, eg information, interpretation and translation, are only applicable to victims based on their role in the relevant criminal justice system or where they are parties to proceedings. This means that some victims may not be able to access information because they are deemed to not have sufficient connection, interest or value to the proceedings.

Other examples of language which can reduce access to rights include 'upon request', 'afford the possibility', unless required for the purposes of criminal proceedings. This language either places a burden on victims to pursue a right and increases the likelihood that victims who would benefit from the right do not access it, or it provides a broad discretion to States and their authorities to limit a right without setting clear parameters.

Indeed, even where language is not vague *per se*, some Articles lack sufficient detail to ensure that they are implemented in the best manner and consistently across the EU. For example, support for victims is essential. The Victims' Rights Directive establishes that Member States shall ensure that victims have access to support services. It also sets out the types of services that should be provided and, in recitals, explains that accessibility means that services should be at a sufficient geographical distribution. In fact, the requirements on establishing victim support services are amongst the most detailed Articles.

However, the diversity of support mechanisms and approaches is such that, today, in one country such as Greece, there is no identifiable organisation that supports all victims of crime whilst, in a country like the Netherlands, they have a national support service which assists more than a million victims per year – without taking into account other support organisations working with, eg victims of sexual violence. In such circumstances, it is hard to argue that the Victims' Rights Directive has resulted in anything close to a level playing field for victims.

The combination of limitations, vague language, insufficient detail and legitimate requirements to leave the method of implementation to Member States has resulted in highly variable levels of implementation across the EU, which cannot be attributed simply to differences in cultures and systems.

B. Challenges at the National Level

At the same time, a number of factors at the national level dramatically influence the extent to which rights are effectively implemented or not. These include:

- Insufficient or poorly drafted victim-specific primary legislation and a lack of implementing rules;
- The siloed development of victims' policies, resulting in inefficiencies, competition, gaps, overlap and inconsistency across different policies and sectors;
- State agencies and Civil Society Organisations lacking mechanisms, structures and technical solutions to facilitate co-operation and co-ordination whilst funding and

decision-making structures often result in, if not directly encourage, unhelpful competition;

- Lack of data, research, oversight and evaluation and change management infrastructure that would support appropriate short and long term decision-making, prioritisation and appropriate allocation of funds and continual, consistent and strategic developments in the field;
- Lack of understanding of roles and relevance of action for victims, resulting in a failure to appropriately prioritise action, a focus on some groups and a failure to act for others, and insufficient incorporation and interconnection of the victims' agenda into wider sectors of relevance, eg education, health, social services, employment. This lack of understanding manifests itself at the individual level amongst practitioners, the public and victims and includes a lack of focus on these matters in the leadership of organisations and in how those entities are organised to address victims' issues;
- Lack of legal remedies and appeal processes for victims to enable them to enforce their rights.

The consequence of not having these systems and rights in place has been researched widely by VSE and other organisations, including the European Agency for Fundamental Rights. As was concluded in the 2019 Vociare synthesis report:

> Worryingly, none of the Articles of the Directive are fully and satisfactorily implemented for all victims across the EU. Neither is there a single country that offers full implementation of the entirety of the Directive to all victims on their territory. The main conclusion of the present exercise remains – that there still remains plenty to be done to make victims' rights a reality for all European victims.[12]

Whilst the drivers of these problems are many, varied and interconnected, victims' policy over the last 50 years has been developed incrementally, driven by passionate people often working on the frontline or who are victims themselves, or driven by short term political priorities or high-profile cases. Services and laws have been set up based on specific agendas to address specific issues in specific contexts, rather than taking a strategic, long term and systems-based approach as we might see with respect to healthcare, justice, policing, etc.

Nonetheless, there have been plenty of successes. In numerous victims' fields, particularly on human trafficking and domestic violence, strategies and co-ordinating structures have been or are being developed. Yet this in itself is a symptom of the problem as policies on different victims' topics, types of crime or victim groups are being developed separately instead of as part of a single, unified and coherent system. Just as our healthcare system consists of many different services and areas of focus but operates under a single umbrella, a single holistic victim care system is necessary.

With this in mind, VSE has developed a series of recommendations and principles to assist decision-makers in the development of a comprehensive victim care system. In the following section, I summarise the essential elements of these policies.

[12] A Ivankovic and L Altan, 'Vociare Synthesis Report', available at https://victim-support.eu/wp-content/files_mf/1564677465VOCIARE_Synthesis_Reportweb.pdf.

II. Key Problems of Implementation and the Way Forward

A. Moving to a Coherent Victim Care System – Defining Success

Given that we know that there are wide ranging problems and that many of these problems have been expressed for decades, how do we move to a situation of effective implementation of rights? The starting point is to understand what success for all victims of crime actually looks like and, of course, we have to want this success for all victims (as opposed to only certain groups).

On that point, I would emphasise that the type of crime a victim suffers is not the sole predictor of harm or appropriate response. Two people can be subjected to the same crime but have very different experiences, reactions, traumas and needs. Nor is it possible to predict who will fall victim to what crimes and when, nor what the repercussions of the crime will be. In a world of multiple priorities and competition for limited resources, it will always be difficult to avoid the need to prioritise and make choices. Nevertheless, we must try to benefit the most number of victims in the most efficient way in order to maximise the benefits and impact of any action taken.

This issue must be at the heart of victims' policy and practice, yet it is questionable whether we have a single clear vision of what success looks like. How in fact do we know if we are getting it right for victims, if we are maximising the impact of all our actions for the most number of people, and does change depend on the field or policy area that we are discussing or operating in?

VSE argues that the core objectives should be to address the impact of crime, primarily on the victim but on wider circles as well, facilitating, as much as possible, their well-being and healing pathway, supporting post-traumatic growth and minimising further harm that our responses may cause.

Of course, it is a legitimate question to ask why, if at all, we should care about the well-being and healing of victims, or indeed why should this be a priority. Whilst there is not enough space in this chapter to explore core criminological theories (and indeed there are better experts for this kind of discussion), I would at least point to historical and modern narratives or philosophies which connect concepts of achieving successful lives as individuals to building successful communities and nations.

From the concept of Eudemonia put forward by Plato, to approaches of Buddhism, and Stoicism, right through to modern pyscho-therapeutic techniques such as cognitive behavioural therapy, there is a recognition of core approaches to helping individuals flourish. At the same time, states are exploring ways to measure a country's success, which go beyond simple economic measures such as gross domestic product and rather look at the wellbeing economy. This change starts to mainstream the objectives of health and well-being into all policies, aiming to strengthen resilience, inclusivity and sustainability. Such models are increasingly explored by States, by the

World Health Organization (WHO),[13] Organisation for Economic Cooperation and Development (OECD)[14] and the European Council.[15]

If, for the sake of argument, we accept core objectives as being to address harm, maximise well-being and minimise further harm, what might be the key approaches to achieve these aims? I would break them down into three parts:

- What are the key elements which should drive the way in which we treat victims?
- How do we work out what actions to take for victims?
- How do we organise ourselves to maximise the chance of success of these actions?

B. Key Elements in how We should Treat Victims – A Victim Centric Approach

With respect to the core elements of how to treat victims, these are set out well via the United Nation's (UN) definition of a victim centric approach, as adopted in VSE's Safe Justice paper:

> a way of engaging with victim(s) that *prioritizes listening* to the victim(s), *avoids retraumatization*, and systematically focuses on their *safety, rights, well-being*, expressed *needs and choices*, thereby giving back as much **control** to victim(s) as feasible and ensuring the *empathetic and sensitive* delivery of services and accompaniment in a *non-judgmental manner* (emphasis added).[16]

What this definition does not explain or cover is the inter-relationship with other fields and other priorities. As such, to these objectives, we have to add a policy analysis or theory of change framework. In simple terms, it is necessary to know:

- What is the impact of crime on victims?
- What are the needs of victims?
- What are the challenges and barriers that victims face in access rights and services?
- What are the challenges and barriers that society faces in meeting victims' needs?
- What adaptations in other sectors, on rights, and services will be required and/ or how might solutions need to be adapted having regard to other priorities or fields?

The main impacts and needs are summarised in Fig 20.1 and detailed in the Safe Justice paper.

[13] See World Health Organization, 'The Geneva Charter for Well-Being (2021)', available at www.who.int/publications/m/item/the-geneva-charter-for-well-being.

[14] European Health Forum Gastein, 'Collaborative Leadership for Health and Well-Being. How to Rise to the Challenge?' (2021), available at www.ehfg.org/conference/programme/sessions/collaborative-leadership-for-health-and-well-being.

[15] Council of the EU, Council Conclusions on the Economy of Wellbeing (2019/C 400/09) [2019] OJ C400/9.

[16] UNHCR, 'Policy on a Victim-Centred Approach in the UNHCR's Response to Sexual Misconduct' (2020) 4; 6.

Fig 20.1 Impact of Crime and Needs of Victims

For brevity I won't detail victims' needs and impact of crime, other than to explain that recognition and respect covers not only treatment of victims but also the ability to identify victims and have them recognised within proceedings – rights bearers with a legitimate voice. Protection covers both physical protection from harm as well as secondary victimisation. Support encompasses all forms of assistance, including information, emotional and psychological, practical, financial and more. Justice means not only the judgment itself but access to justice – the ability to report a crime, participate in the process and some influence over at least key decisions of significant interest to victims. Finally, compensation covers not only financial compensation by the offender and State but also restoration through, for example, restorative justice.

It should also be recognised that victims are not a single homogenous group and responses must be adapted accordingly. This means that impact, needs, challenges and solutions will all differ in some ways between each individual victim. In order to address this effectively but also efficiently, it is important to understand that, broadly speaking, we can identify factors which are common to all victims (those mentioned in Fig 20.1). These factors can then vary based on the type and nature of crime and can also vary based on the personal situation, history, characteristics, etc of the individual.

Knowing this means that, if we want to get it right for every victim of crime, we have to establish comprehensive solutions that address the common needs of all victims and in addition specialised responses which identify group and individual needs and respond to them in a targeted manner. This can mean, for example, having a combination of all-crime (generic) victim support services and specialist services, with an individual needs assessment and referral process that helps victims reach the right type of organisation for them.

Fig 20.2 Common, Group and Individual Needs

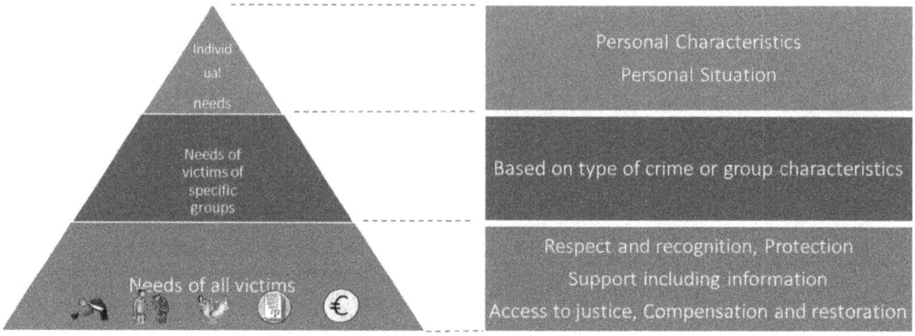

By taking this approach we can assist the most victims possible, co-ordinate solutions across different areas to maximise their impact, and minimise competition and overlaps, whilst reducing gaps. This approach will also help lower costs and maintain specialised responses without leaving any victim behind. Fundamentally, it helps ensure that there is no hierarchy of victims whilst enabling targeted responses.

The above methodology is valuable in understanding how rights and services should be implemented for victims in an effective way. However, this information alone is not sufficient to enable policy-makers to make decisions about what actions to prioritise, what budget to allocate and how to balance potentially competing priorities or competing rights.

C. Ensuring Decision-Making Takes into Account All Benefits of Victim Action

The challenge to effective implementation of victims' rights is that the true value of those actions is not properly assessed and accounted for. This may be because not all benefits are identified. It may be because only short-term benefits are considered. Equally, the cost of crime and its impacts may be underestimated, in particular those relating to psychological, emotional and health harms; these of course have knock-on effects with respect to employment, education, family structures, etc.

Similarly, there tends to be little data on how victims' rights impact justice systems, in particular with respect to effectiveness and efficiency. For example, feedback from support services in Sweden indicated that, where support is provided to victims, the workload on prosecutors is reduced but we do not see statistical measurements of this in efficiency of justice calculations. Equally, where prosecutors have victim-focused training and tools, this tends to reduce workload on victim services. In other words, the combination of the two has multiplier effects, not even accounting for the wider benefits to victims themselves.

The failure to account for wider and longer-term benefits, and interconnections with wider social issues, weakens the ability to make informed choices about the prioritisation of victim action. In contrast to this approach, in a project for the World Bank and the Serbian Government, VSE carried out a cost benefit analysis of the cost of crime and the benefits of establishing and running a national victim support service which accounted for a wide range of benefits.

Whilst data was difficult to obtain, it was concluded that a basic support service would cost around €300,000 to set up whilst a high performance service would cost €19 million. On the face of it, this would be a significant cost to bear. However, the research also estimated that the benefits could range from €84–470 million, which includes savings related to reduced legal fees in trials and reduced costs arising from trauma.[17]

Whilst this data would seem to make the set-up of victim support unquestionable, numerous barriers still discourage policy-makers from investing in support services. For example, the cost benefit analysis had to rely on extrapolations rather than full data sets (since relevant agencies do not tend to collect victim relevant data), costs tend to be incurred in the short term whilst benefits are fully experienced in the long term, and the ministries which incur costs may not be the ministries that experience the benefits.

For this reason, a cost benefit analysis alone tends to be insufficient to persuade policy- makers of the value of investing in victims' rights. Therefore, additional actions are needed to support a change in the prioritisation of victims' rights. In particular, a review of how we measure success in our justice systems is needed, as well as the establishment of decision- making, implementation and oversight mechanisms that focus on co-ordination and long-term solutions.

D. What Makes Justice Successful? Incorporating Victim Objectives into Our Justice System

With respect to our justice systems, the primary objectives over the last decades have been to ensure that they find guilty people guilty, innocent people innocent, ensure appropriate punishment and do this in an efficient manner. Over time, wider priorities have been incorporated, such as rehabilitation and to some extent victim experience or participation.

Yet the safety, well-being, voice and participation of victims tend to be absent from clearly articulated justice objectives. Even where they exist in those terms, they tend to be considered of a lesser priority than defence rights. Thus, for example, in balancing the fundamental rights to privacy and a fair trial (bearing in mind there isn't a hierarchy of fundamental rights), most countries will assume that personal data about the victims must be provided to the defendant. This presumption is based on the belief that knowledge of the accuser is an essential element of a fair trial. Yet, not all information is always necessary for this – in fact, much of it may not be. Moreover, it is possible to protect such information in various ways without compromising defence rights.

[17] Victim Support Europe, 'Costs of Victimisation and Benefits of Victim Support in Serbia (2018), available at https://victim-support.eu/publications/costs-of-victimisation-and-benefits-of-victim-support-in-serbia/.

The question is why should we bother improving protection of victims' personal data? Essentially, because in signing up to the EU Charter of Fundamental Rights, to the European Convention on Human Rights and in claiming the rule of law as an essential value, it is what is required of our States. As such, if there is a fundamental right to privacy, the victims privacy should be presumed from the outset. In other words, there should be privacy by design.

Only in demonstrably necessary cases should this fundamental right be breached or limited. This, in fact, is how defence rights are treated. Limitations to those rights are exceptions with strong rules protecting the processes and circumstances in which a limitation may occur. This same approach does not tend to be applied to a victim's right to privacy – as can be seen in the EU Council's general approach to amendments on the Victims' Rights Directive. Here, there is an outright rejection of even a temporary privacy protection (the so called 'firewall solution') with respect to migrant victim information being submitted to migration authorities for reasons unconnected to the reporting of the crime.

The solution, as VSE proposes, is to review what the purpose and objectives of our justice systems are. Modern and traditional theories of justice encompassing distributive justice, procedural justice, retributive justice, restorative justice and integral justice which take into account politico-legal, societal, cultural, ecological and spiritual/metaphysical issues should be adopted to form a more comprehensive purpose underpinning justice. In this way, we have to conclude that justice systems cannot achieve their true potential of addressing crime and supporting successful, resilient and cohesive societies without including success criteria related to victim outcomes (as defined by the victim sensitive approach).

Given that it is effectively accepted that enabling successful societies is the ultimate goal of criminal justice systems (through the lens of addressing crime), then victim priorities should be seen as being as important as efficiency or defence rights. As argued in the Safe Justice paper:

> Success in justice cannot be claimed while vast numbers of victims choose not to report even the most serious of crimes, while victims feel they are not heard, or while victims do not have a voice. A system which treats victims disrespectfully, which further harms victims or fails to protect them, and leaves them dissatisfied by their experience, cannot be considered successful no matter how efficient it is, nor what the final verdict is. Equally, a justice system that causes vicarious trauma to its actors, in particular witnesses and members of the jury, should not be considered a success story.[18]

This approach does not mean that defence rights are weakened. Rather, victims' rights are established and implemented as a necessary part of a justice system. Where different rights may be incompatible or competing, they should both be examined on their merits and necessity, with the least harmful solution being explored. This contrasts with the current situation, where defence rights are usually assumed to be the priority.

Perhaps a telling example of this is that the original EU Commission Proposal on the 2012 Victims' Rights Directive, Art 4(2)[19] established a right for the victim to be

[18] Victim Support Europe, 'Safe Justice Discussion Paper' (2023) 2, available at https://victim-support.eu/wp-content/files_mf/1699611215SafeJusticeforvictimsofCrime_compressed.pdf.

[19] European Commission, Proposal for a Directive of the European Parliament and of the Council establishing minimum standards on the rights, support and protection of victims of crime, COM(2011) 275 final.

notified of the release of an offender or suspect at least in a case of identified risk of harm to the victim. Subsequent discussions resulted in a limitation where such notification would risk causing harm to the offender (Article 6 (5 and 6)). Of course, it is reasonable to limit such risks. Yet no balancing of risk is established. It seems that harm to the offender is considered more important than harm to the victim.

A shift in mindset is therefore necessary. It means moving away from the quasi-automatic limitations currently imposed on the development of victims' solutions, such as stipulations that these solutions must not prejudice defence rights, must not impact the course of the criminal proceedings, and must only be implemented where practically possible. This is the language repeatedly proposed by Member States in current negotiations and it is a fundamental barrier to achieving the systemic change necessary to fully implement victim rights.

Rather, we must incorporate victim priorities into justice success criteria and adopt a victim-sensitive approach. That is, one where victims' rights and solutions are first developed based on the foundation of a victim-centric approach. Only subsequently should those solutions be adjusted taking into accounting wider priorities, operation of justice systems, balancing of rights, etc.

Yet, even this shift in approach will not be sufficient to facilitate full and effective implementation of rights. To maximise our chances of success, we next need to explore VSE's concept of the national victim support framework and the implementing conditions necessary to enable rights.

E. Developing a Long Term Systems-Based Approach to Victims' Rights

In 2022, VSE published its paper on a National Framework for Comprehensive Victim Support. That paper seeks to take a more holistic and comprehensive view of what our understanding of victim support should be, who should be responsible for supporting victims and the core principles of how a system of support should be organised.

The paper reflects that support starts with the individual resilience of the victim – something that is largely overlooked in policy-making. Equally, a victim's social support network – family, friends, colleagues – can be instrumental in a victim's healing pathway. They can also be highly detrimental and many victims may not have a social network at all. Again, States must recognise this and act to improve the way in which these networks support victims or they must help victims to build a support network.

Beyond this, we reflect on the need to have accessible services specialised in supporting victims (those serving all victims – sometimes called 'all-crime services' or 'generic services' and those focused on a specific group, often called 'specialist services'). Co-ordinated with these services, any entity coming into contact with victims can have a role in supporting them and should therefore have the tools and expertise to do so.

This means, for example, that hospitals should train staff to identify signs of victimisation, ensure that they know how to communicate and advise victims and that they have the tools and mechanisms to refer victims to appropriate services. Similarly, police and prosecution services should have specialist victim solutions, employers should have mechanisms to identify signs of victimisation in their employees and have appropriate mechanisms to address this where it exists.

The reason for this approach is that any person can become a victim of crime at any time in any place. The impacts can be wide-ranging, affecting all aspects of the victim's life and the impacts can ripple outwards to affect many others, including social networks, witnesses, first responders, local communities and the population at large. If we genuinely want to address crime impacts and build resilient societies, a 'whole of society' approach to support is fundamental.

Having in mind these wide ranging impacts, the necessary involvement of multiple sectors and entities, as well as many other complicating factors, eg timeframe for responses, location of crime, perpetrator and victim dynamics, barriers to reporting crime and seeking support, socio-cultural and legal factors, the challenge that the benefits of actions won't always be experienced in the sector which carries out the action, actors operating in siloes – it quickly becomes apparent that effective solutions require a systemic and co-ordinated approach.

This is why VSE has focused not only on what rights are needed but also on a long-term co-ordinated approach which includes what decision-making, implementation, oversight and review mechanisms are necessary.

To illustrate the point, we might consider a victim's testimony in court. Barriers to achieving a high quality testimony include the mental and physical health of the victim, their fear of the perpetrator and of the proceedings, embarrassment, shame or other emotional factors, their trust in various authorities and possibly fear of those authorities, pressure from their life situation, eg the need to work or go to school, care for children, community pressures to not be involved with justice actors.

All of these factors cannot simply be addressed by offering a victim a screen so that they do not need to look at the defendant, or a separate court waiting area. What is required is that out of court and in court, support solutions are offered and accessible. It may require actions to help employers understand their support roles and the importance of providing victims with time and space in advance of their appearance in court. It may involve providing free childcare facilities or ensuring that appointments with social or employment services are organised around the victim's situation. It may require community engagement with groups that are difficult to reach, addressing fear and trust factors. It may simply require practical and financial solutions like a bus ticket or transport to get to the court. And, of course, it implies potential high cost, structural action which can nevertheless have significant benefits on the justice process – such as establishing separate court entrances and waiting areas for victims.

These multiple issues cannot simply be addressed in a piecemeal fashion or, if they are, each solution will be limited and as a result perhaps judged a failure or not cost effective. Without overarching mechanisms to set priorities and ensure that actors work together in a coherent manner, it is inevitable that gaps or overlapping responses arise. By contrast, by developing long term co-ordinated actions to address all factors that support the provision of evidence by victims, we can maximise the value of every action and its impact.

With this in mind, the following recommendations have been made regarding the constituent parts of a coordination framework:

- A national victims' rights strategy: a long-term sustainable strategy should set out key priorities, objectives and governmental activities that will protect and promote the rights of all victims of crime. It should identify key actions for various actors (government, judiciary, societal and private sectors, and civil society);
- A national co-ordinator: a high-level government or civic official responsible for the overall delivery of the framework;
- A victims' commissioner: an independent body in charge of monitoring and challenging government on its policy, which would give recommendations and advice to the government as well as act as the voice of victims and raise awareness about victims' rights and issues;
- A working group or implementation committee made up of senior governmental and civil society representatives, who can develop and implement the National Strategy's policy and procedures, and co-ordinate activities across different sectors. Such implementing committees and bodies should also exist at the local or regional level;
- *Ad hoc* working groups that deal with specific issues relating to victims may also be created – A national advisory council composed of victims and survivors ensures that the voices of victims are integral to the development of policies, procedures and practices, etc;
- A national referral mechanism that ensures that victims are referred to the appropriate services.

Effectively, these recommendations address three types of challenges. On the one hand, we have to make sure that there is a *long-term vision* relevant for all victims. This allows for specific strategies on some groups, but it ensures that different action across sectors and crimes is better co-ordinated. It also allows for long term investments. The term 'it costs too much' can never be correct without a timeline attached to it. A ten-million-euro investment may be impossible in one year, but could be possible in ten years. It is simply a matter of deciding if it is necessary and planning for it.

Secondly, we have to be able to act on that vision, which means planning mechanisms that include all the relevant stakeholders and voices. And of course, planning is nothing without implementation. That means having the capability to carry out solutions in a co-ordinated manner across an entire country.

To guarantee continuous and consistent action across the lifetimes of multiple governments it is also necessary to have in place oversight mechanisms. In line with policy cycle theory wherein policies are evaluated to determine what improvements are needed, it is necessary to have oversight bodies that assess the implementation of commitments. At least some of these bodies should be independent of government and all assessments should be inclusive of victims' views and of all those working with and for victims.

What might such an approach look like in practice? We can look first to countries like Croatia and Portugal, which have adopted national victim strategies. We see

Croatia, Estonia, France and others having multi-sectoral committees that meet regularly to discuss priorities and challenges in implementation. In France, a minister is assigned clear responsibility for the victims' agenda. A law was adopted in 2017 to create an Inter-Ministerial Delegate for Victim support (DIAV), who coordinates the actions of France's various ministries in relation to a whole series of crimes against victims – not quite all crimes but close. As they explain, the DIAV:

> monitors the effectiveness and improvement of the means for aiding victims and coordinates all actions of France's ministries in their relations with victim and victim support organizations. The DIAV organizes meetings of the cross-government committee to aid victims and ensures the guidance, tracking, coordination and support of local committees to aid victims. Lastly, when needed, the DIAV coordinates France's state services to pay homage to victims and hold commemorations.[20]

Multiple supporting mechanisms are also established including the Victim Rights, Justice and Assistance Service and the Office for Victim Support and NGO Policy. Moreover, local co-ordinating committees are established to co-ordinate the implementation of policies at the local level. This approach is also reflected in the establishment of France Victimes, which is a national network organisation of victim support services who together support all victims of crime and operate the national 116 006 victim helpline. To ensure that those services exist and can operate across the whole country, a victims' fund has also been established, which pays not only for these services but also for the victim compensation scheme. Thus, co-ordination, delivery and funding are addressed.

Improved co-ordination and decision-making is also established through community needs assessments,[21] whereby an analysis of needs, existing resources and services, gaps and priorities, is carried out. The process brings together all actors operating in the area of analysis, facilitates conversations and trust between those organisations and aims to develop a single vision for what the community needs for victims.

We also see national referral mechanisms – largely understood in the context of human trafficking but in fact necessary for all victims. This entails setting up a national system to enable police and other agencies to refer victims to the most appropriate support service. It should also result in cross referral between support organisations and others with clear agreements and rules which facilitate speedy access across the entire territory of a country.

To my knowledge, the combination of all these solutions as a comprehensive system do not exist. I would argue a key driver for this is the complexity of some of the issues which necessitates multiple co-ordination mechanisms – which themselves are generally lacking in most countries.

By way of example, the referral of victims from the police to victim support (the provision of victims' contact information to a support service which then directly

[20] See dedicated website page available at www.info.gouv.fr/guide-victimes-en/inter-ministerial-delegation-for-victim-support-diav.

[21] See page dedicated to the AREV project, available at https://victim-support.eu/what-we-do/our-projects/previous/arev/.

contacts the victim to offer their support), seems relatively straightforward but consistently runs into challenges in terms of:

- which organisation should be referred to (type of service, type of crime, way of work, accessibility, waiting lists, etc);
- how to ensure that the system is easy to use by practitioners (how they decide who to refer to and practically how the referral is made);
- how to comply with data protection rules whilst making the system fast, efficient and effective.

On this last issue (data protection), experience indicates that an opt-out system tends to result in the most victims reaching support services. The opt-out system involves a victim being informed that their information will be passed to victim support unless they object. In the Netherlands, victim information is sent directly to Victim Support Netherlands, from the police, through an electronic system. This eliminates administrative burden on the police, removes decision-making and results in fast referrals.

However, this system is not accepted by all data protection authorities with EU data protection bodies being silent on the matter. An opt-in approach which would satisfy some data protection authorities results in far fewer victims accessing services. For example, Victim Support Scotland saw an approximate 70 per cent drop in referrals when their system was moved away from opt-out.

To further complicate matters, the recently adopted violence against women and domestic violence Directive and proposed amendments to the Victims' Rights Directive, are likely to put the optimal opt-out system at risk since it seems the police (competent authority) will have to determine the need to refer based on an assessment – an approach which traditionally doesn't work out well for victims' access to support.

This is a lengthy example, but it illustrates that without the co-ordination of multiple actors at the national and international level, across different fields, it will be difficult to implement effective solutions. Even where there is co-ordination amongst justice actors, solutions can be jeopardised by action in other areas.

Whilst recognising these complications, it can nevertheless be seen that numerous effective co-ordination solutions exist. There are many other examples as well, such as victims' commissioners in England and Northern Ireland, multi-agency centres such as Family Justice Centers in Belgium, etc.

Unfortunately, I am not aware of any country that has the full panoply of solutions in place with an effective co-ordination across different victim priorities and with the inclusion of those priorities across all other sectors (security, economy, mental health, justice, environment, etc).

Such an approach would, in particular, mean ensuring that States explore how actions for victims of domestic violence, child abuse, human trafficking, to name but a few, could be developed together, and could be designed to benefit other victims besides that limited group. It would also explore how all sectors should incorporate victims' priorities. For example, by incorporating resilience, empathy and effective communication education into schools and universities, or ensuring that support for employees victimised in or out of the workplace was part of priorities on the economy.

In other words, returning to the original analytical framework – national and international institutions should address needs and actions common to all, mainstream these perspectives across all policies, and determine the specific needs and actions necessary for different victims, layering these on top of a strong foundation for all.

III. Conclusions

To conclude, if we want to break the decades long cycle of implementing victims' rights in a piecemeal, start stop fashion, if we want to end the litany of reports detailing how we are failing victims and failing to implement commitments made almost 50 years ago, we must have a fundamental shift in thinking.

We must move beyond thinking merely of victims' rights to thinking about a national victim care system, in the same way as we think of our healthcare systems or justice systems. This starts by being clear about what our vision for victim care is and why this matters.

It means approaching all action from the perspective of victims' needs, impact of crime, addressing challenges and operating in a victim sensitive manner. Using those principles for our analytical framework we must establish an infrastructure of long term, strategic, co-ordinated decision-making and delivery. A victim strategy, clearly identified political leadership, co-ordinating committees for laws, policies and implementation at the national and local level are needed. It means establishing funding mechanisms for long term change and, ultimately, it means establishing a strong foundation that addresses the needs of all victims whilst setting up specialised responses for different groups.

There is movement in this direction. More and more states are adopting strategies, coordination mechanisms and more. Yet, this remains a piecemeal approach with different States taking more or less action perpetuating, for victims, decades long differences in standards depending on where you are victimised or residing.

This is why action at the local and state level must be supported by European and International laws, policies and funding. EU institutions have a responsibility to facilitate co-ordinated and meaningful progress. Progress which moves from minor adjustments to a few rights towards a focus on systems, standards, co-ordination frameworks, oversight, review and enforcement of laws.

Together with State actors, there must be a realisation that the success of strategic priorities on prosperity, security, social cohesion and resilience, and much more – as adopted by the European Council and pursued under President Von der Leyen's recent Political Guidelines – will be greatly advanced through co-ordinated, meaningful action for victims and will be hampered without it. To put this in perspective, in the next five years we will see hundreds of millions of people in the EU suffering serious crime. This will impede their productivity, reduce education and work success, increase discord, and weaken resilience and belief in our democratic, rule of law based systems.

The signs, however, are not positive. Member States have comprehensively rejected or diluted EU Commission proposals, which themselves are far less ambitious than those of the European Parliament. There has been a strong push back against the EU 'interfering' in national decision-making, whilst short term perspectives on costs, benefits and infrastructure change seem to drive thinking.

As we approach the anniversaries for the UN Declaration of Basic Principles of Justice for Victims of Crime and Abuse of Power, EU Victims Day and the Charter of Fundamental Rights, we should celebrate our successes. Yet we cannot ignore the reality that crime remains pervasive with many new forms, especially online, exposing ever increasing numbers to new dangers. At the same time, most victims never report the crimes that they suffer, most victims never access support services, and where victims do come forward they are often let down or suffer even more.

In my view, there is little to excuse for this situation. Many of the solutions to these problems already exist, we must now commit to adopting them.

21

Exploring the Emergence of an EU Model for Victims' Rights: Progress and Challenges

CHLOÉ BRIÈRE

I. Introduction

Initial efforts made and actions undertaken by the European Union (EU) in favour of the rights of victims of crime came in the late 1990s and early 2000s. In 1999, in the conclusions of the Tampere European Council, Heads of State and Government considered that 'minimum standards should be drawn up on the protection of the victims of crime, in particular on crime victims' access to justice and on their rights to compensation for damages, including legal costs'.[1] More than 20 years later, a series of legislative instruments have been adopted within and beyond the EU area of criminal justice and the first-ever EU strategy on victims' rights has been adopted (in 2020). It seems, therefore, to be an appropriate time to question whether the evolutions of the EU legal framework have led to the emergence of an EU model for victims' rights that is built on a comprehensive approach ensuring that each victim can receive the assistance needed. Providing an answer to such a question is not an easy task and feels more like embarking on a long and hazardous journey marked with a constant obstacle: the fragmentation of norms and actors that we will aim to unpack in this concluding chapter.

Before moving onto this analysis, two preliminary remarks must be made. First, the idea of an EU model must not be understood as a claim favouring a unique set of standards, functioning as a 'one-size-fits-all' and entailing a full harmonisation of all aspects of national procedural laws relating to victims. Scholars and practitioners alike have repeatedly stressed how essential it is to consider each victim's specific circumstances and the need to rely on the individual assessment of their situation and needs to provide them with the most appropriate assistance and protection. As a result, the set of standards to be put in place should function more like a toolbox that can be mobilised depending on various factors, including but not limited to the following

[1] European Council, Presidency conclusions, Tampere meeting, 15 and 16 October 1999, para 32.

elements: the potential vulnerability of the victims; the type of crime to which they have been exposed (material crime involving physical harm, vs moral crime linked to identity theft and financial loss); the place in which they have been victims of a crime (in their country of residence vs in another country where they are temporarily staying, a country where they understand or do not understand the language of the proceedings), the stage of criminal proceedings (initial reporting of the crime, pre-trial and trial phases, or after a final judgment has been rendered) and any other circumstances likely to impact their access to justice and compensation (eg offender in the same country vs offender located abroad). Such diversity requires the adoption and implementation of various rights, which can be divided into core rights, such as the right to compensation or access to justice to be granted to all victims, encompassing, for instance, the rights of information and interpretation; and peripheral rights, such as the medical and social assistance to be granted to victims following the assessment of their circumstances and needs.

Secondly, the EU model in favour of victims' rights must be based on a clear definition of the notion of victim and include measures enabling the identification of all victims. Behind the easy assumption that the notion of victim is well established, the reality is much more nuanced, and there are often gaps between the theoretical definition and the practical identification and recognition of victims. The definition enshrined in the EU Victims' Rights Directive covers natural persons who have suffered harm which was directly caused by a criminal offence; and family members of a person whose death was directly caused by a criminal offence and who have suffered harm as a result of that person's death.[2] This definition has now been accepted as the point of reference for the EU legislator, and other actors, and it is key to delineate who qualifies as a victim and can benefit from the rights associated with such a status. However, scholars have stressed the gaps existing for those who do not correspond to the 'ideal' victim, and/or who find themselves in complex situations (eg victims of trafficking forced to commit criminal offences as a result of their trafficking, migrants prosecuted due to their irregular migration status, victims of hate crime or violence against women afraid to report a crime due to their fear of homophobic/transphobic/misogynous reactions from the police, etc). Other questions remain regarding the possibility for national legislators to decide which family members can be considered indirect victims, or the representation of interested parties in certain circumstances (eg non-governmental organisations granted the right to intervene as third parties). Hence, the definition of the notion of victim should not be set in stone and should continue to be debated.

Beyond these remarks, to answer the question as to whether the EU has succeeded in elaborating a model for victims' rights, these conclusions will be divided into three parts. First, the particularities of the development of EU law standards in that field will be highlighted and put in perspective alongside developments at international, other regional and national levels. Second, the EU legal framework currently in force will then be analysed to showcase the diversity of the norms relevant to the protection of victims'

[2] Directive 2012/29/EU of the European Parliament and of the Council of 25 October 2012 establishing minimum standards on the rights, support and protection of victims of crime, and replacing Council Framework Decision 2001/220/JHA [2012] OJ L315/57, Art 2(1).

rights and to categorise them in concentric circles. In this way, we will assess whether the current legal framework achieved a certain degree of coherence, or whether any remaining inconsistencies and gaps persist. Finally, in conclusion, future perspectives and suggestions for improvement will be set out.

II. Victims' Rights within the Ecosystem of the EU Area of Criminal Justice

The development of EU standards concerning victims' rights has already been addressed in this volume, notably in the introduction, as well as in literature,[3] either on the occasion of the adoption of the Framework Decision[4] or the adoption in 2012 of the Victims' Rights Directive.[5] The objective of this section is thus to dissect how the adoption of victims' rights standards fits within the EU's area of criminal justice.

Even though relevant texts have been enacted in various policy areas,[6] the issue of victims' rights continues to be perceived first and foremost as belonging to the field of EU criminal law. The latter consists of the corpus of texts and instruments adopted by the EU to support police and judicial cooperation in criminal matters. More precisely, the development of standards on the rights of victims of crime is closely intertwined with the development of standards on the rights of suspects and accused persons and the potential development of rules on the admissibility of evidence. Under Article 82 (2) of the Treaty on the Functioning of the European Union (TFEU), the EU can claim competencies to adopt rules in these three fields, thus participating in the development of embryonic EU criminal procedural legislation.

Victims' rights distinguish themselves as the area in which the EU legislature has been the most proactive, with the adoption of the first instrument, a Framework Decision, in 2001, replaced by a Directive in 2012, and a Proposal for its revision published in 2023.[7] By contrast, the first texts for procedural rights of suspects and accused were only adopted after the entry into force of the Lisbon Treaty in 2009,[8] and

[3] MS Groenhuijsen and A Pemberton, 'The EU Framework Decision for Victims of Crime: Does Hard Law Make a Difference?' (2009) 17 *European Journal of Crime, Criminal Law and Criminal Justice* 43; I Wieczorek, 'The New Proposal on Victims' Rights: Law Enforcement or Safeguard for the Rights of the Individual?' (2011) 2 *New Journal of European Criminal Law* 343; R Lang, 'The EU's New Victims' Rights Directive: Can Minimum Harmonization Work for a Concept Like Vulnerability' (2013) 22 *Nottingham Law Journal* 90; or R Letschert and C Rijken, 'Rights of Victims of Crime: Tensions between an Integrated Approach and a Limited Legal Basis for Harmonisation' (2013) 4 *New Journal of European Criminal Law* 226.

[4] Council Framework Decision 2001/220/JHA of 15 March 2001 on the standing of victims in criminal proceedings (Hereafter '2001 Framework Decision') [2001] OJ L82/1.

[5] Directive 2012/29/EU (n 2).

[6] See, for instance, Council Directive 2004/80/EC of 29 April 2004 relating to compensation to crime victims [2004] OJ L261/15, adopted based on Art 308 TEC (now Art 352 TFEU).

[7] European Commission, Proposal for a Directive of the European Parliament and of the Council amending Directive 2012/29/EU establishing minimum standards on the rights, support and protection of victims of crime, and replacing Council Framework Decision 2001/220/JHA, COM(2023) 424, 12 July 2023 (hereafter '2023 Commission Proposal').

[8] A proposal for a Council Framework Decision on certain procedural rights in criminal proceedings was presented in 2004, but never adopted. C Riehle and A Clozel, '10 years after the Roadmap: Procedural Rights in Criminal Proceedings in the EU Today' (2020) 20 *ERA Forum* 321.

the question of admissibility of evidence, albeit partially addressed in specific instruments and contexts,[9] has not yet been the subject of a dedicated proposal.

Consequently, the standards developed in favour of victims and those developed in favour of suspects and the accused are often compared. Indeed, both strands of legislation share common characteristics and notably participate in the development of the 'rights component' of European criminal law.[10] Such a contribution was not initially obvious since the competence attributed to the EU in Article 82 TFEU reflects a functional approach,[11] under which the adoption of minimum procedural rules shall be 'to the extent necessary to facilitate mutual recognition of judgments and judicial decisions, and police and judicial cooperation in criminal matters having a cross-border dimension'. The Working Group tasked with drafting this provision identified approximation of procedural norms as a facilitator of collaboration between national law enforcement agencies of the Member States (and the EU bodies acting in this field) and as a support to the application of instruments based on the principle of mutual recognition. The mobilisation of the functional arguments to justify the adoption of common procedural standards has been particularly strong in the directives concerning the approximation of procedural rights for the suspects and the accused, thus reflecting the idea that 'EU competence to legislate on the rights of the defence is conditional upon the need to demonstrate that defence rights are necessary for mutual recognition'.[12] Similar arguments have been used to justify the adoption of standards on victims' rights.[13]

However, in both fields, the insertion of references to the rights protected under the EU Charter of Fundamental Rights[14] has led to an important transformation: these EU criminal law instruments now also fulfil 'to a large part self-standing objectives rooted in the fundamental norms and values the EU is based on'.[15] For the directives on procedural rights for the suspects and the accused, their consecration as rights-based instruments has been progressive and intervened notably under the influence of the case law of the Court of Justice of the European Union (CJEU), which expanded their scope of application beyond cross-border criminal proceedings.[16] For victims, a rights-based approach was already noticeable in the 2001 Framework

[9] See, for instance, the provisions in the European Public Prosecutor's Office (EPPO) Regulation, and their implementation (D Brodowski, 'Admissibility of Evidence in EPPO Proceedings' (2023) 14 *New Journal of European Criminal Law* 34), or the case law of the Court of Justice (ECJ, judgment of 30 April 2024, Case C-670/22 *MN (EncroChat)*, ECLI:EU:C:2024:372).

[10] A Klip, 'Fair Trial Rights in the European Union: Reconciling Accused and Victims' Rights' in T Rafaraci and R Belfiore (eds), *EU Criminal Justice* (Springer Cham, 2019) 3.

[11] J Ouwerkerk, 'EU Competence in the Area of Procedural Criminal Law: Functional vs. Self-Standing Approximation of Procedural Rights and their Progressive Effect on the Charter's Scope of Application' (2019) 27 *European Journal of Crime, Criminal Law and Criminal* 89.

[12] V Mitsilegas, *EU Criminal Law after Lisbon: Rights, Trust and the Transformation of Justice in Europe* (Hart Publishing, 2016) 157.

[13] European Commission, Proposal for a Directive establishing minimum standards on the rights, support and protection of victims of crime, COM(2011) 275, 18 May 2011, 2–3.

[14] For victims, see Directive 2012/29/EU (n 2) Preamble, para 66, or 2023 Commission Proposal (n 7) 11–12.

[15] Ouwerkerk (n 11) 96.

[16] I Wieczorek, 'The Emerging Role of the EU as a Primary Normative Actor in the EU Area of Criminal Justice' (2021) 27 *European Law Journal* 378.

Decision on victims' rights, in which the objective of approximation was to 'attain the objective of affording victims of crime a high level of protection, irrespective of the Member State in which they are present'.[17] The 2012 Directive further pursues such an approach given that its purpose, enshrined in Article 1(1), 'is to ensure that victims of crime receive appropriate information, support and protection and can participate in criminal proceedings'. These two fields of EU procedural criminal law thus appear connected. Some authors have pondered their relationship, questioning whether both sets of rights must be equal[18] or whether one set should take precedence over the other one.[19] Others have attempted to draw lessons from the implementation of defence rights, and their potential use and guidance in the implementation of victims' rights.[20]

Yet scholars have also stressed that the adoption of EU standards in the field of victims' rights presents several specificities. Firstly, the traditional perception of the objectives and actors of the criminal procedure emphasised the role of the State, and the impact the exercise of its law enforcement powers may have on suspects, the accused and convicted persons. This led to the development of standards focusing on procedural guarantees to their benefit at national and regional levels, while the victim's position in the criminal justice process remained marginal.[21] The substance of the European Convention on Human Rights and Fundamental Freedoms and the case law of the European Court of Human Rights (ECtHR) were able to draw from existing national legal traditions, with clear synergies, leading to their codification in the directives on the rights of the suspects and the accused. By contrast, as pinpointed by Lorena Bachmaier Winter in this volume, national legal traditions were far less developed with regard to victims' rights. In many countries, victims did not have a say in the criminal procedure or were only involved as witnesses of the facts.[22] Within the Council of Europe, except for the 1983 Convention on the Compensation of Victims of Violent Crimes,[23] the only text elaborated was a recommendation on the position of the victim in the framework of criminal law and procedure, providing very broad suggestions on the information provided to the victims.[24] The case law of the ECtHR was also less developed. It focused mostly on the role of victims as a civil party in criminal proceedings, and the positive obligations that were binding for States' parties had only

[17] 2001 Framework Decision (n 4) Preamble, para 4.

[18] See the contribution in this volume by K Strada-Rozenberga, 'Do Victims' Rights and Defendants' Rights Really Have to be Equal?' in chapter 17.

[19] Klip (n 10) 24.

[20] See the contribution in this volume by L Baudrihaye-Gérard, 'Towards More Rights for Victims to Participate in Criminal Proceedings? Reflections from the Implementation Experience of EU Defence Rights' in chapter 18.

[21] P Bárd and A Borbíró, 'Victims' Rights Developments in the EU' (2015) *Hungarian Yearbook of International Law and European Law* 496.

[22] See the contribution in this volume by L Bachmaier Winter, 'Council of Europe Instruments and the Case Law of the ECtHR: What Influence on EU Law?'in chapter 7. See also contributions by G Conway, 'An Evaluation of the Impact of the EU Victims' Rights Directive on the Scope of Victims' Rights in Ireland' and D Ionescu, 'Victims' Rights in Romania: The Gap between the Adoption of Legal Texts and their Effective Implementation' in chapters 15 and 11 respectively.

[23] ETS No 116.

[24] Council of Europe, Recommendation No R(85)11 of the Committee of Ministers on the position of the victim in the framework of criminal law and procedure of 28 June 1985.

a limited impact on the protection of victims' rights.[25] As a result and in contrast with the negotiation of the directives on the rights of the suspects and the accused, which were intended to codify the case law of the ECHR, the Council was in a very different position when negotiating and adopting the 2001 Framework Decision on victims' rights. The adoption of EU standards in this field not only approximated the few pre-existing national norms but it was also, in many EU Member States, pushing for the introduction of new measures not yet foreseen in national criminal procedural law nor in European standards.

This postponed development of victims' rights is not a European specificity. The procedural dimension of international criminal law was also relatively slow in integrating standards aiming to safeguard the victims of international core crimes. First and second-generation international tribunals did not grant them many possibilities to participate in the proceedings, confining them to the status of witnesses.[26] The Statute of Rome establishing the International Criminal Court (ICC) constitutes a clear shift, with increased references to victims and the establishment of specialised services, and this led to the development of similar provisions before other international jurisdictions.[27] Nevertheless, the recognition and protection of victims' rights in international criminal law remains fragmentary. Victims, or their legal representatives, do not enjoy party status with absolute rights to intervene in the proceedings before the ICC,[28] leading some authors to suggest the right to request a review of the threshold decision not to prosecute.[29] Their compensation for the damages they suffer appears also as a delicate matter, with the offenders often being recognised as incapacitated.[30]

In such a context, two paradoxes can be pinpointed. First, the EU legislator was left with a broader margin of manoeuvre in defining the standards to be applied, and yet it made a choice in favour of a limited degree of detail of the provisions enshrined in the Framework Decision, thus leaving Member States with a considerable amount of leeway. Second, as a result of such wide discretion in implementation, in many cases the transposition of the provisions resulted in no action at national level and no Member State can claim to have fully implemented it.[31] The adoption of the Victims' Rights Directive in 2012, with the involvement of the European Parliament as a co-legislator, did not fully correct such a situation. As pinpointed by Levent Altan in this volume,[32]

[25] See the chapter in this volume by Bachmaier Winter (n 22) section III.

[26] M-L Hébert-Dolbec, 'La reconnaissance des victimes dans la justice internationale pénale : entre rétribution(s) symbolique(s) et incidence rituelle significative' (2019) 129 *Témoigner. Entre histoire et mémoire* 61.

[27] ibid 62. See the contribution in this volume by V Koutroulis and M-L Hébert-Dolbec, 'The Participation of Victims in International Criminal Trials: A Way Forward?' in chapter 8.

[28] C Safferling and G Petrossian, *Victims before the International Criminal Court, Definition, Participation and Reparation* (Springer, 2021) 326.

[29] N Hodgson, 'Victims as Agents of Accountability: Strengthening Victims' Right to Review at the International Criminal Court' (2023) 34 *Criminal Law Forum* 273–94.

[30] Safferling and Petrossian (n 28) 328.

[31] European Commission, Impact Assessment accompanying the Proposal for a Directive establishing minimum standards on the rights, support and protection of victims of crime, SEC(2011) 580, 7.

[32] See the contribution in this volume by L Altan, 'Transforming EU Victims' Laws into Reality for Victims: Developing a Strategic Framework for the Implementation of Victims' Rights' in chapter 20.

and the 2022 evaluation of the Victims' Rights Directive,[33] the 2012 Directive at times retains a form of wording that is too broad or feeble and fails to impose clear obligations on the Member States. Such weaknesses are not compensated by the case law of the CJEU. The latter is far less developed than the case law on procedural rights for suspects and the accused, with only a handful of cases directly concerning the interpretation of the Victims' Rights Directive.[34] As a consequence, even though the EU actions in this field led to further developments of victims' rights, even outside the EU legal order,[35] the degree of approximation reached remains less than the one achieved in other fields of EU criminal law. Additionally, the relevant EU instruments are not solely limited to the Victims' Rights Directive adopted based on the EU's competencies in criminal procedural law. The proliferation of measures on victims' rights in other areas of EU law makes the identification of an EU model more complex and leads to a risk of inconsistencies and incoherence, which we will analyse in the next section.

III. A Complex Multi-Faceted Framework Beyond the Texts Solely Addressing Victims' Rights

A first and superficial examination of the legal framework in force may lead to one thinking that the EU model for victims' rights results exclusively from the Victims' Rights Directive, the Victims' Compensation Directive and policy documents, such as the EU Strategy on Victims' Rights.[36] However, the corpus of relevant texts is broader and multi-layered. The Victims' Rights Directive functions as a cross-cutting instrument, laying down a minimum level of protection for all victims, but it is complemented by sectoral instruments, providing for measures specific to certain groups of victims, and/or defining measures on protection or compensation. Most of them have been adopted within the EU's competencies in criminal matters, but others belong to other areas of EU law. Such a legal framework deserves exploration as it is necessary to fully grasp the content of the norms enacted at the EU level. The exercise is also particularly appropriate as the EU legislator is engaged in a series of negotiations, either revising previous instruments or introducing new texts.

As discussed earlier, the recognition of victims' rights integrates itself in the broader development of the Area of Freedom, Security and Justice (AFSJ), and it is not so

[33] European Commission, Evaluation of Directive 2012/29/EU of the European Parliament and of the Council of 25 October 2012 establishing minimum standards on the rights, support and protection of victims of crime, SWD(2022) 179, 31. See also, as pinpointed by L Bachmaier Winter, the similar definitions of a 'victim' in the Directive and the Council of Europe's Recommendation CM/REC(2023)2.

[34] See the contribution in this volume by A Lazowski, 'The Flood that Never Came: Case Law of the Court of Justice on the Victims' Rights Acquis' in chapter 4. Only three cases referring expressly to Directive 2012/29/EU, namely ECJ, Order of 13 December 2016, Case C-484/16 *Criminal proceedings against Antonio Semeraro* ECLI:EU:C:2016:952; or ECJ, Judgment of 29 July 2019, Case C-38/18 *Criminal procedure against Massimo Gambino and Shpetim Hyka*, ECLI:EU:C:2019:628; and ECJ, Judgment of 1st October 2020, Case C-603/19 *TG and UF*, ECLI:EU:C:2020:774.

[35] European Commission, Evaluation of Directive 2012/29/EU (n 33) 33.

[36] European Commission, Communication 'EU Strategy on Victims' Rights (2020-2025)', COM(2020)258, 24 June 2020.

surprising to notice that the instruments adopted within the AFSJ contain provisions that may participate in the protection of victims even though crime prevention and cooperation in criminal matters are not their main or first objective. All these instruments potentially relevant for victims' rights can be presented in concentric circles ranging from those dealing with the issue in the most superficial way to those closely dedicated to it.

The outermost circle would, for instance, include instruments adopted in the field of migration. The first instruments adopted within the EU's competencies in migration policy concerned third-country nationals being victims of certain crimes and their possibility to obtain a residence permit *if they cooperate with the competent authorities* (emphasis added). Directive 2004/81/EC provided for such a regime for those who are victims of human trafficking and who have been subject to an action to facilitate irregular migration.[37] The trend of mobilising such competencies can also be illustrated through the instruments forming part of the Pact for Migration and Asylum adopted in 2024. The Regulation on the screening of third country nationals at external borders provides for a preliminary vulnerability check that may participate in ensuring the protection of victims of crimes[38] while the Regulation on International Protection also considers the specific needs of victims of crime and the possibility of excluding remote interviews.[39] Similarly, some of the databases set up to register and keep track of the movements of third-country nationals within the EU territory, such as Eurodac,[40] or the Entry Exit System,[41] provide that law enforcement authorities may access the data that they contain to identify people who died violently or build evidence by tracking the travel routes of a victim of crime.[42] While the use of such databases for law enforcement purposes has been strongly criticised in doctrine,[43] the possibility to consult them for the identification of victims is seen as a welcome addition[44] and constitutes a measure taking into consideration the specific circumstances of

[37] Council Directive 2004/81/EC of 29 April 2004 on the residence permit issued to third-country nationals who are victims of trafficking in human beings or who have been the subject of an action to facilitate illegal immigration, who cooperate with the competent authorities [2004] OJ L261/19.

[38] Regulation (EU) 2024/1356 on the screening of third country nationals at external borders [2024] OJ L2024/1356 providing for a preliminary vulnerability check with a view to identifying persons with indications of being vulnerable, of being victims of torture or other inhuman or degrading treatment (Preamble, para 37 and Art 12 on preliminary health checks and vulnerabilities).

[39] Regulation (EU) 2024/1348 establishing a common procedure for international protection in the Union [2024] OJ L2024/1348, providing for special measures, notably to exclude remote interviewing, for certain vulnerable groups, among which are listed victims of trafficking in human beings, or victims of torture, rape or other serious forms of psychological, physical, sexual violence or gender-based violence (Preamble, para 15 and Arts 20 and 21).

[40] Regulation (EU) No 603/2013 of 26 June 2013 on the establishment of 'Eurodac' for the comparison of fingerprints (…) [2013] OJ L180/1.

[41] Regulation (EU) 2017/2226 of 30 November 2017 establishing an Entry/Exit System (EES) to register entry and exit data and refusal of entry data of third-country nationals crossing the external borders of the Member States and determining the conditions for access to the EES for law enforcement purposes [2017] OJ L327/20.

[42] See, eg, ibid Preamble, para 22.

[43] See a.o. C Blasi Casagran, Fundamental Rights Implications of Interconnecting Migration and Policing Databases in the EU (2021) 21 *Human Rights Law Review* 433, or N Vavoula, 'Interoperability of EU Information Systems: The Deathblow to the Rights to Privacy and Personal Data Protection of Third-Country Nationals?' (2020) 26 *European Public Law* 131.

[44] N Vavoula, 'Consultation of EU Immigration Databases for Law Enforcement Purposes: a Privacy and Data Protection Assessment' (2020) 22 *European Journal of Migration and Law* 166.

migrants who may often lack identity documents or may not have their data stored in a national database.[45] Similarly, the Schengen Information System may also be used for preventive purposes as its current legal framework allows for the insertion of alerts on children prevented from travelling due to a concrete and apparent risk of them becoming victims of human trafficking, forced marriage, female genital mutilation or other forms of gender-based violence, or of them being victims of or involved in terrorist offences; as well as on vulnerable adults at risk of becoming victims of human trafficking or gender-based violence.[46]

Turning now to the instruments adopted within the EU's area of criminal justice, or in other terms in the fields of police and judicial cooperation in criminal matters, we can still identify several circles. The least useful instruments are those that only make a slight reference to the victims and usually mention them only in relation to the determination of the best-placed Member State to exercise jurisdiction.[47] The Framework Decision on conflicts of jurisdiction mentions the significant interests of victims among the facts and deserves to be considered,[48] and the invitation is amplified by Eurojust's Guidelines on the matter.[49] In this field, the proposal for a Regulation on the transfer of proceedings[50] marks a subtle but welcome change: it provides an obligation to take the interests of the victim(s) much more into consideration, which may be affected by the decision to transfer the proceedings to another Member State.[51] The draft text not only grants victims the possibility to request such a transfer,[52] but it also provides for their right to a legal remedy against a State's decision to transfer proceedings.[53]

The third circle includes the instruments on the freezing and confiscation of the proceeds and instrumentalities of crime,[54] or asset recovery and confiscation.[55] Both

[45] ibid.

[46] Regulation (EU) 2018/1862 on the establishment, operation and use of the Schengen Information System (SIS) in the field of police cooperation and judicial cooperation in criminal matters [2018] OJ L312/56, Art 32 1)(d) and (e).

[47] See, for instance, Directive (EU) 2017/1371 on the fight against fraud to the Union's financial interests by means of criminal law [2017] OJ L198/29, or Directive (EU) 2018/1673 on combating money laundering by criminal law [2018] OJ L284/22, in which the Member States have to ensure that the exercise of their jurisdiction is 'not subject to the condition that a prosecution can be initiated only following a report made by the victim in the place where the criminal offence was committed, or a denunciation from the State of the place where the criminal offence was committed'.

[48] Council Framework Decision 2009/948/JHA of 30 November 2009 on prevention and settlement of conflicts of exercise of jurisdiction in criminal proceedings [2009] OJ L328/42, Preamble, para 9.

[49] Eurojust, Guidelines for Deciding 'Which Jurisdiction Should Prosecute?', referred to in Eurojust, 'Report on Eurojust's Casework on Victims' Rights' (2022) 13. See also the contribution in this volume by J Carmona Bermejo and E Fréjabue, 'Eurojust's Role in Enhancing Victims' Rights in Cross-Border Criminal Cases' in chapter 6.

[50] European Commission, Proposal for a Regulation on the transfer of proceedings in criminal matters, COM(2023) 185 final, 5 April 2023.

[51] ibid Preamble, para 32. See in contrast the provisions included in the Council Framework Decision on the European Supervision Order [2009] OJ L294/20 which only invite the competent authority of the issuing State to 'take due account of any indications communicated by the competent authority of the executing State on the risk that the person concerned might pose to victims and to the general public' (Art 22 (2)).

[52] ibid Art 5(3).

[53] ibid Art 8.

[54] Directive 2014/42/EU of 3 April 2014 on the freezing and confiscation of instrumentalities and proceeds of crime in the European Union [2014] OJ L127/39.

[55] Directive (EU) 2024/1260 of 24 April 2024 on asset recovery and confiscation [2024] OJ L2024/1260.

texts contain brief provisions seeking to ensure that their implementation does not have a negative impact on the possibility of the victim(s) obtaining compensation.[56] The Directive on asset recovery goes a step further by inviting Member States to take into account the victims' claims within the relevant asset-tracing, freezing and confiscation proceedings.[57] These two instruments, which aim to secure pecuniary compensation from offenders' assets, are particularly interesting considering the limits of the EU legal framework on compensation,[58] and the resistance of some Member States to making State-funded compensation available to victims.

The fourth circle encompasses two instruments adopted to encourage the mutual recognition of protection measures that the Member States are at liberty to provide either through criminal, administrative or civil law mechanisms. As a result, two complementary instruments have been enacted: a Directive favouring the recognition of protection measures in criminal matters[59] and a Regulation pursuing the same objective for measures in civil matters.[60] The two texts have been criticised, notably for their limited added value[61] and their 'sporadic use' in practice, often linked to the diversity of national measures and the lack of harmonisation.[62] The latter has not yet been addressed by the EU legislator: the proposed revision of the Victims' Rights Directive only envisages the adoption of barring, restraining or protection orders during criminal proceedings, to ensure the victims' physical protection.[63] Furthermore, while the Directive on violence against women and domestic violence contains an obligation to foresee the granting of such protection measures in national law,[64] the Member States' discretion is preserved, as the text 'does not oblige the Member States to modify their national systems as regards (their) the qualification (…) as falling under criminal, civil or administrative law'.[65]

The last circle is the most well-known as it integrates the Victims' Rights Directive and all the directives providing specific rights for certain groups of victims, considered to be particularly vulnerable and/or in need of more advanced rights (legal assistance, or medico-social assistance to be provided before, during and after the criminal proceedings for an appropriate length of time).[66] Although it presents an increased risk of fragmentation, the combination of a crosscutting text and sectoral ones has been the model chosen since the early 2000s, and it has been supported by practitioners, supporting 'a combination of all-crime (generic) victim support services

[56] Directive 2014/42/EU (n 54) Art 8(10) and Directive (EU) 2024/1260 (n 55) Art 18 (4).

[57] Directive (EU) 2024/1260 (n 55) Art 18.

[58] L Lúparia and J della Torre, 'Victims of Crime in the Area of Freedom, Security and Justice' in S Iglesias Sánchez and M González Pascual (eds), *Fundamental Rights in the EU Area of Freedom, Security and Justice* (Cambridge University Press, 2021) 316.

[59] Directive 2011/99/EU of 13 December 2011 on the European protection order [2011] OJ L338/2.

[60] Regulation (EU) No 606/2013 of 12 June 2013 on mutual recognition of protection measures in civil matters [2013] OJ L181/4.

[61] Lúparia and della Torre (n 58) 322.

[62] European Parliament, Study 'European Protection Order & Directive 2011/99/EU, European Implementation Assessment' (2017, PE 603.272) 17.

[63] 2023 Commission Proposal (n 7) Art 1(12) proposing a revision of Art 23(4).

[64] Directive (EU) 2024/1385 of 14 May 2024 on combating violence against women and domestic violence [2024] OJ L2024/1385, Art. 19.

[65] ibid Art 19(7).

[66] Lúparia and della Torre (n 58) 319–20.

and specialist services, with an individual needs assessment and referral process that helps victims reach the right type of organisation for them'.[67] Traditionally, the Victims' Rights Directive was presented as being complemented by the sectoral texts applicable for victims of child pornography and child abuse,[68] victims of trafficking in human beings (addressed by Weatherburn in this volume)[69] and victims of terrorism.[70] The number of sectoral instruments has since then grown and now also covers two new groups. On the one hand, we can find victims of fraud and counterfeiting of non-cash means of payment,[71] which include victims of identity theft considered particularly serious due to its economic and non-economic consequences for its victims,[72] and its large scale. On the other hand, a specific instrument governs the measures designed for victims of gender-based violence and domestic violence (addressed by Saenz Perez in this volume).[73] The EU legislature did even tackle the extraordinary circumstances of environmental crimes, for which there is no direct victim, but rather members of the public who may report crimes, benefitting from *ad hoc* provisions.[74]

This last circle constitutes the hard core of victims' rights in EU law and it is worth dissecting further the choice made to combine a cross-cutting instrument providing for a minimum (and minimal) level of protection for all victims of crime, with more specific instruments. This choice is not completely satisfactory for a series of reasons. It leads to a clear fragmentation of the protection measures applicable, creates overlaps and sometimes gaps[75] as well as a differentiation between the categories of victims. Some authors qualified its consequences as a rupture of equality and the source of a difference in treatment between victims of crime depending on their nationality or residence status.[76] It fails to protect some victims who find themselves outside the scope of application of the instruments tackling only the most serious crimes.[77] It also

[67] See Altan (n 32).

[68] Directive 2011/93/EU of 13 December 2011 on combating the sexual abuse and sexual exploitation of children and child pornography [2011] OJ L335/1.

[69] Directive 2011/36/EU of 5 April 2011 on preventing and combating trafficking in human beings and protecting its victims [2011] OJ L101/1, amended by Directive (EU) 2024/1712 of 13 June 2024 amending Directive 2011/36/EU on preventing and combating trafficking in human beings and protecting its victims [2011] OJ L2024/1712.

[70] Directive (EU) 2017/541 of 15 March 2017 on combating terrorism [2017] OJ L88/6.

[71] Directive (EU) 2019/713 of 17 April 2019 on combating fraud and counterfeiting of non-cash means of payment [2019] OJ L123/18.

[72] European Commission, 'Study on Online Identity Theft and Identity-Related Crime: Final Report (Publications Office of the European Union, 2022) 10–11.

[73] Directive (EU) 2024/1385 (n 64).

[74] Directive (EU) 2024/1203 on the protection of the environment through criminal law [2024] OJ L2024/1203, which makes a clear distinction between the rights granted to the victims and those granted to the members of the public concerned.

[75] European Parliament, Study 'The Victims' Rights Directive 2012/29/EU: European Implementation Assessment' (2017, PE 611.022) 19.

[76] M Borraccetti, Human Trafficking, Equality and Access to Victims' Rights, in LS Rossi and F Casolari (eds), *The Principle of Equality in EU Law* (Springer, 2017) 281. The author highlights the difference between victims of trafficking who are third country nationals and those who are EU citizens.

[77] For an illustration of the gaps for those who are outside the scope of the Directive on preventing and combating trafficking in human beings (n 69) and the Employers' Sanctions Directive, see the contribution in this volume by A Weatherburn, '(Human Trafficking) Victims on the Margins of Protection: The (In)coherence of Sectoral Instruments?' in chapter 16.

complicates the identification of the protection regime to be applied, as it is necessary to combine both texts to comprehend the protection granted, and their combination is not always sufficient to fully cover all dimensions of victims' protection.[78]

Additionally, such complexity is amplified by the differentiated timelines of their adoption and revision, leading to a certain disconnect between the rights granted to victims. By way of example, victims of trafficking in human beings and child victims of pornography and child abuse have long (and rightly so) been considered as groups of victims requiring particular attention. Specific instruments governing their rights have been adopted since the early 2000s and they were among the first ones to be upgraded into directives shortly after the entry into force of the Lisbon Treaty. The Directive governing the measures applicable to victims of trafficking was updated in 2024 and a recast of the Directive on combating sexual abuse and sexual exploitation of children was proposed by the Commission in February of the same year.[79] By contrast, directives on victims of terrorism have not yet been revised. This can lead to possible disconnects between the rights granted to victims covered by recently revised instruments and those provided under the general regime of the Victims' Rights Directive. On a more institutional note, such differences may be further emphasised by the lack of coordination among the services of the European Commission: while DG Justice was engaged in the evaluation of the Victims' Rights Directive and the preliminary work for the presentation of its revision, two proposals were prepared and presented by other services: one on the Directive on violence against women and domestic violence, announced by European Commission President Ursula von der Leyen in her State of the Union speech in 2021; and the other to revise the anti-trafficking Directive, focusing mostly on turning into an obligation the criminalisation of the knowing use of the services provided by a victim of trafficking, a measure criticised by civil society organisations.[80]

To conclude our attempt to offer a categorisation of all the relevant instruments in protecting victims of crime, we can stress once more the complexity of the legal framework in place. Such complexity is partially inherent to the multi-faceted nature of victims' protection which requires the combination of diverse preventive, support and assistance measures, often not limited to those enacted in criminal matters. The fragmentation of relevant instruments is further amplified by the way legislation has been developed at the EU level and the choices made by the EU institutions. This has often been illustrated through the example of the 2004 Directive on compensation in cross-border cases,[81] enacted in response to the CJEU's judgment in *Cowan*,[82] based on the flexibility clause (then Article 308 TEC, now Article 352 TFEU). The question

[78] For an illustration and the gap regarding the protection measures to be granted to victims, see the contribution in this volume by C Sáenz Pérez, 'Protecting Vulnerable Victims: An Analysis of the EU Legal Framework for Victims of Gender-Based Violence' in chapter 3.

[79] European Commission, Proposal for a Directive on combating the sexual abuse and sexual exploitation of children and child sexual abuse material and replacing Council Framework Decision 2004/68/JHA (recast), COM(2024) 60, 6 February 2024.

[80] La Strada and PICUM, Joint Statement 'New EU Anti-Trafficking Directive Leaves Trafficked People Behind', available at https://picum.org/blog/new-eu-anti-trafficking-directive-leaves-trafficked-people-behind/.

[81] Directive 2004/80/EC (n 6).

[82] ECJ, Judgment of 2 February 1989, Case 186/87 *Cowan v Trésor Public* ECLI:EU:C:1989:47.

remains as to whether all these different instruments form a coherent set of norms that could be considered as the EU's model for victims' rights. The criteria for assessing such coherence should be the attention paid to the provision of support, protection and assistance adapted to the individual circumstances of each victim, and a possible gradation depending on the seriousness of the offence or the vulnerability of the victim.

IV. Does this Lead to a Comprehensive and Coherent Approach to Victim Protection?

Since the early 2000s, numerous instruments have been adopted to ensure the protection of the rights of victims, and some have already been the subject of revisions. As such, the abundance of texts and provisions, albeit leading to fragmentation, can give the impression that the EU legal framework provides for a full and coherent model favouring the protection of victims' rights. The following section will seek to pinpoint the weaknesses in such a legal framework, focussing on two dimensions: the issues identified at the EU level, and those arising in the transposition and implementation of the EU standards at the national level.

At the EU level, the main weaknesses standing in the way of the development of a comprehensive and coherent approach to victims are linked to the priorities and policy choices made by the EU institutions. The first element lies in the unbalanced attention paid to certain groups of victims, with a clear influence of political considerations and contextual elements in the decision to develop standards targeted at specific groups. The EU's Strategy for Victims' Rights further identifies victims requiring special attention, such as persons with disabilities, elderly persons or victims of crime committed in detention,[83] but, except for the last category,[84] no specific measures are envisaged for these other groups, and the Commission has relied on a reinforced individual assessment to pay due consideration to the needs of these victims. In such a context, victims of hate crimes appear to be particularly neglected. Despite the numerous reports and consensus surrounding the under-reporting of hate crimes,[85] and the difficulties in mobilising criminal justice mechanisms, the legal framework remains patchy. The Victims' Rights Directive provides for the absence of discrimination among the victims of crime and offers protection from discrimination in criminal law to grounds and fields not covered by the EU anti-discrimination directives.[86] However, the Council Framework Decision on combating certain forms and expressions of racism and xenophobia,[87]

[83] EU Strategy on Victims' Rights (n 36).

[84] 2023 CommissionProposal (n 7) Art 5a, with a broad definition of detention facilities including 'in addition to jails, detention centres and holding cells for suspects and accused, specialised detention facilities for applicants of international protection and pre-removal centres, and accommodation centres where applicants and beneficiaries of international protection are located.' Maintained in the Council's general approach.

[85] See the Fundamental Rights Surveys, referred to in the EU Strategy on Victims' Rights (n 36) 4–5.

[86] R Gião Hanek and L Farkas, 'The Potential of the Charter in Fighting Hate: Enforcing International Human Rights Standards through Victims' Rights', EUI Working Paper RSCAS 2020/75, 8.

[87] Council Framework Decision 2008/913/JHA of 28 November 2008 on combating certain forms and expressions of racism and xenophobia by means of criminal law [2008] OJ L328/55.

with a sole and very limited reference to victims,[88] has not been updated since its adoption, and a common legal definition of hate crime, which would, in turn, harmonise the identification of its victims, is still missing.[89] Such a gap can be explained by the necessary pre-requisite of adding hate crime to the list of eurocrimes in Article 83(1) TFEU, and the dead end in which a 2021 proposal remains despite the ambition of the French presidency of the Council in 2022.[90] Additionally, despite measures indirectly relevant in the 2024 Directive on violence against women and domestic violence to address misogynous hate online,[91] there is no sectoral text defining specific measures taking into account the difficulties in reporting such crimes. Similarly, the attention given to certain groups of victims varies over time. Victims of core international crime are now integrated among the victims of targeted and integrated support services in the Proposal to revise the Victims' Rights Directive.[92] And, in reaction to the war in Ukraine, the Council adopted conclusions inviting national authorities to pay due attention to their situation and their needs.[93]

Such political or contextual considerations also imply that several measures, or actions, are not explored or implemented, leaving loopholes in the EU's approach to victims' rights. Listing all the roads not taken by the EU legislator would be too long, but a few examples can be given. A sore point of contention remains the issue of compensation for victims. The 2004 Compensation Directive, criticised for its incapacity to remedy the disparities that exist across the Member States,[94] has not been updated since its adoption, despite the fact that a revision is much needed, at the very least to reflect the evolution of the EU legislation on victims' rights or the case law of the CJEU on its interpretation.[95] Such a delay can be explained by the legal basis of the instrument, used at the time of its adoption and still relevant today. The provision referred to is Article 308 TEC, now Article 352 TFEU, which is also known as the flexibility clause. It requires unanimity within the Council for the text to be adopted and amended, which may be difficult to achieve due to the sensitivity of the question of compensation and its budgetary implications. Within the revision of the Victims' Rights Directive, the Commission had proposed to amend the relevant provision, ensuring the right of victims to obtain a decision on compensation during criminal proceedings, thus deleting the reserve previously referring to States preferring compensation to be awarded

[88] ibid, only reference in the Preamble, para 11 that investigations and prosecutions shall not be dependent on reports or accusations made by victims.

[89] See in this regard the proposals to add hate crime to the list of eurocrimes contained in Art 83(1) TFEU: European Commission, Communication 'A More Inclusive and Protective Europe: Extending the List of EU Crimes to Hate Speech and Hate Crime', COM(2021) 777.

[90] N Franssen and A Weyembergh, 'From Facts and Political Objectives to Legal Bases and Legal Provisions: Incremental European Integration in the Criminal Law Field' (2021) 27 *European Law Journal* 373.

[91] Directive 2024/1385 (n 64) Preamble, para 25 and the criminalisation of cyber stalking, cyber harassment and cyber incitement to violence or hatred.

[92] 2023 Commission Proposal (n 7) Preamble, para 7, and amended versions of Art 9(3)b) and Art 22(3).

[93] Council conclusions on the fight against impunity regarding crimes committed in connection with Russia's war of aggression against Ukraine [2022] OJ C474/31, paras II k) to p).

[94] E Sellier and A Weyembergh, 'Comparative Study – Compensation Schemes for Victims' in E Sellier and A Weyembergh (eds), *Criminal Procedures and Cross-Border Cooperation in the EU Area of Criminal Justice* (Editions de l'Université de Bruxelles, 2020) 390–94.

[95] See the contribution in this volume by L O'Driscoll, 'Being "Fair and Appropriate" to Victims of Violent Crime: Evaluating the Provision of State Compensation in the European Union' in chapter 5.

in the context of civil proceedings, and the payment of the adjudicated amount by the competent authorities.[96] However, the Council decided in its general approach to remove such amendments.[97] As we await the outcome of the negotiations, we can already notice discrepancies in the access of different groups of victims to compensation. The updated Directive on trafficking in human beings invites the Member States to establish a national victims' fund or similar instruments which can include laws that ensure that victims of trafficking in human beings receive compensation.[98] By contrast, the Directive on violence against women and domestic violence only provides that victims shall have the right, in accordance with national law, to claim compensation, and shall where appropriate be able to obtain a decision on compensation in the course of criminal proceedings,[99] while older instruments, like the Directive on victims of terrorism, are drafted in even vaguer terms, merely inviting States to provide them with assistance with claims regarding compensation available under the national law of the Member State concerned.[100] Beyond the question of compensation, we can note a certain reluctance to provide strong obligations with financial implications for the national budgets. This is evidenced by the limits of the victims' right to legal aid, as the relevant provision in the Victims' Rights Directive only provides for their 'access to legal aid, where they have the status of parties to criminal proceedings (and) the conditions or procedural rules under which victims have access to legal aid shall be determined by national law' (Article 13). The proposed revision does not cover this provision and focuses rather on the introduction of a new right to assistance at the court (Article 10a) and the introduction of national protocols drawn up in cooperation and coordination between law enforcement, prosecution authorities, judges, detention authorities, restorative justice services and victim support services.[101] The Council's general approach does not challenge the creation of a new right but rephrases it substantially into a 'right to receive information and emotional support at the court premises', the latter potentially offered by trained volunteers.[102]

The weaknesses of the provisions included in the EU legislative instruments are further amplified by the margin of discretion that they leave to the Member States, either due to the multiple references (and deference) to national laws, or the vagueness of their wording. As a result, their transposition and/or implementation by the Member States leads to increased fragmentation and diversity. The same provision enshrined in an EU directive may have many interpretations and practical consequences. The discrepancies that may exist between different national criminal justice systems have been repeatedly pointed out in reports prepared by the European Commission,[103] the contributions to the public consultations opened and in the academic literature.[104]

[96] 2023 CommissionProposal (n 7) Art 1(7) proposing a revision of Art 16.

[97] Council, Proposal for a Directive amending Directive 2012/29/EU establishing minimum standards on the rights, support and protection of victims of crime – General Approach, doc. 11260/24, 21–25 (hereafter 'Council Proposal General Approach').

[98] Directive (EU) 2024/1712 (n 69) Art 17.

[99] Directive (EU) 2024/1385 (n 64) Art 24.

[100] Directive (EU) 2017/541 (n 70) Art 24(3).

[101] 2023 Commission Proposal (n 7) Art 1(6) proposing a new Art 10a and Art 1(14) proposing a new Art 26a.

[102] Council Proposal General Approach (n 97), Art 1 (6) proposing a new Art 10a, and Preamble, para 8.

[103] European Commission, Evaluation of Directive 2012/29/EU (n 33) 12.

[104] See, eg, Lúparia and della Torre (n 58) 327.

Comparative legal research, whether addressing criminal procedures in general or focusing on some victims' rights such as the chapters on national case studies in this volume,[105] highlights how the adoption of EU standards has not brought all the changes intended. More concretely, in most Member States, diverse budget streams (often insufficient) fund the measures in favour of the victims' rights, and the distribution of competencies across national actors makes identification of the amounts granted, as well as control of their use, difficult.[106] On a more legal note, in many EU Member States, the adoption of EU standards has had a positive influence in modernising the legal framework applicable to the victims, especially in countries in which the national legal traditions did not provide many measures in their favour.[107] However, in none of the countries reviewed for this volume had the Victims' Rights Directive been fully transposed. Certain rights, such as the right to actively participate in criminal proceedings, still vary substantially from one Member State to another, and the situation of certain victims, such as the victims of cross-border crimes or victims of core international crimes, remains almost unchanged.[108]

The adoption of new legislative instruments may not be sufficient to correct such deficiencies, unless the scope of the EU's competence in criminal matters is amended and expanded beyond the adoption of minimum rules.[109] The establishment of EU funding programmes, as described in the EU Strategy on Victims' Rights,[110] can only be seen as a temporary solution, which may also not suffice to correct the imbalances and inequalities aimed at victims, depending on the country in which they are located and the types of crime they face. The question still remains as to whether there are ways to address such issues and achieve a comprehensive approach, achieving a twofold objective of improved coherence between EU instruments and a higher degree of harmonisation in terms of national implementation. A first positive step in such a direction can be found in the case law of the CJEU, with the recognition on 7 November 2024 that the concept of victim must be, in the context of the Victim Compensation Directive, regarded 'as an autonomous concept of EU law, which must be interpreted in a uniform manner in the territory of the European Union'.[111]

V. Are there Reasons to Hope for a Better Future?

To close this concluding chapter, two main remarks can be made. The first one relates to the discrepancies and incoherences pinpointed in the text and the possible remedies

[105] See 'Part III – Selected National Perspectives on Victims' Rights Across the EU: Major Trends and EU Law Impact' in this volume.

[106] European Commission, Evaluation of Directive 2012/29/EU (n 33) 39.

[107] See, eg, the chapters by Conway (n 22) and Ionescu (n 22).

[108] See for instance the contribution in this volume by M Alié and C Samri, 'Victims' Rights in Belgian Law: Significant Progress due to the Influence of EU Law but Still Gaps to be Filled' in chapter 9.

[109] K Zoumpoulakis, 'From the Ground up: The Use of Minimum Rules in EU Procedural Criminal Law and the Question of Member States' Discretion' (2020) 5 *European Papers* 1289, available at www.europeanpapers.eu/en/e-journal/ground-use-minimum-rules-eu-procedural-criminal-law-and-question-member-states-discretion.

[110] EU Strategy on Victims' Rights (n 36) 7.

[111] ECJ, Judgment of 7 November 2024, Case C-126/23, *Burdene* ECLI:EU:C:2024:937 for a discussion of the judgment, see J Burchett, 'Compensation for Victims of Violent Crimes, Narrowing the Member States's Discretion under Directive 2004/80/EC', *VerfBlog*, 2024/11/28, https://verfassungsblog.de/compensation-for-victims/.

that can be identified. Once more, without seeking coherence for the sake of it, it is interesting to pinpoint some initiatives to improve coordination and exchange of information among key stakeholders. Within the European Commission, the position of a Victims' Rights Coordinator was established in 2020. Such a function already exists in other fields, with the appointment since 2010 of an EU Anti-Trafficking Coordinator, whose creation was foreseen in the 2011 Directive on trafficking in human beings.[112] The exact attributions and importance of the post of the Victims' Rights Coordinator are still not totally clear, and the scope of its powers appears confined to the coordination and concertation among the EU actors, without extending to a broader coordination with national authorities.[113] The EU's Strategy refers to its role, and emphasises in particular its function in synchronising the actions of other EU-level stakeholders and ensuring the smooth functioning of the Victims' Rights Platform.[114] Interestingly, the latter serves as a forum for discussion with various EU actors, such as Eurojust, the EU agency on judicial cooperation, whose work on victims' rights appears less known and researched,[115] and stimulates exchanges, for instance among experts belonging to the European Network on Victims' Rights.[116] Such initiatives are worth highlighting as they serve as a basis for increased cooperation across national borders, thus favouring assistance to and support for cross-border victims, and may pave the way for more ambitious coordination mechanisms (such as transnational referral mechanisms, not limited to certain categories of victims).[117]

The second remark relates to the question of the emergence of an EU model for victims' rights. Giving a final answer to such a question is a delicate task, especially at a time when the negotiations for the revision of the Victims' Rights Directive are still ongoing and may have an impact on the degree of ambition reached. While the European elections of June 2024 paused the legislative work, the negotiations will soon resume since the Parliament gave its green light, in April 2024, to the beginning of trilogues with the Council and the Commission.[118] As the key cross-cutting instrument in this field, its final formulation will most certainly determine whether the future rules will partially correct the vagueness of the provisions contained in the 2012 Directive and provide a minimum layer of protection for all victims of crime. Even after its adoption, the question will remain valid as the discrepancies among EU instruments and their implementation at national level may still influence whether a minimum level of protection adapted to the individual circumstances of each victim is ensured.

[112] Directive 2011/36/EU (n 69) Art 20. On the genesis and content of the mandate, see Z Sakelliadou, 'EU Anti-Trafficking Coordinator: Trajectory of a Unique Mandate' in J Winterdyk and J Jones (eds), *The Palgrave International Handbook of Human Trafficking* (Palgrave Macmillan, 2020) 1299.

[113] This contrasts for instance with the role of the EU Counter-terrorism Coordinator, also reporting and collaborating with the Member States within the Council.

[114] EU Strategy on Victims' Rights (n 36) 19–20.

[115] See the chapter in this volume on Eurojust by Carmona Bermejo and Fréjabue (n 49).

[116] See the contribution in this volume by A Ferenczi, 'The Protection of Victims at EU Level: The Need for Cross-Border Cooperation Coordination' in chapter 19.

[117] The obligation to establish a referral mechanism is at present only foreseen for victims of human trafficking (Directive (EU) 2024/1712 (n 69) new Art 11(4)).

[118] See the dedicated page on European Parliament Legislative Observatory, available at https://oeil.secure.europarl.europa.eu/oeil/popups/ficheprocedure.do?reference=2023/0250(COD)&l=en.

INDEX

access to justice:
Belgium, 179–81
ECHR, 131, 249
EU Charter, 83, 180–1, 326
human trafficking and, 319–20, 326, 330–1
international crimes, 179–81
national regimes, 386
aviation: Conventions, 140

balance of rights:
asymmetric situation, 336–8
CJEU case law, 67
coexistence, 338–40
debate, 14–15, 403–4
ECtHR case law, 131
equality issue, 335–49
Italy, 131, 282
practices, 355
public and private interests, 344–8
punitiveness and, 367–8
requirements, 371
victims' role in proceedings, 340–4
VRD, 384
vulnerable victims and, 274
Bangladesh: ICC jurisdiction, 145
Belgium:
access to justice: international crimes, 179–81
civil party status, 174
compensation, 187–92
confiscation and restitution, 188–9
cooperation, 190
cross-border cases, 191–2
existing framework, 188–90
from offenders, 191
gaps, 191–2
state compensation, 189–90
terrorism victims, 189–90
violence victims, 189
cooperation, 127–8, 190
cross-border cases, 186–7, 191–2
definition of victim, 173–6
fragmentation, 174–6
domestic violence, 187
Dutroux case, 173, 176
European protection orders and, 43–4
gaps
access to justice for international crimes, 179–81
compensation, 191–2
cross-border issues, 186–7
protection measures, 185–6
review of discontinued proceedings, 179
gender-based violence, 184
human trafficking, 326–7, 327–30, 332
information: detention/release of convicted persons, 178
injured party status, 174–5
interpretation rights, 177
investigation obligations, 129
legal representation, 357
prison population, 364
protection measures, 181–7
domestic violence, 181–2
during proceedings, 182–3
inadequacy, 185–6, 187
sentencing stage, 183–4
stalking alarm, 182, 185
punitiveness, 367
standing of victims
criminal proceedings, 176–81
EU law impact, 177–8, 184–7
remaining gaps, 178–81, 184–7
strategies, 397
translation rights, 177
Borealis, 327–30, 332
Budapest Roadmap, 19
Buddhism, 387
Bulgaria:
access to justice, 131
civil party rights, 130
interpretation and translation services, 365
Istanbul Convention and, 46

Canada: punitiveness, 367
CEDAW, 46
children
see also vulnerable victims
abuse, 100, 411, 412
EU procedural safeguards, 353
Ireland, 302
Latvia, 243
protection, 112
VRD, 100
civil party rights: ECtHR case law, 128–31
CJEU and victims' rights:
case law, 55–74
compensation cases, 67–73, 75–6, 78–81
Cowan case, 55–6, 57–8, 74
national regimes and, 13
paradigm shift, 96
Pupino, 60–2, 74
role, 4, 6–7
standing, 60–5
state compensation, 75–6
Victims' Rights Directive cases, 65–7
Cluster Munitions Convention, 149
cognitive behavioural therapy, 387
compensation:
Belgium, 187–92
BV, 75–6, 77, 78, 81, 82, 83, 205–6, 223, 306
cooperation, 70, 79, 190, 377
cross-border cases, 68–71, 79, 114, 191–2, 286–7
Directive 2004/80, 412
Belgium and, 190
CJEU case law, 67–73, 75–6, 78–81
cooperation, 190
exceptions, 92
provisions, 77–8
replacement, 87
scope of application, 67–71, 101
ECtHR case law, 130–1
Eurojust role, 114
fair and appropriate, 71–3, 78–81, 92
international criminal tribunals, 166–8
Ireland, 73, 81–7, 299, 306–11, 311
Italy, 69–73, 79–80, 284–7
Latvia, 240, 244–7
law reform, 87–92
2023 Commission proposal, 87–9, 92, 134
Dutch APS, 89–91, 92
minimum standards, 87, 91–2
Lithuania, 259–62
Netherlands, 76, 89–92, 200–2, 205–6
proceeds of crime and, 409–10
public and private interests, 347
right to decision, 32
Romania, 221–4
state compensation, 75–93
see also specific countries
CoE and, 133
EU model, 414–15
VRD, 133
time limits: *Bowes & Brophy*, 84–7
transparency: *Doyle & Kelly*, 82–4
VRD, 77–8, 166, 168
amendment, 76, 76–8, 117
Ireland and, 309–10, 311
state compensation, 133
complaints:
international criminal tribunals, 155–9
Ireland, 293
translation, 26–7
VRD, 25, 26–7, 155–6
conflict of laws, 102–5, 409
cooperation:
Belgium, 127–8, 190
compensation, 70, 79, 190, 377
counter-terrorism, 372–3
Covid-19 pandemic, 374–5
ECtHR case law, 127
ENVR, 373–7
EU-level importance, 372–3
European Investigation Orders, 110–11
European Protection Orders, 111–12
'find my victim support' tool, 375–6
ineffectiveness, 44
Ireland, 304
Lithuania, 265–6
need, 371–7
SCPVOT, 376
video conferencing, 110–11
VRD, 99, 372
corruption: 2003 Convention, 140
Council of Europe
see also specific conventions
assessment of victims' needs, 134–5
Convention no 73, 106
definition of victim, 122–3
fair trial, 361
human trafficking and, 223
protection of victims, 137
Recommendations, 123–6, 134–5, 250
Terrorism Convention, 112
victims' rights instruments, 123–6, 405–6
counterfeiting, 100, 108, 411
counterterrorism *see* **terrorism**
Covid-19 pandemic, 8, 318–19, 371, 374–5
crimes against humanity:
2023 Convention, 140
Draft ILC articles, 140, 149
complaint rights, 158
participation rights, 165

protection of victims, 160–1
reparation, 166, 167
jurisdiction, 143
criminal proceedings:
meaning, 146, 146–7
participation *see* participation in criminal proceedings
transfer, 105–8, 117–18, 409
Croatia, 395–6
cross-border cases:
Belgium, 186–7
compensation, 68–71, 79, 114
Belgium, 191–2
Italy, 286–7
complexity, 96
cooperation *see* cooperation
EU model, 416
Eurojust role, 95–120
casework, 113–16
compensation, 114
competing EAWs, 108–9
EU architecture and, 98–102
European Investigation Orders, 110–11
identification of victims, 113
jurisdiction conflicts, 102–5
multifaceted support, 97–8
transfer of proceedings, 105–8
European Protection Orders: improving implementation, 118–19
gender-based violence, 52, 53
Ireland, 300
mutual recognition, 7
Netherlands, 199–200
Romania, 221, 228–30
transfer of proceedings
Eurojust role, 105–8
proposals, 117–18, 409
VRD amendment, 115, 116–17
cybercrime, 8, 49, 51, 99, 113, 115–16, 374
Cyprus, 366

data protection, 397
databases, 375–6, 408–9
defence rights:
balance of rights *see* balance of rights
efficiency *versus*, 360, 361–3
EU law, 351–69
background, 352–5
implementation gap, 356–60
practices, 355–68
training, 359
fair trial *see* fair trial
punitiveness priority and, 363–8
trial waver systems, 361–3
direct effect doctrine, 59, 61, 66
discontinued proceedings:
Belgium, 179
Ireland, 296
review requests, 29–31
Romania, 217–18
domestic violence:
Belgium: protection measures, 181–2
Citizenship Directive (Art 13), 37–9
compensation, 415
cooperation during Covid-19 pandemic, 375
Directive, 36, 48–51, 53–4, 273, 414
free movement and, 37–8, 52
information strategies, 397
Istanbul Convention, 36, 37, 38, 45, 46–8, 49, 50, 51, 52, 53, 54, 112
Italy, 275–8
Lithuania, 253
national discretion, 410
standing of victims, 63–5
support services, 38, 45

effectiveness principle, 85–6
enforced disappearances: 2010 Convention, 140, 149, 166, 252
Estonia, 265, 396
EU model:
AFSJ framework, 3, 4, 5, 9, 407–8
coherence issue, 413–16
definition of victim, 402
emergence, 417
EU criminal justice framework, 403–7
fragmentation, 413
function, 401–2
multi-faceted complexity, 407–13
prospects, 416–17
weaknesses, 413–14
Eudemonia, 387
Eurodac, 408
Eurojust:
case law, 113–16
compensation casework, 114
cross-border role, 95–120
EPOs, 119
EU architecture and, 98–102
European Investigation Orders, 110–11
European Protection Orders, 111–12
jurisdiction conflicts, 102–5
protection of victims, 115–16
transfer of proceedings, 105–8
VRD amendment, 116–17
Guidelines, 102, 103–4, 109, 115, 409
identification of victims, 113
information on rights, 113–14
methods, 96–8
opinions, 104

recommendations, 104, 107
requests, 104
Victims' Rights Working Group, 101
European Agency for Fundamental Rights, 356, 367, 386
European Arrest Warrants, 61–2, 108–9, 352, 353
European Charter of Fundamental Rights:
access to justice, 83, 180–1, 326
human dignity, 75, 80, 81, 249
impact, 404
requirements, 392
European Convention on Human Rights:
access to justice, 131, 249
ECtHR *see* European Court of Human Rights
fair trial, 123, 282, 352, 366–7
requirements, 392
victims' rights and, 123, 405–6
European Court of Human Rights:
fair trial, 366–7
paradigm shift, 95
plea-bargaining and, 362
Romania and, 226
victims' rights and
case law, 126–32, 405–6
civil party rights, 128–31
EU law and, 132–5
protection in criminal proceedings, 131–2, 136, 137
European Investigation Orders, 110–11
European Network on Vicims' Rights (ENVR), 373–7, 417
European Protection Orders (EPOs):
Directive, 5
Eurojust and, 111–12
gender-based violence, 42–4
improving implementation, 118–19
Ireland and, 311–12
Italy and, 277–8
Netherlands, 204–5
Romania and, 228–9
statistics, 44
Europol, 8, 369
Extraordinary African Chambers, 148
Extraordinary Chambers of the Courts of Cambodia, 148

fair trial:
balance of rights *see* balance of rights
ECHR, 123, 352, 366–7
civil party rights, 129
equality of arms, 282
ECtHR case law, 129, 131
efficiency *versus*, 360, 361–3
EU law, 352–5
implementation gap, 356–60
practices, 355–68
impartiality, 30, 31, 159, 161, 162, 164, 166, 269
punitiveness priority and, 363–8
trial waver systems, 361–3
Fair Trials, 358, 359, 361, 362
family: definition:
international criminal tribunals, 154
Italy, 270
VRD, 147
female genital mutilation, 48, 49, 51, 275, 409
forced labour, 317–19, 329, 332
forced marriage, 48, 49, 52, 317, 409
Framework Decision 2001/220:
definition of victim, 252
legal entities, 271
impact, 59–60
landmark, 4, 58, 59–60, 381
later case law, 62–5
Lithuania and, 250
paradigm shift, 96
poor results, 96
Pupino, 59, 60–2, 74
replacement, 65
VRD and, 21
France:
appeal rights, 130
balance of rights, 355
Cowan case, 55–6, 57–8, 74
defence rights, 360
prison population, 364
Romanian law and, 210
sentencing, 360
victim strategies, 396
VRD impact, 305
fraud:
cross-border cases
Eurojust role, 113, 115–16
identification of victims, 113
protection of victims, 115–16
victims' rights, 100–1, 105, 411
free movement, 4, 37, 38, 40, 44, 53, 111, 289

gender: definition, 46–7
gender-based violence *see* **sexual offences**
genocide, 140, 142, 143, 179
Genocide Network, 143
Greece, 73, 385

harm:
causation, 152–3
community harm, 152
definition, 150–2
transgenerational harm, 152

hearing:
public hearings, 161
right to be heard, 29, 129–30, 217, 296
homophobia, 402
hostages: 1979 Convention, 140
human dignity, 75, 80, 81, 155, 160, 161, 249
human trafficking:
access to justice, 319–20, 326, 330–1
Anti-Trafficking Coordinator, 417
Belgium, 326–7, 327–30, 332
CoE Recommendation, 223
Directive 2009/52, 320–1, 324–6
amendment, 415
failures, 327–30
ineffective implementation, 325–6
Directive 2011/36, 320–4
amendment, 323–4
failures, 326–8
EU legal framework, 408–9, 411
exploitative working conditions, 320–1, 324–6
marginality, 317–33
national strategies, 396
prospects for marginals, 330–2
protection failures, 326–30
protection measures, 112, 319–26
statistics, 317–18
temporary residence, 322, 331
victims' rights and, 99–100, 104, 317–33
video conferencing and, 110–11
Hungary, 46, 63

impartiality, 30, 31, 159, 161, 162, 164, 166, 269
implementation of rights: strategy, 381–99
indirect effect doctrine, 59, 61, 311
information:
Belgium, 178
EU rights, 22–9, 353, 358, 363, 385
Eurojust role, 113–14
Ireland, 293
Italy, 279–80
Latvian rights, 243
Lithuania, 257
margins of appreciation, 24
Netherlands, 196
release/escape of offenders, 24–5, 178, 393–4
right to receive, 23–5
Romanian rights, 214–17
strategies, 397
technology, 117
understanding and being understood, 22–3
international crimes:
Belgium: access to justice, 179–81
core international crimes, 143
early conventions, 140
extraterritorial jurisdiction, 179
material jurisdiction, 142–6
number of victims, 143–4
International Criminal Court (ICC):
complaint rights, 157–8
definition of family, 154
definition of victim, 148
legal persons, 150
harm
causation, 153
definition, 151–2
indirect victims, 153
influence, 140
initiating proceedings, 157–8
jurisdiction, 143, 144–5, 159
number of victims, 143–4
participation in criminal proceedings, 154–5, 164–5
protection of victims, 161–3, 186
reparation rights, 167–8
Trust Fund for Victims, 143, 167–8
victims' rights, 139, 142–54, 406
international criminal trials:
causation, 152–3
compensation rights, 166–8
core international crimes, 142–4
definition of family, 154
harm definition, 150–2
meaning of criminal proceedings, 146–7
meaning of victims, 147–54
participation in criminal proceedings
filing complaints, 155–9
right to, 163–6
substantive aspects, 154–8
protection of victims, 142, 159–63
territorial jurisdiction, 144–6
victims' rights
relevant proceedings, 146–7
scope of application, 142–54
International Criminal Tribunal for Rwanda (ICTR), 143, 154, 161
International Criminal Tribunal for the Former Yugoslavia (ICTY), 143, 154, 161
International Law Commission: Draft Articles on crimes against humanity, 140, 149, 158, 160–1, 165, 166, 167
interpretation rights:
Belgium, 177
EU rights, 22–3, 26–9, 353, 361–2, 385
Ireland, 294
Netherlands, 197
quality of services, 364
intimidation, 103, 159, 160–1, 163, 203, 312

investigation obligations: ECtHR case law, 126. 127, 129
Ireland:
compensation, 73, 306–11
assessment, 314
discretion, 310–11
from offenders, 299, 309–11
legal representation, 307–8
state compensation, 81–7, 307–9, 310
time limits, 84–7
transparency, 82–4, 308
complaint right, 293
cooperation, 304
cross-border cases, 300
definition of victim, 292
domestic violence, 313
English legal influence, 290
information rights, 293
interpretation rights, 294
legal aid, 297
mutual recognition, 312, 313
non-prosecution decisions, 296
proceeds of crime, 299
protection measures, 301–3, 311–13
avoiding contact with offenders, 301
children, 302
during proceedings, 302
individual assessment, 302
investigation phase, 302
privacy, 302
reimbursement of expenses, 298
restorative justice, 297
right to be heard, 296
right to understand, 292
sentencing procedure, 291
support services, 294, 295
training practitioners, 304
translation rights, 294
victims' rights, 289–314
assessment, 313–14
evolution, 290–1
VRD transposition, 291–306
amendments, 305–6
impact, 305
vulnerable persons, 306
Istanbul Convention, 36, 37, 38, 45, 46–8, 49, 50, 51, 52, 53, 54, 112
Italy:
compensation, 69–73, 79–80, 284–7
cross-border cases, 286–7
freezing orders, 285
competent authorities, 273
definition of victims, 268–72
damaged person, 269
direct v indirect victims, 268
family members, 270
injured person, 268–9
legal entities, 271–2
domestic violence, 275–8
information rights, 279–80
legal assistance, 281
mutual recognition, 278, 285
participation in criminal proceedings, 278–84
protection measures, 276–8
during proceedings, 281–3
European Protection Orders, 277–8
Pupino, 60–2
restorative justice, 269–71, 283–4
rights during investigation, 66–7
standing of victims, 64–5
victims' rights, 267–87
VRD transposition, 279–84, 287
vulnerable victims, 272–4

Latvia:
Baltic cooperation, 265
compensation, 240, 244–7
state compensation, 245–7
information rights, 243
participation in criminal proceedings
evidence, 241–2
initiating prosecutions, 239–40
out-of-court models, 244
procedures, 238–44
simplified procedures, 244
private prosecutions, 239
road traffic offences, 245
Soviet law, 235
specially protected victims, 238
victim status, 235–7
EU norms and, 240–1
victims' rights, 233–48
assessment, 247–8
legal framework, 234–8
legal aid:
EU law, 353, 415
European practices, 136, 357–8
Ireland, 297
Lithuania, 256–7
Netherlands, 197–8
rights, 31–2, 136
Romania, 219–20, 226
VRD, 415
legal assistance:
balance of rights, 344
EU right, 362
free access, 32
information on, 23
Italy, 281
Latvia, 240, 243

Lithuania, 256
mutual assistance, 110, 127
national regimes, 136
Romania, 214, 215, 216, 217, 220, 221, 224, 226
VRD, 415
vulnerable persons, 410
legal certainty principle, 70, 107, 179, 260, 384
legal representation:
Belgium, 357
EU law, 353, 361–2
Irish state compensation and, 307–8
Luxembourg, 357
Netherlands, 197–8
Lithuania:
Baltic cooperation, 265
compensation, 259–62
state compensation, 260
VRD impact, 261–2
cooperation, 265–6
domestic violence, 263
information rights, 257
legal aid, 256–7
mutual recognition, 265
participation in criminal proceedings, 255–9
list of rights, 256
VRD compatibility, 258–9
protection measures, 262–6
reconciliation with offenders, 257
victim status, 251–4
domestic violence, 253
injured persons, 252–3
relatives, 252
victims' rights, 249–66
assessment, 266
Ljubljana-The Hague Convention (2023), 140, 148, 159, 161, 167
Luxembourg: legal representation, 357

Mali: cultural heritage, 150
marriage:
definition, 46
forced marriage, 48, 49, 52, 317, 409
same-sex marriages, 46–7
member states *see* **national regimes**
Middle Ages, 346
migration *see* **human trafficking**
misogyny, 402, 414
mutual recognition
see also cross-border cases
EU instruments, 410
European Arrest Warrants, 62
European Protection Orders, 111–12
gender-based violence and, 42–4
ineffectiveness, 7, 44
minimum standards and, 352
security goals, 43
trust and, 352
Myanmar: ICC jurisdiction, 145

national regimes
see also individual countries
challenges, 385–6
comparisons, 416
compensation, 68–71
conflicting national laws, 61
jurisdiction conflicts, 102–5, 409
margins of discretion, 14, 24, 27, 410, 415
overview, 16
transposition delays, 58–9
victim status, 32
victim strategies, 395
nationality discrimination, 55, 308
***ne bis in idem*,** 105
Netherlands:
compensation, 76, 200–2
advanced payment scheme, 89–91, 92
EU law and, 205–6
by offenders, 200–1
state compensation, 201–2, 205–6
statistics, 91
cross-border cases, 199–200
European Protection Orders, 204–5
definition of victims, 194–5
human trafficking, 326–7
information rights, 196, 397
legal aid, 197–8
participation in criminal proceedings, 195–200
personal statements by victims, 198, 207
proper treatment rights, 195–6
protection measures, 202–5
individual assessment, 202–3
investigation phase, 203
prosecution phase, 203–4
protection orders, 204–5
trial phase, 204
vulnerable people, 127
representation rights, 197–8
restorative justice, 198–9
sexual offences, 89
support services, 199, 385
translation and interpretation, 197
victims' rights, 193–208
assessment, 207–8
EU law impact, 205–6
non-discrimination principle, 4, 48, 146, 156, 202, 364, 371, 413
non-prosecution decisions *see* **discontinued proceedings**
Norway: Romania and, 226

Organisation for Economic Cooperation and Development (OECD), 388
organised crime, 79, 98, 105, 106, 108, 110, 113, 164–5

participation in criminal proceedings:
balance of rights, 340–4
civil party rights: ECtHR case law, 128–31
complaints, 25, 26–7
Directive 2012/29, 20–33
gender-based violence and, 49
information rights, 22–9
international trials *see* international criminal trials
interpretation rights, 22–3, 26–9
legal aid, 31–2
original rules, 19–20
review requests, 29–31
right to be heard, 29, 129–30, 217, 296
rights during investigation, 66–7
standing *see* standing of victims
translation rights, 22–3, 26–9
trial waivers and, 363
VRD, 20–33, 163–4
personal statements by victims: Netherlands, 198
plea-bargaining, 362
Poland: Istanbul Convention and, 46
Portugal: victim strategies, 395–6
Prestige oil spill, 104
presumption of innocence, 348, 353, 361
prison rates, 363
privacy rights:
Ireland, 302
Romania, 228
VRD, 160, 228, 392
proceeds of crime, 188, 299, 409–10
protection of victims:
Belgium, 181–7
CoE and, 137
cross-border cases, 115–16, 118–19
development, 122
ECtHR case law, 131–2, 136
impact on EU law, 132–3
Eurojust role, 115–16
human trafficking *see* human trafficking
international criminal tribunals, 142, 159–63
VRD, 112, 160, 163

racism, 364, 413–14
rape: definition, 48–9, 227
Rejust, 218, 221, 228
reparation *see* **compensation**
retaliation, 25, 103, 159, 160, 161, 163, 203, 268, 281
retrospective legislation, 85–6
review requests: non-prosecution decisions, 29–31
Romania:
compensation, 221–4
moral damages, 223
by offenders, 221–2
state compensation, 222–4
confiscated assets, 221–2
cross-border cases, 221, 228–30
civil protection orders, 230
criminal protection orders, 228–30
definition of victim, 212–13
French legal influence, 210
information rights, 214–17
interpretation services, 365
labour migration, 229–30
legal aid, 219–20, 226
legal assistance, 214, 215, 216, 217, 220, 224, 226
participation in criminal proceedings, 210–14
protection of victims, 224–30
avoiding contact with offenders, 227–8
children, 226–7
civil protection orders, 230
criminal protection orders, 228–30
during proceedings, 225–7
individual assessment, 224–5
privacy, 228
video conferencing, 227
reasonable time principle, 222
reimbursement of expenses, 220
restorative justice, 218–19
review of non-prosecution decisions, 217–18
right to be heard, 217
sexual offences: age of consent, 227
support services, 225
training practitioners, 230–1
transposition of VRD, 213–14
victims rights, 209–32
assessment, 231–2
vulnerable victims, 213
rule of law, 285, 392, 398

Schengen Agreement, 105
Schengen Information System, 409
SCPVOT, 376
secondary victimisation, 8, 41, 50, 88, 100, 103, 111, 131, 160, 186. 191, 195–6, 213, 242, 268, 278, 281, 301, 322, 329
Serbia, 391
sexual offences
see also domestic violence
assessment, 53–4
Belgium, 184
child victims, 100, 411, 412

Commission Proposals, 48–51
compensation, 415
cross-border element, 52, 53
cross-examination, 132
Directive proposal, 88–9
EU model, 411, 414
Euro crime, 51–3
European protection orders, 42–4
indirect victims, 153
Istanbul Convention, 36, 37, 38, 45, 46–8, 49, 50, 51, 52, 53, 54, 112
Italy, 275–8
legal framework, 35–54
mutual recognition, 42–4
national discretion, 410
participation in criminal proceedings and, 49
protection, 41, 127
revisiting current framework, 44–6
support services, 45
video conferencing and, 111
VRD, 39–42, 49
slavery: modern slavery, 317–18
Spain:
domestic violence, 63–4
European Arrest Warrants, 127
protection measures, 185
victims' rights: history, 121
Special Tribunal for Lebanon, 148
stalking, 182, 184, 185, 203, 275, 282, 312
standing of victims:
Belgium, 176–81
Council of Europe and, 123–6
development, 121–2, 381
Framework Decision *see* Framework Decision 2001/220
legal persons, 62
Stockholm Programme, 19, 41, 44, 352, 354, 355, 356
Stoicism, 387
strategy:
coherence, 387–8
comprehensive benefits, 390–1
EU Strategy for Victims' Rights, 98–9, 101, 373, 377, 413, 416, 417
implementation of rights
developing, 381–99
key problems, 387–98
national challenges, 385–6
incorporating victim objectives in justice system, 391–3
language, 393
long-tern systems, 393–8
organised crime, 106
victim centric approach, 388–90
vulnerable people, 413
support services:
cooperation, 374–5
Covid-19 pandemic, 374–5
cross-border cases, 97–8
domestic violence, 38, 45
Ireland, 294, 295
Netherlands, 199
Romania, 225
VRD, 156, 160, 385
amendment, 355

terrorism:
Belgium: compensation, 189–90
compensation, 415
conventions, 112, 140
counter-terrorism
cooperation, 372–3
instruments, 411
SCPVOT, 376
EU victims, 412
torture/inhuman treatment:
definition of harm, 151
definition of victims, 149
ECtHR: civil party rights, 129
right to remedy, 166
training:
EU defence rights, 359
VRD, 230
transfer of proceedings:
CoE Convention, 106
Eurojust role, 105–8
proposals, 117–18, 409
transgender rights, 46
translation rights:
Belgium, 177
EU law, 353, 362, 385
Ireland, 294
Netherlands, 197
quality of services, 365
VRD, 22–3, 26–9
transphobia, 402

Ukraine, 129, 158
understanding: right to understand and be understood, 22–3
UNESCO World Heritage Sites, 150
United Kingdom:
balance of rights, 355
defence rights, 360
human trafficking, 366
United Nations:
1985 Declaration, 148, 150–1, 155, 164, 250, 381, 399
human trafficking and, 318
Personnel Safety Convention, 140

Sustainable Development Goals, 44–5
victim centric approach, 388
Universal Declaration of Human Rights (1948): right to remedy, 151, 166

victim status:
Belgium, 173–6
Council of Europe, 122–3
EU law, 365
EU model, 402
Framework Decision 2001/220, 252
harm, 150–2
international criminal tribunals, 147–54
Italy, 268–72
Latvia, 235–7
legal aid and, 32
legal persons, 150
Lithuania, 251–4
Netherlands, 194–5
Romania, 212–13
UN Declaration, 148
VRD, 12, 72, 147, 150, 402
Victim Support Scotland, 397
victimisation *see* **secondary victimisation**
victims:
compensation *see* compensation
definition *see* victim status
direct and indirect, 153
participation *see* participation in criminal proceedings
protection *see* protection of victims
statistics, 7
victims' commissioners, 192, 395, 397
victims' rights
see also specific rights
balance of rights *see* balance of rights
EU model *see* EU model
EU strategy, 98–9, 101, 373, 377, 413, 416, 417
persistent gaps, 6–7
strategy *see* strategy
Victims' Rights Coordinator, 417
Victims' Rights Directive *see* **VRD**
video conferencing, 100, 110–11, 156, 183, 186, 200, 204, 227
VOCIARE, 45, 382
VRD (Victims' Rights Directive)
see also specific rights
2022 Evaluation, 251
aims, 21, 146, 176, 251, 292, 354
amendments, 24, 28, 33, 49
2023 proposals, 87–9, 92, 134, 136, 141, 156–7, 160
assessment of needs, 135
compensation, 76, 87–8, 115
core international crimes, 144
cross-border cases, 115, 116–17
importance, 377
Netherlands and, 207
participation rights, 164
protection of victims, 160
rationale, 368
reporting crimes, 156–7, 159
scope, 355
approach, 405
balance of rights, 14, 384
case law, 65–7
child victims, 100
compensation *see* compensation
complaint rights, 25, 26–7, 155–6
contact with offenders, 45
cooperation, 99, 372
critiques, 6
deference to national regimes, 13
definition of crime, 346
definition of victim, 12, 147, 150, 402
Domestic Violence Directive and, 36
ECtHR and, 133
gender-based violence, 39–42, 49
harm
causation, 152
definition, 150
implementation challenges, 385–6, 416
key problems, 387–98
information rights, 22–9
landmark, 11, 35–6, 96, 140–1
language, 383–5
legal aid, 415
meaning of victim, 147
mutual recognition and, 410
non-discrimination, 413
non-EU citizens and, 12
out-of-court settlements, 363
participation in criminal proceedings, 20–33, 163–4
privacy rights, 160, 228, 392
protection, 112, 160, 163
support services, 156, 160, 355, 385
training, 230
translation rights, 22–3, 26–9
weaknesses, 383–5, 406–7
VSE (Victim Support Europe), 382, 386, 387, 388–90, 391, 392, 393–4
vulnerable victims
see also protection of victims
balance of rights, 274
counter-terrorism, 373
cross-border cases, 100, 111
defence rights, 354
ECtHR case law, 127
EU model, 410–11

EU strategy, 413
Ireland, 306
Italy, 272–4
Netherlands, 217
protection, 35–54
Romania, 213

war crimes, 12, 137, 140, 142, 143, 179, 180, 286, 376
World Bank, 390–1
World Health Organization (WHO), 388

xenophobia, 413–14

www.ingramcontent.com/pod-product-compliance
Ingram Content Group UK Ltd.
Pitfield, Milton Keynes, MK11 3LW, UK
UKHW020846290926
15470UKWH00004B/1577

9 781509 975358